Eyewitness:
Writings from the Ordeal of Communism

Edited and compiled by
Ross Mackenzie and Todd Culbertson

Focus on Issues, No. 15

Freedom House

First published in 1992.

The Library of Congress Cataloguing-in-Publication Data
Eyewitness: writings from the ordeal of communism / edited by
Ross Mackenzie and Todd Culbertson.
463 p.   cm. — (Focus on issues ; no. 15)
Includes bibliographical references.
ISBN 0-932088-77-5 (cloth : alk. paper)
1. Communism—History—20th century. 2. Communism—Soviet
Union— History—20th century. 3. Communism—Europe, Eastern—
History—20th century.   I. Mackenzie, Ross, 1941-   .
II Culbertson, Todd.   III. Series: Focus on issues
(Freedom House (U.S.)) ; no. 15
HX40.E95   1992
335.43'09'04—dc20

Distributed by:

National Book Network
4720 Boston Way
Lanham, MD 20706

3 Henrietta Street
London WC2E 8LU England

Dedication

For Tennant Bryan,
who always has understood

Acknowledgments

Many aided in the completion of this book.

The editors would like to thank especially:

John Barron, Midge Decter and Thomas Henriksen—all of whom helped at the beginning; David Bovenizer, Kenneth Tomlinson, and A. Barton Hinkle, who helped at the end; and Willa Johnson and Jean Vonderlehr, who helped hugely throughout.

Finally, they would like to thank James Finn and Mark Wolkenfeld at Freedom House for their counsel, commitment and abiding patience.

About the Editors

Ross Mackenzie and Todd Culbertson are longtime students of Communism and the Soviet Union. Mackenzie, a graduate of Yale (B.A.) and Chicago (M.A.), is Editor of the Editorial Pages of the *Richmond Times-Dispatch*. Culbertson, Associate Editor of the *Times-Dispatch*'s Editorial Page, is a graduate of Principia College (B.A.) and was a media fellow at the Hoover Institution of War, Revolution, and Peace, Stanford, CA.

Copyright notices

Contents

MENTAL

CAMPS

Foreword

If we are to remember, and understand, the totalitarian phenomenon—and guard ourselves against it—it is crucial that we study the testimonies of those who studied it close up. These include such observers as James Michener and John Barron, both of whom are represented in this volume. It is not the case that you must have lived an experience directly in order to analyse and describe it; if that were so, most historical and scientific literature would be useless. There is no question that we owe some of the best and most insightful reports on Nazi Germany or Soviet Russia, on the level of journalism as well as on the level of historical scholarship, to writers whose every predispostion was to be repelled by what they found but who knew they must try to put their talents at the service of a large public, even though they must have known that they would be greeted with incredulity.

However, it is a special phenomenon of Communism, and Soviet Communism in particular, that it produced two kinds of witnesses from "inside," whose writings, sampled in this volume, constitute an invaluable if excruciatingly painful monument to the human soul's longing for truth and freedom. These witnesses I will call the believers and the victims. These are simple arbitrary terms which the reader will accept or reject as he wishes; that is not of great import. The important point is that these individuals tasted of the revolutionary fruit and were able to reject it before it poisoned them. Their understanding of the nature of the poison is one of the most important historical lessons of our times.

Among the believers were men like Milovan Djilas and Arthur Koestler, who consciously adopted the Marxist thought system and chose to act in accordance with their belief. But ideological choices were not the only ones. In men like Ion Mihai Pacepa, Stanislav Levchenko, an Petro Grigorenko we have sincere and devoted servants of the Communist revolution.

Among the victims—and I know this is a term they would deplore, but what else do you call individuals, however heroic and free of self-pity, whose lives were broken by years in the most oppressive prison conditions — are the likes of Natan Sharansky and Elena Bonner and Vladimir Bukovsky, whom we will never thank enough for their teachings.

We must give a special place in history to the writers and thinkers who, in the deepest depth of the totalitarian night, found in themselves resources of courage and clear-sightedness permitting them to understand and describe in detail the regimes that crushed them. Their personal courage makes them heroes in the fight for freedom and human dignity. They paid the price of their revolt: years in prison, concentration camps, internal exile, unemployment.

But perhaps by even more than their moral greatness, one is moved by the power of their reflection. Where did they find the strength to achieve such insights about this system that did all it could to prevent the truth from emerging, which forbade books from circulating, falsified information, disallowed human contacts and free research, and submitted everyone to incessant barrages of propaganda? Totalitarianism is unlike traditional despotisms or present-day authoritarian regimes: it is not content to control and censor intellectual life or ideas and books it judges to be subversive. Totalitarianism strikes at the very root of thought and feeling, for it wishes to kill the source of intellectual and moral autonomy that each individual has in himself. It wishes to substitute itself for us inside our deepest selves, to reign as master not just over but inside our souls. The ineptitudes of Mao's Little Red Book replaced people's brains during China's Cultural Revolution, even as two ballet-operas produced by the genius of Mrs. Mao replaced the entire tradition of Chinese art.

"Totalitarianism" is not a label that historians came up with after the fact; it was a concept and a program deliberately crafted by a politician, Benito Mussolini, in 1922, and subsequently "perfected," if that is the word, by the Nazis. As to the Communists, they were the pioneers of totalitarianism with Lenin and Trotsky, and they skillfully paved the way for the Stalinist apocalypse.

The fact that men and women imprisoned in these systems were able to save their intelligence and turn it against the machine that was supposed to smash them proves, in the last analysis, that humankind is meant to survive. And the energy and lucidity of these extraordinary dissidents truly ought to astonish us.

There were essentially two kinds of totalitarian systems. There are those whose ideas I will call straightforward, and that makes their aims perfectly clear. Mussolini and Hitler always said they were hostile to democracy, to freedom of expression and culture, to political pluralism and free trade unionism. Hitler, additionally, explained at great length, well before coming to power, his racist, and specifically anti-Semitic, ideology. Therefore, supporters and adversaries of this type of totalitarianism were from the start on opposite sides of a clearly defined line. There were no "disillusioned" Hitlerians: Hitler accomplished what he promised. His downfall was due to external causes.

Communism differs in that it made use of ideological subterfuges. If I may use some Hegelian jargon, I would say that Communism was "mediated by way of utopianism." It is the utopian connection that allowed this ideology, and the political regime that it produced, to proclaim an unending stream of successes even as it was doing the opposite of its declared program. Communism promised abundance and produced misery, it promised freedom and led to slavery, it promised equality and ended up in the most stratified of societies, with a privileged *nomenklatura* such as had not been seen since the age of feudalism. It promised to respect human life and engaged in mass murder, it promised the cultural enhancement of all and led to generalized mental crippling, it dreamed of a "new man" and instead it petrified him. And yet for many years believers accepted all these grotesque contradictions because utopia is always somewhere in the future. The intellectual trap of a totalitarian ideology mediated by utopia is therefore far more difficult to counter than the straight-forward ideology of nazism and fascism because, in utopian thinking, real facts never suffice to prove to believers that the ideology itself is false.

As the devious strategies of totalitarian utopianism have been dissected by the very intellectuals whom they were designed to mislead, and defeated by the very people whom they were supposed to hold in servitude forever, we in the West should recognize our debt to them, our eternal debt.

JEAN-FRANÇOIS REVEL

Introduction

Communism ranks overwhelmingly as the central ordeal of our age, the single searing event. For nearly seventy-five years, installed on the Russian land mass, it dominated—and often terminated—the lives of millions.

Wherever it takes root, Communism rules via terror and terror's routine techniques: atrocity, deportation, and slaughter; contrived famine, imposed scarcity, and slave labor. Its byzantine bureaucracy is at once remote yet invasive, inquisitional, and casually capable of the grisliest enormities. The bureacracy plans everything—at the same time indirectly encouraging indolence and incompetence. As Dante went to such lengths to explain in the *Divine Comedy,* Hell was a thoroughly planned community.

Most in the West possess but the vaguest understanding of Communist realities. Partly that is a result of the deceits that propaganda for rigorously closed societies blandly sells to the unsuspecting. Partly it is a result of indifference and sloth. And partly it is a result—as Alexander Solzhenitsyn has aptly phrased it—of "the desire not to know."

Certainly our broad ignorance of those realities does not derive from a lack of effort by Communism's oppressed to tell us about them. Books by defectors, dissidents, refuseniks, exiles, and escapees—children of a defiant Destiny—fill endless shelves. One might fairly subsume them under the heading "Escape Books," for all the authors have escaped physically, emotionally, or intellectually from The Bear's embrace. Whittaker Chambers' *Witness* is no less an escape book than Walter Krivitsky's *In Stalin's Secret Service,* Armando Valladares' *Against All Hope,* or Solzhenitsyn's monumental *Gulag Archipelago.* Even Arthur Koestler's fictional *Darkness at Noon* is at bottom an escape book— Rubashov's escape from the nightmare of his life coming only by means of a bullet in the brain.

Many of these eyewitnesses have risked much to write books

telling their stories; and indeed books often are the best way to get the stories out. Yet such books impose on the rest of us an obligation to read them—an obligation too few fulfill. What's more, such books typically have small printings and smaller audiences, and soon disappear. In compiling this anthology we have sought, through excerpts, to retrieve some of the best escape books from the edge of oblivion.

The literature of defection, though frequently pedestrian, occasionally contains considerable power. Having read well over 200 books, we present here samples from thirty. Each speaks in its way to the degradation, the loneliness, and the agony—the stifling of even spiritual liberty—that form the heart of defectors' apostasy.

* * *

Just three books have ploughed this ground before, but none in quite the same way.

One is *Verdict of Three Decades,* edited by Julien Steinberg [Duell, Sloan and Pearce]. Another is *The God That Failed,* edited by Richard Crossman [Harper & Brothers]. Both were published in 1950. The Steinberg volume is a mixture of philosophical and first-person accounts documenting the "individual revolt against Soviet Communism: 1917-1950." A key book, it is long out of print, and of course lacks works from its post-publication period.

The Crossman volume contains pieces by six of the West's leading writers who—between the October Revolution and the Hitler-Stalin Pact—had flirted with Communism and spurned it. Wrote Crossman in his introduction: "Our concern was to study the state of mind of the Communist convert..., the journey into Communism, and the return." The book was important to its generation; the pieces were (and remain) sometimes compelling. Yet none of these writers had dwelt under a Communist regime; and none, at journey's end, embraced the democratic capitalism that is Communism's fundamental alternative.

The third book is *Soviet Defectors: The KGB Wanted List,* by Vladislav Krasnov [Hoover Press: 1985]. Comprehensive, heavily statistical, and highly useful, it catalogues data on 670 post-war Soviet-bloc defectors. It nevertheless lacks lengthy excerpts from the works it discusses or cites.

* * *

The present work is limited to books published since the Stalin purges; it also is limited to books by those who have lived in what used to be the contiguous Soviet bloc—that is, the East European satellites and the Soviet Union.

All selections are first-person accounts—except those by John Barron and James Michener, who have written for others; all are non-fiction—except those by Varlam Shalamov and Valeriy Tarsis, whose fictional accounts are autobiographical. Several are by those who believed deeply in the Party and the system, those driven to disillusion by reality; others are by those who simply could not escape history, who in different times would have become one of Pasternak's "nameless numbers"; and still others are by those who never even tried to play the game, whose resistance to the twin temptations of ideology and power began in adolescence or early adulthood.

Certain expected names do not appear here. Few apostate books are produced by practiced writers, and many suffer accordingly; some from translation, others from the leaden prose that inheres in Communism's ineloquence. Some simply were not conducive to excerpting. Some that we wanted to include ran aground in the permissions process. Some were selected (or rejected) for reasons relating to the authors' nationality or to the period of the authors' experience: We sought to show the similarity of experience throughout the fifty-year period and throughout the Soviet bloc. Some (Solzhenitsyn, for example) were excluded in favor of giving space to lesser-knowns.

And all were written in obedience to this observation by Malcolm Muggeridge, who spent time in the Soviet Union as an initially sympathetic journalist during the Thirties:

> The greatest asset of Bolshevik propaganda has been the naive, and quite unfounded, belief...that it is possible to describe the Soviet regime fairly, and in detachment. [Some] like to think that both sides of the question have been set; that the describer is a referee rather than a player; that all the pros and cons have been dispassionately weighed. As a matter of fact, of course, in regard to a thing like the Dictatorship of the Proletariat, there are no referees. Only players. And a player masquerading as a referee, accepted by the spectators as a referee, is worth more to his side than the most accomplished player. The vast army of sympathetic critics of the Soviet regime have done more to enhance its prestige than all its paid agitators and subsidized publications put together. By being sympathetic they have accepted its premises; and once the premises are accepted, criticism becomes irrelevant.

In this century of false testimonies, every argument for the destruction of liberty can be answered from reality. The authors of the books excerpted in the pages that follow are neither trendy celebrities with utopian illusions nor semi-skilled intellectuals who confuse Communism with Unitarianism. Rather, they have been players in the strictest sense: They have lived through the stringencies of Leninist ideology; through the Party *apparatchiks'* ceaseless wars against family, religion, and property; through betrayals by *stukachi* (informers); through seven decades of unblemished brutalization and deceit.

One of mankind's great divides separates those who acquiesce from those who react. One type yields when pushed; the other type—represented here— when pushed, pushes back. These are humble people possessed of spiritual strength. They have borne the burdens of Communism. They have done daily battle against its wardens. They have seen its mendacity and its murder, its crimes against decency, honor and truth. Where possbible, they have left their land to tell their story. (Let it be noted that defections occur almost uniquely from slave societies.)

The book contains reports from several sectors.

• Every-day life of every-day people—plus the luxuries and perks of the *nomenklatura* (the oligarchy, the ruling elite).

• Apostasy: the inception of alienation, the blossoming of dread.

• For the lucky ones, flight (defection).

• For the unlucky, arrest prison and Kafkaesque trial. And for the convicted (as just about all those arrested are, or were)....

• Special-regime psychiatric hospitals, with abuse variously by constraint and/or neuroleptic drugs, or

• The camps, for which everbody is a candidate; the Gulag, where— according to Solzhenitsyn's estimates—perhaps 70 million innocents died in the Soviet Union alone.

* * *

These words are written at a momentous hour: the implosion of the Soviet empire. The satellites have gone their way; the Soviet Union exists no more.

The Socialist Order proclaimed a new humanity, a new man, a new world. It proved a scourge: Party fetters, compelled atheism, enforced deprivation, omnipresent surveillance, moral corruption, unscrupulous rule. It produced a hideous legacy—in Václav Havel's words, "the culture of the lie."

Terror is the highest form of violence against man. The essential terror of Communism is its lawlessness. The Party elevates above "the law" the privileged few who exploit the many; it often employs its "judicial system" to transfer stipulated numbers of citizens to the category of prisoners. It oversees every aspect of the economy and society—even internal movement—to dominate the lives of its people.

These people. Eyewitnesses.

And these are their accounts of the reality of the Socialist Order, the grim gray truth of the lie they have lived. If the Fates finally are gathering to escort Communism down, then eloquent testimonies such as these—from Destiny's children—have done much to pave the way.

Ross Mackenzie
Todd Culbertson
Richmond, Virginia
August 1992

Nomenklatura and Life

Biographies

A native of Montenegro (1911), **MILOVAN DJILAS** joined the Communist Party in 1932.

He helped Tito organize volunteers for the Spanish civil war, and during World War II was active in the Yugoslav resistance. He served for nearly a decade thereafter as one of Tito's top advisors.

His support of the Hungarian anti-Communists in 1956 landed him in jail. Tito extended Djilas' jail term in 1957 following publication of *The New Class*—one of the first, and one of the most devastating, insider critiques of Communist oligarchy.

WOLFGANG LEONHARD sacrificed a promising career in Walter Ulbricht's East Germany in March 1949 by defecting to Yugoslavia. He was twenty-seven.

The son of a German woman who went from Germany to Moscow to work for Lenin's revolution (resulting ultimately in her Siberian exile), Leonhard grew up in the bosom of the Soviet Communist Party.

At the time of his defection he remained a Communist. But he had had his doubts, first during self-criticism sessions in a Comintern school in the early 1940s—an experience recounted in this excerpt from his 1958 book, *Child of the Revolution* [see also his excerpt in the section "Nomenklatura and Life"].

MICHAEL VOSLENSKY, a prominent Soviet historian, graduated from Moscow University. He held many positions in the country, including professor at both Moscow's Academy of Sciences and Moscow's Lumumba University.

The Soviet regime expatriated him in 1977. He moved first to Austria and then to Germany, where he has written widely.

His 1984 book on the Soviet "nomenklatura" remains definitive in its field.

The nomenklatura is the luxuriating Soviet Soviet elite that rules through corruption, terror, and labyrinthine bureaucracy. Propaganda, ideology and elaborate device shield its existence from the Soviet people and from prying foreign eyes.

Yelena Mitroknina was born in Leningrad and became a teacher, translator, and sociologist before moving to Washington. Her husband became First Secretary of the Soviet embassy.

She defected with her two children in August, 1978. Subsequently she took the name **ALEXANDRA COSTA**, earned an advanced degree, and established her own computer consultancy in the Washington area.

Her 1986 book, *Stepping Down from the Star*, relates her reactions upon arriving in America, her life in the embassy compound, her defection—and the aftermath.

In 1980, **LOIS BECKER** began a year of graduate study in the Soviet Union. In Moscow's Lenin Library, she met a freelance journalist—Andrei Frolov.

She had been born and raised in Chicago; he had been born and raised in Moscow. They were married in Moscow in May 1981.

Their jointly authored book, *Against the Odds*, published in 1983, recounts their overcoming the obstacles Soviet authorities put in the way of their marriage and Andrei's emigration.

This excerpt, by Lois, describes an American graduate student's observations of Moscow life.

At the time of his March 1978 defection, Lieutenant General **ION MIHAI PACEPA** was chief of Romania's DIE—the *Departmentul de Informatii Externe* (Foreign Information Department). His defection—the Romanian equivalent of a defection by the head of the Soviet KGB—caused both the disbanding (and subsequent replacement) of the DIE and the largest purge of all Romanian government branches since World War II.

Once in the U.S., Pacepa was debriefed by the CIA for three years. And he survived nearly a dozen assassination attempts.

A constant companion of the late dictator Nicolae Ceausescu, Pacepa relates in his 1987 book, *Red Horizons,* the Strangelovian Ceausescu's methods for repressing his citizens and keeping them under constant surveillance—as well as Ceausescu's role in international terrorism and as a Soviet marionette.

ELENA BONNER is the wife of Andrei Sakharov—a leading Soviet dissident, nuclear physicist, and winner of the Nobel Prize.

She wrote *Alone Together* during six months in the U.S. for surgery, a trip resulting from international pressure.

Her 1986 book recounts her harrowing life with Sakharov during three years of involuntary internal exile in Gorky: It is a testimony to perseverance in hideous existence—constant surveillance (every action filmed), libels, and harassment.

Born in 1931, **VLADIMIR GOLYAKHOVSKY** rose to become one of the Soviet Union's leading orthopaedic surgeons—holding the chair of traumatology, orthopaedics, and military surgery at the Moscow Medical and Dental School. Among his patients were Nikita Khrushchev, Boris Pasternak, and Dmitri Shostakovich.

A non-Communist, he lived in Communism's privileged milieu. And there he witnessed its corruptions, deceptions, stiflings, and contradictions—the abyss between the rulers and the ruled.

He became disenchanted and emigrated—ultimately to the U.S.—in 1979. His book *Russian Doctor,* recounting his disaffection, appeared in 1984.

The New Class

Milovan Djilas

E 1.

verything happened differently in the USSR and other Communist countries from what the leaders—even such prominent ones as Lenin, Stalin, Trotsky and Bukharin— anticipated. They expected that the state would rapidly wither away, that democracy would be strengthened. The reverse happened. They expected a rapid improvement in the standard of living—there has been scarcely any change in this respect and, in the subjugated East European countries, the standard has even declined. In every instance, the standard of living has failed to rise in proportion to the rate of industrialization, which was much more rapid. It was believed that the differences between cities and villages, between intellectual and physical labor, would slowly disappear; instead these differences have increased. Communist anticipations in other areas—including their expectations for developments in the non-Communist world—have also failed to materialize.

The greatest illusion was that industrialization and collectivization in the USSR, and destruction of capitalist ownership, would result in a classless society. In 1936, when the new constitution was promulgated, Stalin announced that the "exploiting class" had ceased to exist. The capitalist and other classes of ancient origin had in fact been destroyed, but a new class, previously unknown to history, had been formed.

It is understandable that this class, like those before it, should believe that the establishment of its power would result in happiness and freedom for all men. The only difference between this and other classes was that it treated the delay in the realization of its illusions more crudely. It thus affirmed that its power was more complete than the power of any other class before in history, and its class illusions and prejudices were proportionally greater.

1

This new class, the bureaucracy, or more accurately the political bureaucracy, has all the characteristics of earlier ones as well as some new characteristics of its own. Its origin had its special characteristics also, even though in essence it was similar to the beginnings of other classes.

Other classes, too, obtained their strength and power by the revolutionary path, destroying the political, social, and other orders they met in their way. However, almost without exception, these classes attained power *after* new economic patterns had taken shape in the old society. The case was the reverse with new classes in the Communist systems. It did not come to power to *complete* a new economic order but to *establish* its own and, in so doing, to establish its power over society.

In earlier epochs the coming to power of some class, some part of a class, or of some party, was the final event resulting from its formation and its development. The reverse was true in the USSR. There the new class was definitely formed after it attained power. Its consciousness had to develop before its economic and physical powers, because the class had not taken root in the life of the nation. This class viewed its role in relation to the world from an idealistic point of view. Its practical possibilities were not diminished by this. In spite of its illusions, it represented an objective tendency toward industrialization. Its practical bent emanated from this tendency. The promise of an ideal world increased the faith in the ranks of the new class and sowed illusion among the masses. At the same time it inspired gigantic physical undertakings.

Because this new class had not been formed as a part of the economic and social life before it came to power, it could only be created in an organization of a special type, distinguished by a special discipline based on identical philosophic and ideological views of its members. A unity of belief and iron discipline was necessary to overcome its weaknesses.

The roots of the new class were implanted in a special party, of the Bolshevik type. Lenin was right in his view that his party was an exception in the history of human society, although he did not suspect that it would be the beginning of a new class.

To be more precise, the initiators of the new class are not found in the party of the Bolshevik type as a whole but in that stratum of professional revolutionaries who made up its core even before it attained power. It was not by accident that Lenin asserted after the failure of the 1905 revolution that only professional revolutionaries—men whose sole profession was revolutionary work—could build a new party of the Bolshevik type. It was still less accidental that even Stalin, the future creator of a new class, was the most outstanding example of such a professional revolutionary. The new ruling class has been gradually developing from this very narrow stratum of revolutionaries. These revolution-aries composed its core for a long period. Trotsky noted that in pre-revolution-ary professional revolutionaries was the origin of the Stalinist bureaucrat. What he did not detect was the beginning of a new class of owners and exploiters.

This is not to say that the new party and the new class are identical. The party, however, is the core of that class, and its base. It is very difficult, perhaps impossible, to define the limits of the new class and to identify its members. The new class may be said to be made up of those who have special privileges and economic preference because of the administrative monopoly they hold.

Since administration is unavoidable in society, necessary administrative functions may be coexistent with parasitic functions in the person. Not every member of the party is a member of the new class, any more than every artisan or member of the city party was a bourgeois.

In loose terms, as the new class becomes stronger and attains a more perceptible physiognomy, the role of the party diminishes. The core and the basis of the new class is created in the party and at its top, as well as in the state political organs. The once live, compact party, full of initiative, is disappearing to become transformed into the traditional oligarchy of the new class, irresistibly drawing into its ranks those who aspire to join the new class and repressing those who have any ideals.

The party makes the class, but the class grows as a result and uses the party as a basis. The class grows stronger, while the party grows weaker; this is the inescapable fate of every Communist party in power.

If it were not materially interested in production or if it did not have within itself the potentialities for the creating of a new class, no party could act in so morally and ideologically foolhardy a fashion, let alone stay in power for long. Stalin declared, after the end of the First Five-Year Plan: "If we had not created the apparatus, we would have failed!" He should have substituted the "new class" for the word "apparatus," and everything would have been clearer.

It seems unusual that a political party could be the beginning of a new class. Parties are generally the product of classes and strata which have become intellectually and economically strong. However, if one grasps the actual conditions in pre-revolutionary Russia and in other countries in which Communism prevailed over national forces, it will be clear that a party of this type is the product of specific opportunities and that there is nothing unusual or accidental in this being so. Although the roots of Bolshevism reach far back into Russian history, the party is partly the product of the unique pattern of international relationships in which Russia found itself at the end of the nineteenth and the beginning of the twentieth century. Russia was no longer able to live in the modern world as an absolute monarch, and Russia's capitalism was too weak and too dependent on the interests of foreign powers to make it possible to have an industrial revolution. This revolution could only be implemented by a new class, or a change in the social order. As yet, there was no such class.

In history, it is not important who implements a process, it is only important that the process be implemented. Such was the case in Russia and other countries in which Communist revolutions took place. The revolution created forces, leaders, organizations, and ideas which were necessary to it. The new class came into existence for objective reasons, and by the wish, wits, and action of its leaders.

2.

The social origin of the new class lies in the proletariat just as the aristocracy arose in a peasant society, and the bourgeoisie in a commercial and artisans' society. There are exceptions, depending on national conditions, but the proletariat in economically underdeveloped countries, being backward, constitutes the raw material from which the new class arises.

There are other reasons why the new class always acts as the champion of the working class. The new class is anti-capitalistic and, consequently, logically dependent upon the working strata. The new class is supported by the proletarian struggle and the traditional faith of the proletariat in a socialist, Communist society where there is no brutal exploitation. It is vitally important for the new class to assure a normal flow of production, hence it cannot ever lose its connection with the proletariat. Most important of all, the new class cannot achieve industrialization and consolidate its power without the help of the working class. On the other hand, the working class sees in expanded industry the salvation from its poverty and despair. Over a long period of time, the interests, ideas, faith, and hope of the new class, and of parts of the working class and of the poor peasants, coincide and unite. Such mergers have occurred in the past among other widely different classes. Did not the bourgeoisie represent the peasantry in the struggle against the feudal lords?

The movement of the new class toward power comes as a result of the efforts of the proletariat and the poor. These are the masses upon which the party or the new class must lean and with which its interests are most closely allied. This is true until the new class finally establishes its power and authority. Over and above this, the new class is interested in the proletariat and the poor only to the extent necessary for developing production and for maintaining in subjugation the most aggressive and rebellious social forces.

4

The monopoly which the new class establishes in the name of the working class over the whole of society is, primarily, a monopoly over the working class itself. This monopoly is first intellectual, over the so-called *avant-garde* proletariat, and then over the whole proletariat. This is the biggest deception the class must accomplish but it shows that the power and interests of the new class lie primarily in industry. Without industry the new class cannot consolidate its position or authority.

Former sons of the working class are the most steadfast members of the new class. It has always been the fate of slaves to provide for their masters the most clever and gifted representatives. In this case a new exploiting and governing class is born from the exploited class.

3.

When Communist systems are being critically analyzed, it is considered that their fundamental distinction lies in the fact that a bureaucracy, organized in a special stratum, rules over the people. This is generally true. However, a more detailed analysis will show that only a special stratum of bureaucrats, those who are not administrative officials, make up the core of the governing bureaucracy, or, in my terminology, of the new class. This is actually a party or political bureaucracy. Other officials are only the apparatus under the control of the new class; the apparatus may be clumsy and slow but, no matter what, it must exist in every socialist society. It is sociologically possible to draw the borderline between the different types of officials, but in practice they are practically indistinguishable. This is true not only because the Communist system by its very nature is bureaucratic, but because Communists handle the various important administrative functions. In addition, the stratum of political bureaucrats cannot enjoy their privileges if they do not give crumbs from their tables to other bureaucratic categories.

It is important to note the fundamental difference between the political bureaucracies mentioned here and those which arise with every centralization in modern economy—especially centralizations that lead to collective forms of ownership such as monopolies, companies, and state ownership. The number of white-collar workers is constantly increasing in capitalistic monopolies, and also in nationalized industries in the West. In *Human Relations in Administration*,* R. Durbin says that state functionaries in the economy are being transformed into a special stratum of society.

---

* New York, Prentice-Hall, 1951.

...Functionaries have the sense of a common destiny for all those who work together. They share the same interests, especially since there is relatively little competition insofar as promotion is in terms of seniority. In-group aggression is thus minimized and this arrangement is therefore conceived to be positively functional for the bureaucracy. However, the esprit de corps and informal social organization which typically develops in such situations often leads the personnel to defend their entrenched interests rather than to assist their clientele and elected higher officials.

While such functionaries have much in common with Communist bureaucrats, especially as regards "esprit de corps," they are not identical. Although state and other bureaucrats in non-Communist systems form a special stratum, they do not exercise authority as the Communists do. Bureaucrats in a non-Communist state have political masters, usually elected, or owners over them, while Communists have neither masters nor owners over them. The bureaucrats in a non-Communist state are officials in a modern capitalist economy, while the Communists are something different and new: a new class.

As in other owning classes, the proof that it is a special class lies in its ownership and its special relations to other classes. In the same way, the class to which a member belongs is indicated by the material and other privileges which ownership brings to him.

As defined by Roman law, property constitutes the use, enjoyment, and disposition of material goods. The Communist political bureaucracy uses, enjoys, and disposes of nationalized property.

If we assume that membership in this bureaucracy or new owning class is predicated on the use of privileges inherent in ownership—in this instance nationalized material goods—then membership in the new party class, or political bureaucracy, is reflected in a larger income in material goods and privilege than society should normally grant for such functions. In practice, the ownership privilege of the new class manifests itself as an exclusive right, as a party monopoly, for the political bureaucracy to distribute the national income, to set wages, direct economic development, and dispose of nationalized and other property. This is the way it appears to the ordinary man who considers the Communist functionary as being very rich and as a man who does not have to work.

The ownership of private property has, for many reasons, proved to be unfavorable for the establishment of the new class's authority. Besides, the destruction of private ownership was necessary for the economic transformation of nations. The new class obtains its power, privileges, ideology, and its customs from one specific form of ownership—collective ownership—which the class administers and distributes in the name of the nation and society.

The new class maintains that ownership derives from a designated social relationship. This is the relationship between the monopolists of administration, who constitute a narrow and closed stratum, and the mass of producers (farmers, workers, and intelligentsia) who have no rights. However, this relationship is not valid since the Communist bureaucracy enjoys a monopoly over the distribution of material goods.

Every fundamental change in the social relationship between those who monopolize administration and those who work is inevitably reflected in the ownership relationship. Social and political relations and ownership—the totalitarianism of the government and the monopoly of authority—are being more fully brought into accord in Communism than in any other single system.

To divest Communists of their ownership rights would be to abolish them as a class. To compel them to relinquish their other social powers, so that workers may participate in sharing the profits of their work—which capitalists have had to permit as a result of strikes and parliamentary action—would mean that Communists were being deprived of their monopoly over property, ideology, and government. This would be the beginning of democracy and freedom in Communism, the end of Communist monopolism and totalitarianism. Until this happens, there can be no indication that important, fundamental changes are taking place in Communist systems, at least not in the eyes of men who think seriously about social progress.

The ownership privileges of the new class and membership in that class are the privileges of *administration*. This privilege extends from state administration and the administration of economic enterprises to that of sports and humanitarian organizations. Political, party, or so-called "general leadership" is executed by the core. This position of leadership carries privileges with it. In his *Stalin au pouvoir*, published in Paris in 1951, Orlov states that the average pay of a worker in the USSR in 1935 was 1,800 rubles annually, while the pay and allowances of the secretary on a rayon committee amounted to 45,000 rubles annually. The situation has changed since then for both workers and party functionaries, but the essence remains the same. Other authors have arrived at the same conclusions. Discrepancies between the pay of workers and party functionaries are extreme; this could not be hidden from persons visiting the USSR or other Communist countries in the past few years.

Other systems, too, have their professional politicians. One can think well or ill of them, but they must exist. Society cannot live without a state or government, and therefore it cannot live without those who fight for it.

However, there are fundamental differences between professional politicians in other systems and in the Communist system. In extreme cases, politicians in other systems use the government to secure privileges for themselves and their cohorts, or to favor the economic interests of one social stratum or another. The situation is different with the Communist system where the power and the government are identical with the use, enjoyment, and disposition of almost all the nation's goods. He who grabs power grabs privileges and indirectly grabs property. Consequently, in Communism, power or politics as a profession is the ideal of those who have the desire or the prospect of living as parasites at the expense of others.

Membership in the Communist Party before the Revolution meant sacrifice. Being a professional revolutionary was one of the highest honors. Now that the party has consolidated its power, party membership means that one belongs to a privileged class. And at the core of the party are the all-powerful exploiters and masters.

For a long time the Communist revolution and the Communist system have been concealing their real nature. The emergence of the new class has been concealed under socialist phraseology and, more important, under the new collective forms of property ownership. The so-called socialist ownership is a disguise for the real ownership by the political bureaucracy. And in the beginning this bureaucracy was in a hurry to complete industrialization, and hid its class composition under that guise.

4.

The development of modern Communism, and the emergence of the new class, is evident in the character and roles of those who inspired it.

The leaders and their methods, from Marx to Khrushchev, have been varied and changing. It never occurred to Marx to prevent others from voicing their ideas. Lenin tolerated free discussions in his party and did not think that party forums, let alone the party head, should regulate the expression of "proper" or "improper" ideas. Stalin abolished every type of intra-party discussion, and made the expression of ideology solely the right of the central forum—or of himself. Other Communist movements were different. For instance, Marx's International Workers' Union (the so-called First International) was not Marxist in ideology, but a union of varied groups which adopted only the resolutions on which its members agreed. Lenin's party was an *avant-garde* group combining an internal revolutionary morality and ideological monolithic structure with democracy of a kind. Under Stalin the party became a mass of ideologically disinterested men, who got their ideas from above, but were wholehearted and unanimous in the defence of a system that assured them unquestionable privileges. Marx actually never created a party; Lenin destroyed all parties except his own, including the Socialist Party. Stalin relegated even the Bolshevik Party to second rank, transforming its core into the core of the new class, and transforming the party into a privileged, impersonal and colorless group.

Marx created a system of the roles of classes, and of class war in society, even though he did not discover them, and he saw that mankind is mostly made up of members of discernible classes, although he was only restating Terence's Stoic philosophy: "*Humani nihil a me alienum puto.*" Lenin viewed men as sharing ideas rather than as being members of discernible classes. Stalin saw in men only obedient subjects or enemies. Marx died a poor emigrant in London, but was valued by learned men and valued in the movement; Lenin died as the leader of one of the greatest revolutions, but died as a dictator about whom a cult had already begun to form; when Stalin died, he had already transformed himself into a god.

These changes in personalities are only the reflection of changes which had already taken place and were the very soul of the Communist movement.

Although he did not realize it, Lenin started the organization of the new class. He established the party along Bolshevik lines and developed the theories of its unique and leading role in the building of a new society. This is but one aspect of his many-sided and gigantic work; it is the aspect which came about from his actions rather than his wishes. It is also the aspect which led the new class to revere him.

The real and direct originator of the new class, however, was Stalin. He was a man of quick reflexes and a tendency to coarse humor, not very educated nor a good speaker. But he was a relentless dogmatician and a great administrator, a Georgian who knew better than anyone else wither the new powers of Greater Russia were taking her. He created the new class by the use of the most barbaric means, not even sparing the class itself. It was inevitable that the new class which placed him at the top would later submit to his unbridled and brutal nature. He was the true leader of that class as long as the class was building itself up, and attaining power.

The new class was born in the revolutionary struggle in the Communist Party, but was developed in the industrial revolution. Without the revolution, without industry, the class's position would not have been secure and its power would have been limited.

While the country was being industrialized, Stalin began to introduce considerable variations in wages, at the same time allowing the development toward various privileges to proceed. He thought that industrialization would come to nothing if the new class were not made materially interested in the process, by acquisition of some property for itself. Without industrialization the new class would find it difficult to hold its position, for it would have neither historical justification nor the material resources for its continued existence.

The increase in the membership of the party, or of the bureaucracy, was closely connected with this. In 1927, on the eve of industrialization, the Soviet Communist Party had 887,233 members. In 1934, at the end of the First Five Year Plan, the membership had increased to 1,874,488. This was a phenomenon obviously connected with industrialization: the prospects for the new class and privileges for its members were improving. What is more, the privileges and the class were expanding more rapidly than industrialization itself. It is difficult to cite any statistics on this point, but the conclusion is self-evident for anyone who bears in mind that the standard of living has not kept pace with industrial production, while the new class actually seized the lion's share of the economic and other progress earned by the sacrifices and efforts of the masses.

The establishment of the new class did not proceed smoothly. It encountered bitter opposition from existing classes and from those revolutionaries who could not reconcile reality with the ideals of their struggle. In the USSR the opposition of revolutionaries was most evident in the Trotsky-Stalin conflict. The conflict between Trotsky and Stalin, or between oppositionists in the party and Stalin, as well as the conflict between the regime and the peasantry, became more intense as industrialization advanced and the power and authority of the new class increased.

Trotsky, an excellent speaker, brilliant stylist, and skilled polemicist, a man cultured and of excellent intelligence, was deficient in only one quality: a sense of reality. He wanted to be a revolutionary in a period when life improved the commonplace. He wished to revive a revolutionary party which was being transformed into something completely different, into a new class unconcerned with great ideals and interested only in the everyday pleasures of life. He expected action from a mass already tired by war, hunger, and death, at a time when the new class already strongly held the reins and had begun to experience the sweetness of privilege. Trotsky's fireworks lit up the distant heavens; but he could not rekindle fires in weary men. He sharply noted the sorry aspect of the new phenomena but he did not grasp their meaning. In addition, he had never been a Bolshevik. This was his vice and his virtue. Attacking the party bureaucracy in the name of the revolution, he attacked the cult of the party and, although he was not conscious of it, the new class.

Stalin looked neither far ahead nor far behind. He had seated himself at the head of the new power which was being born—the new class, the political bureaucracy, and bureaucratism—and became its leader and organizer. He did not preach—he made decisions. He too promised a shining future, but one which bureaucracy could visualize as being real because its life was improving from day to day and its position was being strengthened. He spoke without ardor and color, but the new class was better able to understand this kind of realistic language. Trotsky wished to extend the revolution to Europe; Stalin was not opposed to the idea but this hazardous undertaking did not prevent him from worrying about Mother Russia or, specifically, about ways of strengthening the new system and increasing the power and reputation of the Russian state. Trotsky was a man of the revolution of the past; Stalin was a man of today and, thus, the future.

In Stalin's victory Trotsky saw the Thermidoric reaction against the revolution, actually the bureaucratic corruption of the Soviet government and the revolutionary cause. Consequently, he understood and was deeply hurt by the amorality of Stalin's methods. Trotsky was the first, although he was not aware of it, who in the attempt to save the Communist movement discovered the essence of contemporary Communism. But he was not capable of seeing it through to the end. He supposed that this was only a momentary cropping up of bureaucracy, corrupting the party and the revolution, and concluded that the solution was in a change at the top, in a "palace revolution." When a palace revolution actually took place after Stalin's death, it could be seen that the essence had not changed; something deeper and more lasting was involved. The Soviet Thermidor of Stalin had not only led to the installation of a government more despotic than the previous one, but also to the installation of a class. This was the continuation of that other violent foreign revolution which had inevitably borne and strengthened the new class.

Stalin could, with equal if not greater right, refer to Lenin and all the revolution, just as Trotsky did. For Stalin was the lawful although wicked offspring of Lenin and the revolution.

History has no previous record of a personality like Lenin who, by his versatility and persistence, developed one of the greatest revolutions known to men. It also has no record of a personality like Stalin, who took on the enormous task of strengthening, in terms of power and property, a new class born out of one of the greatest revolutions in one of the largest of the world's countries.

Behind Lenin, who was all passion and thought, stands the dull, gray figure of Joseph Stalin, the symbol of the difficult, cruel, and unscrupulous ascent of the new class to its final power.

After Lenin and Stalin came what had to come; namely, mediocrity in the form of collective leadership. And also there came the apparently sincere kind-hearted, non-intellectual "man of the people"—Nikita Khrushchev. The new class no longer needs the revolutionaries or dogmatists it once required; it is satisfied with simple personalities, such as Khrushchev, Malenkov, Bulganin, and Shepilov whose every word reflects the average man. The new class itself is tired of dogmatic purges and training sessions. It would like to live quietly. It must protect itself even from its own authorized leader now that it has been adequately strengthened. Stalin remained the same as he was when the class was weak, when cruel measures were necessary against even those in its own ranks who threatened to deviate. Today this is all unnecessary. Without relinquishing anything it created under Stalin's leadership, the new class appears to be renouncing his authority for the past few years. But it is not really renouncing that authority—only Stalin's methods which, according to Khrushchev, hurt "good Communists."

Lenin's revolutionary epoch was replaced by Stalin's epoch, in which authority and ownership, and industrialization, were strengthened so that the much desired peaceful and good life of the new class could begin. Lenin's *revolutionary* Communism was replaced by Stalin's *dogmatic* Communism, which in turn was replaced by *non-dogmatic* Communism, a so-called collective leadership or a group of oligarchs.

These are the three phases of development of the new class in the USSR or of Russian Communism (or of every other type of Communism in one manner or another).

The fate of Yugoslav Communism was to unify these three phases in the single personality of Tito, along with national and personal characteristics. Tito is a great revolutionary, but without original ideas; he has attained personal power, but without Stalin's distrustfulness and dogmatism. Like Khrushchev, Tito is a representative of the people, that is, of the middle-party strata. The road which Yugoslav Communism has traveled—attaining a revolution, copying Stalinism, then renouncing Stalinism and seeking its own form—is seen most fully in the personality of Tito. Yugoslav Communism has been more consistent than other parties in preserving the substance of Communism, yet never renouncing any form which could be of value to it.

The three phases in the development of the new class—Lenin, Stalin, and "collective leadership"—are not completely divorced from each other, in substance or in ideas.

Lenin too was a dogmatist, and Stalin too was a revolutionary, just as collective leadership will resort to dogmatism and to revolutionary methods when necessary. What is more, the non-dogmatism of the collective leadership is applied only to itself, to the heads of the new class. On the other hand, the people must be all the more persistently "educated" in the spirit of the dogma, or of Marxism-Leninism. By relaxing its dogmatic severity and exclusiveness, the new class, becoming strengthened economically, has prospects of attaining greater flexibility.

The heroic era of Communism is past. The epoch of its great leaders has ended. The epoch of practical men has set in. The new class has been created. It is at the height of its power and wealth, but it is without new ideas. It has nothing more to tell the people. The only thing that remains is for it to justify itself.

5.

It would not be important to establish the fact that in contemporary Communism a new owning and exploiting class is involved and not merely a temporary dictatorship and an arbitrary bureaucracy, if some anti-Stalinist Communists including Trotsky as well as some Social Democrats had not depicted the ruling stratum as a passing bureaucratic phenomenon because of which this new ideal, classless society, still in its swaddling clothes, must suffer, just as bourgeois society had to suffer under Cromwell's and Napoleon's despotism.

But the new class is really a new class, with a special composition and special power. By any scientific definition of a class, even the Marxist definition by which some classes are lower than others according to their specific position in production, we conclude that, in the USSR and other Communist countries, a new class of owners and exploiters is in existence. The specific characteristic of this new class is its collective ownership. Communist theoreticians affirm, and some even believe, that Communism has arrived at collective ownership.

Collective ownership in various forms has existed in all earlier societies. All ancient Eastern despotisms were based on the pre-eminence of the state's or the king's property. In ancient Egypt after the fifteenth century B.C., arable land passed to private ownership. Before that time only homes and surrounding buildings had been privately owned. State land was handed over for cultivation while state officials administered the land and collected taxes on it. Canals and installations, as well as the most important works, were also state-owned. The state owned everything until it lost its independence in the first century of our era.

This helps to explain the deification of the Pharaohs of Egypt and of the emperors, which one encounters in all the ancient Eastern despotisms. Such ownership also explains the undertaking of gigantic tasks, such as the construction of temples, tombs, and castles of emperors, of canals, roads and fortifications.

The Roman state treated newly conquered land as state land and owned considerable numbers of slaves. The medieval Church also had collective property.

Capitalism by its very nature was an enemy of collective ownership until the establishment of shareholders' organizations. Capitalism continued to be an enemy of collective ownership, even though it could not do anything against new encroachments by collective ownership and the enlargement of its area of operations.

The Communists did not invent collective ownership as such, but invented its all-encompassing character, more widely extended than in earlier epochs, even more extensive than in Pharaoh's Egypt. That is all that the Communists did.

The ownership of the new class, as well as its character, was formed over a period of time and was subjected to constant change during the process. At first, only a small part of the nation felt the need for all economic powers to be placed in the hands of a political party for the purpose of aiding the industrial transformation. The party, acting as the *avant-garde* of the proletariat and as the "most enlightened power of socialism," pressed for this centralization which could be attained only by a change in ownership. The change was made in fact and in form through nationalization first of large enterprises and then of smaller ones. The abolition of private ownership was a prerequisite for industrialization, and for the beginning of the new class. However, without their special role as administrators over society and as distributors of property, the Communists could not transform themselves into a new class, nor could a new class be formed and permanently established. Gradually material goods were nationalized, but in fact, through its right to use, enjoy, and distribute these foods, they became the property of a discernible stratum of the party and the bureaucracy gathered around it.

In view of the significance of ownership for its power—and also of the fruits of ownership—the party bureaucracy cannot renounce the extension of its ownership even over small-scale production facilities. Because of its totalitarianism and monopolism, the new class finds itself unavoidably at war with everything which it does not administer or handle, and must deliberately aspire to destroy or conquer it.

Stalin said, on the eve of collectivization, that the question of "who will do what to whom" had been raised, even though the Soviet government was not meeting serious opposition from a politically and economically disunited peasantry. The new class felt insecure as long as there were any other owners except itself. It could not risk sabotage in food supplies or in agriculture raw materials. This was the direct reason for the attack on the peasantry. However, there was a second reason, a class reason: the peasants could be dangerous to the new class in an unstable situation. The new class therefore had to subordinate the peasantry to itself economically and administratively; this was done through the kolkhozes and machine-tractor stations, which required an increase proportionate to the size of the new class in the villages themselves. As a result, bureaucracy mushroomed in the villages too.

The fact that the seizure of property from other classes, especially from small owners, led to decreases in production and to chaos in the economy was of no consequence to the new class. Most important for the new class, as for every owner in history, was the attainment and consolidation of ownership. The class profited from the new property it had acquired even though the nation lost thereby. The collectivization of peasant holdings, which was economically unjustified, was unavoidable if the new class was to be securely installed in its power and its ownership.

Reliable statistics are not available, but all evidence confirms that yields per acre in the USSR have not been increased over the yields in Czarist Russia, and that the number of livestock still does not approach the pre-revolutionary figure.

The losses in agriculture yields and in livestock can be calculated, but the losses in manpower, in the millions of peasants who were thrown into labor camps, are incalculable. Collectivization was a frightful and devastating war which resembled an insane undertaking—except for the fact that it was profitable for the new class by assuring its authority.

By various methods, such as nationalization, compulsory cooperation, high taxes, and price inequalities, private ownership was destroyed and transformed into collective ownership. The establishment of the ownership of the new class was evidenced in the changes in the psychology, the way of life, and the material position of its members, depending on the position they held on the hierarchical ladder. Country homes, the best housing, furniture, and similar things were acquired; special quarters and exclusive rest homes were established for the highest bureaucracy, for the elite of the new class. The party secretary and the chief of the secret police in some places not only became the highest authorities but obtained the best housing, automobiles, and similar evidence of privilege. Those beneath them were eligible for comparable privileges, depending upon their position in the hierarchy. The state budgets, "gifts," and the construction and reconstruction executed for the needs of the state and its representatives became the everlasting and inexhaustible sources of benefits to the political bureaucracy.

Only in cases where the new class was not capable of maintaining the ownership it had usurped, or in cases where such ownership was exorbitantly expensive or politically dangerous, the ownership surrendered to other strata or other forms of ownership were devised. For example, collectivization was abandoned in Yugoslavia because the peasants were resisting it and because the steady decrease in production resulting from collectivization held a latent danger for the regime. However, the new class never renounced the right in such cases to seize ownership again or to collectivize. The new class cannot renounce this right, for if it did, it would no longer be totalitarian and monopolistic.

No bureaucracy alone could be so stubborn in its purposes and aims. Only those engaged in new forms of ownership, who tread the road to new forms of production, are capable of being so persistent.

Marx foresaw that after its victory the proletariat would be exposed to danger from the deposed classes and from its own bureaucracy. When the Communists, especially those in Yugoslavia, criticize Stalin's administration and bureaucratic methods, they generally refer to what Marx anticipated. However, what is happening in Communism today has little connection with Marx and certainly no connection with this anticipation. Marx was thinking of the danger from an increase in a parasitic bureaucracy, which is also present in contemporary Communism. It never occurred to him that today's Communist strong men, who handle material goods on behalf of this own narrow caste's interests rather than for the bureaucracy as a whole, would be the bureaucracy he was thinking of. In this case too, Marx serves as a good excuse for the Communists, whether the extravagant tastes of various strata of the new class or poor administration is under criticism.

Contemporary Communism is not only a party of a certain type, or a bureaucracy which has sprung from monopolistic ownership and excessive state interference in the economy. More than anything else, the essential aspect of contemporary Communism is the new class of owners and exploiters.

6.

No class is established by its own action, even though its ascent is organized and accompanied by a conscious struggle. This holds true for the new class in Communism.

The new class, because it had a weak relationship to the economic and social structure, and of necessity had its origins in a single party, was forced to establish the highest possible organizational structure. Finally it was forced to a deliberate and conscious withdrawal from its earlier tenets. Consequently the new class is more highly organized and more highly class-conscious than any class in recorded history.

This proposition is true only if it is taken relatively; consciousness and organizational structure being taken in relation to the outside world and to other classes, powers, and social forces. No other class in history has been as cohesive and single-minded in defending itself and in controlling that which it holds—collective and monopolistic ownership and totalitarian authority.

On the other hand, the new class is also the most deluded and least conscious of itself. Every private capitalist or feudal lord was conscious of the fact that he belonged to a special discernible social category. He usually believed that this category was destined to make the human race happy, and that without his category chaos and general ruin would ensue. A Communist member of the new class also believes that, without his party, society will regress and founder. But he is not conscious of the fact that he belongs to a new ownership class, for he does not consider himself an owner and does not take into account the special privileges he enjoys. He thinks that he belongs to a group with prescribed ideas, aims, attitudes, and roles. That is all he sees. He cannot see that at the same time he belongs to a special social category: the *ownership* class.

Collective ownership, which acts to reduce the class, at the same time makes it unconscious of its class substance, and each one of the collective owners is deluded in that he thinks he uniquely belongs to a movement which would abolish classes in society.

A comparison of other characteristics of the new class with those of other ownership classes reveals many similarities and many differences. The new class is voracious and insatiable, just as the bourgeoisie was. But it does not have the virtues of frugality and economy that the bourgeoisie had. The new class is as exclusive as the aristocracy but without aristocracy's refinement and proud chivalry.

The new class also has advantages over other classes. Because it is more compact it is better prepared for greater sacrifices and heroic exploits. The individual is completely and totally subordinated to the whole; at least, the prevailing ideal calls for such subordination even when he is out seeking to better himself. The new class is strong enough to carry out material and other ventures that no other class was ever able to do. Since it possesses the nation's goods, the new class is in a position to devote itself religiously to the aims it has set and to direct all the forces of the people to the furtherance of these aims.

The new ownership is not the same as the political government, but is created and aided by that government. The use, enjoyment, and distribution of property is the privilege of the party and the party's top men.

Party members feel that authority, that control over property, brings with it the privileges of this world. Consequently, unscrupulous ambition, duplicity, toadyism, and jealousy inevitably must increase. Careerism and an ever expanding bureaucracy are the incurable diseases of Communism. Because the Communists have transformed themselves into owners, and because the road to power and to material privileges is open only through "devotion" to the party—to the class, to "socialism"—unscrupulous ambition must become one of the main ways of life and one of the main methods for the development of Communism.

In non-Communist systems, the phenomena of careerism and unscrupulous ambition are a sign that it is profitable to be a bureaucrat, or that owners have become parasites, so that the administration of property is left in the hands of employees. In Communism, careerism and unscrupulous ambition testify to the fact that there is an irresistible drive toward ownership and the privileges that accompany the administration of material goods and men.

Membership in other ownership classes is not identical with the ownership of particular property. This is still less the case in the Communist system inasmuch as ownership is collective. To be an owner or a joint owner in the Communist system means that one enters the ranks of the ruling political bureaucracy and nothing else.

In the new class, just as in other classes, some individuals constantly fall by the wayside while others go up the ladder. In private-ownership classes an individual left his property to his descendants. In the new class no one inherits anything except aspiration to raise himself to a higher rung of the ladder. The new class is actually being created from the lowest and broadest strata of the people, and is in constant motion. Although it is sociologically possible to prescribe who belongs to the new class, it is difficult to do so; for the new class melts into and spills over into the people, into other lower classes, and is constantly changing.

The road to the top is theoretically open to all, just as every one of Napoleon's soldiers carried the marshal's baton in his knapsack. The only thing that is required to get on the road is sincere and complete loyalty to the party or to the new class. Open at the bottom, the new class becomes increasingly and relentlessly narrower at the top. Not only is the desire necessary for the climb;

also necessary is the ability to understand and develop doctrines, firmness in struggles against antagonists, exceptional dexterity and cleverness in intra-party struggles, and talent in strengthening the class. Many present themselves, but few are chosen. Although more open in some respects than other classes, the new class is also more exclusive than other classes. Since one of the new class's most important features is monopoly of authority, this exclusiveness is strengthened by bureaucratic hierarchical prejudices.

Nowhere, at any time, had the road been as wide open to the devoted and the loyal as it is in the Communist system. But the ascent to the heights has never at any time been so difficult or required so much sacrifice and so many victims. On the one hand, Communism is open and kind to all; on the other hand, it is exclusive and intolerant even of its own adherents.

7.

The fact that there is a new ownership class in Communist countries does not explain everything, but it is the most important key to understanding the changes which are periodically taking place in these countries, especially in the USSR.

It goes without saying that every such change in each separate Communist country and in the Communist system as a whole must be examined separately, in order to determine the extent and significance of the change in the specific circumstances. To do this, however, the system should be understood as a whole to the fullest extent possible.

In connection with current changes in the USSR it will be profitable to point out in passing what is occurring in the kolkhozes. The establishment of kolkhozes and the Soviet government policy toward them illustrates clearly the exploiting nature of the new class.

Stalin did not and Khrushchev does not consider kolkhozes as a "logical socialistic" form of ownership. In practice this means that the new class has not succeeded in completely taking over the management of the villages. Through the kolkhozes and the use of the compulsory crop-purchase system, the new class has succeeded in making vassals of the peasant and grabbing a lion's share of the peasants' income, but the new class has not become the only power of the land. Stalin was completely aware of this. Before his death, in *Economic Problems of Socialism in the U.S.S.R.*, Stalin foresaw that the kolkhozes should become state property, which is to say that the bureaucracy should become the real owner. Criticizing Stalin for his excess use of purges, Khrushchev did not however renounce Stalin's views on property in kolkhozes. The appointment by the new regime of 30,000 party workers, mostly to be the presidents of kolkhozes, was only one of the measures in line with Stalin's policy.

Just as under Stalin, the new regime, in executing its so-called liberalization policy, is extending the "socialist" ownership of the new class. Decentralization in the economy does not mean a change in ownership, but only gives greater rights to the lower strata of the bureaucracy or of the new class. If the so-called liberalization and decentralization mean anything else, that would be manifest in the political right of at least part of the people to exercise some influence in the management of material goods. At least, the people would have the right to criticize the arbitrariness of the oligarchy. This would lead to the creation of a new political movement, even though it were only a loyal opposition. However, this is not even mentioned, just as democracy in the party is not mentioned. Liberalization and decentralization are in force only for Communists; first for the oligarchy, the leaders of the new class; and second, for those in the lower echelons. This is the new method, inevitable under changing conditions, for the further strengthening and consolidation of monopolistic ownership and totalitarian authority of the new class.

The fact that there is a new owning, monopolistic, and totalitarian class in Communist countries calls for the following conclusion: All changes initiated by the Communist chiefs are dictated first of all by the interests and aspiration of the new class, which, like every social group, lives and reacts, defends itself and advances, with the aim of increasing its power. This does not mean, however, that such changes may not be important for the rest of the people as well. Although the innovations introduced by the new class have not yet materially altered the Communist system, they must not be underestimated. It is necessary to gain insight into the substance of these changes in order to determine their range and significance.

The Communist regime, in common with others, must take into account the mood and movement of the masses. Because of the exclusiveness of the Communist Party and the absence of free public opinion in its ranks, the regime cannot discern the real status of the masses. However, their dissatisfaction does penetrate the consciousness of the top leaders. In spite of its totalitarian management, the new class is not immune to every type of opposition.

Once in power, the Communists have no difficulty in settling their accounts with the bourgeoisie and large-estate owners. The historical development is hostile to them and their property and it is easy to arouse the masses against them. Seizing property from the bourgeoisie and the large-estate owners is quite easy; difficulties arise when seizure of small properties is involved. Having acquired power in the course of earlier expropriations, the Communists can do even this. Relations are rapidly clarified: there are no more old classes and old owners, society is "classless," or on the road to being so, and men have started to live in a new manner.

Under such conditions, demands to return to the old pre-revolutionary relations seem unrealistic, if not ridiculous. Material and social bases no longer exist for the maintenance of such relations. The Communists meet such demands as if they were jests.

The new class is most sensitive to demands on the part of the people for a special kind of freedom, for freedom in general or political freedom. It is especially sensitive to demands for freedom of thought and criticism, within the limits of present conditions and within the limits of "socialism"; not for demands for a return to previous social and ownership relations. This sensitivity originates form the class's special position.

The new class instinctively feels that national goods are, in fact, its property, and that even terms, "socialist," "social," and "state" property denote a general legal fiction. The new class also thinks that any breach of its totalitarian authority might imperil its ownership. Consequently, the new class opposes *any* type of freedom, ostensibly for the purpose of preserving "socialist" ownership. Criticisms of the new class's monopolistic administration of property generate the fear of a possible loss of power. The new class is sensitive to these criticisms and demands depending on the extent to which they expose the manner in which it rules and holds power.

This is an important contradiction. Property is legally considered social and national property. But, in actuality, a single group manages it in its own interest. The discrepancy between legal and actual conditions continuously results in obscure and abnormal social and economic relationships. It also means that the words of the leading group do not correspond to its actions; and that all actions result in strengthening its property holdings and its political position.

This contradiction cannot be resolved without jeopardizing the class's position. Other ruling, property-owning classes could not resolve this contradiction either, unless forcefully deprived of monopoly of power and ownership. Wherever there has been a higher degree of freedom for society as a whole, the ruling classes have been forced, in one way or another, to renounce monopoly of ownership. The reverse is true also: wherever monopoly of ownership has been impossible, freedom, to some degree, has become inevitable.

In Communism, power and ownership are almost always in the same hands, but this fact is concealed under a legal guise. In classical capitalism, the worker had equality with the the capitalist before the law, even though the worker was being exploited and the capitalist was doing the exploiting. In

Communism, legally, all are equal with respect to material goods. The formal owner is the nation. In reality, because of monopolistic administration, only the narrowest stratum of administrators enjoys the rights of ownership.

Every real demand for freedom in Communism, the kind of demand that hits at the substance of Communism, boils down to a demand for bringing material and property relations into accord with what the law provides.

A demand for freedom—based on the position that capital goods produced by the nation can be managed more efficiently by society than by private monopoly or a private owner, and consequently should actually be in the hands or under control of society exercised through its freely elected representatives—would force the new class either to make concessions to other forces, or to take off the mask and admit its ruling and exploiting characteristics. The type of ownership and exploitation which the new class creates by using its authority and its administrative privileges is such that even the class itself must deny it. Does not the new class emphasize that it uses its authority and administrative functions in the name of the nation as a whole to preserve national property?

This makes the legal position of the new class uncertain and is also the source of the new class's biggest internal difficulties. The contradiction discloses the disharmony between words and actions: While promising to abolish social differences, it must always increase them by acquiring the products of the nation's workshops and granting privileges to its adherents. It must proclaim loudly its dogma that it is fulfilling its historical mission of "final" liberation of mankind from every misery and calamity while it acts in exactly the opposite way.

The contradiction between the new class's real ownership and its legal position can furnish the basic reason for criticism. The contradiction had within it the ability not only to incite others but also to corrode the class's own ranks, since privileges are actually being enjoyed by only a few. This contradiction, when intensified, holds prospects of real changes in the Communist system, whether the ruling class is in favor of the change or not. The fact that this contradiction is so obvious has been the reason for the changes made by the new class, especially in so-called liberalization and decentralization.

Forced to withdraw and surrender to individual strata, the new class aims at concealing this contradiction and strengthening its own position. Since ownership and authority continue intact, all measures taken by the new class—even those democratically inspired—show a tendency toward strengthening the management of the political bureaucracy. The system turns democratic measures into positive methods for consolidating the position of the ruling classes. Slavery in ancient times in the East inevitably permeated all of society's activities and components, including the family. In the same way, the monopolism and totalitarianism of the ruling class in the Communist system are imposed on all the aspects of social life, even though the political heads are not aiming at this.

Yugoslavia's so-called workers' management and autonomy, conceived at the time of the struggle against Soviet imperialism as a far-reaching democratic measure to deprive the party of the monopoly of administration, has been increasingly relegated to one of the areas of party work. Thus, it is hardly possible to change the present system. The aim of creating a new democracy through this type of administration will not be achieved. Besides, freedom cannot be extended to the largest piece of the pie. Workers' management has not brought about a sharing in profits by those who produce, either on a national level or in local enterprises. This type of administration has increasingly turned into a safe type for the regime. Through various taxes and other means, the regime has appropriated even the share of the profits which the workers believed would be given to them. Only crumbs from the tables and illusions have been left to the workers. Without universal freedom not even workers' management can become free. Clearly, in an unfree society nobody can freely decide anything. The givers have somehow obtained the most value from the gift of freedom they supposedly handed the workers.

This does not mean that the new class cannot make concessions to the people, even though it only considers its own interests. Workers' management, or decentralization, is a concession to the masses. Circumstances may drive the new class, no matter how monopolistic and totalitarian it may be, to retreat before the masses. In 1948, when the conflict took place between Yugoslavia and the USSR, the Yugoslav leaders were forced to execute some reforms. Even though it might mean a backward step, they set up reforms as soon as they saw themselves in jeopardy. Something similar is happening today in the eastern European countries.

In defending its authority, the ruling class must execute reforms every time it becomes obvious to the people that the class is treating national property as its own. Such reforms are not proclaimed as being what they really are, but rather as part of the "further development of socialism" and "socialist democracy." The groundwork for reforms is laid when the discrepancy mentioned above becomes public. From the historical point of view the new class is forced to fortify its authority and ownership constantly, even though it is running away from the truth. It must constantly demonstrate how it is successfully creating a society of happy people, all of whom enjoy equal rights and have been free of every type of exploitation. The new class cannot avoid falling continuously into profound internal contradictions; for in spite of its historical origin it is not able to make its ownership lawful, and it cannot renounce ownership without undermining itself. Consequently, it is forced to try to justify its increasing authority, invoking abstract and unreal purposes.

This is a class whose power over men is the most complete known to history. For this reason it is a class with very limited views, views which are false and unsafe. Closely ingrown, and in complete authority, the new class must unrealistically evaluate its own role and that of the people around it.

Having achieved industrialization, the new class can now do nothing more than strengthen its brute force and pillage the people. It ceases to create. Its spiritual heritage is overtaken by darkness.

While the new class accomplished one of its greatest successes in the revolution, its method of control is one of the most shameful pages in human history. Men will marvel at the grandiose ventures it accomplished, and will be ashamed of the means it used to accomplish them.

When the new class leaves the historical scene—and this must happen—there will be less sorrow over its passing than there was for any other class before it. Smothering everything except what suited its ego, it has condemned itself to failure and shameful ruin.

Child of the Revolution

Wolfgang Leonhard

One of the outstanding evils, and one which was frequently the cause of "political collywobbles," was that of the privileges enjoyed by officials. My friends and I who had grown up in the Soviet Union had never known it otherwise, and at first we saw no problem in the preferential treatment given to governmental, economic and Party officials. It was true that as long ago as 1942 in Karaganda, I had thought it not altogether right that there should be such a vast difference in time of war between the great mass of the working class, including many party members who were, in the literal sense of the word, starving, and a small number of party officials who never knew what it was to have the least material anxiety; but then it was only the degree of the officials' privileges that I regarded as excessive, not the fact itself.

A single event made me change my mind. It was in October, 1945, at the beginning of the great campaign for unification. I was just coming out of my office to go to the dining-room of the Central Committee. On the steps I was accosted by a pleasant looking middle-aged man: "Excuse me, Comrade, do you work here?"

"Yes, in the *agitprop* section."

"That's good. I am a K.P.D. official. I have been invited here from the West. I have been given some chits for meals, but I don't know where the dining-room is."

"That depends on what sort of ticket you have."

He looked at me in surprise and showed me his ticket. It was Category II— a ticket for the less important members of staff. I showed him the way.

"But tell me—are the meals different for different members of the staff in the Central Committee?"

"Yes, of course. There are four different kinds of ticket, according to the class of work one is doing. The last two categories are for technicians and clerks."

"Yes, but . . . aren't they all members of the Party?"

"Yes, of course. They are all certified Party members, including the charwomen and chauffeurs and night-watchmen."

He looked at me in astonishment and said, "Different tickets—different meals—and they are all members of the Party!"

He turned and went without another word. A moment later I heard the creak of the front door. My comrade had left the Central Committee building. Thoughtfully, I crossed the courtyard to the dining-room. I went through the rooms in which Categories III and IV—the lower classes—were fed: and for the first time I had an uneasy feeling as I opened the door into the dining-room reserved for our category. Here, at a table covered with a white cloth, the senior members of staff enjoyed an excellent meal of several courses. Curious, I thought, that this had never struck me before!

My thoughts turned to the luxurious villas at Niederschönhausen where Pieck, Grotewohl, Ulbricht, Dahlem, Ackermann, and others lived. I visited them practically every weekend. The whole quarter was fenced off, and the two exits were guarded by Soviet sentries.

"Well, I agree," I said to one of the senior officials who lived there, "I understand the need for security measures, but do they have to—absolutely *have* to—be Soviet soldiers? And of course you need plenty of room to live in; but does it really have to be such a palatial villa? It's not a question of principle, but at a time when everything is short, preferential treatment may well provoke bitter feelings among the population."

The man I was talking to grew serious.

"I should never have expected such antiquated ideas from you. That is simply succumbing to hostile propaganda—it's nothing but a reversion to *petit bourgeois* egalitarianism. Why shouldn't our leading comrades live in these villas? Perhaps you would like to give them back to the Nazis?"

"I never said anything of the kind," I replied. "I am just against these palatial villas at a time when everyone is in such need—in the middle of political controversies in Berlin, where everyone knows that the Social Democrat officials in the West are living on a much more modest scale, and old Kulz, of the Liberal Democrats, is living somewhere in three rooms of a lodging house."

"Sometimes I have the impression that in spite of your responsible position, you are something of a starry-eyed revolutionary idealist."

The words "starry-eyed revolutionary idealist" were spoken in the cold tone of superiority of an *apparatchik*. I said no more. The villas continued, of course; so did the Soviet sentries. Both of them were electioneering points for the S.P.D. in the Berlin elections of October, 1946.

These villas, and the hierarchical grading of the feeding arrangements, were not the only privileges enjoyed by senior officials. The building of the Central Committee in Wallstrasse had been specially equipped, as we came to know at the opening of a Rest Home reserved for members of the Central Committee *apparat*. It was at Bernicke, near Bernau, and it was very luxuriously fitted up for that date. It was surrounded by a huge park, and entirely cut off from the outside world. The feeding there was so sumptuous that it made even the rations at the Central Committee building appear poor by comparison. This was where we used to spend our leave.

Careful attention was paid to rank in the exercise of all these privileges. At first the Rest Home at Bernicke was used by all officials in the Central Committee *apparat*. Not long afterwards, however, a new distinction was introduced: an even more exclusive Rest Home at Seehof was established for the most senior members of the Central Secretariat.

There was also an exact gradation of rank in the distribution of the famous *payoks*, those great parcels of food, cigarettes, tobacco, drinks, and chocolate which we received regularly in addition to our ration cards and our meals at the Central Committee. These *payoks* were not only for middle-grade and senior Party officials, but also for officials in the Government and economic administration, as well as for scientists, specialists, poets and artists: but they were on a sharply graduated scale. Everything depended on the function of the recipient and whether he was a V.I.P.

In Saxony, I met a Party official who worked in the Free German Trade Unions and was well acquainted with the situation in the factories. He trusted me, and was glad to have the opportunity of unburdening himself.

"Between ourselves, we feel our dependence on the Russians much more forcibly down here than you do in higher places, where things are done more politely. For instance, the trouble with these *payoks* —"

"I know what you mean—the workers are feeling bitter about them."

"Yes, they are, but that's not what I meant." He then went on to tell me the story of the fate of a *payok* official in his town.

A loyal party member who had spent years in a concentration camp had come back to his factory, where he was joyfully welcomed by his fellow workers. He soon got an official position again, and came to be regarded as the chief man in his factory. Then came the dismantling of German industry. The Russians told him that he must justify the dismantling to his fellow workers. They promised him that as soon as the dismantling was over, everything would be settled and the workers would be able to go on working unmolested. He believed it, and the workers trusted his explanations. The dismantling was carried out. The workers assumed that everything would now settle down, and they went back to work with great enthusiasm, recovered their machinery from somewhere or other and rebuilt the factory. It was not as good as before, but anyhow the factory was working. A few months passed. The Party official was called to see the Russians again. They told him his factory had to be dismantled again. He remonstrated with them, and reminded them of their promise on the first occasion. He spoke of his own reputation and the prestige of the Party. It was no use. The Russians insisted on the second dismantling. He refused to put their case to the workers. The Russian officer smiled maliciously and said: "If you aren't going to do it, I shall tell your fellow workers what you have been receiving in *payoks* and special privileges." With that, he pulled a list out of his pocket. Every single item that he had received in a year and a half was carefully enumerated. That was when he first began to realize what *payoks* meant. The following day he justified the second dismantling to his fellow workers, but he was no longer the man he used to be: he was completely broken.

It was this story that first taught me that the *payoks* were not merely a generous device for helping loyal comrades, and their purpose was not merely the well-being of the Party cadres.

Translated by C.M. Woodhouse

The Soviet Ruling Class

Michael Voslensky

S 1.

oon after the abolition of food rationing in the postwar period, a book was published in the Soviet Union called *On Good and Wholesome Food*. To the overwhelming majority of Soviet citizens the recipes were useless because of the unobtainability of the ingredients. But it was so successful with the gourmets of the nomenklatura that it soon became a collector's item.

Good and wholesome food is a matter of deep and perpetual concern to the nomenklatura. When one is invited to the home of one of its dignitaries, the variety and quality of the fare is always astonishing. Excellent canteens and buffets are a feature of nomenklatura offices, whether in Moscow or in the provinces, and meals are an agreeable ritual in a nomenklaturist's life.

At the Central Committee of the CPSU, the buffet opens at eleven o'clock and nomenklatura dignitaries soon start dropping in for a second breakfast. All the items in the menu are the best quality and of exceptional freshness; they are also cheap. True, the portions are not lavish, but that has nothing to do with parsimony, for nothing is too good for the nomenklatura; it is simply that the comrades have to watch their waistlines. Black and red caviar is for sale in small saucers, and there are platefuls of salmon or sturgeon. *Kumys*, the celebrated beverage based on mares' milk from the eastern steppes, is always available, the yogurt is as creamy as could be desired, and the sweet cream cheese, always perfectly fresh, melts in the mouth.

At one o'clock, the canteen opens. For a long time this was at October 25 Street, which is now the home of the Slaviansky Bazaar restaurant, with its noisy band and its rather tipsy customers, who drag their feet while dancing. But imagine the place in the days of its glory, when a KGB official in civilian clothes stood close to the big mirror in the vestibule checking passes while carefully selected, reliable waitresses flitted to and fro between the tables, and the majestic and self-satisfied murmur of nomenklaturist conversation filled the rooms.

Though it is not very far from the Central Committee building to October 25 Street—it takes ten minutes on foot and stretching one's legs for that period can be quite agreeable—the nomenklaturists ended by objecting to the fact that they were not sufficiently protected from scrutiny by the outside world during this short transit. They found it intolerable to have to rub shoulders with the ordinary Soviet citizens swarming in the streets around Dzerzhinsky Square, and the unaccustomed promiscuity upset them. Their uneasiness as usual found a convenient alibi in the necessity for political vigilance. They began muttering to one another that a foreign agent might well take photographs of everyone entering the place. Just imagine it, comrades, and the next thing would be that photographs of all the officials of the Central Committee apparatus would turn up in the files of the CIA.

Unsurprisingly, the incontrovertibility of this argument was immediately recognized, and a modern three-story house was built in a narrow street adjoining the Central Committee building where there is a charming seventeenth-century church (the Holy Trinity of Nikitny). This building now houses the canteen. The address is 5 Nikitnikov Street, and nothing on the outside indicates the canteen's existence. Admission is restricted to holders of a Central Committee pass, which a KGB official at the entrance examines with the greatest care. Special passes are issued for persons who do not belong to the Central Committee apparatus but have business in the building. The staff of the Party High School and of the Academy of Social Sciences, attached to the Central Committee, are allowed to use the place an hour before closing time.

On the left inside the huge vestibule there is a kiosk with newspapers and periodicals, and the cash desks are at the back. The cloakroom is on the right. A door near the cash desk provides access to a special buffet at which one can buy every conceivable kind of delicacy. The prices are low, the quality is outstanding, and nothing like it has been seen in ordinary shops since 1928.

A modern-style elevator and a staircase are available to take one to the first or the second dining room. The latter is reserved for customers on a diet. The tables are for four. On a long side table there are kegs containing fruit and vegetable juices and a vitamin-rich drink based on rose hips. One fills one's glass oneself and puts a few kopeks in a saucer provided for the purpose.

The canteen is immediately opposite the building that houses the Central Committee foreign travel department, which is a hybrid organization halfway between the party apparatus and the KGB. It would be inadvisable for anyone to stop here and take photographs.

The cooking is excellent, and only first class produce is used. Here, too, the portions are not large. Consequently, one may well order three, four, or even five items from the menu. The prices are those one would pay for a wretched, unappetizing meal at an ordinary canteen at which workers are lining up for a meal at the same time.

The Central Committee canteen is used both by personnel not entitled to a *kremliovka* and the happy possessors of that privilege. The latter could of course use their cars to go to Granovsky Street or to the "government's house," where, as they say in Russian, everything is available except birds' milk (though to make up for that you can buy in the Central Committee buffets those delicious sweets called "Birds' Milk").

But nomenklaturists endowed with *kremliovka* coupons do not do that, for it is not advantageous. For one of those coupons can be exchanged for a meal that can be taken home; as we have already mentioned, a single portion is enough for a whole family. That is why the Central Committee canteen is used not only by heads of desks, consultants, and other high officials of the apparatus who have *kremliovkas*, but also by powerful heads of divisions of the Central Committee, who are officially senior to ministers of the Union.

The buffet reopens before the end of the working day, and although all the Central Committee officials could go there again, usually they do not. A first-class meal is waiting for them at home, and having a snack at the buffet would be improper. Instead one can go to another place that is also called a "buffet" but is actually a luxury delicatessen where one can pick up things one has previously ordered, just as higher officials pick up their parcels in Granovsky Street.

The canteens of organizations controlled by the Central Committee are similar in style, though rather more modest. They are to be found at the Party Higher School, the Academy of Social Sciences, the Institute of Social Sciences, and the Institute of Marxism-Leninism. The menu may be a little less extensive, but everything else is the same, and the prices are low.

At the hotel of the International Department of the Central Committee, housed anonymously in a building at No. 12 Plotnikov Street, quite near the Arbat, meals are completely free. Foreign visitors can use the hotel restaurant and order whatever they like, including wine and spirits, all entirely free. The same applies to the central committee "hostels" in all the socialist countries; and it is notably the case in the guesthouse of the East German central committee, a sumptuous new building opposite the Märkisches Museum, in East Berlin.

The nomenklatura in the provinces is looked after in the same way. In all the capitals of the Union's republics, in every big regional center, there are central committee canteens to which the public has no access. They are not exact replicas of the Central Committee canteen in Moscow, but successful imitations.

We shall pass over in silence the quality and quantity of the nourishment provided for those at the topmost level of the nomenklatura, who are entitled to a so-called special diet, which is of course provided free of charge. Meanwhile ordinary Soviet citizens have to line up to buy poor-quality food at high prices. Let us repeat that a gulf divides the nomenklatura from the rest of the population.

2.

The width of that gulf is even more striking when nomenklaturist accommodation is compared with that of ordinary Soviet citizens.

For the population at large the housing problem is so acute that it is actually admitted by the authorities. Party and government resolutions, and speeches and articles in the press, agree that, while Soviet citizens enjoy all the good things of life, the exception is the housing problem, which has not yet been satisfactorily solved. "Activity on a gigantic scale" is of course taking place in the building sector, and with every day that passes every citizen has a better chance of improved living conditions. Nevertheless the target announced at the beginning of the sixties, that every citizen should have a room to himself, is still far from having been reached. The Soviet norm is nine to twelve square meters of habitable space per person. In the West, as I have had occasion to note, that figure is generally not understood, or is taken to apply to a bedroom. And particularly rare are those who understand that twelve square meters of habitable space is not a guaranteed minimum, but a permitted maximum; space in excess of the norm was formerly simply confiscated, and in 1984 the rent was tripled. An area of about five square meters per person is considered to be "in a situation of distress in the housing sector" and is put on the waiting list of the housing service of the district soviet. The wait is generally a long one.

None of this applies to the nomenklatura. Our head of desk has no truck with waiting lists or the district soviet, but is given an apartment in a building belonging to the Central Committee. Nevertheless every nomenklaturist is always trying to change his apartment for a bigger and more comfortable one. Conversation in nomenklatura circles continually revolves around moving, i.e., giving up good accommodations for better. Soviet newspapers are delighted when they are able to report that somewhere or other in the Soviet Union "a

32

worker's family has improved its housing conditions." The subject is not new; immediately after the October Revolution the party ceremoniously set about installing working-class families in bourgeois homes. In 1920 the poet Mayakovsky celebrated in verse the installation of a working-class family in an apartment equipped with a bathroom, but no one has yet written a poem about nomenklaturists' moving into bigger and better homes. Meanwhile new and sumptuous residences are built in the best neighborhoods for the central, regional, or town committee of the party or the Council of Ministers, and are shown from a distance to tourists as new buildings reserved for workers.

Housing for the nomenklatura is built under special supervision and is not standardized or jerry-built. Good, solid buildings contain spacious apartments, quiet elevators, wide and comfortable staircases. In Moscow, residential complexes of this type are situated on the Kutuzovsky Prospekt or in the Kuntsevo district. There are also isolated buildings of this type in between ordinary buildings in central but quiet streets in the capital; one of these is the celebrated building in Granovsky Street facing the Kremlin canteen; another is the new building in Stanislavsky Street. In East Berlin there is a district that the Germans call the Volga German district, which means that residential complex is inhabited by Germans who have a Volga official car.

The times have passed when victorious Communist workers emerged from their cellars to install themselves in the homes of the wealthy. Aristocratic homes and districts have reappeared under the real-socialist regime, and carefully selected workmen have access to them only to carry out repairs.

These homes are large; they may have as many as eight rooms. Especially important nomenklaturists may be allotted a whole floor, consisting of two adjoining flats turned into one.

The excessive size of nomenklatura apartments by Soviet standards is revealed by statistics. We quote from an official publication giving the number of inhabitants of the Soviet Union in 1975 and the habitable space available. The total population of 253,261,000 persons occupied 1,798,589,000 square meters of habitable space. The impressiveness of these figures running into thousands of millions no doubt explains why they passed the censor. Simple division shows that the number of square meters per person was seven. As we have seen, the figure of twelve meters per inhabitant is a permitted maximum and not a guaranteed minimum, and there is still a long way to go before it is achieved for all.

In an overpopulated city like Moscow, with its 7.6 million inhabitants (1975), the situation is acute, and the waiting lists of persons admitted to be in a situation of distress in the housing sector, that is, having less than five square meters each at their disposal, are never-ending. In spite of that, the Moscow average is fifteen square meters per person, or more than double that of the rest of the country. This is explained by the large number of nomenklaturists living in the capital. Their spacious apartments make it appear on paper to be the best-off city in the Soviet Union so far as housing is concerned.

Taking into account the habitable space actually available, an average Moscow family of four ought to be occupying an apartment of sixty square meters *now*, and not in a radiant Communist future.

The causes of the Moscow housing crisis are not technical, but social. If the inhabitants of Moscow live in such overcrowded conditions, it is not because the habitable space available in Moscow is too small, but because the nomenklatura occupies too much of it, at the expense of workers who have been on a waiting list and have been living with their families in single rooms for years....

3.

Once upon a time—it was actually before the October Revolution—Russian liberal intellectuals sarcastically translated the phrase *bien-être général en Russie* as "It's a good thing being a general in Russia." Since then the purifying storm of the October Revolution has blown itself out, and nowadays being a general in Russia is even better than it used to be.

But do generals and other highly placed personages really feel they are living in Russia? I have actually heard it suggested in nomenklatura circles that above a certain level in the hierarchy, nomenklatura officials behave as if they were living not in the USSR but in another, entirely different, and special country.

Ordinary citizens are just as carefully isolated from that country which we shall call Nomenklaturia, as they are from foreign countries. It is the country of the special, with special accommodations built by special builders, special country houses and vacation homes, special hospitals, out-patients' departments, and convalescent homes, special products sold in special shops, special buffets and canteens, special hairdressers, garages, gas stations, and license plates, a special information network, special kindergartens, schools, and institutions of higher education, special waiting rooms at stations and airports, and even a special cemetery.

A member of a nomenklatura family can spend his life from the cradle to the grave working, resting, eating, shopping, travelling, talking, or being ill without ever coming into contact with the Soviet people, whom he is supposed to be serving. The barriers that separate foreigners from Soviet citizens also separate the nomenklatura from the mass of the population, with the difference that, while foreigners are not allowed contacts with the citizens of the country, the nomenklatura imposes that ban on itself.

A detailed description of Nomenklaturia would take us too far afield. So let us take a swift bus tour of the geopolitically highly original country of real socialism.

It was discovered by Lenin on October 25, 1918. On that day, accompanied by his sister Maria and Krupskaya, his wife, he went for the first time to the country house that had been made ready for him at Gorky, near Moscow. It had been confiscated from a rich landowner named Reinbot, and it was the first "state dacha" in the history of Nomenklaturia. At the entrance Lenin was ceremoniously presented with a bouquet by the Cheka guards. The discoverers of Nomenklaturia inspected the whole house, "overcome with astonishment," as a journalist noted, "at the sight of the furniture, carpets, chandeliers, and Venetian mirrors in their guilded frames." Lenin ordered everything to be left as it was and settled down comfortably in all this luxury, which he evidently did not find in the least disturbing. He modestly referred to the place as "our dacha," for it would have been embarrassing to call it "our estate" or "our summer palace." Thus "dacha" became the established term to designate the numerous palazzi subsequently built by the nomenklatura.

In 1920, while the civil war was still raging, the incipient nomenklaturists had developed such a taste for luxury that in September of that year a so-called Kremlin control commission was appointed for the purpose of examining "the question of Kremlin privileges" (that was the official term) and, as far as possible, "bringing them within bounds that would be acceptable to every party comrade." This was announced in the *Izvestia of the Central Committee of the Russian Communist Party* (which was what the CPSU was called at the time) on December 20, 1920, that is, between Stalin's birthday and Brezhnev's. The result was modest; the commission and the newspaper that published this news item were abolished, but the privileges were not.

The Eleventh Party Congress, in 1922, settled for a less ambitious objective, namely "to put an end to *great* disparity between the pay scales of differing groups of Communists." In October 1923 a Central Committee circular was even more discreet; it simply criticized the "expenditure of public funds on the equipment and furnishing of the homes of leading figures," "the furnishing of official offices and private dwellings," and the "use of the unbudgeted public funds for the country houses of certain officials." The circular concluded that it was necessary "to increase the salary of responsible colleagues to assure them of a minimum standard of living."

In February 1932 the ceiling on party members' pay (the "party maxi-mum," introduced by Lenin) was done away with, thus eliminating the last obstacle in the way of the nomenklaturists' rapid rise to material prosperity. At the same time, there was an appalling famine in the Ukraine, but by now the nomenklatura was establishing itself as a class, and it began increasing its pay by means of secret decisions.

Here is the text of one of them. It is still top secret in the Soviet Union, but it is to be found in the so-called Smolensk Archive, which was taken from Germany to the United States after the war:

Not for publication. Decision No. 274 of the Council of People's Commissars of the U.S.S.R. and of the Central Committee of the CPSU dated 11.2.1936. *On increasing the salaries of leading district officials.*

The Council of People's Commissars of the U.S.S.R. and the Central Committee of the CPSU resolve that

1. From February 1, 1936, the pay of presidents of district executive committees and of first secretaries of district committees of the party is to be increased to 650 rubles in 50 percent of the districts and to 550 rubles in the other 50 percent, and the pay of deputy presidents of executive committees and second secretaries of district committees is to be increased to 550 and 450 rubles respectively; the salaries of managers of the agriculture, trade, and finance departments, managers of district branches of the State Bank, heads of the cultural and propaganda department of the district committee, and the secretary of the district committee of the Komsomol are to be increased to 500 and 400 rubles respectively,

2. In accordance with a special list to be approved by the Orgburo of the Central Committee of the CPSU the presidents of 250 district executive committees and the first secretaries of 250 specially important party district committees are to be granted a salary of 750 rubles; the deputy presidents of the district executive committees and second secretaries of party district committees are to receive a salary of 650 rubles;

3. These salary increases to be carried out within the framework of the 1936 budget.

The President of the Council of People's Commissars of the U.S.S.R. Molotov.

The Secretary of the Central Committee of the CPSU Stalin.

At the same time, the nomenklatura established special canteens and shops for itself, its excuse being that during the first half of the thirties food and textiles had to be rationed.

Having acquainted ourselves with the living and working conditions that prevail in Nomenklaturia at the present day and seen the apartments and the dachas, let us now take a look at another sector: the hospitals, convalescent homes, and out-patient departments.

There are many holiday resorts in the Soviet Union, but it would be difficult to find one where the Central Committee or the Council of Ministers does not have a sanatorium. Even if our head of desk took it into his head to "bury himself" in a small and out-of-the-way resort such as Berdyansk, on the Sea of Azov, where I was born, he would not have to mingle with the common herd in an ordinary rest home, for the town party committee has a dacha reserved for nomenklaturists. No matter how much he was willing to pay, an ordinary Soviet citizen could not gain admission to a rest home or dacha of that category.

Here nomenklaturists are among themselves. A surprising consequence is the extraordinary license that prevails in these places. Nomenklatura officials who for eleven months of the year maintain a façade of impeccable marital fidelity here make up for lost time, men and women alike. This is generally accepted, and everyone knows that there will be no difficulties with the party when they go home.

A characteristic feature of the nomenklaturist is his concern for his health. According to his own story, he exhausts himself in grueling work, and if you compliment him on how well he looks he replies that appearances are deceptive. But it is not his appearance that is deceptive, but the pretense that he is perpetually overworked.

He and his family are looked after by the Fourth Medical Administration of the USSR Ministry of Health (formerly known as the Kremlin Medical Administration). The family is allotted to the Kremlin hospital and the Kremlin out-patients' department, where they will always see the same doctor. This luxuriously appointed medical complex occupies two buildings on the Kalinin Prospekt at the corner of Granovsky Street and a little road near the Arbat. Malicious tongues say of it, "*Poly parketnye, vrachi anketnye*"—"parquet flooring and doctors picked by questionnaire"; and the doctors are indeed selected for their political qualifications. They are not expected to do much doctoring, but simply to chat pleasantly with their patients. If a nomenklaturist complains of anything that shows signs of being at all serious, he is referred to a consultant. The consultants are eminent specialists, members of the Academy of Medical Sciences of the USSR, and the best of them are personal physicians to the Soviet leaders. In 1952, when Stalin cooked up the famous "doctors' plot," the whole of the Soviet medical elite vanished into the underground cells of Lubianka, the KGB headquarters. The old dictator had no confidence in doctors picked by questionnaire, so when he was taken ill in the middle of the doctors' plot he had no medical attention. He died of a stroke while his personal physician, Professor Vinogradov, was chained in a cell in the Lubianka, where he was periodically beaten by the dictator's own orders.

The Kremlin hospital equipment and pharmacopoeia are imported from the West (the nomenklatura never relies on local medical skill and pharmacology when its health is at stake). The food and nursing are outstanding, and the staff are numerous, well trained, and smiling. This is in striking contrast to conditions in ordinary hospitals, where every corridor is encumbered with beds, the staff is inadequate, and the food so bad that it is impossible to manage without food parcels sent in by one's relatives. Convalescent and chronically ill nomenklaturists are sent to an annex of the Kremlin hospital in the wooded park of Kuntsevo, outside the city.

A Soviet writer, A. Bek, has described the Kremlin hospital in a novel about the life and death of a nomenklaturist. The patient's "room" consists of "an office, a bedroom with a balcony, a bathroom, a vestibule leading directly to a carpeted staircase." This "bright and spacious apartment" is furnished with soft armchairs, carpets, expensive statuettes," and on the wall there are pictures "in massive gilt frames." This apartment is in the semiluxury category. The mind boggles at the thought of what the luxury category must be like.

4.

Let us turn our attention to the transport sector in Nomenklaturia.

We have already mentioned that our chief of desk can live in comfort, work, and rest without ever coming into contact with the Soviet people. Even in the course of his travels across the vast spaces of the Soviet Union he can avoid all contact with his compatriots. He obtains his rail or air tickets directly from the Central Committee transport section, which is accommodated in an inconspicuous little house behind the Central Committee complex. The American journalist Hedrick Smith reports, with naïve Western indignation, an Intourist guide's complaints that places are kept vacant in all hotels, trains, and aircraft in case a high official should unexpectedly turn up. Soviet citizens have long since learned to take that for granted; they know the best places are reserved for the government quota (bronya) and that tickets for them are not sold until thirty minutes before departure time, for a nomenklaturist might turn up at any moment.

Trains and aircraft are always overcrowded. Not till I arrived in the West did I discover that it is perfectly possible just to go to a station and buy a ticket.

In the Soviet Union the lines at the advance booking offices are interminable, and a reserved seat is a great privilege.

Our chief of desk sets out in a black Volga with his ticket in his pocket. Instead of mingling with the vulgar mob at the station, he goes to a private waiting room called the waiting room for deputies to the Supreme Soviet. The officials whose duty it is to look after nomenklaturists are proud of this description, which sounds democratic and in harmony with the spirit of the constitution. No, it seems to say, the place is not reserved for big shots, but is an ordinary waiting room for the representatives of the people to whom we have given our votes. And who is to tell that for most of the time it is nomenklatura officials who use this room, with its upholstered furniture and soft carpets and special staff, and not deputies to the Supreme Soviet, the number of whom who are on the move at any one time is not sufficient to justify the existence of a vast network of such waiting rooms? There was also another problem. How was the existence of these places to be explained to foreigners, who were very conscious of not being deputies to the Supreme Soviet? The answer was simple. The words "VIP Hall," in English, appeared on the panel outside the door. Nobody was likely to be offended by being referred to as a very important person.

Polite staff—very different from those who deal with other travelers—take our head of desk straight to the train or aircraft some minutes before other travelers are invited to do the same; he must be spared the necessity of meeting people on the platform or in the gangways, and in his first-class sleeping compartment or in the first class on the aircraft he is among his fellows again. When the aircraft lands, the mobile steps are first taken to the first-class exit and our man walks down them, to be greeted by an assembly of local bigwigs. Only then are the other passengers allowed to get out. When he gets out of the train, he unfortunately has to mingle with *hoi polloi*, but not for long, for it is only a few paces to the "deputies' waiting room" on the arrival platform. An official car will be waiting for him at the exit to take him to the place where he will be staying in comfortable surroundings ideal for the preparation of his speech to the members of the party on some classical theme such as: "Unity of party and people."

5.

Let us now turn to the subject of education in Nomenklaturia. Here, too, everything is for the best; the children of the nomenklatura have not been forgotten.

Certain difficulties had to be overcome. After the October Revolution it was announced that all children without exception were to have the same schooling. But at the time of the giddy ascent of the Stalinist nomenklatura, at the end of the thirties, special schools were established, making it appear that they did not want their offspring to mix with the children of ordinary folk. The official purpose of these schools was to train future artillery officers for the Red Army of Workers and Peasants (which was what the Soviet Army was then called), but in fact these were privileged establishments that had nothing whatever to do either with workers or peasants or artillery.

This military-proletarian camouflage has since been given up. Nomenklatura children are nowadays entered into special schools where they are taught in a foreign language (English, French, or German); the children of diplomats or other important persons employed abroad are sent to special boarding schools.

Also, at university level the children of nomenklatura dignitaries are saved from having to mingle with ordinary students. That is the reason for the existence of the Higher School for International Relations, in Moscow; here an elitist caste spirit prevails for which the Corps des Pages in the days of the czars provides the only parallel.

A number of institutions of higher education are reserved for the nomenklatura; the Central Committee's Party Higher School, the Foreign Ministry's diplomatic academy, the Academy of Foreign Trade, the Komsomol Central School, the military academies, the KGB Higher School and the Ministry of the Interior's academy. Some of these establishments accept only students who have already completed a course of study and have a certain amount of experience of the workings of the party. That is how the children of the nomenklatura are trained to take over responsible positions in it.

The taste for university degrees is very widespread in these exalted circles and has to be taken account of. Since 1947 there has been an institution in Moscow for granting doctor's degrees to nomenklaturists; this is the Academy of Social Sciences, attached to the CPSU Central Committee. I was for some years a member of the council of that institution, and I can say that in no ordinary university are such efforts made to extract a thesis from the future doctor. Each professor or lecturer has the same number of students as in other universities, but it is the production of doctoral theses that takes up most of his time (all that is required of him otherwise is that he publish one article a year). Admission to the institution is by decision of the Secretariat of the Central Committee of the CPSU at the request of republican or regional party committees. The students' living conditions are first class. They live in a comfortable hostel inside the academy; the canteen food is excellent; their allowances are nearly equal in value to their teachers' salaries; and they are sent abroad for long spells to enable them to gather material for their theses. All this has nothing in common with the life of the ordinary students, who live in overcrowded hostels, hurriedly eat Spartan meals in the university canteen, have a very small allowance, and do not go abroad even in dreams. Nevertheless their theses are on the whole better than those of their privileged colleagues. Everyone knows that theses written at the Academy of Social Sciences are invariably accepted, and that their standard is invariably low.

If the average student at this establishment is less gifted, it is partly due to the fact that selection is solely for political reasons. The special atmosphere that prevails in the place plays an even bigger part in bringing this about. A student who has been recommended by the party and approved by the Central Committee Secretariat knows from the outset that he has been considered in high places as being worthy of being granted a degree. Consequently if he fails to get one it must be the fault of the director of studies. The mere fact that students have already been enrolled in the Central Committee nomenklatura and that after receiving their doctorates they will immediately be appointed to positions of responsibility in the party apparatus results in their looking down on the professors who are feverishly writing their theses for them. The children of the Athenian aristocracy probably looked down on their slave schoolmasters in the same way.

According to these figures quoted by Ilya Zemtsov, who worked for the science department of the Central Committee, 63 percent of the Central Committee staff have a degree, and in the case of the central committees of the republics the figure is 73 percent. A big change from the first generation of a ruling class that boasted of not having finished secondary school!

The nomenklatura officially forms part of the "intermediate social stratum of intellectuals" and makes claims to culture. In a nomenklaturist's apartment one generally finds a full bookcase containing not only the classics of Marxism but also handsomely bound copies of Russian authors (including the *émigré* Ivan Bunin) and foreign authors in translation. It is difficult to tell whether these books are read or are merely decoration, but at any rate they have been bought. Nomenklaturists stick faithfully to their rule of marking themselves off from others by ordering books that are difficult to obtain. But a nomenklaturist's library never includes suspect books. After Khrushchev's downfall, his collected speeches were quickly removed from the shelves, as were copies of the periodical *Novy Mir*, which published Solzhenitsyn in 1962 and 1963. Pasternak's poems (the posthumous edition) or the works of Anna Akhmatova might still be on the shelves, but that is by no means certain. There must be nothing to suggest that the owner of these books has any "unhealthy interests," as it is so charmingly put.

Theater tickets are easily obtainable by nomenklatura officials. But it is not advisable for a nomenklaturist to acquire the reputation of being a theater fan, which would suggest that he was not a serious person and might raise doubts about his taste. Consequently it is the adolescent children of the nomenklatura or relatives and friends who have failed to secure admission to it who chiefly benefit from these theater tickets.

In fact the number of such friends is small, for the sagacious members of the ruling class quickly and correctly interpret the coded instructions that come down to them from above "that for security reasons" they should restrict their social contacts and as far as possible not make friends outside the nomenklatura. They also realize that these instructions are intended not so much to protect official secrets (a point on which in any case all nomenklaturists show the greatest discretion) as to protect the secret of the *dolce vita* led by the nomenklatura.

6.

Let us have a glance at retirement pensions in Nomenklaturia.

Years have passed, the children of our head of desk have grown up and have themselves become nomenklaturists, and the time has come for him to enjoy his "well-earned retirement," as the saying is. Unlike ordinary citizens, he does not have to obtain a whole mass of references to support an application to the local security office for a pension that will not exceed 120 rubles (152 U.S. dollars) a month. A resolution of the Central Committee Secretariat will entitle him to a personal pension on the Union scale, and he will continue to occupy a Central Committee apartment and take his vacations at a Central Committee rest home. A military nomenklaturist of general's rank will live in a dacha of which he is legally the proprietor, and if he wishes to build he will be granted a plot of one hectare instead of the .08 hectare ordinary people are allowed—in other words, twelve and a half times as much. Colonel-generals and generals (to say nothing of marshals) come into what is called the Defense Ministry's "paradise group" when they retire. They retain all their privileges—an official car with driver, an official apartment, an aide-de-camp, free rations and uniform, etc.—without having to do any work in return.

Western readers may well be tempted to object that a four-room apartment, a country villa, an official car, a pension of a thousand dollars a month is not to be sneezed at, it's true, but it isn't a fortune.

The answer is that it is a fortune. Wealth is relative, and no arithmetical figures can be given for it. To the great mass of the Soviet population, what a nomenklaturist receives is a veritable fortune.

Above all, it is a privilege. Man is a social animal; he does not consider his situation in isolation, but in relation to that of other members of the society in which he lives. When you, dear reader, walk down the street, you have no particular feelings about it. But suppose a tyrannical authority forced all people to advance on their hands and knees and subsequently in its kindness allowed you to resume your normal stance; imagine how proud and delighted you would be. You would do everything in your power to "justify the confidence" placed in you, as they say in the USSR.

This way of looking at things is not peculiar to nomenklaturists. I have often noted with interest that Western journalists who have worked in Moscow look back with nostalgia to the time they spent there. There is no objective reason for this: it is extremely difficult to obtain any information apart from what has already been officially published; foreign correspondents are subject to KGB surveillance; they can write nothing that upsets the authorities without exposing themselves to all sorts of unpleasantnesses or sanctions that may go as far as expulsion; contacts with the local population are minimal; all sorts of things, including food parcels, have to be sent from abroad; accommodation is worse than it would be in the West, and as non-Soviet citizens, they are not free to travel wherever they like. Living in Moscow can be interesting professionally to a western journalist, but what is it that makes life there so attractive to him?

The answer is that it is his privileged status. In spite of all the inconveniences to which he is subjected, he is incomparably better off than the ordinary people of Moscow. To the latter, his apartment, though inferior to what he would have at home, represents an inaccessible marvel. They cannot buy things in special shops, and still less can they buy things from abroad. They cannot go abroad and buy things to bring back or have Western books and publications sent them, and they cannot talk politics freely. They creep on all fours while Western correspondents walk on their two feet—even though they have to bend—and this privileged status acts like a charm on their memory.

It is this privileged status that is all-important to the nomenklatura, though its material advantages must of course not be underrated.

We have looked at this very special country that is Nomenklaturia from the point of view—neither too high nor too low—of the head of a Central Committee desk. Now, Nomenklaturia is a mountainous country characterized by the fact that the higher the altitude the more fertile the soil and the more succulent the fruits.

The difference between the head of a desk and a deputy head of a division in the Central Committee leaps to the eye as soon as you enter their offices. You walk into the former's office straight from the corridor; it is comfortable, but small and characterless. The *zam. zav.* (deputy head of a division) has a smart office with a vestibule and a secretary who, to avoid any possibility of scandal or gossip, is generally no longer very young (the most exalted officials have male secretaries). When the head of a desk needs transport, he sends for an official car from the Central Committee pool, while the *zam. zav.* has a car and driver to himself. He does not go to a holiday home, but to a comfortable dacha suitable for use all the year round, with staff provided; and naturally he has a higher salary, *kremliovka* coupons of the first category, and a better apartment. Mounting still higher in the hierarchy, we reach the level of first deputy head of a division, who no longer belongs to the nomenklatura of the Central Committee Secretariat, but to that of the Politburo. So he has still greater privileges.

The first secretary of a regional party committee is a kind of omnipotent satrap, the other secretaries being merely his assistants. All these people not only have higher salaries, official residences and dachas, cars, free food, and special hospitals and convalescent and rest homes; they also have practically unlimited opportunities of drawing on the material wealth of their region. Now, the territory of a region is almost as big as that of an average European country.

The head of a Central Committee division perhaps enjoys fewer material advantages than these regional satraps, but he has one foot on the ladder to the top leadership of the nomenklatura. The head of a big division is also a secretary of the Central Committee and is thus one of those who take their place on Lenin's tomb and wave to the crowd on special occasions; he is one of those whose faces are recognized in press photographs and on television.

He is far higher in the world than our head of desk, and the two are not reunited even in death. When the latter dies, *Pravda* will print a brief announcement in a black border, or a brief tribute signed by a "group of comrades." The merits of a deceased head of a division or a first secretary of a regional committee will be the subject of a long obituary, accompanied by his picture and the signatures of members of the Politburo. But our head of desk will have no cause for complaint. His widow will not have to apply to a trade-union committee that will reluctantly give her twenty rubles (26 U.S. dollars) for the funeral expenses, but will be given a state funeral, a convoy of Chaikas and black Volgas will follow the hearse, speeches will be made at the so-called lay funeral service, and after the return from the cemetery Armenian brandy will be drunk to the memory of the departed. In front of the luxurious bier, a brass band will strike up the famous

You bravely fell in the terrific fight
In the service of the workers
You gave all to bring them well-being and light . . .

The desk head's burial will not take place in a cemetery for ordinary mortals, but in a special one at the Novodevichy monastery, where the remains of nomenklaturists lie in splendid stone tombs. Among them are those of Stalin's wife, Alliluyeva, and her relatives, Kosygin's wife, and Khrushchev. The widow, who will have completely taken over her husband's way of thinking, will complain bitterly that he never reached the highest level of the nomenklatura, which would have entitled him to burial in the Kremlin wall in Red Square; and she will note that dead generals are given military honors here in the Novodevichy cemetery, while her husband did not get them, though he loved nothing so much as pomp, power, and honors.

7.

And how do the highly placed comrades live who greet the crowd from the top of Lenin's tomb and are later buried in the Kremlin wall? A nomenklaturist who moved in those exalted circles once told me that they lived like the richest American multimillionaires.

The salaries of the Soviet leaders are top secret. But there are rumors that the salary of a secretary of the Central Committee of the CPSU, and even the Secretary-General is about a thousand rubles. That is of course much better than the average worker's 181 rubles a month but is far short of the multimillionaire level. So how is the difference made up?

In the first place, each of these people also has his pay as a deputy to the Supreme Soviet, as well as other fees. Much more important is that he has an open account at the State Bank that enables him to draw on public funds for any sum that he may need at any time. Secondly, he has no need to draw on that account or on his salary, as he does not need money, for at this level everyone lives in luxury at the state expense without opening his purse. The *gensek* (Secretary-General) has only to pick up his vertushka and tell the head of the Central Committee administration to have a house or dacha built for him. He will have to sign a party decision to this effect, and some time afterward his new home will be fully furnished with every modern convenience, ready to move into, and carefully guarded.

The Secretary-General will thus be much better lodged than a big company chairman in a capitalist country. An idea of how "they" lived at the time is not to be obtained from Henri Barbusse's description of the little house in the Kremlin in which Stalin received him—while laughing behind his

45

mustache at so much naïveté. But two houses in Moscow dating from the Stalin period enable one to see for oneself.

One of them, now the Tunisian Embassy, on the Sadovaya Ring, near Vosstania Square, used to be Beria's palace, and at the time it was inadvisable to walk along the big gray stone walls with bricked-up ground-floor windows—not that there was any inducement to do so with all those grim-looking individuals in civilian clothes standing about. Pedestrians used either to cross to the opposite pavement or at least walk in the roadway. Nowadays ordinary Soviet citizens still cannot enter the place because of the same grim-looking figures, now in militia uniform. But even if one is invited to an embassy reception there, it gives one a grisly sensation to walk through those parquet-floored rooms where revolting orgies took place with terrified girls taken there by Beria's bodyguard. In the basement, Beria himself tortured prisoners who were brought there for his entertainment. A selection of specially prepared and carefully looked-after instruments of torture were found there after his downfall. There are a number of small cells in the basement with heavy iron doors fitted with spy holes in which citizens of the country of the victorious socialism were kept and tortured by a member of the Politburo with his own hands, because he enjoyed it. There is also a small door that is kept firmly barricaded. Either it conceals some dreadful secret or, as rumor maintains, it provides access to an underground passage to the Kremlin.

Another, less macabre building was opened to the public about twelve years ago; this is where Maxim Gorky lived, and it has been turned into a museum. If after thirty years of hesitation it was at last decided to open to the public this baronial mansion that was the home of a proletarian writer, it was because the master of the house was, according to his own confession, only a "literary master craftsman" and did not belong to the ruling elite of the nomenklatura. But the brilliant chandeliers of the Gorky palace reveal the truth about its lifestyle even then. Stalin and members of his Politburo came here as guests, and they did not do so just to escape from their cramped apartments for a few hours and be able to stretch their limbs in comfort.

There is also in Moscow a monumental relic of the post-Stalin period, the Cuban Embassy, in the Pomerantsev Pereulok. Malenkov was not satisfied with what the old dictator provided for the members of the Politburo, that is, two apartments in Moscow: one in the Kremlin and the other in Granovsky Street, opposite the Kremlin canteen. So he had himself built a supplementary residence or, rather, a large palace, which later turned out to be big enough to house an embassy, complete with offices, reception rooms, and ambassador's residence. If he never benefited from all this, it was because Khrushchev unceremoniously threw him out.

But the nomenklatura did not exactly languish in poverty in Khrushchev's time either. Before Stalin's annihilation of Lenin's old guard, a cooperative estate of dachas, all of them small and simple wooden buildings, had been built for old Bolsheviks. It was called *Zavety Ilyicha* ("Lenin's testament"), but the people of Moscow ironically gave the same name to the palaces built on the Lenin Hills, behind Moscow University, for Khrushchev's "collective leadership."

There is a high, cream-colored stone wall with a heavy iron gate behind which are the guards. A house in the middle of a big garden is almost invisible from the street. Unless it is desired to have dealings with a *toptun*, which is what KGB guards in civilian clothes are called, loitering here is not advisable. But if you are one of the elect, your driver merely flashes his lights and the iron gate is opened. You advance through the garden, followed by the suspicious eyes of uniformed KGB officers, and you enter the palace through a heavy door. It is a huge, massively constructed building, decorated with wood carvings, marble statues, glass chandeliers, and open fireplaces. The reception rooms are on the ground floor, there is another suite of big rooms on the second floor, and the bedrooms are at the top. That was how the leaders of the party and the government were accommodated under Khrushchev. And how are they accommodated today?

The Lenin's Testament estate on the Lenin Hills is still unoccupied. The houses, furnished in neutral official style, are now used for distinguished foreign guests. The leaders of the party and the government have left their palaces for democratic apartments. One of them is theoretically secret, but the secret is known to everyone. A militiaman in uniform demonstratively stands guard outside No. 26 Kutuzov Prospekt, a Central Committee building. Next to the entrance there is a small red panel saying No Standing—Parking Prohibited. Leonid Brezhnev occupied a five-room apartment there with his wife, Victoria Petrovna, and the rest of his family, and his neighbor was said to be Yuri Vladimirovich Andropov, then president of the KGB. The numerous wings of the building accommodate the families of middle-grade Central Committee officials. Ordinary citizens were actually allowed to cross the big courtyard without being subjected to an identity check. They could also rejoice that under the new Ilyich there was a return to the Leninist taste for simplicity.

In fact Brezhnev practically did not live there. The apartment was registered in his name, the domestic staff were in residence, and members of the family and Victoria Petrovna were sometimes to be seen there. But, like the other members of the governing elite, the supreme overlord lived in an official dacha near the village of Usovo, not far from Moscow, and the town apartment served the same purpose for him as the Kremlin cell served for Stalin. The Usovo dacha, incidentally, belonged to Stalin. It is known as the *dalniaya* (distant dacha), to distinguish it from the *blizhniaya* (near dacha), near Kuntsevo, where Stalin died. Khrushchev was the next occupant of the "distant dacha." As he had a sense of publicity, he allowed photographs of this two-story white palace, with its colonnades, balconies, and suites of reception rooms, to be published in the Western press....

8.

This lifestyle results in a special mentality. I myself had occasion to savor it for a few days in Sofia in the summer of 1970, when I was there with M. D. Millionshchikov, first vice-president of the Academy of Sciences of the USSR and president of the supreme soviet of the Russian Soviet Federated Socialist Republic (R.S.F.S.R.), and A. P. Vinogradov, the vice-president. We were accommodated in a government palace that had belonged to the sister of Czar Boris of Bulgaria and later to Vasil Kolarov, the former Bulgarian Communist leader. It is in a quiet street near the center of the city. Everything is as it should be: a wall with a heavy iron gate, guards by the entrance, and a shady garden at the back. To the right of the front door two Chaikas with governmental license plates and dignified chauffeurs waited. There was a large staff, but we had dealings with only one of them, no doubt the chief steward. You could ask him for anything you liked, and the dish, the wine, or brandy you wanted would be produced immediately. In a small office next to the drawing room there was a telephone—the Bulgarian vertushka. When we had enough to eat and drink, we had only to beckon and a Chaika drove up immediately; an agent of the security service opened the door and off we went through Sofia, keeping to the middle of the road and dutifully saluted by the police. After the meetings, banquets, and receptions the Chaika would reappear and whisk us back to the palace. A few days of this made one feel completely detached from real life. I very soon found this intolerable and started going for walks. But it is of course perfectly possible to get used to it. A man as dynamic and sociable as M. D. Millionshchikov, who lived in a single-family house in Moscow and always stayed in government residences when he traveled in the various republics of the USSR or in the countries of the Eastern bloc was capable of spending hours sitting in the garden in the warm Bulgarian sunshine without being worried in the least by this splendid isolation.

Yes, it is perfectly possible to get used to it, but it ends by blunting one's sensibilities and completely insulating one from humanity and ordinary life.

Stalin tried to find a remedy by watching films that—so he believed—showed him the life of the people. At the Twentieth Party Congress, Khrushchev made fun of him for having no sources of information other than films, but soon we learned that he relied on them himself, though they were newsreels. In fact neither Stalin nor Khrushchev really knew how the people whom they governed lived. Svetlana recalls that Stalin was completely ignorant of current prices and knew only prices of the prerevolutionary Russia.

The Stalin tradition of ruling the people without having even an approximate idea of how they live remains intact. Contact between the leaders of the nomenklatura class and the people are limited to official visits to the federated republics or to the regions in the course of which they are—not unwillingly—shown Potemkin villages by zealous subordinates. If banquets and meetings leave any time for this.

The nomenklaturists have dug a gulf between themselves and their subjects. With their hearts full of anxiety and contempt, they shelter themselves behind their sevenfold fences and the KGB, talking in the meantime about their "links with the masses" and denouncing as renegades those who publicly express their dissatisfaction with the nomenklatura regime. But isn't it the nomenklatura class, the class of *déclassé* officials, that by reason of its nature and lifestyle has become a class of outsiders? What else is one to call a class of persons that actually live like foreigners in their own country?

That, then, is how the nomenklaturists live. There is no point in comparing it with the way of life of the privileged classes in the bourgeois West. The essential feature of capitalist society is not privilege, but money; in real socialist society it is not money, but privilege. This makes the nomenklatura both arrogant and nervous, for it is well aware of the reactions that the constant growth of its privileges rouse in the population. The nomenklatura are beginning to feel anxious; like rulers whose reign is terminable without notice, more and more they fear a fatal outcome. The following joke went the rounds of the nomenklatura in the seventies.

One day the mother of a Central Committee official, who lived in a kolkhoz, came to visit him. She was shown his luxurious Moscow apartment and his dacha and was given excellent *kremliovka* meals. Unexpectedly she wanted to go home as quickly as possible.

"What's the matter, Mother?" her son asked. "It's lovely here; why don't you want to stay?"

"Yes, it's certainly lovely here," the old woman replied, "but it's dangerous. Suppose the reds come?"

Translated by Eric Mosbacher

Stepping Down from the Star

Alexandra Costa

We arrived at Washington's Dulles Airport on August 24, 1975. Our friend Gennady met us at the airport. My very first impression of America was a feeling that I had stepped into a sauna—I was unaccustomed to the heat and humidity that is typical of Washington's summers. Although summer temperatures in Moscow occasionally reach 90 to 95 degrees, the climate there is much dryer and the heat is more tolerable. It was a relief to get into an air-conditioned car (another alien thing, since Soviet-made cars do not have air conditioning). The size of the car was impressive, and I thought briefly that it must require quite an effort to handle it. Watching Gennady handle the steering wheel with what appeared to be just one finger, I could not help but ask him how he managed to do it.

"It's not me." He laughed. "On cars of this size, the steering and brakes are electrically enhanced. It only gets heavy when the electrical system is out of order, which is not often."

The car slid smoothly out of the airport onto the Dulles Access Road and then took a turn to the Capital Beltway. Things got more and more confusing. I expected to see an "industrially developed" country, as it is traditionally described in the Soviet press: buildings crowding each other, heavy smog. Instead I saw mostly open space, clusters of trees, occasionally high-rise buildings and small houses, and very blue sky. I asked Gennady how far away from the city we were.

"We *are* in the city," he replied. "Just about in the middle between the center and the outer bounds." He caught my puzzled look and added, "It'll take some getting used to, but we'll guide you through the first days. It happens to everybody who comes here for the first time. We all help newcomers to adjust."

The embassy had arranged for us to stay in the apartment of an embassy family on vacation in Moscow at the time. That way we had a couple of weeks to find an apartment and arrange for other necessities and still be comfortable, rather than having to live out of suitcases in a hotel. There were other Soviet families in the apartment complex in Riverdale, the Washington suburb where we were to stay, and one of them volunteered to assist us in the transition. The apartment was ready for our arrival. Gennady and his wife had even done some grocery shopping for us, and we found that the basic necessities such as milk, eggs, and baby formula were already in the refrigerator; on a coffee table was a box of disposable diapers for our baby daughter—another new thing! Gennady only waved back when we offered to pay for the groceries. "Forget it," he said. "What are friends for?"

Within minutes of our arrival, the apartment was filled with people from the embassy, each bringing something for the table, and we had a welcoming party. We were prepared, too. Before we left Moscow, we had been told that certain simple things from home, such as black bread, salted herring, and smoked salami were always in demand in the Soviet colony abroad, and we brought a generous supply with us. We put it all on the table as our contribution, and I saw the nods of approval from the people around us. We had done our homework and made the first step toward being accepted in the community. The party lasted several hours, with people coming and going. Although we were completely exhausted from the long flight, our friends explained that they were keeping us up intentionally in order to break the jet lag. Otherwise the eight hours' time difference would be felt for days. The trick worked—we were so tired the next morning we slept late and got up at the normal Washington morning hour.

Gennady arrived soon after breakfast to take Lev to the embassy for introductions and a discussion of future arrangements. Before they left, he said, "First thing you have to do is buy a car. Without it, you are helpless here. I will make arrangements with our senior mechanic to take you to the dealership tomorrow."

The men left. I cleaned up the apartment and tried to get familiar with the things in it. I figured out fairly quickly what a few containers on the kitchen counter were for. Most appliances were familiar. The stove did not look all that different from the one we had in Moscow, although I would have to get used to the fact that I did not need matches to light it—Soviet stoves do not have pilot lights. The toaster on the counter was similar to the one I used in Moscow. Earlier, Gennady had shown me how to use a coffeemaker.

As I started to do the dishes, I remembered that nothing on the counter seemed to be a dishwasher liquid. Perhaps the apartment owners had run out of it before they left. I took the soap from the bathroom and used it for the dishes. It also seemed strange that there was no rack or some other place to put clean dishes to dry. I started looking in the cabinets, and discovered that one of them had several rows of drying racks. Some still had glasses and plates on them. I put the dishes in and called my new acquaintance next door, a woman named Valentina, to tell her I was ready to go shopping. She came over and we started making a shopping list. I mentioned the washing liquid. "But you have a whole box of detergent, right here," she said, and pointed to one of the boxes that I thought to be a clothes detergent. "You should not use liquid in the dishwasher." Seeing incomprehension in my eyes, she laughed. "Of course, I forgot," she said. "You know, after you spend several years here, you begin to forget all the things that do not exist back home." She opened what I thought was a cabinet with the racks. "This is a dishwasher. Here you don't have to do dishes by hand." And she showed me how to use the machine.

My first reaction was embarrassment. The rest of my feelings were more difficult to sort out. What else was in store for me on my first day in this strange country? Here I was, a worldly woman by Moscow standards. Lev and I were very well off back home. Our apartment was well equipped, or so I had thought up till now; we had access to special stores and many things that were out of reach for most of my countrymen. I travelled to several foreign counties as a tourist, and Lev had visited many counties, including the United States, as a member of scientific delegations. He had often told me of his travels and of the different things he had seen. And yet I could not figure out some of the obviously everyday things in this rather modest apartment. What next?

"Next" turned out to be the supermarket where Valentina took me after we had finished the list. The shopping trip turned into a guided tour. At least half of the items simply did not exist in the Soviet Union. The produce and household goods aisles were most confusing. I did not even know that so many varieties of fruits and vegetables existed on earth, let alone on supermarket shelves. The household goods took at least half an hour to go through while Valentina patiently explained the merits of such things as plastic wrap, various detergents, "quickie" floor mops, and the myriad of other items. I had already been introduced to the wonder of disposable diapers the night before, but the selection of baby food and instant baby cereals stopped me dead. In Moscow, having a baby meant hours of labor every day: washing diapers, cooking cereals, grating and mashing fruits and vegetables by hand. All of a sudden it occurred to me that having a baby here did not mean being tied up in the kitchen for half a day. What a wonderful surprise!! I remembered my American friends who had visited us in Moscow. When they had mentioned that they had six children, it had sounded unbelievable to me that a charming woman such as my American acquaintance would want to spend her life between the kitchen counter and the clothesline. Now I realized that in this country you could have more than one child and still have time and energy for other things in life.

Another incredible thing was that I could buy everything in one place, have it packed in bags, loaded into the car, and be home in an hour! In Moscow, I often had to go to several different stores to do my grocery shopping: the bakery, produce store, general grocery store, and on and on. Without a car I had to make several trips to complete my shopping because I could only carry so much in two bags. Even in larger stores that had produce and bakery departments, each department had its own counter and, naturally, its own line. I decided that someday I would calculate how many years of my life I had spent standing in lines and doing household chores. Even without exact calculations, I knew that this country was already giving me the greatest gift I could dream of—my time.

But the most amazing thing was the profusion of color. Color, color everywhere. Things *looked* pretty. Soviet life is essentially colorless. The consumer products are generic and often scarce. An item may be produced by hundreds of factories through the Soviet Union, and will look the same everywhere. A bar of low-grade household soap is invariably brown; a better hand-soap is always pink. A typical grocery shelf in the Soviet Union looks like a generic brand section in the supermarket—plain paper with dark lettering on everything. There is no need to make things attractive. First, if you need something, you buy it no matter how it looks; second, the factories are compensated by the quantities they produce. Whether an item is sold later or not, and whether things produced by one factory sell better than from another, is not the concern of the factory directors. Many things such as butter, sausage, and sour cream, are not packaged at all but sold by weight. If the item is solid, it is cut, weighed, and wrapped in plain paper at the counter. For things that cannot be wrapped—such as sour cream—it is necessary to bring a container from home. All this weighing and wrapping at the counter is time-consuming and creates those infamous lines so often described in the Western press. In many instances, however, the lines are not the result of scarcity but simply inefficient organization.

The scarcity of man-made color does have at least one positive effect. The Russians are very appreciative of the beauty nature provides and try to make it a part of their lives as much as possible. The first fragile flowers appear on the streets of Moscow early in the spring, sold on the street corners by private entrepreneurs from the southern republics. From then on, there are tiny flower markets everywhere until the end of fall. The flowers are not inexpensive since most of them come from private sources, but people buy them anyway. In Moscow it's not the migrating birds that signal the spring; it's when you see people in the crowd carrying the first bunches of yellow mimosas.

The lack of color partially explains the fascination Russians have with foreign goods. Not only is the product better; it also looks pretty and brightens up your apartment. It is not unusual to keep empty containers from foreign-made hairspray in the bathroom, or a dishwashing liquid in the kitchen, long after the contents were used up, just for decoration. When I was a student of foreign languages, I often worked as an interpreter with foreigners and received a lot of small gifts, especially cosmetics, and my friends always asked me to give them the empty containers.

By the time we got home from the supermarket, my head was spinning from all the new information I was trying to absorb. And, as though everybody conspired to finish me off, Gennady had already made arrangements for us to go buy a car the same afternoon.

Buying a car in the Soviet Union was an experience that could rival anything Kafka ever put on paper. You have to live through it to believe it. It has to be planned long in advance, much as young families here plan for their dream house. My particular encounter started in 1967, when the Soviet Union put in operation an Italian-built plant in Togliatti which was to produce a Soviet version of the Fiat-124 called the "Zhiguli." The local newspapers announced that on January 20 the automotive store in Leningrad, where I lived with my parents, would be "signing up those citizens who desire to purchase a car." It also announced that any previous signups through the automotive club and other semiofficial groups would not be honored—strictly first come, first served.

There was only one automotive store in Leningrad, a city with a population of four million. There is no need for another—the cars are allocated by quota throughout the country. This store's annual quota was six hundred cars.

The line started to form on the eighteenth. In order to prevent blocking in the street, the sign in the store window directed people to the back door, where it had a large empty lot capable of holding crowds.

By the time we arrived in the evening of the nineteenth, our number in line was something over twenty-five hundred. Volunteers from the line were keeping track of arrivals and conducting roll calls every hour. Anybody who missed the roll call was struck out from the list. It was about twenty below, and almost impossible to stay in place. People were bundled in several layers of clothing and used their ingenuity to keep themselves warm—some with coffee mixed with brandy, some with vodka straight from the bottle. Most came in families, with family members taking turns out in the cold while the others were warmed up in shelters—heated staircases of nearby buildings, or for the lucky ones with older cars, inside their cars parked on the street with motors running. There were only two of us—my mother and I, but we struck a deal with a couple next to us to take turns on the roll call for each other so we could spend less time exposed to the cold.

By seven in the morning the crowd had grown to over four thousand people and the police closed the entrance to the street to everyone except the residents and store employees. The store opened at eight. Signup cards were distributed quickly. All we needed to do was to fill in our names and addresses, hand the card over, have the number assigned to us, and go home. Within three hours, our turn came. Our number was 1856—apparently some people left the line during the night or missed the roll call. I was jubilant—in three years I would be able to buy a car. It did not matter that I did not have 9,000 rubles—I doubted that many people in the line did either.

For three years, once a year I received a postcard from the store requiring me to appear in person to confirm my registration. Finally, in 1970 a notification arrived that I could purchase my car. By then I was living in Moscow. Luckily, as a graduate student, I had only a temporary registration for Moscow residence. My permanent address was still in Leningrad and I was eligible for car purchase.

I still did not have 9,000 rubles, however. My father could cover about half the sum, but he was happy with his old car and did not want to spend money on a new one. Finally, after lengthy negotiation he agreed to lend me the money. I was planning to marry Lev, and it was obvious that he had the means to repay the debt. Under the worst circumstances, I could resell the car. It just did not make sense to go through what we had for registration and not take advantage of it now.

The Soviet Union has no financial system from which people can borrow money—banks, credit unions, or anything like that. There is a State equivalent of a savings bank where people can keep their money and earn 2 percent interest, but you cannot withdraw more than you put in. The only source of financing is friends, and money is constantly borrowed and repaid between friends—sometimes "till the paycheck," sometimes "until needed." It is always a gentleman's agreement, and no interest is charged, although I've heard of loan sharks who do it for profit. Primarily, the habit developed from the fact that most major purchases cannot be planned in a timely manner, but depend on supply and luck. It was not uncommon to get a phone call from a friend who found herself at a store at a time when an imported refrigerator or piece of furniture was announced to be available for sale, and was strapped for money. Since most of those rare commodities sold out in a matter of hours, the only way to cope with it was to get a cashier's reservation, usually for an hour or so, and start calling friends to see who had money on hand. A couple of times I had to catch a cab and deliver money to a friend in need at the other end of the town. It goes without saying that my friends did the same for me more than once.

Therefore it did not take long to collect the necessary amount—we had only one week from notification date to claim the car—and soon I was the owner of a shining new Zhiguli. For two weeks I happily drove it around Moscow. Then Lev and I broke up. Angry and frustrated, I contacted a friend of mine who was not an unfamiliar figure in the Moscow black market and asked him to help me to sell my car, splitting the profit fifty-fifty with him for his services as a mediator.

Selling a car in the Soviet Union is an easy way to make a profit, since there are always people who want to buy them but cannot do so legally, either because they live in remote places where the allocation of cars is next to nothing, or because they have illegal income, which quite a few Soviet people do—from moonlighting or taking bribes. Of special value are cars won in the State lottery. The ticket is often purchased for twice the value of the car since the owner can claim that he won the car in a lottery rather than having to explain to the authorities where in the world he had gotten that much money on a grocery clerk's salary. Another way for reducing the official value of the car is to sell it through the State-owned consignment store. Since the seller names the price at which the car is consigned, the purchase price can be officially low. The store takes 7 percent commission and does not ask any questions. The rest of the money for the actual price agreed upon is paid on delivery, in cash. It took my friend only two days to find a buyer who was willing to pay 19,000 rubles for my Zhiguli. A week later I paid off my debts to my friends and spent my share of the profit on a nice Phillips stereo system in a consignment store for foreign goods. Soon Lev and I reconciled and decided to get married. I had my fiance back, but the car was gone.

Obviously I did not expect to find anything close to that car-buying nightmare here, but I did not expect what I saw either.

Oleg, the embassy senior mechanic, took us to an Oldsmobile dealership where the embassy bought most of its official cars. It did not occur to me to question the choice. At the time I could not tell the difference between one car and another. I had seen American cars parked in front of the American Embassy in Moscow, and they all looked the same to me—long, sleek, and elegant. Gennady drove a Delta Royale, and it certainly looked good enough for me.

The salesman, introduced as Derek, greeted Oleg as an old friend—which he almost was, since he was in charge of car purchases at the embassy. We walked to the new car lot, and there I got my second shock of the day. There they were, rows of long, sleek, shining cars—just walk in and pick one.

"I want a silver one," I managed to say. The salesman started to explain the standard features, most of which did not make any sense to me. Finally he said, "What options do you want on you car?"

Options?

I was saved from total humiliation by Oleg, who said, "We'll take it out of stock, and there is only one silver car." He then launched into the price negotiations, which made me feel even more confused. Finally the salesman started to write a long bill of purchase. Out of the long list I made out the word "discount." Was it because the embassy was getting a special consideration?

"You can pick up the car tomorrow morning," the salesman said.

"We'll pick it up in three hours," Oleg replied, and, without listening to Derek's protests that it was not enough time to prepare the car properly, shook hands with him, took me to his car, and drove away.

Against the Odds:
A True American-Soviet Love Story

Andrei Frolov and Louis Becker Frolova

I was one of eleven American students who had come from all over the United States for a year's worth of research in the archives and libraries of Moscow. Once before, at the age of seventeen, I had traveled to the Soviet Union, but this time around everything was to be different.

The first time I had come with my parents, brother and sister. We spent two weeks in the Soviet Union as tourists, our time split between Moscow and Leningrad. The foreigner who does not know the Russian language and who comes to the Soviet Union for only a short while is given a very limited glimpse into Soviet life. He or she stays at special "Intourist" hotels where only foreigners and special Soviets live. The quality of the rooms and restaurants surpass anything available to the regular Soviet. One must show a pass in order to enter an Intourist hotel. The guards at the doors have an excellent eye for spotting Westerners and Soviets attempting to pass as Westerners. The foreign tourist is shuttled about on special tours in special buses all designed to show the visitor the best view of Soviet life. A common stop on these tours is at a *Beriozka* store—a special store for foreigners. The Soviet officials hope that the foreigner will plunk down some of their "hard" foreign currency—*valuta* in Russian—in exchange for items that are not found in ordinary stores for Soviet citizens. After a busy day of sightseeing and shopping the foreigner will take in an evening at the Bolshoi or the Mariinsky Theaters, tickets for which are impossible for the ordinary Soviet citizen to obtain without using connections and paying exorbitant prices.

Foreign visitors might complain about certain shortcomings in their accommodations, about how the quality and variety of their meals decrease as the tour continues, and about the lack of acceptable souvenirs to choose from. But they have been given the first and best of everything. It clouds their vision. They make judgments on the Soviet Union based on what they have been shown: the closed stores, the closed hotels, the special seats to the theater. They have no idea how distant all of that is from everyday Soviet reality. It is a trick like that played on Catherine the Great by one of her ministers and lovers, Commander General Potemkin. When Catherine went on a royal tour to inspect the reforms being undertaken in the countryside, the good General had scores of impromptu villages built along the road that the Empress traveled upon, thus giving her the impression that the Empire's money was well-spent and the conditions of her serfs' lives were improving. Similarly the foreign visitor is treated to a show of "Potemkin villages," as the Russian expression goes.

This time, however, at age twenty-seven, I had come to the Soviet Union for nine months to gather research for my dissertation. I would be living and working amongst Soviet citizens. I was excited at the prospect of seeing the Soviet Union behind the Potemkin villages set up for tourists. Yet, despite close contact with Soviet citizens I was not to be in the mainstream of Soviet life. Over and over again I found that being a foreigner was all-important; it determined my living conditions and my relationships with people. "Foreigner" was my official status and my social position. In every way we foreigners were privileged and apart from the rest of Soviet society. Some Soviets refer to foreigners as "whites" and themselves as "blacks." Evoking visions of our own not so distant past in America, they joke about the closed "Intourist" hotels and *Beriozka* shops where entrance is "for whites only." As exchange students we were not given the luxuries reserved for foreign tourists, but nonetheless we received the special treatment that the Soviet Union offers its own most important citizens.

We were given accommodations in the dormitories at Moscow University, for twenty years considered the best that a university student could aspire to. The campus grounds are extensive, but the majority of offices and classes and all of the dormitories are in one monstrosity of a building. Its dimensions are massive with four wings and a main corpus. There certainly are taller and larger buildings in the United States, but this building is of solid stone and its every line emphasizes its significance. It was built in the famous Stalinist "wedding-cake style" with various tiers and ornate carvings leading up to the red star on the top of a spire. Standing in front of Moscow University one cannot help but feel dwarfed and overcome by its granite might. Its wings stick out from the central corpus like legs on a spider and the individual feels like a fly in its midst.

We Americans lived two to a *blok* : in other words, we shared a toilet, shower and sink and each had our own room. The room was small, long and narrow, perhaps six feet by twelve feet, and the bathroom had long ago been taken over by large, slow-moving cockroaches. It was not paradise but it was assigned to me alone and that constituted its luxury to Soviet students. On the other side of the dormitory and on the floors where there were no foreigners from capitalist countries, Soviet students often lived two, and in some instances as many as four, to a room. Only the cream of the crop and those living in close proximity to foreigners were granted the privilege of their own living quarters.

Besides these living arrangements, my income also was provided by the state. As a foreign student from a capitalist country I received a living stipend of 220 rubles a month—almost two and a half times the stipend of a typical Soviet student of my age and training. The 220 rubles were barely adequate for us Westerners. I have no idea how the Soviet student got by on his 90 rubles a month, which is the equivalent of half a pair of blue jeans, the student uniform in the Soviet Union.

In such a privileged position, I was left only with the problem of obtaining food—the greatest everyday concern of Soviets. They spend an incredible amount of time and energy in the pursuit of nutritious and appealing foods, often taking off from work in order to stand in line. People travel to Moscow and other major cities to acquire the basic foodstuffs that are not available in other parts of the country. We students got by on the regular methods and by taking advantage of a number of sources open to us as foreigners.

Every floor of the dormitory had two kitchens, thirty people to a kitchen. Thirty people cannot share one kitchen. It is difficult to feel a strong sense of responsibility for a facility used by so many people and the kitchen was usually filthy. The alternative was to eat in the student cafeteria which, like all Soviet cafeterias, is a hit or miss proposition. On some days the food was quite nice, hot and filling. On other days it was abysmal, inedible and appetite-depressing.

I took to eating bread and chocolate, both of which are quite delicious in Moscow, if bought fresh. For nourishment I ate at people's homes, a fairly frequent occurrence. Any invitation by a Soviet results in a meal.

It is amazing what people will serve in their homes. Moscow food stores offer so little: cabbage, carrots, potatoes, meat of poor quality, canned fish. And yet in one home after another the foreigner is treated to a feast, from appetizers to dessert. In the beginning I asked: "How is it possible? I didn't see any of these foods in the stores?" Some people smiled in answer, some people laughed.

Soviets had long ago formed other outlets. A huge illegal or semilegal market in food still exists. People establish their own networks for getting food, food that is skimmed off the top of government stocks and sold at great profit. You can read about it in any political science text but you can only understand it when you go to a friend's apartment and sit down to eat *blini* (Russian crepes) with black and red caviar and lingonberry jam for dessert after you have spent an afternoon running after eight mealy apples, a can of sardines and a half-kilo of macaroni.

While I did not use these illegal outlets I soon received instructions on how to better my diet. I went to the open air market where farmers brought the fresh fruits and vegetables they had raised on their own small land parcels that the state had granted to them for private use. The prices were very high, but I had the money.

I also had the option of using my hard currency at the diplomatic grocery store. In this store the Soviet government itself has skimmed from the top of its stocks in order to provide its foreign guests with edible produce, in exchange for *valuta*. Here the food is expensive, but there are no lines and the variety and quality are vastly better than in the stores for Soviets. For some reason the liquor was cheap, a liter of Stolichnaya vodka, which is not available to Soviet citizens, came to $4.50, so I always brought liquor to greet my hosts who fed me.

We students were feeding only ourselves and not a family. We had money, the diplomatic store and frequent invitations to dine at people's homes. Still, despite our advantages, we experienced the pressure involved in obtaining food. We stood in lines, in crowds with people pushing from all sides, everyone trying to get just that much closer to the counter even though the number of customers ahead in line remained the same. We witnessed fights erupting over places in line. We came to master the system of standing in more than one line at a time. And finally we came to understand that tense, glum look of Muscovites as they pushed and shoved and bustled down the street, ever-pressured by the problem of providing for themselves and their families with the basic necessities and a few touches here and there.

Of course, a country is most keenly experienced through contacts with its people, but again my status as a foreigner determined with whom I had relations and the nature of those relations.

Russians say that Americans think only about money, that Americans use one another and act solely out of self-interest. I found much of this avarice in the Soviet Union, as well as much of its opposite. In every society one gets by on a developed sense, an instinct based on experience about who wants what from whom. In the Soviet Union the rules of the game were so different that in the beginning I had no sense, no instinct to rely on. Like the fly before the spider, at times I felt overwhelmed and helpless.

Dormitory life in Moscow presented an odd mix of people. Our floor was filled with students from capitalist countries—America, England, West Germany, France, Holland and Japan. There were a few Russians on the floor as well but most of the other inhabitants were either from Soviet Central Asia or from Arab countries. There was a veritable platoon of Palestinian Freedom Fighters and their families. For some reason the Palestinian students liked to congregate in the center of the floor. Day or night, as I stepped out of the elevator I was met by a group of Palestinians playing backgammon on the couch next to the floor phone.

Half of the Americans had been placed at one end of the floor where several students from the British Isles had already been living. They seemed quite happy to see us and the first introductions took place a half hour after our arrival. There was a Welshman, an Englishman and a third fellow they called the "Lord." The "Lord" had bright red hair and a striking face, was a bit overweight and spoke in the most beautiful upper crust English. He smiled when his colleagues joked about his aristocratic heritage, but we had no reason to distrust the truth of what they said.

We stood in the corridor, these three fellows, my roommate, and I, gabbing on and on. We had a myriad of questions, technical questions, such as where certain university offices were located, what were the procedures for acquiring all the necessary ID's and passes. We then began to speak in general about conditions in the dorm and in Moscow. They wanted to know what sort of things we had brought with us—if any of them would serve us well in exchange for rubles. The Welshman did most of the talking. He kept poking the Lord in the side and saying: "That's right, isn't it?" The Lord did not respond directly. He spoke about the importance of improving our Russian, how we could best do this, and what cultural events we ought to attend.

The Welshman became more animated. He seemed to be chuckling, enjoying a private joke. Finally he came clean.

"So where do you think the Lord is from? Where did he get his schooling?" he asked.

Judging by his impeccable English I was tempted to say Oxford, but the Welshman broke in.

"Here. He's from here! He's a Sov!"

Sure enough the Lord had received his excellent training in Moscow. I had never heard anyone speak English as a second language that well. I was impressed. But why had we been talking about selling things in front of him? Why had he asked about our friends in Moscow?

The Lord was the only Soviet who lived on our side of the floor. He was always polite and helpful. A week never went by when he did not knock on our door with an offer of tea and a "heart-to-heart" in English. We talked a lot about Soviet theater and film and student life. He was curious about my other acquaintances in Moscow: "Oh really, you went to see that new film on Dostoevsky? With whom?"

Our conversations rarely rolled around to politics. He acted as if politics did not interest him and everything in the political realm had long ago been understood and decided. He casually asked about life in America, as if that did not really interest him, when actually he was bursting to hear about the size of my apartment and my car. Occasionally he would interject a question about the availability and cost of certain items in the United States—items that interest any student of any country: sporting equipment, photographic equipment, motorcycles and cars. I would answer these questions explaining the various models and alternatives that exist, to which he invariably replied, "Yes, you have so much in America, but no one can afford to buy anything."

My first week in Moscow also brought a visit from Vladimir, a "business-man." A knock at my door and he introduced himself.

"Well, hello. So this year's crop of Americans has arrived. I've been waiting for you."

He was in his late twenties, well dressed, with short clipped hair and a breezy, familiar manner of speech. He proceeded to run off a list of names of Americans he knew from previous exchanges. He seemed to know someone from every university that we represented, and it was comforting to hear him speak the names of people we knew. He invited us out, to parties, to restaurants closed to the general public. It seemed that every few nights he was entertaining a group of Americans. He always had lots of money, even dollars.

He was a shady figure, an expression that is identical in Russian and in English although the Soviet context has invested this expression with added meaning. I began to avoid him and none too soon. One night Vladimir arranged a big party at his apartment in one of the new sections of Moscow. Several of the American students went. After they had dined on shrimp and beer the police came to the door and arrested the lot of them for disturbing the peace. It was only 9:30 P.M. Vladimir was furious. He paraded around the police station making indignant speeches and bringing up his father's name at every possible occasion. (As it turned out, Vladimir's father was a major official in Siberia.) After a three hour wait everyone was released. We later learned that the apartment was not Vladimir's—he was not even registered to live in Moscow, but somewhere in Siberia. However, Vladimir was not thrown out of the city. Every now and then he would show up even though everyone now went out of their way to avoid him. He asked a lot of questions and was already in possession of a lot of the answers.

I eventually understood that Vladimir was a *fartsovshchik*—a person who speculates in foreign goods. In the Soviet Union one has to "obtain" almost everything, that is, either buy goods on the black market or through acquaintances. All Soviets live by a system of contacts, from the salesclerk at a store to a famous writer or actress. *Fartsovshchiki* and speculators, those who deal more exclusively in Soviet items, can help in everything; they can obtain all the necessities, depending on their specialties. Some specialize in clothing, others in stereo equipment and recordings, others in books and art, and others in theater tickets or entrance into exclusive restaurants. A large part of their business depends on foreigners, and the items and currency they bring into the country.

If a foreigner does not intend to do anything more illegal than selling a few pairs of blue jeans, then *fartsovshchiki* are harmless. Still, it is often with their help that the Soviet authorities bring foreigners under their control. Many of them cooperate with the police or with the KGB, depending on the category of foreigners and goods with which they deal. As long as they do not work at cross purposes with the government their association with foreigners is not dangerous for them, and the security forces will continue to ignore their illegal activities.

Vladimir was an obvious case of a long-time *fartsovshchik* who enjoyed government sanction of his activities. Less obvious but more disturbing was my friendship with a woman named Nina. Nina was thirty years old and she lived with her ten-year-old son from her first marriage. She was very hospitable, always inviting me over and feeding me well. Her refrigerator was stocked with delicacies. Her son was clever and playful—amused by the fact that an adult could speak Russian no better than he and eager to give me language lessons. Nina and I talked about clothes—she was terribly interested in Western fashions—and about men, another strong interest. It was pleasant to gossip idly in a language I had so long used only for reading the most serious materials. I enjoyed her company and we became friends. I came to confide in her and ask her advice.

Nina was a clothes designer but from what I could tell she went to work only a couple of days a week. She was always on the phone. As soon as she put the receiver down the phone rang again. Nina "arranged things," she brought people together. If she could not get something for you then she would find someone who could. She was a *fartsovshchik* and a speculant. This alone did not bother me; I had already met so many *fartsovshchiki*, dealers in antiques, in rare books, in furniture. Many of them had amassed fortunes and Nina seemed like a small fish next to them. However, as I began to understand my way a bit better I was haunted by the fact that I was only her most recent in a string of "close" foreign friends. She asked a lot of questions, she wanted to know where I had been, and with whom. At first I just wrote this off as her nature, but later I felt that she was not asking out of simple curiosity. Much of what I was to tell Nina came back to me; government officials had information on me and it seemed that she provided it, although I had no positive proof.

The strong distinction in Russian between the words "acquaintance" and "friend" became clear to me. In the Soviet context it means a great deal to be a friend. It is a title that must be earned and it means that you are trusted. In my carefree and naive American manner I too quickly accepted Nina as a friend.

Not all of my relationships in the Soviet Union turned out to be so disappointing. Most of all I enjoyed associating with relatives of Soviet emigres that I had met in the United States. I often went to see the relatives of a woman I knew in Chicago. I was very fond of her. She gave me all sorts of gifts for her relatives and friends: records, books, umbrellas, razors, etc. I contacted them soon after I arrived in Moscow. They greeted me warmly, although they were disconcerted that I had called from a phone on the university grounds. We set up a meeting at a metro station and there we instantly recognized one another as if we ourselves were relatives. Back in their apartment, I told them all the news of my friend, news that they themselves had read in her letters, but it meant so much to hear it again from someone who had actually seen and talked to her. They knew that they would most likely never again see their relative, and I was the only available substitute, a part of their relative's new life.

There were many other invitations. It is always prestigious to have a foreigner at a party. It is a sign of protest that results in nothing and usually threatens no consequence. I met many young people in Moscow who held their anti-state views just as one might wear eccentric clothing or engage in the newest fad. For such people, association with foreigners, especially intellectuals and students, was a great status symbol which, like their anti-Soviet speeches pronounced in small kitchens in small apartments, was not something that the state expressly forbids.

As a foreigner, I could easily have spent my time going from one party to another gracing them all with my presence, but this "movie-star syndrome" held little attraction for me. Except for relatives of friends at home, the people

I knew were people who had special vested interests in dealing with foreigners. They associated almost exclusively with foreigners. They were fun and entertaining, but they were not the Soviet mainstream I had hoped to be a part of. I did not want to close myself off further, but I did not like playing this game in which I did not know the rules, in which I felt both privileged and taken advantage of. So, I decided to concentrate more time and energy on my research.

I was studying Alexander Herzen, a writer and revolutionary of the mid-1800s, and his relationship with the famous writer Ivan Turgenev. It was a romantic, literary topic. An American professor had once called it "sexy." The Soviets liked it. It was not political and it dealt with two bona fide greats of Russian culture. My Soviet advisor, a world renowned historian, thought it very promising.

I started to attend my Soviet advisor's seminars in order to see how my counterparts were trained, but most of all I was mesmerized by this professor. He was very intelligent and insightful and he treated his students and me with the greatest respect. At Stanford I had been told that this professor spent fifteen years in a labor camp. He had been arrested along with millions of others in the great terror of the Stalinist thirties and forties. Once released he forgave his jailors and reasoned that they had simply made a mistake in his case. I sat there in class and unwittingly stared at him. I had read, even taught Soviet history, but here it was sitting in front of me.

Most of my work I did in the Lenin Library. We foreigners had the privilege of studying in the first hall, which brought two main advantages: first, I could sit by myself and did not have to share a desk with someone as was the case in the rest of the library, and second, the first hall had a reserved coat check so that I did not have to stand in line to hang up my coat before entering the library. At crowded times that might save me a half hour.

Only academicians, professors and foreign students could use the first hall and the result was an odd blend of people. Men and women in their 50's, 60's and 70's, all hunched over from years of study at these very same tables, all dressed in the same brown and gray suits, baggy at the elbows and knees, the women looking much like the men. Interspersed were young students in blue jeans, sweatshirts and bright woolen mufflers wrapped around their necks. The foreigners wore the mufflers because they could not adapt to the habit of "airing the hall." Twice a day the windows that looked out on the golden spires of the Kremlin were flung open and left open for 45 minutes, every season of the year.

Red Horizons: Chronicles of a Communist Spy Chief

Ion Mihai Pacepa

Ceausescu had long ago set this date for his visit to the exhibit arranged for him and Elena by the Securitate's DGTO (*Directia Generala de Technica Operativa* or General Directorate of Technical Operations). It was set up in a couple of large rooms next to Ceausescu's office at the Communist Party's Central Committee headquarters in Bucharest.

The DGTO is a huge outfit. It conducts microphone and telephone intercepts and mail censorship throughout the country and makes surreptitious entries into private homes and public institutions. It also covers all Western embassies and other Western representations in Romania, including their radio and telex communications, and it monitors the NATO communications in the area.

Created in the early 1950's by the KGB, the DGTO has grown enormously in the last ten years. Ceausescu considers it his most important weapon for controlling the domestic population, much more effective than the hordes of Securitate agents created within every Romanian organization and the "block" and "street" committees of informants covering all social, economic, and residential areas. He has always been deeply interested in all of the DGTO's activities, but he has a special thing about microphones.

1.

Ceausescu's fascination with microphones was born in the early 1950's, when he was the military forces' political commissar, responsible for replacing the Romanian capitalist army with a new, Communist one modeled after the Soviet Red Army. The Directorate for Military Counterintelligence, known as Directorate IV, was among the first intelligence units the KGB set up in Romania. Microphones were in those days the most efficient weapon Directorate IV had, and it is still true today, when over 90 percent of the Romanian officers have their offices and homes electronically monitored at least periodically. When in 1954 the Moscow-educated General Ceausescu became secretary of the Communist Party in charge of military and security forces, he was intensively instructed several times by Nikita Khrushchev himself in the use of microphones.

From my position in the Ministry of Interior, I myself saw how the instructions Khrushchev had given to Ceausescu were gradually put into action. In 1965, when Ceausescu became the supreme leader, population monitoring grew into a mass operation of unprecedented scope. Hundreds of thousands of new microphones were silently put to work from their hiding places in offices and bedrooms, starting with those of the Politburo. As in the Soviet Union or any other Communist country, corruption and prostitution reigned at the highest levels in Romania, and the microphones relentlessly recorded everything. Like Khrushchev, Ceausescu also ordered a monitoring room built behind his office, so he could personally check on the take from the microphones. They were the key to his power.

The number two man in the Romanian hierarchy, Gheorghe Apostol, who had once been a general secretary of the Party himself, was Ceausescu's main rival. The microphones on him showed Apostol to be a devoted Marxist-Leninist with nothing to reproach him for except not having enough regard for Ceausescu. Coincidentally, however, they also revealed that Apostol's wife, a young actress, was throwing frequent parties with her colleagues, very rarely attended by Apostol himself. His new minister of interior presented Ceausescu with clandestine photographs of these parties. Ceausescu then personally dictated an "anonymous" letter, written as if from a friend of Apostol's, in which Apostol was described as a bourgeois whose conduct was incompatible with his position as number two in the Party. Ceausescu ordered that the letter be handwritten, put in an envelope together with several clandestine photographs, which he personally selected, and "mailed" to the first secretary of the Romanian Communist Party–Ceausescu himself. On December 10, 1967, during a break at the National Conference on the Romanian Communist Party, Ceausescu confronted Apostol with the "anonymous" letter and asked him to resign from the Politburo. Fearing an obstinate refusal, Ceausescu immediately convened an emergency meeting of the Politburo. After a 20-minute discussion, the Politburo, caught off guard by Ceausescu's aggressiveness and the unusual "evidence," agreed to remove Apostol temporarily from his position and to appoint him as chairman of the national trade union organization. Once he was no longer number two, Apostol was finished. In May 1977 he was demoted for his "bourgeois lifestyle" and appointed ambassador to Argentina. When Ceausescu gave me the order to have microphones installed in all his rooms there, he remarked in an aside, "Apostol might save us a lot of trouble if he would just become a victim of the terrorist wave" that was overwhelming Buenos Aires at that time.

Once Apostol was replaced in the Politburo with a Ceausescu supporter, the rest was not difficult for the ambitious new leader. He convinced the number three man in the Party hierarchy, Chivu Stoica, a former president and prime minister, that he had a drinking problem that might make him an embarrassment to the Party. Stoica resigned on Ceausescu's promise that he would be held up as an honorary figure for the rest of his life. On February 18, 1975, however, Stoica was called in by the Central Committee and accused of having sexual relations with a 22-year-old niece. He quickly realized that he had microphones in his own home. That night Stoica committed suicide by firing his hunting rifle into his mouth. A suicide letter addressed to Ceausescu was found on his desk and given to the addressee. Its contents were never disclosed; however, after he read it, Ceausescu was said to have ordered first alcohol for his hands, and then champagne.

A few other leaders from the "old guard" were blackmailed, recruited, and finally installed as the "new guard." Compromising materials and microphones were kept hanging over their heads like swords of Damocles to ensure their loyalty. The most important of them was a four-star general, Emil Bodnaras, who was a member of the Politburo, former minister of national defense, and Ceausescu's mentor. Blackmailed for his personal admiration of Stalin and for his secret membership in Lavrenti Beria's state security organization, Bodnaras agreed to transfer his loyalty to his former subordinate. The microphones installed all around him proved that he really did remain loyal the rest of his life.

In 1967, Ceausescu replaced the former 17 Romanian administrative regions with 39 smaller districts, thus killing three birds with one stone: new leaders came in on the regional level, each of them had far less personal power, and Romania as a country looked larger than ever. The whole group of army senior commanders were also replaced. It was the most dramatic turnover of power since the Communists had taken over the government. The real and only reason for these changes was Ceausescu's policy of putting his own men in everywhere, a strategy designed to last until the end of his life, and until that of the dynasty he envisions passing the scepter to.

In March 1974, Ceausescu finally removed the last pawn from the old guard. He blackmailed his prime minister, Ion Gheorghe Maurer, with "anonymous" letters condemning his liberal views and his wife's behavior and persuaded him to resign for reasons of health.

Soon after he came to power, Ceausescu decided that every member of the old guard, whether removed or kept in office, should be electronically monitored for the rest of his life. He also secretly ordered that new Politburo members and government ministers be covered by microphones in their offices and homes from their first day until their removal, when they would be treated like the old guard. "We should not trust anyone, family members included, before checking on their thoughts," Ceausescu said to me in 1972, when he appointed me to supervise the unit monitoring the Politburo and the "old guard."

Based on the knowledge I have gained from experience, I can find no substantive differences in the way Ceausescu became leader for life and the way it was accomplished by Leonid Brezhnev, Todor Zhivkov, Janos Kadar, and the other Soviet bloc leaders. But the way Mikhail Gorbachev has gone about seizing absolute power in the Soviet Union today truly makes him look like Ceausescu's alter ego. Like Ceausescu, when Gorbachev became supreme leader he was the youngest member of the Politburo, with only domestic experience. Ceausescu's only expertise was in military and security matters, as an instant general; Gorbachev's was in agriculture, as an engineer without on-the-job experience. Their views on foreign policy were unknown. Soon after Gorbachev's nomination, rumors were heard in Moscow that Grigory Romanov, his main rival for supreme power and the number two man in the hierarchy, had a penchant for the easy life, and that Catherine the Great's dinner service, borrowed from the Hermitage Museum, had been smashed at his daughter's wedding party. Then Romanov was tacitly demoted from the Politburo and has since disappeared from public life.

Premier Nikolay Tikhonov "resigned" for reasons of health, and Andrei Gromyko, whose name was far better known abroad than the new leader's, was "promoted" to an honorary job, without executive power. Almost half of the members of the new cabinet were replaced in Gorbachev's first year. A new generation of military and naval commanders took over, constituting the most rapid turnover at the top of the Soviet military since 1945. Over 40 percent of the regional Party first secretaries on the oblast or kray level were replaced between March and December 1985. The explanations for the changes were exactly the same as Ceausescu's: old age, poor health, a need to end corruption, a desire to make the economy more efficient. There is also a startling similarity in the way the two dictators have portrayed themselves to the West. Both Romanian "Horizon" and Soviet glasnost depict a supposedly liberal and reasonable Communist dictator with whom the West should think it can do business.

Monitoring the thoughts of the entire Romanian population has been Ceausescu's major domestic policy goal, for which he has spared no expense or manpower. When he came to power in 1965, the Romanian security forces had one central and 11 regional KGB-designed electronic monitoring centers and five central mail censorship units around the country. The new exhibit showed that the DGTO had, as of March 1978, ten central and 248 peripheral automated electronic monitoring centers, plus over 1,000 "portable" units covering small towns, vacation resorts, and the picturesque, historical monasteries favored by Western tourists, as well as 48 mail censorship units.

When I arrived at the exhibit, only Generals Ovidiu Diaconescu and Istichie Geartu were there. Both electronics engineers, the former was the commander of the DGTO, and the latter the chief of its huge research institute. Geartu was a scholar, living with and for his inventions. Diaconescu, in contrast, was a sly old fox who had spent all his life in the electronic monitoring business. I had gotten to know Diaconescu better in February 1972, when we both went to Moscow for discussions with the KGB. Our schedules in the Soviet Union contained a visit to Leningrad together, including a day at the Hermitage Museum and an evening at the Kirov Ballet to see Ulanova herself in Swan Lake. On our arrival in Moscow, however, we got the unpleasant news that the Leningrad trip had been canceled and replaced by a visit to some kolkhozes. At the end of the first day in Moscow, when we got back to the KGB's luxury guest house, we asked for Armenian cognac. For over two hours, we both pretended to get increasingly inebriated, as we loudly speculated about why our trip to Leningrad might have been canceled, winding up with the drunkenly brilliant conclusion that it was Brezhnev's hatred of everything cultural that had stood in our way. The next morning we were unexpectedly taken for a short meeting with KGB Chairman Yuri Andropov, who told us that the Leningrad visit was on again, apologizing for the actions of some stupid bureaucrats. Diaconescu was in seventh heaven. "Microphones are the most efficient intelligence weapon there is," he said, repeating his favorite maxim.

2.

Ceausescu came in at ten o'clock, on the dot as usual, together with Elena. Ungainly in the military uniform he seldom wore because of the secrecy of his job, Diaconescu stepped up and said, all in one breath, "Comrade Supreme Commander of the Romanian Armed Forces, the exhibit 'DGTO in 1984,' set up according to your personal order, is ready to be presented. I am the commander of the DGTO, Lieutenant General Ovidiu Diaconescu."

Although Ceausescu loves to hear these formal reports and his title of supreme commander, omission of which can ruin his whole day, he made a modest sign with his hand, as if to say that all this was not necessary. "Time is precious. Stop talking and let's get to work," he said.

Diaconescu, who was as good a judge of human nature as he was an engineer, continued unperturbed. "Comrade Supreme Commander and Highly Esteemed Comrade Elena, the theme of our exhibit is the future development of the DGTO, so as to carry out your orders to monitor the entire population of our beloved country, the Romanian Socialist Republic."

"I like your accent. Where are you from?" asked Elena, smiling broadly with all her yellow teeth.

"Oltenia. Not far from where the Comrade and you were born," answered Diaconescu, discreetly wiping the perspiration from the back of his neck, after all the effort he had put into loading his first few words with every hint of Oltenian accent he could muster up.

"Your general's sweet," Elena whispered to me.

"This is a telephone device that has been perfected by the DGTO after ten years of work," Geartu started out slowly and methodically, in sharp contrast to Diaconescu's rapid manner of speaking. He held an innocuous looking, beige colored telephone. "This is not just a normal telephone. It also serves as a very sensitive microphone, capable of recording all conversations in the room where it is installed. If this telephone is approved as the only kind legally allowed in Romania, it will open a new era of broad-scale electronic surveillance, without the tedious need for surreptitious entries into private homes to install microphones."

"Could it have different models?"

"We have three models and five colors, and we can have as many as you wish to order."

"That's what I've been waiting for. How good is it?"

"Excellent," broke in the fast talking Diaconescu. "Much better than anything we've seen to date. We have samples of similar instruments discovered in our embassies abroad—American, British, and West German-made. Ours is clearer. Please listen to these comparative tapes."

"Can we use it on a wide scale?" asked Ceausescu, ignoring the request that he listen to the tapes.

"We are only waiting for your command, Comrade Supreme Commander."

"Approved. Starting today, March 28, 1978, this is the one and only telephone approved for use in Romania. Period. How many old telephones do we have in use today?"

"More than three million," Diaconescu promptly replied.

"Replace them with the new ones," Ceausescu ordered.

"I don't understand, Nick. What's the difference between this one and the black one I have in my office?" Elena asked, a little embarrassed. She knows nothing about how the tapes are made that she so avidly listens to in the back room of her office.

"The d–difference is t–that *you* will never have the new one, neither in your office nor at home," Ceausescu answered, winking toward us. He also stutters when pleasurably excited.

"May we do a demonstration, Comrade Supreme Commander?" asked Diaconescu.

"Go ahead," approved Ceausescu, with a large smile on his face and a glow in his eyes. Being addressed as "Supreme Commander" is even more exciting for him than having sex, or so Diaconescu had told me a few days earlier.

"To this portable monitoring center we have hooked up four phones that are installed in four different, randomly selected apartments. Two are the kind we use now, and two are the new model. The monitoring center is voice-activated, so it will automatically start recording when any one of the phones is in use. It's recording one conversation right now," said Diaconescu, pointing to a moving recorder. The conversation could barely be heard in the exhibit room when he pushed a button. "The recorder stops when the conversation is over, as it just did. That's all we can record with the old phones. But now let's listen to the new one."

Diaconescu dialed a number and asked if it was the National Theater. "Wrong number" came from the other end of the line, but the tape recording did not stop after the telephone had been hung up. A woman's voice could be heard asking who had called. "Some idiot who put his finger in the wrong hole. Let me finish what I was listening to on Radio Free Europe about the trip the Dictator and his old bag are making to the United States," the man's voice replied, before being cut off sharply. Diaconescu's hand, darting out faster than a snake, had flicked off a switch. He always did have good reflexes.

The deadly silence was interrupted when Diaconescu flicked another switch. A fuzzy noise together with heavy breathing and short yelps came suddenly out of the speaker, but Diaconescu's quick hand immediately shut it off.

"Turn it back on," Elena ordered with a biting voice. Her experienced ear was almost as good as Diaconescu's. "They should be arrested," she ordered, after listening a few more minutes. "At eleven in the morning, working people should be out working, not making love."

73

Ceausescu moved along a few steps. Geartu was holding up a normal-looking telephone outlet, explaining that inside its plastic body there was a concealed mini–microphone, which could not be found without the outlet's complete destruction. It was to be used in other rooms that did not have the telephone device in them, so that a whole apartment could be covered. The same display contained several other new pieces of equipment designed by the DGTO for use in villages where people often had no telephone. Ceausescu's eye was caught by a television set with a built-in transmitter that could be activated by a remote control matching its code.

"We propose introducing this microtransmitter in all television sets that are to be sold in rural areas. One advantage with having it is that it would have a constant source of power, eliminating the need for batteries. And for another thing, a television set is silent eighty percent of the time." Romanian television programs are on the air only a few hours a day.

"If we're going to use this hocus-pocus, we could even shorten the daily program. Some news and a film about the Party is all the people need, isn't that so, Nick?" asked Elena.

"Approved," Ceausescu said, moving on to a display showing monitoring equipment for restaurants. The ceramic ashtrays and flower vases caught his attention. Geartu reported that, by the end of the next five-year plan, every restaurant would be equipped with only ceramic ashtrays and vases containing thin, battery-activated micro-transmitters. They could be turned on by any surveillance officer or waitress-agent, who needed only to pull out a needle-like pin.

First invented by the Soviet KGB, ceramic ashtrays and flower vases containing microtransmitters are now secretly used by all East European security services for monitoring discussions in restaurants and hotel lobbies. The American journalist Hedrick Smith humorously describes what he witnessed in a Soviet hotel by the Caspian Sea, when word came down that a delegation of foreign ambassadors was about to make a visit there. "Like the provincial bureaucrats of Gogol's rich satire *The Inspector General*, the staff scurried about in a frenzy to make the hotel more presentable....The regular glass ashtrays disappeared from the dining room tables and new, more decorative ashtrays appeared. Large, white carnations were placed on each table." It evidently did not occur to Smith that the new ashtrays and flower vases were not only for show. Their use as portable monitoring devices is still one of the best kept secrets within the Soviet bloc.

Ceausescu and Elena went slowly from one display to the other, listening with growing interest about new ways of performing electronic monitoring, daytime and nighttime clandestine photography, indoor and outdoor video-taping, and faster and more complete mail censorship. Then the Ceausescus came to a display of equipment designed for use abroad. Geartu and Diaconescu began presenting the prototype of a new electronic monitoring center for use in Romanian embassies, along with passive systems, lasers, and encoded ultra-high-frequency transmitters for installation in such targets in the West as government institutions, military units, and private homes.

"Show them to Arafat and 'Annette.' To Gadhafi, too," he whispered into my ear." "And give them as many as they want."

3.

It was noon when the Ceausescus arrived at the end of the exhibit. Taking a noisy deep breath, Ceausescu looked around and asked: "How many people will we be able to monitor simultaneously by the end of our next five-year plan?"

"I can only report, Comrade Supreme Commander and Esteemed Comrade Elena," replied Diaconescu, "that, if our proposals are approved today, then as of January 1, 1984, we will be able to monitor ten million microphones simultaneously. Assuming that our population will keep the same rate of increase in the next five years as in the last five, our estimate is that every single family could be periodically monitored during each calendar year, with the suspect ones continuously covered."

"How many children do you have, comrade?" Elena interrupted Diaconescu.

"One, Comrade Elena. One soldier for the Party."

"That's why our population isn't growing. You should have at least four soldiers for the Party, dear comrade. Add a ten to fifteen percent population increase to your estimates, General. By 1984, Romania should have at least thirty million inhabitants. I'll take care of that, and you take of your micro-phones."

Ceausescu sucked in air between his teeth several times, then began. "We are now building a beautiful life for the Romanian people, comrades. A new and independent life, which our people deserve, after two thousand and fifty years of struggle and humiliation." Elena led the applause. "For the past decade, each year has marked something new in our Communist history. Let us make 1984 another cornerstone. Let us again be unique in the Warsaw Pact. Let us be the first in the entire world, comrades. In a very short time we will be the only country on earth able to know what every single one of its citizens is thinking. Five years is all that separates us today from a new, much more scientific form of government." He looked meaningfully at his audience before continuing.

"Why is American imperialism so unpopular? Because it does not know what its people think, because it is not scientific. What you are doing here, comrades, is the real science of government. It is a true public opinion survey. The Communist system we are creating together is the most scientific ever, I repeat, comrades, *ever* to be put at the service of mankind."

Diaconescu opened the applause. Ceausescu raised his arms, asking for silence. "It is too bad that we cannot tell our working people how the Communist Party is looking out for them, comrades. Wouldn't the miners go out and dig more coal, if they could just be sure that the Party knew what their wives were doing every single instant? They would, comrades, but we cannot talk about our system today. The Western press might accuse us of being a police state. That's imperialist propaganda, comrades. We do not have a police state, and we will never have a police state. We are a proletarian dictatorship preserving our ideological purity. Communism is the only real democracy, and history will attest to that for generations to come." Applause.

"But someday we *will* be able to talk about what we are doing here. Someday, when our proletarian world revolution defeats the capitalist hydra, and our red flag is flying everywhere on earth!" Ceausescu finished dramatically....

4.

To the ordinary Romanian people, the word *nomenclatura* means the elite, a social superstructure recognizable by its privileges. *Nomenclatura* people do not travel by bus or streetcar. They use government cars. The color and make of the car indicate its owner's status in the hierarchy: the darker the color, the higher the position. White Dacias are for directors, pastel colors for deputy ministers, black for ministers; black Audis for Nicu; black Mercedes for the prime minister and his deputies; and black Mercedes 600, Cadillac, and Rolls-Royce limousines for Ceausescu. *Nomenclatura* people do not live in apartment buildings constructed under the Communist regime. As I did, they get nationalized villas or luxury apartments that previously belonged to the capitalists. *Nomenclatura* people are not seen standing in line to buy food or other necessities. They have their own stores, and black car people can even order by telephone for home delivery. *Nomenclatura* people are not seen in normal restaurants fighting for a table or listening to a disagreeable waiter saying, "If you don't like it, stay home." They have their own special restaurants, and they can even go to the ones for Western tourists. During the summer, *nomenclatura* people are not seen on Bucharest's crowded, sweaty beaches. They either go to special bathing areas or have weekend villas in Snagov, a resort located 25 miles outside Bucharest. *Nomenclatura* people do not spend their vacations packed like sardines into Soviet-style colonies. They have their own vacation homes.

The darker the car, the closer the house is to Ceausescu's vacation residence, and black car people also get cooks and servants. They do not stand in line outside Soviet-style polyclinics, where treatment is free but you are yelled at by everyone from the doorman on up and may not spend more than 15 minutes with the doctor, who has to see at least 30 patients in his eight-hour shift. They do not go to the regular hospitals, where people may have to double up two to a bed. They have the luxurious, Western-style Hellias hospitals, built as a private foundation in the days before Communism.

The microphone coverage on top members of the *nomenclatura* is without doubt the best kept secret in the Soviet bloc. "For us, only Comrade Brezhnev is tabu," KGB Chairman Yuri Andropov told me when I was visiting Moscow in 1972. "Keeping a close watch on our *nomenclatura* is the KGB's most delicate task. Take Shchelokov, for example." General Nikolay Shchelokov was the Soviet minister of interior. "We all respect him, but through the microphones we learned that he was drinking too much. I reported it, and Comrade Brezhnev is now trying to help him. The same thing happened with Ustinov." Marshal Dmitry Ustinov was the Soviet minister of defense.

The KGB's *nomenclatura* coverage is imitated throughout the whole Soviet bloc. Every East European country has its own top secret "Iosif's unit," where a faceless army of little security people record everything for the supreme leader, even the way a *nomenclatura* man moans when he is making love.

Translated by Alexander Cook

Alone Together

Elena Bonner

Iwould like to tell the story of our car. It's an old one, born in 1976. And the KGB has subjected it to its persecutions, too. As soon as it was widely known that Andrei and I were planning a hunger strike to get Liza an exit visa, the car was stolen—this was in the fall of 1981. Rumors were spread around Gorky that I had driven the car to Moscow and hidden it, so that we could accuse the state of stealing it. When we were on the hunger strike and not leaving the house, afraid of being grabbed on the street and forcibly hospitalized, it was suddenly found, and the traffic police kept calling us to come for it. Andryusha said that we didn't care about the car now, but they argued that it was so valuable a possession that our hunger strike could be interrupted. But at last, unable to lure us out of the house with the prospect of getting our car back, they simply broke down our apartment door and took us by force to separate hospitals.

After Liza's departure, the car was returned to us, but only its remains—everything that could be unscrewed had been taken, and the tires were replaced by bald ones. Half the parts had been removed from under the hood and everything taken out of the interior—even the ashtrays. Liza left on December 19, but we did not get the car back into shape until May. In the years that followed a strange situation developed with this inanimate object. Whenever the authorities did not like something, it was our car that suffered. Either two tires would be punctured, or a window smashed or smeared with glue. This was how we knew that we had done something bad by their standards: perhaps we managed to talk to someone on the street or at the market, or had gone to the wrong place, or refused to see Dr. Obukhov or another doctor.

There are many sins and only one car, so it suffers, poor thing. And as the limitations on us increased, they reflected on the car. That first summer we decided to go for a swim in the Oka river—exactly twelve kilometers from our house. We swam and sat on the shore. As we were driving onto the highway from the river road, I was stopped by a traffic policeman, which surprised me as I had not committed any violations. Then I saw that there was also another police car next to the traffic vehicle. Snezhnitsky (then a captain, now a major) got out and headed toward us.

Here I have to mention another episode involving him. This was at the very beginning of our life in Gorky. On February 15, 1980, Yura Shikhanovich came to see us on my birthday. He was immediately dragged off to the "point for the protection of public order," where Snezhnitsky began questioning him and working him over. Andrei and I burst in. The agents started pushing us out, and I slapped Snezhnitsky. We were dragged out, of course, and dropped in the corridor—we were like beaten dogs. Then there was a trial which I did not attend. (Perhaps it wasn't a trial, but something administrative.) I was fined thirty rubles. I had the occasion to tell Captain Snezhnitsky that it wasn't expensive—thirty rubles for the pleasure of slapping him. Incidentally, history shows that in the years of Nicholas I the police chief in the central part of Nizhni Novgorod* was a certain Snezhnitsky—perhaps it's a family profession.

On this summer day, Snezhnitsky came over to us and declared that Andrei had violated the rules of his regime by going beyond the city limits. He wrote out a report which Andrei refused to sign. However, we no longer went there together. I went by myself quite often, because the local Sovkhoz has a stand there, and three times a week they sell very good cottage cheese and sour cream. Andryusha would wait for me on the side of the road inside the city limits. Once it was pouring, and the traffic police (they're not all KGB) invited Andrei to wait out the shower in their little booth.

That also happened when I gave an old man with a Leo Tolstoy beard a ride to the bus station in the rain, while Andryusha sat in a traffic police inspector's car. He waited for me once when I decided to take a look at what was on the other side of the big Volga bridge. But I did not enjoy driving alone; it was lonely and I felt sorry for Andrei. That is why I never went to Pushkin's estate Boldino nor to the village of Vyezdnoye, where the Sakharov family originally came from. I naively expected better times when we could go together. But from the moment that I signed an agreement not to leave the city, I stopped going too.

In those early years we often gave lifts to strangers. Then, without any explanation, we were forbidden to do that. At first the ban was not total—that is, when I was driving alone I could pick up people, but if Andrei and I were both in the car, I couldn't.

—————————

* Gorky was called Nizhni Novgorod until 1932.

The authorities underscored the ban by puncturing our tires and that sort of thing. Then, seeing that we still did not understand fully, they began hauling passengers forcibly out of the car. I remember one horrible scene when Andrei was driving. He took in two women—one was very elderly and could barely shuffle. As soon as he started the engine, our escort ran over, stopped the car, and with shouts and curses pulled the two passengers out. The old woman was so frightened she could have died on the spot. We were forced to drive away.

Another incident occurred in the summer of 1985, when I was without Andryusha. A man stood by the side of the road holding a screaming child of four or five. I stopped. The boy had a broken leg, which the man was supporting. I started to help them in. My guards ran over and began pulling the man from the car. I think he would have fought with them if he weren't holding the child. Everyone was screaming—the child, the man, the KGB agents. And I started to yell louder than everyone, scaring them. I rushed at one of the guards, and I think I was prepared to kill him or die. I shouted for him to get in the car and drive. I think my behavior frightened the KGB man. He got in the front seat with me. I put the man and boy in the back and we drove to the first-aid station near our house. When the man and boy were gone, the KGB man said to me: "You are not allowed to stop. You know that, and if you try it again, you can say goodbye to your car." I did not reply, simply slamming the door. I shook for a long time.

Another incident was funny. Tires do go flat occasionally, a car's a car. It's hard for me to change them, so when I get a flat I tell the KGB escorts that I will flag down a truck. Any driver is happy to do it for three rubles. Sometimes the KGB man will give me permission on his own, sometimes he radios for advice. When I have permission, I flag a truck. Once the van driver was surprised by my request, since he saw a strapping young man near my car. When he was done and I offered him a three-ruble note, he said: "Don't bother, Mother, but you should teach a kid a lesson. What's the matter with him, is he sick or something that he can't change a tire?" "He's not mine, he belongs to the Committee,"* I replied. "Ah . . ." said the driver, and hurried back to his van. I still don't know what he thought. But at the last moment he gave me a look that made me think he knew who I was.

Our guards talk to us in the language of breaking or taking our car. They also speak in another way—the language of the loss and subsequent return of other things. A pair of glasses disappears and then resurfaces in a place where we both have looked. At first, I used to hiss at Andrei that he was being

---

* Euphemism for the KGB—the Committee of State Security.

forgetful and that the KGB had nothing to do with it. But then it started happening with my things too. I began keeping notes. For instance, this silly notation: "My toothbrush is gone, and both Andrei and I have looked in the bathroom in the glass," with the date. Then more than a week later: "Hurrah, the toothbrush is in the glass," with the date. Obviously we are not crazy. Books have vanished like this, and so has Andrei's dental bridge, which turned up when Andrei was released from the hospital. When I was alone for ten months I often felt an inner anxiety from the knowledge that they were constantly entering the apartment when I was out. They were doing things, looking for things. What would they take away? What would they leave? The sentence from my trial vanished, and various papers disappeared during Andrei's absence. This whirlwind of moving objects creates a feeling of a Kafka-esque nightmare on the one hand and on the other that you are on a glass slide of a microscope, that you are an experimental subject.

Translated by Alexander Cook

Russian Doctor

Vladimir Golyakhovsky

In my opinion, alcoholism is a phenomenon of physiological preconditions on a background of social conditions. Alcoholism is an individual illness, but in certain social conditions it becomes a mass phenomenon, a national epidemic.

The roots of the tendency toward alcoholism have their beginnings for Russians in their wild forefathers, the Scyths. We know from ancient history that the Scythian tribes who populated southern Russia and the Ukraine more than one thousand years ago were all uncontrollable in everything. They were subject to a passion for alcoholic drinks, and this passion was combined with the wildness of mass orgies. For example, they turned the funerals of their leaders into general drinking bouts. The whole tribe would get drunk, and then all of the men would make love with the leader's wives, after which these wives would be killed and buried with the leader.

During the course of ten centuries of Christianity in Russia and the Ukraine, these closely related nations were distinguished by their immoderate consumption of alcohol. The peasants in the villages always drank moonshine, and when the working class began to form in the eighteenth century, almost all of the workers were drunkards from the very beginning.

The famous Russian czars Ivan the Terrible and Peter the Great were alcoholics, and all of their noble court constantly participated in royal orgies. Many great people of Russia were chronic alcoholics and died prematurely from alcoholism.

The three most numerous groups of alcoholics in Russia are the factory workers, the village peasants, and the military officers. Alcoholism is less developed among the intellectuals in general, but there are a lot of alcoholics in the arts—actors, painters, writers, and musicians. Among the 129 Soviet nationalities, three—the Russians, Byelorussians, and Ukrainians—are the most vulnerable. These three nationalities have a common ethnic background.

There are also a lot of alcoholics among the Latvians, Lithuanians, and Estonians. The fewest are among the Moslem nationalities—the Tadzhiks, Uzbeks, Kirgiz, Tatars, and Turkmen—because of the tradition of the Koran, which forbids alcohol, but gradually many of them are also turning to drink. As a rule, this happens under the influence of Russian friends.

Nobody knows how many alcoholics there are in the Soviet Union, but according to the most modest calculations, they include half of the adult population and a fifth of the adult female population, which adds up to at least 50 million people. Two factors in the life of Soviet society contribute to such a mass spread of alcoholism—economic difficulties and moral depression caused by propaganda. The low average wage (150 rubles, or about $225 a month), the high cost of absolutely all goods, and the inadequate quantity of goods chronically undermines the material position of the average family. As a result, people develop a chronic dissatisfaction with their daily lives. The desire "to drink from sorrow" appears more and more often. To this is added the depression from the influence of ceaseless propaganda in the newspapers, radio, and television, in the movies and in the magazines, in the books and theaters. The whole population has to occupy itself with the study of Marxism-Leninism and listen to political lectures at work and participate in meetings every week. Under the influence of this unbearable, boring propaganda, against which people cannot object because they are afraid of political accusations, they become angry and find their only diversion in alcohol.

The Soviet rulers do not do anything to cut down the alcoholism in the country. To the contrary, through their domestic policies, they increase it all the time. Premier Nikita Khrushchev and President Leonid Brezhnev themselves were chronic alcoholics. I saw with my own eyes how they drank cognac from large glasses when I had dinner with them. Almost all the other members of the Politburo are also alcoholics. Even the single woman among them, the Minister of Culture, Yekaterina Furtseva, was a chronic drunk.

Occasionally, the government begins a campaign against drunkenness and the newspapers publish long directives that nobody reads. The lines in front of the vodka stores do not get any shorter because of these directives.

Translated by Michael Sylwester and Eugene Ostrovsky

Apostasy

Biographies

For biographical information on **WOLFGANG LEONHARD** see excerpt in the section, "Nomenklatura and Life."

A cipher clerk in Canada's Soviet embassy working coded message traffic between Ottawa and Moscow, **IGOR GOUZENKO** defected to Canadian authorities in September 1945. He took with him 109 documents from the embassy safe.

His revelations of several parallel Soviet spy networks in the Western Hemisphere shook the Western world. Canada and the U.S. had assisted the Soviet Union amply during World War II; here was incontrovertible evidence that the Soviets were conducting espionage to acquire the atomic bomb. The evidence resulted in the conviction of several atom spies.

The Soviets sentenced Gouzenko and his wife to death in absentia. In 1948 his *Iron Curtain* appeared—detailing Soviet collectivization, purges, famine, slave labor, and the Party's opulent lifestyle.

Gouzenko died in 1982 near Toronto.

Born in 1907 in New York City, **JAMES MICHENER** is one of the nation's most prolific and most respected writers.

During Hungary's October 1956 Revolution, Michener went to Andau. There he assisted many of the 20,000 Hungarians who fled their bleeding country across Andau's bridge—to Austria, and to freedom. Later he spent six weeks in Austria interviewing Hungarian refugees.

The Bridge at Andau, published in 1957, is Michener's portrait of Hungary under Soviet domination—drawn by the people whose ordeal it was.

Born in a small town in the Urals in 1942, **VLADIMIR BUKOVSKY** early saw through the Soviet miasma. He was still in high school when first arrested; in 1961 he was expelled from the University of Moscow.

He spent twelve of his first thirty-five years in prisons, camps, or mental wards. Bukovsky was one of the first to draw attention to the USSR's abuse of psychiatric medicine.

His "crimes" included political demonstrations and public readings of banned poets. In 1976, he, his mother, sister, and nephew were expelled from the USSR in exchange for the Chilean Communist Luis Corvalan. He studied biology at Cambridge and has written numerous books and articles about the Soviet Union. He lives in England.

To Build a Castle—My Life as a Dissenter, an account of Bukovsky's years of imprisonment and his resistance to totalitarianism, was published in 1979.

VIKTOR BELENKO, born in 1947, spent his childhood in Soviet squalor—first in the Caucasus and then in Siberia.

He was awakened to another world by a librarian in Siberia who gave him books by American authors; he read voraciously.

Later he joined the military and became one of the country's top jet pilots. Yet the system palled, and he grew disillusioned. While on a routine mission in September 1976, Lieutenant Belenko veered off course and flew his top-secret Mig-25 to Japan and requested asylum.

Ultimately he came to the United States.

John Barron, a leading American writer on the Soviet Union—notably the KGB—wrote Belenko's story in the 1980 *Mig Pilot*.

A KGB major, **STANISLAV LEVCHENKO** was top Soviet spy. His specialty was disinformation; he fronted as a Soviet freelance journalist in Tokyo.

Growing increasingly disenchanted with the Communist system for which he worked, he found himself deceiving his friends and hating himself. And his job was destroying his marriage.

In 1979 he defected to American officials in Tokyo, who flew him to the United States. The Soviet Union sentenced him to death.

In chronicling his life, *On the Wrong Side* (1988), is a testimonial to his protracted alienation from the ideology he served.

Child of the Revolution

Wolfgang Leonhard

The summer of 1942 in Ulfa had given me a clear indication of the difference between the life of a privileged official and that of an ordinary person. It was quite clear to me that much that I had been able to say and do as a Soviet student or a member of the *Komsomol* was no longer permissible in my present environment. On my arrival at Kushnarenkovo I had made up my mind to adjust myself to the new way of life. It was by no means only a matter of refraining from saying anything about my past, or from mentioning my real name. That did not turn out to be at all difficult. What caused much more difficulty was a fact which no one had ever told me, and which I was now to learn for myself: that every word is politically significant.

That sentence is not lightly set down. It means exactly what it says. Every word is politically significant. This was something entirely new to me.

When one was a student and a member of the *Komsomol* in the Soviet Union, it was good enough in normal times—the years of the purges from 1936-1938 being naturally an exception—to stick to the correct line when talking of political affairs, to voice no opinion on any subjects that had not yet been dealt with in *Pravda*, and to present one's political views in such a way that even the stupidest and most malicious listener could not distort them into anti-Soviet utterances. Apart from this, there were contexts of a completely non-political character in which one could say more or less what one wanted.

The difference between my previous life and the life which now awaited me was one which I had not completely understood in my first few weeks at the school. When talking of non-political subjects, I used to say freely and cheerfully whatever came into my head. So did all the other younger Party members in our group. We were all fundamentally in accord with the system, but that did not prevent young students like ourselves from criticizing certain aspects of it here and there, and even making jokes on some subjects. Above all, it did not prevent us from feeling completely free and uninhibited when talking of non-political subjects, just like any other young people of our age anywhere else in the world. But it was just this that was forbidden, and this was the beginning of the criticism and self-criticism of which I was to be the first victim.

We were frequently made to undertake manual work, usually on jobs which had to be done in the vicinity of the school. Occasionally we were required to do agricultural or other labor outside the school grounds. One afternoon we were called together accordingly and told: "This afternoon's lessons are canceled—our group is to unload a cargo steamer."

Half an hour later we were on board the ship, where we had to unload huge bags of flour. Otto, from Hamburg, who was strong as an ox, missed no opportunity of teasing us younger ones because we could only carry one sack at a time, whereas he could easily handle two. One of the younger members of the group, named Stefan, who was small and feeble and short-sighted, suffered particularly from Otto's ridicule. Stefan had guts enough to stand up to Otto, however, and the result was a fight in which Otto hit the wretched little Stefan in the face with his powerful fist. I was standing close by and I let myself go in a fury of indignation.

After lunch the following day, the three of us were notified that we were required to report to the Director at 7 o'clock. I presented myself without any anxiety, imagining that Otto was going to be severely ticked off and that I was required only as a witness. But things turned out quite differently.

As I came into the Director's room I had a surprise. Two long tables were set at right angles to each other. Besides the Director sat the Chief of Cadres—a man we seldom saw and still more seldom heard speak—and also a woman official who was said to be a member of Dimitrov's secretariat, together with Paul Wandel, and most astonishing of all, Emmi Stenzer, a blue-eyed girl of nineteen who was totally ignorant of all matters connected with political theory, but was very good at forming "people's committees" on them. There was a grave and solemn silence. It might have been an investigation by the Inquisition.

Against the wall stood a couch and three chairs. We were told coldly, almost in a whisper: "You can sit on those chairs."

Silence followed for several minutes: nothing whatever happened. An oppressive feeling came over me, although I still assumed that the discussion had nothing to do with me. After some time, Mikhailov said in a voice that was entirely unfamiliar to me: "I think we can now begin."

Paul Wandel was the first to speak. He reconstructed the whole incident, and to my surprise I began to realize that the episode of the sacks of flour was really a matter of serious political importance. My surprise was even greater, however, at finding that Klassner's account of the matter put the blame considerably more on the victim, Stefan, than on the aggressor, Otto. Stefan was accused of having been provocative.

"The behavior of our younger comrades seems to require a thorough review," I heard Paul Wandel (Klassner) say. As he went on, my name was more and more frequently mentioned. His tone became sharper and sharper, but there was no anger in it and his voice was never raised. He spoke coldly and factually in clear, precise language. The others followed one after another, but I had difficulty in following what they said. All I heard over and over again were the words: "behavior unworthy of a Bolshevik . . . lack of serious-mindedness . . . presumptuous arrogance."

I sat dumbfounded. I had never known anything like it before. What made it worse was the complete calm with which everything was conducted; the pauses in which not a word was spoken, while the nightmare atmosphere in the room never lifted for a second.

I could not make up my mind what to think. What could it all mean? What was it all leading to? Why had I never been told anything before? What was going to come next?

About an hour had already passed since we began, and still nothing concrete had been said about what I had really done. Yet already I was beginning to feel myself guilty. I felt that I must have done something wrong, but the very fact that I did not know what it was made me feel even more helpless. Nor did I yet realize that this was only the beginning.

After a short pause—one of those ghastly minutes of silence—I heard the words: "I think Comrade Emmi Stenzer would like to say something."

The girl got up. She was no longer the helpless creature I had seen in the seminars when she was unable to answer political questions. She rose confidently, calmly, with a complete sense of her own power. Automatically she imitated the cold, severely factual tone which the others had used before her. She had a piece of paper with notes on it in front of her. From time to time she picked the paper up, and then went on speaking. Her notes were the points of indictment against myself.

I was in such a state of excitement that I could not follow everything, but there was one thing which I have never been able to forget from that day to this—the exact detail in which the indictment was formulated against me. Every opinion that I had expressed at any time or in any place from the first day of my arrival in the school had been carefully noted down to be used against me as evidence now.

"On the 23rd September at 11:30 in the morning, as we were coming out of the seminar room, Linden said..."

"On the 27th September at 6 o'clock in the afternoon, as we were leaving the folk singing, Linden stated..."

It was all so petty that anyone who did not know that atmosphere at this kind of school would only have laughed at it. The remarks quoted had not the slightest connection with politics.

Suddenly Emmi raised her voice. "When the lecture about Alexander Nevsky was announced, Linden told us that this was a question which interested him very much and he had studied it in some detail at the Institute in Karaganda. He was anxious to see whether the lecturer would have anything new to say."

The prosecutors put on a solemn face at this, and eagerly made notes. The woman sitting at the table shook her head dubiously. It was clear that this remark was one of grave significance. There followed a number of other remarks that I made. I tried desperately to remember the points in the indictment, but the whole atmosphere had had such an effect on me that I was unable to do so. The indictment seemed to be endless.

"When we came back from wood cutting on the evening of the 6th October at about 7:30, some comrades from the Spanish group passed by us. Linden then said to Förster that some of the Spanish girls were very pretty." There was more scribbling at the tables, and the eagerness with which the prosecutors made notes showed that this remark, too, was one of exceptional gravity.

At last the indictment came to an end. Otto was now quite at his ease on his chair. The whole thing seemed to be over now as far as he was concerned. Stefan, who was sitting next to me, looked at me from time to time with anxiety in his eyes, although his name was now very seldom mentioned. Next there spoke in turn the woman from the secretariat of the Comintern, the Chief of the Cadres, and Mikhailov himself. The points in the indictment recited by Emmi Stenzer were now only occasionally mentioned in their speeches; they served simply as starting points for the main indictment.

Today, when I look back on this first evening of criticism and self-criticism, I no longer find any difficulty in understanding the system. Every kind of remark—innocent, trivial, completely non-political—was exaggerated and distorted on a gigantic scale, so as to reveal peculiarities of character and political notions. Then these political notions, which one had never formulated, were equated with political actions which one never committed, and so finally the monstrous consequences were brought to light. This was achieved in something like the following way:

"Comrade Linden says that he has already studied the question of Alexander Nevsky at Karaganda. He says he was anxious to see what viewpoints the speaker would have to bring up. What is the significance of that? The significance lies in his belief that he already knows everything and that he has no need to learn anything new. This is an expression of the kind of presumptuousness which has already brought about the downfall of many Party officials in the past."

There followed examples, tragic and shocking examples in the clandestine struggle, of the way in which personal arrogance had caused officials to neglect security measures, so that trusted comrades had fallen into the hands of the enemy; examples of the way in which difficulties had been underestimated through arrogance, with the result that important tasks had not been fulfilled, and even that "if one follows the matter out to its logical conclusion, the officials concerned can be said from an objective point of view to have been accessories to the murder of trusted comrades and in that way to have served the enemy."

It was the same with my remark about the pretty Spanish girls at the school.

"One has only to look at the facts. In the middle of the war, when we are engaged in a life-and-death struggle against the Fascist criminals, when the entire Soviet people is sacrificing everything to achieve victory in the struggle for freedom and national independence, the Party gives Comrade Linden the opportunity of studying and preparing himself for the struggle ahead under ideal conditions. The Party has a right to expect that Linden's every effort will be directed to that purpose, that all his strength will be devoted to that goal; that every minute will be used for his studies and that all his thoughts will be concentrated on the coming struggle. And with what are Linden's thoughts in fact occupied? He is thinking of pretty Spanish girls and thus setting the interests of his own ego above the interests of the Party. Once again, it is not the first time that it has happened."

There followed further examples, each as shocking, startling and tragic as the other: of clandestine officials who had forgotten their duty through love affairs and thus gambled away into the hands of the enemy not only themselves, but also the whole of their clandestine group; examples from Italy, from Hitlerite Germany, from Franco's Spain and from Horthy's Hungary followed one after another.

Each time the conclusion was recapitulated, that this was the consequence of arrogant personal opinions. It all seemed so logical that by this time I felt myself guilty of having committed the same crimes. This impression was all the stronger because I had never yet experienced anything of the kind. At Soviet schools I had always been a model pupil and twice received certificates of merit as an exceptional scholar. As a student, I could point to more than one examination which had earned me a scholarship. As I had had no previous experience of criticism and self-criticism, and as there had never yet been a single critical remark about my conduct here at this school, the present massive indictment was a shattering blow.

At last, Mikhailov, the last to speak, had finished. Suddenly I heard him say: "Comrade Linden will now speak."

I remember making a few disconnected remarks to the effect that I considered the criticisms justified and I would try to improve myself. I could not make a consecutive speech—I simply stuttered.

Then came the summing-up, again by several speakers. The keynote was the same as before; Linden's statement is an evasion—Linden has not grasped the kernel of the problem. His statement shows his superficiality. It would be premature to believe a statement of this kind, made on the spot. There then followed further examples—examples of officials who had been accused of some fault or other and had made an immediate, facile confession of their fault, but had not made any real change, and had continued on the same pernicious path as before. Suddenly, completely to my surprise, I heard Mikhailov's voice: "I think we can now close."

No conclusion had been reached, no resolution passed, no measures had been decided upon. I was not even given the slightest indication what I now had to do. After lasting several hours, this terrifying session had ended just as unexpectedly as it had begun.

It was now night and all was quiet in the house. Everyone had gone to sleep. Slowly I climbed the rickety staircase to my bedroom. For hours I could not get to sleep. I had no idea what the whole thing meant. Would I be removed from the school? Would I be dismissed from the *Komsomol*? Would I be sent back to Karaganda? I was not so much disturbed by my immediate personal fate as by my sense of guilt and the apparent impasse in which I found myself. I was sincerely prepared to admit my faults; but now I had done it—and that too was wrong. Restlessly I turned over from side to side in my bed. Just what was I to do? Never before, not even in the Kazakhstan desert, had I felt so helpless as I did that night in the Comintern School.

Next day the usual instruction went on. Nothing seemed to have changed at the school. No one seemed to know anything about last night's session of criticism and self-criticism in the Director's room. I found it hard to follow the lessons, but I knew that since the evening of criticism and self-criticism, my conduct was going to be even more carefully watched than before. I wrote out my lessons, but it was nothing but a mechanical process. My thoughts were still back on the previous evening and on what the future had in store for me. The only thing that I was clear about was that the episode was not yet closed.

On my left sat Emmi, who seemed completely unmoved by anything. I suddenly found myself surprised by the thought that the way she had behaved, noting down everything so precisely, was something contemptible. Without any intention on my part, my thoughts went farther: was this, after all, the right way? Was it really necessary to use such methods to train Party members into officials? Certainly, I thought, I have many faults and of course the Party at the school has not merely the right, but the duty, to help me to overcome my faults and my weaknesses. But is this the way it ought to be done, in an atmosphere grimmer even than that of a court of law? Would it not have been possible to do it differently and to give me some friendly advice from time to time?

I recoiled from my own thoughts, but it was now impossible to suppress them. Is our whole relationship at the school what it ought to be between Party members? There came back into my mind other critical thoughts, which I had had earlier in the period of the purges. Critical conversations came back to me, and I was frightened of myself. If I had already expressed critical thoughts like these, what was the end likely to be?

I made up my mind in future to be much more cautious in what I said and to keep it to the minimum necessary. I would think out every sentence and every word before I uttered it. But again there came doubt. Must it be so? Was it really honest? If not, what ought one to do? How could one be honest if every innocent word, looked at objectively, was to be treated as a hostile utterance?

Again I shrank back from my own heretical thoughts. The previous evening, my admission of guilt had been completely honest. I was convinced that evening that the criticism directed at me, severe as it was, had been completely justified. I had been really anxious to improve myself, but the statement I had stammered out in all sincerity had been rejected. If that evening of self-criticism had gone just a little differently, if everything had been cleared up by my admission, possibly my heretical thoughts would never have arisen, or anyway not until much later. Possibly, in that case, that evening would have contributed, as it did with so many Russian and non-Russian officials, towards turning me into an unreasoning and compliant tool of the Stalinist Party leadership. But as it was, the evening had achieved the opposite.

True, I was still completely involved in the system. I wanted nothing more passionately than the victory of Soviet arms. I still believed firmly that Socialism had been realized in the Soviet Union, and that such of its manifestations as were unattractive to me personally were not the result of the system, but were explicable by the fact that it was in such a backward country as Russia that the Socialist order had first been established. I already saw these faults and defects quite clearly, but I did not yet see that they were linked by a logical connection. To me, they were still lapses by local officials; the childhood diseases of a new society; measures that had to be accepted as an inevitable consequence of backwardness; episodes of an essentially transitory character. But although this evening of self-criticism did not rob me of my faith in the Soviet Union, nevertheless it did contribute towards reinforcing my critical attitude.

The most important consequence of that evening was that, from then on, I reflected carefully upon every word and sentence I uttered, and quite consciously kept my thoughts to myself on any questions, to conceal my real feelings and opinions. But at that time my acceptance of Stalinism had much greater weight than my sense of criticism. What was likely to be the result, however, when more and more critical opinions intruded on the thoughts which I kept to myself and cautiously suppressed? Today I believe that this was the beginning of a road which was to lead seven years later, after a severe internal struggle, to my break with Stalinism and my escape from the Soviet Zone of Germany.

My reflections in the morning made me feel somewhat calmer and more secure. In the afternoon it was announced that that evening a period of criticism and self-criticism would take place in our German group. Nothing was said about the subject, but the same solemn atmosphere prevailed as in the Director's room the day before. The result was again an extreme accentuation of the tension and nervousness of everyone present.

First Wandel began to speak. The whole story was repeated: the description of the episode on the steamer, the shifting of the burden of guilt on to Stefan and myself; and finally the main barrage of criticism was again directed at me. Although this was the second time I had heard the whole story, I was just as tongue-tied as before. The critical reflections of that morning receded farther and farther into the background as every minute passed, and soon I felt again as helpless and guilty as on the previous evening. But it was not exactly the same. There were moments when I was not so completely the prisoner of events, for this time I did not lose my head, and I even felt a recurrence of my heretical thoughts.

Wandel spoke for about an hour. He explained that this complex of questions was so important as to require a further serious discussion of them in the framework of the whole group. There followed the same equation of trivial, insignificant utterances with political theories and actions. At the end of his speech he mentioned that the previous evening Linden had made an entirely unsatisfactory statement, and that now it was the duty of all members present to "define their attitude."

One after another all the members of our group then spoke. Everything went exactly according to plan. Even my best friends had now to condemn me—and they did so. The substance of the matter had been precisely prescribed in Wandel's speech, and every member of the group conformed to it. Only in the tone of their remarks was there some variation. Some of them wanted to exculpate themselves by condemning me even more severely than Wandel himself had done. Others linked their accusations against me with a personal self-criticism in which, although they had not been required to do so, they convicted themselves of similar faults. One of the students tried out of friendliness to spare me by not mentioning me at all, treating the matter entirely theoretically; thus he began with a general disquisition on the danger of defects of character—but he did not get away with it. He was sharply interrupted by Wandel and accused of deviating from the serious questions which were now under debate. Thus even this loop-hole was closed.

Several hours passed. Finally the moment came when I had to speak myself. This time I spoke more calmly and factually. I admitted my fault again, but I added at the same time that it was my intention to reflect seriously and in greater detail on the whole matter. On the first point, I was being quite honest, but the second was a tactical move which I felt myself obliged to make. After all, I already knew from the previous evening that an immediate admission of my faults was not well received. The evening then came to an end with a statement and a few closing words from Paul Wandel.

Once again no decision was reached. I still did not know whether everything was now finished or whether further measures would follow. Before long, however, it became quite clear that everything was in fact now finished. It was the first case of self-criticism in our own group. In the following weeks and months we had many further examples of this performance, until finally practically every student had been through the mill of criticism and self-criticism.

The first self-criticism was responsible for a change not only in myself but in all the other students of our group. We became more serious, and above all more cautious in everything we said. There was no more of the boisterous greeting, the uninhibited storytelling, the happy shouting. Although we were still young people between nineteen and twenty-two years of age, we behaved like staid veteran Party officials, coolly and thoughtfully choosing their words.

Translated by C.M. Woodhouse

The Red Army

Igor Gouzenko

1.

T hings at the front were going from bad to worse. Proud Rostov-on-Don surrendered to the Germans and a great despondency settled over us. I felt the news keenly because happy memories of my aunts and uncles and cousins were still very much alive. In a way, it was good that grandmother had passed away. Her fine big heart would be bleeding for her "flowers without motherly watering."

Shortly after news of the surrender reached us, our chief called us together and with troubled expression read from an official paper.

"This," he began, "is an order from the Commander-in-Chief, Marshal of the Soviet Union and Comrade Stalin."

He cleared his throat. We were straining forward with bated breath. Never before had a Stalin order been read to us.

"Having surrendered Rostov, the Red Army has besmirched its banners for centuries. The commanders had every opportunity to save Rostov yet they failed. I have ordered all commanders immediately responsible removed from their posts and their ranks reduced. We must learn from the enemy. In order to raise the standard of discipline in the Red Army I order the formation of penal battalions for officers and penal companies for the ranks. The penal companies will be stationed in the front lines in order that the guilty officers and men may redeem their fault with their blood."

"Secondly," the Stalin order continued, "I order the formation of 'restraining companies' to be composed of trusted detachments of the NKVD armed with machine guns. These 'restraining companies' will be stationed behind weak and spiritless regiments with explicit instructions to shoot to kill if the regiments show signs of faltering from their front line positions.

"The Germans have organized 'penal' and 'restraining companies.' We must do the same because the German standard of discipline is higher than ours. In contrast with the Germans, however, the Red Army has the basic support of the honorable idea of freeing their fatherland. The Red Army is fired with the noble inspiration of defending a righteous cause. From that inspiration must rise iron discipline.

"Those who have completed their sentence in the penal battalions will be exonerated of past blame and reinstated in their former rank and service. Only the most trusted and exceptionally exacting younger officers are to be placed in command of the guarding battalions."

The Stalin order concluded with a stern sentence:

"The Russian people curse the Red Army which is retreating and leaves them in slavery with the Germans."

As we walked away, subdued and worried by this harsh message from our idol, somebody ahead remarked in a loud whisper: "Compulsory bravery!" Another snapped back: "Good soldiers don't retreat!"

Almost immediately an extensive campaign of Russian patriotism began in the newspapers, on the radio and in the motion picture theaters.

The seriousness and danger of the situation was stressed. Lengthy articles, filled with emotional appeal, frankly stated the fatherland was in peril. An ingenious propaganda note that escaped me at the time was injected during this period.

The words "communism" and "Soviet" disappeared. Instead everything was spoken of as "Russian." Marxism was forgotten. Communism versus Fascism was forgotten. Everything carried the "Defend Russia!" theme. Military heroes were described or dug up from ancient graves. "Russian soil" was repeatedly mentioned. Ilya Ehrenburg, later the subject of drooling admiration during a tour of North America, disappeared temporarily from the pages of the newspapers, because somebody suddenly remembered Ilya was not a Russian.

Press articles set a new high in frankness. For example, one article by government-favored Gorbatov described how an old woman watching the retreating soldiers cursed the Red Army.

The effect of such unprecedented frankness impressed on the people how things had changed, and that they were now all one family. There was a reversion to old Russian traditions, to Russian folklore. Russian folk songs, Russian patience and endurance, Russian common sense, Russian bravery and self-sacrifice. All were emphasized in the newspapers, while stories of the bravery of modest Russian heroes were given major prominence.

Marshal Koulik was reduced to Major-General for surrendering Rostov. Ten generals whose names were mentioned in a Stalin order were cashiered. Koulik's name abruptly disappeared from the news. When last I heard of him, he was handling an unimportant administrative task in the Department of Defense.

There were many such discredited generals working in the "administration nothing" sections of the Red Army, as the war progressed. Usually they were given to drunkenness. Major-General Yevstigneiev was typical. One morning on Frunze Street I saw him reeling, holding to a railing while trying to adjust his persian lamb hat. He was cursing loudly. The militia watched him in perplexity from a distance. Drunken officers were subject to arrest, but a general had complete power, even to shooting ordinary soldiers.

A general's uniform was very resplendent and generals were forbidden to travel on streetcars. However, since generals were easier to make than automobiles, many of them had to walk while subordinates rode by on streetcars.

None of us liked to walk along Frunze Street, Gogol Boulevard or Comintern Street, because generals and colonels were so plentiful our saluting hand was never lowered. In theaters, the best seats were reserved for generals because they were forbidden to sit farther back than the sixth row.

All this was done to increase the power and authority of high command personnel, yet an ordinary workingman in the United States or Canada is living in a home incomparably better than that of the Russian general. The workingman's home outside of Russia also has conveniences the general has never imagined existed.

The wife of a Canadian worker never had to stand in a long queue waiting for an onion, and only an onion. Yet the wife of a Russian general learned she could excite envy and interest by obtaining an onion. It meant a privileged position.

The Russian general, too, always has the threat of Siberia hanging over him. Stalin has authority to order it without question, and the general usually has more opportunity for displeasing Stalin than anybody else in the Soviet Union.

One day at Intelligence Headquarters we were awed to find an unexpected visitor in our midst. It was Kalinin, premier of the Soviet Republics.

We knew he must have something very important to say because, in the Soviet Union, only people of importance are permitted any freedom of speech.

There were few preliminaries. Even the usual introductions, filled with lavishly exaggerated praise, were omitted. Kalinin's voice was so low that those in the rear couldn't bear him.

"The Red Army is in retreat," he said, "leaving Russian towns and Russian people behind it. Never before has Russian soil borne such shame. Our Red Army appears inferior to the German army, our officers appear inferior to the German officers, our general staff appears decidedly inferior to the German general staff. We have apparently over-estimated ourselves and under-estimated the enemy."

We listened with unbelieving ears. We had expected fire and thunder, or inspiration from the powerful Kalinin, member of the *Politburo*. Instead, we saw an apparently dejected and pessimistic man. Although we were not aware of it at the time, this Kalinin performance marked a deliberate reversal of Soviet leaders' tactics. Abruptly faced with the realization that abstract, high-sounding phrases had failed to evoke expected surges of patriotism, the leaders decided to abandon their aloofness. They decided to identify themselves with the hardships and misfortunes as co-sufferers with the common men and thus remove the impression of relentless dictators whose brutal system had been basically responsible for most of the hardships and misfortunes.

The finale of Kalinin's dour message was even more depressing.

"But the worst feature of Russia's present plight is that our people don't know how to die." He gazed around for a moment before continuing. "They have not learned to die. I speak not as a member of the government but as a simple Russian whose heart is sore. But I tell you this, although the Red Army has shown weakness the Party will find strength to pull Russia through."

On still another occasion we were formed up to hear another "Secret Order" of the Red Army read to us.

The order noted that officers and soldiers had recently abandoned military equipment in the field of battle when in retreat. This had been specially noted in the case of artillery men, who, in running away to save their lives, had left their heavy guns, cannon, howitzers and trench mortars on the field of battle. In addition, theft of state property was reportedly becoming more frequent.

The order dealt with the situation tersely.

"I order that those guilty of leaving military equipment on the field of battle shall be shot on the spot without trial. For any theft of property I set one form of punishment—immediate execution by firing squad.

"This order is to be read to all regiments, details, garrisons, schools and units of the Red Army."

It was signed: "Commander-in-Chief, Stalin."

A subsequent follow-up order reminded commanders who did not act promptly as commanded that they would be "punished with the greatest severity." Stalin further demanded that every weapon and piece of military equipment would be charged to a definite individual and in the case of his death would become the full responsibility of the next lower in rank. Officers in command of guns were ordered to defend same with their lives.

"It is better to die defending the guns than to surrender them and live," the order stated.

From these extreme measures and their urgent tone, it was clear that so

100

much equipment had been thrown away that the situation was extremely serious. A higher value was now placed on guns than on human life.

Stalin then commanded a check-up of all military equipment to be made and completed within two weeks, and the results reported without delay.

The press and radio news suddenly featured reports of German machine-gunners being found chained to their guns. This propaganda twist was apparently double-edged. For the public, it helped explain why the Germans were fighting so well against our supposedly invincible Red Army. For the Red Army, it was a subtle warning about things to come if desertion of weapons continued.

From the commander of the Kazan garrison came a report that startled our section considerably. The report was only twenty-five words long. I read it over so often in unbelieving amazement, that the words still remain impressed on my mind.

"Major-General Ivanov issued an extra ration to an officer who was leaving for duty elsewhere. I have ordered Major-General Ivanov to be shot."

Most of us knew Major-General Ivanov by sight at least. He was a popular, kindly man not usually associated with the cruel, tyrannical type of Red Army general. He had a ready, contagious laugh and was particularly well-liked by members of his staff. On one of the two occasions on which I had to speak to him, he treated me more as an associate of equal rank than as an awed lieutenant.

It seemed likely that Major-General Ivanov's kindliness had proven his undoing. Poor fellow, he had very bad luck, because ordinarily nobody would pay serious attention to an extra ration, especially when issued on the authority of such a high and respected officer. There were whisperings that he had really committed a more serious offense, and the incident of the extra ration was used merely as a pretext, but such whisperings weren't uncommon after sensational executions.

If it was the Soviet Government's intention to use his death to place stress on a campaign against thefts of military property, the execution was a complete success. Its immediate effect in our school ranks was to cause us to keep a desperately close watch on our suitcases. In common with others, I had my share of enemies among those seeking choice posts at Intelligence Headquarters, and realized the current situation presented unrivaled opportunity for my disposal by planting some piece of equipment in my suitcase and informing on me. I made a habit of checking several times daily.

Among the students was one, Lieutenant Ivan Tourkin, who was a village schoolteacher before becoming a political director in the army. He was subsequently sent from Moscow to Mexico, where a determined undercover organization was being affiliated with the Military Attaché's department.

Tourkin had a distinguished career in the army. Before being wounded he had worked his way to the command of a battery of artillery and it was of intimate experience with the Red Army at the front that he often used to talk.

All sections of the front were in retreat, he once told us, and the heavy guns made retreating in order extremely difficult. Others were abandoning their guns, but not Tourkin. Even when a column of German cavalry passed down the road, his battery, hidden in the woods, courageously opened fire and blasted the Germans heavily. However, this gave away their hiding-place and they in turn were badly battered by German artillery.

Their line of retreat led to a river, the Dneiper, and when what was left of Tourkin's battery arrived there, the near bank was crowded with Red Army officers and men milling up and down the bank. A demolished bridge was under steady bombing and strafing attack. The river could be swum only by most expert swimmers, which made the plight of most troops serious, and that of the wounded, hopeless.

Tourkin had suffered a shattered arm and was quite weak. There was another bridge two kilometers away but nobody knew whether it was still intact. Anyway, he doubted, after losing so much blood, if he could walk far. Finally he decided to try crossing by swimming with one hand close to the demolished bridge. In that way he would have piers and twisted girders on which to rest. He would take a chance on the accuracy of the German aerial attack.

Inching his way across was a nightmare. Tourkin described how he would reach a pier and weakly grab for a hold through the maze of soldiers already holding on there, only to be shoved off. His wounded arm meant nothing. It was every man for himself.

A twisted girder saved his life in one spot because be couldn't have made it to the next pier. A buckled strut allowed him another precious breather. The cold water, however, must have had a stimulating effect. Eventually he stumbled on and up the other bank, where he saw some wounded being carried into a large wooden shack. Tourkin lurched inside but the conditions were so bad and the stench so sickening he went outside again, preferring to shiver in the cold air. He found a clump of trees some hundred yards away and sank down there for a rest. As he did so, a bomb hit the wooden shack and blew it and the wounded to pieces.

This crossing of the Dneiper later became known throughout the Red Army as "Operation Sokolovsky." Nobody seemed to know just why. The general opinion was that the episode had been a terrible disgrace, wherein

Russian soldiers had lost all semblance of discipline and allowed a defeat to become a panic-stricken rout. So strong was public feeling about "Operation Sokolovsky," that some students treated Tourkin with open contempt, despite his having been wounded in action.

The Tourkin episode taught us that even a brave war record meant nothing in the face of any adverse opinion the Communist Party wished to encourage—or condone. The Party, it seemed, always made the most of any opportunity to slap the army down.

The German invasion of Russia on June 21, 1941, came in the nature of a shocking surprise. Throughout the summer there had been rumors of the Stalin-Hitler non-aggression pact developing frayed edges. But, like the Allied peoples, we were inclined to regard such rumors as part of Hitler's "war of nerves." After all, it did seem irrational that Hitler, with England falling steadily, would establish a 1,700-mile battlefront from the Arctic to the Black Sea.

When Hitler did announce that Russia and the Reich were at war, commenting that "Russia, Great Britain and the United States have been continually trying to throttle Germany," the Red Army was already retreating steadily. The same army that had made such a dismal showing in the Finnish war was then reported to be fighting "with tremendous bravery," yet it was apparent that the Red Army was failing to engage the Nazis in anything resembling a battle.

The field regiments, staffs, NKVD detachments, Intelligence Sections, propaganda organizations and Party bodies in such cities as Riga, Lvov, and Bielstok, simply packed up in a mad rush and fled for Moscow. Wives and children of responsible workers were often placed on trains within hearing of the artillery bombardment.

2.

Years later, Gorshkov, a fellow member of the Soviet embassy staff at Ottawa, told us he had been working in Bielostok at the time. He managed to get his wife and all their transportable belongings on to a crowded train, and followed in a crowded official auto, for the Soviet Union.

Weaving their way through crowded streets and highways packed with every kind of vehicle, Gorshkov finally arrived at Minsk to find the city still in the throes of panic caused by the German air raid on the morning of June 21st. On reporting to the Intelligence Section, he was mobilized with all other available manpower, to quell the panic and "exterminate diversionists."

With drawn pistols they marched into a mob milling in front of the railway station. A German had been caught in the uniform of a Russian militia man. Gorshkov and his companions put the German under formal arrest and were just about to lead him away when a Nazi plane dropped a stick of bombs across the area. When Gorshkov managed to crawl from the debris of a collapsed wall, he found the prisoner had escaped. But even as he looked around there came a cry:

"The German! The spy!"

An army captain had spotted the German weaving uncertainly across the smoky, dusty street. The captain drew his revolver and shot the German through the head.

Minsk became an absolute chaos. Gorshkov and seven others were crowded into a car and ordered to get to Moscow as quickly as possible. But just outside Minsk the traffic snarled into a solid, motionless mass. A general came rushing along and yelled at Gorshkov.

"In the name of the military Soviet you must take action at once. This movement of automobiles must be halted and the highway cleared for the army."

Rather uncertainly, Gorshkov drew his revolver and pointed it at approaching cars. Some stopped, others speeded through. In the thick of the new bottleneck, a woman in the uniform of a captain of the Medical Services began shrieking at a colonel. She used the word Saboteur repeatedly. The colonel replied with a coarse epithet.

Abruptly, the woman drew her revolver and shot the colonel dead!

A lieutenant in the colonel's party flashed out his revolver and fired. The woman's face went blank, she pawed at her chest, then plunged to the road—also dead.

The general rushed from beside Gorshkov and yelled at the lieutenant: "Why did you kill this woman?"

The lieutenant pointed with his still smoking revolver at the two bodies: "Because she killed the colonel," he answered in a tense voice.

The general ordered the lieutenant's arrest and the latter was handed over to the Special Section.

The episode served one good purpose. It quelled the traffic uproar and allowed the bottleneck to be cleared and traffic was efficiently re-routed.

3.

As the Germans approached the town of Gryaz a new high in ruthless thoroughness was established by the loyal Communist Party committee. A list of names of townspeople was drawn up; people who, it was suspected, would collaborate with the Germans on their occupation of the town. The list was based, in the main, on quick expressions of suspicion by one or more Party members. As evacuation of the town finally got under way, armed officers of the NKVD speedily visited the addresses allotted them. They would sharply ask the family name, then the first names. If any names corresponded with those on the list, the shooting was done right there—in full sight of the family.

I have no way of knowing how many executions were thus carried out, but semi-official statistics reported disposal of "thousands of potential collaborators."

This procedure won such commendation from the NKVD heads that it became standard practice in all urban locales subject to immediate evacuation. The term "to meet all contingencies" appeared frequently in conversations of Party men.

There was no attempt at any kind of probing before placing a person's name on the death list. If you were a Party member your suspicion was enough to have a fellow inhabitant shot, and I once heard a Party man comment dryly that the most had been made of "a splendid opportunity to purge loud-mouthed nuisances."

In the cases of jails and concentration camps, the Army transferred the inmates if time permitted. Otherwise mass executions were performed to prevent those inmates from possible alliance with the German invaders.

Later, when exactly similar stories of "German outrages" were published in the controlled Soviet press, I marvelled at the crocodile tears shed by many of the same Party members who had approved such action by the NKVD and Red Army firing squads among their own people.

The whole transplanting of entire population groups from the German Autonomous Republic was carried out with unbelievable cruelty in spite of the fact that these people were real Soviet citizens. But the Soviet Government decided not to risk the chance of this Republic supporting the Germans, and ordered the mass exodus to be carried out under NKVD supervision.

The unfortunate people were given twenty-four hours to gather only such belongings as each could carry. They were formed into columns and marched to the nearest railway stations, each family being responsible for any ailing members, as well as children.

The villages were left absolutely bare. The cows, unmilked and unwatered for days, bellowed until they weakened and died. There was practically nothing alive by the time the first of the refugees poured in from German-occupied districts. These residents from Soviet Union points were settled in villages and towns of the Republic and given full ownership of the homes of the expelled citizens. In this way, the flow of refugees was stopped and the Germans found "true" Soviets in the urban points. But no NKVD report ever attempted to explain the senseless and wanton destruction of the cattle at the time when foodstuffs were so vitally needed.

The same "transplanting" procedure was performed later in two other "autonomous" Republics—the Checheno-Ingoush and the Crimean-Tartar Republics.

Where German occupation did not follow immediately or, in some cases not at all, this installing of tens of thousands of refugees in the ruined and ravaged areas merely resulted in a series of crises for the Soviet administration. These refugees had to be fed or they would be wonderful subjects for German propaganda when the Germans did come. So an emergency relief program had to be organized with supplies sorely needed by the country in general, for people of the Republics made desolate by the Soviet "transplanting"!

In Intelligence Headquarters it was privately admitted by some officers that a fantastic series of blunders had been committed. At one time an "exhaustive survey" of our documents was made by Red Army Intelligence men and we noted they seemed only interested in removing anything pertaining to the "emergency executions" and transplanting of Republic populations.

Yet, so effective is Communist Party preaching when extended from cradle to grave that at the time I sincerely regarded this Stalin-ordered blood-bath of our own countrymen not as a bloody blot on Russian history, but rather as awesome evidence of Stalin's power.

Our leader had demonstrated, through determined use of his Red Army and the NKVD branch operating within the Red Army, that he could ruin even Republics as effectively as he had gained control over them.

4.

By the time I returned to Moscow, mother and sister had been through experiences that would have killed an average man. But somehow they survived and I found them in 1942 back in their same little room again. Both looked old beyond their years and mother in particular brought a lump to my throat. Her brain had evidently wearied, the alertness was going. It was obvious, too, that she was starving.

When the Scientific Research Institute where sister worked had been hurriedly evacuated to Sverdlovsk in the Urals, she, in desperation, took mother along.

Several people died on the way from the innumerable hardships. Later, cold, rain and disease took so many lives that morale hit an almost impossible ebb. The Scientific Research Institute was moved back to Moscow.

Mother no longer spoke critically of Soviet authority. But she did say repeatedly that Russia must conquer the Germans.

"And then, please God," she would invariably add, "things may be better."

A rule by fear was now in full force in Moscow.

Keynoted by Stalin's speech approving what he called stern action on "a healthy suspicion," important arrests were being made throughout the Soviet Union during working hours. This was designed to work a psychological effect on the public in general, and fearful whisperings never lose anything in repetition.

The wave of purging, as inspired by Stalin himself, made normal existence perilous.

In the *Politburo*, even long before the war, a "healthy suspicion" was publicly expressed. Kaganovich attacked Andreyev, Commissar of Railroad Transportation, with venom never before heard among members of the *Politburo*. The accusations linked Andreyev with the opposition party, although this had happened a long time previously. However, Andreyev was speedily replaced by Kaganovich. Now, from what I read, Andreyev is back in favor with Stalin so it should be interesting to see what happens to Kaganovich.

The major danger behind the Stalin "suspicion" craze lay in petty political individuals making charges against rivals to protect themselves, a ruse not at all difficult where proof wasn't essential. And, in the Soviet Union, then as now, the road from suspicion to concentration camp or firing squad was very short.

What astonishes me in retrospect is the obvious fact that the "healthy suspicion" tactics caused more harm to the Soviet Union than a whole army of spies and saboteurs. What the spies and saboteurs were unable to do, no matter how skilful, the scheming, self-protection, Party leaders and bureaucrats accomplished with great success. In at least three cases, I knew of Dynamo engineers being removed from their posts because "healthy suspicions" had been voiced against them. On all three occasions their assistants were appointed to the vacancies as rewards for informing!

The damage caused among young minds by this "healthy suspicion" complex is incalculable. It became noticeable that honest, conscientious workers were more and more frequently the victims of such attacks. It was also noticeable that more and more young workers were openly figuring in accusations, appreciating, no doubt, the double opportunity presented of not only speeding their own way to the top, but also of establishing their own staunch loyalty to the Soviet.

For four consecutive years, the hunt for "enemies of the people" continued with unabated fury. The hunters of yesterday became the hunted of today. It went to such preposterous extremes that Stanov, a member of the *Politburo*, recommended at one of the Party congresses that we should classify our enemies under three categories:

"Enemy,"

"Lesser Enemy,"

"Insignificant Enemy."

We all began seeing enemies on every hand. Party secretaries were behaving like people sitting on hot bricks. The situation grew ludicrous as almost every member of the Regional Committee, the district Soviet organization and most Party members became periodically objects of suspicion or counter-suspicion. The main thing was for you to speak your bit first, but after your prestige was established, somebody was sure to knock you.

A lecturer, whom most of us personally admired, proved a classic example. He evidently made some remark one day that could have been construed two ways. The wrong way was immediately reported to the principal who in turn reported it to the NKVD. Speed was essential, because if somebody else reported to the NKVD first it might look as if the principal didn't take care of his staff. In this instance I know the principal didn't even take time to check with the lecturer, who was arrested in the lecture hall before our eyes. Somebody told me he was freed after some time but never returned to the Institute.

This sort of thing extended even to institutions far removed from the political sphere. For example, if the hairdressers' organization had been going along for some time without "suspicions" being directed at them an official opinion would eventually develop that the hairdressers were being "protected" by the Regional Committee. There was such a charge as "political shortsight-edness" that took care of almost any such exigency.

During those days a knock on the door was enough to make one's knees tremble. The first thought would be: "What have I done?" When no answer was forthcoming, you'd next ask yourself: "What am I being accused of ?" and, of course, there was no answer to that one.

The NKVD became a thoroughly hated body of men—their forage caps with light blue top (called "Cornflowers"), a symbol of mixed fear and savage scorn. When occasion presented itself for a safe expression of opinion in a crowd setting, you'd hear individuals muttering such epithets as:

"Huns! Traitors! Murderers!"

Yet, it seemed, the more such hatred was expressed the more satisfaction they seemed to derive from their despicable work. Stalin himself repeatedly approved of this antagonism between people and NKVD, realizing, no doubt, that with the NKVD more hated than even the Tsar's Okhrana, the constant search for subversive groups would be much more effective. Dissatisfaction among workers was naturally more quickly and effectively suppressed when the NKVD watch-dogs were looking for reason to act—and not sympathetically.

Selection for the NKVD was and still is made from people who are rough, who recognize force only and act with force. Once in their clutches it was impossible to figure what would happen. Their great weapon lay in making annoying people "disappear." They would arrest your brother and when you would go to inquire about him his name just wasn't on the record.

"You must have made a mistake," the NKVD official was sure to say, with a cold eye that suggested you watch your step.

The suspicion mania embraced almost every human action. This was best exemplified at the temporary school to which we cadets were sent when Moscow was in danger. It had been a Forestry Technical school and was situated in a forest almost totally isolated from the rest of Russia. The women cleaners were brought from a village which was some miles away, along a road fit only for oxen. This village was a thousand kilometers from Moscow and far removed even from a railway station. Practically the entire population was illiterate, dull and apparently half-starved. Yet one day our chief, Colonel Ershov, called us to a meeting and solemnly warned us to exercise extreme caution with these cleaners from the village because he had been warned that some of them might be "spies" and "diversionists."

From that moment we looked at the poor, plodding old women with ill-concealed suspicion. We even locked our classroom doors while studying. The thought of those precautions now makes me smile. But I believed it then.

It surprises me to realize how utter nonsense was made to look reasonably acceptable, the same nonsense which is still being forced down Russians' throats as truth.

A group of us made one trip—and one only—to the village. What we saw left us abjectly depressed.

We arrived at the lunch hour and found peasants of the local Kolkhoz at the mess hall waiting in queue for a piece of bread about the size of a fist. The queue wound into a cabin that was thick with tobacco smoke and soot. There was a sound of quarreling and some shouting. Apparently, a man had pushed somebody ahead of him and the distributor had refused the man his share.

Once the bread queue had been passed, the peasants moved on to another queue where they were handed a dirty wooden bowl into which muddy-looking liquid was ladled. This combination of "soup" and bread represented a meal that would cause a riot in an average penitentiary.

I thought of the way we had grumbled about our food at Headquarters and felt inwardly ashamed. Beside this peasant fare our eating was in the luxury class. Within me, once again, I, as a son of peasant stock, felt burning anger that these poor human beings should be forced to live so close to the animal fringe. But, as quickly as the anger rose, it was suppressed by the training that compels one to abstain from critical observations on anything associated with the Soviet system. I didn't dream there was any country in the world where free speech on such matters could be attempted without fear of concentration camp—or death.

Communist training ingeniously educated us when seeing such evidences of maladministration to think how much worse off these peasants would be under the capitalistic system. Later I often remembered those shuffling lines of peasants in ragged coats, nondescript caps, their faces dirty and haggard. Some were patient and humble, others made pathetically nervous gestures of impatience. They returned to memory whenever, here in Canada, I read propaganda pamphlets featuring the glowing benefits offered the "underprivileged" by Communism.

At the school we cadets also went hungry most of the time. Often we had pea soup, sometimes three times a day, without anything else. Whispers had it that Colonel Ershov and his friend, Commissar Krylenko, received generous rations for us, but converted most of the food into drink by trading it. Certainly they both looked well fed and we were all aware of frequent parties. They certainly got the liquor somewhere and had to pay for it with what? Vodka was never sold, it was used for bartering.

In the cities, such as Moscow, there was curious evidence of the Soviet government's actual encouragement of the black market. I've never been able to figure out the reason but I've seen enough evidence to be sure of it.

Whenever vodka was sold at the official stores, the queues were always the longest because, as all officials knew, it could be exchanged for bread, soap, milk and other products. The original purchasers seldom, if ever, drank it. Officers gave their vodka to their wives for bartering on the market in exchange for groceries.

I never allowed an opportunity for obtaining vodka or wine to pass. On one such occasion I managed to get a few bottles and thought of Nina Grouyeva. However, knowing how degraded the unfortunate girl had become, I knew she would probably drink them. I exchanged the bottles for two bars of soap. I had no trouble finding her address—the police had it officially recorded by this time. I enclosed a note:

"A little present for old time's sake."

Over all this constantly hovered the dread NKVD with the most savage weapon of all, the threat of cutting rations. And, too, they had the greatest prize of all—an extra ration.

Yet, even as these Russian people starved and fought like dogs for crusts, there were outrageous contrasts. Anna's brother, Gousev, worked at one time as supply agent for the mess at the plant *Tsagi,* a large aircraft factory in Moscow engaged mainly in the construction of experimental aircraft.

It happened on one occasion that the distributing point from which he usually obtained the food products for the mess had run out of its stock. As the factory was of prime importance and the workers could not live without food, some high personage permitted an issue of food to be made from a Government provision supply base.

Gousev was instructed to accompany a truck driver to an address on Highway No. 10. It sounded wrong because the section was practically barren of housing, much less warehouses. However, they drove as directed and found themselves at a shack. But the street number was on it. Gousev rapped on the door, which was opened by an armed soldier. He asked to see the credentials of both Gousev and driver. After a careful check of documents, the soldier pointed to a narrow, almost indiscernible road off the highway into the forest.

"Drive along that road until you're stopped," he said.

They turned into the forest and after a quarter of a mile of bumpy road were halted by armed guards standing before a gate leading through a barbed-wire entanglement.

Their credentials were again checked and, as a double precaution, one of the guards telephoned the permit bureau in Moscow. Apparently he was told that Gousev and the driver were there legally for provisions, because he opened the gate and told them where to report.

The provision supply base was subterranean and astonishingly extensive, but their eyes almost popped with what they saw stored along the sides.

There, in full view, were stacks of smoked fish, thousands of smoked hams, mountains of sugar sacks and flour sacks, canned goods of almost every type, tons of edibles which Gousev and the driver had heard about but never tasted. The warehouse was so big and the supplies so vast it seemed as though the wealth of Russia was here assembled.

Gousev told me afterwards the height of so much food while Russia was starving beyond the walls seemed obscene. The amazement on his face apparently amused the warehouse manager.

"What's the matter with you?" he laughed loudly. "Not hungry today?"

For a moment Gousev gazed at the warehouse manager, uncomprehending.

"Do you mean…" Gousev stuttered, "we can eat some of this?"

"Eat all you want," the manager waved in the direction of the supplies, but added in stern tone, "Carry away all you want as long as it is in your bellies. Don't try taking anything out beyond what your official order calls for."

Gousev and the driver went a little berserk. They ate their fill for the first time in years. As they began loading the truck Gousev became sick. His stomach was not used to such generous feeding.

The warehouse manager saw Gousev leaning against the truck vomiting. He roared with laughter.

"That's what I get for being kind to him!" he boomed at the guards. "Now he wasting our good food."

Meanwhile, the "common" people in that particular district were getting one small piece of bread a day, which they apportioned so that it might last the day. This required strong will-power with hunger constantly gnawing at their insides. Some people managed to fight off the temptation, but most ate their bread in the morning and went hungry the rest of the day. Still others would use extra rations and find themselves without any bread whatsoever for the last three or four days of the month.

Of course, bread could be obtained on the black market. White bread cost 120 rubles a pound, black bread 100 rubles. But this was beyond the reach of the ordinary worker, who was lucky to receive 300 rubles a month. In fact, I saw many plant workers sleeping at the plant because they lacked the strength to walk a long distance home.

A child's life meant little. The small tots were dying like flies from undernourishment.

Meanwhile, throughout the hungry years, the representatives of Soviet bureaucracy, then as now, displayed a great zest for squandering public money. We grew to long for the time when we would achieve a position entitling us to participate in the banquets which where held on the smallest pretext. The birthday of the district secretary of the Party, for example, was always the occasion for a very special orgy.

It was entirely in keeping with our Communist twist of mind that waiters' whispered stories, about wasted food and episodes resulting from celebrants getting entirely drunk, failed to shock us.

During the war, I would read those colorful press stories of Soviet dinners given to visiting political and military dignitaries, including Winston Churchill and the late President Roosevelt, and realized they followed the same pattern all the way down the line to the minutest official. Lavish feasts were the bureaucrat's privilege, while starvation raged outside the very windows!

The lesser bureaucrats, including all kinds of secretaries of regional and town committees, in emulating the higher authority, do not restrict themselves to food and drink in living literally at the expense of the nation. Even their furniture comes from public funds.

Never before has Russian soil supported such a class of parasites. They compose a whole class of society, a debauched and unprincipled layer of hypocrites living at the expense of the Russian people, who no matter what propaganda is poured out to the world, are at this moment living in the utmost degradation and poverty.

These people, the great masses of modern Russia, must stand in queues for the merest pittance of bread. Clothing means rags to the overwhelming majority. But what is worse, they have no hope of ever being able to live better. And while this condition exists, the bureaucrats bring finery from abroad for their wives.

On one occasion in Moscow there was considerable merriment caused in official circles over a long sweeping gown worn by an important secretary's wife at a large banquet. He had brought it back with him after a flying mission to London. It had obviously cost a lot of money and was certainly very beautiful but, to the chagrin of the secretary and his wife, they found during the party that it was a nightgown!

During the war all kinds of groceries were sent to Russia from the United States, but the ordinary Russian people saw very few of these. Mainly they were allocated to the innumerable stratas of bureaucrats. Thus American generosity helped this "authority" to live without hardship during the most severe period of the war.

At a dinner arranged by a general shortly after Stalingrad, I saw a table loaded with American canned goods, vodka and delicatessen products. What would have fed ten Russian families for a month was eaten there by a small group of well-fed guests. But the most unhappy aspect of it was that this group ate with complete conviction that they had a right to it. Their consciences were absolutely clear. The sufferings of the people were not their concern.

Therein lies the iron hold of the Soviet system.

The vast horde of big bureaucrats and little bureaucrats are vigorously loyal because of what it means in food, drink, homes and parties. The vast army is loyal for the same reason it stayed loyal during Russia's grimmest war years—you eat well in the army. Even when conditions were at their worst, the shrewd Soviet organization kept rations at peak-best in the front lines, so much so troops in the rear lines continually asked to be sent up front. There used to be a saying among front-line troops:

"While you live you eat well."

The control of food is a power you people in democracies have never had to think about very seriously. But you would, if the state punished a critical public utterance or failure to pay some taxation by decreasing the food ration for your family.

There are vast hordes of other privileged classes such as the *Komsomols.* And, at the top, there are, I calculate, some 5,000,000 official members of the Communist Party.

113

Most Americans and Canadians I have met seem to think all Russians are Communists. Such is not the case. Membership in the Party is much sought after because of the privileges and better chances it offers for top jobs. And it isn't so easy to become a member. It took me two years to obtain the required three signatures of Party members for membership in the *Komsomols*.

Members are hesitant about vouching for a candidate because there is always a harsh kick-back if the new member doesn't pan out well. I shudder to think what happened to the three who vouched for me!

With regard to a candidate for membership in the Party, there are three stages. First comes that of sympathizer, then candidate and finally member. Observation is exceedingly intensive and promotion from one stage to the next happens only after careful consideration. However, you may readily appreciate that the 5,000,000 members represent a staunch supporting element for the Soviet system, a loyalty held by special privileges, special rations and fear of death and suffering if higher-up displeasure is incurred.

Still another steel band handcuffing the people of Russia is the omnipresent and entirely ruthless NKVD and their vast array of "special committees." A conspiracy against the Soviet is utterly impossible as long as the NKVD is operating. It is all so very simple. In a nation haunted by thoughts of rations, dreaming of more rations or fearing less rations, everybody knows that giving valuable information to the NKVD means privileges.

If any two people got together to hatch the overthrow of the Soviet system, it is most likely that one of them would come around to the thought of reporting the other to the NKVD. If the conspiracy grew larger, it is unthinkable that somebody wouldn't weaken—thinking the conspiracy couldn't get anywhere anyway and he might obtain a minor bureaucrat job through betraying his fellows.

So it goes all the way to the top, where any man who puts his hands in his pockets in the presence of Stalin is liable to be shot instantly. The same goes for standing behind Stalin.

But even if a plot against Stalin succeeded there is, from my personal observation, little or no chance of a change coming from within. There are big men such as Molotov ready to take over and no organization in world history, even the Nazi machine, has ever been more proficient at shoving national heroes out of the spotlight.

Did you ever stop to wonder what ever happened to the great Russian generals of the heroic post-Stalingrad days?

As soon as the necessity for keeping them in the headlines was gone, Stalin saw to it that these popular war heroes were shifted to remote commands. Like the pretty girl who always chooses a homely girl as a chum, Stalin never allows himself to be obscured by popular personalities.

There were Germans, they say, who used to pray for defeat in the hope of having kind and just liberators take over Germany. I feel that many who still pray in Soviet Russia, pray along the same line. Frankly, with full appreciation of the awful consequences, I have long since reached the conclusion that such is Russia's only hope, unless more men like me make a decisive move toward breaking down the iron curtain behind which the Soviet "shelters" its millions from exposure to democracy.

5.

On returning to Moscow, I found very few of my friends left. Many of them were at the front. Of the girls I used to know two had married. The husband of one was the commandant at one of Moscow's railway stations and, she confessed confidently, he was able to bring home sacks of flour at fairly frequent intervals. She left me to figure out how he got them.

Another girl I had known for several years lived next door to where mother and sister resided. On entering her room on a visit a sickening stench hit me. It was coming from something cooking on the stove, something that looked like thick paste of a greenish-gray color. The girl, now haggard and unattractive, was obviously embarrassed. She hastily covered the pot and sat down. Conversation was awkward. She seemed to resent my neat uniform. When I asked personal questions about how she was getting along, she snapped:

"Not so well!"

I tried to shift the conversation to pleasant memories but she remained silently staring at me. Finally, I left without my old friend even saying goodbye.

Many of the people I had known intimately were so changed in appearance I failed to recognize them. Some openly castigated me for what they charged was deliberate ignoring of them. Others seemed frightened by the uniform, answered in monosyllables when I spoke to them and left me in a hurry. The "healthy suspicion" epidemic was at its peak and the poor frightened people had already learned there was no longer such a thing as dependable friendship.

Even in my mother's home, conditions were no longer pleasant. The filth of the house and the foul smell of dirty clothes on mother and sister made my clothes burn into my self-consciousness. There just wasn't any soap with which to wash and, when I sat down to supper, there was only soup that smelled so bad I just couldn't swallow it.

Sister laughed shortly and said to mother:

"Surely you know he gets much better food where he is!"

115

Mother tried to smooth over the remark, but I held no resentment; their ghastly thinness told the story. I asked if they would like to split my soup between them and both reached at once.

I visited the Architectural Institute and found the food situation was having a disastrous effect on the teaching staff. Their sole source of food was in the mess, and food there was exceptionally bad. They got no fats and the soup was as weak as water. They had become so emaciated I failed to recognize some of them, particularly a lecturer on planning and designing who had been one of my favorite professors. He had become a skeleton and it was plain he was dying as he sketched on a blackboard. But he was getting old. He had entered the category of the *lishnetzy*. His usefulness to the USSR had faded. We realized it was inevitable that he would be starved systematically. The decrease in his rations was normal official procedure and there was just nothing to be done about it. A few months later, I heard with some relief of the kindly old fellow's death.

It was during this period that Liubimov, a veteran now taking the cipher clerk course, related an incident that had happened while he was serving on the Caucasian front.

The Red Army had been pushed back to the outskirts of Tuapse, a town noted only because it contained one of Stalin's "summer houses." Even with the Germans so close, detachments of NKVD troops guarded all entrances to the large estate which contained a series of buildings spread through groves of shady trees.

Liubimov was helping move the wounded back and witnessed a grim scene at the main entrance to the Stalin grounds. The doctor in charge of the wounded noticed the buildings inside the grounds and asked the NKVD guards to let him pass. One guard rasped:

"Entrance to these premises is forbidden."

The doctor impatiently waved his arms and cursed at them. He attempted to push his way by the guard but they shoved him back.

"This is a government house. If you come one step further you'll get a bayonet through you!"

The doctor was pale with rage. He said no more, but signalled the column of wounded to proceed along their course. He finally commandeered a number of half-demolished houses and the wounded men were left there. Those who couldn't stand were stretched in rows on the floors.

When Liubimov told me about the episode in Tuapse he was greatly disturbed.

"It was the most shameful thing I ever saw," he said hoarsely. "Of course," I commented as sincerely as possible, "Stalin didn't know about it. If he had known he would have welcomed the wounded into his summer home. Liubimov studied my face, then nodded. "I think so, too," he said.

116

The Bridge at Andau

James Michener

The promises of communism were so inclusive and so cleverly worded that in 1944 Gyorgy Szabo, who was then exempt from military service because he was working in the munitions part of what was later to be renamed after the contemporary communist leader, the Rakosi Metal Works, secretly joined a cell of communists. In this exciting and dedicated group of men, Szabo imagined himself to be working for a communist Hungary in which the vast promises of his party would be fulfilled.

In the spring of 1945, when Szabo was twenty-four years old, the communists launched a major propaganda drive which was destined to end in their controlling Hungary. Szabo says, "It was very exciting. Of course, we understood that not all the promises could be put into operation right away, because Hungary had to be rebuilt after the destruction of the war. And it was explained to us that we needed Russian guidance for some years, since they knew what communism was and we didn't."

So although Russian planes and guns had destroyed much of Hungary in freeing it from the Germans, Gyorgy Szabo and his communist friends had to buckle down under Russian leadership and repair the damage. Promises were also suspended because of the various economic plans, during which every worker had to work about one-third more time each day for no extra pay, just in order to fulfill the plans.

Szabo, a good communist, understood the necessity for such overtime. "We were told that we had only a short time to make ourselves strong before the capitalists and reactionaries would try to capture Hungary and revive the bad old days."

Nor was Szabo immediately disturbed when he realized that each month the norms which determined how much work a man should do were being

117

quietly upped. "I didn't worry about it because I had become a Stakhanovite and had even won a medal for doing more work than any of the men on my shift."

Looking at Szabo's powerful hands and strong physique, you can believe that he led the pack. He would be a good worker under any system, and with little imagination you could picture him at the Boeing works in Seattle or on the Ford assembly line at River Rouge.

"I have always loved my job," he admits. "It was good work and until I got married I didn't realize how little money I was getting paid. But when I did take a wife, I asked for a vacation and was told I was too valuable and could not be spared. Then I saw that all the people who got the paid vacations at Lake Balaton were the same types that used to get them before. The managers got the vacations, and the Russian advisers, and the AVO spies and the party bosses. But the workers rarely got there.

"And the same types of people had the automobiles, and the fur coats, and the good food. I did not speak to anyone about this, for I was beginning to be afraid of the AVO spies. But one day a friend of mine from the Rakosi Bicycle Works, without saying a word to anyone, escaped to Austria. The AVO picked me up on suspicion of having helped him, and for two days it was pretty bad. They beat me almost all the time, but in the end I convinced them that I had nothing to do with his escape. After the beating they gave me a little card with three phone numbers, and if I ever heard anything about my friend, or anything else, I was to call one of those numbers and report it. Every once in a while the AVO would check to see if I still had the card."

By this time Gyorgy Szabo had discovered that being a member of the party really didn't help him very much. He was forced to work harder than ever before in his life, for less money, and with less chance to make a protest. Nor did being a good communist protect him from AVO beatings. It didn't get him vacations on Lake Balaton. It didn't get him a better house.

"In fact," he asked himself one day, "what does it get me?"

Only more work. Sometimes two or three nights a week he would have to stay in the plant after work to hear long harangues about the glories of communism. "Always things were going to be better in the future," he says ruefully. "What made me angry was that we were always harangued by men who weren't doing any work themselves."

Then there were the enforced protest meetings. "We marched for the Rosenberg trial, for the workers of Paris, for the Koreans. During the Korean War we had to contribute four extra days a month of unpaid work to help the Chinese communist volunteers, and we protested against the American use of germ warfare.

"There were some weeks," Szabo says, "when I hardly saw my family. And when I did see them, I had hardly a forint to give them. For all this work I received only 1,000 forints a month, not enough for a suit of clothes—I could never even save enough money ahead to buy one suit of clothes." Gyorgy Szabo's meager funds—his rewards from communism—went mostly to buy his children's clothing.

Inside Gyorgy's family a quiet protest had begun against such a defrauding system. It had been launched accidentally by Gyorgy's wife, who had begun to ask questions. "Why is it?" she first asked. "You're a good communist. You attend party meetings and march in parades. Why can't we buy in the good stores?"

"You can buy anywhere you like," Gyorgy said. "Only have enough money."

"No, I mean in the good stores, where the prices are cheaper."

"Look," he snapped. "If you want to go into the big stores in Pest, you can go."

"But the stores I mean are here in Csepel." And she told him of the three good stores into which she couldn't go. First there was the very good store for Russians only, and here the best things produced by Hungary were on sale at eighty percent reductions. Second were the stores that were almost as good, for Hungarian officials and AVO men, where the reduction sometimes amounted to seventy percent. Next came the stores for minor communist officials, where the goods were of fine quality and the prices reasonable. "And when everything good has been used up by those stores," Mrs. Szabo complained, "what's left is placed in stores for us workers, and we pay the most expensive prices. Why is this?"

Gyorgy said, "It's that way with everything, I guess."

But his wife persisted, "I thought you told me that in communism everybody was going to be equal."

"After they get things properly worked out, everybody will be equal."

"Until then, Gyorgy, will you please see if we can buy in one of the better stores?"

But in spite of his good record and his unquestioned loyalty to the party, Gyorgy found that no ordinary worker could possibly buy in the good stores. "They're for the big bosses," he was told. "You wouldn't feel at home in big stores like that."

That night Gyorgy spoke to his wife in the secrecy of their home. "We're worse off than we used to be," he confessed. "Before, we never had any money either, but we could dream, 'When I get a lot of money I'll go into the biggest store in town and buy one of everything.' But now they don't even let you in the stores."

One of the most moving stories of the revolution concerns the manner in which this hard-core communist finally took arms against the system. It was not because he was a reactionary, for he had fought in defense of communism. It was not because he was a devout Catholic, for he never bothered with the church. Nor was it because he had intellectually weighed communism and found it to be a fraud. It was because of a football game, and as one listens to his account of this memorable game, one suddenly realizes that all over Hungary, in those bitter days, men were discovering the nature of the deception that had been practiced upon them but always as the result of some trivial occurrence.

"It was a fine day in Budapest," he recalls, "and I was walking down Voroshilov Street to the big new stadium. Even if a man didn't have enough money for a new suit, he set aside a few forints for football, because it was a pleasure to go into the stadium. You cannot imagine how beautiful it was. It was about the only thing the communists accomplished. I have been told it's the biggest in Europe and the most beautiful in the world."

Hungarians' love for sport is legendary. In a nation with about the same population as metropolitan New York City, a completely disproportionate number of world champions has been produced in fencing, swimming, riding and track. For example, in the Helsinki Olympics of 1952, Hungarians copped an improbable number of first places and as a team ranked third among nations. But in recent years it has been soccer which gladdens the heart of a Hungarian, especially the Csepel man. This intricate game reached Hungary long after it had thrived in England and France, yet in the matter of a decade the Hungarians were world champions, sometimes thrashing their more famous competitors by large scores as to lead one foreign expert to charge, "If magicians were driven out of England at the time of Merlin, I know where they went. To Hungary."

"This day there was a great game," Szabo recalls. "A championship team had come over from Vienna, and we won. Of course, we usually win, but what was unusual at this game was that I sat behind some visitors from eastern Austria who spoke Hungarian and I told them their team was going to lose. We talked a little and I said, 'If you have come all the way from Vienna, why do you sit in the cheap seats?'

"They said, 'We're workmen, too.'"

"And I asked, 'But how can you afford such good suits?' Then I asked many more questions. 'How can workingmen save the money for a trip all the way to Budapest?' 'Where do you get so much extra food?' And there were other questions that I didn't ask them—why they weren't afraid of the policeman who came by, and why they laughed so much, even though their team was losing." Big, tough Gyorgy Szabo stares at his hands and adds, "From that football game on, I never stopped asking questions as to why dirty capitalists in Vienna could have such things whereas good communists in Budapest couldn't."

When Gyorgy Szabo returned to the bicycle works after the football game, he began asking new questions. "Where do all these bicycles go that we are making?" They went to Russia. "Am I making more money than when I worked for the capitalists?" He was making less. "Have the prices of things gone up or down?" They had gone far up. "Why are all these Russians still here?" They were here to police Hungary.

Finally he asked the most damning question of all: "Am I any less a slave now than I was then?" The answer was terrifyingly clear: "Then I was free. Then I was not afraid to laugh or to speak my mind. It is now that I am a real slave."

From then on Gyorgy Szabo, "the classical communist worker," began to speak openly. He found that most of the men in the Rakosi Metal Works felt as he did. He says, "We said to hell with the AVO. If they arrested all those who complained, they would have to arrest us all."

He stopped going to party meetings. He refused to march in fake processions. He allowed his work norm to drop back to what a human being might reasonably be expected to perform. And he began to tell his children that they, and their father and mother, were caught up in a hopeless tragedy. "I taught them to hate the regime," he said. "It sits on the necks of the workers."

It was in this frame of mind that grim-lipped Gyorgy Szabo heard, on October 22, 1956, that some students were going to stage a demonstration against the government. Without telling his wife where he was going, he went into the heart of Pest and made inquiries as to where the meeting was to be. He was told that some students had gathered in the Technical High School in Buda. He crossed the river and walked up to the brightly lighted building. Inside, he listened in dismay as one clever young man after another delivered what seemed to be pointless talks, and he thought to himself, "This won't get anywhere."

But then, from the rear of the meeting, a man in a brown windbreaker like his own rose and said, "I should like to ask one question. Under what right are Russian troops stationed in our country?" The question electrified Szabo, and in the following minutes he was overjoyed to hear young men who spoke well expressing all the doubts and hatreds he had accumulated against the regime.

"Something big is going to happen," he muttered to himself, and then another workman, from another part of the hall, spoke Szabo's mind for him. "I don't have the good language you men have," this man said haltingly. "I'm a worker, from Csepel. Men like me are with you." At this announcement there was cheering, and that night Gyorgy Szabo went home determined that if "something big" did happen, he was going to play his part.

Late the next afternoon he was working at the bicycle shop when news arrived that students had begun marching in the streets. Instantly he told his fellow workmen, "There'll be trouble. They'll need us." The same thought had struck many workmen in Csepel that afternoon, and at dusk they marched forth. Of 15,000 workmen in Szabo's immediate area, all but 240 ultimately joined the revolution. Of these 240, two hundred were assigned by the revolutionists to guard the plants against sabotage, meaning that out of 15,000 workmen on whom communism depended for its ultimate support, only forty remained loyal.

It would be repetitious to recount in detail Gyorgy Szabo's actions during the three stages of the revolution. In the attack on the radio station, it was a truckload of arms and ammunition that he had helped dispatch from the Csepel ordnance depot which turned the tide. The young fighters who holed up in the Corvin Cinema used Csepel guns and were in large part Csepel workers. The Kilian Barracks, having little ammunition of its own, depended upon Csepel equipment and Csepel men to use it. Throughout the victorious battles of those first days Gyorgy Szabo and his fellow workmen provided the sinews of the revolution. Gyorgy himself was shot at many times, helped burn tanks, and in general proved himself to be the firebrand that most once-dedicated communists turned out to be when they finally took arms against their oppressors.

In the second, peaceful stage, he performed an even more important task, for it was under his guidance—he being an older man than many of the Csepel workers—that the Csepel workers developed their plan for the utilization of the Rakosi Metal Works in the new Hungarian state. Their plan was certainly not reactionary, and many people in America could surely have deemed it archcommunism, but for the Hungary of that day it seemed a logical and liberal solution. "What we proposed," Szabo says, "was a nationalized factory, owned by the state and supervised by it, but run in all working details by workers' committees. Our engineers would set the norms in terms of what a human being should perform. Norms would not be handed down by some boss in an office. There would be no AVO, nor anyone like an AVO, allowed in the plant. And any of the good things, like vacations and doctors, would be shared equally. We were very certain about that."

122

By the afternoon of November 2, Gyorgy Szabo and his committee had concrete proposals to offer the government. Szabo also had suggestions for what pattern the government itself might take. "We thought a liberal-labor party would be best, one which stressed the production of things for people to use and to eat. No more munitions for Russia. We wanted personal freedom, courts, political parties, newspapers and a free radio. And we insisted upon one right which we wanted very badly, the right to travel to other countries. We wanted to see what workers were doing in other countries." As for the general spirit which ought to guide the new Hungary, Szabo proposed, "We don't want the aristocracy returned, or any selfish capitalists like the kind we used to know. If the Church won't meddle in politics, it ought to come back the way it was before. We should all work for a decent government and we should try to be like Austria or Switzerland or Sweden."

When these fine dreams were destroyed by the Soviet batteries on Gellert Hill, whose shells ripped through the Rakosi Metal Works, Gyorgy Szabo found himself in the middle of the prolonged and bloody battle which marked the third part of the revolution. It was a determined workers' army which faced the Russians, for Szabo was joined by every available Csepel man, and this sturdy group of workers was to give the Soviets their toughest fight in the battle for Budapest. Szabo himself used guns from the Csepel armory, helped spray Csepel gasoline on Russian tanks, lugged ammunition to the antiaircraft gun that knocked down the Soviet plane, and thought up one of the neatest tricks of the campaign. Whenever a group of Csepel men found an isolated tank which they could not destroy, some young workers of incredible daring would leap upon the turret, where no gun could fire at them, and plant there a Hungarian flag. If the Russians inside opened their hatches in an effort to dislodge the flag they were killed and the tank immediately destroyed. But if they allowed the flag to fly, the next Russian tank they met would blaze away at a supposed enemy and blow it apart. Obviously such a trick could work only a limited number of times, but until the Russians caught on, it was a beautifully simple maneuver.

But finally the Soviets triumphed, and with the annihilation of Csepel the situation of Gyorgy Szabo and his men was desperate. As we have seen, they quietly melted into the countryside and escaped capture. What they did next forms a heroic chapter in the battle for Budapest, and in order to appreciate their heroism we must pause to analyze the situation they faced.

The Russians dominated the city, and through a puppet government made decisions of life and death. All food supplies were under Russian control, and only those Hungarians whom the Russians decided they could pacify were fed.

The Russians also controlled the police, the health services and every operation of the city's existence. Anyone who dared oppose this Russian control ran the risk of starvation, imprisonment or execution.

In addition, the Russians had another horrible weapon, one which the Hungarians feared more than any other. On the afternoon of November 6, while the fight for Csepel still continued, Russians began rounding up Hungarian men, tossing them into trucks, and carting them off to secret railway depots where they were herded into boxcars for shipment to perpetual slavery in Siberia. Possibly by plan, Russians allowed a few such deportees to escape so that news of this inhuman punishment could circulate throughout Hungary. To most Hungarians, such deportation to Siberia was truly worse than death, and many resisted it to the death, as their bullet-riddled bodies were later to testify.

So all of what Gyorgy Szabo accomplished in the days following the termination of actual fighting he did under threat of death, starvation, imprisonment by the reincarnated AVO and deportation. Here is what he accomplished.

On November 11, the workers of Csepel reported for work. Both the Hungarian government and its Russian masters had made earnest entreaties to the workers in heavy industries to resume production lest the country collapse in a runaway inflation. Communist leaders tried to cajole miners and electrical workers into producing their prerevolutionary norms, and were promised food and full wages if they did so.

Szabo met these government enticements by helping to organize a general strike. He was only one of many to whom the idea occurred at roughly the same time, but in his factory he did have the courage to stand forth clearly as the leading spirit. He knew that the AVO spies who had been replanted in the works would report him as the instigator, but he no longer cared. "We will work long enough to replace the 3,000 bicycles stolen from freedom fighters by the police," he announced, "then we will quit."

In other plants similarly brave men stood up and made similar proposals. All over Hungary the strike proved to be amazingly successful, even though the leaders were constantly threatened with death.

The economic life of the nation was brought to an absolute standstill. Trains were halted and no industrial electricity was provided during critical hours. Truckers refused to bring food into the starving city if it had to be turned over to the communists for distribution, and women would not work at cleaning buildings. Factories in Csepel lay idle, and those in nearby Kobanya worked only enough to provide minimum essentials to the workers themselves.

The government raved and made new threats. Then it pleaded tearfully, "Dear workers, please go back to work. Don't let inflation destroy us." When this appeal failed, wage increases were offered, then additional issues of food to "workers who were loyal to the cause of workers' solidarity and world peace."

No appeal made the slightest impression on the men of Csepel, and with consummate insolence they even refused to answer the government's proposals. Szabo says, "We had reached a point in which not a man cared if he was shot or starved to death. We would not cooperate with our murderers." They even published a poster which read, "Wanted. Six loyal Hungarians to form a government. The only requirement is that they all be citizens of Soviet Russia."

Day after fatal day the strike continued. From Csepel it spread to other regions of the city, and from there to the countryside. In no section of Hungary was greater bravery shown than in the coal mines of Tatabanya. Here men who could be easily identified for future retaliation and torture refused to go into the mines to bring out the coal required for heating and lighting the new communist paradise. Against these miners the frantic Russians brought their full power of coercion. Food was cut off from Tatabanya, and any stray young men who wandered from the crowd ran the risk of being picked up for Siberia. Troops were moved in, and tanks, but to no avail. The mines stayed shut. The Soviets, having run out of ridiculous promises by which to lure these stubborn miners resorted to threats of death, but the miners replied, "Shoot one man and we'll flood the mines."

At this point it is appropriate to consider the meaning of this general strike. There had always been, during the three stages of the Hungarian revolution, a chance that Soviet propaganda might eventually turn a crushing moral defeat into a shabby victory. They could claim that reactionary forces had led the revolution. They could tell uncommitted nations in Asia and Europe that broken-down nobility had tried to engineer a coup d'etat. They could and did point to Cardinal Mindszenty's speeches as proof that the Church was about to seize control of Hungary. And they could claim, legalistically but spuriously, that a legitimate Hungarian government—the Janos Kadar puppet regime— had specifically invited them back into Hungary to put down a counterrevolution. They could also claim, spuriously, that under the terms of the Warsaw Pact of 1954 they were not only entitled but also obligated to return. Finally, in order to explain away the participation of students, writers, youths and workers in the actual fighting, they could, and had already begun to, feed out the official line that the students were impetuous, true, but underneath it all really dedicated communists; that the writers were nervous types who didn't know

125

what they were doing; that the youth were misled by evil adults; whereas the workers acted on the spur of the moment out of hot-headed but understandable patriotism. I regret to say that such excuses would probably be accepted in India, parts of France, parts of Italy and Indonesia, where they would accomplish great harm.

But no propaganda, no matter how skillfully constructed, can ever explain away the coldly rational, unemotional strike of the Csepel men. It was conceived by workers, and by workers in heavy industry. It was carried out without the aid of writers, students or churchmen. Of greatest importance was its duration and determination, proving that it was neither hastily conceived nor emotionally operated.

The Csepel strike was a solemn announcement to the world that the men whom communism is most supposed to aid had tried the system and had found it a total fraud. Most of the leaders of this Csepel strike were members of the communist party. They had known it intimately for ten years and had, in some cases, even tried to help direct it along the promised channels. There was not, so far as I can find, a single excited intellectual or daring philosopher of freedom involved in this strike.

This was communism itself, rejecting itself. This was a solemn foretaste of what communists in India or Italy or France or Indonesia would themselves conclude if they ever had the bad luck to live under the system. This was, for Soviet communism, a moral defeat of such magnitude that it cannot be explained away.

When the world propagandists for communism have explained everything to their satisfaction, how will they explain the fact that of 15,000 workers in one Csepel area, only forty remained true to the system? How will they explain the fact that the other workers fought Soviet tanks with their bare hands? And how will they explain the behavior of a man like Gyorgy Szabo, who, when there was no hope of further resistance, was willing to stand forth as the leader of a general strike against the Soviet system?

For example, what sensible man, knowing the facts of Budapest, could possibly accept the following explanation which the trade unions of Soviet Russia offered to fellow workers in Europe as an excuse for the massacre of a city? "You know, dear comrades, that Soviet troops upon the request of the Hungarian government came to its help in order to crush the counterrevolutionary forces and in order to protect the basic interests of the Hungarian people and peace in Europe. The Soviet armed forces could not remain aloof because to do so would not only have led to further blood-shed but would have also brought tremendous damage to the cause of the working class. The Soviet trade unions wish to bring to your attention the fact that the Soviet army has never fought for an unjust cause."

When such lies became intolerable to the men of Csepel, and when the puppet government dared to announce that all the trouble in Budapest had been caused by discredited members of the nobility who were trying to impose their will upon the simple communist workers, Gyorgy Szabo and his men could stomach the nonsense no further. They had posters made which announced, "THE 40,000 NOBLEMEN OF CSEPEL, EACH WITH A CASTLE NEAR THE RAKOSI METAL WORKS, AND WITH NUMEROUS SERVANTS, DEFY THE GOVERNMENT." Then, to make their intention crystal clear, they announced, "We have mined the buildings in Csepel and if you try to take them over or to make us work, we will blow them to pieces."

The importance of the resistance in Csepel did not lie, however, in the unparalleled heroism of the workers. Rather it lay in the slow and methodical manner in which it was conducted. The world had time to hear of it and could marvel at the total rejection of communism voiced by these men of communism. Had there been no strike, the Soviets could have argued, as indeed they tried, that although there had been an unfortunate uprising, no real workmen were involved. If the revolution had ended abruptly or in obscurity, any reasonably logical interpretation could have been promulgated in Rome and Paris and New Delhi. But with men like Gyorgy Szabo doggedly striking, and in the very teeth of communism, day after day until the stoppage lasted a month, and then on into the second month—that could not be brushed aside as accidental. That was a rejection of communism which was irrefutable. As this book goes to press, toward the end of January, 1957, the methodical, unemotional workers of Csepel are still showing the world what they think of communism. They have now entered their fourth month of protest.

In my recent life I have witnessed many brave actions—in war, in Korea, in municipal riots, and one which I shall speak of later when I write of the bridge at Andau—but I have never seen anything braver than the quiet, calculated strike of the men of Csepel. I have long suspected that raw courage, like that required for blowing up a tank, is largely a matter of adrenalin; if a man gets a strong enough surge of it he can accomplish amazing feats, which the world calls courage. But courage such as the workers' committees of Csepel exhibited is not a matter of adrenalin, it is based on heart and will. Voluntarily these men signed manifestoes, although they knew that their names were being collected by the Russians. Without protesting they permitted themselves to be photographed, although they could be sure that these photographs would be filed and used to identify strikers for later retaliation. They were willing to stand forth undisguised and to demonstrate their contempt for their Soviet masters. I call that the ultimate in courage.

On November 22, when the strike was at its height, Gyorgy Szabo returned home from an exhausting meeting in which he had publicly argued for a continuation of the strike "no matter what the Russians do."

As soon as he entered his grubby home he realized that his wife was distraught. "Gyorgy," Mrs. Szabo said in a trembling voice. "The Farkas boy was deported last night."

"Sooner or later we'll all be deported," he said, sinking into a chair.

Mrs. Szabo twisted her hands nervously, then blurted out, "I think we ought to escape with the children to Austria."

Gyorgy said nothing. Dropping his head into his hands he tried to think. For some days he had known that this question was going to come up, and twice he had forestalled discussion of it. Now he said bluntly, "I'm a Hungarian, not an Austrian."

His wife's voice rose in both pitch and intensity. "I am too. But I can't bring my children up in Hungary."

"This is my home," Szabo argued stubbornly.

"Gyorgy," his wife pleaded, her voice growing urgently gentle. "They need men like you in Australia. Today the BBC said America was taking refugees."

"I don't want America—" he began.

His reply was interrupted by a terrible scream. Mrs. Szabo had risen from her chair, her hands in her hair, and was shouting hysterically, "I can't live here any longer. I can't live here and listen with dread for fear an auto will stop outside our house at night and the police—" She fell back into her chair and sobbed, "Gyorgy, in a few days they'll take you away."

One of the children, hearing his mother's screams, had come into the room. "You must put your clothes on," Mrs. Szabo said in grimly excited tones. "And tell your brothers to put theirs on, too."

Gyorgy Szabo, the good communist, the trusted worker in heavy industry so dear to communism, looked stolidly at his wife. There was no arguing with her now, so he stalked into the cold night air.

The scenes about him were familiar and warm. This was his Csepel. He had defended it against capitalists, against Nazis and against the Russians. He had grown up here as a boy and had grown to love the sprawling buildings and the things they produced. This factory in the darkness, he had helped to build it, helped to protect it against the Soviet tanks. Within its ugly walls he had known much comradeship and happiness. This was a good island and a good land. Maybe things would work out better…later on.

A car's lights showed in the distance, and instinctively he drew into the shadows, for under communism an auto meant danger. Only the police and the party bosses had automobiles, and such men usually meant trouble. Flashing its spotlight here and there, the car approached and Gyorgy could see the glistening rifles of police on the prowl. He remained very silent and they failed to spot him. Slowly the car went about its duty, and in the darkness Szabo acknowledged finally how terrified he was.

"I was afraid," he admitted later. "For many years I had been living in a world of bleak hopelessness. I had no chance of saving for things I wanted to buy. No chance at all. But worse was the emptiness inside. All the big promises that I had lived on as a boy were gone. Not one thing the communists had promised had ever been fulfilled. You can't understand how awful it is to look into a hopeless future. At the start of the revolution lots of us were brave, but do you know why? Because we didn't care whether we lived or died. Then we had a few days of hope, and we spoke of a new, honest system, but when the Russians came back I knew the bleak days would start again. That time I was brave because I didn't give a damn about Siberia. It couldn't be any worse than Csepel, because in Siberia you admit you're in prison. That's why, when I hid in the shadows afraid of the automobile and heard my wife's screaming in my ears, I finally said, 'If there's a better life in Canada or Australia, I'll go.' I was afraid."

A man who had destroyed tanks by spraying them with gasoline from a hose, a man who had stood forth as the announced leader of the strike, beat his face with his hands and said, "I was afraid."

Using only the shadows, he returned to his home, where he found his wife and the three boys bundled up in all the warm clothes they could muster. Mrs. Szabo was no longer crying, for she had made up her mind to leave Budapest this night and walk to the Austrian border whether her husband joined her or not—to do anything to escape the terror under which her children had been living and would live for the rest of their lives if they remained in Budapest.

Szabo looked at his wife, reached for his own heavy clothes and said, "We'll leave right away."

So Gyorgy Szabo and his family left Hungary. They carried with them one small handbag of food for their children. After ten years of dedicated service to communism this gifted workman had as his worldly possessions one small bag of food and a legacy of fear. When he fled from Csepel to the mainland and then across the bridge from Pest into Buda, he did not bother to look back on the beauty of Pest, for he knew that it had been destroyed.

To Build a Castle

Vladimir Bukovsky

1.

Two particularly painful and shameful episodes from my school life I now recalled most often of all.

Most of our class was taken into the Pioneers when we were eight years old, and nobody asked our permission. They simply announced that on such and such a date there would be a ceremony for entry into the Pioneers and they would accept the ones who were fittest for it. On the appointed day we were taken to the Museum of the Revolution, which fortunately was just around the corner, on Gorky Street, and lined up in one of the big rooms. A banner was solemnly carried in and each of us had to swear an oath before it: "I, a Young Pioneer, solemnly swear before my comrades that I shall stand fast for the cause of Lenin and Stalin and the victory of communism," and so on. Then you had a red scarf put around your neck and the master of ceremonies, standing by the banner, declaimed: "Young Pioneers, be prepared to struggle for the cause of Lenin and Stalin!" "We shall always be prepared!" we replied in unison.

In fact, I had nothing against being a Young Pioneer. When you were old enough you became a Young Pioneer, then a member of the Komsomol, and then a member of the Party.* It was as simple as that. That was what happened to everybody, just as you moved regularly from class to class. But things turned out worse than I had expected. There were regular Pioneer assemblies, marching sessions, and parades, and while the fortunate non-Pioneers made their way home to amuse themselves and kick their heels, we had to sweat it out at exercises, discuss such topics as our classmates' study performance and behavior, attend political information sessions, and so on and so forth. Our

---

* The Young Pioneers and the League of Communist Youth, or Komsomol, are a kind of Soviet equivalent of the Cubs and Brownies, Boy and Girl Scouts, except that they come under the direct control of the Communist Party and are openly manipulative in their practices. (Translator's note.)

instructors took every opportunity to reproach us: "You are a Pioneer, you're supposed to be more obedient and not to do this and that." And we were all given social tasks to perform: issuing wall newspapers, preparing reports, keeping stragglers up to the mark, and, above all, educating others and one another, and admonishing classmates who got low marks or misbehaved. All of us were obliged to censure wrongdoers. Thus we found ourselves arrayed on the side of the teachers, which seemed unnatural and even ignoble. From the point of view of our classmates it was a betrayal.

The result was a kind of schizophrenia. Some of us turned into sneaks and were heartily hated as a result. But most of us simply lied and feigned ignorance, saying we had seen and heard nothing.

All of this became crystal clear to me a year or two later, when I was ten and, as one of the best students, was made chairman of the Pioneers in my class. I was the one who had to call the confounded assemblies, make sure all the other Pioneers carried out their instructions, attend meetings of the Pioneer leadership of the whole school, and so on. The teachers would tell me quite bluntly who was to be discussed at the next assembly, who should be expelled from the Pioneers, or punished in some other way. And then I personally had to participate in reprimanding the stragglers and mischief-makers.

One day a teacher summoned me to carry out one of reprimands. I was supposed to give my erring classmate a dressing down in the teacher's presence. I started off with the standard arguments and said that he was letting the side down, that he would have to reform himself in order to help the country build communism. Then, suddenly, I had a bright idea: this boy's name was Ulyanov, the same as Lenin's, and I began telling him that he was bringing disgrace to our leader's name, that with a name like that he ought to be studying the way Lenin studied, and I added something to the effect that Lenin himself would have been most upset if he knew of this boy's behavior. I must have been very eloquent and convincing, and also offensive, because all of a sudden he turned red, scrunched up his face, and burst into tears.

"You bastard!" he said. "You swine!"

The teacher was delighted with this result but I really did feel like a swine. I didn't at all feel that the boy was bringing disgrace to anybody, and I wasn't in the least angry with him. But I had grown used to parroting the words expected of me, and everyone I had spoken to before had realized I didn't mean what I said and merely did it to get it over with. Nobody had taken offense and I was on friendly terms with everybody; more than that, I was respected, because I never ratted on anyone and always pretended I hadn't seen anything. Now I had caused this boy real distress and I was stunned.

131

I realized I couldn't and wouldn't play this idiotic role any longer. I resigned. They tried talking me round, upbraided me, censured me, but I stuck to my guns. I didn't explain the reason for my resignation—I don't think I could have done so—but from then on I stopped even wearing the red scarf. (Lots of others didn't either: you carried it in your pocket, and if a grown-up noticed, you simply slipped into the toilets and put it on. You could always say it had got dirty and your parents hadn't had time to wash it.)

I was ten years old at that time. When I was fourteen, which is when they start taking everyone into the Komsomol, I refused to join. "What's the matter? Do you believe in God?" they asked me curiously, but I refused to give any explanation. They pressed me for a very long time, because I was a good student and it was the accepted thing for all the good ones to be in the Komsomol, but they didn't get anywhere and in the end gave up. "Watch out," said my friends, "you'll find it harder to get into the university."

2.

The other, equally shameful, episode occurred during my Pioneer years. In 1952 we heard about the "doctors' plot," which coincided with a wave of anti-Semitism.* Hatred of the Jews was growing all the time, and now there was a lot of talk about the Jews being deported because they were enemies who wanted to kill Stalin. For every single one of us, Stalin was greater than God, a reality in which it was impossible not to believe; he thought for us, he was our savior, he was responsible for our happy childhood. There could be nothing higher in the scale of human values. It was impossible to imagine an act of greater barbarism than killing Stalin.

I took these developments extremely hard. Several times I dreamed the same persistent dream: I was sitting in an enormous auditorium, full of people who were clapping and shouting; Stalin was on the platform, giving a speech and being interrupted by the applause. He reached for a pitcher of water, poured some into a glass, and was about to drink it. I was the only one there who knew the water was poisoned, but I could do nothing. I cried out: "Don't drink it; don't drink it!" But my voice was drowned by the ovations and shouting. I wanted to run to the platform, but there were so many people that

---

* By January 1953 nine prominent physicians, most of them Jewish, had been arrested on orders from Stalin and accused of attempting to poison members of the Politburo, whose medical attendants they were. Two of them were beaten to death during interrogation, and there was talk of banishing all Jews to Siberia, but the case was terminated on the death of Stalin two months later, and the doctors were rehabilitated. (Translator's note.)

I couldn't get through. The nightmare of Stalin being killed haunted me and made me literally ill.

In our school there were only two Jewish boys. One, Iosif, was a rather unpleasant fellow. I didn't like him and we were never friends. As for the other one, nobody but I knew he was a Jew, for he had a Ukrainian name. He lived next door to me and we used to walk to school together. I had seen his mother and father and knew that they were Jews. We weren't friends, and our relations began and ended with the walk to school, but now I was tormented by the question: Is it possible that his parents want to kill Stalin too?

One morning in the school playground things came to a head and the other boys started beating Iosif up. A big crowd gathered and everybody tried to kick or punch him. No explanations or incitements were needed. Everybody understood that it was all right to beat him, that nobody would be punished for it. But for some reason the unhappy Iosif, instead of going home, staggered into the school and tried to show that he was a stout fellow, one of the boys, not in the least offended. The upshot was that he was beaten again during the next break and during the one after that; but he insisted, with a pathetic smile, on sticking to his friends, and the more they beat him, the more he seemed to invite them to continue. After every break he would stagger into the classrooms covered in blood, with swollen lips, still trying to talk as if nothing in the world were wrong. Each time he believed that it was all over now, everything was finished and would be as before. All the teachers did was say to him impassively: "Go to the cloakroom and wash yourself." And asked no questions.

I didn't join in. He was so revolting, with that pitiful, cringing smile on his broken lips, that I couldn't bear to go near him. I just waited miserably for it all to end. If only he had the gumption to go away, or if they even killed him or something! I knew perfectly well that Iosif had nothing whatever to do with Stalin, was incapable of even thinking of murder. So why didn't I try to stop it? Worse still, the next morning I stopped walking to school with the boy next door, contriving to leave just a little bit late. Whether I felt shame or disgust, I do not know.

3.

Stalin's death shook our life to its foundations. Classes virtually came to a halt, the teachers wept openly, and everybody went around with swollen eyes.

One man shouted from a window of the eye hospital in a sobbing voice: "Stalin's dead and I'm here!"

The rows and fights in the yard stopped too, and enormous unorganized crowds streamed through the streets to the Hall of Columns, where Stalin lay in state. There was something awe-inspiring about these immense, silent, gloomy masses of people. The authorities hesitated to try to curb them and simply blocked off some of the side streets with buses and trucks, while the waves of people rolled endlessly on. We boys managed to make our way via attics and rooftops to the roof of the Hotel National. The crowd below us surged forward and backward, like waves in the sea, and then suddenly, in one of the side streets, a bus shivered, toppled over, and fell, like an elephant rolling onto its side. This vast procession continued for several days and thousands of people perished in the crush. For days, Gorky Street was littered with buttons, handbags, galoshes, and paper. Someone had even stuffed a pair of galoshes into the mouths of the lions at the entrance to the Museum of the Revolution.

On the day of Stalin's funeral, factory sirens shrieked and wailed and cars and locomotives hooted. Something terrible and irreparable had occurred. How would we live from now on? Our Father, to whom have you abandoned us? People said quite openly: "Who is there to die for now? Malenkov? No, the people won't die for Malenkov!"

But the years passed, and we went on living just the same, or at any rate no worse, which was itself sacrilege. Life did not come to a halt. The grown-ups went to work and we went to school. Newspapers continued to appear, the radio to broadcast, and the yard went back to the old shouting and fighting. Stalin was mentioned less and less. And I was bewildered: Hadn't God died, without whom *nothing* was supposed to take place?

Like threatening clouds, rumors began to spread about executions and tortures, about millions of Russians ill-treated in the labor camps. The doctors were released, Beria was executed as an enemy of the people, and another rumor spread like an obscure muttering: "The biggest enemy of the people of them all was Stalin!"

It was amazing how quickly people believed this, people who two years before had stampeded to his funeral and been ready to die for him. Now his misdeeds were announced at the Party Congress, and all the newspapers and radio stations, books and magazines, films and textbooks that had lauded his genius began to condemn his "mistakes" and "distortions."

All those people whose business it had been to praise Stalin for so many years now assured us they had known nothing about this terror or, if they had, had been afraid to say so. I didn't believe the ones who said they had never known: How could you fail to notice the deaths of millions of people, the deaths of your neighbors and friends? Nor did I believe the ones who said they were afraid—their fear had brought them too many promotions. You might keep quiet from fear, you might run away or lie doggo, you might even humor the person you feared, but did fear oblige them to compose odes and dithyrambs, to become generals and members of the Central Committee? You don't get Stalin prizes and country houses if you're afraid. It was said that at the Party Congress, someone sent a note up to Khrushchev: "Where were *you* at the time?" And that Khrushchev asked over the microphones: "Who wrote this note? Please stand up!" Nobody, of course, got to his feet. "All right," said Khrushchev, "I was where you are now." Many people liked that answer, but I despised both Khrushchev and the author of the note. They both knew the truth; yet neither had the guts to say so openly. And neither of them was obliged to be in a public position where guts were needed; no one had forced them to be in that hall, so close to power.

How could it happen that people were still afraid to stand up? How could one man, or say ten men, seize power and keep all the rest in fear and ignorance? When did it all begin? Khrushchev seemed to think that he had explained everything, that he had given answers to all the questions. According to Khrushchev they had got to the bottom of it, released the innocent, spoken well of the dead, and life could go on. But for us, and especially for my generation, the questions were only just beginning. We had just had time to be taught that communism was the world's most progressive doctrine and Stalin the incarnation of its ideas when presto, Stalin turned out to be a murderer and a tyrant, a terrible degenerate no better than Hitler! So what was the nature of the ideas that had produced a Stalin? What was the nature of a Party that, once having brought him to power, could no longer stop him? What difference did it make now whether they had been afraid or simply ignorant? After all, even now, when all had been revealed, they were still frightened to stand up and be counted. The first conclusion was self-evident: a system based on a single-party government will inevitably produce Stalins and then be unable to get rid of them, and it will always destroy all attempts to create an opposition or an alternative.

At that time a lot was said about inner-Party democracy, but this struck us as unconvincing. Why should democracy be limited to the Party? Did that mean that the rest of us weren't human? We didn't elect the Party—they elected themselves. Did this mean that the same people who had produced and supported Stalin were again undertaking to establish absolute justice by introducing democracy among themselves? Were they planning to speak in the name of the people again, though the people had not elected them to do so? The same rogues who had lied about Stalin for thirty years would carry on about party democracy? Who would believe it? If today, if for the time being, they had ceased killing millions of people, where was the guarantee that this wouldn't

135

happen again tomorrow? It was the same system, and the same people. No one had even been punished or put on trial.

But who could they try? Everyone was guilty: those who did the actual killing, those who gave the orders, those who approved the results, and even those who kept silent. Everyone in this artificial society had carried out the role assigned to him, for which he had been rewarded. Take my own parents, for example—modest, quiet, honorable people. But they were journalists, writing the very propaganda that had so vilely deceived me, that was created to justify the murders or hush them up. One long essay of my father's had been praised by Stalin, and on his personal instructions my father had been made a member of the Writers' Union—had become a writer! This had happened only recently, it seemed like yesterday. Everybody was delighted and congratulated him. The essay was broadcast over the radio and printed in *Pravda*, then published as a separate book. But what was there to be so pleased about? He had played his subordinate role and the chief executioner had rewarded him. What difference did it make to me how they justified their complicity, even if it was by the need to feed me and my sister?

And was I any better myself? It wasn't just that I ate their bread. I had been a Pioneer, I had participated in the work of this terrible machine whose end product was either hangmen or corpses. Did it make it any easier that I hadn't realized what I was doing? Does a man feel better when he learns that by accident, without knowing it, he has been an accessory to murder? I recalled Iosif, whom I had not defended, and Ulyanov, whom I had tormented by invoking his namesake. I might have gone on like that, from rung to rung, from the Pioneers to the Komsomol and then into the Party; forty years later, perhaps, I would be waving to the masses from a platform or signing arrest warrants. And as I grew older, my children would say to me: "Where were you, Papa? Why were you silent? How could you allow all that to happen?" And my bread would stick in their throats.

Naturally I started reading voraciously, anything I could lay my hands on. And of course, one of the first to come to me in my darkness was Vladimir Ilyich Lenin. Ah, our beloved Ilyich, how many people has he lured into the darkness, how many supplied with a justification for their crimes! But to me he brought light.

Some years later, I had some friends I often used to visit—a couple and their little daughter; their grandmother lived with them too. They were a quiet, lovable family which talked for most of the time about art and painting. One day I was surprised to find the entire family, including the ancient grandmother, engaged in a violent argument about Lenin. Each had their own understanding of what Lenin wanted, what he believed in, and what principles he preached. They had no liking for Lenin, they were Christians, and I had never known them to take any interest in Lenin's views before. The thing that amazed me was that they were quoting Lenin, and each new quotation refuted the one before. I had never suspected such erudition in them. The following day I saw them again, and again they were arguing about Lenin. What the devil had got into them? And so it continued for a couple of weeks. The peaceful haven where I had been able to refresh my soul was destroyed. That's all it needs, I thought. This Lenin enters into people like Satan and sets them at loggerheads!

All of a sudden the whole thing was resolved. It turned out that because of the shortage of toilet paper, they had taken the complete works of Lenin into the toilet. Naturally, each of them saw different pages of this opus, taken from different articles and sometimes from different periods, and of course they couldn't reach a consensus on what his beliefs were. And that is typical of Lenin and his dialectics. Just try it. Hand out his works to different people and ask their opinion afterward: hardly two out of a hundred will agree. It is not surprising that there are dozens of Marxist-Leninist parties in the world, and all of them genuine. Lenin had but one principle—to supply a theoretical basis for each concrete step that he took.

Still, I derived much benefit from reading Lenin. First of all, it was a living history of the crimes of the Bolsheviks. The libraries wouldn't let Soviet citizens read the files of *Pravda* of twenty years before, yet here was the entire Revolution, the entire Civil War, still living in Lenin's notes and comments! And knowing our later history, it was easy to see where it had begun.

From Lenin I went back to the Russian thinkers of the nineteenth century and stumbled across an amusing characteristic of theirs: all of them, sitting on their estates or in their city apartments, loved to hold forth about the people, about the latent unplumbed forces of the people, and about how the people would one day awaken from their slumbers and resolve everything, pronounce the ultimate truth, and create a genuine culture. It is understandable that they couldn't know what would happen in the following century—how the people would demonstrate their worth—and they made their judgment on the basis of their coachmen and yard sweepers. That was the birth of the idea of a proletarian culture as somehow higher and superior.

To us who had grown up in the communal apartments and backyards of this selfsame proletariat, living among them as equals, not masters, the term "proletarian culture" sounded grotesque. For us, it meant no mystical secret, but drunkenness, brawling, knife fights, obscenity, and chewing sunflower seeds. No true proletarian would have called this culture, because the distinguishing feature of the proletariat was a hatred of all culture, combined with a sort of inexplicable envy. Culture was a witch they stoned. "Intellectual" was an insult hissed venomously by your neighbors.

With great curiosity I read further, devouring as many of the socialist utopians as I could find. I was astounded: all their utopias had truly been realized by us! Realized, that is, as far as they could be by mere mortals. We simply turned out to be the most conscientious and consistent exponents of these utopias. Please note that all these theories presuppose a special type of people whom the ideal state will please, people who are exclusively honest and objective, with the commonweal at heart—I wonder what happens to all the scoundrels in their utopias?

Furthermore, it is considered self-evident that people who are born and grow up in the new conditions will be quite different from before, the sort of people, in short, who are needed for the new order. And this is their fundamental error. They regard man as being born into this world completely empty, like a vessel, and as malleable as wax, and therefore they assert that there will be no more crime, dissatisfaction, envy, or hatred.

The amazing, naïve, and inhuman faith of all socialists in the power of re-education transformed our school years into a torture and covered the country with concentration camps. In our country, everybody is being "re-educated," from the cradle to the grave, and everybody is obliged to re-educate everybody else. Conferences, meetings, discussions, political-information sessions, surveillance, checkups, collective measures, Saturday work, and socialist competition. For the ineducable, heavy physical labor in concentration camps. How else could you build socialism? All this was clear to me as a fifteen-year-old lad. But ask any Western socialist what should be done with people unsuited to socialism and he will reply: Re-educate them.

In the Soviet Union they even made a serious attempt to turn apples into pears, and for fifty years based biology on that belief. It is said that for twenty years an eccentric Englishman cut the tails off rats in the expectation that they would produce tailless offspring, but nothing came of it and he gave up. What can you expect of an Englishman? No, that's no way to build socialism. He lacked sufficient passion, a healthy faith in the radiant future. It was quite different in our country: they cut off people's heads for decades, and at last saw the birth of a new type of headless people.

This dream of absolute, universal equality is amazing, terrifying, and inhuman. And the moment it captures people's minds, the result is mountains of corpses and rivers of blood, accompanied by attempts to straighten the stooped and shorten the tall. I remember that one part of the psychiatric examination was a test for idiocy. The patient was given the following problem to solve: "Imagine a train crash. It is well known that the part of the train that suffers the most damage in such crashes is the carriage at the rear. How can you prevent that damage from taking place?" The idiot's usual reply is expected to be: Uncouple the last carriage. That strikes us as amusing, but just think, are the theory and practice of socialism much better?

Society, say the socialists, contains both the rich and the poor. The rich are getting richer and poor poorer—What is to be done? Uncouple the last carriage, liquidate the rich, take away their wealth and distribute it among the poor. And they start to uncouple the carriages. But there is always one carriage at the back, there are always richer and poorer, for society is like a magnet: there are always two poles. But does this discourage a true socialist? The main thing is to realize his dream; so the richest section of society is liquidated first, and everyone rejoices because everyone gains from the share-out. But the spoils are soon spent, and people start to notice inequality again—again there are rich and poor. So they uncouple the next carriage, and then the next, without end, because absolute equality has still not been achieved. Before you know it, the peasant with two cows and a horse turns out to be in the last carriage and is pronounced a kulak and deported. Is it really surprising that whenever you get striving for equality and fraternity, the guillotine appears on the scene?

It is all so easy, so simple, and so tempting—to confiscate and divide! To make everybody equal, and with one fell swoop to resolve all problems. It is all so alluring—to escape from poverty and crime, grief and suffering once and for all. All you have to do is to want it, all you have to do is reform the people who are hindering universal happiness and there will be paradise on earth, absolute justice, and goodwill to all men! It is difficult for man to resist this dream and this noble impulse, particularly for men who are impetuous and sincere. They are the first to start chopping heads off and, eventually, to have their own chopped off.

> Do not fear ashes, do not fear curses,
> Do not fear brimstone and fire,
> But fear like the plague that man with the rage
> To tell you: "I know what's required!"
> Who tells you: "Fall in and follow me
> If heaven on earth's your desire."

They are the first to put their head on the block or go to prison. Such a system is too convenient for scoundrels and demogogues, and they are the ones, in the final analysis, who will decide what is good and what evil.

You have to learn to respect the right of even the most insignificant and repulsive individual to live the way he chooses. You have to renounce once and for all the criminal belief that you can re-educate everyone in your own image. You have to understand that without the use of force it is realistic to create a theoretical equality of opportunity, but not equality of results. People attain absolute equality only in the graveyard, and if you want to turn your country into a gigantic graveyard, go ahead, join the socialists. But man is so constituted that others' experiences and explanations don't convince him, he has to try things out for himself; and we Russians now watch events unfolding in Vietnam and Cambodia with increasing horror, listen sadly to all the chatter about Eurocommunism and socialism with a human face. Why is it that nobody speaks of fascism with a human face?

Mig Pilot
The Final Escape of Lt. Belenko

John Barron

Why? Of all officers, why Belenko? Nowhere in the recorded history of his life and career was an answer discernible. None of the conventional causes that might motivate a man to abandon homeland, family, comrades, and privilege could be found. Belenko was not in trouble of any kind. He never had associated with dissidents or manifested the least ideological disaffection. Like all Soviet pilots, he underwent weekly medical examinations, and physicians repeatedly judged him exceptionally fit, mentally and physically. He drank moderately, lived within his means, was involved with no woman except his wife, and had the reputation of being honest to the point of fault....

On a wintry Sunday afternoon a light aircraft crashed near the truck factory. The wreckage was still smoldering and ambulance attendants were taking away the body of the pilot, wrapped in a sheet, when Viktor arrived. The scene transfixed him, and he stayed long after everyone else had gone. Like a magnet, the wreckage kept drawing him back day after day, and he contemplated it by the hour.

Why did he die? Why did I not die in the fire when the mine exploded? Is there a God who decides who will die and when? They say that God is only the product of superstition and the whole world happened by chance. Is that so? Do the trees and berries grow, do the cockroaches scoot, does the snow fall, do we breathe and think—all because of chance? If so, what caused chance in the first place?

No, there must be some Being, some purpose in life higher than man. But I do not understand. Maybe that is the purpose in life—to try to understand. The pilot must have tried in the sky. What he must have seen! Someday I will take his place and see for myself. Some way I will give life meaning. I would rather that my life be like a candle that burns lightly and beautifully, if only briefly, than live a long life without meaning.

This embryonic ethos foreordained Viktor to conflict. He wanted to find meaning, to dedicate himself to some higher purpose, to be all the Party asked. Yet he could no more give himself unquestioningly to the Party on the basis of its pronouncements than he could give himself to his grandmothers's God on the basis of her chanted litanies. He had to see and comprehend for himself. As he searched and tried to understand, his reasoning exposed troublesome contradictions between what he saw and what he was told.

His inner conflict probably had begun with the announcement in school that First Party Secretary Nikita Sergeyevich Khrushchev delivered a momentous and courageous address to the Twentieth Party Congress. The political instructor who gravely reported the essence of the speech suddenly turned Viktor's basic concept of contemporary Soviet history upside down. Stalin, the father of the Soviet people, the modern Lenin, Stalin, whose benign countenance still looked at him from the first page of each of his textbooks, now was revealed to have been a depraved monster. Everything he had heard and read about Stalin throughout his life was a lie. For the leader of the Party himself— and who could know better?—had shown that Stalin had been a tyrant who had imprisoned and inflicted death upon countless innocent people, including loyal Party members and great generals. Far from having won the war, Stalin had been a megalomaniac who had very nearly lost the war.

The revelations so overwhelmed and deadened the mind that for a while he did not think about their implications. But as the teachers elaborated upon the Khrushchev speech and rewrote history, questions arose. *It must be true; else they would not say it. But how could Stalin fool everybody for long? Khrushchev worked with Stalin for years. Why did it take him so long to find out? Why did he take so long to tell us? If everything the Party said before was untrue, is it possible that what it is saying now is also untrue?*

Khrushchev returned from his 1959 visit to the United States persuaded that corn represented a panacea for Soviet agricultural problems. In Iowa he had stood in seas of green corn rising above his head and seen how the Americans supplied themselves with a superabundance of meat by feeding corn to cattle and pigs. The American practice, he decreed, would be duplicated throughout the Soviet Union, and corn would be grown, as the radio declared, "from ocean to ocean." Accordingly, corn was sown on huge tracts of heretofore-uncultivated land—uncultivated in some areas because soil or climate were such that nothing would grow in it.

But the most stupid kolkhoznik *knows you can't grow corn in Siberia. I have seen it with my own eyes. It is not even a foot high, a joke. How can the Party allow something so ridiculous?*

The effort to amend the laws of nature by decree, combined with adverse weather, resulted not in a plethora of corn but rather in a dearth of all grain, which forced the slaughter of livestock. Serious shortages of meat, milk, butter, and even bread inevitably followed. Nevertheless, the radio continued to blare forth statistics demonstrating how under the visionary leadership of the gifted agronomist Khrushchev, Soviet agriculture was overcoming the errors of Stalin and producing ever-larger quantities of meat, milk, butter, bread, and other foodstuffs.

If we have so much bread, why am I standing in line at four a.m., hoping I can buy some before it runs out? And milk! There has been no milk in all Rubtsovsk for five days and no meat for two weeks. Well, as they say, if you want milk, just take your pail to the radio. But why does the radio keep announcing something which anybody with eyes knows is not true?

The population of Rubtsovsk included an abnormally high percentage of former convicts because most inmates of the surrounding concentration camps were confined to the city for life upon completing their sentences. Many were irredeemable criminals habituated to assault, robbery, rape, and murder. Armed with knives or lead taped to the palms of their hands, they killed people for no more than the gold in their teeth and robbed men and women of the clothes off their backs in broad daylight. Innocent citizens lost their lives in theaters or on buses simply because criminals in card games sometimes used as their stakes a pledge to kill somebody, anybody.

One Saturday night Viktor rode homeward from a skating rink on a bus with passengers so jammed together that it was hard to breathe deeply, and he had room to stand on only one foot. At a stop the front and back doors swung open, people poured out as if a dam had burst, and Belenko was swept outside with them. From within the bus he heard a heart-rending scream. "They have cut her up. Police! Ambulance!" Lying lifeless on a seat was a young woman, a large wet crimson splotch on her thin pink coat. There were no public telephones on the street and calls for help had to be relayed by word of mouth or runners. The police arrived about an hour later. They could do nothing except haul away the body.

Viktor examined the newspapers the next day. They did not mention the murder, as he was almost certain they would not, for crimes of violence in Rubtsovsk never were reported. They did report the rising crime rate in Chicago along with the rising production of soviet industry and agriculture.

Of course, I know there are many criminals in Chicago and everywhere else in capitalist countries. How could it be otherwise? They always are having one crisis on top of another. The people are exploited and poor and hungry and plagued by all the other ulcers of capitalism. We don't need the newspaper to tell us that. We need to know what's going on here.

Why do we have so many criminals, so many people who don't want to live openly and honestly? They say the criminals are the remnants of capitalism. But the Revolution was in 1917. That was nearly half a century ago. All these criminals grew up under communism, not capitalism. Why has our system brought them up so poorly?

Having fractured his wrist in a soccer match, Viktor took a bus to the dispensary for treatment. Although his wrist hurt, he recognized that his condition did not constitute an emergency, and he thought nothing of waiting. Ahead of him in the line, though, was a middle-aged woman crying with pain that periodically became so acute she bent over double and screamed. Her apprehensive husband held her and assured her that a doctor would see her soon. Viktor had been there about an hour when a well-dressed man and a woman appeared. A nurse immediately ushered them past the line and into the doctor's office. The husband of the sick woman shouted, "This is not just! Can't you see? My wife needs help now!"

"Shut up and wait your turn," said the nurse.

If we are all equal, if ours is a classless society, how can this happen? And why do some people get apartments right away, while everybody else waits years? And look at Khokhlov [son of a local Party secretary]. He's a real murderer and robber; everybody knows that, and everybody is afraid of him. But every time he's arrested, they let him go. Why does the Party pretend everybody is equal when everybody knows we are not?

One of Viktor's political instructors, the teacher of social philosophy, genuinely idolized Khrushchev as a visionary statesman whose earthy idiosyncrasies reflected his humanitarian nature and his origins as a man of the people. Khrushchev had freed the people of the benighting inequities bequeathed by the tyrannical Stalin, and by his multifaceted genius was leading the people in all directions toward a halcyon era of plenty. On the occasion of Khrushchev's seventieth birthday the instructor read to the class the paeans published by *Pravda*. Everyone could be sure that despite advancing years, the Party leader retained his extraordinary mental acumen and robust physical vigor. *We are lucky to have such a man as our leader.*

Some months later the same instructor, as if mentioning a minor modification in a Five-Year Plan, casually announced that Khrushchev had requested retirement "due to old age." For a while nothing was said in school about the great Khrushchev or his successors. Then it began. Past appearances had been misleading. Fresh findings resulted from scientific review by the Party disclosed that Khrushchev actually was an ineffectual bumbler who had made a mess of the economy while dangerously relaxing the vigilance of the Motherland against the ubiquitous threats from the "Dark Forces of the West." Under Brezhnev, the nation at last was blessed with wise and strong leadership.

This is incredible! What can you believe? Why do they keep changing the truth? Why is what I see so different from what they say?

Recoiling from the quackery of social studies, Viktor veered toward the sciences—mathematics, chemistry, physics, and especially biology. Here logic, order, and consistency prevailed. The laws of Euclid or Newton were not periodically repealed, and you did not have to take anybody's word for anything. You could test and verify yourself.

He shifted his reading to popular science magazines about biology and medicine, aviation and mechanics. At the time, Soviet students were required to study vocational as well as academic subjects, and those who excelled could participate in an extracurricular club the members of which build equipment and machinery. Viktor designed a radio-controlled tractor which was selected for a Mosow exhibition displaying technical achievements of students through-out the Soviet Union. As a prize, he received a two-week trip to the capital.

The broad boulevards of Moscow, paved and lighted; subway trains speeding through tiled and muraled passages; theaters, restaurants, and museums; ornate old Russian architecture; department stores and markets selling fresh fruits, vegetables, and flowers; traffic and official black limousines—all represented wondrous new sights. Collectively they elated him while they inspired pride in his country and hopeful questions.

Is not the Party right after all? Does not what I have seen prove that we are making progress? Will not all cities someday be like Moscow?

The final morning he joined a long line of women waiting four abreast outside the Kremlin to view the perpetually refurbished body of Lenin. The Kremlin with its thick red walls, stately spires, and turrets, connoted to him majesty and might, and upon finally reaching the bier, he felt himself in the presence of history and greatness. He wanted to linger, but a guard motioned him onward. Leaving reverently, he asked the guard where the tomb of Stalin was. The answer astonished him. They had evicted Stalin from the Lenin mausoleum. *Why, they've thrown him away like a dog!*

While telling his classmates back in Rubtsovsk about Moscow, Viktor heard disturbing news. The KGB had arrested the older brother of a friend for economic crimes. He remembered how admiring all had been the year before when the youth had bribed a Party functionary to secure employment in the meat-packing plant. There, as everybody knew, a clever person could wax rich by stealing meat for sale on the black market, and procurement of the job had seemed like a triumph of entrepreneurship. *He will be imprisoned. He will be one of them in the trucks. He will be a zek.*

The specter shocked Viktor into recognition of a frightening pattern in the behavior of many of his peers. Some had taken to waylaying and robbing drunks outside factories in the evening of paydays. Others had stolen and disassembled cars and machinery, to sell the parts on the black market. A few, sent to reform school for little more than malicious mischief or habitual truancy, had emerged as trained gangsters, who were graduating from petty thievery to burglary and armed robbery.

They are becoming real criminals. They never will be New Communist Men. Nothing is going to fix them. How did our communist society do this to them? I do not understand. But if it can make them that way, it could make me that way. That I will not allow. It is as Father said. I must make my own way. I must start now before it is too late.

Always Viktor had received good marks in school without especially exerting himself. He attended to his homework dutifully but quickly so he could devote himself to his own pursuits. Frequently in class, particularly during political lectures, he read novels concealed behind textbooks. Now he resolved to strive during the remainder of school to earn the highest honors attainable, to obey all rules and laws, to try to mold himself into a New Communist Man. Through distinction, he would find his way out of Rubtsovsk and into the sky.

Faithful to his vows, he disassociated himself from most of his friends, studied hard, and parroted the political polemics, even when he believed them absurd. As part of the final examinations in the spring of 1965, he artfully wrote three papers entitled "Progress of the Soviet System," "Crisis of the Western World," and "Principles of the New Communist Man." They faithfully regurgitated the dogma of the day and were brightened by a few original flourishes of his own. The teacher, who read portions of "Progress of the Soviet System" aloud, commended his selection of the tank as the best exemplification of the supremacy of Soviet technology. Although Viktor achieved his goal in social philosophy, a perfect grade of five, he was not entirely proud because he suspected that not all he wrote was true.

Certainly, his assessment of the crisis of the Western world was valid. The grip of the Dark Forces which controlled governments, policies, events, and the people of Western societies was weakening. The Dark Forces, that shadowy cabal, comprised of the U.S. Central Intelligence Agency, the American military, the Mafia, Wall Street, corporate conglomerates and their foreign lackeys, clearly themselves were in retreat and disarray. Everywhere in the West, signs of decay and impending collapse were apparent.* However, he was not so sure that the progress of Soviet society was as real and fated as his paper asserted. And he doubted the perfectibility of the New Communist Man, whose evolution and character he delineated in detail.

Maybe it was guilt that caused him to speak out to his detriment. His Russian literature teacher, in some casual comment, said that light is matter. "Of course it isn't," Viktor interjected. "That's basic physics."

What began as a polite discussion degenerated into an angry argument, and Viktor embarrassed the teacher before her class by opening his physics book to a page that stated light is not matter. She ordered him to report to her at the end of the day.

His excellent work, she noted, ordinarily would entitle him to a grade of five. But literature taught, among other things, proper manners. She could not in good conscience award a perfect mark to a student so unmannerly. The difficulty could be eliminated were he to acknowledge his error, recant before the class, and apologize for his impertinence.

No! Why should I say I am wrong when I am right? In science, at least, you must be honest. I will not be dishonest.

The teacher gave him a grade of four, and as a consequence, he was graduated with a silver medal instead of a gold. Still, he had his academic degree, a diploma certifying him as a Grade 3 Mechanic (Grade 6 being the highest), and a letter from school attesting to his good character and ideological soundness. He also had a plan.

The Soviet Union maintains a military auxiliary, the Voluntary Society for Assistance to the Army, Air Force and Navy, which is known by its Russian acronym DOSAAF. Among other functions, DOSAAF provides young volunteers with technical military instruction preparatory to their entry into the armed services. Viktor learned that the branch in the city of Omsk, 380 miles away, offered flight training. By finding a job in Omsk to support himself, he reasoned, he could learn to fly through DOSAAF.

His farewell to his father and stepmother was awkward, for all pretended to regret that he was leaving home, while each knew that everyone was relieved. His father gave him a note to a cousin living in Omsk and, shaking hands,

---

* Sometimes the Russians also used the term "Dark Forces," which Belenko heard throughout his schooling and military career in the Soviet Union, to denote in a narrower sense only the CIA or American intelligence.

pressed twenty rubles into his palm. He did not know whether his father wished to conceal the gift from Serafima or whether he simply was too embarrassed to make it openly. He did realize that his father could ill afford the gift, which equaled roughly a sixth of his monthly take-home pay....

Toward the end of the six months of basic flight training at Grozny, Litvinov and Belenko were changing clothes in the locker room. As Litvinov picked up his flight suit to hang it in the locker, a thick little book, small enough to be hidden behind a man's palm, tumbled out of a front flap pocket onto the floor. Belenko glanced down and saw the title of the book: Holy Bible. Litvinov's eyes were waiting to meet his when he looked up. They asked: Will you inform? Belenko's answered: Never.

Neither said anything, nor was the incident ever menioned subsequently. Belenko thought about it, though. *It's his business what he reads. If the Bible is full of myths and fairy tales, let everybody see that for himself. Everybody knows that a lot of what the Party makes us read is full of shit, we can see and prove that for ourselves. Why not let everybody read anything he wants to? We know our system is the best. Why be afraid of other ideas when we can show they are not as good? Unless...unless, of course, we're afraid that our ideas aren't the best.*

The schedule stipulated that the cadets would study the MiG-17 for two months back at Armavir preparatory to the final phrase of training. But the two months stretched into four because an emergency had sprung up in the countryside—another harvest was nearing. Each weekend and sometimes two or three more days a week, officers and men alike were packed into buses and trucks to join the battle of the harvest. For Belenko, it was a pleasant diversion. They mostly picked fruit and ate all they wanted. Because the schools and colleges of Armavir had been closed for the harvest, many pretty girls worked and flirted with them in the orchards. The farmers were hospitable and slipped them glasses of cider and wine. And at night they went back to the barracks, a good meal, and a clean bunk.

Yet Belenko despaired at the acres and acres of apples, tens of thousands, maybe hundreds of thousands of apples, rotting because nobody had arranged for them to be picked in time. He remembered how precious apples were in Siberia, how once in Rubtsovsk he had paid a whole ruble to buy one apple on the black market.

Why doesn't anything work? Why doesn't anything change? It's barely ten years before 1980. But we're no farther along toward True Communism than we were when they first started talking about it. We're never going to have True Communism. Everything is just as screwed up as ever. Why?

In April 1970 Belenko was assigned to a MiG-17 training regiment seventy-five miles northwest of Armavir near Tikhoretsk, whose 40,000 residents worked mainly in canneries and wineries. Although not accorded the privileges of officers, the cadets now, by and large, were treated as full-fledged pilots. They arose at 4:00 A.M. for a bountiful breakfast, then flew two or three times, breaking for a second breakfast around 9:30. The main meal at noon, which always included meat and fruit, was followed by a nap of an hour or so. They attended classes from early afternoon until early evening—tactics, future trends in aerodynamics, technology of advanced aircraft, military leadership, political economics, science of communism, history of the Party, Marxist/Leninist philosophy. Passes were issued on Saturday nights and Sunday, unless they were called to clean factories or work in the fields on weekends, requests which occurred roughy every other week.

Fortune again gave Belenko a good flight instructor, Lieutenant Nikolai Igoryevich Shvartzov, who was only twenty-four. He longed to be a test pilot and was able enough; but he had given up this ambition because he had no influence in Moscow, and nobody, so it was believed, could become a test pilot without influence. At the outset, Shvartzov gave Belenko only two instructions: "Let's be completely honest with each other about everything; that way we can trust and help each other," and, "if a MiG-17 ever goes into a spin, eject at once. You can pull it out of a spin, but it's hard. We can always build another plane. We can't build another you." Throughout their relationship, they were honest and got along well.

The MiG-17, light, swift, maneuverable, was fun to fly, and Belenko had confidence in it. Vietnam had proven that, if skillfully flown at lower altitudes, it could cope with the American F-4 Phantom. Should he duel with an American pilot in an F-4, the outcome would depend on which of them was the braver and better pilot. It would be a fair fight. That was all he asked.

Every four or five weeks the regiment received a secret intelligence bulletin in reporting developments in American air power characteristics, strengths, weaknesses, numbers to be manufactured, where and for which purposes they would be deployed. The bulletins were exceedingly factual and objective, devoid of comment or opinion and dryly written.

Reading quickly, as was his habit, Belenko scanned a description of the new F-14 fighter planned for the U.S. Navy and started another section before the import of what he had read struck him. "What?" he exclaimed aloud. "What did I read?" He reread the data about the F-14. It would be equipped with radar that could detect aircraft 180 miles away, enable its fire-control system to lock onto multiple targets 100 miles away, and simultaneously fire six missiles that could hit six different aircraft eighty miles away—this even though the F-14 and hostile aircraft might be closing upon each other at a speed up to four times that of sound.

Our radar, when it works, has a range of fifty miles. Our missiles, when they work, have a range of eighteen miles. How will we fight the F-14? It will kill us before we ever see it!

Belenko put the question frankly to an aerodynamics professor the next afternoon. The professor stammered, equivocated, evaded. Every aircraft has certain weaknesses. It is only a question of uncovering them and teaching how to exploit them. It may be possible to attack the F-14 from close range with superior numbers.

Shit. That's ridiculous. Besides, if what our own intelligence says is true, the F-14 still could outfly anything we have even if we got close to it.

The professor who taught the technology of advanced aircraft was respected for his intelligence and technical background, so Belenko asked him openly in class. He answered succinctly. We presently have nothing to equal the F-14. We are experimenting with something that could be the answer. It is designated Product 84.

Subsequently Belenko read details of the F-15 being built as an air-superiority fighter for the U.S. Air Force, then accounts of the planned B-1 bomber, and they were still more devastating to him. The F-15 would fly at nearly three times the speed of sound and climb to altitudes above 60,000 feet faster than any plane in the world, and at very low levels, where metallurgical problems restricted the speed of Soviet fighters, it could hopelessly outdistance anything the Russians had. The capabilities of the B-1 seemed other-worldly. A thousand miles away from the Soviet Union, it could commence firing missiles armed with decoys and devices to nullify radar and nuclear weapons to shatter defenses. Then it could drop to tree-top level, beneath the reach of radar and missiles, and, at speeds making it impervious to pursuit, skim over the target area. Having unleashed a barrage of nuclear bombs, it could skyrocket away at extreme altitudes, at 1400 miles an hour.

The professor of technology again was candid. He said that presently there was no known defense, practical or theoretical, against the B-1 should it perform approximately as designed. The history of warfare demonstrated that for every offensive weapon, an effective defensive weapon ultimately emerged, and doubtless, one would be developed. The broader difficulty lay in Soviet technological deficiencies. The Russians still could not develop an aircraft engine that for the same weight generated the same thrust as an American engine. They were behind in electronic transistors, and microcircuitry. And all technological difficulties were compounded by the comparative inadequacy of their computer technology. Cadets should not be discouraged by these handicaps but rather consider them a further stimulus to becoming better pilots than the Americans.

But if our system is so much better than the Americans', why is their technology so much better than ours?

Again, though, the thrill of flight, the excitement of personal success diverted him from the concern and skepticism such questions inspired. In July 1971 he passed his final flight examinations, receiving both the highest grade of five and a commendation. The 258 cadets remaining from the original class of 360 were ordered back to Armavir to study for the state examinations. But Belenko knew these were meaningless. It was over. Having brought them this far, the Party did not intend to lose any of them. He had done it. For more than four years he had done all the military, the Party, the Mother Country demanded. He had done it on his own, despite the oppressions, brutalities, risks, and stresses of cadet life, despite multiplying heretical doubts about the Party he was sworn to serve. He was about to be what since boyhood he had aspired to be. And he was proud of himself.

The professors now tacitly treated the cadets as officers, and Belenko for the first time learned of all the benefits and perquisites bestowed on a Soviet pilot. To him they were breathtaking.

Whereas the average Soviet doctor or scientist was paid 120 to 130 rubles a month, and an educator only about 100, he would earn 300. The typical young Soviet couple waited seven to eight years, and often much longer, for an apartment, and the majority of Soviet dwellings still were without indoor plumbing. As a pilot Belenko was guaranteed an apartment with bath and kitchen, wherever stationed. Food constituted the largest item in most Soviet family budgets; meat and fresh vegetables frequently were unavailable; shopping was arduous and time-consuming. Pilots, wherever based, were entitled to four excellent free meals a day seven days a week, ordinary citizens were allowed two weeks of vacation; pilots forty-five days. Additionally, during vacation, pilots could fly anywhere in the Soviet Union on Aeroflot for a nominal fee. Normally a Soviet citizen did not retire before sixty-five; Belenko could retire at forty, receiving two-thirds of his regular salary for the rest of his life. There was more—the best medical care, free uniforms and shoes, little preferential privileges, and enormous prestige.

Belenko had known of some of these benefits. But their full range was kept secret, never published or discussed. *No wonder! If people knew how much more we get, they would detest us instead of liking us....*

In April 1976 Belenko's squadron commander asked him to take a truck and pick up a shipment of office supplies from a railroad freight terminal thirty miles north of Vladivostok, paper and office supplies being essential to the functioning of the squadron. It was a task that should have been performed by the deputy squadron commander, but he never stayed sober enough to be trusted with the truck.

The morning was bright, the dirt road empty and not yet dusty, and forests through which he drove were awesome in their natural, unspoiled beauty. They reminded him of man's capacity to despoil nature and himself and of delicious hours in other forests.

Starting back, Belenko saw a frail, ragged figure walking along the road, and the man looked so forlorn he decided to give him a lift. The hitchhiker, who had few teeth, gaunt eyes, sparse hair, and a sallow, unhealthy complexion, looked to be in his sixties. He explained that he worked at the freight terminal and walked or hitchhiked daily to and from his hut eight miles down the road.

"How long have you been here?"

"Almost twenty-five years. After the war I spent ten years in the camps, and ever since, I've worked around here, doing whatever I could find. I am not allowed to go back to the Ukraine, although I miss my home very much. I have relatives, but it is too expensive for them to visit me. You know how life is. The first years were very hard for me because it is so cold here. The Ukraine is warm and sunny, you know, and there are flowers and fruit. I wish I could see it once more before I die. But I guess I won't, I have no passport." *

"How old are you?"

"Forty-seven."

"Are you married?"

"Oh, yes. She spent eight years in the camps. She's also from the Ukraine. Her relatives were exiled. They've all died now, and there's just the two of us. We thought about children, but we were afraid we couldn't take care of them. It's not easy to get a good job if you're an exile. You know how life is."

"What did you do? Did you kill someone?"

"No, I gave bread to the men from the forest." **

---

* To legally travel from one locale to another, each Soviet citizen must possess an internal passport which is issued or denied at the discretion of the authorities. Denial or withdrawal of a passport effectively confines a person to the area of his residence indefinitely.

**The "men from the forest" were Ukrainian nationalists, followers of General Stefan Banders, who allied themselves with the Germans in World War II and afterward tenaciously continued guerrilla warfare against the communists until they were largely wiped out in the late 1940s. Bandera escaped to West Germany but was killed there in 1959 by a KGB assassin.

What can he do, that poor man, to our country? Look at him. He hardly has any teeth; he won't live much longer. What kind of enemy is he? What kind of criminal? Whatever he did, ten years are punishment enough. Why not let him go back to his home and die? Why be so hateful? What kind of freedom do we have here?

Belenko was sent to a training center near Moscow for a few weeks' intensive study of the MiG-25, and when he returned in mid-June, a state of emergency existed in Chuguyevka. A dysentery epidemic had disabled fully 40 percent of the regiment, two soldiers had committed suicide, at least twenty had deserted, there had been more hunger strikes, and the enlisted men now were verging on open mutiny. Fuel shortages had prevented pilots from flying as much as they needed to master their new aircraft. American reconnaissance planes, SR-71s, were prowling off the coast, staying just outside Soviet airspace but photographing terrain hundreds of miles inland with side-angle cameras. They taunted and toyed with the MiG-25s sent up to intercept them, scooping up to altitudes the Soviet planes could not reach, and circling leisurely above them or dashing off at speeds the Russians could not match. Moscow was incensed, and Commandant Shevsov lived in terror of an investigation. Already they had been notified that the regional political officer was flying in next week to lecture all officers of the regiment.

Shevsov announced that a pilot from each squadron would have to speak at the scheduled assembly, present an assessment of the regiment's problems, and propose solutions. He instructed his political officer to pick those likely to create the most favorable impression. The regimental political officer was not from the political directorate of the armed forces; rather, he was a pilot who in the frenzied formation of the regiment just happened to be saddled with the job. He thought as a pilot, and he was the only popular political officer Belenko ever knew. When asked, Belenko told him bluntly and in detail what he thought was wrong and what should be done.

"Well, I agree. You will speak for your squadron. If you say just what you said to me, maybe it will shock them into letting us do something."

The regional political officer, a corpulent, perfumed man with bags under his eyes, appeared in a resplendent uniform bedecked with medals that made the pilots smile at each other because they knew that no political officer had ever participated in battle, except perhaps at a bar.

"Comrade Officers, your regiment is in a serious situation, a desperate situation.

"Around us the SR-71 is flying, spying on us, watching us in the day and in the night.

"The Chinese are a day's walk away from us. We should not let the Chinese frighten us. We can massacre them any time we want. They have a few nuclear bombs, but they can deliver them only by donkey. Their planes are so old we can wipe them out of the sky. But we cannot underestimate the Chinese because there are so many of them, and they are fanatical, mad. If we kill a million of them a day, we still will have three years of work ahead of us.

"So the Party requires that you increase your vigilance, your readiness, your discipline in order to defend our Mother Country. You have been given our country's best interceptor. It has the highest speed and the highest altitude of any plane we have. It is a very good weapon. Yet your regiment is in such disgraceful condition that you cannot use this weapon properly. Your soldiers and, yes, some officers, too, are drinking the alcohol for the planes, and your regiment is too drunk to defend our Mother Country."

We know all that. We've heard all that. It's as if they sent us a recording instead of a man.

Belenko was the fifth member of the regiment to speak, following Shevsov, the deputy regimental commander, and two other pilots.

"We must consider our problems in light of the principles of Marxism/Leninism and the science of communism," he began. "These principles teach us that man is a product of his environment. If we examine the environment in which we have placed our men, we can see the origins of our problems and perhaps, in the origins some solutions.

"On the kolkhoz I have seen livestock housed better than our men are housed. I have seen pigs fed better than our men are fed. There is no place for our men to wash themselves. That and the filthy mess hall are why we have so much dysentery. There is no place for our men to play, and they are forbidden to do almost anything that a normal young man would want to do. We have created for them an environment from which any normal person would want to escape, so they try to escape through alcohol.

"We must change that environment. First of all, we must build decent barracks, a decent mess hall, a decent latrine, and a bathhouse with fire for hot water. There are nearly eight hundred of us here. If we all went to work, officers, sergeants, soldiers, we could do that in a month. If there is not enough money, let us go into the forest and cut the logs ourselves. If every officer would contribute 30 rubles from his salary, we would have more than six thousand rubles to buy other materials.

"We should organize social parties at the base and invite students so that our men can meet nice girls in a normal way. It is unnatural and unhealthy to try to keep our men from seeing girls.

"The forests and streams are full of deer, elk, rabbits, ducks, geese, quail, and fish. We should take our men to hunt and fish. It would be enjoyable for them, and the game would enrich their diet. We should start our own garden and plant our own potatoes right here on the base.

"Each weekend officers should be appointed to take groups of men on the train into Vladivostok and let them just walk around the city. We can ride the train free, and we can sleep in the station, and we can take up a collection among the officers to buy them some sausage and beer instead of vodka. It will give them something to look forward to. It will show that we care about them.

"When we can, we should build a football field and a library so the men can improve their professional skills and education. And if they want to read detective stories, why not let them? That's better than having them drink alcohol.

"If we demonstrate to our men that we are loyal to them, that we respect them, then they will be loyal and respect us and obey us. If we give them alternatives to alcohol, most will take those alternatives.

"Comrade Colonel, I have spoken frankly in the hope that my views will be of use to our regiment and our Mother Country."

As Belenko sat down, the officers clapped their hands, whistled, stomped their feet, pounded the table until Shevsov stood and silenced them.

The visiting political officer, who had been taking notes, rose, his face fixed with a waxen smile.

"Comrade Officers, this has been a productive gathering. I find some merit in what each of you has said. I find that underneath, this regiment is imbued with determination to eliminate drunkenness, to enforce discipline, and to serve our Mother Country. That is what I shall report.

"But to you, Comrade Belenko, I must say a few words frankly, just as you spoke frankly. You do not ask, 'What may I give to the Party?' You ask the Party to give, give, give; give me utopia, now. You show that you lack the imagination to grasp the magnitude of the problem, much less the difficulty of solving it. You do not understand that our country cannot build complex aircraft, modern airfields, and barracks all at the same time, and your priorities are exactly the reverse of what they should be. You spoke of the principles of Marxism/Leninism. I urge you to restudy these principles until you understand that the Party and the people are one and that, therefore, the needs of the Party always must be first. We will do everything in time, step by step, and the Party wisely has decided which steps must be taken first, threatened as we are by the Chinese and the Dark Forces of the West."

The faintest of hopes, the finest flicker of light sparked by Belenko's speech evaporated. Nothing would be done. They filed out silently, Shevsov among them and for once one of them.

Pig! No, that is an insult to a pig. In the order of the universe, a pig serves some useful purpose. You and all you stand for are to the universe like cancer.

I wish I could put you for one night in those barracks and see how you feel when someone shits in your boot. I wish I could march you into that mess hall where a maggot would retch. Oh, there you would learn the science of communism.

Well, go back to your fresh fruits and meat and perfume and lying while our men lie disabled by dysentery, cholera, and alcohol, while the Americans look down and laugh at us from the skies. But you leave me alone.

All my life I have tried to understand, tried to believe you. I understand now. Our system is rotten, hopelessly, incurably rotten. Everything that is wrong is not the result of mistakes by bureaucrats in this town or that; it is the result of our system. I don't understand what is wrong, but it is wrong. It produced you. You, not the Dark Forces, have kidnapped our Mother Country.

Soon after this climactic and decisive intellectual rebellion, Ludmilla announced that she was leaving. They had tried as best two people could; they had failed; it was pointless to try anew. Her parents were overjoyed by the prospect of having her and Dmitri with them in Magadan, and they could guarantee Dmitri's future and hers. She would stay until October, when her commitment to the dispensary expired. But after she left it would be best for all if he never saw her or Dmitri, who would only be confused by his reappearance.

Her statement was so dispassionate and consistent with previous demands for divorce that Belenko could find neither energy nor desire to try anew to dissuade her. Besides, she was right about Dmitri.

Conditions at Chuguyevka were not atypical of those throughout the Far East. Reports of desertions, suicides, disease, and rampant alcoholism were said to be flooding into Moscow from bases all over. In late June, Shevsov convened the officers in an Absolutely Secret meeting to convey grave news. At an Army base only thirty-five miles to the southwest, two soldiers had killed two other soldiers and an officer, confiscated machine guns and provisions, and struck out through the forest toward the coast, intending to steal a boat and sail to Japan. They dodged and fought pursuing patrols several days until they were killed, and on their bodies were found diaries containing vile slanders of the Soviet Army and the grossest misrepresentations of the life of a soldier. These diaries atop all the reports of trouble had caused such concern in Moscow that the Minister of Defense himself was coming to the Far East and to Chuguyevka.

The career of every officer would depend on his impressions, and to make a good impression, it would be necessary to build a paved road from the base to the helicopter pad where the Minister would land, about four miles away. The entire regiment would begin work on the road tomorrow.

It never was clear just where in the chain of command the order originated; certainly Shevsov had no authority to initiate such a costly undertaking. In any case, the Dark Forces, the SR-71s, the Chinese, the desirability of maintaining flying proficiency were forgotten now. Pilots, engineers, technicians, mechanics, cooks, everybody turned to road building—digging a base, laying gravel, pouring concrete, and covering it with macadam.

It's unbelievable. For this we could have built everything we built—everything, barracks, mess hall. Everything. We could have built a palace!

But the crowning order was yet to come. Within a radius of about a mile, the land around the base had been cleared of trees to facilitate takeoffs and landings. The Minister, it was said, was a devotee of nature and its verdancy. He would want to see green trees as he rode to the base. Therefore, trees would have to be transplanted to line the mile or so of road.

You can't transplant trees here in the middle of the summer! Everybody knows that!

But transplanted they were, hundreds of them, pines, spruces, poplars, dug up from the forest, hauled by truck and placed every fifteen yards along the road. By the first week in July they were dead, shriveling and yellowing.

Dig them up and replace them. So they did, with the same results.

Do it again. He may be here any time now.

So again saplings and some fairly tall trees were imported by the hundreds from the forests. Again they all died. Finally acknowledging that nature would not change its ways for them, someone had had an idea. Leave them there, and just before he arrives, we'll spray them all with green paint. We'll drive fast, and he won't know the difference.

It all was to no avail. In early August they were advised that illness had forced cancellation of the Minister's inspection. He, wasn't coming after all. It was time to fly again.

To fly well and safely, a pilot must practice regularly. His skills, like muscles, grow flabby and can even atrophy through disuse. Because of fuel shortages and preoccupation with the road, they had flown little since May.

The second day they resumed, a pilot suffered vertigo as he descended through clouds preparatory to landing. In his disorientation he panicked and ejected himself. Scrub one MiG-25 and the millions of rubles it cost.

Subsequently a MiG-25 malfunctioned at takeoff. The runway was conspicuously marked by a line and guideposts. If a plane was not airborne upon reaching this line, the pilot was supposed to abort the takeoff, deploy

157

his drag chute immediately, brake the aircraft; if he did, he could stop in time. But on this morning the pilot neglected to abort soon enough, and the MiG-25 plunged headlong off the runway. By terrible misfortune a civilian bus was passing, and like a great steel knife, the wing of the MiG sheared off the top third of the bus, decapitating or dismembering five children, three women, and two men and badly injuring other passengers. When Belenko went to help, he saw three soldiers from the rescue party lying on the ground, having fainted at the horror of the sight.

The crashes might have occurred in any circumstances, even if the pilots had been flying regularly, even if they were not fatigued from working twelve hours a day seven days a week on the road. But Belenko did not think so. *It was murder.*

That night he knew it was futile to try to sleep, futile to try to postpone a decision any longer. A fever of the spirit possessed him, and only by a decision could he attain relief. He told Ludmilla that he had to return to the base, and through the night he wandered beneath the moonlight in the forests.

For hours, thoughts, recollections, apprehensions—half-formed, disjointed, uncongealed, contradictory, disorderly—tumbled chaotically through his mind until he realized that, as in other crises, he must gather sufficient strength, courage, and poise to think logically.

I cannot live under this system. For me there can be no purpose or meaning to life under this system. I cannot change this system. I cannot overthrow it. I might escape it. If I escape it, I might hurt it.

Why should I not try? I will have no family. Mother I have not heard from in twenty-five years. Father I have not seen for eight years. They are not like father and mother to me anyway. Ludmilla does not want to see me again. Dmitri, maybe I could see him a few times in my life, but we would be strangers. Privilege, yes, I have privilege; I could retire in 1987. But was I born to think only about whether I eat meat and white bread? No, I was born to find my way, to understand; to understand, you must be free.

Is there freedom in the West, in America? What would it be like there? I don't know. I know they have lied about everything else, so maybe they have lied about the West, about the Dark Forces. I know that however bad it is in the West, it cannot be worse than here. If the Dark Forces are the way they say, I can always kill myself; if they are as bad as they say, there is no hope for the world or mankind.

All right. I will try. And I will try to hurt this system as badly as I can. I will try to give the Dark Forces what this system most wants to keep secret from them. I will give them my plane and all its secrets.

On the Wrong Side

Stanislav Levchenko

During all those years in Japan, I could never be the friend to my country that I wanted to be, a fact that saddens me still. Oh how I studied Japan: its decision-making mechanisms, its way of life, its national psychology, its moral values, its culture. The more I studied, the more I loved Japan. But the sad fact is that all this knowledge and experience was a tool with which to stab Japan in the back in my role as a KGB officer.

My life was divided into four separate and unharmonious parts. The first, and of necessity the major part, was the time spent in the KGB's Tokyo residency, a place no different from the KGB headquarters in Moscow—same office intrigues, same militaristic discipline, same piles of paperwork. The second part was spent in employing all of my professional skills to induce contacts and agents to work against their own country. The third part was maintaining my cover by functioning as a journalist. Only when I was interviewing Japanese politicians or journalists for the *New Times* magazine did I feel good about myself. It was a straight job that had nothing whatever to do with my intelligence-gathering work.

The fourth part was at home with my family, the crumbling mortar that had to fit between and bind together my other three identities. All too often I had nightmares of meetings with strange, threatening people or of being caught by Japanese counterintelligence. At other times, gratefully, I'd slip into more tranquil dreams of my homeland.

We went back to Moscow on periodic visits for vacations, and the cold realities of my homeland refuted the sweet stuff of my dreams. Every time we went home, the first thing I'd have to do was report to all of my superiors at KGB headquarters. On each visit I'd hear the same litany of questions: "Why can't you recruit more? Why couldn't you get such and such information? When you get back, do this! Do that!"

Yet life outside KGB headquarters seemed even gloomier and darker than inside. I'd look into the faces of pedestrians and be stung by the sadness, the concern, even the anger I'd see in their eyes. I couldn't help comparing those faces with the ones in Japan, which broke into smiles and laughter at little provocation. And the corruption in the Soviet Union! Each time we visited Moscow it was worse, growing like a cancer out of control.

On one visit Natalia wanted to buy some knitting worsted to take back to Tokyo with us, so she asked her sister if such yarns were very expensive.

"No," was the answer, "but they'll still cost you quite a bit of money."

"Why?" Natalia asked. "That doesn't make any sense."

"Oh, you'll have to slip the clerk a bribe or she'll swear up and down that they don't have any. It's that way everywhere. You want the best bread, you bribe the baker. You want good meat, you bribe the butcher."

I found that to be true all over Moscow. I was once stopped by a policeman for a minor traffic violation, one for which I should have been given no more than a mere caution. "Oh, come on," I pleaded. "I've been in Japan for years, and this is a new regulation. Why can't you just give me a warning and let me go?" "What will you give me from Japan if I do?" he asked. I searched around in my overcoat pocket and found one of those trick match folders that have little three-dimensional cards fastened to their backs for advertising various bars or cafés. When they're riffled, they give the effect of motion pictures. This one advertised a bar in Tokyo called the Friendly Lady and showed an innocuous winking girl. He was delighted with it and forgot all about my traffic violation.

I was furious with the Soviet leaders who had failed to establish anything close to prosperity, who never intended to establish any semblance of democracy, and who fed their people nauseating propaganda to alienate them from people in free societies around the world. Every time I returned to Tokyo, I was stirred to the core just knowing that I once again stood on free soil. Each time I returned, I was sadder and more discontented. I was filled with self-loathing and contempt at what I saw myself doing: planting stories in newspapers, spreading malicious rumors that sometimes reached (and hurt) high-ranking officials, and constantly recruiting more agents from among the Japanese.

Since the evening I watched that TV show with my son and when I admitted to myself that there had to be a better way to live, a little worrisome doubt lay at the back of my mind. Sooner or later, I'd have to face facts. When I finally got down to facing those facts, the process was unbelievably painful. I had to admit that I was by nature a workaholic; Natalia would have been the first to agree. As a result, my work had always been at a high-performance level and nearly nonstop. For the first years of my Tokyo assignment, I'd worked hard

160

because I was convinced that what I was doing would benefit my people. I finally realized that I was indeed helping my people, but I was only helping them to become more deeply enslaved by the Soviet system. By the time I'd realized that, I was already into the job. I worked on and on like an automaton, trying not to notice what I was actually doing by the simple expedient of working harder and harder. It was stupid, no doubt, but it almost worked, for much of the time I was too tired to notice.

My KGB career had flourished, it's true, but I was nearing the end of my tour of duty in Japan. I was due to be recalled to Moscow any time after October 1979, and there were those in Moscow who had mixed feelings about me. In the first place, I'd be assigned to the Seventh Department of the KGB's First Chief Directorate, and the deputy director of that department was Vladimir Pronnikov, a declared and dangerous enemy. Feeling as he did that I was different from other KGB officers, he had tried his damnedest to slow my promotions while we were in Tokyo. I had no doubt that he would do the same or worse if I were under his command again in Moscow.

Though my KGB career was established and my professional record was exemplary, by 1977 I had grown to hate my decision to become a KGB officer. I hated having fallen for the argument that I should become a "courageous warrior and do a man's work" for the Soviet Union. Gradually, agonizingly, I admitted my eternal regret for what I'd done to Japan. Somehow, I knew I'd have to find forgiveness.

At the age of thirty-seven, I finally comprehended that I was on the wrong side.

Sometimes I still see Russia in my dreams—majestic pine groves, quiet silky rivers, magnificent old churches, icy patterns painted on the windows on frosty days. In those dreams I feel a longing for the country of my birth. But sometimes those dreams turn into nightmares in which I see hordes of people herded into labor camps and priests struggling to keep their faith and dignity in wretched prisons. I know that I'll have these dreams and nightmares for the rest of my life.

When one loves his countrymen as much I love mine, it's a wrenchingly painful thing to decide that everything one has done to help them has been in vain. I knew only too well that what benefits the Soviet system does not benefit Soviet citizens. People are pawns in the game, as far as the KGB and the Politburo of the Communist Party are concerned. Once the blinders fell from my eyes, I knew that to continue the work I was engaged in was impossible.

The next step was to decide what I could do about it. It was a long time before I could articulate it. Even to myself, I couldn't easily bring myself to say the words, "Stanislav Levchenko, you are going to have to request political asylum in the United States of America." Like anyone anywhere, I tended to confuse loyalty to a country with loyalty to the regime and therefore to wonder if the act of becoming a political refugee were not an act of treason against my people. Before I could do another thing, I had to answer that question to my own satisfaction.

At first I considered the possibility of trying to fight the Soviet system from within, as many dissidents do. But as a KGB major, I realized that what happened ultimately to dissidents would necessarily happen to me as soon as I spoke the first dissenting word. I'd be slapped into prison or locked in a mental institution. That's what they do in the Soviet Union to those who speak out against the system. The logic they use is that anyone who opposes the system is demonstrably insane. Once in the mental institution, the dissident is "treated" by means of brainwashing. If he persists in his deviant behavior, he is pronounced incurable. The treatment for incurables is a regimen of drugs that eventually reduces them mentally to vegetables.

I recalled that moment in my childhood when my father, tormented and disillusioned by the revelations of the Beria trials during Stalin's reign, had cried out in anguish over his disbelief that a Soviet leader could commit such atrocities against his own people. I remembered my early realization, never quite eclipsed by the mists of time, that the Russia my father loved—that all Russians love—and the Soviet Union were not the same thing at all. I summoned up the image, unfading, deeply alive, of the real Mother Russia, she of the courageous, long-suffering, spirited people who deserve far more than their leaders are giving. And I had my answer.

"Oh, no," I finally thought, "I'm not the one who is the traitor. If I leave the Soviet Union to live in another place, I'll not be the betrayer. If people want to know who the real betrayers of the Russian people are, let them look to the Communist party and its new elite."

I'd reached a turning point in my life, and I'd never felt more alone. Never let anyone tell you that it's easy to leave the country where you were born and raised and to go into voluntary exile. It isn't. I could confide in no one, seek no one's advice. There was nowhere I could turn to discuss my discontent. I knew that if I undertook this course, I'd have to do it alone and remain alone, never seeing loved ones and friends again. The agony of mind caused by this knowledge was so intense that I came close to deciding that the price I'd have to pay for my freedom was too high.

Aleksandr, my little son, was in school in Moscow. I didn't dare mention my feelings to my wife. As devoted as she was to the Soviet Union, it wouldn't have been safe. Our marriage had reached a point where divorce was inevitable, so I was reasonably certain that even without her extremely strong patriotism, Natalia would never have considered coming with me to the United States. My greatest concern (and justifiably, as it turned out) was for Natalia's and Aleksandr's safety in the Soviet Union should I change sides.

In assessing the situation, I considered two things. Aleksandr was a child. "Even the KGB doesn't prey on children," I told myself. Next, there was Natalia. Her credentials with the party were impeccable, both through her family's long history of absolute loyalty and her own record. I was certain the KGB file on Natalia was at least as complete as my own dossier. I also knew that Natalia would never have made a move that could have suggested any disloyalty on her part.

"Yes," I reasoned, "Natalia and Aleksandr will be safe." In all honesty, if I could go back to those initial days when I was reasoning this through, knowing what I know now about what happened to those two dearly loved people, I'm not at all sure that I'd make the same decision.

But at the time, I felt as if I was submerged in cold water. Nothing could make me feel warm even in the humid heat of the Tokyo summer. I needed tenderness, just as I had as a wrongfully punished child. And I tried to find that tenderness in brief romantic affairs with members of the Soviet theater and dance groups that visited Japan.

I had a brief affair with a woman who worked for the Soviet puppet theater, and later I reflected on the irony of the situation. She was a famous puppeteer. Her puppets made people laugh, made them sad, happy, or angry. When a puppeteer is good, many people in the audience forget that they are seeing dolls. They see the dolls as people. I reflected that I was just like a puppet, except that my manipulators were thousands of miles away in Moscow, in the KGB headquarters. Even they were manipulated by master puppeteers whose offices were located in the Kremlin.

Another romance I had was with a beautiful, tall, blond ballerina who came to Japan with an amateur group. She became very interested in me in a matter of days, and I got involved in this romance rather deeply. One night I drove five hundred miles from Tokyo to Osaka where the group was performing, just to spend a couple of hours with her. But this short-lived love left a bitter taste. I knew that my new girlfriend admired me not for my human qualities, but because she was fascinated by my profession. She was convinced that there was no better job than to spy for the Soviet motherland, and she thought I was a hero. She loved me for what I most despised about myself. Another disappointment!

Meanwhile, my professional life went on as usual. The internal intrigues in the residency had cooled down after Pronnikov was recalled to Moscow in 1977. We all hoped that his elevation to a higher rung on the career ladder would keep his interest centered in Moscow, so that we could breathe a bit in Tokyo. As we were to learn, however, his interests were everywhere. Those of us he'd left behind in Tokyo were far from forgotten. My one source of satisfaction about my problems with Pronnikov was the fact that his superior, Deputy Director of the First Chief Directorate Major General Popov, held me in high esteem and considered me to be an accomplished intelligence officer. When I was moved to active measures in Tokyo residency, I was apparently accepted as an officer capable of implementing sensitive actions. In 1978 I became one of four or five officers in the KGB residency's think tank.

Although my tour of duty in Japan was scheduled to end in October 1979, if I had stumbled the least little bit or made some embarrassing political blunder along the way, I could have been yanked out and sent home at a moment's notice. I also knew that time was slipping away entirely too fast for me to delay much longer, but I simply wasn't yet ready to make a final commitment. Then something happened that made me realize just how short the time was getting.

I was in the resident's office one morning when his secretary buzzed through on the intercom. The resident listened a moment, then said, "Send him in."

"Shall I leave?" I asked.

"No, this will only take a moment."

The door opened to admit an officer whom I knew by sight only. I think he worked in communications somewhere.

"Come in, come in," said the resident with what I thought was a false heartiness. "We've just received a special message from Moscow, and they need you back as soon as we can get you there. Here's your plane ticket. There's a driver waiting downstairs to take you to the airport."

"What about my family? Will I be coming back? What—" he sputtered before the resident interrupted him.

"Just call your wife. Tell her you're on your way to Moscow and that she and the children will follow in a few days. We'll see to packing and returning your household effects. Now, you must hurry. Maybe you'd better wait until you're at the airport to call. You mustn't miss that flight."

As soon as he had hurried from the room, I asked, "A promotion?"

"No," he explained, shaking his head sadly, "the poor devil's in serious trouble of some kind. He just won't know it until he walks into headquarters."

I too could be returned to Moscow at a moment's notice. I'd just seen it happen to another with my own eyes. As a consequence of that incident I took pains to maintain my high level of work. I was under the sword of Damocles; I had to keep all risks to a minimum. By late spring and early summer Pronnikov was so firmly entrenched in the Seventh Department in Moscow that those of us in Tokyo were often made aware of his interest in us. I was particularly aware of his far-reaching and unsympathetic interest in me. I knew that the caliber of my work could not falter, or I would be whisked back to Moscow before I could have a chance to think through my personal dilemma. I had no intention of becoming one of the expelled officers. Even if I were to return to Moscow in the normal rotation, Pronnikov was still there gunning for me. As events unfolded during my last months in Japan, I became increasingly aware that he was just waiting to pounce.

Flight

Biographies

SIMAS KUDIRKA was a Lithuanian radio operator aboard a Soviet trawler working U.S. territorial waters off Martha's Vineyard. In November 1970 he leapt from his ship to the U.S. Coast Guard ship *Vigilant* and requested political asylum.

On orders from an American admiral, Soviet seamen were allowed to board the *Vigilant*, find Kudirka, beat him, bind him, and drag him back to the trawler.

The incident created a public outcry that forced a revision of U.S. immigration regulations. In the Soviet Union, Kudirka was charged with treason and sent to Siberian labor camps. After it was learned his mother had been born in Brooklyn, Kudirka was released in November 1974, and—with his family—flown to the United States.

For Those Still at Sea, his story written with Larry Eichel, appeared in 1978.

VALERY PANOV was born Valery Shulman in Lithuania in 1938. He began studying ballet at age six and in 1958 joined Leningrad's Maly Ballet.

After changing his name to Panov in 1963, he joined the Kirov Ballet and soon became the company's outstanding dramatic dancer. ("I couldn't join the Kirov Ballet until I called myself Panov," he explained years later. "I managed to change my passport from Jew to Russian. Many dancers are Jewish but they don't admit it. Even ballet is ruled by politics here, though it seems far from ideology.")

Despite the excellence of his dancing, only once—in 1960—was Panov allowed to accompany the Kirov on a foreign tour. Even then he was called home—on the pretext of a family emergency. He applied his talents to choreography—creating "Pugachev," a ballet based on the leader of a peasant revolt. When Kirov officials demanded that he modify some scenes, he refused.

In 1972 Panov and his wife, Galina Ragozina, applied to emigrate to Israel. His application inspired denunciations of him as a traitor to Russian art; the Kirov dismissed him and demoted Galina, a soloist, to the corps.

Western balletomanes took up Panov's cause—aided considerably by Senator Henry Jackson. In June 1974 the Soviets issued Valery and Galina exit visas. They flew to Israel and since have danced with many of the world's leading companies.

To Dance, published in 1978, recounts Panov's career and struggles, with particular emphasis on the intrigue poisoning Soviet ballet.

For biographical information on **STANISLAV LEVCHENKO**, see excerpt in the section "Apostasy."

For Those Still at Sea

Simas Kudirka & Larry Eichel

I

1.

n 1959, after I had become a ship's radio operator and had married Gene, I tried to learn to be happy in Lithuania. All I wanted was an apartment for my family and a seaman's passport for myself. Was that so much to ask?

At the time of our marriage, we lived in a single room in a drab clapboard barracks in a section of Klaipeda called Fishtown. The neighborhood was a slum, a center for drinking, mugging, and prostitution. A giant fish-processing plant was just a few blocks away, and when the wind came off the Baltic Sea, as it did every afternoon, the stench was unbearable. We did what we could to make this room a real home. But there was nothing we could do about the paper-thin walls that let the chill of the winter wind and the raucous voices of drunken neighbors come right through. We had no running water. There was just a pump outside and a filthy outhouse about seventy-five yards away. To cleanse our bodies, we had to take the cross-town bus to the public bathhouse, a trip which could consume the better part of a day.

We had our first child, Lolita, in 1960. On winter days when I was out to sea, Gene would awaken in the freezing room at 6:00 A.M., hop out of bed, clean the dead ashes out of the stove, load in fresh wood, and start a fire, hoping to warm the room before the baby woke up. Then she would breast-feed Lolita, put together a package of diapers, and, just before 8:00 A.M., drop her with a neighbor before running off to her job at the store. Several times a day she hurried home to nurse the baby. When Gene's workday finally ended at 11:00 P.M., she would drag herself home, pick up Lolita, and leave the crying child bundled up in the carriage while she worked feverishly to get a fire going and warm the room, which had been unheated since morning. Then after undressing the child, feeding her, and putting her to bed, she boiled the next day's diapers, chopped the next day's wood, and went to bed at 2:00 A.M., looking forward to four precious hours of sleep.

169

The arrangement was becoming unbearable, and the room was just too small. As soon as Gene could stop breast-feeding, we took our daughter to Griskabudis to live with my mother and stepfather. We vowed to bring Lolita home as soon as we got our apartment. But in the Soviet Union, which has a chronic housing shortage, a man and a woman cannot just go out and walk the streets in search of an apartment. They must put their names on a list and wait for their names to get to the top. I would have to wait thirteen long years.

Every time I came back from a voyage, before I went back to the barracks, I checked the all-important list; and every time I found that my name had moved up only a few notches, or not at all. At this rate, I would have a grandchild before I had an apartment. My child would grow up hardly even knowing her mother and father. I wanted to find the people who were responsible for this travesty of a list and knock their teeth down their throats. Who were those bastards, dozens of them, who managed to jump ahead of me on the list? Who were the sons-of-bitches who got apartments without even appearing on the list? What gave the privileged few—government officials and party bigwigs—rights that an ordinary working stiff didn't have? I would swear and curse and yell so loudly that Gene feared the police would come.

Once I went to see the great and exalted housing supervisor to try to get an explanation. I was admitted into his office after a long wait, and I was made to feel as if I had been granted an audience with the king on his throne. This man had a huge apartment of his own, a chauffeur-driven car, a generous salary, and all sorts of other privileges. And when I asked for his help, he said he was sorry, there was nothing he could do. I asked him why. He said that was not for me to know. I felt as if he had stabbed me in the gut and poured boiling vinegar into the wound. What could he know about living in a barracks room? You come back from a month at sea, and you want to make love to your wife. How can you do that and enjoy it when the door has no lock and could fly open any time and the walls are so thin that the neighbors can hear the bed creaking?

At first, we tolerated the situation. We told ourselves we only had to suffer a few years there. But as the years went by, we couldn't fool ourselves anymore. We were probably going to be living in this squalor forever.

On board ship, I took out my mounting frustration by listening to the forbidden Western radio stations—the Voice of America, Radio Liberty, and British Broadcasting. The more I listened, the more my hatred for the Soviet system grew. I heard talk of a Russian writer named Alexander Solzhenitsyn and a physicist named Andrei Sakharov, men who called themselves dissidents. At first, I paid them no mind; they were after all, ethnic Russians. Besides, what could those Moscow intellectuals know about finding an apartment in a provincial town or getting a passport? Gradually, though, I sensed that they were all complaining about the same conditions—the lack of respect for union rights and human dignity.

As the years passed my frustration grew into a rage that I had to fight at all times to suppress. Once it totally overwhelmed me. In full view of other sailors, I screamed at my ship's political officer, denouncing him, the fishing fleet, the collective farming system, Lenin, Stalin, and the inability of the system to provide a simple apartment for a hard-working man and his family. After that outburst, I was confined to shore for six months and lost six months' salary, a loss I could ill afford with a second child on the way (our son, Evaldas, born in 1966, joined Lolita in Griskabudis with my mother). I knew I could not risk another day of rage. But by the end of the 1960s, as I entered my second decade of waiting for an apartment, my patience was disappearing. My outbursts were becoming more frequent and harder to control. I saw myself walking down a long gangplank. One day soon I would reach the end of it and fall into the ocean, where the sharks were waiting to rip me to bits.

Then one day, in the spring of 1970, just before my fortieth birthday, I received a short telegram at sea from Gene. At long last, we had been assigned an apartment. I felt all the tension disappear in an instant. I got drunk that night, and I celebrated again when I got back to port and saw the apartment for myself. The living room alone was bigger than our old barracks room. It was no palace. It needed work. But that was the kind of work I had been waiting to do all my life, work that would create a real home for my family.

I thought my problems were all behind me. But it was not to be. I asked for a permanent job in port so that I could enjoy my new apartment all the time. My supervisor said no. And if I didn't go back to sea, he said, he would make sure I never got any kind of a job ever again. He even threatened to have the apartment taken away. So nothing had changed, not really. The system would never allow me to be the master of my own destiny. Unless I did exactly as I was told, I would lose everything I had worked so hard to get. So I did what I was told, hating the system more than ever. I had no choice. On November 5, 1970, against my will, I left Klaipeda as the radio operator of the factory ship *Sovetskaya Litva,* not knowing the ship was bound for the coast of North America.

2.

The short, husky man in the brown wind breaker stood on the third deck of his ship and stared out over the rail. The gray skies were low and thick. The air was unseasonably mild, the winds gentle, and the sea almost calm.

For weeks, Simas Kudirka had eagerly anticipated this day—November 23, 1970. His ship, the *Sovetskaya Litva,* a floating factory that processed the catch of the Soviet fishing fleet, was at anchor one-half mile off the island of Martha's Vineyard in a gentle curve of American water called Menemsha Bight. There the Soviet ship and her crew of 160 awaited the arrival of an American Coast Guard cutter. The American ship would be carrying a special delegation of angry Massachusetts fishermen who wanted to protest that the Soviets were harvesting too many fish from New England waters. But Simas did not care about the substance of the meeting. He was a radio operator, not a fisherman. He just wanted to see the Americans close and maybe talk to them for a few minutes. As a child growing up in Lithuania, he had dreamed of visiting America, as his grandfather had done so long ago. Now, as a man entering middle age, he felt certain that this brief encounter would be as close to America as he would ever get.

He turned his head and watched the chalky white American cutter, so tiny in comparison to his own ship, approach from astern. As the cutter drew closer, he could make out its name—*Vigilant.* Soon the men on both ships began mooring them together with thick sea line. They rocked back and forth in the gentle swells, six feet apart one moment, ten feet apart the next.

The smiling American seamen waved wildly and shouted their greetings. Simas looked below him down to the main deck of the *Sovetskaya Litva.* There the Soviet sailors stood in silence, their teeth clenched, their arms folded in front of them, lining the deck like robots. He had feared it would be this way. Soviet sailors were always rude and aloof to Westerners, not because they liked being rude but because they valued their careers. Only a fleet officer could safely offer an American a smile and a handshake and only in a situation staged for a photographer's benefit.

Yet when the lines were secured and the two ships linked, the atmosphere changed. The American good cheer proved irresistible. As the American fishermen were hoisted across from the *Vigilant* to the *Sovetskaya Litva* for the meeting itself, the American sailors bombarded the Soviet ship with gifts in a spontaneous cultural exchange. They hurled boxes of cigarettes, cans of beer and soda, belts, pennies, and dark blue baseball caps with VIG for *Vigilant* sewn across the front in gold letters. The Soviet sailors caught the gifts, waved in thanks, and threw their own belts, caps, and cigarettes in return.

"Come on aboard!" one American shouted to a Soviet seaman.

The smile on the Soviet seaman's face disappeared, and he quickly drew his finger across his Adam's apple, as if slitting his throat. There was a moment of uneasy silence. Then he burst into laughter, and the relieved American laughed with him.

Soon the deck of the *Sovetskaya Litva* was littered with debris, mostly magazines and the magazines just lay there, their pages riffled by the breeze. The Soviet sailors were in no hurry to pick them up. Smoking an American cigarette or wearing an American baseball cap was one thing. Reading a piece of capitalist propaganda was quite another.

On the third deck, about four feet down the railing from Simas, Emilius Gruzauskas, the ship's first mate and chief political officer, was watching the exchange with professional interest. It was his job to vaccinate the men of his ship with constant doses of Soviet ideology, to immunize them against the Western ideas they would encounter on their voyages. He had been enjoying himself until the Americans started throwing magazines. Those glossy magazines, so full of dangerous ideas, were a threat to him and his work. He knew that he was about to find out how effective his vaccinations had been. He anxiously surveyed the main deck. Suddenly, his eyes locked into a cold, hard stare.

"Look," he said to another officer. "Watch this."

Simas, overhearing the conversation, looked too.

Two young crew members, a man and a woman, had stooped to the deck in an area that was covered with magazines. They slipped a few under their jackets and hurried below to hide their treasures. The vaccinations had not taken on everyone.

Gruzauskas turned to the officer. "Those two will never go to sea again," he said.

3.

I heard those words and inside I blew up. "I'm finished," I said to myself. "I've had it." I wanted to turn around and really let Gruzauskas have it. Those two poor kids! You walk a tightrope between staying alive and dying and then one careless, meaningless gesture can throw you off. One wrong word, and it's all gone for the rest of your life, I knew. I had fallen off the tightrope once long ago. And I had paid for it dearly. Wasn't that slip the real reason I had still not received a seaman's passport? Wasn't that the reason I had had to wait thirteen years to get an apartment big enough for myself, my wife, my daughter, and my son? Now this pair would have to endure the same suffering I had endured. They would be booked on voyages and then taken off at the last minute by the border police without ever knowing why. They would always be threatened with the loss of their right to work. And for what? In the instant they picked up those magazines, their lives melted into mine and mine melted into meaninglessness. We were victims—all of us. We were trapped on a floating jail.

I had to do something to break out of it. The idea of jumping to the American ship flashed into my mind out of nowhere. The idea felt right, and I never questioned it. I guess I had a rocket inside me just waiting for the right spark to light the fuse. No salary, no feeble promise of getting passport someday was going to stop me. I was going to jump. I was going to defect to the United States of America. I didn't know much about American law or American society. I didn't know a soul in the whole country. I knew only what my grandfather had told me, and that was sixty years out of date. I knew only a few words of English. But I had a clear conscience. I would find someone who would listen to my sorrows, someone who would understand me and give me a job. I would work hard. I would get my family out of the Soviet Union. It wouldn't be easy—I knew that—but in three or four years I could do it. I could pull them out into freedom, and any wound I had caused them would be healed.

My mind was set, I was going to jump.

4.

On the *Sovetskaya Litva*, Simas was getting ready to jump. He was sitting in the ship's tiny radio room, where he had reported for duty at mid-afternoon. All the Americans had returned to the *Vigilant*. Soon the moment for the jump would be upon him and there would be no time for second thoughts. He would just have to do it or the chance would disappear. He would be ready. He had spent the afternoon sorting through his belongings, knowing that he would have to travel light. He would leave behind everything except a packet of newspaper clippings, radiograms, and letters from home which he had stuck in the breast pocket of his blue flannel shirt.

And he had picked out the spot for his jump. He planned to leap directly from the main deck of the *Sovetskaya Litva* to the flight deck of the *Vigilant*, eight feet across and three feet below. If all went well, he would not even get wet. At the spot where he hoped to land, the *Vigilant's* flight deck had a railing made of three horizontal cables about a foot apart. As he hit the rail, he would grab for the top cable with both hands. If he missed, he would grab for the second or the third. If he missed all three, he could snag the edge of the flight deck or the deck below.

He stared at his watch and waited for the voice of the ship's captain, Vladimir Popov, to crackle over the public address system, ordering all hands to prepare to shove off. The minutes passed. No order. What could be going wrong? He threw his headset down on the table. He had to see what was happening outside. He headed toward the staircase that led down to the main deck, but before he got to the top of the stairs, he saw Captain Popov approaching down the hall.

"Simas," Popov said. "What are you doing out here?"

"I was just looking for someone who would know whether we're going to be leaving soon."

"We are. I was just on my way to the bridge to give the order."

Simas followed Popov to the bridge and saw him pick up the microphone. The moment for the jump had arrived.

He hurried down the first flight of stairs and stopped on the landing for an instant. He heard nothing, saw no one. Convinced he was not being followed, he ran down the second flight and the third, turned right, and went out the door. He was outside, on the main deck, facing the *Vigilant*.

He walked down the deck, heading for his spot. It was 4:25 P.M., dusk, and there was a stiff, chilling breeze in the air. But he was not going to be in the air long enough for the wind to make any difference.

"Hi, Simas," a passing crew member said. Simas was too nervous to reply. He kept on walking. In a few seconds, he was standing at the spot. He had played the scene out in his head all afternoon. He clasped his hands in front of him in an instant of prayer. Then he lifted one leg over the rail and then the other. He was standing on the ship's giant rubber bumper. Freedom was eight feet away. He looked to either side. No one was watching.

He bent his knees and dove across the abyss, his body parallel to the water, his arms extended, reaching desperately for the railing up ahead. For an instant, he was sailing in between, free of the Soviet ship and not yet touching the American. Then he felt the palms of his hands slam into the top wire cable. Instinctively, he closed his fingers around it and held on tight as both feet landed hard on the edge of the deck. It took a second or two for him to realize that he had a sure grip on the *Vigilant*. He had arrived.

Pushing off with his feet, he vaulted over the railing and tumbled onto the flight deck of the American cutter, landing on his right shoulder. He crouched down to avoid hitting his head against a hanging lifeboat, rolled under it, hopped up, and ran to an open doorway four steps away.

He ducked through the doorway and started up a steep, narrow staircase on his right. Then he stopped. He saw a pair of shoes descending the steps, and the shoes became a man—stocky build, thick face, brown hair. He immediately recognized Ivan Burkal, the acting commander of the Soviet fishing fleet and the host for the meeting with the American fishermen. Unknown to Simas, Burkal had insisted on a brief tour of the *Vigilant* when the fishing meeting broke up. His tour was just ending.

Simas clung to the left rail and burst up the stairs.

"Kudirka! What are you doing here?" Burkal yelled.

"Excuse me," he said as he bolted past. "I don't have time."

Simas got to the top of the steps, whirled to his left, and kept running. He ran past four closed doors, turned left again, and bounded up another flight of stairs, which brought him inside the pilothouse. For an instant, he stood silently at the top of the steps, his chest heaving, his presence unnoticed by the half-dozen Guardsmen who filled the small room. He saw the officer who had caught his cigarette pack.

"Good evening," Simas said in English.

The officers turned from their work and stared at him. For a few seconds, there was silence.

"Good evening," Lundberg said, and the silence erupted into a hubbub of handshaking and hugging and voices all talking at once.

"Comrades!" Simas yelled, hysterical with happiness. "Thank you!"

Simas tried to tell them that Burkal knew he was on the *Vigilant*. But he could not make himself understood.

"Did you jump?" Lundberg asked.

Simas did not understand.

Lundberg crouched, extended his arms in front of him, and pretended to grab a railing. "Jump? Jump?"

"Yes," Simas laughed, mimicking Lundberg's crouch. "Jump!"

He tried to explain who he was, "I sailor in Russian fleet. I Lithuanian, not Russian. I try long time to get sailor's passport and nothing, nothing, nothing. . . . I not alone. I have family—two childs, girl, Lolita, boy, Evaldas."

After a few minutes, he was led to the rear of the pilothouse, through a metal door, and into a storage closet called the "stick." He was instructed to stand inside the closet behind a padded yellow stretcher. And there he waited for the *Vigilant* to start its engines and take him to American soil.

5.

Ralph Eustis forced himself to knock on the door of the watch-stander's head. "This is the commander," he said as he opened it. His face was ashen, and his forehead was dotted with beads of perspiration. "A Russian delegation would like to speak with you."

"No!" Simas shouted. "Twenty years of speaking with Russians and nothing. Enough! Enough!"

"The Russians say that you have stolen some money, stolen some money."

Simas frantically ran his hands through his pockets, across his chest, and down his legs, denying the charge by frisking himself.

"Nothing, nothing!" He pointed to the papers he had given Eustis earlier. "Nothing, nothing!"

Eustis nodded, then pulled a handkerchief from his pants pocket to mop the perspiration off his forehead.

"Dear Captain, please not giving me again, again," Simas pleaded, his hands clasped in front of him. "For me is Siberia. Siberia is death."

Eustis turned, walked out, and closed the door behind him. He couldn't bear to tell Simas that his request for asylum had been refused. He staggered down the stairs and informed Fleet Commander Burkal that Simas would be given back.

Burkal offered no words of thanks. "I request that you take measures to return the sailor to our ship," he said through his translator.

Somehow, all evening Eustis had managed to avoid thinking about the mechanics of the return. Now that he did think about it, he had visions of a terrible brawl—of American sailors chasing Simas, beating him into submission, and then carrying his bruised body to the Soviets. He could not let that happen. But Eustis knew that he could not convince Simas to go back on his own, and so now he asked Alex Obolensky, the Russian-speaking translator who had accompanied the Massachusetts fishermen, to try. He escorted Obolensky to the head and introduced him to Simas.

"The captain is requesting that I translate the following to you," Obolensky began in an emotionless tone of Russian. "Asylum has been refused to you and the captain has orders from his superiors to return you to your ship. He has no right to detain you further. You have to make a choice of how you wish to leave the ship."

Simas's spirits wilted. He had expected the bad news. Still, it hurt to hear it, especially from a man whom he had never seen before.

"I will not return! I will not return!" Simas yelled. "I will jump in the water first. If I jump, what are my chances of being rescued by the Americans?"

"The captain will make every effort."

"Do the Russians have the right to pick me up?"

"Yes."

"In that case, I will not jump."

Obolensky did not react. Simas was infuriated by his indifference.

"I cannot return!" he yelled. "Do you understand? You obviously

177

understand the language, but do you understand what I am saying?" Perhaps this new man did not comprehend how serious he was about defecting. "The Soviets asked me years ago to inform against my cousin, who was a hero in resisting the Russian takeover of Lithuania. But I refused. And even though that happened twenty-two years ago, I have suffered ever since. Every other member of the ship's crew has a seaman's passport. Not me. They won't let me leave the ship in a foreign port. Ever! Do you understand what that does to a man? I will not return. Siberia waits for me if I do."

"Yes," Obolensky said, nodding his head. "I see. Still, the captain has no right to keep you on this ship any longer. You must decide how you wish to leave."

"No! I will not return!"

Obolensky left. Simas burst out of the head and paced the length of the hall outside, panting, quivering, and clutching his stomach. Seaman Fowlie, who had been posted in the hall as a guard, watched in helpless bewilderment.

"Do you have knife?" he asked Fowlie excitedly, pronouncing the word kah-nee-fay. "I making hara-kiri." He pretended to stab himself in the gut to make sure he was understood.

"No, I don't have a knife," Fowlie lied.

"Revolver—you have pistol? I must die."

"No."

Simas heard footsteps and voices on the stairway. He raced back into the head and slammed the door.

The door opened. Eustis was there. He was not alone.

"I believe you know this man," Eustis said to Fleet Commander Burkal, a short, pot-bellied man with dark, wavy hair.

Burkal stepped up into the doorway. "Now, Simas," he said in a patronizing tone of Russian, "can you look me straight in the eye and tell me you know what you're doing?"

"Yes, I can," said Simas, his voice cracking just a little.

"I advise you, reconsider—come back on your own before it is too late."

"Let's not waste time."

"Simas, how can you shame us so much? Do you know what this means?"

"Yes, I know. And I am not coming back."

"Why did you do this thing?"

"Because I am sick and tired of your eternal lies, sick and tired of your meaningless political instruction classes, sick and tired of your Leninisms. You have lied and lied and lied and today I am putting an end to the lies—for myself!" He pounded his right fist into his left palm. His face reddened. His voice quickened. "You have inflicted incurable wounds, and I am leaving in the hopes of healing some of them. Your system is not worth the shit on a dog's tail. All you have done is trample on everything. Today I have chosen to say goodbye to all that. You can go on and build your empire, but you are going to do it without me!"

"I don't understand," Burkal said with a hard edge in his voice.

"What were you lacking? You had a job, a family, an apartment. That society you attack has educated you, clothed you...."

Simas began to fumble with his life jacket. "I defecate on your society!" he shouted. He leaped out of the life jacket and hung it on the wall behind him. Then he tore off his shirt and threw it at Burkal's feet.

"Here!" he shouted. "I'm giving you back everything the Soviet Union has given me." He began to unbuckle his pants.

Burkal backed away from the head entrance and up stepped Gruzauskas, the political officer whose remark about the sailors picking up magazines had put the idea of defecting into Simas's head. He spoke in Lithuanian. "Have you given any thought to the position you put the captain and me in?" he asked.

"You put yourselves in that position."

Someone accidentally turned on the hand-drier, forcing everyone to shout to be heard.

"What about the position in which you put your wife, your children, your mother?" Gruzauskas asked.

"Listen. Don't bait me with my family. You have sucked the lifeblood out of everyone who is near and dear to me." Simas was trembling. "I worked twenty years and for what? All your damned money buys is tears for the eye and acid for the stomach. I can earn more bread in the United States cleaning out places like this than I did as a sailor for you. We have talked about all this before, but this is the last time we will talk."

"You will be sorry," Gruzauskas said, still calm. "But then it will be too late."

Burkal tapped Gruzauskas on the shoulder. "Let's get out of here. You can feel the anti-Soviet atmosphere." They turned and walked down the steps, followed by Eustis.

On the way down the steps, through the translator, Burkal told Eustis: "The only way to bring him back will be by force."

To Dance

Valery Panov

1.

The early light of March 21, 1972, illuminated our bedroom like sun shining through stained glass. I got up and inhaled the morning's sweet sorrow of leaving.

When Russian sailors heard their ships were steaming into battle, they rushed below decks to change. It was important to die in clean underwear. This happy association came to me when I realized I was putting on my Belgian suit. Anything could happen to us.

But I didn't believe it. Serious trouble seemed farfetched in the rare blueness of the early spring day and in my happiness. The luxury of acting on my deepest impulse had washed away the hesitations, half measures, and compromises. At last I was taking an unequivocal, unretractable step that allowed me to respect myself. I felt liberated already.

I was going to inform the powers this morning by asking the Kirov for a statement of our character, attitudes, and job performance. Since we wanted to leave the country, not apply for a new job or for membership in some organization, this lightly camouflaged security evaluation was an absurd irrelevancy in our case. According to normal reason, the greater a would-be emigrant's "deviations" from the norm, the better for Soviet society to dump him onto the ideological enemy. But the iron rule was that this document, known as a *kharakteristika*, had to accompany all visa applications. The authorities simply ordered the candidate's place of work not to provide it when they wanted an extra obstacle. But the request for it was decisive, for it declared your intentions—and on paper.

At the theater I went directly to Rachinsky's Command Post, as he liked to call it. His secretary was guarding the office from her usual place. For her delicate mastery of the bureaucratic arts, the old girl was known as the bulldog. She understood the relationship of power to paper shuffling better than the many directors she had served. The bulldog always stiffened at the faintest whiff of political complication in any paper that neared her desk. After setting down our request as if it were a declaration of war, she stared straight ahead and said nothing.

I went upstairs to change for the morning class. Midway through it, the assistant to the theater's Party Secretary entered. He was so frantic that he kept bumping into the chairman of the Komsomol* organization, who accompanied him. Both kept adding "immediately" and "without the slightest delay" to their hoarse whispers that I was wanted in the Party office.

An emigration application sent wheels spinning with amazing speed. Four dark-browed men were indeed waiting. They aimed black stares at me, as if to announce what agency had dispatched them here so quickly. Their prologue was establishing that I was in fact Panov and had actually submitted "this terrible request." They tried to inform me I couldn't be serious about it but were hampered by an aversion to pronouncing the name "Israel."

"That militaristic, fascist country. And you're not even a full Jew!"

Later their leader took charge. "Let's drop this horseplay. You tell us what's bothering you. Are you dissatisfied with something?" I tried to suppress my smile. "Dissatisfied" was not exactly how I'd have put it, but there would be no sense in trying to explain anything to the present company. "What's troubling you, that's what we can't understand. You're picking up the top Kirov salary, and a packet in Vilnius to boot. So what is it—your apartment? You want a better one; we'll give you a better one. Just say the word."

I restrained myself. "Let's just say that I want to join my people," I said. "It's time for me to live in my own homeland."

After the long pause this earned, the leader of the quartet was first to find his place again. "You're hurt because you haven't been going on foreign tours. That's ridiculous. Millions of people don't go abroad, and they don't commit suicide. But don't worry, we'll fix up even that."

As the agents' faces grew angrier, they pulled their chairs closer. Obviously, their orders had been to make "that bastard dancer" retreat from his villainous deed. "Do you realize what might happen now? Why ruin you career, finish your life?"

Of course, it wasn't *my* career that worried them, but their own. As always,

---

* Young Communist League

someone would have to pay for the trouble. The punishment would fit the unforgivable publicity of two Kirov principals, supposedly the happiest people on earth, asking to depart. And this was the team directly responsible for protecting the theater from ideological subversion.

At last they gave up. The Party Secretary scurried after me as I walked down the corridor. He looked as if Count Albrecht had lowered his leotards in front of a full house. "For heaven's sake, why? You have...we have... we want to help you get your choreographic ideas on the stage." He realized this wouldn't work even before I said *Pugachev*. Shifting ground, he said that I was "no kid" any longer. "You don't understand how these things work. There are always ways of getting around obstacles. You just have to—"

For the first time that morning I interrupted. "Why don't you save yourself lots of trouble and just let me go?"

Class had ended, but the pianos seemed to rear on their hind legs as I walked past the studios. I smiled at the good old Russia I was leaving, where everything was secret, but word-of-mouth news traveled faster than teletype. Wide arcs were negotiated around me in the corridors. Coaches peered from behind cracks in doors, as if I had amputated my own legs. Members of the orchestra looked at me as if I were the first aborigine in Europe.

Cleaning women were the first who actually dared say farewell. Their red eyes flowed with tears for the wretch who was about to be cut off from Mother Russia. Their children stared at me as if I were going to my beheading. "My God, those poor people!" one granny actually wailed.

A hypnotist had obviously convinced most of my fellow dancers that I didn't exist. Someone I'd known since the Academy would pass me as if I were air. If I'd put out my hand and said my name was Valery, he would not have believed me. I was no longer the person he once knew.

As eyes full of compassion or horror followed me constantly over the next days, whispers of "Israel!" and "Jew!" went along. They sounded in the same half-frightened, half-disgusted tone as used for "Third Reich!" and "Nazi!" The company had been so laced with propaganda that most perceived Zionism and Hitlerism as roughly the same evil and the same threat. This partly explained the avoidance of me. Something had stirred in the Kirov's swamp of compromises, intrigues, and half-truths. Now the thing had emerged and was trying to...leave!

At the top, furious consultations went on about what measures to take. Every other matter in the life of the great theater was dropped, while Rachinsky rocketed back and forth to Moscow like a steam-powered shuttle-cock. "What a selfish bastard you are," his assistant sputtered. "This damn emergency, the unbelievable trouble—all for *you* and your terrible unfairness. A real comrade would never think of giving us so much work."

The Personnel Director had a more personal complaint. Frantic because of a favorable recommendation of me on the latest KGB questionnaire, she screamed about my heartlessness. "I called you a *Soviet* person. I put it in *writing*. Now look what you've done to me."

Rachinsky's every return from Moscow increased the feeling that retribution was coming, but no one took any action while senior politicians were deciding what it should be. The few members of the company who continued to see me were fully conscious of their valor. Driving me home one day, a colleague suddenly became apprehensive for his new Moskvich. "Be a pal, and hop out at the next light, okay? They might be fixing up a crash for you. Why should an innocent buggy take it on the chin?"

Another young friend gave a straightforward answer to my teasing. "Yeah, I *am* scared. Which proves *I'm* not crazy."

Oleg Vinogradov of *The Mountain Girl* was one of the exceptions who offered sympathy, although he disagreed with my decision. Losing dancers was a personal blow to him. And he knew more defections would follow. "Ye gods, how stupid it is. How opposite everything in art. Where is our crudeness leading us?"

The plan Rachinsky finally returned with from Moscow was to isolate me entirely from the Kirov in preparation for expelling me. I was to have no contact, no coaching, above all, no performances. But I had already given one. Months before, I had been scheduled to dance *The Creation of the World* on March 27. No stand-in for the Devil was available, and rather than cancel the ballet, I danced this final time.

High Party and KGB officials stuffed the boxes that evening. They had come to be outraged in person by the dancer who was trying to defile Soviet art. What was the animal that had committed this terrible crime? Why had the responsible comrades allowed it to happen—in the Kirov of all places? But another part of the audience sensed they would never see me again and felt that *this* was the disgrace. The interaction of bureaucrats controlling their fury and admirers controlling their sorrow generated its own electricity.

The current reached me as I waited beneath the stage, from where the Devil first emerges. When I realized that this was going to be my final appearance in Russia, nostalgia and love surged through my system. I wanted to hold the props, the wings, the set against my face.

Hell blazed above me in the form of pyrotechnic flames. A small elevator lifted me through the Devil's trapdoor. Applause of a kind I'd never received before filled the Kirov.

For the first time since Batumi, I heard my old music, telling me I could dance again. My muscles themselves had stayed sound during this deathly season. Now that my reflexes were back, everything worked as well as it used to. But this wasn't enough. I wanted to be truly extraordinary and show the Party bosses what they were losing. Something else also summoned. The part of me that would always belong to the Kirov demanded tribute to ballet while I was still there.

Crowds of dancers, stagehands, and the entire administrative staff watched me from backstage. Instead of the customary "Fantastic!" and "Marvelous!" when a soloist exited to the wings, I received silence. A hundred eyes burned my back as I walked alone to my dressing room.

As word of my swan song spread, people rushed to buy flowers at stalls just outside the theater. It was a Kirov tradition to present each performer with his bouquets at the curtain calls following every act. Although Rachinsky could do nothing about the farewell cheers, he took decisive action to prevent a non-Soviet rat from receiving visible evidence of public esteem. This further disgrace would have been too much while district, city, and regional overlords watched, beady-eyed, from Tolstikov's boxes. I wasn't even given an individual curtain call after the second act, but this was a kind of compliment.

Yuri Soloviev was dancing God with his usual brilliance, and Mischa Baryshnikov was a genius as Adam. Our styles were too different to speak of a "winner" in our friendly competition, but miracles were taking place. I amazed myself. I leaped higher than ever, did more turns in the air than during my experimental rehearsals. My Devil risked his own special steps—double assemblé while spinning horizontally in the air—with a charmed immunity to physical hazards. This is how I wanted to be remembered; it was the way I wanted to remember what Russian ballet had given me. Chaliapin's bells tolled for the first time in years.

My flowers were again withheld after the final curtain. The enormous pile lay out of public sight, like offerings for a secret funeral. But the applause almost became a demonstration.

Several weeks later the middle-aged official responsible for scheduling Kirov performances was summoned to a stern Party meeting. "Comrade Ukhov, why didn't you *prevent* it?" Ukhov tried to protest that in the absence of instructions, he could only wait, together with everyone else.

"No. In a terrible case like this, your duty was to have foreseen all possibilities. You should have had a spare Devil to substitute…for him."

Ukhov's defense was useless. Rachinsky had indeed brought back his orders too late from Moscow. And since *someone* had to answer for the mistake thousands had seen on the Kirov stage, Comrade Ukhov was severely reprimanded and told that his Party card might be recalled. He had a heart attack.

2.

Not even the elderly props man dared visit me after my last performance. Galya was home from the hospital, but not strong enough to have danced her She-devil role. She and I were alone in my dressing room when the door was opened and the floral mountain dumped inside. Fear was lurking, threatening, growing in the aftermath of the exhilaration on stage. But Galya gazed at the luxurious bouquets as if nothing else existed in the world. "Just think," she whispered. "The whole audience knew. It's even a little exciting, don't you think?"

What I thought was that we'd had a taste of what awaited us. The theater's willingness to flout its solemn traditions for petty slaps at us showed what the great machine of state could do to "enemies." But this didn't occur to her. Having decided what was right and acted upon it, she was free of all anxiety. "Look at our flowers, how beautiful they are."

For the hundredth time in our few years together, her innocence soothed me. Whatever form the battle would take, it would be easier with her as my partner. Throughout the coming years, her "Let them say what they want about us, we know what counts" would save me again and again.

3.

Even while he was commuting to Moscow for instruction on how to handle me, Rachinsky knew what to do about Galya. He sent Party ballerinas to work on her while she was still in the hospital. In his first free moment he himself was at her bedside, his voice tender. "I don't believe it! There's some kind of silly paper on my desk. Why should that oddball ruin *you*? What on earth does a Russian girl have to do with Israel? Let him go; nobody cares about him anyway. But you're our darling." I was a lost cause, but she was savable and *must be saved*. "You know how the people who matter feel about you. It would be tragic to lose the fantastic career and the marvelous life that are awaiting you."

A Party ballerina called to chat about what fun it had been having three husbands. The next visitor simply had to tell Galya what a terrible husband I was. I had exploited all my Kirov mistresses very selfishly, she said, and now was trying to work a new nasty trick on Galya.

Galya and I wrote to Rachinsky, with a copy to Party headquarters. We asked to be spared such advice in the future, which, since the marriage was sanctified by Soviet law, could qualify under the criminal code. However, this only fed their efforts. The instinctive reaction to try to split us up seemed more than just tactics. It was the first lunge of revenge.

The first official shots were notices that began appearing on the company bulletin board. "A reprimand to V.M. Panov is hereby announced for being five minutes late for a rehearsal of *Hamlet.*" (The average delay in getting to rehearsals was a good half hour, and no one had complained before.) "A reprimand is hereby announced to V.M. Panov for having performed *The Creation of the World* without a wig." (I had dispensed with the thing a year before.)

Then an order not to notice me must have been issued, for people started pretending I was a sheet of glass. When Galya returned to class, everybody looked straight through her, too, and her teacher didn't even glance in her direction. But after a few days of this she suddenly became a princess for whom every door was opened. The exaggerated courtliness to her was intended to underscore that she was the maiden of pure native stock, sadly corrupted by an evil foreigner. No one spoke to her without emphasizing her "Russianness" in every other sentence, while whispers of "Jew, Jewish" followed me everywhere.

I also heard rumors of a "court of conscience" being planned on orders Rachinsky had brought home from his last Moscow trip. Passing me in a corridor, one dancer whispered that I'd "better be careful: a Party meeting has decided on your condemnation—by the collective." I supposed this meant an article in our wall newspaper. There was nothing to do but keep calm and hope the attacks stayed harmless.

Two days after Galya's first class following her hospitalization we arrived at the theater early to avoid more rebukes for tardiness. Galya went to her dressing room, and I to the men's, which was several degrees more frigid than previously. Yuri Soloviev was particularly out of character. He had remained an exceptionally decent man who simply couldn't do anything devious. His stunningly tragic suicide a few years hence would remain a mystery, but it must have grown out of Kirov disappointment; in this sense, it could be called an internal defection and added to the list of those who escaped abroad. Now it obviously distressed him to have to avoid my eyes.

I changed and went upstairs to Kaplan's class in Studio Number One. Still early, I was one of the first to begin limbering up. Just as I started, a young Jewish boy whispered, "Watch out!" and hurried away. Then Alexander Pavlovsky, the man who had been graduated from the Academy the year before me and never fulfilled his promise, announced he found it "shaming and disgusting" to be near me. It was certain that something was brewing. If not keyed up for it, Pavlovsky would never have had the courage.

After five minutes of warming up, I was ready for work. After ten, I wondered whether the class had been canceled. The Party Secretary nervously stopped me on my way to find out. "If you'd please wait just a minute more. You're...er, needed here."

Needed? I had an image of Colosseum lions clawing at human meat. Just then Galya crossed the studio on her way to the one next door, where the women trained. After the missed days in the hospital, practice called her even more insistently than usual. She went toward it with the same determination on her face as when I first saw her at the competition.

A few minutes later the thunder of a driven pack shook the corridor. They weren't lions, but they didn't sound like dancers either. The doors burst open. A vanguard of Party activists rushed in, followed by the entire company, with administrators, accompanists, and coaching staff. Almost three hundred people spilled around the studio's perimeter, pushing me against the piano in the far corner. Then I heard voices trying to pry Galya loose from her warming up. Her impatient face finally appeared among the crowd at the door, opposite me.

The silence was as if a conductor's baton had been raised. A dancer who divided his time between lyric roles and Party work strode to the center of the studio and assumed the pose of an opera hero attacking a tragic aria. His deeply melodramatic voice echoed off the mirrors. "Despicable...treachery ... has...been...committed...in...our...Temple...of...Art...and...of...Love...for... Humanity...I...call...upon...the...collective...to...drive...the...traitor...out."

Then Maltsev had the floor. "Shulman, a Jew, has submitted an application to go to Israel. Having fattened himself like a swine on the art of the Soviet people, he now wants to sell it elsewhere. But that's not all. If he goes, foreign newspapers will carry the stink of his slander and lies. We must stop our enemy from carrying out his hateful intentions."

Few had heard of our recent split. Everyone knew that he had been my best friend. And despite the preparation for this "court of conscience," despite the universal knowledge of Maltsev's outside work, people gasped. Private life was something separate and sacrosanct, even—or especially—under Soviet conditions. This language from a man who had shared so much of my life was startling.

After ten more minutes nothing startled anyone. One of my neighbors in the old Rossi Street apartment confessed his shame for having borrowed bread from me there. His roommate, a young corps dancer I sometimes fed and with whom I had worked for months on his stage presence, said he wanted to "vomit up all the putrid leftovers Panov gave me." Pavlovsky shook while announcing that "Panov and Ragozina have sold themselves to a foreign intelligence service. We must fix a punishment for them usually not provided for in humane Soviet law. We must exile them to Siberia for the rest of their lives."

The calls for vengeance followed in smooth succession. It was absolutely clear that the Party had planned the order and the content of this nightmare, but for whom? I looked at Galya and froze. Her face was a pool of shame and distress. Everyone else was staring at her and waiting.

A character dancer named Korrstantin Rassadin was now explaining that "Panov wants to betray the greatest art in the world for the West's dirty degradation. We are revolted by this cheater who never understood that the only true art is Soviet. If he wants to sell what the Soviet people gave him, he is a thief and must be punished. If he wants to trade the best ballet in the world to rummage in moneymaking garbage, he is an animal, and we must treat him as such."

Fighting instinct told me to hit back at the same level. But the Party activists growled orders for me to hold my tongue. Obviously the program did not include an answer by me.

Next, People's Artist Irina Kolpakova described her reaction when she first heard of the "loathsome betrayal....But what really hurt was a young girl's surrender, a Russian girl agreeing to go to Israel with him. This disgusting scum befouling our theater—I wanted to throw up. Now I want to spit in their direction. Out! I say. Out forever, you Zionist fascists. And may your traitorous feet never again defile our sacred studio."

After Party stalwarts had led the attack, Komsomol activists eager to get ahead and abroad marched right behind them. I observed this with a surprising detachment, trying to decipher what it might mean for our future. A major article about me by Suzanne Massie in the *International Herald Tribune* was less than a year old, and the tappers knew we sometimes talked on the telephone. I'd been hoping that her access to the press on top of my other foreign contacts would persuade the authorities to let us go quietly. I had underestimated their desire for revenge.

Maybe these Stalinist-style accusations were the prelude to this kind of punishment. Or maybe the one good discharge of resentment—and the scare for my fellow dancers—was the climax of the campaign: a sign that we *were* about to go. But the flush-faced accusers had warmed too happily to their roles. The stage-managed speeches were going beyond the call of duty, building up a thirst for personal vengeance. The increase in pressure boiled away my analytical coolness. All I had left was an urge for self-protection.

Not hacks were yelling now, but dancers with whom I'd worked closely and I had learned to respect. "We took him into our ranks and gave him a title," shouted a ballerina who had kept coming to see me after my divorce. "Now let's throw the bastard out." My old friend and frequent partner Gabriella Komleva demanded that I "tell us once and for all what you did in America. Tell us what filth you're preparing to write about our art." While these spontaneous threats came from the sidelines, corps de ballet boys with eyes full of unrehearsed menace muttered, "Israel," "Shulman," "enemy."

The hatred spread like fire. Everyone welcomed it for settling every kind of score: women who had liked me; men who sought my roles; Kirov patriots who had always despised my style. For the first time I felt the power of a mob kicking a fallen man. The front ranks seemed about to lose control and actually started doing this. My eyes sought out Galya's. She was rigid and white.

Enough hysteria had been whipped up so that the people would "demand" a "fitting" sentence. This *was* Stalin's legacy, but the collective hatred also had older roots. The attackers' common ground was anti-Semitism. The dislike of me as an outsider had all come down to this. While the Party fanned it, the spirit of the pogroms filled the studio.

Kaplan had to say what he did to demonstrate *he* wasn't really a Jew. Another reason was to stay on a tour of Spain starting in two weeks. But despite the extra pressure on him to prove himself, despite his terrible training under Stalin, Kaplan's reaction was dismaying. When the order went out, he had stopped looking at me. For ten years he had lived for me. In one instant I had become Judas.

Several years before, he had written the scenario for a ballet based on Gogol's *Taras Bulba*. All Soviet textbooks treated the hero's murder of his son, who had committed a political betrayal, as a splendid act. Kaplan found his answer in this. "Taras Bulba tells us what we must do. We gave birth to Panov. Now we must kill him."

4.

When I was finally allowed to speak, so much needed answering that I couldn't think of any logical order. I said that since my American trip my working conditions seemed designed to keep me depressed. After thirteen years as an outcast I wanted to leave, and my company called it treason. But this was a specific crime under Soviet law. If applying to emigrate was indeed treason, I should be tried.

I had started as a Young Communist who believed as much as most. With suspicion, slander, scapegoating, the state did everything it could to destroy my belief. Not one official I had turned to since 1959 had given me the truth. Now it was time to end the hypocritical courtesies. I mistrusted the Soviet regime as much as it mistrusted me. The solution was a quiet parting.

I had somewhere to go now, my historical homeland. I would not be an outsider there. The speeches just delivered were the best evidence that I did not belong where I was....

Jeers went up at "historical homeland" together with catcalls of "*Shulman!*" I said that my right to leave was written into the Soviet Union's own laws and international agreements it had signed. I broke off when this brought more laughs and boos.

My comments had been a mistake. I hadn't developed them into a forceful whole, had not, somehow, even got to the main points. I knew how to move, not how to talk. But at least I'd stopped the assault. A tense quiet descended. As on the stage, each minute seemed like ten. Party people were evidently not fully satisfied with their presentation either. "Who wants to add something?" they coaxed.

Suddenly the ballerina who had led the attack on "the traitor's accomplice" broke the sick silence. Others had called out to Galya to "leave the Jew" and "divorce that criminal," but Ninel Kurgapkina, a respected principal and teacher, had been the most explicit. "We can't expect anything from *him*, he's a Jew. But a Russian girl agreeing to leave with someone she can't respect or love is a terrible thing. Great days can be yours in the Kirov—if you free yourself of his foul influence."

That had been near the beginning. Now Kurgapkina, was calling for Galya's answer. "You, Ragozina, why are you standing there? Speak up and say something—like a Russian girl."

This was the finale I had been praying wouldn't come. I knew what the company was demanding. It was the Soviet way, perhaps based on Russian tradition, to beg forgiveness and re-instatement into the "collective." Enormous psychological pressure for public confession and repentance pressed on any Russian who stood alone. The Party had to be seen as flawless by showing how woefully the doubter had erred.

Galya's nose was crimson. Veins swelled beneath her transparent skin. Kurgapkina's third call was like Svengali's command. My hypnotized bride detached herself from the far corner. Tears from her swollen eyes spotted the floor. Losing her this way was the worst thing that could happen to me. I could already hear her pronouncing the compulsory apology: "Save me, comrades, I didn't know. You have opened my eyes to the monster he is." Shame and misery twisted Galya's teenaged face. "It's all right, I understand," I said to myself. The ballerinas who cursed me had been her idols since she could remember. They were crushing her like a doll under a tank.

She had reached the center of the floor, hesitated there. I wanted to run. But she did not kneel down. I saw her advancing to me like a stricken Giselle, from some realm of purity. She did not try to speak. She stopped at my side and soundlessly laid her head on my chest. I kept myself from crying. I had never been so happy in my life.

She was what ballet was meant to be about. The grace and loyalty of her gesture in ballet language said a hundred times more than my attempted speech. The "judges" were stunned.

Just a Few More Steps

Stanislav Levchenko

On October 24, I could not sleep until about 4:00 in the morning. Natalia was sleeping in another bedroom and, as far as I know, hadn't even heard me come in. When I got up at about 8:30, she had already left for her job at the embassy. Thoughtful to the last, she left me a big breakfast, and while it was hard to force food down, I ate. I knew I'd need every scrap of strength I could muster for what I was going to do.

I intended to behave exactly as I always did, to appear as normal as possible until the very last moment. My usual habit was to leave the apartment near mid-morning, giving me time that I usually used to read the papers. But on October 24, 1979, I used the morning instead to consider all of the uncertainties and unanswered questions I faced.

Foremost among the questions I couldn't answer with total certainty was the one I had asked myself when I analyzed the roster in the Active Measures office: had the KGB penetrated American intelligence at a sufficiently high level to allow the Soviets to recapture me if I tried to leave? I'm not afraid to die now, and I wasn't afraid to die then. But I was afraid, and still am, of what the Soviets would do before I could reach the welcome oblivion of death. I know enough about the degradation, the dehumanization, the brutal tortures meted out to such "traitors" in Lefortovo Prison in Moscow. I remembered vividly the photographs shown to us during our training of a KGB colonel, drugged and bound in a straitjacket, being hauled aboard a Soviet plane in Istanbul after he had tried to defect. He was taken, we were told, after Harold A.R. (Kim) Philby, a Soviet agent in British intelligence, had warned them in time. I wasn't going to delude myself: it could happen again, and to me, if the Soviets had penetrated American intelligence.

My exhaustive search of the residency network hadn't turned up such an agent in Japan. I didn't believe there was one. As for the CIA headquarters in Virginia, I couldn't be certain.

Assuming my reasoning was correct, another question presented itself: were the Americans sharp enough to receive me promptly, to protect me sufficiently as they checked my authenticity, and capable enough to get me out of Japan quickly? To this series of concerns, I could only shrug and say, "I'll soon know."

I had long since checked out the Hotel Sanno, the place most often frequented by U.S. embassy personnel, military officers, and various dignitaries. It was a place where people could socialize and where groups could hold receptions and luncheons or dinners. I'd known for a long time that when I made my move, the Sanno was the place I'd go. On October 24th, however, I set about first convincing anyone who might be watching that I was going about my life as usual. I left my apartment about 11:00 A.M. dressed in casual beige slacks, open-necked shirt, and a brown tweed jacket. I stopped at the Press Club and examined the wire service teletypes. Then I began weaving my car through the heavy traffic and drove into the suburbs, turning often into side streets to make sure I wasn't being followed. I went back downtown, parked, and walked for a while, stopping occasionally to browse in the bookstores or to look at antiques. In a small café I attempted to soothe my nerves with a cup of tea.

Finally, at about 8:00 P.M. I climbed the steps to the Hotel Sanno and went in. I could've sworn there was a lump of ice in my stomach as I walked across the lobby to the desk. "The reception?" I asked, taking a wild chance that there was one.

Luck held. I was directed down the hall toward a large room where a military sentry stood posted at the door. I spotted a U.S. Navy commander in the crowd and singled him out as my target. "Would you tell the commander there that I wish to speak to him, please?" I asked the sentry.

"Certainly, sir," he said, saluting smartly before disappearing into the room. I watched as he whispered to the commander, who then looked over at me, obviously curious, before striding out to meet me. "May I help you?" he inquired politely.

"My name is Stanislav Levchenko. I'm a Tokyo correspondent of a Soviet magazine called *New Times*. I urgently need to talk to an American intelligence officer."

For a long moment the commander hesitated. Then he said quietly, "Come with me."

He led me down the corridor to an empty room. "You can wait in here," he said before disappearing. In just a second or so, two military men entered the room to take up guard positions on either side of the door. I waited. For interminable, silent, stressful moments, I waited.

"What is taking so damned long?" I wondered.

In something less than half an hour the door opened to admit an aristocratic-looking gentleman. "Wait outside, please," he said to the guards. Then, turning to me with a courteous smile, he spoke. "My name is Robert. Now, can I help you in any way?"

"I apologize," I said. "I mean no discourtesy, but may I see some credentials or some I.D.? I must know who you are, you see."

He opened his wallet to disclose his identification. In a sharp wave of relief I said at last the words which I'd mentally rehearsed so often. "I'm not only a correspondent of *New Times*," I said. "I'm also a major in the KGB, and I formally request political asylum in the United States."

"My God!" Robert exclaimed in shocked amazement. "I've heard your name, of course, but I had no idea that you were KGB! And I'm supposed to know every KGB officer in Tokyo." He simply stood there, drop-jawed, then finally added, "Can you prove your claim, Mr. Levchenko?"

"I have no documents with me," I responded. To my own ears my voice sounded expressionless, almost indifferent. "And I have no time. I'm in danger, and we both know that the danger increases with each passing second."

"Yes. Well...I must report to Washington, of course. We have to be certain, you understand. Now, try to help me, will you? Who is the Soviet resident?"

"Oleg Guryanov."

"And who was the previous resident?"

"Dimitri Yerokhin."

"Who is the chief of Line PR at the present time?"

"Krarmy Konstantinovich Sevastyanov. He hates his first name, by the way. It's formed of the same letters as the acronym for 'Red Army.'"

"Does he have a nickname?" Robert asked.

"Yes. He asks his friends to call him Roman."

"Why?"

"I don't know why he's chosen that name."

"Do you know Vladimir Pronnikov?"

"Yes."

"What's he like? Describe him."

"He is the single most dangerous bastard in the KGB."

"Good! Well said!" Robert smiled broadly. "Now, I must leave you for a bit while I dash over to the embassy. Don't worry at all. I'll be right back."

The wait for Robert's return was more stressful than the first had been. Now is when I'll find out if American intelligence has been penetrated, I thought. If this Robert is a double agent, he'll take me out of here and turn me right over to the KGB. I'd be lying if I said I wasn't worried about exactly that possibility.

In about twenty-five minutes, a pretty fast trip for him to accomplish all that I knew he'd have to do, Robert was back. He was accompanied this time by a second American. I tried to read his face as he came in, but he revealed nothing. Again, he asked the guards to wait in the corridor. When the door closed behind them, Robert turned to me, his face serious.

"The United States of America formally grants you political asylum," he said with absolute formality and solemnity. My knees actually shook as relief washed over me.

"Thank you very much, of course. I'm very grateful, but I'm also concerned. We both know how difficult the Japanese can be if they decide to cause trouble. If I'm not out of Japan before the KGB discovers that I'm missing, the pressure exerted by the Soviets on the Japanese government will be indescribable. Speed in getting me away is essential. Let me just disappear. Take me to Atsugi, to your air base. Fly me out, anywhere, so long as it's out of Japan!"

"I'll try my best to get them to do exactly that, but the decision isn't mine, you understand. For now, let's just get out of here."

We left the Hotel Sanno without any difficulty whatsoever and got into an unobtrusive, unmarked car. Robert took the wheel. I liked the way he set about clearing the way, carefully and professionally. At last we turned into a fashionable suburb, and Robert parked the car. We walked four or five blocks to a large house set back a little way from the street behind a garden. A charming woman of indeterminate age greeted us.

"Come in, Robert," she said to my companion. "It's been a long time since you've been here."

"And I've brought a friend with me this time." Turning to me, he added, "This lady is our friend, and a good one she is, too."

"Dinner is almost ready," Robert's "good friend" told us. "You've just time to wash up and have a drink beforehand. Come along, and I'll show you to your room." She led the way to a comfortable room with a bath, saw that we had towels, and went away after telling us to come down when we were ready.

Later we were given aperitifs and an excellent dinner; then the lady disappeared. I never saw her again.

Soon the American who had accompanied Robert to the Hotel Sanno arrived. "I've hidden your car," he said to me. "It's to-hell-and-gone on the other side of Tokyo. Do you want your keys back?"

"I won't be needing them."

Both Americans laughed. "You're OK, Stanislav," said the second American, who then told Robert, "So far everything's going well."

It was a tense night. Robert was on the telephone almost constantly, talking in code to the American embassy. Around 3:00 A.M. he came over to where I was slumped in a chair. "I'm going to have to go over there for a little while. I don't know what it is," he said. "Something too ticklish to discuss on the phone, even using double-talk." He must have seen the alarm in my face because he added quickly, "Now quit worrying. You're ours now, buddy! My friends and I will never give you back. Never! And that's a promise!"

When Robert returned at daylight, his news was extremely disturbing to me. "Washington has turned down the proposal to let you fly out on a U.S. military aircraft."

My heart sank. I knew I wasn't yet safe and that the long tentacles of the KGB could still pull me back in.

"If they knew as much about the KGB as they ought to know, they'd realize how much danger they're putting me in this way," I burst out. "The safest way out for me is on an American plane. That way I could just disappear."

"Stan," said Robert, quietly and reassuringly. It was the first time anyone had ever addressed me with the Americanized nickname of Stan. No one ever calls me by any other name now, and I've gotten used to it. "Now, Stan, it's going to work out OK. It really will. Look what's been done. Here's your passport back, officially stamped, with your visa. Here's a first class ticket on Pan Am for a flight leaving today. And here's my ticket. I'm going with you. It's an honor to be your escort."

"There will be trouble at the airport," I predicted morosely. "There'll be trouble."

When we got to the airport several hours later, we checked in and cleared customs without incident. With the first-class departure lounge in sight, it seemed as though my fears were groundless. Then it happened. With only a few feet to go, I came face to face with two Japanese counterintelligence officers. I recognized them at once, and they certainly recognized me.

"We're in for it now," I told Robert. "Those two will alert all of their forces. They'll notify the Ministry of Foreign Affairs, and you can bet your life that as soon as the ministry knows, the KGB will know, too."

"OK," said Robert. "So we're in for a spot of trouble. Just stay calm, and we'll handle it. You've coped with worse."

I wasn't sure that I had. If the KGB succeeded in getting Japan to hand me over to them, I was a dead man.

In no time at all the first-class lounge was jammed with a dozen Japanese, quickly followed by five or six more. One man, obviously the senior officer in the group, approached Robert and spoke to him in English.

"I must speak with the gentleman with you, sir," he said

"I'm sorry," Robert replied, "but we have no time. We are leaving in ten minutes for the United States."

"We must speak with this gentleman before you can leave," the senior officer repeated.

"Why?" demanded Robert.

"Official business," the Japanese officer answered.

"I'm traveling with a valid American passport, and my friend is traveling with a valid U.S. visa. There are no irregularities, so there's absolutely no reason for a delay."

"So sorry." The Japanese official bowed politely. "I'm sure that you do not need to be reminded that this is Japanese territory, sir. Excuse me, also, but we mean to question him alone. You may neither listen nor participate."

Without my quite realizing how it was done, I was suddenly effectively blocked in by Japanese men while Robert and another American were inexorably backed across the lounge and into the remotest corner.

"You will be seated, please," the Japanese officer ordered. It was politely done, but it was an order all the same.

"Just one moment," I spoke angrily. "I'm not going to talk to you or anyone else until I know who you are."

"Some of us are from the Chiba Prefectural Police Headquarters, and some of these officers are security officers whose duty it is to protect you."

"Am I being held as a witness to a crime of some sort?"

"You are not being held at all. We merely want to ask you a few questions.

"Am I accused of a crime?"

"No, no, of course not."

"Has anyone threatened my life?"

"Not to my knowledge." The officer was beginning to show his annoyance.

"Well, then," I said in as reasonable a tone as I could muster, "there is no reason why I should talk with you at all. You are all policemen or security agents. You have interfered with me while I'm trying to conduct my personal business. I'm not a criminal. I have neither committed nor witnessed the commission of a crime. And since you say no threats have been made against me, I think I can take care of my own security."

"I sincerely apologize for the inconvenience," he said, still maintaining his polite stance, "but if you wish to leave Japan, you will talk to us. Who are you?"

"You know who I am."

"What is your job?"

"You know that, too. I'm a journalist, the correspondent for *New Times*, a Soviet publication."

"Are you a KGB officer?" he demanded.

"I'm a correspondent for a magazine. I'm going to the United States with the permission of the American government, and you have caused me to miss my plane. It's just left."

"I'm sorry, but you aren't suffering in any way. You are sitting in a luxurious lounge in all comfort, and there are other flights today. So, to proceed…who are you?"

That was the pattern. Over and over the same questions were asked. Meanwhile, the first plane had gone, the second plane took off, and the seconds kept ticking past. Finally I exploded.

"I insist that I be released or arrested!"

"There is no question of arrest in this case," I was assured. "But we have a consular agreement with the Soviet Union. We must guard against offending them. We must notify them and give them the chance to meet with you and talk with you before you go."

All the time the questioning had been going on, the lounge had become increasingly crowded. I noticed a number of American businessmen waiting for flights to the United States, and though we had begun our session in a somewhat isolated corner of the lounge, more and more people were now within earshot of my interrogation. One little Japanese man in particular was close enough to hear every word, but with characteristic good manners, he appeared not to hear anything at all. I turned my attention back to the senior officer.

"I find that very interesting," I said as sarcastically as I could. "I had no idea that it was the function of the police to guard against hurting the Soviets' feelings. I really thought that was the function of the Ministry of Foreign Affairs."

He reddened at that. "People from the ministry are on the way," he said sheepishly.

"Then you can damned well let them do their own questioning," I said. "I'm going to the restroom."

Four or five Japanese escorts surrounding me. "Damn it to hell! I don't need any help from you. By God, I do think I can manage to urinate all by myself."

They came along, nonetheless. Robert came into the restroom while I was there. By that time, he was seething with anger and openly dared the Japanese to interfere.

"Our embassy is calling the Japanese deputy foreign minister right now," Robert whispered, "and he's threatening Japan with mayhem. Keep up the good work, now."

I pulled one nasty little trick of my own on my captors. Knowing that they couldn't drink while on duty, I later ordered champagne and made an elaborate show of enjoying every ice-cold mouthful. But I really tasted nothing. It could have been day-old tea as far as I was concerned. I won't lie about it: I was getting more scared with every passing moment.

When we went back into the lounge, there was a party of people from the Japanese Ministry of Foreign Affairs, and I could almost feel the relief of the Japanese official who had kept the interrogation going until they got there. "Ah," he said when he saw the ministry representative, "you can't object to official questioning now." "Oh, can't I?" I thought. "I object like hell." Sure enough, the same old pattern was repeated.

"Who are you?"

"Now I've told you people that until I'm blue in the face, and nothing can change anything I've said. When you ask me something new, I might answer you, but I'm not going over that old ground any more."

"You are in no position to tell us what you are going to do. This is my country, not yours, and you do not make the rules." He had obviously decided to get ugly.

"One of the things I've always admired about Japan is that you have laws here. What you are doing right now isn't lawful, I don't think. At least these other gentlemen were polite, which is more than I can say for you," I retorted.

About that time an attendant from the Pan Am desk approached us and, calling the most recent interrogator by name, said, "Excuse me, sir, but there is a telephone call for you. You can take it right here," she said, plugging an extension phone into a jack near one of the overstuffed chairs. If I had to describe the way he walked over to the phone, I'd say he marched.

I watched him as he listened, but I couldn't tell who was calling or what was being said. It was obvious, though, that this smart-ass foreign ministry officer was being humiliated and chagrined. He put down the phone, muttered something to an aide who was standing beside him, then turned to me. "You may go," he fairly barked at me. "You are free to go."

"Thank you very much," I said mildly.

Surrounded by twenty or so Japanese policemen, Robert and I were escorted from the terminal, across the tarmac, to the waiting plane, Flight 2 on a Pan Am 747. As we left the lounge, the group of Americans whom I'd noticed for the last four or five hours seemed to decide that they weren't waiting for a plane after all. Most of them left. A few unobtrusively joined the crowd of Japanese around us.

As I mounted the last step of the boarding platform, I felt a wave of relief that left me weak. I was on my way to a new land, and all I owned in the world were the clothes I was wearing, about $30 in yen, and $100 that one of the Americans, who had pushed through the crowd of Japanese, had pressed into my hand. "That's for luck," he called to me. "You're a brave son of a gun, Stan. Good luck and God bless."

All the way across the tarmac and as we were getting on the plane, one Japanese policeman kept calling. "Please, sir. Please don't go until you tell me. Please, who is the KGB officer who is working against Japan? Please, who is it? Don't go until you tell....Please, sir....Who is the biggest threat to my little country?"

Once we were safely aboard and just before they closed the door, I leaned out, and there he was, still pleading, "Please, sir...."

I called to him: "Hey, you want to know who's the biggest threat to Japan? It's that bastard Vladimir Pronnikov!" The last I saw of the policeman, he was running down the tarmac after the plane, saying

"Thank you, thank you, thank...."

Standing inside the plane, I looked at Robert. "That was close!"

"Yes, sir, that was a bit close all right!" Then, with his quick, friendly smile, he added, "But look at this way—you're home free!"

Those words were the first of many American slang expressions I was to learn. But to me they are neither slang nor colloquialism. I learned that they refer to a children's game, hide-and-seek, where one player is the "seeker" and must find all the other players who are in hiding. If one of the hidden players manage to slip back to his home base without being caught, then he's immune from having to be the seeker next time. He is "home" and "free."

How apropos! How neatly the phrase fit me. Just a few more steps, and I, Stanislav Levchenko, former KGB officer, would at last be "home free."

Prison

Biographies

Born in 1939, **LEONID PLYUSCH** lost his father during the war. He, his mother, and his sister lived with his grandmother in the Ukraine. He taught in a village school, and after marrying undertook advanced studies in mathematics and philosophy.

His participation in the movement to preserve the Ukrainian language and culture displeased Soviet authorities. He was imprisoned in a mental hospital; his wife fought to win his release. In 1976, the two were allowed to emigrate to the West.

Plyusch considered himself a true believer and says, "I am still a Marxist by conviction." But the revelations of Stalin's crimes shattered his faith in the Soviet system.

Plyusch describes *History's Carnival*, published in the United States in 1977, as "neither a confession nor a literary biography. It is an account of one more road to freedom, a description of how the Soviet Union appears in the eyes of a citizen whose fanatic faith in the Soviet system gave way to a struggle to free himself of its illusions, slavery, and terror."

In 1937 **EUGENIA GINZBURG**, a thirty-one-year-old university lecturer, was convicted for being a "counter-revolutionary." Although a member of the Communist Party, she had defended a colleague arrested during Stalin's purges. Her trial lasted seven minutes.

She spent the next eighteen years in various camps. The first volume of her memoirs, *Journey Into the Whirlwind* (published originally in samizdat), covers her arrest and initial years in prison. *Within the Whirlwind* completes her story.

"When you can't sleep, the knowledge that you did not directly take part in the murder and betrayal is no consolation," she wrote in *Within the Whirlwind*. "After all, the assassin is not only he who struck the blow, but whoever supported evil, no matter how: by thoughtless repetition of dangerous political theories; by silently raising his right hand; by faint-heartedly writing half-truths. Mea Culpa and it occurs to me more and more frequently that even eighteen years of hell on earth is insufficient expiation for the guilt."

Eugenia Ginzburg was released in 1955 and died in Moscow in 1977. Her son, the novelist Vassily Aksyonov, lives in the United States.

VIKTOR HERMAN was born in Detroit in 1915. When he turned sixteen he and his family moved to the Soviet Union; his father had been hired as a manager in a Ford auto plant in Nizhni-Novgorod. (Born in czarist Russia, the elder Herman escaped to the U.S. in 1909 after having been arrested for revolutionary activity.) In 1938, the Soviets arrested Victor.

He spent eighteen years in camps and internal exile. He married while in Siberia, and had two children. Even after his release from incarceration, the Soviets did not allow him to return to America. Finally, in 1976, he came home. His wife and daughters joined him in Michigan, where he died in 1985. He often wrote of other Americans held captive in the Gulag.

*Coming Out of the Ice,*published in 1979, tells his story. Herman describes how the camps pitted the prisoners against each other and how—once the guards found a person's vulnerable point—they attacked it relentlessly. CBS turned *Coming Out of the Ice* into an acclaimed TV film.

Born in Donestk in 1948, **ANATOLY SHARANSKY** studied at the Moscow Institute of Physics and Technology. He became active with various dissident causes, particularly on behalf of Jewish "refuseniks." In 1974, he married Natasha Stieglitz. After she emigrated to Israel—where she took the name Avital—he was arrested for treason and spying.

Avital never gave up campaigning for his release. Sharansky himself went on hunger strikes to protest his treatment. In 1986 he won his freedom and joined Avital in Israel, where he changed his name to Natan.

Fear No Evil, published in 1988, opens with his arrest and closes with his arrival in Jerusalem. His devotion to Avital, which gave him strength to endure physical and mental torment, is an oft recurring theme.

For biographical information on **PETRO GRIGORENKO,** see excerpt in the section "Mental."

The end of World War II found twenty-one-year-old **JOHN NOBLE**, a native of Detroit, in Germany. He and his family—American citizens all—had spent the war interned as enemy aliens in Dresden. When the Red Army occupied the city, Noble was arrested as his family was attempting to escape to Germany's Western-occupied sector.

After passing through various prisons, he was assigned to the labor camps in the coal mines of Vorkuta, fifty miles north of the Arctic Circle. In the early 50s he witnessed the prison revolt following Lavrenti Beria's death.

He was released in 1954 and reunited with his family in New York on January 17, 1955. *I Was a Slave in Russia,*his memoirs of his years in the camps, was published in 1958.

Born in 1939, **EDWARD KUZNETSOV** studied philosophy. In 1968 he married Sylva Zalmanson. They lived in Riga.

In 1970, he, Sylva, and several friends were charged with treason for planning to hijack a plane to fly them out of the USSR. Kuznetsov and Mark Dymshitz were sentenced to death; Sylva and the others received prison terms of various lengths.

After her release in 1973, Sylva moved to the West and continued to press for her husband's freedom. In 1979 Kuznetsov, Dymshitz and three others were freed in exchange for two Soviets convicted of spying in the United States.

Prison Diaries is Kuznetsov's periodic record of the time he served. He wrote in secret. The text was smuggled out of the Soviet Union and published in the United States in 1975.

Born in 1938, **ANATOLY MARCHENKO** spent twenty of his forty-eight years in Soviet prisons or camps. He grew up in a small town between Omsk and Novosbirsk in the Siberian lowlands. In 1958 he was sentenced to two years' imprisonment for participating in a dormitory brawl (he was trying to stop the fight). He escaped after a year.

He was rearrested while trying to leave the USSR via Iran—and sentenced to six years for treason. Following his release, he was arrested several times on questionable charges.

In 1973 he married Larisa Bogoraz. In 1975 he was sentenced to internal exile, and in 1979 was given the option to emigrate or go to prison.

In 1981 he was sentenced to ten years in the camps and five in internal exile. A beating by guards damaged his health, and in 1986 he went on a hunger strike demanding the release of all political prisoners and the punishment of the guards responsible for his injuries.

Marchenko died in prison in December 1986.

My Testimony, published in 1969, includes some of the most graphic descriptions of life in Soviet prisons ever written. To Live Like Everyone was published posthumously in 1989, with a foreword by Andrei Sakharov and an afterword by Marchenko's wife.

ELINOR LIPPER was born in Holland. While studying medicine at the University of Berlin in the 1930s, she became interested in Socialism—partly as a reaction to Fascism—and joined the Red Student Group. She left Germany in 1933 and moved to the Soviet Union in 1937.

Two months after taking a job in a publishing house specializing in foreign literature, she was arrested. Her release came in 1948.

Eleven Years in Soviet Prison Camps, published in 1951, tells of her journey through the Lubyanka and Butyrka prisons and countless transit camps, and Kolyma.

History's Carnival: A Dissident's Autobiography

Leonid Plyushch

1.

I fell into bed. An impatient, insolent ringing at the door awakened me. The agents rushed in like bandits with frightened expressions. Why were they always frightened? No one was throwing bombs at them yet. Were they pumping themselves up with courage for their work? As the search got under way, I made malicious comments about the lieutenant's actions in the bedroom. He replied with jokes. The agents searched the rooms carelessly, certain that they wouldn't find anything. They had never found anything before, and thick smoke hung in the air. "Have you burned everything?" they asked when they saw the pail in the lavatory.

"Yes, I did."

"Then you must have had something to burn."

"Yes, Rabindranath Tagore's books, for example."

The lieutenant feverishly leafed through my diary for 1957 and 1958 and read an entry aloud.

"Are you trying to ascribe megalomania to me and to lock me up in a *psikhushka*?" I asked.

"How can you say that, Leonid Ivanovych? We don't send people to mental institutions. Only psychiatrists do that. And you're perfectly normal."

I remembered that it was KGB men, not psychiatrists, who had diagnosed me as schizophrenic in 1969, when Oleg Bakhtiarov's case was under investigation.

"You dreamed of creating a revolution in mathematics and philosophy?" the lieutenant asked.

"Look at the date on the diary entry," I replied. "I was eighteen then."

"Yes, you're quite right. Everyone dreamed of creating a revolution in mathematics and philosophy?" the lieutenant asked.

"Look at the date on the diary entry," I replied. "I was eighteen then."

"Yes, you're right. Everyone dreams of glory at that age."

The telephone rang again and again, but I was not permitted to answer. Tanya and friends from Moscow were probably calling. The KGB men whooped with joy from time to time when they found something. The witnesses had expected to see guns and were disappointed until they realized how much forbidden literature was being piled up. This proved that I was thoroughly anti-Soviet. One of them began to read the literature on the sly and gave me compassionate looks, but he frowned when he saw the Western edition of the *Ukrainian Herald*: it left no doubt that I was an enemy. For his benefit I started to wage anti-Soviet propaganda by arguing with the lieutenant about Stalin and 1937.

When my older son, Dima, came home from school, he looked at the men and pretended not to understand what was happening. I told him in a whisper to telephone his mother so that she could warn our friends. I hoped that she would drop work and rush home. If the KGB did not allow us to say goodbye, I should have to wait God knows how long for a meeting in prison.

The lieutenant realized that he would not find anything interesting in my study. It was full of books on fairy tales and games and folders marked "History of Games," "Psychology of Games," and "Myth and Games." But he did not put aside a folder containing Mykhaylyna Kotsyubynsky's manuscript on Shevchenko. I urged him not to confiscate it. "The search warrant mentions anti-Soviet and slanderous literature. This is philology and has nothing to do with the Soviet regime."

"We shall look through it just in case and return it to Kotsyubynsky," the lieutenant replied.

"It'll be awkward for you. After all, she's related to Mykhaylo Kotsyubynsky and Yuriy Kotsyubynsky. The film *The Kotsyubynsky Family* was shown recently. What if the West learns that you're accusing the Kotsyubynskys of being anti-Soviet?"

"That's all right, Leonid Ivanovych. We're not afraid of the West."

And yet they were afraid when they blackmailed Tanya and then begged her not to inform the West when and how I would be released.

The lieutenant picked up a folder with notes on Shevchenko and, without looking through it, put it aside for confiscation.

"Why do you need notes on Shevchenko?" I asked.

He looked through them and with a laugh read aloud, "'Even Tychnya, who sold out Ukraine and her culture, said on his seventy-fifth birthday about Peter the Great: "I wanted to shit on this jack-booted tyrant."' Did he really say that?"

"Yes, when the Leningrad Writers' Union gave him the Leningrad medal, The Bronze Horseman. You'll have to agree that it wasn't a very pleasant award for a Ukrainian. After the Battle of Poltava, Peter the Great flooded the town of Baturyn with the blood of civilians and then built Petersburg-Leningrad on Ukrainian bones."

Suddenly Lieutenant Colonel Tolkach gave a cry. The other agents rushed to him, but I remained where I was. Well, so what if they had found something more? But Tolkach called me over, too, hoping to shock me with his discovery of my hiding place. I had made bookshelves with plywood and boards and had concealed *samizdat* in them. When I was leaving for Odessa, Tanya had cleaned the house, and one of the shelves had moved slightly. As luck would have it, it was the *samizdat* shelf.

Tolkach leafed through the papers with a malicious grin on his face. "Aha, an article about how to make a printing press! You wanted to set up a print shop?"

"No. I copied that from an article in *Khimiya i zhizn* [*Chemistry and Life*] about how printing was done in the underground before the Revolution. I wanted to write an article about the difficulties then."

"And those leaflets?"

"They're not anti-Soviet. One is an appeal to Shostakovich to support Soviet political prisoners. The other is an appeal to Kosygin about Grigorenko, Gabay, and Dzemilyov."

"Who wrote these leaflets?"

"Two students were distributing them at the State Department Store in Moscow."

"And how did you get them?"

"I went in there to buy something."

Tolkach read the leaflets but could not find anything anti-Soviet in them. Nevertheless, he telephoned the KGB to send a photographer. Aha, I thought to myself, they're going to have a noisy campaign in the press. For the average reader a hiding place is the best possible proof of clever and malicious enemies. The KGB had photographed a wall decorated with original mosaics in Svitlychny's apartment as proof of his "Ukrainian bourgeois nationalism."

Tanya still hadn't come home. I was beside myself at the thought that she had been arrested and was being interrogated. Klara Gildman arrived and whispered to me that Tanya telephoned her. I was both pleased and angry to see her. A woman agent was immediately summoned to search Klara. When Klara returned, she was trembling with anger and humiliation. I tried to calm her down and told her about Tanya's search. "They're only degrading themselves," I explained. "We're still human beings, but they're turning into beasts." Klara was infuriated by my Tolstoyan forbearance toward the KGB agents and the witnesses. I thought of Dzyuba and the way Tanya and I had shouted at the men who were searching him.

Ira Pievsky arrived in the evening, and finally Tanya came home, accompanied by Ira's husband, Serhiy Borshchevsky, and Volodymyr Yuvchenko, a history teacher who had been dismissed the previous year for "propagating Tolstoyism and pacifism" and forbidden ever to work with children. Tanya explained that she had gone around to all our friends. When she visited Alexander Feldman, she walked into a middle of a search and barely got away. We said good-bye to our friends quickly: they were being led away for further searches at their own homes. Klara protested vehemently. Her mother had had several heart attacks, was partially paralyzed, and would not be able to withstand a search.

The search went on and on, and Tanya and I said our good-byes until six o'clock in the morning. Tolkach asked me to verify the entries in the search record, but I told him that I wanted to be with my wife. The witness goggled at us and the searchers. One witness recognized Tanya—they had taken part in fencing competitions together at school—and now he felt very awkward in the presence of such "anti-Soviets."

Tanya and I went over the last four years. Yes, they were worth going to prison for. If we had not joined the opposition movement, we should never have come to know Olitskaya, Surovtseva, Grigorenko, Svitlychny, Sverstyuk, Dzyuba, and dozens of other splendid people. We had been happy these four years; we had been able to respect ourselves. I was going to prison not for the sake of abstract ideas, but for the sake of respect toward myself and others.

It was time to go. The KGB men were polite and quiet, like beasts that had eaten their fill. The children were asleep. I tried to wake up Dima—he had asked to be awakened when I left—but wished me *bon voyage* in his sleep. Half an hour before leaving I wrote Tanya a coded message of love and best wishes, understanding that this good-bye was for a long time. The KGB men studied the note and puzzled over the literary nonsense—Fox, Rose, Prince. "Who is this Prince?" one of them asked.

"The French writer Saint-Exupéry wrote a story called *The Little Prince*."

"Ah, yes, I've heard of it. A good book."

2.

When I arrived in prison, I could not be admitted because the warden was absent. Tolkach left me in his office, assuring me that the prison was clean and the food good and that I was merely being detained, not arrested. I was indifferent to everything and only wanted my KGB well-wisher to let me sleep. I actually fell asleep on his desk, and when he tried to wake me up several times, jabbering something incomprehensible, I just stared at him.

Finally someone led me to another room, where my pen, watch, and notebook were taken away from me with the promise that they would be given to my wife. A jailer undressed me in a special cell called by the English word "box," felt all the seams in my clothing, and peered into my anus. Voltaire's pirates had looked for jewelry in women's private parts, but what was my jailer looking for—*samizdat*, explosives? For whereas Voltaire's pirates had searched for alienated labor in the form of gold and diamonds, my captors were looking for alienated words and ideas. I felt neither degradation nor pain and was only sorry for the boy who was searching me. Here was a human being with a soul who used it merely to engage in socialist piracy.

I was led to cell number 40 and fell on the bed without undressing. I had an idiotic dream: the searcher and the prison warden Lieutenant Colonel Sapozhnikov were trying to rape me. My subconscious was attempting to make sense of the search procedure. I woke up with Sapozhnikov's salacious smile in my mind, and from then on thought of my first dream in my first prison cell whenever I saw him.

When I awoke, I heard an old woman calling out that she had brought dinner. Still half asleep, I took from her a bowl of slops and a bowl of burned porridge with threadlike objects in it. I was horrified to think that I would have to eat it. Later I realized that it was just that the porridge had been burned and something had fallen into it by accident on that first day. I fell asleep again and was awaken by a shout: "Lights out! Go to bed!" I undressed and fell into a heavy, dreamless sleep, a world where there was no KGB, no wife, and no children.

Journey into the Whirlwind:
The Investigators
Have Conclusive Evidence

Eugenia Ginzburg

I have often thought about the tragedy of those by whose agency the purge of 1937 was carried out. What a life they had! They were all sadists, of course. And only a handful found the courage to commit suicide.

Step by step, as they followed their routine directives, they traveled all the way from the human condition to that of beasts. Their faces, as time went by, defied description. I, at any rate, cannot find words to convey the expression on the faces of these un-men.

But all this happened only gradually. That night, Interrogator Livanov, who had summoned me, looked like any other civil servant with perhaps a little more than the usual liking for red tape. Everything about him confirmed this impression—the placid, well-fed face, the neat writing with which he filled the left-hand side (reserved for questions) of the record sheet in front of him, and his local, Kazan accent. Certain turns of speech, provincial and old-fashioned, reminded me of our nurse Fima and aroused a host of memories of home.

In that first moment I had a flash of hope that the madness might be over, that I had left it behind me, down there, with the grinding of padlocks and the pain-filled eyes of the golden-haired girl from the banks of the river Sungari. Here, it seemed, was the world of ordinary, normal people. Outside the window was the old familiar town with its clanging streetcars. The window had neither bars nor a wooden screen, but handsome net curtains. And the plate with the remains of Livanov's supper had not been left on the floor but stood on a small table in a corner of the room.

He might be a perfectly decent man, this quiet official who was slowly writing down my answers to his straightforward, insignificant questions: Where had I worked between this year and that, where and when had I met this or that person...? But now the first page had been filled and he gave it to me to sign.

What was this? He had asked me how long I had known Elvov, and I had answered, "Since 1932." But here it said, "How long have you known the Trotskyist Elvov?" and my reply was put down as "I have known the Trotskyist Elvov since 1932."

"This isn't what I said."

He looked at me in amazement, as though it really were only a question of getting the definition right. "But he *is* a Trotskyist!"

"I don't know that."

"But we do. It's been established. The investigators have conclusive evidence."

"But I can't confirm something I don't know. You can ask me when I met *Professor* Elvov, but whether he is a Trotskyist, and whether I knew him as a Trotskyist—that's a different question."

"It's for me to ask the questions, if you please. You've no right to dictate to me the form in which I should put them. All you have to do is answer them."

"Then put the answers down exactly as I give them, and not in your own words. In fact, why don't we have a stenographer to put them down?"

These words, the height of naïveté, were greeted by peals of laughter — not, of course, from Livanov but from the embodiment of lunacy which had just entered the room in the person of State Security Lieutenant Tsarevsky.

"Well, well, what do I see! You're behind bars now, are you? And how long is it since you gave us a lecture at the club, on Dobrolyubov?* Eh? Remember?"

"Yes, I do. It was very silly, I agree. What could you possibly want with Dobrolyubov?"

My sarcasm was wasted on the lanky, tousled youth with the face of a maniac.

"So you want a stenographer! No more and no less! What a joke! Think you're back in your editorial office?"

With quick, jerky steps he went up to the desk, ran his eyes over the record, and looked up at me. His eyes, like Vevers's, were those of a sadist who took pleasure in his work, but there was also in them a lurking anxiety, a latent fear.

"So you're behind bars," he sneered again, in a tone of hatred as intense as though I had set fire to his house or murdered his child.

"You realize, of course," he went on more quietly, "that the regional committee has agreed to your arrest. Everything has come out. Elvov gave you

---

* Nikolay Dobrolyubov, 1836-1861, radical journalist and critic.

211

away. That husband of yours, Aksyonov—he's been arrested too, and he's come clean. He's a Trotskyist too, of course."

I mentally compared this statement with Vevers's about Aksyonov disowning me. Yes, Lyama was right. They really were brazen liars.

"Is Elvov here, in this prison?"

"Yes! In the very cell next to yours. And he's confirmed all the evidence against you."

"Then confront me with him. I want to know what he said about me. Let him repeat it to my face."

"Like to see your friend, eh?" He added such a scurrilous obscenity that I could hardly believe my ears.

"How dare you! I demand to see the head of your department. This is a Soviet institution where people can't be treated like dirt."

"Enemies are not people. We're allowed to do what we like with them. People indeed!"

Again he roared with laughter. Then he screamed at me at the top of his voice, banged the table with his fist, exactly like Vevers, and told me I'd be shot if I didn't sign the record.

I noticed with amazement that Livanov, so quiet and polite, looked on unmoved. Obviously, he had seen it all before.

"Why do you allow this man to interfere with a case you're in charge of?" I asked.

His smile was almost gentle.

"Tsarevsky's right, you know. You can make things better for yourself if you honestly repent and make a clean breast of it. Stubbornness won't help you. The investigators have conclusive evidence."

"Of what?"

"Of your counter-revolutionary activity as a member of the secret organization headed by Elvov. You'd much better sign the record. If you do you'll be treated decently. We'll allow you to have parcels, and we'll let you see your children and your husband."

While Livanov spoke Tsarevsky kept quiet in readiness for his next attack. I thought he had just happened to come into Livanov's office. But after the two of them had been at me for three or four hours, I realized that it was part of a deliberate technique.

The blue light of a February dawn was casting its child on the room by the time Tsarevsky rang for the warder. The same words ended the interrogation as those of Vevers the day before, but Tsarevsky's voice rose to a falsetto:

"Off to the cell with you! And there you'll sit until you sign."

Going down the stairs, I caught myself hurrying, back to my cell. It seemed, after all, that I was better off there, in the human presence of a companion in misfortune—and the grinding of locks was better than the demented screams of un-men.

Translated by Paul Stevenson and Max Hayward

Coming Out of the Ice

Victor Herman

1.

You did not know it was morning until they rang the bell. Only by the bell could you mark the intervals of time—for the light never changed—and how long does it take for the body to forget the pulses that are natural to it? Not very long—and in Cell 39 less time than that.

All that night the Elder turned the men—and I turned with them, sleepless until the morning bell. He turned them four times that night, and not long after the fourth time a guard came in and used his key, whipping the thing with remarkable force. I saw it all—and heard it—saw the door open, the guard enter, stepping on the men until he found the one he wanted, a man four down from me—and then I heard the guard announce the infraction: "Both hands in view!" and heard the first blow hit.

Iron on flesh makes a terrible sound.

I shut my eyes and then I opened them. I saw it all. It was like looking into that mirror during the surgery on my liver—it was something I had to see—to know what it was, this thing that sometimes happens between men, what one man will do to another.

Yet all the men were fed that morning—despite the rule the Elder said was so. The bell rang and everyone took his place again, even the old man on the floor, going back to his curl under the shelf opposite, and everyone took up the position again, and I followed suit just like them all.

What would it be? Eggs? Scrambled? Fried? My stomach howled for anything save that porridge—and the long night had made me ravenous, hungry in a way I'd never quite been before.

I sat in the position—and, like the rest, I waited. But after a while I wondered if I was the only one waiting. Could it be that no food would come?

Several times I had to check myself from leaning forward and making some sort of motion to the Elder—I could raise my eyebrows and make feeding motions to my mouth. Or I could just rub my belly and smile. Or maybe raise my eyebrows and rub my belly, perhaps that would be better. Or better still, I could make chewing motions—wouldn't that be the least infraction of the rule? What if I went to the pot? That was allowed. I could go to the pot and make chewing motions. But I would not go to that pot. No, that would take time yet, to get me near that thing.

Was it possible to use it without looking inside? I thought about how I would go about using the pot when I could resist it no longer. I kept trying to figure out some sort of eye and hand movement that would keep me from the worst of it. It was a good thing to think about, this problem— something worth giving some study to. That's what I needed—something to think about—other than food and when they would call me to tell me what the charges were or that the charges had been dismissed or that a mistake had been made or to ask me questions that I wouldn't know the answers to or to tell me that I was going to be shot or to hear me tell them that I was an American citizen and that I wanted to be released this instant or to ask me why I had eaten an apple while falling from the sky—and what would I say to *that*?

I need something to *think* about—so I wouldn't think about the kinds of things that I *was* thinking about—and above all I needed *not* to think about food.

But how exactly does one do that when it is hunger and hunger and hunger that is all that his body feels?

I waited.

I sat in the position.

I studied the problem of how I would do it when I had to do it, had to go to that pot and lift the lid that had a kind of furriness on it. And if that's what the top had on it, what was on the other side?

I heard it. Again. That same soft noise, the dragging, metal on padding? And there it was, the general stirring out there that seemed to accompany the dragging. It was what had preceded the last feeding. How long ago had that been exactly? The last feeding—had I missed a day?

I had to get possession of myself. It made me panic to think that I could have perhaps missed a day and not known it. I got dizzy just thinking that— and I had to get better control of myself. This would never do. I had to get something inside my belly, something like scrambled eggs maybe and a good glass of milk—because if I kept on this way, I'd never make it.

I sat there.

I tried not to think.

I could sense something restive in the men—but I dared not look to make sure. Surely they were not moving, but I could sense some sort of unexpressed motion in them, a kind of general urging forward.

The noise outside! That was it course, and they knew it was coming—food!

How long would it be in coming—and when it came, what would it be? But first of course there would be the bowls sent in—or dishes this time—of course, dishes for eggs—and then we'd have to get utensils—so it would all take take time. I must be patient. It will take time for the thing to get set up—time to dish out the eggs and the rest—time to handle each man's serving and how he'd like his coffee or tea fixed or whether he'd like milk instead.

The dragging was at the door now—that much I could tell. I was learning fast—and perhaps in time you found yourself hardly remembering when you needed to talk to get things understood or needed to stand up or walk around to feel good. A man could get used to anything in time. Hadn't I got used to Sam coming home bloody and torn? And what about boxing? Hadn't I gotten used to getting hit—and hitting? Of course I had—and that hadn't been so easy at first. And think of all the other things I'd gotten used to—and that really required some doing. Flying a plane for instance and jumping out of one. Hadn't that taken a tremendous amount of getting used to? Just imagine! And going on a ship for the first time and not getting seasick. Hadn't I done that? If I had done all that, what couldn't I do? I could learn to keep my mouth shut and to listen and never miss a trick! Why, I'd probably hear a thousand times more than I'd ever even known existed! And hadn't I been sitting in the position all morning and not even noticed it once? I didn't even feel like leaning my back against the wall, it was that easy to do, and who even thought of it?

The feeder moved! And they were pushing something through! If the sequence was the same as it had been at the last feeding, then I'd get the first dish!

I looked and saw the Elder pulling through a bowl.

All right. I was ready.

It was passed down to me—and it wasn't empty.

It had water in it. Hot water.

Of course!

For bathing. For washing your hands. Washing your face?

I watched the others. I knew the rules. No man does anything until every man is ready, and then everyone does it together.

I watched to see what they would do.

But when every man had his water, they began drinking it—drinking the hot salty water—and when I saw them do it, I did it too.

2.

That was breakfast—the second day—and breakfast for a year of days thereafter. And lunch was another bowl—only with this wooden bowl you also got a wooden spoon. And this time the bowl held more hot water—only flavored in some way, a fishy smell or a grassy smell—and there were always a few bits of leaves in it—and you were glad there were.

Supper the same—the ball of dry porridge.

And those were your meals—all three—and you never got any other food. One year!

In the morning, the feeding was "tea"—the bowl of hot salty water.

The second feeding was "soup"—the hot water flavored this time, and always a few bits of leaves on the top, and these you were glad to chew.

The third feeding, the cereal—never more than that little ball.

And there would be a fourth item, but you never knew when it would come —a bit of soggy black bread, very sour—and when you got it, it was very good.

It got so I loved that bread. I can taste it even now—and, even in memory, I want it and I love it.

3.

Will a man get used to anything? Some will.

Many won't—and many die. When it gets bad enough, most die.

It is what I saw.

But the bread was good—very heavy and sour—and you'd always find something in it—a bit of twig or some bark. I don't know how they made that bread—but those things were always in it, something like that, something that came out of the forest.

And this is what a day was—the position, the three feedings, and then the position on the floor. A day was this—and nothing more.

And the light was always the same.

4.

But there were four exceptions in the days that you lived—and these are what they were.

Every ten days there was the bathhouse.

Every ten days two men could leave the cell if they were willing to empty and scrub the Parasha.

You could get up and use the pot when you wanted.

The fourth exception was the beatings.

And these had two names—"punishment" and "interrogation."

5.

It was the third day—night.

The door was opened sometimes during the middle of the night.

Who will be beaten? Whose hands are not both in view?

But on a word from the guard and a signal from the Elder, the sixteen of us were made to rise—and the old sick man did it too. They marched us out of there and in a single file we filed down the padded walkway—but Nesterov fell before we got to the stairs, and two of us had to drag him. He was happy to be dragged. You could tell. Wherever we were going, he want to go. So we dragged him. It never occurred to me to think he had a choice anyway. By now I had learned that much. There were no choices.

We were marched down the stairs and through several doors and came out into the prison yard—and they walked us to a corner in that open area—and you could see when you came out into that area that there were lights on in the tiers of barred windows all around you and lots of noise coming from those windows and even men hanging their arms out and calling through the bars. It was a hot night. It was July—and it was a shock—all that noise and humanity in motion and the sense you had of a kind of ribaldry in the air.

It was monstrous, the contrast between what I had just come from and the carnival atmosphere out there in the prison yard. I knew from the stillness behind me, from the gross quiet of the place and the two times I'd been along the walkway, that back there hundreds of men, and possibly women too, sat as we sat, in Spets Korpus, in the position, in silence, behind the muzzle. Whereas it was clear from what I was hearing and seeing out there in the prison yard that life was immeasurably different for the rest of the prisoners, for the thousands of men and women the other six buildings must have, in the aggregate, housed.

We stood outside a wooden structure squeezed into a corner of the yard, a ramshackle affair dwarfed by the massive red brick buildings rising all around it. We stood in a group, the men of Cell 39, two guards off to the side eyeing us. I tried to calculate the time—but there was no telling. I figured it was about three in the morning. Why were we waiting there? And what were we waiting for? I still had no way of knowing what this was all about—and it even passed through my mind that we might be going to some sort of group interrogation. But how could that be? How could you question a group of men all at once? Did that make any sense? But why try to make any of this make sense? Is craziness a logic too?

The door to the wooden structure opened, and in single file we followed the Elder inside. I had to shut my eyes, the light was so powerful—or at least it seemed to me powerful after the bleak constant light of 39. The floor of the room we were in was alive with human hair from wall to wall. It made you want to vomit, the thickness of it and the filth.

I watched the Elder for instructions, but it was the guard that came in with us who gave us the command to strip everything off. When the Elder got his clothes off, he hung them on a rack that was at the other end of the room, and I saw all the rest of the men do the same. I got out of my purple T-shirt and unknotted my trousers and, like the rest of them, I took off my tennis shoes, and all these things I put where the others had placed their clothing. When everyone had his things on that rack, a man came through the door on the other side and pulled the rack back out that door with him.

If this meant we were going to get prison clothing, that was all right with me. It would be good to get into something clean—and certainly it would be good to have the rest of the men in 39 in clean clothes too. The rags they wore were wretched—and if the Parasha had not been there to overwhelm it, the smell from the other men would probably have been almost as bad.

"Line up!" the guard with us called, and when we had gotten ourselves in order, a man came in through the door the rack had gone out of. He carried a large pair of clippers, and he went to the end of the line and he began.

His method was designed to give him maximum speed. Beginning with one side of the head of the first man, he cut the hair there, and then, his clipper going without being raised from the man's body, he went down one side, cutting the hair from one side of the man's face, under his arm on that side, then down over his chest on that side, across his groin, down over one leg and then up the other leg, to the chest, under the other arm, to the face, then back up to the other side of the man's head and then onto the next man, repeating the same procedure, and in this manner all sixteen of us added the hair from our bodies to the sea of hair that matted the floor, a mess of human growth of every texture and shade pressed by the men who walked there into something like a nightmare's idea of a carpet. And if you looked, you could see things crawling in it, their nesting places disturbed.

We still stood in line, all of us revealed to an extreme beyond nakedness, the terrific light overhead a white-hot poker that probed you and poked you all over. You had stinging places all over you too—from where the clipper had cut you or from where the barber had lost patience with the dull work and had yanked the hair out.

Two of us had to hold Nesterov up the whole time, and even in the July heat and that light overhead, the old man was shivering. On the order to march forward, we dragged him with us into the bathhouse. You got to it through the other door, and I could see another group leaving just as we entered the place—and in time I found out that's how it worked, all the political prisoners in *Spets Korpus* run through the hair-cutting and the showering at night, each cell every ten days.

In the bathhouse Nesterov just got down on the floor. He found a place under one of the spouts and just lay down there in his characteristic curl, his legs drawn up and his elbows wedged in against his stomach.

There were spouts set into the ceiling, and you stood under one of them waiting for the water to come. The guard left you and closed the door behind him, and you stood there waiting, and when the streams of water came they were either one way or the other, a bolt of ice or a scalding flame.

There were about twenty spouts sticking out from the ceiling, and under them the men were leaden in their movements, no matter what the water was like or how it suddenly changed from one impossible temperature to another. They stood under the slamming water and rubbed themselves, and even Nesterov was making little rubbing movements, one leg against the other and the same way with his arms—like an insect.

"No," the Elder said when he saw me opening my mouth to catch the water from the spout I was under. "Don't," he said, and it was startling to hear someone's voice, a man other than a guard. But I had heard Sergeyvsky before—when he had stood at the pot and whispered the rules.

Did the rules not hold anymore? Could you speak here, here in the bathhouse?

"The water is not safe," he said, and I said, "All right," and I nearly jumped at the sound of my own voice. How long had it been since I had heard myself speak? "We can talk here?" I said.

The Elder nodded—but held his finger to his lips.

"Then why aren't the rest of them talking?" I said.

"What is there to talk about?" the Elder said.

I looked at the man. Was he serious?

"You are the flyer," he said. "You are Victor Herman."

I nodded my head yes. "I am an American," I said. "I don't belong in here. They made a mistake. What are you doing in here—and the rest?"

"My father is in the church," the Elder said, "so I am a spy. Those two there, they are wreckers—they blew up the Gorky bridge. Twenty-five years for that, for each of them—and that one over there, also twenty-five years—another spy. You, Victor Herman," the Elder said, winking at me, "you are a spy?"

"Are you crazy?" I said. "I am an American. And those men didn't blow up the Gorky bridge—because I drove across it just a little while ago—and those two were here when I got here!"

The Elder raised his finger to his lips again. "Softly, please," he said. "You are a spy, Victor Herman—and those men, they are engineers and they built that bridge and they blew it up a year ago. They are wreckers and their sentence is twenty-five years. The others I don't know about—but I know about you, Victor Herman."

"How?" I said. "How do you know anything about me?"

"I know your name, yes? But of course everybody in Gorky knows your name and what you look like. You are the Lindbergh of Russia, Victor Herman—a famous man and a spy."

But then Sergeyvsky laughed, very softly, and I tried to laugh too—but I couldn't.

"How old are you, Victor Herman?" he said, now rubbing himself again, the water steaming off him.

"Twenty-three," I said.

The Elder said nothing in reply—and his question and then his silence left me feeling a kind of sentence had been pronounced. It was ominous, what he had asked and his silence when I had answered.

"Is there soap?" I asked, to throw off the feeling that had settled on me. But I knew there wasn't any soap, and the Elder did not bother to reply.

Soap? What a question!

6.

The water was shut off, and the guard came back in, and this time he was accompanied by the other guard who'd been with us when they'd marched us out and then down the stairs and across the yard. We went into another shed, going out a door across from the one we'd entered by, and as we stood inside that place the rack was wheeled back in and our clothing was on it. But none of the men was going for his clothing. They stood there, waiting and I did not know why until one of the guards shouted, "Dress!" and all the men went to do it, and I did too.

If the water was hot, it was nothing compared to the scorch you got when you got back into your things. But you did it, no matter how hot they were, and though the rubber on your tennis shoes had been baked sticky and was flame to the touch, you got into them, you got into everything that was yours, Nesterov too, and we had to help him to do it, and he screamed as the clothes went on him.

This was the work of *Zharo Kamera*, the toaster—meant to kill the lice and the crabs and the vermin that flourished on our bodies and in the things that had been on them, and I eventually learned that our cell got the same kind of treatment in our absence, the walls and floor and boards dowsed with carbolic acid from top to bottom. Not that this ever got the smell of vomit off the boards or ridded them of the stains of blood that gave them all the pattern of maps. As for the tiny parasites that fed on the sixteen men that were the human population of 39, by morning they were among us again and thriving. The hardiness of these creatures is nothing less than wondrous, and it is no less remarkable the great number and variety of verminous life that will all find a little something to satisfy them somewhere on the flesh of one man. You would sometimes wonder where all these things came from—and it sometimes seemed that they came from nowhere else but inside you, that it was you who had given birth to the tiny cannibal horde that fed on you openly as you sat helplessly in the position.

We were marched back in the same fashion we had come, another group waiting at the door to the barber's shed as we started back through the yard, and probably a third group inside that shed and a fourth under the spouts now.

Even before the door was locked on us again, most of the others seemed already asleep in their positions on the floor. I could hear Nesterov groaning a little from his position next to Sergeyvsky, but then he was quiet and only snored, the distinctive wheezing sound that told you it was him.

It was my third night in 39. The other two, I'd lain sleepless until the morning bell, still tormented, when it rang, by all the questions that had come welling up in me during the long, terrifying nights. Nothing I wanted to know had been answered, and it was gradually being disclosed to me that maybe nothing ever would.

I slept that third night. I slept the little time remaining between our return from the bathhouse and the crack of the morning bell. I know I slept—because the man next to me had to wake me to turn me the one time left—and then I was waked a second time, and it was the first time I waked to the bell, a sustained shrilling, a sound gone mad.

The bell was just a short burst. But for minutes and minutes it renewed itself inside your head. It was like a nail introduced into your ear in three distinct stages, each accomplished by a smart blow with a hammer—one, two, three—until a shaft had been opened all the way through to your brain—and then the hammer was turned and the claw was used to grip the nail and draw it out.

7.

Nestorov died after the bathhouse. A month later Sergeyvsky died too—in the first case, death came from some kind of choking, and in the second the man just fell over and there was blood running out of his ears.

It was onto the lid of the pot that the Elder fell forward from the position and the blood from his ears streamed along the disc of wood and then spilled into the Parasha below.

I tapped it out. And perhaps the message went from cell to cell.

Maybe it was what my mother had—a stroke, a bleeding in the brain.

But between the time that Nesterov died and the time that Sergeyvsky followed him to the grave, I was called.

They called me out—for interrogation.

"G!" came the shout from the guard through the feeder. "Get ready!"

It must have been about midnight—about two hours after the second bell.

I got up and went to the door. I got up and stepped between the men lying there and positioned myself at the door. And it is extraordinary what happened to me, how I quite suddenly changed inside. I could feel myself trembling all over—but it was not from fear. It was rage—it was anger that was going through me, and eagerness—and as I stood there waiting for the door to jerk open, I began to feel incredibly renewed—an energy waiting to get loose. I could scarcely contain myself—and I began to rehearse all the things I would say, the wrath I would explode with when I finally confronted my captors. My arms and legs were actually buzzing with the fever that was building in me. The shout through the feeder was "Get ready!" and that's what I was, the heat in me terrific. I could feel it in my face, the skin on my face and my neck warm with it, actually itching. There's no other way to say it—I was seething. I stood there burning up with rage. And still I waited and the door didn't open—and I thought that maybe I should call out, "Herman is ready! I'm ready!" But I didn't do it.

I just stood there—and when the door was finally opened, thrown back with that powerful abrupt movement that seemed routine to me now, I took a hard look at the guard and stepped forward and then all the way out of Cell 39, feeling myself utterly restored to the man I had been the day I had entered that small hell behind me.

I stood on the padding in the walkway and waited with rising indignation while the guard heaved the door closed and worked his gargantuan key in it.

"What time is it?" I asked.

"No noise!" he wheeled on me and shrieked it and then flipped the key back and forth in my face. "Head down, prisoner—hands behind back, no noise!"

I did as I was told and when my head was down, he pushed me along the walkway, and I moved ahead with him following....

"Where are we going?" I said, and I turned when I said it to make sure he heard me—and he just smiled in reply, and I could see how he had dog teeth and one of them was rotted.

We were on the first floor now, and since he gave me no directions, I kept to the same route that I was used to, the one that led out into the yard and the bathhouse. He let me go. He didn't stop me—and then I realized what a mistake I'd made—*don't go outside* —whatever it is, it would be better to stay inside!

But we were in the yard now, and there was a van there, just like the one that had brought me here, and I started heading toward it, and still the guard let me go.

"Up!" he said when I was within ten feet of the van.

I got in—and when I was struggling to make it up with my hands still behind me, the guard shoved me from behind.

He pulled up after me—and I could hear him breathing hard. There was another guard in there, but he seemed to be paying no attention to us. The first guard turned me to the only locker door that was open. Were all the others occupied? Were people already in there? "In!" he said, and when he said it, the other guard was right behind him and together they pushed me down and in.

They pushed me so that my face was rammed against the metal in front of me and away from the vents in the locker door. I was stuck like that. I couldn't move—and one of my arms was taking too much of my weight. But then the van bounced—I guessed it was the first guard jumping off—and the rear doors banged closed—and immediately the van pulled ahead—and the motion tilted me in a way that I could move a little strain on my arm. But there was no reversing my position in the locker, and even though I knew I had air enough, it made me uneasy to be turned away from the vents.

I tried to concentrate on interpreting the features of the drive—listening and feeling for hints—and it wasn't hard to do—because everything matched another set of things remembered, only this time it was all going backwards, and we were going down the steep hill instead of up it—and I knew that when we stopped and the door opened and they got me out, it would be in the courtyard behind the building on Vorobevka Street.

I was going there! Was it to receive an apology? Was that it—they would make their excuses and release me directly from there, from NKVD headquarters in Gorky? Was that their jurisdiction, this business, this mess that had been made? But why at this hour of the night? Why, if you wanted to make amends, would you take a man out in the middle of the night and stuff him into a locker to get him where he would receive your apology?

We stopped. But my door did not open. I heard another locker rattling and a man getting out. I could hear him fall down as he walked through the aisle toward the rear of the van. And the van doors opened and then they closed. In a little while, another locker opened—and it was the same thing, the van doors opening and then closing again. There was an interval of about five minutes between each of these exits—and I quickly multiplied five times thirteen—to get an idea of how long I was going to have to wait. If I was the last man in, then I would be the last man out—and if all sixteen lockers had been filled, then it followed that I'd have to wait over an hour to get out.

I settled back into a slump to wait. My arm hurt again and my nose and lips were flush against the back wall of the locker. It was very cold.

But there was motion right behind me and then I heard the door move and felt myself being pulled back by the shoulders. I backed out and stood in the aisle, and, with my arms behind my back, I tried to rotate my shoulders to loosen the stiffness in my neck.

"Head down, hands behind back, no talking." It was a new guard. I followed him to the rear of the van, and when the doors flew open, I jumped down. I was pleased with the way they did that, pleased that my legs held and that I didn't go over onto the pavement. I could see the cobblestones, but not the building, not where we were going. I could see a guard's boots ahead of me and I could see the cobblestones, and I followed the backs of his boots. But I didn't have to see the white building to know. These were the same cobblestones.

I could see we were getting to a doorway. The guard in front of me said, "Stop!" Another guard's boots came into my field of vision—and I heard "178," and then my elbow was taken by the new guard—and I followed him inside. We went all the way to the end of a corridor on the first floor and then we climbed a flight of wooden stairs and came out into a hallway, and I followed him all the way to the end of that hallway on the second floor to another flight of stairs. We climbed these to the third floor and again came out into a hallway and started along it toward the other end, but this time the guard in front of me paused at each doorway on the right side, a pause of several seconds for each doorway. At last we were at the end of the hallway on the third floor, and again we climbed a flight of wooden stairs, and it was the same on this floor, always that pause at each door on the right side, until we came to one and stayed there.

I stood waiting. I raised my bead a little. There was a whitewashed stencil on the door—it gave the numerals 178.

I waited.

I heard an unbelievable scream. It was the first time I had heard anything like it. It was the kind of scream you imagine a woman makes in childbirth. It was a scream like that, not hysterical, but more a stupendous howl of exquisite agony with relief mixed into it.

I looked up. The guard said, "Head down."

I waited. I tried to decide where that scream had come from. What had made it—a man or a woman? It was that kind of scream—beyond gender—but a perfectly human sound. In fact, I remember thinking that it was the most human sound I had ever heard—what I mean is that it seemed to suggest a declaration of something at the very bottom of what it feels like to be human. That's all I can say about it—that sound.

It was remarkable. It was truly unbelievable, and I have never heard anything like it since. Even though I came to see men and women in states of appalling torment, I was never again to hear anything like this—that one transfigured scream—and on either side of it silence, a perfect silence.

No, I must correct that. There something even worse. But it did not come out of a man or a woman. It came out of a girl—and it was not a solitary perfection of the sort I am trying to tell you about. It was worse and it was different—and there were many of them, those sounds that girls made. They went on for a long time.

The door in front of me opened, and I heard the guard say, "Prisoner Herman." And then: "Do you need me?"

The voice that answered was not hearing. It wasn't loud and it had a high voice, very pinched, very like the voice of an adolescent boy—or the kind of voice a woman will sometimes have if she has a great deal of man in her—it was a voice like that, hoarse, damp, as if the throat needed clearing, a breathy, wet contralto.

The voice said, "No," and the guard pushed me forward—and I entered that room and when I made those three or four steps forward it was like stepping onto a wing and taking a mouthful of the rushing air, getting a good mouthful of the rushing air, getting a good mouthful inside me, and then pushing, pushing myself out from what held me up, and jumping, going out there into whatever would catch me, and it's air itself that does it, it's the air itself that embraces you, and you let go and go limp and careen through it all the way down, deadfall.

I looked up when the door closed behind me. I had already seen the highly polished boots—and I could tell from the size of them and the legs that went into them—that he was big. But I was not ready for how big he was. He was about the height of Sergeyvsky, but broad—heavy thighs, and a wide waist, and very meaty in the chest and shoulders.

He wore the brown woolen trousers of his uniform, and they were tucked into the tops of his boots and the material was pulled very tight. His jacket was off, and even though it was cold in the room, his sleeves were rolled up past his elbows. His arms were hairless, and the skin was white, the meat in them dense. That's what they looked like, his arms, as if they had a kind of ponderous weight.

He turned away from me before I could see his face. He was striding now, walking to the desk that stood in front of the wall opposite. There was a window behind the desk, and a chair. And there were chairs on either side of the desk, like the chairs I'd seen in schools back in Detroit. In fact the chairs on either side of his desk were exactly the same kind of chairs I'd seen in the principal's office at Cass Technical High—and certain teachers had the very same kind of chair.

He went to the window and looked out. It was dark. What was he looking at?

Then he turned and took up a position behind his arms supporting his weight as he hunched forward on it. It was no problem seeing his face from where I stood just inside the door. The light was strong in the room—and from where I was I could see his lips weren't right. When you got a better look, you could see that it was really the lower one that was off, the skin sort of scrambled and puffed out and lopsided, as if a razor had sliced straight down and the ends of the separated flesh had been yanked together, one over the other, and then sewn up. In the light from the little lamp that sat on his desk, his whole face looked disorganized because of that lower lip. But when he pushed himself erect and stepped around and into the light that came from overhead, I could see that his face was otherwise very ordinary. It was just the lip that wasn't at all right, and the place where it was pleated was very red. It looked raw—and it glistened in the light.

He still had not spoken. He just studied me, his face without expression. He had his arms folded, and he just stood there looking me up and down. He seemed two, three times my size, his total bulk. I stand about five-eight. This man was more like six-three and I guessed his weight was well over 200, solid. I tried to recollect my weight when I'd last gotten on the scales at Spartak. I used to weigh myself there every morning I trained—and sometimes when I got finished in the afternoon I'd do it again. But I was always the same—a little over or a little under 135.

What did I weigh after the meager diet of Cell 39? I had no way of knowing. I could only tell how much I'd lost by the longer and longer tails to the two ends of my waistband that I knotted to keep my trousers up. I was suddenly aware of my clothes. It was as if I had actually forgotten what I'd had on all these weeks since July 20th. Somewhere back there in those weeks I'd begun to lose sight of a kind of catalog I suppose we all keep on ourselves, a kind of everyday accounting—what you wear, what you eat, how you feel, a list of how and what, a whole array of routine things that you're more or less not mindful of during the course of the day and yet they constitute the index to that day.

I wore what I'd been arrested in—except I had no belt in the loopholes of my trousers and no laces in my tennis shoes. And my fly was open—the buttons there had been cut off—and I could only hide myself by overlapping the ends of my pants when I tied the knot to keep them up.

Still he did not speak. And I began to think, well, it is a contest again— who can keep silent longer? And then I thought, goddamn it, now is the time to speak things straight! I began to think what my first statement should be— and although I was not entirely satisfied with it, I thought I had a clever one. It would leap us ahead in whatever exchange was coming up. I was going to say, "I demand to know who's told lies about me!" I was going to say that—and I was holding it in me a while longer to give it further consideration for just an instant more, to make sure it wasn't something that would trip me up, to make sure it was precisely the best statement to open with. But before I could get it out, the man spoke. It was that same curious voice—a notably unpleasant voice. Not the attitude that underlay it—that was not what was so unpleasant. It was instead that the voice did not go with the man that had it. And when you heard it, you wanted to clear your throat—or say something to the man about it, perhaps suggest to him that he cough out the phlegm that was making him sound like that.

He said, "I am Belov." Just that one statement, and then he made a half smile, and it resulted in something hideous, because you could see his lower lip wouldn't stretch enough, and his effort to smile aggravated the distortion you saw in his face.

It is astonishing what one will say in certain situations. Later on, you're amazed at what comes out of you. You say something that has nothing to do with the things you've been getting ready to say. It is not that you don't say the right things—because that's the point. In a kind of way, what you say is exactly right—too right—as though one were reading from a worked out in advance.

I said, "Good evening, Comrade Belov."

And I stood there waiting. When he said nothing more, I turned slightly, one way and then the other, and gazed at the room. It was just a whitewashed room, nothing at all on the walls—across from me the desk and the three chairs, perfectly balanced, and behind, the one window. Did it give out onto

228

Vorobevka Street? Onto the courtyard in the rear? Or was it a side window?

I thought to go to it—to do something to break the crazy silence and waiting. If the window showed Vorobevka Street below, then I might see people out there, even at this hour, and that would be pleasant, it would be wonderful. Would I recognize someone? It is true, I was four stories up, but even so I might see someone familiar to me. After all, this was Gorky— I'd lived in this region for over seven years—and wasn't there a *Dynamo* gymnasium nearby? I might see someone I knew even at this hour. Were there streetlights out there?

I started to make a move toward the window and then I stopped myself and acted as if I had just been shifting my weight and, when I did that, the corner to my left and behind me came into view.

It was not whitewashed, like the rest of the walls. The rest of the walls glowed white, empty of everything and white. But the corner to the rear and to my left, it was painted dark blue—an area about four feet out into either wall and about seven feet high was painted a very dark shiny blue, and I could see from the flash where I was that it was an enamel. It was so shiny that it looked like an enormous right-angled tile had been pushed across the floor and leaned into the corner.

I looked away from this as if I had seen nothing of note. I studied the window again. It was barred. What harm, then, if I walked over to it and had a look outside?

But I stayed where I was.

I just kept looking at the window across the way and waiting for the man to say something else. It was the usual kind of window you saw in big Russian buildings in those days, doubled, to protect against the cold, the exterior glass opening out and the interior glass opening in—and between them there were bars.

Was he never going to talk again? Was this perhaps how it worked? An interrogation? Or whatever this was? You just stood a while together, not speaking, and then it was over with? Could it be that he was judging me in some kind of subtle way? Could that be it? That this is how they made up their minds about you—they put you into a room with a man and he looked you over closely and then he went out and told them what he thought?

And then my mind started turning against me—and I could feel myself losing control. I began to think that perhaps he had already spoken a great number of sentences—and that I simply had not been paying close enough attention. It startled me, this thought. Was it possible? Had the man—what was his name?—had he already asked me dozens of questions, already given me every opportunity to clear myself, to get myself out of this, and I had not heard, had instead been looking out the window or at some blue design in the corner?

Had I already missed it all? And failed some kind of test? Could this have happened to me—had my mind done this to me? Had those weeks and months in 39 driven me insane? Made me deaf? Delivered me into some kind of waking trance?

What had he said? He'd given his name!

It was…Belov!

I swallowed with relief.

Belov! He said—*I am Belov.*

Who talks like that?

What a queer way to talk.

And, that's right, I had *answered*—I had said. I had said…

I had said something stupid, something dull.

I had said—it was amazing—how long ago?

I had said: *Good evening, Comrade Belov.*

I waited.

I tried not to look at his face, at his lip.

Was that it? They stood you here and the test was to see if you could *look* at his lip? Or *not* look at it?

I couldn't decide. It seemed to me that perhaps this made sense—it had to be one or the other. But I could not decide which you were expected to prove.

I tried to look at his desk—to see if there was anything on it.

I couldn't tell.

And then I looked at his face. If that's what they wanted, I would do it— and it was then that I noticed something else. The man was slightly drunk. I could see he was looking at me. It's something that if you're not a drinker you get used to spotting in people—and I could spot it in this Belov. The man was slightly, or maybe more than slightly, drunk.

Perhaps this accounted for the man's silence. Perhaps he was drunker than I surmised. Perhaps he was asleep on his feet.

And then he spoke again.

"I am your interrogator."

And that was all he said. I waited for more—but nothing came. I repeated the phrase in my head, tried to say it the same way he'd said it, figuring I could make up my mind about how drunk he was.

It was the ensuing silence and my distraction perhaps that led me into saying the second crazy thing I said. But what was I to say?

I said, "Thank you for telling me that."

I had to say something—and what should I have said? I am Victor Herman? I am an American? Did he not know these things? Was it not better to be extremely formal, extremely civil? To let the statements follow some sort of ceremonial pattern that only this man could guide us through?

He dropped his arms from where they were folded in front of him and took a step closer to me, moving his hands behind his back as he came. He stood about three or four feet from me now and the deformation of his lower lip seemed to glare in the light, it was that inflamed even though you could see it was something that had happened to him long ago.

I couldn't take my eyes off it now. He blocked my view to the window across the way and there was nowhere else to fix my eyes. I could have looked down to his chest—but wouldn't that have appeared guilty or servile? Wasn't this the test to establish my innocence? Wasn't the imperative thing that my bearing, my least gesture, my every move all convey the testimony of a man who is without the slightest guilt? I should look this Belov right in the eye! But when I tried to do it, that twist of flesh drew my attention as if it were a wound I myself had inflicted—and it was impossible! It would be a wretched mistake to gape at that tortured lip—yet I could not take my eyes from it. So I stared—knowing as I did it that this was a critical misstep, that clearly the man must be sensitive about such a thing, such an ugliness to have on a face. Who could not be uneasy over such a thing, even if he were born with it? No man could ever get himself indifferent to a malformation like that!

The lip moved! He was saying something.

In that womanish voice, very breathy and very hoarse, this Belov said, "You will tell me about your counterrevolutionary activities. I will hear every one."

What?

Could this be what the man had said?

Could I trust my hearing anymore?

But that is what he said, and I for the third time said the wrong thing. To begin with, I hesitated. It was in my mind to show the man that I was giving his question serious study, that I was a prudent fellow, that he could rely on me, that I would of course weigh my words for gravity and precision before speaking—when I simply should have laughed in the man's face.

At last, and with great composure, I think, I said, "No, I have done nothing counterrevolutionary. I am, of course, an American—and this is not my revolution. I have nothing to do with it, one way or the other. But you have my word on it, in any case. Really, I have done nothing counterrevolutionary. I don't think in such terms, really. I am not a political person, you see. Perhaps

231

you don't know, but I'm a sportsman. I'm not at all interested in politics, one way or the other, I promise you."

All through this speech, I kept trying to stop myself. The first sentence would have been enough. Certainly by the finish of the second sentence, I'd said all that simply carried me forward—into what seemed to me further qualifications that were necessary. And then I could see that he wasn't listening to anything I was saying, and that made it all worse, just added to my uneasiness with what I'd already said and urged me on into the next sentence and the next, trying to work myself up into a sentence that would compel his attention to what I was saying, and anyway, it was so good to be saying anything, to be talking at all.

But it would have all come out the same, in any event—no purity of language or impression of candor would have improved my claim in the slightest. Nor would indignation have helped me, the anger I had so pleasurably held in store.

In time I was to learn that only guilt would help me—and it's no good learning that when you're innocent.

"Turn around," Belov said.

I did it immediately.

"Walk into that corner there, the blue one."

I took a few steps forward and stopped.

"Keep going!"

I started up again, slowly now.

"Stand two feet from the corner!"

I reached what I took to be two feet from the corner and stopped.

"Face the corner."

I stood there. It crossed my mind that something like this must have happened to me in grade school. It had happened to all the boys at one time or another, so it must have happened to me at least once—but I could not remember. Didn't they put a dunce's cap on your head—or something like that?

I stood there. I could tell he had not moved.

All right, then I will stand here.

Should I turn around and say, "See here, Mr. Belov, I demand to be put in touch with the American consulate! With a lawyer! With a judge! With your Mr. Stalin! With the President of the United States! With my father, Mr. Samuel Herman, a tireless and dedicated Communist like yourself! With my mother! That's right, my mother! I promise you, *she* will explain how all this happened! Call my mother, goddamn it!"

I stood there. I faced into the corner. There was nothing to see but that dark blue enamel. It was painted right out from the corner onto the floor beneath my feet.

My trousers had loosened and I reached to knot them tighter. But I never got my hands there.

He came fast when he came. For a big man and a man I judged at least moderately drunk, he moved with surprising speed. I could hear every brisk step he took, those boot heels reporting his heavy rapid march across the wooden floor.

He never hit me anywhere but in the kidneys. He would hit three times on the right side and then pause. And then he would hit three times on the left side and pause. He always took his time. No matter what happened, he was never hurried and he always paced himself, three times here, but slowly, one ... two... three. Then a longer pause—and now three times over here, one... two ... three. And after a series of three, he would return to one of the chairs and sit a while. Sometimes he would sit for as long as half an hour—drinking a bit from a bottle he had, beer sometimes, whiskey sometimes—and then he would rise—I could hear the weariness in it, in his motions—but as soon as he was standing, he came across that floor very fast—and then it would be another series of three, on the right, then on the left, always in the kidneys.

It would start always after twelve, sometime after twelve o'clock, and it would not finish until dawn. I would go in the van, in the locker, and we would climb the four flights of stairs, always pausing on the last two floors at each of the doors on the right side of the corridor, and then we would stand before the door marked 178 and wait. We would wait sometimes ten minutes, sometimes more, and then I would go in.

Belov would say, "You will tell me about your counterrevolutionary activities. I will hear every one."

And I would answer.

And he would say, "Go to the corner."

And I would go there. And after the first time, he used manacles or cord. After the first time, I could not raise my arms. I could not put my hands up to ease myself into the walls. After the first time, I just went into the walls.

After the eighth time, he tied my fingers together—one finger from each hand. Maybe this gave him more room to move in, a better target, with my hands fastened together in front of me.

The first night I did not fall.

But I fell the second night—and after that I fell every night. But falling did not matter.

There was just the one question—every night I walked into that room, the same question—and then I would go to the corner and stand.

But Belov never tied me or manacled me. A guard did that—and then the guard would leave the room.

He never took my shirt off, either.

When I think back on it, I think this Belov did not like to touch me. It is the impression that I have—that the man could not bear to touch me.

But the eleventh night he did.

With the tips of his fingers he felt along my back. He inched along from side to side and from top to bottom, pressing as a doctor does—and asking, "Hurt? Hurt here?"

But I never said yes.

Still, he found the place where I winced—and then that's where he hit.

Do I owe God that this Belov did not like to touch me? Do I owe God that my shirt was never taken off me? Is it God I owe that the scar where they healed my liver stayed hidden from Belov? Or is it God I owe that Belov lived to hurt me?

He hurt me for fifty-five nights.

From sometime after twelve until dawn, that man hurt me—and then he would call the guard to take me down and pass me along to another guard to walk me to the van, and in the van there was a third guard to put me in the locker—and I would walk out of Room 178 and down those four flights of stairs—*head down, hands behind back, no noise*—and ride the van back to *Spets Korpus*, Cell 39, and I was always there in time for the morning bell.

Those fifty-five mornings I gulped my hot water down. It did not matter how hot it was—I gulped it—and I was grateful to be on time. I never missed that first feeding. I always made it back before the first bell—and fifty-five times I made it back.

After fifteen mornings, they shared. It is one of the memories that makes me cry. Of all the things I will remember, of all—the things that are printed onto my thoughts until I will think no longer, only three or four make me cry.

This is one of them—that they *shared* with me, all those mornings from fifteen to fifty-five, each giving a little, until I had a second cup.

Yes, I owe God for that—and admit it. Or I owe man—both my gratitude and my hate.

What is it I should remember? Those fifty-five nights? Or the mornings when they shared?

Fear No Evil

Natan Sharansky

1.

On my third morning in Lefortovo the food trap opened with a clang and a guard pointed at me with the cell key—a key as thick as the barrel of a gun.

"Name!" he demanded. He checked my name on his form. Then, "To a summons!"

This I learned, was the procedure for taking a prisoner to an interrogation, and during the hundred and ten times I was questioned, it never varied.

In the center of the prison, where the four corridors of the letter K converged, stood a signalman with a red flag. His job was to ensure that no two cells were ever opened simultaneously. When he waved the flag once, my cell door could be opened. A second wave meant I could proceed.

After being searched, I walked slowly down the long corridor with my hands behind my back. The guard followed, snapping his fingers as loudly as possible or banging two keys together. This was a warning: I am with a prisoner.

Then it was up a winding staircase, where I crossed over to the investigative department and into an entirely different world. Whereas the prison was dark and all the guards wore uniforms, here there were windows and telephones and men in business suits.

From time to time, when a similar finger-snapping was heard from the other end of the corridor, they locked me in a special closet that resembled a telephone booth. If there was no closet nearby, I might be taken up or down to another floor, or even back to my cell. But this was rarely necessary.

The signalman and the other precautions were there to enforce a basic rule of prison life—that no prisoner awaiting trail could know who else was being held. (This was why the guard always asked your name and never said it himself, for if he happened to make a mistake, you might inadvertently learn the identity of a fellow prisoner.) If you passed another zek in the corridor, there was always the possibility that some quick message or gesture might be exchanged. Or you might see a witness from your own case who would somehow let you know that he wasn't cooperating with the authorities, even if your interrogators insisted that he was.

At some level, every Soviet citizen lives in fear of the consequences of his actions, for he knows there is no presumption of innocence on the part of the KGB. That is what makes interrogations so sinister.

At the same time the nature of these sessions has changed enormously since the Stalin era. From my older friends, and from samizdat memoirs, I knew about endless nocturnal interrogations in Lefortovo, as well as crude beatings and more refined tortures to pressure the accused into signing a confession and giving "testimony," which was then used against his companions. In some cases, prisoners were brought to Lefortovo and summarily shot. Now, however, both quick executions and torture are officially forbidden, and the KGB is a paragon of Soviet legality.

Lefortovo is no police station: officially, fists aren't permitted here, and they don't yell at you. True, they can torture you with the cold and hunger of the punishment cell, but even there they address you formally. The prison guards called me Citizen Sharansky, and the KGB officers, including my interrogators, always addressed me as Anatoly Borisovich, which was more polite and less ceremonial. Never in my life was I addressed so often by that honorific, which normally wasn't used for people my age.

Years later, in a prison camp, I learned that I had been one of the lucky ones. As they led me down the deathly silent corridors of Lefortovo, I had no idea that next to the freight elevator was a room lined with rubber. If "state interests" demanded it, and if the KGB was certain that Western public opinion had no interest in their victim, they would bring him here, where the beatings were carried out by the very same officers who addressed me politely. And while my interrogators tried to assure me that our Helsinki Group reports on Soviet psychiatric abuses were false and slanderous, in the very next office other interrogators were showing my fellow prisoners terrifying pictures of people whose faces were distorted by pain, and telling them, "If you don't want to spend the rest of your life on a cot in a lunatic asylum, you'd better testify."

Where they had once used force, the KGB now preferred to engage you in long conversations, which often lasted the whole day. They kept you here for weeks, months, even years, trying to manipulate you with explanations, threats, promises, hints, and more threats. The point of these incessant interrogations was twofold: first, to create an aura of legitimacy to mask what was still a legal farce, and, second, to induce you to reveal as much information as possible, even if it was already known to the investigators. Everything you told them was written down in the protocol, which you would then be asked to sign. Later, carefully selected and twisted excerpts could be used to pressure the next person: "You see? Sharansky has already told us all about this."

2.

My first interrogator, Major Anatoly Vasilievich Chernysh, seemed to be in his early forties. He was only slightly taller than I, and almost as bald. Chernysh was clearly concerned about losing his hair, and one day he asked whether I had ever tried to restore mine. For me, however, this topic had been moot since the age of twenty-two.

Chernysh had a small head and tiny eyes, but they were observant and, I must admit, intelligent. At first he reminded me of a hamster—later, a rat. His office was long and narrow, and he sat behind a large desk, beneath the hammer-and-sickle insignia. I sat near the door, behind a small table. Between us, along the drab wall, was a bookshelf filled with the standard works of Marx and Lenin, assorted legal volumes, and professional and party journals. There were portraits of Lenin and Brezhnev, and of Felix Dzerzhinsky, the first head of the Soviet Secret Police.

Chernysh began by informing me that a team of eleven investigators had been set up to handle my case. (Later, the number grew to seventeen.) Hearing this news, I felt overwhelmed and depressed. Why so many? Instead of closing my case, they were apparently gearing up for something enormous. "If this is how the KGB uses its personnel," I replied sarcastically, "then there's obviously no danger of unemployment."

"What can we do?" replied Chernysh. "You and your accomplices were engaged in criminal activity over many years, and now we have to investigate it all." He said this calmly and politely, but every word heightened the tension. I realized I had better get used to the idea that from now on my friends were "accomplices," and that our struggle to emigrate to Israel constituted "criminal activity."

Then Chernysh repeated the question that Galkin had asked me when I first arrived: "What can you tell us about the essence of the charge?" I gave my same reply, but in contrast to Galkin, Chernysh calmly recorded my answer and read it back to make sure he had it correctly.

Only then did he try to pick apart my response: "You say you 'informed international public opinion,' and that you 'drew attention to...' By what means?"

I hesitated briefly to make sure my reply conformed to the principles of my tree.* "I organized press conferences and met with Western correspondents and politicians. I also sent letters to the appropriate Soviet organizations. This was all done openly, and the material I transmitted was designated exclusively for public use."

"Who else participated in this activity?"

"I refuse to answer because I don't want to help the KGB prepare a criminal case against any other Jewish activists or dissidents who, like me, have committed no crimes."

"If you really committed no crimes," said Chernysh, "then what are you afraid of? If your activity was open, speak openly. You're forcing me to think there was something secret in all this."

"Our activity was open and public," I replied. "You have copies of letters with our signatures that we wrote for publication. If you want to know who was involved, you can read the names yourself. But for some reason you need *me* to testify about the participation of others. Why?"

Chernysh politely reminded me that he was the one who was asking the questions. He continued: "Exactly what kind of letters and appeals were sent? When and to whom did you send them?

Again I had to pause: What kind of answer did my tree indicate? While I didn't plan to deny any of my activity, I also had no intention of helping the KGB prepare a dossier on us.

"I refuse to answer," I told Chernysh, "because I don't want to help the KGB draw up criminal cases against Jewish activists for their legal and open activity."

He duly recorded my reply, read it aloud, and then launched into a little speech. He didn't want to frighten me, he said, but it was his unpleasant duty to explain my situation. He had handled several previous cases that resulted in *rasstrel*—execution—although he always hoped to avoid such an outcome.

And now, as he looked at me and thought about my various talents, about my young wife who was waiting for me in Israel, and my elderly parents who had pinned so many hopes on me—at this moment, despite our ideological differences—he found it difficult as a fellow human being to think that I might be executed. The didn't want to encroach on my views or change them, but I had to understand that my fate now depended on only one thing—the nature of my testimony.

—————————————

* That is, his own set of priorities regarding how he would respond to questions.—Ed.

Chernysh had been pacing around the room, but suddenly he grabbed a chair, sat down at my little table, and looked me right in the eye. I was leaning back with my arms folded over my chest, trying to appear calm and indifferent. Inside, however, I was trembling with anxiety. It was that word *ras-s-strel*—especially the way Chernysh pronounced it, with a hissing sound—that grated on my ears and made my knees shake. Each time he said it the muscles tensed up in my chest and shoulders and I had to clench my teeth to hide my tension.

Some people associate *rasstrel* with a firing squad, but for me the word has always conjured up a different image: a prison official leads you down to the basement, and when you get to the bottom of the stairs he shoots you in the back of the head. That's how things were done in Stalin's time, and that's what I thought of every time Chernysh uttered that terrible word.

Over the next few weeks Chernysh diligently sought out ways to insert *ras-s-strel* into the conversation. When I asked for my Hebrew-Russian dictionary, which had been seized during the search of my apartment, he expressed surprise: "What do you need that for? Given your conduct, they're going to shoot you anyway." When Brezhnev delivered another speech denouncing the Americans after Cyrus Vance's unsuccessful visit to Moscow at the end of March, Chernysh said, "See for yourself. It's right here in black and white that we won't permit any interference in our internal affairs. The Americans won't save you from *ras-s-strel*."

Back in the cell, Fima would tell me about his case and ask about my own. The conclusion of his stories was always the same: Don't let them smear your forehead with iodine. There it was *ras-s-strel*, here it was iodine. I just wanted to left alone.

I lay down, covered myself with my overcoat, turned toward the wall and fell asleep. On days when there were no interrogations, I slept right through except for meals and exercise. When interrogations were scheduled, I fell asleep as soon as they were done. By law there were no sessions past ten at night—this was one of the post-Stalin reforms, along with the official ban of beatings and torture—but when the interrogation dragged on past noon and they brought me back to the cell for lunch, I used the time to doze for another forty or fifty minutes. When I returned to Chernysh's office I was barely able to suppress a yawn.

Chernysh was convinced I was faking and trying to appear indifferent, but my fatigue was real. Never in my life did I sleep as much as during those first three weeks in Lefortovo. I had never needed much sleep, but ever since the *Izvestia* article appeared I was exhausted, and now I was sleeping as much as fifteen or sixteen hours a day. I would doze off immediately, but it was fitful sleep, as my mind was filled with interrogations, both past and future, and with anxiety over friends and loved ones. Mostly I thought about Avital. Where was she now? What was she thinking about at this very moment? What was she doing? What was the weather today in Israel? And Mama—how was she coping with all of this? And what about Papa, whose health wasn't all that strong to begin with?

One morning, about twenty days after my arrest, I woke up and suddenly realized that I no longer wanted to sleep. Instead of feeling crushed or tired, I was full of strength. I even did exercises and doused myself with cold water from the sink, although our cell was so chilly that Fima and I slept in warm underwear and covered ourselves with a blanket and an overcoat.

It wasn't that my problems had disappeared. I still felt weighed down by a sense of responsibility and by the uncertainty of my situation. But now, for the first time since my arrest, I felt determined and ready to struggle.

Invigorated by this new energy, I decided that my first priority was to sort out my feelings. Why was I so anxious before each interrogation? I invariably expected some terrible surprise—a mysterious document, perhaps, or the unexpected testimony of a close friend that would finally make clear why they had accused me of treason. But nothing of the sort ever happened. Instead, Chernysh would ask a few questions and then launch into a long discourse about the hopelessness of my situation.

Before my arrest I had trained myself not to pay attention to the threats of the KGB interrogators I occasionally met with. Instead of answering their questions, I told them only what I wanted them to hear. In their presence I felt like a chess player facing a much weaker opponent. They did exactly what they were supposed to, and I knew all their moves in advance: their threats and warnings, their attempts at blackmail, their flattery and their promises.

But now my former confidence had disappeared. So far, at least, I hadn't said anything I regretted. But who knew what would happen later, when they switched from the opening artillery barrage of all these general questions to a more detailed, frontal attack?

Analyzing my first few sessions with Chernysh, I came to the obvious conclusion that I hadn't been psychologically prepared for a charge of treason—and especially for the horrifying possibility of *rasstrel*. My only hope was to quickly become accustomed to that idea, to steel myself against it. Just as the skin on my feet used to toughen up every summer during my childhood, when I walked around barefoot, I now had to toughen up my ears and my heart until the sound and the prospect of *rasstrel* meant nothing to me.

As a dissident, I had gradually grown accustomed to words like "arrest" and "exile," which no longer had the same dramatic power over me as they once did. Now I had to get accustomed to the word *rasstrel,* but I had to do so on my own—and fast. Any word loses its mystique when you use it often enough, so I started talking about *rasstrel* with Fima at every opportunity. As for Chernysh, I still remember how amazed he was the first time I turned the tables on him and blurted out, "What's the use of all these conversations when you're just going to shoot me anyway—*rasstrel?*"

He was shocked. Until now this word had been his exclusive weapon, while I had avoided any mention of it. Chernysh seemed to think I was testing him, and he began to ramble on about how these were not empty threats, and how his duty was not to coerce me but simply to explain the situation. But the atmosphere had changed. At first it was awkward, but as we went along I was able to insert *rasstrel* into almost every conversation, whether it was appropriate or not. Before long my plan began to pay off, and neither the word itself nor our conversations about it caught me off-balance. Within weeks, *rasstrel* had become a word like any other.

While the interrogations had their own routine, there were occasional surprises. One morning Chernysh brought in excerpts from the treason laws of Western countries. "You see?" he said. "Acts that go against the interests of the state are prosecuted everywhere. And there's no point in alluding to the West because their guidelines are even stricter."

I glanced at the pages he showed me, but I couldn't see much difference in the formulations. "I don't understand all the legal terms," I said, "but I know this—if the Western nations had an equivalent to our laws on 'anti-Soviet activity,' then the Communist Party would be outlawed in these countries, and all their members would be arrested."

Chernysh took a moment to think this one over. "Of course it ought to be that way," he conceded, "but the capitalists tolerate the Communists because they're afraid of the people's anger." This idiotic answer—the same moronic drivel I used to hear back in kindergarten—reminded me of how primitive my adversaries could be.

Chernysh's next tactic was to tell me about two other prisoners he had recently dealt with who had decided to cooperate with their investigators. They were both foreigners, a Dutchman and a Frenchman, and were arrested for passing out dissident literature. As I could see from the protocols of their interrogations, each had loudly insisted on his rights, but soon recanted. Then, after returning home, both men had repudiated confessions, and the Dutchman had even written a book about his imprisonment. Chernysh's message was obvious: Recant, and you, too, will be released. Then you can say whatever you like. "Goddamn foreigners," I muttered. "How glibly they recant and write books."

Chernysh didn't mention Yakir and Krasin, but they were on my mind a great deal. In 1973, when I first became an aliyah activist, dissident circles in Moscow were in shock from the confessions of Pyotr Yakir and Viktor Krasin, two leaders of the democratic movement who had survived Stalin's labor camps. At a major press conference that was broadcast on radio and television, Yakir and Krasin condemned their own dissident activities, including *Chronicle of Current Events,* the journal of the human rights movement. Both received conspicuously light sentences, while their friends and colleagues who did not recant were punished more harshly. Although I later witnessed many cases of prisoners cooperating with the KGB, the case of Yakir and Krasin was the first time I had seen this process in sharp relief, and it remained with me.

Sitting in my cell, I asked myself the obvious question: Why not recant and then repudiate it after I was released? But I already knew the answer. First, any confession I made would mean betraying my friends. When Yakir and Krasin decided to cooperate with the authorities, it was enormously demoralizing for the dissident community. I had no desire to undermine the movements I believed in, or to do anything that would leave my fellow refuseniks and dissidents with an even greater feeling of hopelessness, or of the KGB's omnipotence.

Second, I knew that the only reason the world paid any attention to a small group of Soviet dissidents and Jewish activists was our strong moral position. While collaborating with the KGB might be understandable, it would severely compromise that stance. The moral righteousness of our struggle was our greatest asset, perhaps our only asset. To cooperate with the KGB would mean letting down our growing number of supporters in the free world and undermining their continued determination to help us.

Finally, on a more practical level, I knew that each time the KGB made a political arrest, it required permission from the political leadership. If I recanted, it would only make it easier for the KGB to receive permission to initiate new repressions and another round of arrests.

Recalling these arguments in my cell, I found them as compelling as ever. But even if none of them was true and I could somehow surrender to the KGB without any damage to my friends and our supporters, I still couldn't confess to crimes I hadn't committed. For behind all these valid and rational arguments was a barrier of the spirit that blocked all roads to surrender.

To put it simply, there was no way I could ever return to my former life as an assimilated Soviet Jew, a loyal citizen who said one thing but thought another as he tried to act just like everyone else. That was all behind me now. For the past four years I had been a free man, and it was unthinkable that I would ever give up the marvelous sensation of freedom that came over me after I returned to my roots. For now I had purpose, I had perspective, I had peace of mind.

And although we were separated by time and space, I had Avital.

Memoirs

Petro G. Grigorenko

On April 19, 1964, a commission of experts presided over by Academian Snezhevsky, with the special participation of a Professor named Lunts, determined that I was insane. They did not, of course, tell me this, but I had no doubts that the commission's decision would confirm previous ones. However, I wanted to hear this directly and therefore asked for a meeting with Lunts and Taltse. Neither received me. Previously they had seen me any time I so requested. It was probably to avoid such an encounter that they sent me to prison the next morning.

After being told the decision I did not return to the Lubyanka. They had closed it down and thus took me instead to Lefortovo, where I was put in cell number 25. I was taken to neither questionings nor conversations. I could read and think in peace. I demanded more walks in the fresh air and received permission to go from one to two hours. A few days after I entered Lefortovo they allowed me a visit with my wife.

The visit was unusual. After lunch they called me out for a walk. A few minutes later I felt ill. I asked them to take me to my cell. They said they would, but didn't. I felt I was going to fall asleep while I was in motion. Once again I asked them to take me to my cell. Again they did not do so. Just before the end of the walk period, the escort guard appeared and led me away. On the way to my cell we encountered the duty officer. He announced, "You have a visitor."

I tried to pull myself together as best I could and went along with them. I remember nothing about the visit; nor do I remember returning to my cell. Later my wife told me that I made grimaces, that I shouted out "Rot front!" and jerked like a marionette. At one point I tossed a note to her, which fell short. Bending in front of the guard, I picked up the paper and reached into her pocket. When the meeting came to an end the guard demanded the note of her.

She gave him something but found when she returned home that she had the note. I don't have the right to disclose the art of this deception; while there are still prisoners they must be allowed their special secrets.

They then informed my wife that she had been invited to see the interrogator. At that moment it dawned upon her that our visit had been staged. The interrogator would want to know what she thought. Did she now believe that her husband was insane? Understanding this, she nearly hurled herself upon the interrogator when she entered his office, demanding to know what they had done to me and whether they had given me drugs. When she said that she was going to complain—to let the whole world know—the interrogator offered to let her visit me again the next day.

The next visit went very well. My wife told me a great deal of family news. I kept looking at her; I felt I couldn't get enough of seeing her. Then she asked me, "Do you remember my last visit?"

"No! I went to sleep afterward, and in the morning everything that had happened the day before, beginning with my walk, seemed to have happened in a fog. I remember asking them to take me inside. Everything else is like a dream—I don't know whether it really happened or not."

If judged by events, my life flowed on monotonously, but a human being lives not by events alone. Always, and especially in prison, one is introspective, concerned with the past, relationships, politics, and the spiritual world. More and more, I returned to the question of defense against the tyranny of the ruling authorities. My belief that it is possible to achieve something only by open and daring struggle grew even stronger. People love truth, nobility, and honor. They follow with fascination the example of a bold, heroic battle for justice and good; against evil, falsehood, and deceit. It is the duty of all who are capable to openly set such an example. Then the army of the heroic, honorable, and just will grow.

What form of organization must this movement take? I thought about this for a long time and then firmly decided, none at all. In the first place, as soon as even small groups came together they would be liquidated by the KGB. In the second place, I did not belong to the party. I was through with parties! Each assures the death of the cause it stands for. A party is a struggle for power; it replaces communication with bureaucratic intrigues, and is necessary simply as a forum in which to struggle against what you would never accept for yourself.

Such thoughts were not new to me. The Alliance for Struggle for the Rebirth of Leninism was an unorganized organization. In essence I continued to support the concept of a chain—except that the chains I now foresaw would not be secret and would unite all honest, just, courageous people on the basis of love and on the basis of the inseparable rights given us by God.

In prison quiet the past unfolds before the mind's eye in an incessant stream. Books are read in a new way: What interests you is not so much the plot as the author's philosophy, and light reading simply does not satisfy. One takes a different attitude toward events. Nothing is insignificant.

My first evening at Lefortovo prison, I heard a bell that aroused memories of my childhood, my father, my Uncle Alexander, Father Vladimir, Sima, Valya, church holidays, and in particular Christmas, Easter, and church services. At the time I was an agnostic—indifferent to the teachings of religion. Now I heard the voice of the church. During the war I had spent almost two months in the chief military hospital, in the very same district in which I was now serving time in prison. Then I had not heard the bells. When I heard them ringing for the first time, I was astonished. I wanted so much to be in that church. No, I did not believe in God, but in my heart that church was a living being emitting a living voice. Right then I decided that if I was freed, I would go there. (I did so after my release. A friend, Grigory Alexandrovich Pavlov, told me that the bells I'd heard were from the Church of Peter and Paul, a church built by Peter the Great for soldiers. Together we attended a beautiful service.) While in Lefortovo I had come to know when the bells would ring and would put everything else aside to listen. The first chime always brought blessedness into my soul, and each time the ringing stopped I was terribly sad.

Translated by Thomas P. Whitney

I Was a Slave In Russia
An American Tells His Story

John Noble

I knew little about theoretical Marxism at that time, but in this attitude toward death I sensed the gulf that separated these MVD officers from the Christian civilization to whose extinction they are committed. They believe that man is an animal, no more. To kill a man is no more significant than to kill a highly trained horse or a cow. If the beast becomes unmanageable, it is killed. If the man-beast becomes unmanageable, he is killed.

Although death sentences were passed every court day, the executions were carried out once a month. This was more efficient than shooting the people one by one, as sentenced.

A prisoner sentenced to death was put on half rations; since humans are animals, there is little sense in giving full rations to one that is about to be destroyed.

The squad assigned to bring the prisoners to the place of execution consisted of a junior-grade MVD lieutenant and two enlisted guards. Their procedure was standardized and, like the sentencing itself, almost casual. When the guards came to a cell where a sentenced prisoner was, they ordered him to remove his clothes. In some cases they forced him to take off everything, in others, an undershirt might be worn. Clothes that were taken from prisoners were heaped on the corridor floor. A guard would poke through the piles and pick out the good articles. The rest were turned over to me to distribute.

While the undressing went on, guards and officer would joke and laugh, usually over what they thought the prisoners might do to their underwear if permitted to wear it to their death. What a waste of laundering it would be, they laughed.

In that joking was summed up a startling difference between these guards and the Nazi death squads about which those prisoners who had known both sometimes spoke. The Nazis, they said, killed viciously, because they were convinced that the people being killed were actually their enemies. The Russians killed because, almost literally, a number had been drawn from a hat, because some meaningless document in some meaningless proceedings had said to snuff out the candle. No ferocity attended the executions. The reasons for the killings were as remote and irrelevant to the Russian guards as was the concept of death itself. Their joking, then, was not forced. When they patted a prisoner's shoulder, the action came easily. Life had to end for certain integers in the state table of statistics. That's all, comrade. Nothing personal, comrade.

Horribly, the laughter of the guards marked those days more than did the sounds of the killings themselves.

The process of execution, about which the guards sometimes boasted because it was so "humane," was simplicity itself. After a condemned prisoner had undressed, he was led to a partly shattered wing of the prison. As he rounded the comer into a corridor of the wing, a guard shot him in the back of the head. It was "humane," because it came without warning.

As each prisoner was shot, his body was dragged to the end of the corridor. By the end of a day's killing, a stack of sprawling bodies, naked or in undershirts, stood in the dark and dirty hall. A guard doused the bodies with gasoline and tossed on a match. The flames from the pyre made a light that often was seen by prisoners in other parts of the building. A guard, if questioned, would explain that trash was being burned.

As the smoke from the burning bodies drifted from the execution corridor into other parts of the prison, it was difficult to make anyone believe that it was anything but exactly what it was. On execution days, in many cells not even the pitiful scraps that passed for rations were eaten.

One execution day the flames from the cindering corpses rose higher than usual, perhaps because of an extravagant drenching with fuel. From the burning bodies the flames licked up and caught the wood trim, moldings, and sashes of the corridor. The guards, idly watching the blaze till now, ran for aid. My helper and I were called out to haul a hose up to extinguish the flames, but we were not permitted to turn the corner into the corridor itself. The guards carried the hose into the death corridor and flushed the flames from the grisly torch they had set.

To some prisoners the walk in the corridor probably was a relief, as humane as the Russians said it was. These were the prisoners who had been tortured. For some time, I had known only the sounds of torture. But I learned, as I came to know more about the prison during my records-keeping job, what it was that produced the shrieks and sobs.

The most common form of torture was the beating with strips of thick, lead-wrapped, electric installation pipe, covered with heavy insulation. They were about one third of an inch wide and two feet long. It was not uncommon to see guards strolling around with these whips in their hands. In the interrogation rooms, however, the pipes were put to their harshest use.

The questioning involved the victim, an investigating MVD officer, and an interpreter. Oddly enough, it also usually involved the proposition that the victim was innocent of whatever charge the Communists had brought against him and to which they wanted him to confess. The regularity with which this was true seemed at first a nightmare, without rhyme or reason. I soon learned, though, how sensible it was, from the Communist point of view. If a person was indeed guilty of something, the Communists usually had little trouble proving it. At least, they had facts enough at hand to warrant a passable charge. But if the person was innocent, the whip would pound and lash the desired "guilt" into the person's back muscles, nerve fibers, mind, and consciousness.

I helped to carry one of the beaten prisoners to his cell. He had been whipped with his shirt on. His skin was laid open from the ridge of his shoulders all the way to his belt line, and the shirt had been ground into the raw meat of his back. For an hour, with the doctor who also was a prisoner, I picked bits of shredded cloth from the wounds, trying always to pick bloody cloth rather than the slivers of split red flesh. When we had finished cleaning his back, we wrapped him in strips of toilet paper, the prison dispensary's gesture toward providing medicine for the man.

More complex and subtle, and I always have thought more damaging, was the torture of the disinfecting cabinet. This was a large, boiler-like metal cabinet in which, under the German prison administration, mattresses had been disinfected—a cleanliness undreamed of in any Russian-administered prison at that time.

Prisoners being moved through the corridors or going about prison work were able to see this looming presence, with its high-pressure steam pipes and valves. What they did not know, if they were new and had not circulated among the veteran prisoners, was that the disinfecting tank was no longer connected to receive steam. It was these new prisoners that went to the tank for their torture.

A prisoner was thrown into the tank by guards who were being purpose-fully rough to intimate that severe punishment was underway. Inside, the terrified prisoner watched the steel hatch swing shut and beard the booming clang as the locking mechanism turned and the bolts seated themselves in their slots.

In the total interior darkness, the prisoner could only expect a searing jet of steam or a choking cloud of poisonous gas to be pumped in. And so he would be left for a full day or two, the door never being opened.

After this ordeal, several prisoners were taken from the tank completely mad. No person ever emerged without serious nervous consequences. Most came out of it with hair turned gray. All were willing to confess to whatever the Communists wished them to confess.

Another psycho-physical torture method was used of which I had heard, although I never saw the place where it was carried out. I have, however, seen prisoners brought back from it. A deep pit, possibly used at one time as part of a drainage or garbage-disposal system in the prison, was filled with water to knee height. The victim was placed in this pit, standing with his clothes on. Every half hour a pail of water was thrown over him. First there was the tense waiting, and then the wet shock. Both grew progressively worse. As the water level rose, by pailfuls, from knees, to hips, to waist, a slow horror welled within the man. Finally he was ready to confess anything that was expected of him.

The very system of Communist arrests inevitably led to a system of torture that was as much mental as physical. Arrests were made to terrorize the citizens, in sweeping, indiscriminate raids. Men were arrested as they walked the streets, as they dined or sat in the homes of friends. They were arrested anywhere, anytime, without explanation. Everyone in the city was kept poised on the edge of terror.

There was a plan to it all, and it was remarkably effective even beyond its terrorizing results. When a load of prisoners newly yanked from home and street was thrown into cells, the first topic of speculation naturally was, "Why was I arrested?" They would search their memories for minor infractions and even for unvoiced thoughts antagonistic to the Communists. A cell full of prisoners might talk for hours about these things, elaborating upon point after point, seeking always a clue to their arrest. There was, of course, no clue. But in every cell was a Communist police informer, patiently listening as the prisoners spelled out possible grounds for Communist charges. It was the unfortunates who could find absolutely no reason whatever for their arrests that were passed on to the body-and-mind-racking torments of lash and tank and pit.

A torture of humiliation for us all was the regular weekly search, when guards would sweep through the prison and pick over our personal belongings. These had been thrown to the floor, and contraband or any article that might seem desirable to the guards was taken. We then were forced to kneel down and sort out our pitiful belongings. To see the paltry scraps of one's only personal life—shreds of soap, a wad of toilet paper, a saved crust, an extra pair of torn socks—thrown on the floor and then to have to scramble for them was a brutalizing experience. I came to dread it as others must have dreaded an expected new ordeal with the whip.

The severity of these searches depended upon what day of the week they were carried out. In midweek they were routine and without incident. The guards came in, belongings were heaped, and the recovery scramble began.

But if an additional search was held, on Friday or Saturday, beatings and other abuses were added. This was a result of the MVD indoctrination course. Every Friday, all MVD officers and guards were assembled for ideological lectures. After the lectures, the guards toured the cells, grabbing prisoners at random, asking incredible questions, and administering beatings to any who could not answer—and no one ever could. If, during these sessions, a search was ordered, every man could expect a hard time. The guards would take special pains to rip and tear the articles they threw to the floor. They walked over things, crushing, perhaps, a treasured pair of glasses or other breakable objects. When prisoners stooped to pick up their things, the guards might kick them. Prisoners were thrown bodily from cells and smashed against walls.

There seemed to be only one defense at these times of special abuse. Prisoners who cringed before the guards were kicked, beaten, spat upon. Prisoners who suddenly turned on the guards and struck out at them were taken away for hours of extreme torture or were killed. But those men fared best who went through the indignities calmly and stoically, without cringing or losing their tempers, apparently with an inner conviction that the Communist animal terror could not break them. The Communists could not cope with men, it seemed to me, who insisted on remaining more than the animals which Communists regard men to be.

Day after day I witnessed the torment and terror dealt out to my fellow prisoners. I, myself, being too useful to be submitted to more than the common humiliations, never knew when my turn might suddenly come. My work kept me busy from 7:00 A.M. to past midnight, and I had little time to let my thoughts wander too far back or too far ahead. I was aware, of course, that I never could leave this prison without undergoing the investigational process. On the one hand I dreaded to see it come, because it was bound to involve terror and ill treatment. On the other hand, I preferred an end, with fear, to fear without end.

Prison Diaries

Edward Kuznetsov

13th December

The trial is the day after tomorrow. Yesterday morning I changed my mind and began to write out a draft for my speech in court, in case I should decide to use it, after all. I've been scribbling non-stop for two days and I've only just now finished (10 o'clock). I haven't yet determined how I shall act in court. The fact that I have prepared something could very well be the decisive factor.

14th December

I have decided to copy my speech into this diary. While I am doing this I will be able to remove all the sharper political edges, and thus keep it down to a bare minimum. Here it is:

Before recounting the circumstances leading up to my attempt to leave the confines of the USSR illegally, I should like to draw the attention of the court to an exact description of the offence committed by myself and my friends. We were a prey to quite abnormal passions, and without a detailed analysis of all the motives that led to our being at the airport on the morning of 15th June, it is quite impossible to understand our case.

I ask the court to be patient, for I intend to be as thorough as I can.

So as not to digress, I shall keep to the text of the charges made against me:

"*Being* of anti-Soviet disposition, Kuznetsov entered, during the years 1969-70, into a criminal conspiracy with Butman...," then a little lower down: "Being convicted of anti-Soviet activities in 1962 and upon the termination of his punishment, he again began to involve himself in anti-Soviet activities..."

Concerning this sham invocation, "being...", which is used not unintentionally by those who have compiled these charges against me, I would like to reveal, albeit imperfectly, my true state of mind, which is here described with such ominous significance.

I was born in 1939; in 1956 I finished school, worked at a plant as a turner, served in the army, then studied at the Moscow University faculty of philosophy; in 1961 the KGB, considering that my social activities went beyond the bounds of those laid down by law, arrested me and estimated that the degree of digression of my behavior from that required was seven years. At first, on account of my naivete and youthful inability to comprehend the needs of the state, I was, I must confess, extremely taken aback by such a severe appraisal of the danger I was considered to represent to the state. A product of Soviet education, I had never gone farther than criticizing the Soviet regime within its own terms. A victim of youthful daydreaming, of searching for my own identity, and to some extent a prey to my own stormy passions and the schoolboy's understanding of ideology, I was still the tragic-comic victim of a system of myths. In no other way can I explain my lack of understanding of the severity of my sentence. A feeling that I had been wronged in *principle* by the injustice of this sentence played a not insignificant role in the formation of the views which I admit to being anti-Soviet.

But even in the concentration camp the ever-vigilant eye of "justice" did not leave me in peace. I do not mean the innumerable punishment cells and biannual sojourns at Vladimir prison; I refer to the breaking of the principle which is the cornerstone of any legislation, namely, that one cannot be tried twice for one and the same crime. In the spring of 1963, the Moscow City Court, for some reason which I do not know, reviewed my case and, "taking into account the prisoner's personality," sentenced me to be kept until the end of my term in a special regime camp, although, according to my first sentence, I had been sentenced to a restricted regime. A substantial difference, permit me to point out. Perhaps nine months later I discovered that this was an infringement of practically half-a-dozen articles. The decision of the court was quashed and I was given strict regime, which was again an infringement of those same half-dozen articles. But by this time I no longer looked for human logic in the action of the organs of repression.

Here it may be in order to characterize briefly my views, which I explained thoroughly during the investigation; the court may learn of them by reading the case documentation. I long ago grew out of active dislike of the existing regime. I think that the essential characteristics of the structure of the regime are to all intents and purposes immutable, and that the particular political culture of the Russian people may be classed as despotic. There are not many variations in this type of power structure, the framework of which was erected by Ivan the Terrible and by Peter the Great. I think the Soviet regime is the lawful heir of these widely differing Russian rulers. A Jew, with neither any inclination towards the wielding of power, nor with any love for meek resignation, nor nourishing any hope of seeing a radical democratization of an essentially repressive regime in the foreseeable future, and considering myself responsible—however indirectly—as a citizen of this country, for all of its abominations, I decided to leave the Soviet Union. I consider it not only impossible but unnecessary to fight against the Soviet regime. It fully answers the heartfelt wishes of a significant—but alas not the better—part of its population.

My mother, Zinaida Vasilyevna Kuznetsova, is a Russian, my father, Samuil Gerson, died in 1941 and was a Jew. It's very curious, but it was in 1953 precisely that my mother changed our family name—and therefore mine as well since I was a minor and under her tutelage—and took her maiden name, Kuznetsova.

Could I, a 16-year old brainless Young Communist, foresee how double-edged my yielding to my mother's insistence that I register (on receiving my internal passport) as a Russian would prove to be? Having observed the symptoms of antisemitism endemic among the people, and sometimes even foreseeing how these symptoms coincided with government policy in certain respects, I grew mature enough to form my own opinions and felt it essential that I personally join the ranks of the oppressed.

I grew up in a Russian family and had practically no knowledge whatso-ever of Jewish culture, nor did I know anything of the influence it had had on nearly every culture in the world. Therefore, my choice to live and be a Jew was dictated in the early stages by emotional considerations rather than by a conscious feeling of physical identity. Tsvetaeva says something of this: "Is it not a hundred times more worthy to be a wandering Jew? For the pogrom is as life itself to any human being who is worthy of the name."

About two months before I was freed from Vladimir prison I put in an application to the prison governor that I be registered as a Jew in the documents I would receive on leaving the prison. But my application was rejected on the grounds that my internal passport had been withdrawn upon my arrest. Later I asked the police to change the note in the paragraph on nationality, but at first they refused because I was under special surveillance, and then because I still had a criminal record and this could only be done after eight years had elapsed.

It fully suited the assimilators, of course, to treat me as a Jew, but nevertheless to count me as a Russian.

I will not conceal the fact that during the seven years I spent in confinement, I had become mentally exhausted, and when I was released my only wish was to be left alone. But then what? I was followed, supervised, summoned by the KGB, by the police, forced to take shelter where I could...I was registered in Strunino, Vladimir district. Sometimes the Strunino police gave me written permission to go and see my mother on Sundays, whereas the Moscow police advised me "not to be seen anywhere near her." So during these infrequent, though apparently quite legal, visits home I was compelled to hide myself and stay the night with friends. This was supposed to last eight years. Do not the motives behind my attempted emigration, which, with such crude tendentiousness are described in the charges against me as, "Being of an anti-Soviet disposition,"' now appear a great deal clearer?

In January, 1970, I went over to Riga to see my wife. In February we received our invitation from Israel, and we had to set about collecting the necessary documents to hand in to the Ovir* for obtaining permission to leave the country. The greatest problem of all was obtaining the employment reference: (can (not) cope with work, does (not) participate in communal life, morally (un)stable, ideologically (un)sound...) I know not whether this was an unconscious effort to humiliate us on the part of the great bureaucratic state machine or whether it was simply the fruit of the labor of one particular Party official. Whatever it was, every alternate word uttered by a specific number of the most sullen of Soviet citizens was to be my reference.

There are many different reasons for withholding this reference. One man is refused because he is in the army (Wulf)** ; a second—because he is studying at the VUZ*** , (Israel)****, and if he just so much as mentions this reference, he is likely to be expelled and packed off into the army, and neither during his military service nor for at least three years afterwards dare he bring up this subject; a third (Sylva) is refused—because she's just finished studying; a fourth—is just refused and no reason given. The most frequent method is that, in the absence of a written request for the reference from the Ovir, they cannot help you, and the Ovir refuses to send you this since, "it's you that need the reference not us". I personally know of a considerable number of people for whom the very word "reference" has become almost

---

* Soviet department of emigration.
** Vulf Zalmanson.
*** VUZ—Institute of Higher Education
**** Israel Zalmanson

a vulgarism. But an even larger number of people who wish to emigrate do not have sufficient courage to let it be known publicly. I am not speaking now of the inevitable dangers of such a course of action, for these remain only too clearly in people's minds and they are afraid of a repetition of those dark and dreadful pages of history.

Everybody knows well enough the inevitability—even though next time it may not be so overt—of repressive measures against the potential "traitor" (the men to whom you may bellow the length of a train compartment, "Why the hell don't you get off to your bloody Israel!" while everybody in the compartment looks on, and smiles their approval). As soon as your desire to emigrate becomes common knowledge, whether at work or in your apartment block, or in the police station, they don't let you forget it. Someone will say the word "Israel" and make an obscene gesture, or wedge a pencil into the dial of your telephone. How people split their sides whenever they hear the old joke: "Jews leaving for Israel, your train will depart from the *northern station!*"

At my place of work in Riga I could not get the reference I needed: I hadn't been working there long enough, they told me. I went to Moscow, then to Strunino, as I thought I had surely worked there long enough by now to be eligible for this necessary bit of paper. When I told the chief personnel officer I had come all the way from Riga especially for this reference, he was dumbfounded and said they could easily have sent it to me by post. "The trouble is that the institution which is asking for a reference insists it should say on it, 'For emigration and permanent residence in Israel.' " (The reason for this incidentally is quite simple—the reference as such is not particularly difficult to obtain.) I shall not bother to describe the reaction of the personnel officer to this, only that I was ordered to appear the next day before the chairman of the factory committee, who, after asking me a whole series of stupid questions like, "Why are you going to Israel?" and, "What are you going to do when you get there?" suddenly caught me unawares when he asked me, "What would happen if tomorrow my son was sent to fight for the Arabs: what would you do—shoot him?" I felt there was nothing I could do but answer him in kind: "Oh, has your son come back from Czechoslovakia already?" I didn't get the reference, need I say.

What do you do when you are everywhere so blatantly humiliated? You can wait year after year—which many people do—living in your suitcase and going through all the difficulties of trying to obtain the necessary documents, give them to the Ovir, and then explain in writing how you have relatives in Israel, Israel is your real homeland, that you have spiritual—national aspirations—and then receive answers like: "You are guaranteed living-quarters and work here, you are materially independent of your relatives who live in Israel, and therefore you have no grounds for permission to emigrate."

I was not prepared to accept this. In my opinion I had been denied my right to emigrate and felt I had the moral right to reply to a sequence of illegal acts by my infraction of the law as expressed in Art. 83, Criminal Code of the RSFSR. I have in mind illegal emigration, punishable by a term of up to three years. I declare that we have been falsely charged. We are charged with premeditated *activities to the detriment of the security of the USSR*. It is quite evident that the intention of each of us was emigration. During the preliminary investigation I attempted to explain as clearly as I could to each of my three investigators in turn, and to Procurator Ponomarev, exactly what the security of the USSR meant in this specific situation. Despite all their fantasies, I realized that their major concern was the harm that might be caused to the prestige of the USSR, for our escape might have been seized upon and made use of by hostile propaganda. Well, firstly, to be influenced in one's mode of conduct by attempting to forestall the slanderous propaganda of one's so-called enemies is not a very worthwhile occupation; and secondly, had any single one of us ever contemplated that the prestige of the USSR might have been increased by our actions, not one of us would have wavered for one moment. Neither the USSR nor its prestige ever had the slightest bearing on our activities or our intentions.

I have very little knowledge of jurisprudence (this is only my second trial, after all!) and when I was held in isolation during the investigation I was categorically refused any legal literature (I cannot even obtain the Constitution of the USSR!) and, therefore, I cannot give you any references or quotations. I would, however, like to direct the attention of the court to the book, "Especially Dangerous State Crimes", which was published in 1965 (its place of publication I do not know), in which it is stated that treason can be accomplished only with the express intention of causing detriment to the national security of the USSR. The investigation did not establish any such purpose in our case.

As far as our situation is concerned one can speak only of the eventual intent which, in my opinion, precludes treason.

Any government that has ratified the "Universal Declaration of Human Rights" (as the USSR has done) is obliged to guarantee these rights to each of its citizens in realistic terms, including Arts. 13, 14 and 15. It was only because my human rights were flagrantly denied me that I decided to flee abroad. It was above all an act of desperation.

We have not collected any information about the military potential of the

USSR, nor have we stolen any state secrets…I maintain that we should not be tried on any supposition as to how we might have acted abroad and as to how the propaganda of any foreign governments might have treated our flight. If one must speak of the prestige of the USSR then I have no doubt that any responsibility for impairing this must be borne by those who, having deprived us of the possibility of emigrating legally, provoked our attempt to emigrate illegally, and who now accuse us of treason. It is they who, by the very act of accusing us, must bear the weight of responsibility for any loss of prestige to their country. For in all civilized countries those who cross the frontier illegally are not considered as anything other than minor criminals. There can be no doubt that every government has the right to inflict punishment for any activity it considers hostile to itself, but to inflict punishment only as the result of concretely incriminating acts and irrespective of how those acts may be termed at some future date.

In the book *The Nuremburg Trial of the Nazi Judges,* published in 1970 by "Legal Literature", it is apparent that the officials of Hitler's judicial and legislative apparatus were tried, among other things, for sentencing to death people who attempted to flee from the Third Reich. Walter Brehm, ex-vice procurator-general, "People's Tribunal," admitted they had tried people who had attempted to flee abroad, solely on the supposition that they might, once having attained their destination, engaged in military operations harmful to the Reich. And this was in time of war! These people were tried on the supposition that they would act hostilely towards the Reich as soon as they had the opportunity of doing so.

The Military Tribunal recognized that the wide definition of treason operative in the Third Reich gave Nazi judges the opportunity of pronouncing death sentences for actions constituting only a minor offence in the eyes of the rest of mankind; the Military Tribunal recognized that such a definition of treason was a military crime and against mankind.

Without denying the fact that we attempted to flee the country, I categorically declare that we cannot be considered traitors and I affirm that such an accusation is the result of an illegally widened definition of treasonable activities.

Concerning Art. 93-I of the Criminal Code of the RSFSR (on large-scale misappropriation of state property). Not one of us had the intention of misappropriating the aircraft. We were convinced that it would have been returned to its rightful owner. Therefore there can be no question of misappropriation! The crime in question was the attempted temporary removal of state property, and this is certainly not misappropriation. If somebody in a rush to attend a Komsomol* meeting were to take possession of another person's motor vehicle and then, on attaining his destination, were to leave it in the middle of a square on the presumption that it would soon be discovered and returned to its owner, then this does not constitute stealing. Although until recently this was considered stealing, a special article appeared in the Criminal Code concerning responsibility for taking possession of another person's car.

In our case the hijacking of an aircraft can be considered a similar action if one takes into consideration the relationship of the subject of the crime to the object. One might object that up to now there has been no article about hijacking aircraft, but it must surely appear soon...And what about steamships, steam engines and small space rockets? Yes, so far there is no relevant article. But this does not mean one can apply an article by analogy, for this was recently forbidden by Soviet legislation. To be specific, it was recognized that the practice of condemning car-hijackers as misappropriators was a mistake. Our case is analogous. It is true that there are no articles about hijacking aircraft. This means that there operates in effect the well-known Roman principle, "Where there is no law there can be no crime."

I demand that we be tried for what we did—attempting to hijack an aircraft—and not for stealing, which we never even contemplated.

In order to illustrate my approach to the matter I will be so bold as to impose upon the court a little parable I have invented, though bearing in mind that fact that, while it cannot possibly exhaust all aspects of the case under discussion, it may nevertheless help to throw a little light on it:

A man was told that he had the right to receive a certain sum of money, but that he would never be allowed to even wish to lay his hand upon it. Be that as it may, he once came to the bank. The cashier rudely reprimanded him as though he were some impudent villain and promptly slammed the window shut in his face. This happened seven times. The man was not, however, imbued with the correct measure of Christian humility and forgiveness and, still hoping to receive the money owed to him, made an attempt to break into the cashier's office and finally broke his door down, with the assistance of, shall we say, the office door handle, the property of the establishment in question. Just when he was at that stage in his crime, he felt his hands being forced behind his back. He, poor wretch, had never imagined, and certainly couldn't have cared less if he had, that the accountant in the office next door had been plotting against the cashier and might turn any insignificant scandal to his own advantage. The criminal considers himself guilty only of being over-credu-

---

* Communist Youth Organization

lous, of taking too seriously any rumors he might have heard concerning his right to receive a certain sum of money, and of being annoyed when he discovered that this right was merely fictitious, as long as he were not prepared to show the necessary humility. He is, however, charged with aiding and abetting the hostile accountant, treason towards the establishment, and stealing an office door-handle. When he is tried he does his best to defend himself, but, of course, is unable to.

For myself, I am charged, in addition to keeping and duplicating anti-Soviet literature, with intent to subvert the political regime of the country. Well, I have spoken already of my attitude towards the Soviet regime and of the reasons why I never had any intentions of trying to subvert it. I will add only the following. The regime of this country is, in my view, a tyrannical religion with the state as its God. It would not be fitting for me to speak now of the possibility of secularizing Russia. I can speak only of the mixture of pagan cults which exist in this primarily religious atmosphere. For every religion is characterized by violence at the very dawn of its existence; later it matures and is content only with burning its heretics, in a figurative sense. It is unintelligent to encourage the substitution of a younger religion for an already decadent one.

A handful of intellectual oppositionists—a phenomenon as characteristic of Russia as it is alien to her national traditions—cannot and will not change things.

The number of rebels will grow, or diminish, as the political barometer changes. These may be mostly young people, attempting to compensate for something they feel is lacking in their lives and who finally find fulfillment in marriage or a suitable reservoir into which they can drain all their languishing energies. Or old men, gone grey on the field of battle. One simply cannot prevent people loving freedom. If today a man looks down at those who read "Samizdat", (underground writing), then tomorrow, if he knows his friends can be locked up for reading it, he will also take to reading it...For that part of society which thinks looks with disgust at the prostitution of talent and ability.

Should anyone ever have told me he had similar views on the existing situation I would have quite understood his desire to leave holy Russia. Do you really understand me? I am a Jew and I want to live in Israel, in the land of my forefathers, in the land of the greatest of all nations. This does not mean Russia is not my homeland, but Israel is my homeland too, and it is Israel I have chosen. For, you see, in my hierarchical system of values, the question of which is my homeland is not uppermost. Uppermost is freedom, and this is why Israel draws me—it is my *Homeland and my Freedom*.

I am accused of keeping and propagating two books: *Memoirs* by Litvinov,* and *Russian Political Leaders,* by Shub.** But I had Lenin in my library too. Yet for some reason I am not accused of propagating Leninism in order to consolidate the regime. I have read Lenin, I have read Litvinov and Shub and many more besides. I have read them because I like reading, because I have by nature an inquiring mind; I have read them neither to subvert nor to consolidate anything. Therefore, if you consider these books to be slanderous, then you must try me for keeping, reading and propagating them only under Article 190-I. Although I have never seen any list of forbidden books, I readily agree that Shub's book is anti-Soviet, but only to the extent that any book on the apostles and saints of the Revolution is bound to be such.

I am inclined to refer Litvinov's *Memoirs* to that category of books which are "not recommended" (apparently such do exist) to be read by the loyal Soviet subject; in which case I would recommend the court to apply only the Lithuanian equivalent of Art. 190-I, Criminal Code of the RSFSR, which differs from Art. 70 only in its inclusion of eventual intent to subvert the Soviet regime.

I do not regard these books as truly anti-Soviet, and this is partially borne out by the fact that I printed them on a machine, an example of the print of which was secretly taken on the orders of the KGB Lieutenant Fedotov by A.V. Prokhorov (agent's designation—"the student"), who was resident up to November, 1969 in Apartment 4, Ordzhonikidze Street, Strunino.

Permit me to sum up briefly:

I can only regard it as just if I be charged under Articles 83 and 72 of the RSFSR Criminal Code, and under the relevant article in the Lithuanian Code, which is equivalent to Art. 190-I RSFSR Criminal Code.

How can one not approve the UN's demand that hijacking be combatted on the condition that all member-states do not stand in the way of those citizens who wish to leave their country, even in times of peace?

The generally accepted definition of air piracy is that of an action in which an aircraft is seized in mid-air thereby creating an extremely dangerous situation for crew and passengers. Our intention was to seize the aeroplane on the ground, remove the pilot from the controls and take off with no outsider on board—only "traitors", only our own people.

My only real fault is that I do not want to live in the USSR. Why do you need me here? Why do you need me to gather in your wonderful harvests, to

---

* Forged "Memoirs" of Maxim Litvinov, published in the West.
** David Shub, "Portrait of Political Leaders...", New York, 1969.

reap the gains of your brilliant successes, to share in your heroic exploits in outer space! Let me go, let me go!

I am sure the cement of Communism is sufficiently tainted with my blood (figuratively speaking, of course!); nor could I possibly object if you gave me a place in any detailed history of Russia that was to be printed.

Karamzin, in his *History of the Russian State,* gives passing mention to some exceedingly conscientious but powerless historical individuals, "Prince V. Ya. Borovsky, who did not wish to remain in Russia after such a disaster, left for the land of Lithuania."

Much of what I have said is perhaps verbose, confused and beside the point. I am sure there is much in it that is unnecessary, superfluous, perhaps there are too many literary allusions…At the moment I cannot criticize what I've written—the umbilical cord tying me to my notes still throbs painfully. There's no point in worrying too much. Lights out.

My Testimony

Anatoly Marchenko

Once more I was taken back to prison, to my cell. To tell the truth, the length of my sentence made no impression on me. It was only later that each year of imprisonment stretched out into days and hours and it seemed that six years would never come to an end. Much later I also found out that the label of "traitor to the Homeland" had crippled me not for six years but for life. At the time, however, I had only one sensation, and that was that an injustice had been committed, a legalized illegality, and that I was powerless; all I could do was to gather and store my outrage and despair inside me, storing it up until it exploded like an overheated boiler.

I recalled the empty rows of seats in the chamber, the indifferent voices of the judge and prosecutor, the court secretary chewing on a roll the whole time, the silent statues of the guards. Why hadn't they let anyone into the court, not even my mother? Why had no witnesses been called? Why wasn't I given a copy of the sentence? What did they mean: "You can't have a copy of the sentence, it's secret"? A few minutes later a blue paper was pushed through the little trapdoor for food: "Sign this to say that you've been informed of your sentence." I signed it and that was that. The sentence was final, with no right of appeal.

I went on hunger strike. I wrote a statement protesting against the trial and sentence, pushed it through the food trap and refused to accept any food. For several days I took nothing into my mouth but cold water. Nobody paid any attention. The warders, after listening to my refusal, would calmly remove my portion of food and soup bowl and bring them back again in the evening. Again I would refuse. Three days later the warders entered my cell with a doctor and commenced the operation known as 'forced artificial feeding'. My hands were twisted behind my back and handcuffed, then they stuffed a spreader into my mouth, stuck a hose down my gullet and began pouring the feeding mixture—something greasy and sweet—in through a funnel at the top. The warders said: 'Call off your hunger strike. You won't gain anything by it and in any case we won't let you lose weight.' The same procedure was repeated on the following day.

I called off my hunger strike. And I never did get a reply to my protest.

Several days later a warder came to fetch me. He led me via a staircase and various corridors to the first floor and directed me through a door lined with black oilcloth. A little nameplate said: "Prison Governor." In the office inside sat the prison governor at his desk, beneath a large portrait of Dzerzhinsky;* on the couch were two men familiar to me from the investigation of my case, the legal inspector of prisons and the head of the investigation department. The fourth man was a stranger. One glance at him and I shuddered, so unnatural and repulsive was his appearance: a tiny little eggshaped body, miniscule legs that barely reached to the floor and the thinnest scraggy little neck crowned by an enormous flattened globe—his head. The slits of his eyes, the barely discernible little nose and the thin smiling mouth were sunk in a sea of taut, yellow, gleaming, dough. How could that neck hold such a load?

They told me that this was the Deputy Public Prosecutor of the Turkmen Republic, and invited me to sit down. The conversation was conducted in an informal and familiar tone. They asked me how I felt and whether I had ended my hunger strike. Thanking them for their touching delicacy and interest I informed them that it was ended and asked in turn: "Can you tell me, please, when and where I will be sent?"

"You are going to a Komsomol** site. You'll be a Komsomol worker,' answered the monster, absolutely wreathed in smiles as he enjoyed his little joke.

I felt unbearably revolted. On me, who had been sentenced by them for treason to my country, it somehow grated to hear them utter these words here, in this office, and to see their cynical sneers. They all knew perfectly well what it meant. And I knew too.

Back in my cell I thought of the various sites I had worked on. Outside every one there had been a camp, barbed wire, control towers, guards and "Komsomol workers in reefer-jackets." *** I recalled how as a nineteen-year-old youth I had been sent on a two-month assignment to Bukhtarma power station. The quarters where we free workers lived were at Serebryanka, some way

---

* Founder of thee Soviet secret police, called the Cheka, then GPU, in his time.
** The Komsomol is the Soviet youth organization.
*** Reefer jacket is the ironic term used for the flimsy cotton-quilted jackets issued to prisoners.

away from the site, and the camp was there too. Both we and the camp convicts were taken to each shift and back again by train. The "free" train consisted of five or six ancient four-wheeled wagons. It used to stop about 50 yards from the guardhouse and then we would show our passes to the soldier on guard duty and walk through the entrance passage. After this they would open up the gates and the endless train with the cons on board would roll straight inside the site perimeter. This one was not like ours with its hopeless little four-wheelers, but consisted of big, strong, eight-wheeled cars into which the cons were packed like sardines. On every brake platform sat a pair of tommy gunners and the rear of the train was brought up by an open platform full of soldiers. The soldiers would open the doors, drive out the cons, herd them away from the cars and line them up five deep. Then began the count by fives: the first five, the second, the third, the fifteenth, the fifty-second, the hundred and fifth…counting and recounting. Suddenly there would be a mistake and they'd start counting all over again. Shouts, curses and yet another recount. After a thorough check the cons would go to their work places. Then, when the shift was over, the same thing would take place in reverse order. I had worked side by side with them, these "Komsomol workers in reefer-jackets." I used to get my pay, go to dances on my days off and never think a thing of it. Only one incident had embedded itself in my memory.

One day at the beginning of August one of the watch towers had suddenly started firing in the direction of the river Irtysh. Everybody downed tools and ran to the river bank, crowding up against the fence, with the free workers and cons all mixed up together. They tried to drive us away, of course, but we stayed put and gaped. A swimmer was already more than halfway across the river, closer to the opposite bank. We could see clearly that he was having difficulty swimming and that he was trying to go as fast as possible. It was a con. It seemed he had bided his time till the dredger stopped working and then had crawled through the pipe and plunged into the Irtysh some way out from the shore. They hadn't noticed him at first and by the time they had opened fire, he was already a long way off. The guard launch had already set off in pursuit and now was about to catch up with the fugitive; it was only about a dozen yards behind, but the officer with the pistol in his hand was for some reason holding his fire. "Well, if he shoots and kills him and the con goes to the bottom, how's he going to prove afterwards that he hasn't escaped?" explained the cons in the crowd. "He's got to have either a living man or a body to show them."

Meanwhile the fugitive reached the far shore, stood up and staggered a few steps. But the launch's bow had already struck the stones and the officer leapt out and found himself within two paces of the con. I saw him raise his pistol and shoot him in the legs. The con collapsed. Some tommy gunners ran up and as they stood there and in full view of the crowd on the opposite bank the officer fired several times into the prostrate prisoner. The crowd gasped and somebody swore obscenely.

The body was dragged over the stones like a sack and tossed into the launch. The launch set off downriver in the direction of the camp.

Now I couldn't help but think of Bukhtarma and this incident, and also other sites. No matter where they sent me now I would always be a "Komsomol worker," I would be soaked and frozen during the checks, I would live behind barbed wire, I would be guarded by armed guards with sheepdogs; and if I couldn't bear it and tried to escape, I would be shot down just like that fellow in the Irtysh.

Translated by Michael Scammell

Vladivostok Transit Camp

Elinor Lipper

1.

Prisoners whose destination was Kolyma in northeastern Siberia were shipped to Vladivostok from prisons all over the country, and were kept in the transit camp until they could be sent on to Kolyma by freighter. But between December and May all communication by water with Kolyma is cut off by ice, and since every ship can carry "only" seven thousand prisoners, the prisoners often have to wait half a year and more at the transit camp. I spent six and a half months at Vladivostok.

The transit camp was a highly instructive place to be, especially for those who still held the illusion that the mad fury of the purges was only a local excess. Here, in this reservoir for prisoners from all over the country, was palpable proof that not a corner of the Soviet Union had been spared in the mass arrests. Everywhere the same methods of interrogation were being applied. Everywhere the same arbitrary procedure was followed: the first to be arrested were the erstwhile functionaries of governmental, economic, and military agencies, then everybody who had had official or friendly relationships with them, and finally everybody who was related to them by blood or marriage.

In the eyes of every prisoner you could read the question, Why? and none of them had the answer. In the Moscow prison the faces of people had worn a look of frightened astonishment, of incredulous amazement that men could so torment their fellow creatures, that men could be so cruel to one another and inflict such shame upon the innocent. Here in Vladivostok the characteristic expression was different; it was an expression of fear and bitterness.

It was not only my own fate that filled me with bitterness, nor was it only shame at the recollection that but a year and a half ago I had praised and defended this Soviet system as progressing toward paradise on earth. More strongly than anything else I felt the gnawing pain of helpless pity for these patient Russian, Caucasian, Tartar, Central Asiatic, Mongolian, and Siberian villagers who accepted their uncomprehended fate with the dumb submissiveness of beaten animals. "No one is ever safe from prison or the beggar's bowl," was all they could say about it. That ancient Russian proverb has kept its tragic applicability to this day.

There were two zones in the Vladivostok transit camp, one for criminals and the other for counterrevolutionaries. The criminals were assigned to all types of labor, received better food, lived in heated barracks, and each one had a cot, a straw mattress, and blankets of his own. Some of them were given passes and could move about with relative freedom. The zone for the counterrevolutionaries was divided into several smaller zones, each of which was surrounded by a cluster of barbed-wire fences. The wooden gate was always shut and there were watch towers at the corners of the enclosure. At night brilliant floodlights illuminated the entire area and patrols of guards incessantly made the rounds with their trained dogs.

In the unheated and frequently unlighted barracks the counterrevolutionaries slept on two or three decks of unplaned planks and had no mattresses or blankets.

Hygiene was out of the question. The criminals had access to water at all times, but a far too small number of counterrevolutionaries were assigned to the water detail. Water was brought in pails from a distance of a hundred to a hundred and fifty yards, and only once a day. The tiny water ration for each prisoner was scarcely adequate for drinking, let alone for washing. Now and then the female prisoners were able to beg a few extra pails, and then furious battles for water broke out among them. Screaming hysterically, they fell upon the pails, snatched them from each other, pulled each other's hands, and wept. And always the same group would look on sadly, standing at a distance, gazing at the water with timid longing; and always the same tough customers were the ones who got it.

Two or three times a month we were sent to the bath, where again there was a battle for the insufficient tubs. Those who seized one first were again the strongest and most forward women. They were able to wash in peace, while the others waited cursing, for by the time their turn came the water had usually been turned off. Often we had to go out into the dressing room with our bodies still covered with soapsuds. Meanwhile our clothes were being deloused. But since the disinfection chambers were run by criminals, who have careless work standards, the temperature was never brought up to the hundred degrees centigrade which is necessary to kill the lice. Usually the heat in the disinfection chambers was just right to make the lice feel comfortable and stimulated.

In the end we became so louse-ridden that we gave up trying to kill the lice. Now and then we would reach under our blouses when we could no longer endure the itching, fish out a handful of the vermin, and throw them away. As often as not they landed not on the floor, but on other prisoners.

Since lice are carriers of spotted typhus, a frightful typhus epidemic broke out in the camp in 1938. It carried off thousands of prisoners. The camp infirmary was so crowded with the sick, who lay on every cot and along all the floors of the wards and corridors, that any kind of care was impossible. Some of the women from our barrack were called in to act as nurses. Their chief occupation was counting the dead who had escaped the misery of the gold mines which awaited the others.

In silence we stared through the barbed wire at the hearses which drove out of the camp every night. Piled high with naked bodies, the load tied on with cord and covered with canvas, the trucks drove out, carrying the victims to eternal freedom. As usual there was a reaction from Moscow only after the epidemic in Vladivostok had cost tens of thousands of lives. Then the camp commandant was arrested. His successor carried through a thoroughgoing delousing program so that the epidemic gradually subsided in 1939.

Few Soviet citizens are fastidious as far as bedbugs are concerned. Their presence is taken to be in the order of nature, for there is scarcely any place in the country that is not overrun with them. But the bugs in Vladivostok transit camp became a legend which was told with vivid details to future groups of prisoners, who had never been through that camp.

The barracks were so overrun with the bedbugs that sleep was almost impossible at night, when the creatures are most active. From the walls and the planks, above and beneath us, they came crawling; they fell upon the tormented bodies of the prisoners, who twisted and writhed at the stinging bites and tried to catch them. But no matter how many were crushed, they were always replaced by new hordes and the struggle would last until dawn, when the exhausted victims were at last able to sleep. In spring, when it got warmer, the hordes of bedbugs attacking us increased steadily, until at last we decided to sleep on the ground outside the barrack. And then there took place a spectacle that we watched with speechless horror. From the empty building the hordes of bedbugs marched in close formation, a long, dark, crawling procession crossing the threshold after their sickened, incredulous victims.

Those were the bedbugs of Vladivostok; they multiplied without let or hindrance.

Everyone in the transit camp of Vladivostok had to resign himself to being shipped off to Kolyma sooner or later. Nobody knew anything about the place. "The end of the world," some said, "completely cut off from everything." Then one day a geography book found its way into our barrack and was passed from hand to hand. We skipped over the material on fisheries and the fur-bearing animals in which the Kolyma district was rich, and we paid little attention to the fact that there were gold and silver mines in the area. What was impressed upon our minds forever were the three sentences about the cold. "Even in summer the earth here thaws out only to a depth of eight and a half inches. The lowest temperatures on earth have been recorded in this region. In winter the temperature drops to minus seventy degrees centigrade (-94 degrees F.) and even lower."

We became very quiet and thoughtful after reading that. Next morning I saw the girl who slept next to me, a young pianist from Moscow, busily searching through her suitcase. After a while she came up with a pair of thick woolen stockings which she offered to me. "You must take them," she said. "Last night I had a dream about you with frozen feet."

The following winter, when I tramped through the snow in Kolyma, I returned again and again to the gratifying thought that I still had Lillian's woolen stockings. I kept putting off the day for wearing them on the theory that I could still endure the present cold and it might get still colder. The presence of those stockings, the mere possibility of wearing them, comforted and warmed me. Finally the day came when I opened my knapsack—improvised out of a piece of blanket—to get the stockings. The stockings were gone; they had been stolen long ago. From that day on I felt the cold worse than before.

Lillian and I were separated in Vladivostok. One of her legs was shorter than the other, and she was among the group of invalids and cripples who were to be sent back to Mariinsk in Central Siberia, an invalid camp where such prisoners were permitted to die slowly. There is no camp drearier and more hopeless than an invalid camp, as I heard later on from many eyewitnesses. A medically certified invalid does not have to work, but he receives only fourteen ounces of bread a day. Mad with hunger, the cripples will battle over a fishhead in the garbage heap of the camp kitchen. Unlike all other prisoners whose only thought is how to get a day off from work, the invalids report to work again and again, hoping in this way to receive a little more bread. But they are always sent back by the foremen on the grounds that they are unable to do the work.

Transfer to an invalid camp does not mean that a prisoner serves the rest of his term there. Medical commissions regularly comb the invalid camps, declare some of the inmates fit for work, and send them to the general camps. These in their turn send their waste human material to the invalid camps, so that there is a constant interchange between the two types of camp.

I do not know what became of Lillian. She had an eight-year sentence for "counterrevolutionary Trotskyist activity" because she had been briefly acquainted with a young cellist, a German exile who had spent three years in Nazi camps for illegal Communist activity and had then escaped to the Soviet Union in 1936. In 1937 he was arrested and convicted as a Trotskyist. Lillian's husband, a resident of Moscow, had repudiated her. Nevertheless, she never doubted for a moment that he still loved her and she bore him no ill will for the repudiation. She knew what it would have meant had he refused to do it: the sacrifice of his artistic career as a composer and teacher of music at best, prison at worst. Lillian was one of the few prisoners who received a package from home during the winter of 1938 in Vladivostok. Among all the wonderful things her mother had solicitously packed was a tiny package wrapped in letter paper and marked "Vitamin C." That was all. But this tiny notation in her husband's handwriting, on his letter paper, meant as much to her as a long, ardent letter; it was a silent message from a suffering man that he still loved her.

When the invalids departed for Mariinsk, those of us who remained behind lost our last hope of escaping Kolyma. During the spring sowing a few hundred prisoners were sent to the nearby *sovkhoz* (state farm) of Dubininsk to plant potatoes, but they returned to the camp a few weeks later. They came back late at night, a queer, stumbling, groping procession of people all clinging to one another, for most of the women had been struck with night blindness. The doctors eventually located some cod-liver oil and this mass attack of night blindness was cleared up.

Early in May 1939 the first rumors of a ship waiting for us at the port trickled through. It was the steam freighter *Dalstroi,* and one bright, warm day we vanished into its hold. There were seven thousand prisoners, among them five hundred women in a separate, partitioned-off section.

During the entire voyage, which lasted a week, no member of the guard or the ship's crew ever entered the prisoners' hold. They were afraid to, especially when a large number of murderers and bandits were being transported, since they were an insignificant, though heavily armed, minority compared to the number of prisoners. They stood with raised guns, ready to fire, when the prisoners were let out on deck in small groups to use the toilet. None of them took any account of what went on below decks. As a result, during all such voyages the criminals put across a reign of terror. If they want the clothing of any of the counterrevolutionaries, they take it from him. If the counterrevolutionary offers any resistance, he is beaten up. The old and weak are robbed of their bread. On every transport ship a number of prisoners die as a result of such treatment.

In the course of every voyage some counterrevolutionaries attempt suicide by jumping overboard. Usually they drown quietly. Some of them attempt the leap while the ship is passing through the narrow Strait of Tartary, a few miles from Sakhalin Island. Here they may manage to swim to shore or be rescued by a fishing vessel. In such cases the ship is stopped, and if the fugitive cannot be picked up, he is shot.

In the fall of 1939 the freighter *Djurma* went to sea with a shipment of prisoners. The criminals succeeded in breaking through the wall of the hold and getting at the provisions. They robbed the stores and then, to wipe out the traces, set the storeroom on fire. There was a frightful panic among the prisoners who were locked in the hold of the burning ship. The fire was held in check, but the *Djurma* entered port still burning.

Early in December 1939 the freighter *Indigirka*, the last ship of the season, left the port of Magadan. There were a number of free citizens on board as well as prisoners who were being released from Kolyma. There was a Russian woman prisoner among them, and there was also a German Communist named Erna D, former secretary of Ernst Thalmann and Wilhelm Pieck, who had been sentenced by a Moscow military tribunal to fifteen years of penal servitude and who was now being turned over to the Nazis in honor of the Stalin-Hitler pact of friendship.

But the Soviet and the German police waited in vain for their victims. The *Indigirka* never arrived in the port of Vladivostok. Lashed by gales, it went off its course and was finally wrecked on the underwater portion of an iceberg. A Japanese steamer saved two hundred of the passengers. Erna D was not among them; she had been washed overboard and drowned. But the workers in all countries have a short memory. Who wonders about the thousands of sincere antifascists who did not die in the war or in Nazi concentration camps, but in Soviet prisons and camps?

The people who were rescued by the Japanese were taken to Vladivostok and turned over to the Soviet authorities whose first action was to subject them to a severe interrogation concerning their stay aboard the Japanese vessel. The Russian woman prisoner told about the adventures of the *Indigirka* to the prisoners awaiting transportation from Vladivostok, and they in turn brought the story to us at Magadan.

In 1944 several hundred young girls came to Kolyma. They were the so-called ukazniki, sent out here for unauthorized absences from a war factory, or for some similar minor offense. During the war the number of guards was cut down everywhere, and on the ships as well; moreover, the guards had to put on civilian clothes during the passage through Japanese waters, since the Japanese would allow no military personnel to pass. The criminals, who formed the greater part of the human freight aboard this ship, had an absolutely free hand in the hold. They broke through the wall into the room where the female prisoners were kept and raped all the women who took their fancy. A few male prisoners who tried to protect the women were stabbed to death. Several old men had their bread snatched from them day after day, and died of starvation. One of the criminals, who appropriated a woman whom the leader of the band had marked for his own, had his eyes put out with a needle. When the ship arrived in Magadan and the prisoners were driven out of the hold, fifteen were missing; they had been murdered by the criminals during the voyage and the guards had not lifted a finger. The upshot of this particularly glaring scandal was that after the facts became known in Magadan, the commander of the ship's guard was called on the carpet and arrested.

We lay squeezed together on the tarred floor of the hold because the criminals had taken possession of the plank platform. If one of us dared to raise her head, she was greeted by a rain of fish heads and entrails from above. When any of the seasick criminals threw up, the vomit came down upon us. At night, the men criminals bribed the guard, who was posted on the stairs to the hold, to send over a few women for them. They paid the guard in bread that they had stolen from their fellow prisoners.

Mental

Biographies

Born in Moscow in 1953, **ALEXANDER PODRABINEK** worked on the text of *Punitive Medicine* for more than three years—beginning in 1973; at the time he was a paramedic in the Moscow Ambulance Service. The secret police confiscated the final version with documentation; in the late 1970s, for this work being smuggled to the West, Podrabinek was exiled to Siberia.

In the foreword, dissident Alexander Ginzburg says the book summarizes "these inhuman experiences, these experiments conducted by animals on human beings."

Alexander Solzhenitsyn has described such treatment as "psychic murder [and] a variation of the gas chamber and yet even more cruel, for the torments of the debilitated are more insidious and more lasting."

Podrabinek's 1980 *Punitive Medicine*—a history and factual accounting of psychiatric repression—has done perhaps more to expose the abuses of "special psychiatric hospitals" to crush resistance to Communism than any other book.

Born in 1907 to a Ukrainian peasant, **PETRO GRIGORENKO** grew up as an ardent, idealistic Bolshevik. A beggar, he rose quickly to privileged positions in the Communist hierarchy—joining the Party in 1927 and the Red Army in the 1930s; in World War II he was a much-decorated general.

Following Stalin's death, Grigorenko moved from being an uncritical apparatchik to being an undeviating critic of the Soviet regime; he openly declared himself opposed to Khrushchev's policies.

The Party stripped him of his rank in 1964 and confined him for five years in special-regime psychiatric hospitals.

In 1977, while Grigorenko was on a trip to the U.S. with his wife Zinaida, the Party revoked his citizenship. He died in New York in 1987.

His book *Memoirs* appeared in 1982.

A native of Kiev, **VALERIY TARSIS** was born in 1906. He made his living as a writer and translator.

His novel *The Bluebottle* appeared in England under a pseudonym. Two months after its publication, Tarsis was arrested and confined in a Moscow insane asylum. A furor ensued in the Western press, and the authorities released him.

Tarsis continued to write—living on the meager earnings of his wife and daughter. Shortly before the fall of Khrushchev, he managed to smuggle the autobiographical novel *Ward 7* out of the country for publication in 1965.

Punitive Medicine

Alexander Podrabinek

1.

Punitive medicine has two types of compulsory treatment—that in special psychiatric hospitals (SPH's) and that in general psychiatric hospitals (GPH's). Let us follow a prisoner on his way to these institutions and then back to freedom. Let us imagine ourselves walking on the wide, well-trodden path of punitive medicine—the path to an SPH.

Everything begins with the arrest. Until the decision of the pretrial investigation official to order an examination, our prisoner is just an ordinary prisoner, one among thousands. While he is answering the interrogators' questions, or evading them, or refusing to answer any questions at all, the investigators are industriously amassing evidence of his mental incapacity. Sometimes it happens that only during the course of an investigation does the KGB decide to put the prisoner away in an SPH, and then the collection of evidence begins later, and the investigation drags on slowly. But it also happens that, even before his arrest, the man is already destined for an SPH, and then the successful collection of evidence depends on his behavior from the very first steps of his life as a prisoner. For an experienced Soviet psychiatrist, it does not matter *how* the prisoner behaves; the charming advantage of Soviet psychiatry consists precisely in the fact that any form of behavior can be interpreted as "clearly abnormal." Indeed, one needs skill and experience, but the savants of the Serbsky Institute of Forensic Psychiatry have plenty of that.

At the time of the arrest, our protagonist will not exclaim Solzhenitsyn's "Me? What for?" As a rule, he already knows "what for." Having collected his will and strength, he will protest, he will appeal, he will demand that legality be observed. In the near future his behavior will certainly be evaluated as "litigation delirium," but—he does not suspect what is going on—not yet anyway. At times our protagonist knows that they will come to take him, and he is prepared to be arrested. He does not demand justice, observance of the law; he does not bristle; he silently accepts what is happening, for he understands its inevitability. Perhaps he already sees himself in an SPH, but he thinks it unworthy of his dignity to demand humaneness from these *unpeople*. Indeed, his silence will shortly be evaluated as emotional poverty, pathological subjectivity (autism); but what can he do? The officials experienced in these procedures do not chase after symptoms but instead cleverly twist the interpretation of any gesture in the direction needed.

The arrest is followed by a search. The search can also supply the investigation with some required materials. After confiscating banned Samizdat literature, the investigator sees, for instance, a handbook on psychiatry in the bookcase. That's just fine! Interest in psychiatry can be a symptom of a serious mental illness! Or, God forbid, a Chekist will stumble upon a personal diary. This represents an accumulation of symptoms and is the best evidence of a severe mental illness, even for a mediocre medical punisher! Many things, unsuspected by the uninitiated, can be extracted during a search for the needs of punitive psychiatry.

After the arrest and lengthy search, our detainee is put in a windowless van and taken to a pretrial incarceration cell or to a prison, say the Lefortovo Prison in Moscow. This prison is called "the committee jail" (from the "Committee for State Security," which is what "KGB" stands for). People arrested on political charges are held there, as well as currency speculators since the day the KGB began investigating illegal currency operations. The Lefortovo Prison (a four story building shaped like the letter "K") enjoys a reputation as "the model prison," and for good reason. Most cells (7.3 by 16.5 feet) are designed for three people. Each cell has a toilet bowl (not a *parasha*!) and a radiator for central heating. The prison also has a good library where one can occasionally even find banned publications which were mistakenly not eliminated, as well as some antiquarian volumes. Black bread is provided in Lefortovo in unrestricted quantities. According to one source, the Lefortovo Prison is primarily investigative (pretrial); according to another source, it is a term-serving prison. Both are probably correct. Prestigious criminals and foreigners do their time in Lefortovo. The average enemy of the people stays there only during pretrial investigation. From any point of view, the Lefortovo Prison is considered the "best" Moscow prison. As one of its former inmates wittily put it, "Once in this jail, you don't ever wanna leave." Leave for a concentration camp, not freedom, is what he meant.

Three days after incarceration, our detainee is officially charged with anti-

Soviet agitation and propaganda or dissemination of slanderous fabrications, and the like, and from now on he is referred to as "the accused."

He is taken to interrogations, confrontations, investigative experiments. His fingerprints are taken; he is photographed frontally and in profile. The investigator tries to persuade him to tell everything because they "already know everything anyway." The investigator explains that only a candid confession can alleviate his lot. He urges the accused to think about his relatives. Sit back, relax, and have a cigarette. Maximum attention and care. A KGB interrogator is the best friend of the accused. Those who bought it bitterly regretted it afterward. They forgot that today's KGBist is a kid brother of yesterday's Chekist whose hands were in blood up to his shoulders. The kid brother is not allowed to hang the person under investigation on the rack and pull his fingernails out with pliers, but he is required to come up with "good results." Having obtained even insignificant information from the accused, the investigator stops playing placid games and starts using this information to blackmail his victim. He declares to the accused that he "cracked" and nothing would make any difference now. His honor is besmirched, and he will not be spared. Now tell us everything and instead of seven years of severe regimen, you will get a year in exile—it's not all that bad, is it? Some people do tell everything. Those who have any courage left deny everything they said during an interrogation at the trial, because they suddenly realize what an abyss has opened up in front of them. No matter what, the information is used by the KGB. Now the investigator may blackmail, promise to arrange a "happy life" for the relatives of the accused, or Article 64 of the national *Penal Code* and the death penalty.

It is at this point that the fate of the accused is decided: camp or SPH. Of course the best way not to say something that one will regret later is not to say anything at all. That is precisely what some people do. But an investigation without testimony of the accused, without his signature on interrogation records, looks unpresentable even in a Soviet court. That is why it is tempting to send the stubborn accused through the channels of punitive medicine. In this case, it is easy to put up with the absence of testimony, because such absence is explained by the mental instability of the accused. The only requirement is a decision by the examination commission. The obliging professors of the Serbsky Institute are always ready to write such a decision, and the fates of those not intended for SPH's from the very beginning are decided in this way.

Those who were meant to go to an SPH even before they were arrested are dealt with in a much simpler way. A brief interrogation is enough to interpret every word of the accused as a manifestation of mental illness. If the accused is intransigent, so much the better: this is an unmistakable sign of abnormality. The investigator will definitely summon the relatives of the accused and ask them if they have ever noticed a certain peculiarity in his behavior. Were there any cases of mental illness in the family? Did his grandmother suffer from schizophrenia? Did he have a concussion during childhood? Does he get along with his wife? Did he have a mistress? If not, this is suspicious: is he really normal? If he is a bachelor, this is also suspicious: why doesn't he get married? Then the investigator summons his apartment neighbors and his co-workers. He asks them if the accused is sociable. How is he getting on with his job? What does he do in his free time? Who are his friends? Who doesn't he want to be friends with? And so on and so forth. It is not even all that important for him to know the answers. "The Serbsky guys" will certainly know how to process them correctly.

Approximately a month after the arrest, the accused is again locked in a windowless van and taken away. He has no idea where he is being taken. No one showed him the investigator's order concerning his examination, and he is not supposed to have a lawyer. But his uncertainty lasts only for about a half an hour, until the van drives through the gate of an institution at Nine Kropotinsky Lane. This is the infamous Professor Serbsky Central Scientific Research Institute of Forensic Psychiatry. It is here that he will be hospitalized for a forensic psychiatric examination.

Actually, he does not have to be hospitalized. Psychiatrists could have talked with the accused in his cell or in the investigator's office. This could have taken a few minutes or a few hours. But that would not look too impressive in our day and age, and therefore it does not usually happen this way. More often than not, hospitalization is required for an examination.

The prisoner is escorted to the third floor of the Institute, to the Fourth Department. In charge of this department is Yakov L. Landau, a worthy successor to KGB Colonel Daniel R. Lunts.

The Serbsky Institute with its Fourth Department is one of the most dismal places in our country. This institution is in the same category as such focal points of communist terror as the Lubyanka Prison, the Lefortovo and Vladimir Prisons, and the Vorkuta and Kolyma camps. It is the crossroads of punitive medicine. It is from this institution that people are sent for compulsory treatment; through it they are released. The expressive Gulag language abbreviated the name of the Institute to "the Serbsky," and the Serbsky is where people are sent for psychiatric examination; the Serbsky is where the discharge commission comes from; the Serbsky is where the prisoners fates are decided. Those sentenced to death pray for the Serbsky; short-term prisoners are afraid of it; the innocent hate it. The name of Professor Serbsky, who dedicated his labors to the implementation of the non-confinement principle, who advocated leniency toward the mentally ill, has become the most dreaded symbol of psychiatric terror in the USSR.

The accused who finds himself in the Serbsky Institute frantically plans his tactics. How should he act? What should he say so that he will not be pronounced insane? Usually the accused decides to act naturally and reasonably, and with dignity. I can say with certainty that the results of the examination do not depend on the behavior of the examined. Only newcomers and people who know little about the Soviet penal system might have the impression that objective and impartial decisions are made at the Institute. A forensic psychiatric examination in the Fourth Department is only one stage in the long show of legality put on during the investigation and in court. Bored with monotony, the Serbsky comedians do not even play their parts well. They have long since stopped pretending that they are interested in finding the truth. The conscience of an SPH physician has been replaced with the cynicism of a Chekist. There is no examination in fact. A few formal conversations with the accused are enough to forward the case to the commission for a conclusion. These conversations are usually conducted by the so-called "acting physician," who is, as a rule, an insignificant employee of the Institute. In some cases, the accused has only one or two talks with the acting physician. However, doctors like to have a chat with certain prisoners to find out about the most recent political news. Prominent people can often be encountered among the patients. Conversations about philosophy and politics are not only used for examination purposes but are also stimulating for the doctors. Not everything human is alien to them, and prisoners under examination are often reputable specialists in various areas. However, this does not prevent physicians from signing false examination decisions, prescribing medication, and obtaining information required by the KGB by means of "tongue-loosening" drugs.

In conversations with fellow inmates and physicians and in receiving medical treatment, our protagonist spends thirty days under examination. If the examiners do not have enough evidence, or if the KGB needs some more time, examination terms can drag on for up to three months.

The internal regimen is quite decent here, and my statement that the Serbsky Institute is one of the most dismal institutions in the country is due to the fact that, for many, this is where the tormented road begins to compulsory treatment in the special psychiatric hospitals of the Ministry of the Interior. It is here, in this quiet lane, that thousands of people are condemned to physical and psychological torture, despair and hopelessness, illness and death.

The day of decision by the examination commission has arrived. The prisoner is taken into a large room at the end of the corridor. In this room at a round table and along the walls five to ten people are sitting . They do not introduce themselves but always introduce the prisoner by his first name and patronym. Professor Lunts—short, plump, respectable looking, with a kind face, golden rims of his glasses glistening—is quietly saying something. He is echoed by V.G. Morozov, a corresponding member of the Academy of Medical Sciences of the USSR—a huge man, baby-faced, with childish, radiant eyes. M.F. Taltse is getting her words in—she is petite and not frightening at all. These nice people ask our protagonist harmless questions for ten or fifteen minutes. After various topics of conversation are exhausted, they ask him to please leave the room and then sign their decision dooming him to torments without term at a special psychiatric hospital.

No one informs our protagonist about the results of the examination. He leaves Nine Kropotinsky Lane without knowing what to expect—a camp or an SPH?

He is brought back to his prison cell to await the trial he will not be invited to attend.

According to Soviet legislation, the term of pretrial investigation must not exceed three months. In "exceptional" cases, the prosecutor's office can extend the term of pretrial incarceration to the maximum sanctioned by the attorney general of the USSR: nine months. However, there are cases where pretrial incarceration has exceeded nine months (e.g., A. Tverdokhlebov, V. Krasin, P. Yakir). Therefore, the accused may spend as much time as the KGB wants in pretrial incarceration, despite the requirements of the law. Weeks and months will have passed; the trial which he will not attend will have been over; and then he will finally find out from his lawyer that an SPH awaits him. Or else there will be no meeting with a lawyer. M.I. Kukobaka spent a whole year in Vladimir Prison after the trial in which he was sentenced in abstentia to compulsory treatment without knowing anything about his legal situation. Long before the accused was turned into a defendant, the defendant was found guilty, but "exempted from punishment because of the necessity of compulsory treatment." He will learn of his sentence only after the warden tells him to take his things—only then will he understand that he is in transit.

I do not know how the truly insane are transported, but our prisoner is transported along with healthy prisoners. It is difficult and boring to follow the script to the last detail. "He is a perfectly healthy fellow," prison officials reason, "let him go with the healthy guys." One night he says farewell to the Lefortovo Prison and is taken to be transported to, say, Kazan. Later in the night he is brought to the station which is between Sokolniki and Krasnoselskaya Streets, or to the transit station at Krasnaya Presnya, stuffed into a wagon with dozens of other prisoners, and transported eastward. He spends a few days in the barred wagon among thieves, murderers, burglars, and civil offenders, listens to endless stories, and then relates his own. Just as it happened two, three, or four decades ago, the escort throws them salted fish, and our prisoner's throat dries up from thirst, his lips are chapped; there is not enough water for all.

Kazan welcomes him with German shepherds straining to break their leashes and submachine guns aimed at his face. Again a "lobster neck," a road, uncertainty, and finally, his abode for many years to come—the special psychiatric hospital (be it the Kazan, Orel, Leningrad, or any of the other fifteen SPH's known to me).

As a rule, the first couple of months are spent in the quarantine unit where psychiatrists and Chekists get acquainted with him and his case and decide in which unit to place him. In most special psychiatric hospitals political prisoners pass through all units—from the most severe to the most lenient ("discharge") unit. Their behavior and their strength or weakness determine the time that will be spent on this tormented route.

Almost always it is the chief physician of the unit who will be in charge of the prisoner's treatment. The chief physician is the one who is most trusted by the authorities. His actions are coordinated by the military chiefs of the SPH and accountable to the KGB. The chief physician is almost always an officer, ranking from lieutenant to major. If the KGB approves of the way he treats the prisoners, he can count on a promotion, a new star on his epaulets. He holds no personal or "class" hatred towards the patients he is tormenting with medication. He is doing it because it serves his personal interests. These interests may vary. In most cases, he simply wants to gain favor. At times it happens that the physician is interested in holding a political prisoner in his unit as long as possible, if the prisoner is "important" and his case is supervised by Moscow or some other influential office. In that case, the physician has to deal with high-ranking KGB officials, and this very fact strengthens his social position and raises his significance in the eyes of his colleagues and the local authorities. I know cases in which, because of such considerations, physicians opposed discharging a prisoner, even though the KGB thought it possible to stop the compulsory treatment.

Some physicians receive payoffs for cancellation of drugging, relaxation of regimen, or an early discharge. Bribery is widespread in the SPH's.

Our prisoner's situation depends largely on the physician's mood and disposition. One untoward look at the physician is enough for the prisoner to be prescribed haloperidol, or sulfazine injections, or some other punishment. Open protest against the hospital regimen is interpret-ed as a psychotic outburst, a manifestation of an acute condition, and entails severe punitive measures such as transfer to the "violent" unit and cancellation of discharge recommendations.

Our prisoner's life passes in wanderings from one SPH to another. If he is quiet and opportunistic, he can reach the discharge unit in one and a half to two years. But it takes only one wrong move to fall to the bottom of this precipice and start the excruciating climb upward all over again.

Our prisoner always has one way out at his disposal, a way that promises decent conditions and freedom—"repentance." It does not have to be done in writing, publicly or vocally. It is enough just to say at the next colloquy with his physician: "Now I feel much better" (that is, he did not feel well before!) and "I will not repeat my mistakes in the future" (that is, there were mistakes before!); and the physician, proud of his victory, will speedily report to the KGB people that the prisoner is broken, that he repented, and that he can be released soon. The repentance will be recorded in the patient's medical file and will have to be repeated at the session of the discharge commission. That is the price of get-ting out of the SPH "at any cost."

Not to idealize victims of punitive medicine, I must admit that some people use this venerable "rational" method. Some have even tried to justify it as the only feasible means of getting out. I have not yet been through an SPH. Therefore, I have no right to condemn this position. But, for the sake of justice, we should remember those who remained intransigent in difficult situations and did not "repent" in exchange for freedom. I will not mention any names; I will only say that there are many such people. Some of them are still in SPH's, and the names of many are unknown to me.

So far so good. Our prisoner has spent two, five, ten years in an SPH. Either his repentance, or a wave of protests (alas, from the West primarily), or some other circumstances have forced the KGB to speed up his release.

Discharge commissions, according to the official norms, are supposed to convene once every six months. In fact, these commissions are called once every eight or nine months, sometimes even less frequently. The Commission is headed by a representative of the Serbsky Institute in charge of this particular SPH. The decision of the commission is then presented to the court which ruled on the case. A session of the court decides on the question of changing the type of compulsory treatment. In theory, the court may terminate compul-sory treatment, but in practice this never happens. Only the regimen is changed: our prisoner is transferred to a general psychiatric hospital, usually in the vicinity where the prisoner lives. Several months will pass between the decision of the discharge commission and a court decision. The appeal deadline will pass; SPH administration will process discharge papers; and our prisoner will feel a slight breeze of freedom which accompanies transfer to a general psychiatric hospital.

SPH's are under the jurisdiction of the Ministry of the Interior, whereas general psychiatric hospitals are under the jurisdiction of the Ministry of Public Health. This has advantages and disadvantages. Our prisoner, who has just been transferred here from an SPH, will be quickly able to appreciate both. The internal regimen of an SPH is much stricter, but one cannot say that that is the biggest disadvantage. In an SPH, the prisoner knew what he could and could not do and what he would be punished for. Medical subordination was strongly supported by military subordination. The limits of arbitrariness were precisely defined and distributed among various branches of the punitive apparatus. In a general psychiatric hospital, personnel are civilian. For this reason, all personnel in GPH's are free to be even more arbitrary than their SPH colleagues, and they are no less corrupt.

In short, GPH's are less rigid. Inmates themselves have some freedoms which are unthinkable in SPH's. Visits are allowed not only for relatives but for others as well, without restriction. Food packages, books, and money are also allowed. But SPH inmates are not the only ones to wind up in a GPH. People are also brought there in accordance with the well-known *Instruction on Urgent Hospitalization of the Socially Dangerous Mentally Ill*, as are those whose hospitalization is not politically motivated.

"Treatment" continues—at times no less tormenting than an SPH. Abuse by attendants, nurses, and orderlies is often even more formidable than in SPH's (e.g., the dreadful regimen in the GPH in the city of Alexandrov).

The fate of the transferred prisoner depends entirely on his new physician (who is also the chief unit physician in most cases). The KGB, having agreed to discharge the prisoner, does not bother much with him anymore. Doctors know this as well as they know that the patient's situation is entirely up to them. Usually they do not try to aggravate the prisoner's condition. Most trouble comes from lower level medical personnel. A great deal depends on the hospital itself —its tradition, administration, location, and relations with the authorities.

The situation of those committed to GPH's on the basis of the *Instruction on Urgent Hospitalization* is entirely different from those committed by a court ruling. For them, the hospital is not an intermediary stage between an SPH and freedom. They must undergo "treatment" here, and they are released only when the KGB deems it possible. Only their relatives are allowed to visit them and only two or three times a week for one or two hours at a time. After the SPH, our hypothetical prisoner would spend about six to eight months here, whereas the people who were sent here by a court order are often held for a much longer period of time. However, political prisoners are more often then not sent to SPH's. Cases are known where, at a general psychiatric hospital, people were not drugged at all. Besides, general psychiatric hospitals are designed for treatment, not incarceration; they are not directly connected with the KGB. Like most hospitals, they have a shortage of available beds. For these reasons, there are no long terms in these hospitals. This route of punitive medicine is shorter and much less tragic than the SPH route.

However, the ways in which people are committed to general psychiatric hospitals in accordance with the *Instruction on Urgent Hospitalization of the Socially Dangerous Mentally Ill* are truly eccentric and unpredictable.

In Moscow, Leningrad, Kiev, and other major cities, compulsory hospitalization is performed by first aid stations with the assistance of the militia and psychoneurological centers (PNC) and with the consent of the chief municipal psychiatrist or a psychiatrist on duty. In locations where there are no stations for emergency psychiatric aid, hospitalization is administered by any psychiatrist (from a PNC, a hospital, a clinic, or a medical sanitary unit) jointly with the militia and with the consent of the chief psychiatrist or a psychiatrist on duty. In cases with which I am concerned the KGB is always backed by the militia.

In Moscow, compulsory hospitalization of dissidents is elaborated to the last detail. There is even a special vehicle for house calls, a vehicle which not only calls for dissidents, but for high-ranking government officials (those victims of internal squabbles) as well. This special punitive medicine car is not outwardly different from other cars on the streets of Moscow. Until recently, it was a regular black Volga (GAZ-24), without special medical identification signs, license number 47-10 MOK. It belonged to the depot of the "first medical aid" and was washed and repaired in the garage underneath the Elektrozavodskoy Bridge. It was on duty at the first psychiatric aid station of the Gannushkin Hospital (Three Poteshnaya Street). The crew of this car was from the personnel of the station, but it was the elite personnel: old psychiatrists and assistants, screened and rescreened, capable of holding their tongues when needed, all party members. Recently the car has been replaced with a white Volga, and its garage is in Bezbozhny Lane. But it is doing the same job: house calls, visits to public places, ministries, and other Soviet institutions. Dissidents are also transported in regular Rafik or Uaz vans—ordinary ambulances.

The *Instruction on Urgent Hospitalization* provides for the compulsory hospitalization only of those mentally ill who are dangerous to those around them or to themselves, such as those with aggressive behavior resulting from a persecution complex, a hallucinatory-paranoid condition, or a suicidal tendency. Punitive medicine interprets these points of the *Instruction* in its own way.

For example, in the town of Elektrostal, Alexi Bubnov, a young worker, was committed to a general psychiatric hospital after he publicly renounced his party membership at a Communist Party meeting.

Irina Kristi was committed to the Kashchenko Psychiatric General Hospital No. 1 in Moscow for her attempt to enter the courtroom where the public trial of her friend, Kronid Lyubarsky, was being held.

Dr. Nikitenkov's wife was committed to a general psychiatric hospital after an unsuccessful attempt to enter the U.S. Embassy in Moscow in order to ask for political asylum.

Y. Brovko, a physicist, entered the Swedish Embassy in order to find out about the possibility of emigration to Sweden. Upon his exit from the embassy building, he was detained by KGB agents and compulsorily hospitalized in the Kashchenko GPH.

Mindaugas Tamonis, a construction engineer, refused to participate in the restoration of a monument glorifying Soviet soldiers and demanded to build a memorial for the victims of Stalinism in Lithuania. For this he was committed to a general psychiatric hospital where he was held for three months and underwent insulin shock treatments.

There are many similar examples. As I have already mentioned, representatives of the authorities take part in compulsory hospitalization. In addition to the directive for hospitalization issued by a psychiatrist, an authorization is issued by the militia. The authorization states that citizen X is found to be socially dangerous by a psychiatrist and has been detained by the militia to be directed to compulsory treatment in accordance with the *Instruction* of August 26, 1971. Any sign of indignation, any protest against compulsory hospitalization, will be evaluated by psychiatrists as evidence of mental illness. The situation is absolutely hopeless. This circular device is wearisome for all: you cannot defend yourself because you were pronounced insane; you cannot lodge a formal protest with the authorities because you were not arrested; you cannot appeal because you were not sentenced.

There are also other ways, even quieter and shorter. It is very inconvenient for the KGB to come after its victim at home or work; this might attract the attention of neighbors, colleagues, or passerby. It is much easier to summon the undesirable dissident so that he will come of his own accord. But where is he to go? If they summon him to the KGB office, this will immediately become known to his friends and might also be inconvenient for a number of other reasons. A neutral, unsuspicious place would be better—a military registration office, for example. If the person is on file with a psychoneurological center, he could be summoned to come there, presumably for a chat. He can even be summoned to a militia precinct—under any inconspicuous pretext. The latter method has become rather popular in recent years.

It is curious that in the PNC summons one is instructed to bring "10 unaddressed, stamped envelopes." They are required for mailing letters from a psychiatric hospital. This phrase alone provides evidence of the fact that hospitalization has already been decided upon, talks or no talks. Here is a copy of one such summons, the name of the person summoned has, of course, been deleted:

Citizen................
You are asked to come see Dr. Katorgin at the psychoneurological center (48 Donskaya Street). In case of failure to appear, the militia precinct will be notified.

The physician's office hours are: Monday, Friday, Saturday—9 a.m. to 12 noon; Tuesday, Thursday—2 to 7 p.m.

Bring 10 unaddressed, stamped envelopes.

Tel. 232-14-00
January 16, 1976
(Signature)

After his arrival at a psychiatric hospital, our "lunatic" must be examined by three psychiatrists within the next twenty-four hours. After the diagnosis has been confirmed, the psychiatrists approve the hospitalization. This is just a formality, but even this formality is seldom observed, and understandably so. Why would the physicians burden themselves with unnecessary talks and waste their time if they knew in advance that this "patient" is being hospitalized in compliance with orders from the KGB?

Usually our dissident spends a few months in a general psychiatric hospital receiving injections of halperidol, aminazine, insulin, sulfazine, and other drugs.

Preventive compulsory hospitalizations occur much less frequently now. Earlier, potentially "dangerous" and undesirable dissidents were committed to mental hospitals before visits to the USSR by foreign dignitaries, before Soviet anniversaries, and before party congresses. Relaxation of this policy is due to the recent protests of Western governments against repression in the USSR.

After serving his KGB-determined term at the hospitals, our dissident comes back home, exhausted from drugs and despair. His stay at the psychiatric hospital, especially in the SPH, will leave its permanent mark on his life. His hardships are not over.

The court that released him from compulsory treatment can pronounce him legally incapable. He is stripped of civil rights granted to him by the law. He is under guardianship now. A healthy, independent adult male now depends on his guardians' will, a will that often goes against his convictions. The guardians are often his relatives, people who may mean well, but who may be unable to understand or respect his principles or aspirations.

A medical commission pronounces him a second-class invalid, and he is given 45 roubles a month as a pension. This is the only direct expense of punitive medicine, but it has negative, rather than positive, consequences. A second-class invalid is not eligible for most jobs, and it is impossible to live on 45 roubles a month. If he renounces his pension, there is a chance that after a while he can obtain a reevaluation as a third-class invalid and find an acceptable job. In any case, he is banned from jobs in aviation and education; he cannot be a driver; and there are many other jobs for which he is not eligible. He is also banned from studying at a college.

Besides the official ban on certain occupations, there are also unofficial bans. In order to obtain a job, one must be screened by the personnel department, which performs a detailed check on all biographical data. First of all, he must show his "work-book," which indicates, for example, that he has not worked for five years. The most recent entry in his work-book says that he was fired on the basis of Article 29.7 of the *Labor Law Code* (which stipulates a court sentence as cause for a breach of work contract), and adds in parenthesis: "arrested." No personnel department would hire this person without requesting his release notification which, in his case, says that during these years he was undergoing compulsory treatment because of his crime in accordance with Article 70 or 190.1 of the Penal Code of the RSFSR. The personnel department official will pale with horror. He will immediately call the KGB to ask what he is supposed to do. But even if the KGB has no objections, the administration would not want to hire such an abominable troublemaker.

You just can't win! Even if you managed to obtain a new work-book or emend the old one, what are you going to do with your passport?! The passport is issued on the basis of the same release notification or some other document concerning your stay at the SPH. Besides, any personnel department official will be able to find out about the disloyalty of the passport owner from its number and serial letters. It is hard for our protagonist to set himself free from the indefatigable supervision of the KGB and the militia. He will wander from one temporary job to another, suffering poverty and misery. If his friends fail him, he will live in hunger, paying the price for his past courage.

But this is not enough. His every step is also closely watched by the regional psychoneurological center. Everyone who has been discharged from a psychiatric hospital is on file with a PNC. The PNC is supposed to conduct periodic examinations and regularly record its observations. The PNC physicians often regard this as a formality, since they understand its medical uselessness. However, if signalled by the KGB, the PNC assumes a rigorous position with regard to the person under observation. The PNC, not providing a special punitive service, is in an ambiguous situation. On the one hand, it is difficult and dishonest to emphasize nonexistent psychopathological symptoms of the "patient." On the other hand, the PNC file must be in such a condition that the "patient" can be hospitalized at any time, should the KGB demand it.

The KGB often puts pressure on the ex-inmate of a psychiatric hospital through the PNC. PNC psychiatrists tell him to stop a certain activity if the KGB is unhappy with it by unambiguously threatening him with compulsory treatment or another trial and another term in an SPH. This person can be hospitalized simply because he was once in a psychiatric hospital.

Thus, the life of our ex-prisoner is spent in reflecting and weighing carefully his every step, under constant threat of rehospitalization.

The roads of compulsory treatment which I have traced here are only the arterial roads. Everyone who has been through a psychiatric hospital can tell you about his own unique hard road. He can tell you about unknown paths and dark alleys of punitive medicine. I have attempted to give only a general idea of what compulsory treatment is all about.

2.

Most SPH ex-inmates claim that if it were a matter of choice, they would prefer labor camps, where they might lose their physical health, but would preserve their intellectual and emotional capabilities.

Those who have been held at both labor camps and special psychiatric hospitals claim a certain similarity between the internal conditions of these respective institutions.

Most special psychiatric hospitals are situated in prisons or former prisons. SPH territory is surrounded by a wall about twenty feet high, with barbed wire carrying high voltage current. Near the wall on the inside is a path for a guard, then a six- to eight-foot-wide restricted area. In the corners of the hospital yard are towers with searchlights and sentries around the clock.

There have been instances of escapes from SPH's. According to V.E. Borisov, two inmates were killed during their attempt to escape from the Blagoveshchensk SPH. Unfortunately, I do not know their names or their mental conditions. Sergei S. Alexeyenko, a navy captain, attempted to escape twice: first from the Leningrad, then from the Orel, SPH—both times unsuccessfully.

The security of SPH's (as well as of prisons) is carried out by officers and soldiers of the internal troops. They recruit informers, organize brainwashing "political colloquies" and "pursue watchfulness." Thus, SPH's have two administrations—military and medical; and there are two directors—a military SPH commander and a chief physician.

SPH's usually consist of ten units; and, as noted above, a prisoner has to go through each of them, from the most restrictive unit to the most lenient "discharge" unit. Regimens vary in these units, and I will describe here a certain average, or medium, regimen—not too harsh and not too lax.

First, some preliminaries concerning the terminology. According to Soviet legislation, compulsory treatment is not a punishment, and therefore SPH inmates are officially referred to as "patients," not as "prisoners." I do not see any significant difference. In view of the fact that the mentally healthy are also held in SPH's, I think that the term "prisoner" is more appropriate. The authorities were less fastidious in the 50's, when SPH's were called "PPH's" (psychiatric prison hospitals); and their inmates were referred to as "patient-prisoners." According to official terminology, the same applies to cells that are referred to as "wards" by SPH authorities. However, these "wards" are usually just prison cells. In the Leningrad SPH, according to V.E. Borisov, the "wards" are exact replicas of the cells in the St. Peter and Paul Fortress. I call these things by their proper names: cells will be referred to as "cells," and prisoners, as "prisoners," even though they are "exempted from criminal persecution" (the standard court formulation) and held there by court order, not by sentence.

A standard cell usually contains about ten people. Mainly they are mentally ill people who committed violent crimes. In the Kazan SPH, according to N. Gorbanevskaya, almost 90 percent of the prisoners were convicted on the basis of Article 102 of the *Penal Code*—murder with aggravating circumstances. (Not all of them are mentally ill. Perhaps this is the way that Soviet justice complies with the "plan to decrease crime." A lunatic's actions are not a crime.)

The authorities have a policy of not putting political prisoners, especially healthy ones (or as they are also called, "the conscious ones"), in the same cell. Insane cellmates are often disturbed and aggressive people; they talk deliriously at night, making it impossible for others to sleep. The environment of the cell is an important factor in a prisoner's life. Living constantly among the insane is hardly bearable for any mentally healthy person. Among prisoners, fakers are often encountered; some of them overdo it and cause a great deal of trouble for the healthy.

Cell walls are bare plaster. Windows are small and barred and often completely covered by wooden boards or "muzzles."

The lights in the cells are on all night long (as in a prison). The light bulb is covered by wire netting and in some cases a red shade is put over it. Newcomers have a hard time adjusting to it; it is very difficult to sleep with a bright light on—especially if the light is red. Prisoners sleep on metallic or plank beds.

Bathing and washing are done once every ten days. Only hospital clothes are allowed. In winter, it is often very cold in the cells and in the yard, but the prisoners are usually not permitted to have their own clothes.

The lavatory is situated either in the cell itself or in the corridor. Often one is not allowed into the corridor (different units have different regulations). If this is the case, one has to ask the warden to unlock the door every time one requires the use of the lavatory. Tobacco products can be restricted or completely banned (as a form of punishment).

Freedom to move about is mostly limited by the cell walls. Food is served through a window in the cell door. In some units, prisoners are taken to a common dining hall.

The quality of the food is repugnant, even to the most undemanding palate.

Theft is commonplace. Foodstuffs are stolen by many doctors, nurses, assistants, orderlies, and wardens, not to mention kitchen personnel. And in addition, all SPH personnel eat their meals in the general dining hall, practically at the prisoner's expense. Mealtimes are haphazard and unorganized, to say the least.

The only thing that can improve the prisoner's nutrition is food parcels from home. Those who do not receive such parcels often suffer from starvation. However, many prisoners share their parcels with their less fortunate cellmates. The permitted number of parcels is often limited; in some SPH's they are completely forbidden, and in others there are no restrictions. The weight of a parcel, as a rule, must not exceed eleven pounds. Certain food stuffs are not allowed.

One can mail letters (of limited format) twice monthly, but only to relatives. It is permitted to receive any number of letters from anyone. Outgoing, as well as incoming, correspondence is censored, and, if need be, filed in the prisoner's record. That is how army prisoner's letters "disappear." Many incoming letters do not reach their addressees, and all correspondence can be banned as a form of punishment.

Only relatives' visits are allowed—as a rule, no more than once a month for two hours. Those who live far away can be allowed four-hour visits once every two months. A warden is present during all visits. Visitors are separated from the prisoners by a very large table with a wooden panel down to the floor. Sometimes a two-foot-high artificial glass screen is on top of the table. Many topics of conversation are not permitted (just as in a prison). If visitation rules are violated, or as a punishment for other types of misconduct, the visit can be cut short or even canceled completely.

Traveling for a visit entails well-known monetary difficulties, especially if the SPH is far away and the prisoner is the father of many children and the main provider of the family. Even those who receive monetary help from Western charitable organizations, or the (underground) Russian Fund, or private sources experience considerable material hardship. The situation for those who live in the provinces and have no connections with these organizations is incomparably worse. They live in total psychological isolation, and their former friends are not only afraid to lend them money for the trip but even to recognize them on the street.

A prisoner is allowed to have money from outsiders deposited in his account at the SPH. Often there are no limits on the account, and prisoners can shop in the hospital store; however, there is almost nothing worth buying there. In certain SPH's, a personal account is limited to ten roubles, and one is not allowed to spend more than three roubles a month. Prisoners are also not allowed to carry money, and forms of exchange (illegal) between prisoners are quite primitive.

One two-hour walk in the hospital yard is allowed per day. In winter, the duration of such walks is decreased, but many prisoners are even happy that this is so, because it is too cold. In some cases, walks are compulsory, and refusal to go for a walk is punishable. If a prisoner enjoys his daily walks, they can be banned—as a punishment. This punishment is quite harsh, especially in summer, when cells are burning hot and the often clogged toilet bowls give off an unbearable stench.

Occupational or work therapy is compulsory in some SPH's, whereas in others it is merely encouraged by the administration. Many healthy prisoners are happy to work, and in that case SPH authorities have yet another means of punishment—banning work. Most prisoners, however, do not wish to work, since this work is incompatible with their interests and professions. Prisoners work in cardboard and weaving workshops, book binderies, sewing rooms, and other workshops. They are paid beggars' wages for their work—two to ten roubles a month which are transferred to their personal credit accounts. Their labor is extremely profitable for the SPH's. Products made by SPH prisoners bring huge profits because their retail prices are ten times higher than the pay received by the exploited prisoners.

M. I. Kukobaka, a former prisoner of the Sychevskaya SPH, writes: "The so-called 'work therapy' has turned into a very profitable business for the authorities. Machines are set up with no regard for sanitary norms. There is very little room. Ventilation consists of a few *fortochkas*. Patients are directly or indirectly forced to work from morning till night. During the summer months, people are forced to work even after supper. Supposedly work is voluntary. But just try not to go! A 'change' in your 'condition' will be immediately discovered, and you will be tortured by various injections, harassed by the orderlies, etc."

Many units have TV sets, and movies are shown regularly. Even though the same trash is shown as on the outside, many prisoners enjoy these occasions—they are happy to forget SPH reality. According to P. Starchik (the Kazan SPH), however, movie viewing can be compulsory. This is very depressing for those whose esthetic standards cannot be met by Soviet cinematic clichés.

Hospital libraries are filled with the usual Soviet pap literature. The only solution for avid and discerning readers is to receive books from the outside. But only books published by the State may be received.

SPH's are manned by military personnel, medical workers, regular citizens, and criminals. A number of duties (guarding, supervision of physicians' activities, etc,) are performed exclusively by the military—Ministry of the Interior (MVD) employees, internal troops, and the KGB. All unit chiefs and many other doctors have officers' ranks. In many SPH's, head nurses and unit assistants also have military ranks. As a rule, orderlies are recruited from among criminals (mostly civil offenders) or, occasionally, from the patients themselves. In many instances, there are no clear boundaries between the duties of the military administration and the medical administration. This is understandable, especially in view of the process of militarization of the medical personnel. It is difficult to determine who is a professional military man practicing medicine and who is a professional physician wearing epaulets.

If, on a doctor's instructions, a patient is receiving injections, he is also subjected to mockery and beatings from the orderlies. Embittered criminals who receive their "schooling" in labor camps, given a little authority, use it beyond all reasonable limits, on both the sick and the healthy.

The following are M. I. Kukobaka's recollections about an orderly at the Sychevskaya SPH:

A certain Sasha Dvorenkov, a little over twenty years old, a brawny fellow, below medium height, with light-blue eyes and a nice-appearing face. Always happy, a little noisy. An ordinary Soviet man, a Komsomol member, in the camp—an IOS (Internal Order Section) member.

Sasha is not even a criminal: he drove a tractor and wrecked it because of negligence. His unofficial duty was to introduce newly hired orderlies to their responsibilities. He did it with pleasure, in a happy and relaxed manner. He would walk, for example, into a ward with a new orderly and say: "So how are you doing, guys?" He walks over to one of the patients: "How come you put your left leg on your right leg? Get up, you! Come over here!" The patient comes over, cautiously. Sasha (with a sweet smile): "Closer, man, don't be scared." And without changing his sweet expression—zap! —hits him in the face once, twice. The patient instinctively covers his face with his hands. "Put your hands down, you!" Sasha yells angrily, and his face somehow becomes pointy, small, rat-like. "Hey, Vitya," he says to the new orderly, "give me a towel." He throws the towel around the patient's neck. "Come on, give him a squeeze," he says to his buddy. The patient's face becomes purplish, and he falls to the floor like a sack of potatoes. An abrupt blow to the abdomen. The man moans— the sound is long, unnatural—and passes out. A grin of satisfaction appears on Sasha's face. He and his new buddy leave the ward, slapping and kicking patients on their way. Now the new orderly is "introduced" and knows his rights and responsibilities well enough.

Unfortunately, most of them were like the blue-eyed sadist.

... a certain Chuprin, with his pals, liked to practice his "right hook." They would make people in the ward stand in a row and then have a competition to see whose punch could more efficiently knock a man off his feet.

Among the controllers, Corporal Pushkin was known for his sadism. When a patient said something against the authorities in his presence, he pulled him down from his bed and began to trample him with his feet.

B. Yevdokimov (alias Sergei Razumny), an ex-inmate of the Leningrad SPH recalls:

Building Two has its landmark: Viktor Valerianovich or simply Valeryanych. He is a medical assistant by profession, a sadist by calling. His name is surrounded by legends. When he is on duty, the whole unit moans in complaint. There has never been a case when, passing by a patient, Valeryanych would not stick his key in between the patient's ribs. But this is nothing. Valeryanych's primary pleasure is to summon two patients to the bathroom and make them beat the hell out of each other. Now this is real fun! Valeryanych is laughing, his hands on his hips. Usually Valeryanych does it every morning. He would also not miss an opportunity to do it himself. He beats until he draws blood, till you lose consciousness, but he doesn't beat those who "violate the regimen" or contradict him—no way. He beats weak and delirious patients who are safe to beat, who will never seek revenge. The chief physician and all the doctors know about Valeryanych's "artistry"...As far as SPH commander Colonel Blinov is concerned, Valeryanych is his protege, his favorite.

I heard about this Valeryanych from other prisoners of the Leningrad SPH as well. I also heard that the prisoners beat the daylights out of him in the same bathroom. He apparently became a little quieter after that. But for how long?

Every SPH has its own Valeryanyches—assistants or orderlies. They beat prisoners, steal from them, or if they are physically weak, they use the measures of punitive medicine—injections, shocks, straitjackets, and other punishments. If an orderly, a nurse, or an assistant complains to the doctor about the "incorrect behavior" of a patient, or writes it down in the "observation book" which is checked daily by the doctor, punitive measures will follow immediately.

V. L. Gershuni says that one can be punished for refusing to speak with the doctor, or even for looking angrily at him.

V. Bukovsky told an Associated Press reporter about SPH's in an interview on May 13, 1970:

They were beating one Ukrainian every day; they would tie him up and kick him in the stomach. At times they would put patients in soundproof isolation cells and beat them without interruption. I know a few instances where people died after these beatings, and the isolation cells were never empty.

M. I. Kukobaka writes about the Sychevskaya SPH:

The largest ward in our unit was No. 3. Patients with serious mental diseases were held there. Anyone could be put there, as a punishment. I, myself, was put there several times. During my first time there, I noticed that orderlies often came in at night, woke up some patients (usually the most harmless ones) and took them out to the toilet. It seemed curious to me. At first I did not believe what I heard. So I decided to find out for myself, and when one more patient was brought back from the toilet, I took a good look at him and asked him some questions. As a result, I found out the orderlies used patients for sexual perversions. This was no secret to anyone, either nurses, nor orderlies, nor physicians. They often joked about it.

Yury Belov also relates atrocities at the Sychevskaya SPH. On New Year's Eve (1975), here in the fourth unit, Georgy V. Dekhnich, a political prisoner, was brutally murdered. Dekhnich was then twenty years old. He was committed to the SPH for dissemination of anti-Soviet leaflets in the Ukraine. First, he was severely beaten by two orderlies at the request of Margarita V. Deyeva, a nurse, whom he had called "a commie bitch." Shortly before this, Dekhnich had had an ulcer perforation. After the beating, the stitches came apart. No one called the doctor, and the nurse, Deyeva (whom the prisoners of the Sychevskaya SPH nicknamed "Elsa Koch"), said: "By morning, we won't be bothered by him anymore." In the morning, Dekhnich died.

Gennady Yefremov was brutally beaten for his remark about frequent thefts by the medical personnel, again at Deyeva's request. (Yefremov was committed to the SPH for dissemination of false fabrications which denigrated the Soviet state and social system—Article 190.1 of the national *Penal Code*).

Vladimir A. Solovyov, a prisoner of the Sychevskaya SPH, was frequently beaten for his Russian Orthodox faith. His jaws, ribs, and arms were broken; his teeth were knocked out.

On July 24, 1975, in an attempt to escape from the Sychevskaya SPH, Anatoly I. Levitin was killed. The attempt failed at the very outset, for Levitin got caught in the barbed wire, and it was easy for the guards to reach him. They did not intend to kill him; however, the physician in charge of the second unit, Nikolay P. Smirnov, who came to the site of the incident, ordered the guards to shoot Levitin, and the guards complied with the order: they shot Levitin at point-blank range.

In the same SPH, in 1976, the chief physician of the seventh unit, Viktor Yefimovich Tsarev, set violent lunatics on a sixty-year old political prisoner, Alexi N. Kotov, a Russian Orthodox believer and a free-lance reporter for the *Messenger of the Russian Christian Movement*. Kotov was murdered.

PUNITIVE MEASURES
Medical Measures
Prescription of haloperidol, sulfazine, aminazine, trifluoperazine, insulin, and other injections. Increased dosage of drugs already prescribed.

Corporal Measures
Beatings and Poundings
    "Fixation." In Soviet psychiatric language this is called "compulsory immobilization" (including the "wet wrap"). A prisoner's hands and feet are tied to a board or bed frame. He can be held in this position for a few hours or a few months.

The bonds are not released even for elimination. Cases are known where prisoners in solitary cells were not even given a bedpan. While the prisoner is crucified on his bed, he will develop bedsores and his muscles and joints will atrophy. Only the care of his friends (if they are there) will save him from unbearable pain and possible death.

Wet Wrap. A prisoner is wrapped tightly in a wet bed-sheet, spire by spire coiled around his body. In drying out slowly, the bed-sheet squeezes the body gradually. The pain is so intense that the prisoner screams. These screams are heard throughout the unit, as if in warning to those who would dare stand up to the brutality wrought by the hospital authorities.

Regimen Measures

Ban on walks.

Ban on work or, vice versa, compulsory work, depending on the attitudes of the prisoner.

Ban on watching TV and movies.

Ban on the use of the hospital library.

Ban on smoking; confiscation of tobacco products.

Ban on correspondence.

Ban on visits.

Transfers to the "violent" unit.

Cancellation of discharge recommendation.

The arsenal of punitive measures is immense. If I have not enumerated all types of punishment, these are certainly the main ones. In different SPH's the punishments vary—depending on hospital traditions, SPH authorities, and the specific physicians.

Recently opened SPH's usually have the most lenient regimens. They do not yet have enough experience in punitive medicine. The regimen and attitudes toward prisoners become more severe as time passes. Militarization of SPH personnel also leads to severity.

Memoirs

Petro G. Grigorenko

I arrived at the Lefortovo prison in a semiconscious state. On admission I went through the customary frisking, the deposit of my possessions in the checkroom, and the receipt of bedding. I reached cell number 6 at about one in the morning—four, Tashkent time. Despite this they made me get up with the rest of the prisoners at 6:00 A.M.

After breakfast I was told to gather up my things and surrender all government issue items. I was then led out of my cell and frisked again. Because of the way the jailers looked at me I decided: the Serbsky Institute. A trial would be publicity. Thus they would not permit me to go to trial. They had only one way out—to label me insane. They'd been mistaken in Tashkent. Berezovsky had thought he could work up a case against me. Therefore he failed to understand the significance of the psychiatric diagnosis and had not selected the experts' commission that would have diagnosed me without fail as insane. As a result a situation had arisen that required Moscow's intervention.

I had been expecting this intervention and a second diagnosis. I knew that this time they would not take any chances but would send me directly to the institution that existed for the purpose of transforming sane people with whom the KGB was not pleased, but who had not committed any crimes, into "lunatics dangerous to society."

I emerged from the car that delivered me to the Serbsky Institute so embittered that I refused to speak with anyone. Thus my second stay there began. My first days demonstrated that fears I had were well founded.

They took me straight to solitary confinement, locked me in, and put a special guard at my door who was under instructions not to allow any of the political prisoners to get near me. Everyone else in the department—both the ordinary prisoners and the political prisoners—was registered under his own name. My name was known only to the doctors. The nurses and other personnel had been told only my first name and my patronymic. All of this put me on my guard, of course. But I firmly decided not to give any causes for psychiatric pestering and to conduct myself calmly. During my stay in solitary confinement no medical tests were conducted on me, except for the customary analyses of urine and blood. The physician, Maiya Mikhailovna Maltseva, came to talk to me on one occasion. I told her that I did not want my replies to her questions set forth in her uncontrolled transcription. "I will conduct any conversation," I said to her, "but only on the condition that I write out my own replies." Past experience had taught me that this was necessary.

Unfortunately, legitimate demands such as this one often played right into the doctors' hands. My desire to record my own answers in interrogations could be twisted by them into a manifestation of paranoia, as could my complaints about wiretapping, being tailed, and other abuses. I was beginning again a struggle against a method of repression extremely advantageous to the authorities. And this method had been "improved," made even more barbaric, since my first experience with it in 1964.

My solitary confinement came to an end within a week, and tests began. On the first day, I was invited to talk with the head of the ward, Professor Lunts. Maiya Mikhailovna Maltseva was also present. In accordance with an agreement I had reached with Lunts, after we finished talking I set forth in writing exactly what I had said. This written record is a part of the case history and speaks for itself. One item I did not write down was the question of why illegal government repressions had descended on me in 1964 and in subsequent years, which I answered by reminding Lunts of the fact that the Serbsky Institute had drawn two separate conclusions about me after my first stay. One of them, which straightforwardly diagnosed me as insane, was for the court. The other was for the government. The latter, I supposed, stated that I had been diagnosed as insane for humanitarian reasons—taking into account my services, my age, and my health—but that in actuality I was sane. The second conclusion, I said, probably had been oral.

Lunts tried to prove to me that I was mistaken, that the institute had reached only one conclusion—that I was insane, I then asked him, "How then do you explain the fact that an insane person was deprived of the pension he had earned and subjected to other cruel repressions? After all, only people who themselves have injured psyches can take such an action. But I do not want to believe that we are ruled by insane people, and therefore I insist: The government received a different conclusion than the court did. Do you not agree with me?"

Lunts only muttered, "The institute did not reach any other conclusion."

This conversation cost me dearly. The day I arrived at the institute I had felt a strange ache in the back of my head, which I'd reported. I was told that a therapist would see me the next day, but for some reason I didn't see her then; and since the therapist received patients only once a week, I had to live with this pain. Nervous tension did me in, and before the week was up the ache became unbearable and I collapsed. The night nurse measured my blood pressure and gave me a shot of magnesium and I managed to go to sleep. The day after, October 30, the ache intensified and I began to feel nauseous. The therapist finally examined me and prescribed some medicine. In a couple of days the ache diminished and the psychiatric examination was resumed.

It was conducted by a man of about my own age whom Maiya Mikhailovna addressed as "professor." One other woman was also present—evidently an assistant—and she wrote incessantly in her notebook. The conversation with this professor was ridiculous. Perhaps such a conversation is required when examining a person who has lost possession of his faculties and fallen into senile dotage. But in my case, almost anyone would immediately have seen its inappropriateness. The professor himself grasped it and seemed embarrassed, no less so than I. From past experience I knew wherein lay the essence of a psychiatric examination, and I wanted to reject it. I am not going to recount all of our conversation, but I will cite the two questions I consider the most intelligent of all that were put to me.

First, I was told to keep subtracting 17 from 200, and call out the remainder after each subtraction. I did this, but when I came to the last remainder, 13, it seemed incorrect to me and I said, "I think I made a mistake somewhere."

"Can you check it out?" asked the professor.

"Yes, of course," I replied. I divided 200 by 17 and found that 13 was indeed the correct answer.

Second, he showed me a drawing, evidently from the humor magazine *Krokodil*, of a desk behind which were sitting on one side a woman and opposite her a man, both of them looking at a man who stood by the chairman's armchair. All three were officials. In the chairman's upraised hand was a ticket for a paid resort vacation from a ticket benefit intended for workers. Beneath the drawing was the legend: "To whom shall we allot the fourth?" The professor asked me to explain the situation. So as not to insult the reader I will not cite my reply to the question. I will only note in passing that I replied with all seriousness, like a schoolchild.

After this Maiya Mikhailovna summoned me twice. I do not know what she wished to speak with me about the first time, because Lunts summoned her to his own office before she had completed the verbal preliminaries and they sent me back to the ward. During the second conversation she informed me that soon a commission would meet to discuss my case. This brought to an end my preliminary meetings with the doctors, though regular visits continued to occur twice a week. During all visits they asked the same question: "How do you feel?" My only reply was: "Just as usual."

In addition to conversations with the physicians and routine laboratory analyses, they carried out the following tests on me: an X-ray of the chest area; an X-ray of the backbone, on the basis of my own complaint; and two encephalographs. On the second occasion the encephalograph lasted two hours, though it usually takes only fifteen minutes. They brought it to an end only after I declared that I could not stand it any longer. Deep dents had been made in my hairless scalp and I had an intense headache. My feet hung off the end of the bench, swollen.

So after twenty-eight days of so-called clinical examination—from the day I arrived in the institute, October 22, to the day of the commission meeting, November 19—the only test result the commission received in addition to the materials from the Tashkent commission was my last encephalograph.

The session of the forensic psychiatric expert commission took place in a large room filled with office tables, one of which was placed in the center of the room. Behind it sat four people. In the chairman's position sat a rather young-looking, brown-haired man. He, I learned subsequently, was Morozov, the director of the Serbsky Institute of Forensic Psychiatry, and Corresponding Member of the Academy of Medical Sciences of the USSR. To his left sat Lunts. On his right was a man in a brown suit whom I have christened for the purpose of this account "the man without a doctor's smock." Opposite the chairman was Maiya Mikhailovna. They motioned me to a chair to the side of the table, near the chairman. I sat down in it and looked about. I saw many people I knew, but of my old acquaintances only Dr. Lunts and a doctor sitting by the window whom I had met in Leningrad in 1964 when the question of my release from the Leningrad Special Psychiatric Hospital was being decided were present. All the rest were ward doctors whom I had met only recently.

I realized that those behind the central table constituted the commission.

The rest were there to learn. They were seated behind the tables by the walls in the following sequence, starting at the chairman's left hand side: Zinaida Gavrilovna; Yakov Lazarevich, my Leningrad acquaintance; Lyubov

Osipovna; and at the door, Albert Alexandrovich. Albert Alexandrovich was the one who escorted me back and forth to the ward. I call attention to the fact that I knew only Lunts's last name. By law the institution was supposed to give me the names of all the experts and I was supposed to have the right to exclude any with whom I was not pleased. This law had been observed in Tashkent. But here in the Serbsky Institute the insignificant prisoner did not even have the right to know the names of the high priests who were deciding his future.

The meeting was begun by the chairman: "Well, how do you feel?"

"I do not know what to answer. Probably I feel most of all like an experimental rabbit, but one capable of understanding his situation."

"No, I don't mean that. I want to know whether you feel any different-ly today from the way you felt when we diagnosed you in 1964."

"I do."

"How?"

"Well, at that time I could not even imagine such a trick as transforming the defendant in a criminal investigation into an insane person. I was astonished when I discovered this and I began to look upon the personnel of the institute as inveterate criminals. I believed in 1964 that I had been brought here for a diagnosis which would assure my imprisonment in an insane asylum to the end of my days. Therefore, my attitude toward all of the officials here was one of hate—and as a result I was extremely aroused, irritable, did not wish to observe any of the institute's rules, and devoted most of my time to the political enlightenment of the patients around me. By all of this I evidently made a strange impression on those around me and may have given some small cause for being considered insane."

"Lunts told me that you said that what took place at that time seemed to you as if it were in a fog," the chairman said.

"Yes, and I still say essentially the same thing. My realization of why I was here so shocked me that even today I perceive what took place as a horrible nightmare."

"What about what's happening to you now?"

"Things are different now. In the first place, psychiatric diagnosis is no longer a surprise to me. In the second place, in the years since my last incarceration I have come to know many honest psychiatrists and I realize that even in a criminal situation, human beings are employed along with the monsters. In all life situations I have decided to concern myself particularly with those who are decent. Therefore I am completely calm right now and I see around me not merely doctors but human beings in me as well." I smiled at him.

"Yes, but everything which you say is bound up with the events of the diagnosis itself, and after all there are actions which would compel us, even without doctors, to doubt your sanity."

"I do not know of any such actions."

"But in the protocol of the commission which determined the possibility of termination of your detention in the Leningrad Special Psychiatric Hospital it is stated that you admitted your actions to be mistaken."

"I admit the same right now."

"How is the one thing supposed to jibe with the other?"

"Very simply," I said. "Not every mistake made by a person is the result of malfunction of his psyche. My mistakes were the consequence of my incorrect political development—of unsophisticated Bolshevik and Leninist indoctrination. I believed that the only correct way was as Lenin had taught. Therefore when I encountered conflicts between what Lenin had written and life, I saw only one way out: back to Lenin. But that was wrong. During our lives changes have taken place and no one has the strength to return to 1924, let alone to 1953. We must use today as the platform from which we move ahead, making creative use of Lenin's heritage, taking into account all accumulated experience. In the past I did not understand this and that was my principal error. I first began to think about these things when I realized I was wrong in some of my actions. At the time I did not disclose my mistakes and those at the institute did not question me on that matter. Therefore, the fact that my mistakes could not be corrected by the interference of psychiatrists remained unclarified."

"How then are we to explain that after the intervention of psychiatrists you conducted yourself properly for a year or a year and a half and then once again took up your old ways?"

"Psychiatrists have no connection with my so-called 'normal' conduct. I imagine what you are alluding to is the fact that I did not write anything for dissemination?"

At this the chairman nodded, and I continued; "I did not write in 1965 and 1966 for two reasons, neither of which had anything to do with psychiatrists. The first was that I had no time. I had to work as a stevedore in two stores in order to get food for myself and my family. For those jobs I was paid a total of 132 rubles—just about what I had paid in income tax from the salary I used to receive in the military academy. The work was very hard, twelve hours each day, and I had no days off. I was therefore always exhausted. The second reason was that during this first year and a half I still hoped that I would succeed in getting the pension which I had earned and which was unlawfully taken from me. If I had succeeded in this, we would not be talking here, since back in the Leningrad

Special Psychiatric Hospital I had remarked that when freed I would concentrate on writing a history of the Great War of the Fatherland. I longed to do this, but experience then showed me that the illegal repressions were rapidly increasing as time went on. I was deprived of the possibility of any employment at all and insulting illegal surveillance of me and my family was carried on at all times. These facts showed me that the time had not yet come to retreat into an ivory tower and devote myself to pure science. Until our country has a reliable defense against the tyranny from within, it is every honorable person's duty to take part in the creation of such a defense—no matter how this threatens him. I therefore joined the ranks of the warriors against tyranny. But you are mistaken when you say that I have taken up my old ways. What I have done in the last two years bears not even an outward resemblance to my old ways."

At this point I was interrupted by the man without a doctor's smock.

"What's the difference? It's only a different tactic, but it is essentially the same."

"No, the essence is different. Before, my actions were typically Bolshevik: I created a strictly conspiratorial illegal organization and disseminated illegal leaflets. Now there is no organization and there is no dissemination of illegal leaflets—but instead open, bold statements against acts of obvious tyranny, against lies and hypocrisy, against the distortion of truth. Before, there was a summons to the overthrow of the existing regime so that we could return to where Lenin had left off. Now there is a summons to liquidate the obvious ulcers of society, a struggle for strict observance of existing laws and for the realization of the constitutional rights of the people. Before, there was a call to revolution. Now there is an open struggle within the framework of what is permitted under the law—for the democratization of our public life. What common tactics or essences are shared here? Of course, if you believe the only normal Soviet person to be one who obediently bows his head before any bureaucratic tyranny then, indeed, I am 'abnormal.' I am not capable of such submissiveness—no matter how much I am beaten.

"I said then and I say again: in nineteen sixty-three through nineteen sixty-four I made mistakes. But in their correction I did not require the help of psychiatrists. In my most recent actions I also see mistakes—but again they are not such as can be corrected by psychiatrists."

"What are your current mistakes?"

"It is my impression that this is not the subject of today's conversation. To effectively analyze my recent mistakes I would have to work with people who think like me. You are not in that category, and I am incapable of speaking of all this as though I were repenting. Even if I had things to repent of, I would not do so when I had the axe hanging over my head. I consider it wrong for a person to repent under threat of punishment and death."

"Thank you, Pyotr Grigoryevich. Everything is clear to me. Do you have any questions?" the chairman directed himself to the man not wearing a smock, who during our entire conversation had remained sitting to my side, while constantly turning his face toward me but covering it with his left hand. For some reason this man interested me very much, and while talking to the chairman I kept trying to look at him. But I did not succeed. So when he declared that he had several questions I was pleased at the thought that at last I would see his face. But even when talking directly to me he managed to hide his face. Bending far down over the table, he asked his questions while looking at me out from under his left arm. I never did get a good look at him.

"How do you picture your future?" he asked.

"It's hard for me to answer that question. Right now, I cannot see beyond my trial."

"Do you mean you want to be tried?"

"Unfortunately, the answer to this question does not depend on me. I, of course, would rather have the case terminated at the stage of the preliminary investigation. But this, I repeat, does not depend on me."

"But after all, treatment can bypass a trial."

"I have no need of treatment. And I have no intention of faking illness in order to avoid responsibility. I am prepared to answer in full measure for whatever I have done."

"But if you are convicted you will be deprived of your pension."

"There is a Russian proverb which says: 'A man who has lost his head doesn't cry over his hair.' Whether I am convicted or whether I am imprisoned in a special psychiatric hospital, I lose first of all my freedom. Why should I then grieve for a pension? And for that matter, why is it certain that they will convict me? I do not consider myself guilty and I will try to prove that to the court."

"Just what does that mean—that you intend to defend yourself?"

"I am not quite certain what you mean. I do not intend to lie or to be evasive. I will speak out honestly about my actions and explain them as best I can. But even if I do not succeed in proving my innocence, the maximum I can receive under the applicable code section is three years. Thus by the time the verdict comes into effect I will have only two years left to serve. So-called treatment is not going to take less time. On the other hand I will spend those years not in a sheltered prison, but in a corrective labor camp working in the fresh air and among normal people. And then too they might give me less than three years, and maybe even merely exile—there are precedents. In that case I would not lose my pension. Finally, we must not exclude the possibility of amnesty on the occasion of the hundred-year anniversary of the birth of Lenin, an amnesty which might even involve me if I am convicted. Under 'treatment' this possibility is excluded. No one grants amnesty to an insane person."

This is how my second forensic psychiatric diagnosis of 1969 and my second encounter with the Serbsky Institute of Forensic Psychiatry came to an end.

The conclusion of the institute was that I was insane. But at the time, the formal decision was not announced to me. I could only guess at the outcome until I saw my lawyer, Sofya Vasilyevna Kalistratova.

On December 4 I pointed out that the period of sanction for my arrest had come to an end November 6. The authorities panicked and that same day carted me off to Domodyedovo and put me on an airplane. On December 5 I was once again in the isolation prison of the Uzbek Republic KGB branch. Here I made a formal declaration that until I had been presented with the sanction for lengthening my detention I would let them put me in my cell only by force. They found the sanction, dated October 21, granted by the deputy prosecutor general for a period up to December 31.

Then Sofya Vasilyevna Kalistratova arrived to defend me. We met in the prison reception room. This was the first time in nearly eight months that I had seen a face from my own world. And what a face it was! I had never seen one more beautiful. "A ray of light in the kingdom of darkness," I said to her, quoting Ostrovsky. I will never forget the tangerines and chocolates she brought to the meeting. I do not like chocolate, but the chocolate she brought me was the most delicious thing in the world.

She told me about my case and I told her about the investigation and the diagnosis. She said she would insist on a third commission of experts being present in court. She was pleased with the diagnosis of the commission of experts in Tashkent. It was competently and objectively written. The Serbsky Institute diagnosis was tendentious and incompetent. The Tashkent commission gave her a good basis for defense, but still it was difficult to hope for success. The very manner in which such cases were reviewed was tyrannous. In one trial, two mutually exclusive questions were decided, that of insanity and that of guilt. The court could not consider the first question correctly because the judges were not specialists and because they more or less had to go along with the conclusion of the experts. This conclusion was presented as part of the prosecution's case. All the court could do was rubber-stamp it. If the accused was classified as insane, there was no problem: An insane person had committed God knows what, so let him be treated. Every crime of the investigation was thereby covered up by the conclusion of a commission of experts created by the prosecution, a conclusion not subject to appeal.

Sofya Vasilyevna told me not to be too hopeful. I knew the outlook was bleak, but I also knew that she would wage a struggle. And she did. Her petition, "On the demand for supplementary medical documents by a commission of experts in court at a court session of February 3, 1970," is a document of extraordinary power.

How resoundingly she began that day: "You have two documents, dear sirs, not just one; each of them has identical force under the law and must obligatorily be considered. You, respected sirs, do not have the necessary knowledge for this and therefore you are obliged to create a third commission of experts for whom I have already chosen the candidates."

And then, between the lines: I know very well that you are not going to do anything of the sort, and that you are going to rubber-stamp the conclusions of the Serbsky Institute. And therefore from here on in I am going to destroy that conclusion and by this subject all of you to universal ridicule.

Indeed Sofya Vasilyevna was able to destroy that conclusion. Her own conclusion was as follows: "All this taken together gives a full basis for affirming that the conclusion of the in-patient commission of experts on the *insanity of* the patient is *mistaken. Everything set forth here gives the defense a basis for insistently requesting the appointment in this case of a third forensic psychiatric examination by a commission of experts for a solution to the question of the psychic state and sanity of P. G. Grigorenko.*"

"The Petition of Attorney Kalistratova" is the best example of how it is possible to struggle to a victory even while in the maw of a totalitarian monster. Both Sofya Vasilyevna and I knew that I would not be immediately removed from the hell of the insane asylums. But her petition had to be made so that the court would be compelled to face the fact of the entire Soviet system of forced treatment. Sofya Vasilyevna's document began the exposure of the foulness of Soviet psychiatry. This document was among the materials sent to western psychiatrists by Volodya Bukovsky in 1971 and it was present at the World Psychiatric Association convention in Honolulu in 1977. It acquires particular significance for me now after I have undergone examination by the most important American psychiatrists, all of whom came to the same conclusion as Sofya Vasilyevna—that I do not have any psychic illness and that I never did. Sofya Vasilyevna's document is destined to have a long life. For years and years it will be a weapon in the struggle to liquidate criminal psychiatry.

The "trial" ended February 5, 1970. Once again Sofya Vasilyevna visited me. The judge tried to refuse her this right, but she proved her right and came.

The judge got back at me for this by refusing to let my wife see me on the grounds that my lawyer had been granted the visit. More than eight months had passed since I had seen Zinaida.

During Sofya Vasilyevna's second visit, we talked about the sentence, which with insane persons is called a "determination." They had "determined" that I should be given forced treatment in the Kazan Special Psychiatric Hospital. I asked Sofya Vasilyevna to ask my wife to petition Pyotr Mikhailovich Rybkin, the chief psychiatrist of the ministry of Internal Affairs, to reassign me to the Leningrad Special Psychiatric Hospital.

When Sofya Vasilyevna and I parted, I estimated that in a week or two I would be closer to Moscow. Days, weeks, and months passed, and it was only on May 11—in other words, one year and four days after my arrest—that I was transferred. I presumed I was being sent to Kazan. I traveled in a Stolypin car* in solitary confinement in an individual cell escorted by a special convoy commanded by that same Major Malyshev who had taken me to the Serbsky Institute and back. The four soldiers under his command took turns standing guard at my compartment, certainly a slap in the face of the regular convoy guard on the car. I had so longed to see the out-of-doors and nature that during every daylight hour of the entire journey I stood at the door of my compartment and looked through it and through the corridor window at the sands, the villages, and the Mohammedan graveyards, which looked like dead villages. I was such an important "insane person" that not only was I accompanied by my own personal convoy guard, but personal checkups were conducted along the way, twice each day.

We arrived in Orenburg after dark. An elderly KGB major entered the car, came up to the door of my compartment with Major Malyshev, and motioned to me through the bars. I approached him and he whispered, "Your last name?" I made a sign to him to put his ear close to my mouth and I whispered directly into it, "I don't know. Ask the major. He knows everything."

---

* The term "stolypin car"—widely used in the Soviet Union—describes a railway car fitted by the KGB for the transportation of prisoners. During the Stolypin reforms in the early part of this century before the revolution, special resettlers' railway cars were created for migration. They had two sections: one for passengers, analogous to a Soviet third-class railway car, and one for transport of livestock, agricultural tools, equipment, and so on. The migrating peasant family received a sort of home on wheels. After the Bolshevik coup d'etat there were no more resettlers and the cars were useless, until someone in the KGB (then, the Cheka) decided to use them for transportation of prisoners, whose number was growing every day. The passenger section was turned over to the guards and the cattle section was left to the prisoners. This use of the cars thereby compromised the name of one of the most remarkable of Russian reformers, P. A. Stolypin-P. G.

At first the captain was taken aback. Then he began to try to persuade me to tell him my name, but I walked away from the door, sat down on the bench, and ignored him.

When our train arrived in Kuibyshev, I was unloaded so that I could be put on the train for Kazan, which, as it turned out, did not leave for several days. They put me in a preliminary detention cell at the railway station. It was well lit and clean, but instead of cots it had sleeping benches. We arrived there after dinnertime, but they gave me a simple, filling meal of thick vermicelli soup with meat. After I had eaten the police chief came and said he was sorry that they would not be feeding me three times a day; that those in the preliminary detention cells are fed only once a day. I refused to accept his apology and told him, "I am not concerned with what you usually do here. I am supposed to get fed three times a day."

In an hour and a half the chief of the province KGB came and apologized for my being put in the preliminary detention cells. He said they had no suitable hospital cell in their prison, but that his own personal aide would bring me breakfast, lunch, and dinner.

I have to give the devil his due. In May 1970 they had an excellent cook at the dining hall of the Kuibyshev KGB. I was served a varied and tasty menu. The fried potatoes were particularly good. Even the macaroni and vermicelli—things I had been unable to eat all my life—were cooked in such a way that I ate them with great relish. My four days in Kuibyshev were like being in a rest home. The conduct of both the KGB and the police led me to believe that they had received special instructions about me from up top.

We resumed our journey late in the evening of the fourth day. I knew right away that we were heading toward Moscow, though Malyshev kept assuring me that we were proceeding to Kazan. Perhaps my wife had gotten them to transfer me to Leningrad. In Moscow they put me up at the Butyrka prison for four days. On the fifth they sent me off via the Byelorussian station—that meant Chernyakhovsk (then called Insterburg), the main city of East Prussia, which was further from home than Kazan.

When Zinaida learned from friends of my stay at the Butyrka in Moscow, she asked to be permitted a visit. At first the authorities acted astonished at her request: "What makes you think he is in Moscow?" When they realized she really did know I was there, they promised her a visit but dragged things out until finally I was sent to Chemyakhovsk. The city's hard labor prison had been transformed into the special psychiatric hospital at which I arrived on May 28,1970. Once again my life in the kingdom of the KGB psychiatrists commenced.

More than a year had passed since I had been arrested, and I'd spent that time in the cellars of the KGB, in prisons like other Soviet prisons—ordinary Soviet torture dungeons. But now here I was at the gates of a "hospital," a special psychiatric hospital—another chapter in the history of my "illness." Here they "treated" me for forty months, after which they sent me to an ordinary insane asylum for nine months. Here I was supposed to "complete my treatment"—to be sure, in a special ward made up of those sent there by a court determination.

What can I say about those forty-nine months? Not long before my arrest in Tashkent, in the autumn of 1968, this new arrest hovered over me and I decided that I had to prepare for it, particularly for a return to an insane asylum. Why this specifically? Because I had not violated any law and thus there was nothing for which they could try me. But to the authorities I had become a persona non grata.

I had been exposing government lies and tyranny and by this had set an example dangerous to the authorities who felt they had to scare my possible imitators and shut my mouth. I realized this and knew I had to warn the public of this imminent reprisal and expose the reasons behind it. With this purpose in mind, I wrote a brief note to my friends about the likelihood of my arrest and at the same time wrote an essay entitled "On the Special Psychiatric Hospitals," which I disseminated via samizdat. Natalia Gorbanyevskaya included it in her book *High Noon*, and from there it was reprinted in the collection *Those Punished with Insanity*. In this way it became widely known.

In my essay I wrote: "The concept of special psychiatric hospitals does not in itself contain anything bad, but there is nothing more criminal or more antihuman than our specific implementation of this idea."

Nowadays I am profoundly sorry for having written this misguided and harmful sentence. But it was how I saw the matter after my fifteen months of ini-tial exposure to the system of forced psychiatric "treatment." It took another five-year stay in the hands of jailers and "psychiatrists" for me to grasp that there was evil not only in the implementation of this idea but in the concept itself. The implementation depends greatly on the location of the hospital and on its staff. In 1964-65, I was "treated" at the Leningrad Special Psychiatric Hospital. After this the one at Chernyakhovsk seemed a real hell. I completed my "treatment" in the fifth Moscow city hospital—the "Stolby"—which has the worst of all reputations in Moscow. But to me, after Chernyakhovsk, it almost seemed like a resort. But there were things in Dnepropetrovsk that were unknown in Chernyakhovsk. And Sychyovka and particularly Blagoveshchensk are incomparably worse in terms of horrors committed than even Dnepropetrovsk.

So the implementation varies. But the variety itself is born of the original concept, which deprives the prisoners of special psychiatric hospitals of all rights. They are entirely in the power of the personnel of these "hospitals," people who need answer to no one.

In his book on the Nuremberg trial of twenty-three SS men, *Das Diktat der Menschenverachtung (The Dictatorship of Misanthropy),* Mitgerlich writes that for him the most striking thing was the merging in one person of a doctor and an SS man. He writes that "from this union came the cold inhumanity which permitted such doctors to experiment on their fellow human beings."

Where is the boundary between "simple service" in an institution that is created to suppress heterodoxy and that cultivates irresponsibility and illegality toward its patients, and the total merging of this institution with a criminal organization of political terror?

I mistakenly gave a positive value to the concept of special psychiatric hospitals, because I drew my conclusions from my stay in the one "hospital" in which I was confined during my first imprisonment. Yes, and I drew my conclusion not on the basis of the purpose of that institution, which is concealed from the eyes of outsiders, but from the composition of the body of prisoners. In order to understand the real purpose of such "hospitals" as these it is necessary to return to their origins.

The first psychiatric prison hospital was created in Kazan before World War II for the imprisonment of dangerous political opponents of the regime—or, as they were called "enemies of the people." At the time it was said that this was a political prison and that only political prisoners were confined within it. In 1952 an analogous prison was created on Arsenal Street in Leningrad. Once again it was stated that this prison was solely for "enemies of the people."

Then Stalin died and rehabilitation commenced. The psychiatric political prisons in Kazan and Leningrad were emptied. But nature abhors a vacuum and someone at the top was unwilling to give up the concept of using psychiatry to suppress political protest. So in order to prolong the existence of both these "hospitals," a small contingent of genuinely mentally ill people who had committed serious crimes such as murder, rape, and robbery were admitted into them. Thus the cadres of the psychiatric political hospitals were preserved.

But there were those who did not wish things to come to a halt after the halfhearted measures of the Twentieth Party Congress, and who had not reconciled themselves to the attempts of the Central Committee to partially rehabilitate Stalin and the Stalinist system—in other words, people not in agreement with efforts to halt society's movement toward new life, movement that had begun only after Stalin's death. There was nothing illegal in their attempts at renewal. Indeed, they rose from the party line of the Twentieth Congress. Consequently it was impossible to try the proponents of this movement under the law. Here is where the psychiatric political hospitals come in. But they were filled with psychologically ill criminals. To clean the hospitals of this element and to replace it with only political prisoners meant to risk the accusation that psychiatric methods were being used against political dissenters.

A way out of this was swiftly found—the political prisoners would be put right in with the psychologically ill. Everything would then be in its place: there would not be, as there had been under Stalin, psychiatric hospitals solely for political prisoners. There would be merely "special psychiatric hospitals" for socially dangerous patients who required a particularly strict guard.

In the meantime the number of political prisoners whom it was undesirable to try in courts kept growing and there was not room for all of them in the two psychiatric special hospitals. To make places in these hospitals for the political prisoners by releasing those who had committed heinous crimes in a state of insanity would have exposed the whole plan. Consequently, new special psychiatric hospitals had to be created, each of which would be mostly filled with the insane but would also have a certain number of places for normal political prisoners.

A special psychiatric hospital was opened in Sychyovka in Smolensk province. Then another in Chernyakhovsk. Things moved swiftly. In the late sixties and seventies the special psychiatric hospitals sprouted like mushrooms after a rain. I know about more than ten: Kazan, Leningrad, Sychyovka, Chernyakhovsk, Dnepropetrovsk, Oryol, Sverdlovsk, Blagoveshchensk, Alma-Ata, and a "special psychiatric sanatorium" in the Poltava-Kiev area. In addition, departments for forced treatment were set up in all of the provincial psychiatric hospitals. Thus were created widescale opportunities to scatter mentally stable political prisoners among a mass of seriously ill patients.

To implement this plan it was necessary to have a cadre of doctors who could openly be told: "Classify so and so as insane," doctors with diplomas or other qualifications who would invent scientific-sounding formulations for diagnosing normal people as insane. All who have encountered this problem in the USSR agree that such criminal medical men—"doctors" and "scientists"—do exist. All those who have written on this subject recognize as chief among them Doctor of Medical Sciences Professor Daniel Romanovich Lunts (now deceased) and Corresponding Members of the Academy of Medical Sciences of the USSR, Georgi V. Morozov and Viktor M. Morozov. Member of the Academy of Medical Sciences Andrei V. Snezhnevsky is, for example, considered a kind and decent person. I myself met Snezhnevsky. He was chairman of my first experts commission and had a noble and kind appearance. Who would not be touched by this, especially in a hostile milieu? I also thought highly of Professor N. N. Timofeyev. In my case he conducted himself honestly, even courageously. He sought to get me liberated, restored to party membership and to my rank as general, and also to get me the pension to which I was legally entitled.

But it is probably wrong to judge such people on the basis of only a personal impression. The kind smile and the friendly look of Snezhnevsky did not prevent him from signing the experts commission conclusion on me, which was the equivalent of a death sentence—if not worse. And when Snezhnevsky declared to an *Izvestiya* correspondent that psychiatry in the USSR was on such a high level that *a mistake in diagnosis* by even rank-and-file psychiatrists was *"absolutely excluded,"* and that he, during his fifty years of psychiatric practice, did not know of even *one case* in which a normal person had been classified as insane, it became clear to me that he was an active participant in the forgeries of the experts commissions. Yes, and he could not have been anything else. He was the spiritual father of the present trend in psychiatric diagnosis of political prisoners, the ideologist of the expanded interpretation of schizophrenia and of other neurological illnesses.

And Professor N. N. Timofeyev appeared in quite a different light in the stories of V. Borisov and V. Fainberg. Timofeyev understood that the men before him were normal, but he made no haste in releasing them and he tried to break them. I could not and did not want to believe my friends. But when I saw Professor Timofeyev's signature beneath a false reply to Western psychiatrists, on a document that affirmed that in the USSR not a single normal person had been imprisoned in a psychiatric hospital, I realized that he was exactly the same sort as Lunts, the Morozovs, and Snezhnevsky. His attitude to me was singular and can be explained both by the vagueness of the situation after the removal of Khrushchev and also by corporate considerations— *General* Timofeyev defended *General* Grigorenko.

Thus the special psychiatric hospitals and the psychiatric experts commissions headed up by a single organ of political terror constitute a well-planned system for the classification and treatment of a particular category of normal people as lunatics.

Wouldn't it be simpler just to convict these people and to send them off to prison, camp, or exile, or maybe even to shoot them? After all, that's what was done under Stalin.

Yes, but things had changed. Now it was necessary to have at least some semblance of an accusation or an admission by the accused of his own guilt. The laws under which political prisoners are tried are not very convincing since what qualifies an action as criminal under them is extremely dubious. For example, if you keep a book with undesirable political content in your library, you can get seven years of severe regime camp plus five years of exile. You can be subjected to the same kind of punishment for oral expressions of dissatisfaction with various aspects of Soviet life. Such writings as diary entries and letters to your friends and relatives can also be qualified as criminal under these laws.

The classification as criminal of political literature, writings, and conversations depends entirely on the investigatory organs or, more simply, on the arbitrary will of the investigator.

For example, when they searched my apartment they confiscated two samizdat essays entitled "Stalin and Ivan the Terrible—Two Sides of the Same Coin," and "Stalin and Hitler—Two Sides of the Same Coin" only because of their titles. They then confiscated all typescripts and manuscript texts they found, giving as reason the fact that they had been issued privately. Near the end of the search, they confiscated two suitcases of newspaper and magazine clippings that they believed I must have been collecting for some specific use. They even started to confiscate the Soviet magazine *Inostrannaya Literatura (Foreign Literature)*, until one searcher informed the rest that it was an official publication.

Among things categorically classified as subversive is everything published abroad: books of philosophy and history, the majority of works of belles lettres, religious books and so forth.

Thus the door to jail is wide open for any thinking person in the USSR. With laws like this it would seem the authorities would need to establish special methods of repression. But Soviet state security organs have concluded that the old methods of prison and camp incarceration have lost their effectiveness. A new generation has entered the political arena and it is not infected with fear. It is a generation not of revolutionaries but of lovers of truth and justice, proponents of law and order, defenders of the inalienable rights of people, unwavering opponents of tyranny and violence. These people will not violate the laws of the country, even the laws they do not like. But they are stubborn in their defense of their lawfully established rights.

This is the tragedy of our people. Many of the most important laws of the Soviet Union are solely for show. Anyone who tries to exercise freedom of speech or of the press will be repressed, and if he then declares that our people do not possess these rights, he will be labeled anti-Soviet and a slanderer. And the government cannot openly try this person. After all, he has committed no crime. Thus it is necessary to convict this person in such a way that though there appears to be a trial, in fact there is none. Such a person must first be processed by a commission of psychiatric experts who pin on him the label "lunatic." And then he can be tried on a "lawful" basis in a closed trial at which he is not even present.

Everything happened clandestinely, and everything was faked. If the organ of Terror had sentenced you to the special psychiatric hospital, the experts commission was an empty formality. They only formulated a pseudoscientific diagnosis of you—and if by chance they couldn't find an appropriate one, then they would lie. Sometimes by chance a lie was revealed. Once the Serbsky Institute director, Corresponding Member of the Academy of Medical Sciences G. B. Morozov, gave an interview to the correspondents of the magazine *Shtern* and showed them "my" case history, which he also had shown to foreign psychiatrists. This "case history" was beyond a doubt a forgery, because the *Shtern* correspondents copied from it a list of illnesses from which I never suffered. For example, I was supposed to have had cerebral thrombosis in 1952 with loss of speech and paralysis of the hand.

And take my trial in Tashkent. From the twenty-one volumes of the case file that allegedly contained three hundred criminal documents, they cited only three in court, and not one was closely examined. During the investigation, 108 witnesses were interrogated—but only 5 were present at the trial. The basic witnesses were not even summoned to the trial, since their testimony would be on my behalf. And while the testimony of the 5 who were present was not essential, none of them testified against me, either in regard to my criminal case or my alleged insanity.

Given such trial conditions, abuses are likely. And the political prisoners are not the only normal people in the special psychiatric hospitals. There are also people whom the prosecution was positive had committed a heinous crime but whose guilt they had been unable to prove. Or else the prosecution doubted that a person had committed a crime, but proof against him was so irrefutable that he was threatened with execution. And in a humanitarian sense the prosecution found it difficult to aid and abet the execution of a man who might be innocent. In a case of this sort the special psychiatric hospital could serve to cover up the failure of the investigator to complete the case.

There were also people within these institutions who were trying to escape punishment for a crime they'd committed. I knew two such. One of them, thanks to protection he received, got off with eight months in the special psychiatric hospital for a heinous crime—the corruption of a juvenile. The other was a KGB official. For beating up a policeman while drunk he was hidden by the KGB itself in the Chernyakhovsk Special Psychiatric Hospital for a lengthy examination by an experts commission. In the end he was declared sane and was freed from detention under special amnesty terms.

Sometimes these institutions were transformed into temporary dungeons. In the Leningrad Special Psychiatric Hospital I met an Azerbaidzhanian smuggler. The authorities had been trying to catch him red-handed, but he outsmarted them and the booty turned out to be two empty suitcases, at which point they decided to extract a confession from him by torture: They beat him up and then set specially trained dogs on him. He never did confess but they maimed him so badly that he could not be brought into court. He was "sentenced" to a special psychiatric hospital, where they began intensive treatment of his terrible wounds and fractures. It took more than a year before he looked relatively normal again and a second experts commission met and he was released for the duration of the investigation. I do not know his subsequent fate.

Among the normal patients of the special psychiatric hospitals were a certain number of paid informers—perhaps even KGB staff members. I met one in the Leningrad Special Psychiatric Hospital—Vasil Vasilich. I first heard about him from other patients who warned me not to talk carelessly in his presence. I ignored their warnings, having always considered this kind of talk to be a sign of delirium. I became even more firmly convinced of this when I met Vasil Vasilich. Without beating around the bush, he announced be was a senior lieutenant of the KGB. By the standards of the asylum this was a clear sign of a sick mind. We had all kinds of "high-ranking" lunatics in our section: "emperors," "kings," "generals," and even one "generalissimo." So a mere "senior lieutenant" caused me no astonishment. But he quite lucidly explained that he had been assigned here for four years with the rank of lieutenant soon after completing the KGB school. While in the hospital he had been promoted to senior lieutenant, and when he completed his term here, he would get the rank of captain. He was receiving credit for his service years just as if he were at the front in wartime—one year for three. He told me that he could fix it so that I would never get out of here, but that he could also get me released in half a year. I laughed up my sleeve but pretended to listen seriously. However, he quickly realized that I did not believe him, and this hurt his feelings: "Very well then! You don't believe me? Just watch what I will do. In spite of everything, this next experts commission will release me and I will leave right after the commission meets, without waiting for any court decision, since I have already completed my term of service here. Anyway, another person has already arrived to take my place."

I still did not believe him. Yet I could not be surprised by the fact that only he was able to escape punishment for all kinds of rowdy acts, Three days before the experts commission he did things to a nurse that by rights ought to have meant he could not dream of being released. But all they did was lock him up—up till then he alone out of the whole department had walked freely about the corridor and visited other cells as he pleased—and prescribe two shots of sulfazine. The commission released him without any rebuke. Two days later he left. Before he departed, having changed to civilian clothes, he came out into the yard while our ward was having its walk—something none of those being released were permitted to do. He offered me his hand and said, "Well, now do you believe me? There are other things you don't know about that go on here. But I did you no harm."

There are other ways in which normal people get put among the insane. For example, there are those who simulate mental illness and manage to get in there through pull or bribes. These were all people who, as a rule, were deceived by the term "hospital," and who felt that anything was better than a prison or a camp. How they later repented! The regret of those who came here from camp was especially bitter. They tried and tried to prove that they had only been simulating illness. But the way back was closed. "Soviet psychiatrists do not make mistakes in diagnoses."

When people talk with me—foreign correspondents, for example—they do not ask direct questions about my sufferings in the psychiatric hospital. But in little ways they show me how much they really want to hear about this. However, I have no desire to talk at length about my experience in the hospital. I am even a bit ashamed of stressing "my experience," since I knew many who were much worse off than me.

In the ward in which they put me in late May 1970, I met a teacher from Minsk who had been there for seven years, a Pole named Genrikh Iosifovich Forpostov. He had tried to cross the border to return to his homeland but had been caught by the border guards and while under detention had expressed opinions on the Soviet system. As a result they had tried him not only for his attempt to cross the border but also for anti-Soviet propaganda. He was a very intelligent and erudite man, and, like myself, he was deprived of all opportunities to work with his mind. In addition they hindered him in all his efforts at communication. For all the years of my imprisonment, we were in the same ward. I left but he remained. Around May Day in 1975, I received a post card from him from Gomel; but he did not give his address. From this I concluded that he had been transferred from the special psychiatric hospital to the psychiatric asylum of the Ministry of Health. And if he had sent the post card from an asylum, he had been imprisoned among the mentally ill by that time for thirteen years.

Apropos, this is a reply to those who doubt the effectiveness of public protests. I spent five years and two months in prison. In that same Chernyakhovsk Special Psychiatric Prison there was a man named Paramonov who was undergoing forced treatment, having been arrested along with other sailors for participating in the Alliance for Struggle for Political Rights. Paramonov was arrested, as I was, in May 1969. By September 1973 I had been transferred for completion of forced treatment—to the psychiatric hospital of the Ministry of Health; but Paramonov spent two years more in Chernyakhovsk. It was only after Gavrilov, the former leader of the Alliance, or, in other words, the chief defendant, after serving out his six-year term in a severe regime camp, had sent a petition pointing out the inconsistency in a situation in which a rank-and-file member of the Alliance had been imprisoned longer than himself, that they finally transferred Paramonov to an ordinary asylum.

These, of course, were by no means all of the political prisoners of the Chernyakhovsk Special Psychiatric Hospital. Because I spent my entire period there in solitary confinement, I was unable to learn about many of them. In 1973 I was informed that in the Special Psychiatric Hospital there was a total of twenty-one political prisoners.

Each person's torments were different. If you happened to get a doctor who was a bit more humane things were already improved. If, as in my case, there was some sort of publicity attached to your case, things also got easier. In Chernyakhovsk, I saw orderlies and custodial staff beating individual patients. Two patients committed suicide during the years I spent there. One man hung himself and another cut his throat with a dull piece of iron—not so much cutting as tearing. There was one horrible case of vengeance. A certain patient was frequently beaten by orderlies. On leaving his job of nailing crates together, he took a hammer, found one of his tormenters, and dealt him a blow on his head. From doctors I learned that the orderly survived—as a total idiot.

The chief of the ward responded to all my protests against beatings and mistreatment of patients. Evidently he feared publicity. He was afraid I would tell my wife stories that she would in turn pass on. All the patients remarked that the atmosphere in the ward had changed since my arrival. When the court decided that I could be transferred to an ordinary asylum, I was congratulated by almost every patient, but those "chronic patients" who had spent many years in the hospital added sadly: "So now you will depart and once again everything will return to what it was before."

Forpostov, in telling about his arrival at the Chernyakhovsk Special

Psychiatric Hospital, said, "It was as if I had fallen into a dark, deep pit. And I had no hope of ever making my way out of here." Forpostov had no family and so he had no connection with the outer world.

It was also impossible to "recuperate." After all, the "illness" and the "crime" of politicals are one and the same. If you say to the interrogator that there is no freedom of the press in the USSR, that means you are a slanderer, a criminal. If you say the same thing to a doctor-psychiatrist he says that this is delirium, a mental illness. If you say to the interrogator that elections should be made elections and not just theatrical productions of unanimity, that means that you are a criminal, you are against the Soviet system, you are anti-Soviet. If you repeat the same thing to a psychiatrist he will ascribe to you "concepts of reformism," and if in addition you also, and God forbid you should do so, say that things cannot go on this way for long, then they will add "prophecy" to the ever-growing list of your illnesses. And so you have a whole clump of symptoms of schizophrenia. In order to be cured of such "illnesses," you have to renounce your own convictions, trample on your own throat. You have to morally stomp on yourself.

And if you are unwilling to thus recuperate, you will be subjected to an indefinitely long "treatment"—lifelong. This gives you something to think about. Thus I am not surprised that there are persons who "repent." The alternative—imprisonment for life—is terrifying.

People advised my wife to persuade me to "repent," and these were people whom I esteemed and who themselves would probably not have "repented." But they did not feel that they had the right to demand what they would have done themselves from an old man already sufficiently wounded by life. I am grateful to my wife for not conveying their advice to me. It would only have made things more difficult. Even now I am not as surprised that anyone repented as that so few did. I do not condemn anyone who repented, and I do not feel that anyone has the right to condemn them.

It is more abnormal for a mother who has been taken from her small children to voluntarily accept life imprisonment than it is for her to return to her children by means of an untruthful "repentance." It is not her own shame but the shame of the system that puts a mother face to face with such a choice.

I am going to dwell a little more on those details common to all special psychiatric hospitals, beginning with *the effect of medication* on patients. Much has been written about this, especially in connection with the savage impact of medication on Leonid Plyushch in the Dnepropetrovsk Special Psychiatric Hospital. Therefore I limit myself only to certain personal observations.

The most widely used medication is aminazin (similar to Thorazine), administered both internally and intramuscularly. I was astonished at the quantity prescribed to be taken internally—literally a cupped handful of pills at a time. Those who regularly took it lost the color in their palates and tongues and lost their sensation of taste. Their mouths were constantly dry and their stomachs burned. If they refused to take the pills then intramuscular injections were prescribed. When I first saw the effects of these injections I was astounded. More than once at the front I had seen buttock wounds categorized as severe. But what I saw at Chernyakhovsk and subsequently at the Fifth Moscow City Hospital was more awful than anything I had seen at the front. Both buttocks were slashed all over by the surgeon's knife. And in both hospitals, nurses in charge of the treatments explained to me that this was the result of forced injections of aminazin. The drug is not readily absorbed into one's system, and many patients' muscles refuse to accept it. Painful nodes form that prevent the patient from walking, sitting, sleeping, and that can be removed only by surgery.

The next most widely used medication was haloperidol (similar to Haldol). Those taking it cannot maintain a single position for any length of time. They jump up, run, then come to a halt and return....One of the patients in the Fifth City Psychiatric Hospital, Tolya, would go into spasms each time he took this medication. He would open his mouth and could not close it for more than an hour at a time. His breathing was interrupted and his eyes bugged out. His face looked tormented and he constantly struggled with asphyxia and body tremors.

After my release from the psychiatric hospital I read a beautifully published Hungarian prospectus for haloperidol. Perhaps it is a fine medication when properly prescribed. But even the most remarkable medication can backfire when taken incorrectly.

The impact of the hospital regime on prisoners was significant. In all special psychiatric hospitals everyone is deprived of the possibility of occupying themselves with mental labor. Not only did they refuse to let me have paper, a pen, or a pencil but they would not even permit me to keep in my cell a half-centimeter piece of pencil lead that I wanted to use to mark the margins of my own books when something in the text attracted my attention. One time the duty officer, a jailer, and a duty nurse burst into my cell, got me up, and carried out a search without telling me what they were looking for. They left without finding anything. But out in the corridor the nurse kept saying, "I saw him using it myself." After a time they reentered and asked me directly for my piece of pencil lead. Once again the nurse asserted she had seen me marking my book, and once again they searched me, but I decided not to tell them that I was not using a pencil point but my fingernail. I was afraid to tell them—they'd cut off my fingernail.

And how much trouble those books cost me! At first I was told nearly every day that I had too many books. So I went to the ward chief, taking the books with me. I demonstrated to him that not a single one was unnecessary. A new shift came on and once again I heard, "A patient is allowed to have only one book." Once again I was forced to prove that they were necessary. Finally they decided that I would be permitted to keep five books in my cell and would have to turn in the rest. This, too, I argued. In the first place, I was studying German. This meant I needed the two books that made up my text, then four volumes of the German-Russian and Russian-German dictionaries, a Russian-German phrase book, plus one literary work in German—a total of eight books. Besides this, I had decided to study mathematics logic, which meant I needed one more book, and I wanted at least one magazine of the four to which I subscribed. Thus I required in my cell twelve books at the very minimum. I had to go and prove this repeatedly.

There were all kinds of *humiliation*—dress, for example, and insults received regularly from the staff. At the same time it was believed that political prisoners should be educated at every available opportunity. The "education" was on the level of the newspapers, but our "educators" were ignoramuses. I did not have to put up with their lessons. They seemed to consider me a well-informed person and always turned to me for clarification of whatever was incomprehensible in international and domestic events. They even appealed to me for help in preparing synopses of Communist party politics. I consented to write them, and the lectures based on them were subsequently recognized by the leaders of the study groups as models.

Forpostov, however, caught it in all respects! He was the first political prisoner in Chernyakhovsk. The philistines set right to work creating a situation in which they could break him. They wanted to prove to the center that they could be entrusted with the "reeducation" of political prisoners. But Forpostov held out. The more I came to know this man, the more I realized that he was really a martyr and a hero. Though isolated he maintained a proud and independent personality through the hell of the Chernyakhovsk Special Psychiatric Hospital and thereby lightened the lot of all those who came after him. It was in particular by watching him that I learned how to fight for certain rights, for example, for books and for walks outdoors.

On the question of walks I immediately came into conflict with the staff. The dangerously insane patients were not taken out at all. When I began to demand to be taken out, in accordance with the schedule, I was told by the duty nurse and the jailer that none of the patients under guard wanted to go out for walks and that they would not consider taking out just me. I summoned the duty officer and then appealed to the chief of the ward, so they began to take me out. The schedule stated that the outdoor walk was supposed to last two hours; they would end my walk period, particularly when it was cold, after only thirty or forty minutes. We argued over this almost every day and they found every possible reason for shortening the walk periods. No matter how nauseating it was I simply had to keep on complaining. If I fell silent they would go right back to the old situation. Finally I got what I wanted. Toward the end of the second year an order was issued stating that I was to be taken out even if no one else wanted to go out. In fact they never did take me out all alone. Most of the patients under guard always chose to go out, and all of them supported me, even though the staff members kept trying to incite them against me.

The orderlies' attitude toward the prisoners included both esteem and fear. During all the years during which I was under guard, a man named Boris Gribov was, too. Boris was aloof and seemed totally out of contact with his surroundings; he lived in some sort of an internal life of his own, conversing with himself and laughing. I had heard that before he became ill he had studied in a technical school. His family consisted of himself, his mother, and his younger sister, whom he loved dearly, and who had died suddenly. Boris had gone to the funeral, outwardly calm. After the funeral he decided to return immediately to school. His mother went to see him off. On the way there he choked her to death.

He was an athlete, still very strong when I knew him. He was nice to me, probably because of my age. I felt a deep, fatherly affection for Borya. He had one unfortunate trait—when alongside a member of the custodial staff, an orderly, or a nurse, he might strike without warning. They beat him as well, and perhaps he struck out at them because of that. He liked to sit on the floor beside or under his cot. One day, as one of the orderlies passed him, he kicked him hard in the face with his boot and badly injured him. I had directed a plea to the chief of the department earlier with a request to give the custodial personnel, the nurses, and the orderlies directions not to treat Boris in this manner. And now an incident like this!

In this case I asked the orderly whether he had really struck Borya. He responded with a challenge: "Sure it was me! So what!" I lost my temper and karate-chopped him on the throat with the side of my hand. He fell to the floor. After that they didn't touch Borya, and those criminals—in other words, the orderlies—began to treat the patients with more respect. I must say that among the orderlies there were a few decent people who were naturally sympathetic to the patients.

Insofar as the average medical staff members went, their attitude to me depended first of all on what wind was blowing from the top. The wife of the hospital chief was extremely influential. The nurses, who certainly knew how to poison daily life, played up to her. What hurt me most was when they hissed at me: "Don't get worked up!" This specific psychiatric expression referred to lunatics in whom the process of mental deterioration had sharply accelerated. All I had to do was make one remark, let's say, protesting against ending the walk ahead of time, and one of them would snap: "Don't get worked up!"

This was psychological pressure; the physical pressures were more tangible. For the first two months they confined me in a cell of six square meters with a delirious patient who had committed a heinous murder. It is not pleasant to spend the whole day staring into the face of a man who either sits motionless with a blank expression or speaks incessantly. It is even less pleasant to awaken and see this person poised over you ready to hurl himself upon you. They removed him from my cell only after I had had to tear him off me and throw him back on his cot one night at 2:00 A.M. I did not call for help, but the door to the cell was immediately opened and they took him away. What that means is that they were watching the whole struggle through the peephole, giving me the opportunity to become thoroughly frightened.

After this I remained in my cell alone until I left the hospital. They put a new lock on the door and stored the key in the guardroom of a different building. They nailed shut the food slot—the sliding window in the door through which meals were passed. These two measures were supposed to intensify my isolation. Their side effects were also tormenting. For example, in summer the air coming through the window was like air from an oven. Before the food slot had been nailed shut, I could signal to the jailer and he would open it. There would be some cross-ventilation in the cell and it would be easier to breathe. Now I felt like a fish on a river bank. I began to have heart paroxysms. They would not permit medication—neither validol nor nitroglycerin—in the cell. Previously when I'd had a heart paroxysm, I'd signaled for medication through the food slot, but now the door had to be opened; and the key was in the guardroom with the duty officer. When the key was needed, the duty officer might be making his rounds in the ward. Sometimes it took an hour to find him.

My isolation was unpleasant in another respect—in the use of the toilet. It was rare that I could not manage to wait to defecate. But urination was, of course, a frequent need. It might happen that by the time they found the duty officer and he came with the key I had waited too long. If this happened systematically I fell into a state of general incontinence. It got to the point where I couldn't think about anything else except not being tardy at signaling to them. Then I got to the point where I would immediately have an intolerable desire to urinate if I pressed the call button for any reason, even if I had just returned from the toilet. A conditioned reflex had been established. And how could it be otherwise? This situation went on for more than a year and a half. They could have given me a toilet in the cell. But someone evidently liked it the way it was.

One more torment was the so-called *release* commission. Twice a year the question of whom to release was allegedly decided in these commissions. In fact, nothing was decided. For one thing, the commission didn't have time. In my ward alone there were from ninety-four to ninety-eight patients. The commission would begin its work at 10:00 to 10:30 A.M. and finish by 1:30 P.M., less than two minutes per person. And within those two minutes the commission chairman, Serbsky Institute professor Ilinsky, was supposed to diagnose the patient better than his attending physician! The physician might recommend release but Ilinsky would decide: "Continue the treatment." What magnificent erudition and how swiftly it manifested itself—an excellent illustration of Snezhnevsky's claim that Soviet psychiatry was on such a high plane that "mistakes in diagnosis were absolutely excluded."

Ilinsky had received directions from Moscow on each political prisoner. All they had to do was give him a list of those to release—and everything was clear. The rest were not to be released. Here, indeed, mistakes were impossible.

But the special hospital prisoners kept on hoping, becoming excited as early as two months before the commission. The cell for prisoners under guard would fill up and two or three more cells would be transferred to the status of prisoners kept under guard. After the commission had met, it would take another month for the prisoners to quiet down. In other words, since there were two commission meetings a year the prisoners were kept in a situation of unusual stress six months of the year.

Even the political prisoners who knew the commission was powerless could not escape this situation. No matter how brief the commission session, it always found time to talk to the political prisoners. To the young who were not yet famous, they talked rudely. And with those like me who had a name they talked ideologically.

I am never going to be able to list all the torments. But I must mention briefly one of the most heinous crimes of the system of "forced measures of a medical character"—one that underlines the antimedical nature of these measures and which none of my predecessors has touched upon: Both the sane and the rest of the patients in the special psychiatric hospitals are totally deprived of a sex life. Even in severe regime colonies and camps there are personal visits, however wretched. In the special psychiatric hospitals there are none. Young people are separated from their wives and fiances. Families are broken up and peoples' lives are destroyed. I speak of young people, whose fate is the most tragic of all, but the elderly, too, are deprived of their last years of the joys of marriage.

Lunatics' Avenue

Valeriy Tarsis

> Everyone tries to be as unlike himself as possible. Everyone takes
> his appointed master for his model. There are other things to be
> read in the destiny of man but no one dares to turn the page. The
> laws of imitation are the laws of fear.
>
> —Andre Gide

1.

Perhaps for Valentine Almazov the worst was simply the slow, empty passing of time. Nothing seemed to be happening anywhere, not that he expected anything more to happen in this one-sixth of the world, which the Soviet way of life had gradually shrunk to the size of a sixty-sixth. He had long believed that even the Princedom of Monaco must be roomier than this walled-in concentration camp, once the land of Holy Russia's turbulence, her faith, her hopes, her disappointments and her struggles.

Tall, dark-eyed and fair-haired, young for his fifty disreputable years and as usual talkative, he was strolling with the geologist Zagogulin and the violin-ist Zhenya Diamant in "Lunatics' Avenue," a corridor, its far end lost in the early morning dimness, which ran the length of Section 39 of one of the largest Soviet mental hospitals.

It was still very early. The corners of the wards were shadowy and silent, the night staff still nodded on their sofas and chairs. The pale yellow blurs of the street lights swung on the frosted window panes; but lorries loaded with tins and bottles were beginning to rattle outside and janitors to call to one another from the doorways; you could hear them through the open window vents while inside, locks screeched and keys jangled as usual.

Nurses and ward-maids hurried along the corridor, some at a run, others at a waddle, among them "Aunt Lina" who weighed twenty stone and was everyone's favorite. Just back from the early service at St. Nicholas, she was cheerfully greeting the patients and made the sign of the cross three times on Almazov's forehead; she assured him that she prayed for him every day and had special prayers offered for him on Sundays.

It was the hour of the patients' morning exercise. The so-called sick were at first glance indistinguishable from the healthy and the only difference apparent upon closer observation was that many looked more spirited, un-bending, uncrushed and unfit for the existence of slaves.

Tired out by insomnia, inactivity and the boredom of their ghost-like existence, they strolled singly or in groups, or did their morning jerks out of the way of the traffic, while the bugbear of the Section, Leonard Sokol, was as usual shouting that he was famished and demanding the key of the cupboard in which the patients' food parcels were kept. His triple chin shaking with indignation as he advanced upon the frightened nurse, he looked forty instead of twenty-two. No one knew much about him; he had given a dozen versions of his background and passed in turn for a student, a journalist, a cinema producer and a police spy—but his harassed father, who flattered and was intimidated by him, was a high government official. The fact that he was the spoiled only son of a powerful bureaucrat was Leonard's only real trouble. Like many others, he had first entered the hospital in order to evade military service, but he had come back to it after a brief but dramatic career of speculation, hooliganism and rape.

It was getting near breakfast time and the Avenue was growing busier and noisier. At last the pretty waitress Masha opened the canteen hatch and began to hand out the plates, each with its portion of sugar, sliced bread and minute pat of butter, while the orderlies ran through the wards, shouting "Breakfast!" and unceremoniously pulling the blankets off those of the patients who were still in bed.

The only genuine patient in the entire Section of 150 men now made his appearance. Karen was as fat as Leonard but his opposite in character. Gliding in the dim light of the Avenue and preceded by a belly as large as a football came the oval head with its black hair, tight crimson cheeks and everlastingly dreamy, radiant, almond-shaped eyes, while the hands were as usual weaving their intricate patterns in the air.

All the tables in the dining-room were already occupied but Karen immediately found a seat. People liked him and were sorry for him. He had had meningitis at fourteen and had since spent thirteen years at the Kanatchikov Villa, as the hospital was popularly known. He talked ceaselessly, nearly always about himself and always in the third person.

"Here is Karen, good Karen, the poor doomed Armenian," he informed

Almazov. "And what are you doing here? Haven't you any better place to go to?"

"Where would be better, Karen?"

"Better at home. Karen's Mummy came yesterday, she brought Karen a shirt, but she wouldn't take him home."

As always when he mentioned his mother, he smiled beatifically. Once, when Leonard had said with a smirk that his mother was pretty, Karen had given him a bloody nose. Dinah, the tall nurse with a Byzantine profile, told him not to fight.

"Why not? He's horrid. But you're nice, you're pretty," said Karen, showing a spontaneity of judgment and a capacity for love and hate which filled Almazov with admiration.

"Breakfast! Breakfast!" Strunkin, the orderly, was shouting. "Need a special invitation, Salmdelov?" Shoving and prodding a crumpled little old man who seemed always on the point of tears, he sat him down at one of the tables and called for the oatmeal.

"For God's sake, Mikhail Samoilich, I can't eat. I'll just have some tea," Samdelov implored.

"You'll eat what you're given." Dipping a tin spoon into the bowl, he held it to Samdelov's mouth with one hand and used the other to unclench his teeth. "Eat, you fool, or you'll go to Section 5." The threat was effective: Section 5 was for the violent and its inmates could be beaten into unconsciousness without any questions being asked.

Samdelov was a well-known bibliographer. Like several other patients, he had been committed by his relations who needed his "living space" (in view of the acute housing shortage, this was not an uncommon practice). There was nothing wrong with his mind, but to be in Section 39, the section used for the further training of doctors, was a great privilege.

No one in it except Karen was the victim of anything except his lot as a Soviet citizen. The presence of Karen among all these healthy people was a mystery. Some said that he was kept as the students' only teaching aid, others that his wealthy parents (both were well-paid scientists) had bribed the administration. But for whatever reason he was there, he alone, among all the prisoners serving their sentence, was completely happy. The melancholy moods in which he called himself the doomed Armenian were vague and fleeting; the rest of the time he sang or talked cheerfully to himself, convinced that he was living in the best of all possible worlds and untroubled by the preoccupation of sane men with improving their own fate even if they could not improve that of the world. Everyone loved him and treated him to snacks and sweets (he had a gargantuan appetite). Even Strunkin called him by affectionate nicknames and never laid hands on him. He was never depressed and only occasionally so excited as to need an injection of aminodin to calm him down.

"For the first time in fifty years I see a really happy man in our God-forsaken country," Valentine Almazov told his friends.

Almazov was relatively a newcomer. He was in Ward 7 and had bed No. 13 in the corner by the window. The window panes were opaque, immovable and invariably curtained, in order to make sure of obliterating the street with its young poplars, flower-beds, cars and passersby, and with it the very notion of life going on outside. But if Almazov had long felt that the chaos of its daily existence had dried up every source of life in the country, he—like all the more sensible of his compatriots—possessed an inexhaustible spring of life in himself. His imagination, which had sustained him throughout the darkest years of his country's captivity, kept before him, day and night, the vision of the full, untrammelled, seething life in the free world; because he was cut off from it, he imagined it as much more beautiful than it really was.

For him as for his friends, the yardstick of beauty was freedom. After four terrible decades they, like other honest Russians, found that their sense of good and evil was blunted; to be more exact, everything appeared to them to be evil, and the good only a remote memory, a lost paradise in the minds of a few old men.

Almazov realized that without goodness there could not be life, but he also realized that freedom must come first: the country must be liberated from its monstrous yoke, swept clean of the monsters who had imposed it—only then, by the light of freedom, could it discover its new ideals and follow them.

At the moment Valentine was entangled in a political argument with Vasily Golin. A colorless individual of uncertain age and profession, all he knew about him was that he came from Kamyshin on the Volga. Golin had evolved a theory of the "liberation of the Soviet mind from the shackles of Stalinism" and was convinced that, once the present rulers were converted to it, everything would be set right.

"But don't you see," stormed Almazov, "that the conflict today is different from any other in history? It's nonsense to talk about peaceful co-existence—what is at stake is not a political regime or a system of balance of powers but the one all-important issue: whether man as an individual, as a person, is to exist or not. Personal freedom is the one unarguable good on earth. The communists have put forward another: not man but the collectivity, not the individual but the herd. But do you imagine that humanity will ever con-sent to be a speechless and endless herd? It would much sooner be destroyed! What the West and the whole free world is trying to prevent is *man* being turned back into a communised anthropomorphic ape. It took thousands of years for the individual to emerge from the herd. Now the atavistic instinct has revived—significantly, among the 'proletarians,' the spiritually destitute who, naturally, are led by blinkered fanatics. All great thinkers have been aristocrats of the spirit, and not one of them, from Heraclitus to Nietzsche, could have fathered the wretched doctrine of that bearded German philistine Marx—nor does anyone follow him except our blockheaded talmudists and the demagogues who make up our ruling junta. But I firmly believe that man will triumph and not the ape. I believe that Russia will enter the new century liberated and renewed in spirit and that by then communism will only be a nursery bogey to frighten our grandchildren. This is why I take no stock in all these pious doctrines of modesty, self-sacrifice, peaceful co-existence, the reduction of all human gifts and potentialities to a single operation on the conveyor belt and of all mental and material needs to a pauper's ration. They are nothing but hypocritical puritanism masquerading as revolution, a new scholasticism more dead than the medieval, a new captivity more terrifying than Babylon. . . ."

"Aren't you overstating your case?" said Golin in his sleepy voice; even his eyelids drooped whenever he argued for longer than a minute.

"What difference does it make if I do? Don't you see that the so-called facts about our way of life are soap bubbles—a bunch of nursery balloons strung on a thin thread? Don't you think that if it weren't for the millions of policemen to guard them, the people would have cut the thread long ago and let these pretty bubbles of illusion be blown away, together with their makers and distributors? How can you over- or under-estimate the qualities of a soap bubble? They depend on what your imagination makes of them. To face the truth, your imagination has to be very rich and daring—unfortunately yours, Vasily Vasilyevich, keeps you trailing after old-fashioned ghosts. You float in the air, completely cut off from reality, and you can't come down to earth. You are as naive as Don Quixote and none of your efforts can get you further than the madhouse. God! the number of useless victims there are! The crowds of Isaacs climbing on to altars of their own free will— not even on their fathers' initiative—and lying down like lambs under the sacrificial knife instead of snatching it up and sticking it into the fat priests!"

After breakfast it was time for aminodin. The patients obediently queued up for their pills: the alternative to a pill was a painful injection. Whatever their alleged illness (the doctors, trained in practice to act as stooges for the police, established whatever diagnosis they fancied) the treatment was the same. Neurotics, schizophrenics, paranoiacs, the manic and the depressed, all were principally treated with aminodin, a remedy as universal as the castor oil in Chekhov's *Ward 6.* *

After the aminodin, it was time for the doctors' rounds and the patients went back to their wards. The maids dusted and scrubbed floors. The patients in their striped pyjamas lay on their beds, waiting, talking, cursing the food, the staff, their life and the world.

It was autumn. Crimson and yellow leaves were spinning in the gold-blue air outside, and somewhere far away, beyond the sunset, people were living: living and not only existing. But here you could only fill your belly, talk of life in which you had no share, and at the end of the day take a double dose of sedative and hope to sleep.

Ward 7 was a Noah's Ark in which every variety of creature was represented. Very roughly, they fell into three main groups—firstly, the failed suicides, classified as lunatics because it was assumed (by doctors and politicians, writers and ideologists) that anyone dissatisfied with the socialist paradise must be a lunatic, and the doctors had conveniently produced the theory that only a lunatic was capable of making an attempt on his own life: not, therefore, the inhuman conditions but individual cases of mental disorder accounted for the suicide rate. They were treated with aminodin for months, sometimes for years. Some took to it and were unwilling to leave. "It might be a lot worse outside," they said darkly. Except for Samdelov, they were all under thirty: almost without exception, suicide was attempted by the young.

The next largest group were the "Americans": people who had tried to get in touch with a foreign embassy—usually the American, hence the nickname—or with tourists from the free world. The boldest had expressed the wish to emigrate.

Finally there was the less clearly defined category of young people who had failed to find their proper place in our society and who rejected all our standards. If they didn't always know what they wanted, they knew exactly what they didn't want: to begin with, to be in the army. They were disgusted by the very thought of military drill and of listening all day long to the official truths which they regarded as pious falsehoods. Discipline was odious to them. They refused to submit to authority in any form and were sickened by reminders of the motherland and of the social tasks which they were nevertheless forced to undertake as most of them were members of the Komsomol (admission to the University depended almost as much on a Komsomol ticket as on finishing

———————————

Ward 6: story by Chekhov about a provincial hospital in the 'eighties, where the doctor in charge himself ends up in the psychiatric ward.

school). A stay at the Kanatchikov Villa meant exemption from military service and, for those who wanted it, a chance to think, to look at things from outside and to take their time over the choice of a career, as well as a holiday from home and the detested authority of their parents. One student was almost in tears the day he was released.

"It bores me to study," he complained to Almazov, "and still more to get a job. Here, nobody forces me to do anything. There are plenty of interesting people. There's conversation, there's chess—I've been exercising my mind. Whereas out there, everyone is busy with such futilities! And my parents don't give me a chance to live. You can't imagine what a dreary, tiresome lot most parents are! And the more progressive, educated, knowledgeable they are, the worse! My *Papachen* is a professor, he's got several decorations; as a result, I've had enough moral maxims dinned into me to drive me clean out of my mind. Officially of course there is no child-parent problem in our society: the children happily follow the heroic tradition of their fathers. But that's another of those official lies. In fact, the children think that the tradition of their fathers leads to a dead end. At best they laugh at them, at worst they send them to hell. What Papa says to me goes in one ear and out the other. It's true that there have been heroes among people of his generation. But either they were killed by Stalin or else they're sitting in a madhouse or some other such health resort. And I'll tell you honestly: their children are worth a lot more than we are. They know what to think of the past and of the present, and they know what to do about it."

"And what's that?"

"You shouldn't ask. You've taught me quite a lot about it yourself."

Like several of the older patients such as Samdelov and Zagogulin, these young people had fetched up in the asylum through the intrigues of their families and, since they were there against their will, they took their status as prisoners for granted.

Apparently this was also taken for granted by the doctors, for, poor though their training was, they knew enough to realize that they were not dealing with sick men. In fact, there were neither patients nor doctors but only jailers in charge of inconvenient citizens. Not only was this true of Section 39 but, in varying degrees, of the hospital as a whole, which incidentally had been built before the revolution for a maximum of a thousand inmates and now held a population six times as large. In Ward 7 and in others after it the doctors *(vrachi)* came to be known as the enemy *(vragi)*, and the day began with a hymn sung to the tune of the "International":

Arise ye starvelings from your slumbers,

Arise ye psychic slaves of woe:,
For reason in revolt now thunders
Against the psychiatric foe…

The doctor in charge of the Section, Lydia Kizyak, a woman of indeterminate age and appearance but of unmistakable police functions, felt sure that all such songs were composed by Almazov and accused him of spreading anti-Soviet propaganda. He looked in astonishment at her boot-button eyes and the overalls which seemed to conceal a papier mache body faintly scented with eau-de-Cologne.

"Do you really imagine I would waste my time on such nonsense?"

"Nonsense or not, you do yourself no good by it."

"The Government's anti-Soviet propaganda for the past half-century has been so effective that I wouldn't dream of entering into competition with it."

Taken aback, she left the room and avoided visiting Ward 7 after this incident. In general, she was afraid of the patients, never saw them alone and pretended not to hear when they tried to speak to her as she hurried through the corridor.

A similar functionary, though more highly placed, was Professor Stein. As a good Marxist, he believed that all mental disorders were caused by a mysterious malfunctioning of the body and refused to have any truck with the soul: the very sound of the word had something anti-Soviet about it. Arrogant and ill-mannered, he was detested by the patients. Most of the staff conformed to the Stein-Kizyak pattern. Among the happy exceptions were Professor Andrey Nezhevsky, chief consultant to the Ministry of Health, and a youngish doctor, Zoya Makhovha, who was deputy head of the section.

2.

"I wish it were *fin du globe,*" said Dorian, with a sigh. "Life is a great disappointment."

"Ah, my dear," cried Lady Narborough, putting on her gloves, "don't tell me that you have exhausted Life. When a man says that one knows that Life has exhausted him…"

—*The Picture of Dorian Gray,* Oscar Wilde

Nearly everyone Almazov knew was exhausted by life. Few of them reached the end of the journey. Kept kicking their heels in purgatory, they gave up their hope of heaven, and as the purging fire was getting more and more like that of hell, they often smouldered away to ashes before learning the final judgment of fate.

Yet Almazov, at fifty, felt young. True, his forehead was furrowed and his hair pepper and salt, but his soul was as young, violent, inconsistent and ardent as when he was seventeen. This indeed was his tragedy. The only thing he felt sure of about himself was that he would still be seventeen even if he lived to be a hundred. He had not the shadow of sophistication or "experience." Everything life had taught him seemed to him increasingly uncertain. Even the people he knew best, his closest friends and relations, appeared to be scarcely more than acquaintances. "What do they want with me?" he asked himself when they walked unceremoniously into his room and offered him advice on his affairs. Yet they were kind, affectionate and well-intentioned.

He had lost all sense of what was currently known as good and evil, principles, convictions, faith. It seemed to him that they had long since vanished from his mother country, a country which he now thought of as a wicked stepmother. He found it as difficult to assess his own actions as those of others and, as a consequence, unbelievably painful to live. All he knew was that the only way of life offered him was intolerable, unworthy of men, fit only for insects.

All the words in current use had lost their resonance, their impact. Language had to be renewed if anyone was to be convinced of anything. There had been a time when words had had a meaning! He even thought of composing a new grammar and a new syntax, and of abolishing all punctuation except perhaps dashes and dots, so that the words should come at the reader in waves, in jostling fighting crowds, breaking their way through to his heart and mind. So that language should have power and beauty—not the beauty of elegant restraint but of power and passion. Dostoevsky was never elegant—there was not a landscape in his books to compare with Turgenev's or Prishvin's or Paustovsky's* —but what power he had! So should a writer's words burn the human heart and leave their meaning in it. Used by politicians, journalists and the various pimps, prostitutes and hangers-on of Soviet literature, they were nothing but the stale sound of hypocrisy and fraud.

Almazov thirsted for action, he saw it as sacramental. His duty as a writer was to speak new words, and his worst fear was of uttering words which failed to become acts, failed to become God transfiguring our wretched, terrifying, bankrupt world.

He had searched for years. He had prayed in churches, he had joined the Party, but had scarcely noticed the difference between Party and church: everywhere he found the same hypocrisy, the same self-interest. There were many gods but never the one God, no one knew Him, least of all himself—

---

* Prishvin and Paustovsky: Soviet novelists.

and he longed with an insane intensity to find Him, to be guided to Him out of his dark night.

There were many signposts, many stars, including those on the Kremlin Towers, but none that led anywhere except to darkness and the void.

Alone and clearly aware of his destiny, he repeated daily the lines of his beloved Pasternak:

> But the order of the acts is planned
> And the end of the way is inescapable.
> I am alone, all drowns in pharisaism.
> To live a life is not as simple as to cross a field.*

But he was not alone, or he could not have lasted a day. With him were companions, a few doomed seekers: Heraclitus, Plato, Zeno the Stoic, Ovid, Claudian, Shakespeare, Bacon, Pascal and, above all, Dostoevsky who of all men had drawn closest to God but had not had time to finish saying what he knew of Him. Lucky or unlucky but certainly enviable, Almazov secretly believed that his own lot was to add to the revelation, to point the way for others.

"The madman is tormented by his thirst," an Indian sage had said (the wise are always madmen to philistines). "It grows ever sharper, it clings to him like bindweed, it follows him as he goes from life to life, like a monkey from tree to tree in search of refreshing fruit. I too was a monkey searching for fruit in the forest but finding only poisonous berries and breaking my bones but also the boughs."

Almazov's thirst was indeed unquenchable and so tormenting that he sometimes felt as if it would choke him. He kept notebooks of quotations in several languages and in his worst moments it gave him a strange and almost physical joy to read them aloud to himself. As powerful as incantations, they gave him not only comfort but the strength to live.

"Live as though you were on the point of death, as if every moment were an unexpected gift," he read in Marcus Aurelius.

This indeed had been his life for a long time past and especially in recent years, ever since he had realised that Communism was a form of Fascism and that Russian literature had ceased to exist: it was then that he handed over a batch of his manuscripts to a visiting British journalist whom he met by chance. His publishers urged him to use a pseudonym but he refused,

---

* From the poem "Hamlet" in *Doctor Zhivago*.

although he knew what awaited him. He cared nothing for the official version of public opinion, and no genuine public opinion was left: for years, no one in Russia had said what he really thought.

"If you knew the source of public judgments, you would cease to strive for approval and praise," Marcus Aurelius had said.

It was with bitter shame that Valentine recalled his years as a Party member. Why had it taken him so long to realise that his "comrades," particularly those who were officials, secretaries, members of the party bureau, were nothing but policemen? Now he held the proof of it. Acting openly as usual, he had made no secret of the fact that he had sent his manuscripts abroad. As soon as this was known, the secretary of his Party committee rang him up. "Drop in tomorrow at noon, Valentine," he said in a honeyed voice. "Let's talk it over. We'll do our very best to help you."

Almazov went. The secretary met him in the hall. Bald and with vacant, watery eyes but usually talkative and self-assertive, he shuffled and rubbed his hands with an embarrassed air.

"Ah, my dear fellow! Come in...There are some comrades from State Security waiting to see you...I'm sure you understand. We thought we'd put our heads together about how to help you best... Let me introduce you..."

The two Chekists,* one short, fat and bald, the other tall, thin and grey, were wandering about the room, plainly ill-at-ease.

Almazov had one of those rare moments of illumination when a man suddenly sees clearly what, for years, was hidden from him. He scarcely heard what the agents were saying; their voices were drowned by the hammering in his head. How was it possible that for so many years he had mistaken this gang for a band of idealists?

"You are in a very serious predicament," mumbled the fat one. "If your book comes out abroad, we'll have to lock you up."

"It's certainly going out, and others after it, so you'd better go ahead." Almazov grinned. "So Khrushchev's assurances of socialist legality are so much wind!"

"Why be coarse? We hope that you'll recall your manuscripts. This is plainly your duty as a communist . . ."

"Yes, I see..." He was thinking that he must hurry up and send the rest of his manuscripts abroad. So ended his affair with the Party; it had been a shameful *mésalliance*.

He remembered the words of Oscar Wilde:

---

* Members of the Cheka, now known as the K.G.B.

But he never fell into the error of arresting his intellectual development by any formal acceptance of creed or system, or of mistaking, for a house in which to live, an inn that is but suitable for the sojourn of a night, or for a few hours of a night in which there are no stars and the moon is in travail.

Certainly, Almazov's night was dark enough, and starless, but he was filled with shame to think that, even for a time, he could have let himself mistake the Kremlin's pentagons for stars and a thieves' den for a house to live in.

But he had never indulged in the morbid contemplation of his sufferings. Now he knew that the sooner he shook the dust off his feet the better: he wrote to Khrushchev and asked permission to go abroad, frankly stating his reasons.

There was no answer for a long time. After a month or two, he assumed that as usual when bureaucrats are addressed without flattery there would be none. But the answer came.

Enchanted by the fading but still lovely August evening, Almazov was writing a description of it in Italian, inspired by the first yellow leaves drifting in the blue and golden sunset. There is a kind of sweet sadness in the barely audible first messages of autumn, awaited with troubled hope. As a man grows older he no longer looks forward to fiery passions and catastrophic splendors in spring, though he still foresees disappointments in autumn. But when every illusion has been dispelled and drifts away in the raw air, he no longer mourns them as in his youth. His heart, grown spacious, all-embracing and enduring, holds their memory but not their venom and he writes about them—always in verse and so headily that his own head spins.

Almazov was writing variations on Leopardi's theme, the "tragedy of everyday life," when that very tragedy broke into his room in the person of two policemen, the head janitor who, like all head janitors, was employed by the police, and a nosy woman who, according to the head janitor, represented the "community" destined in future to replace the organs of the State.*

"Sorry to trouble you, Valentine Ivanovich," said the senior of the two policemen, looking embarrassed. "But the police superintendent wants to have a word with you. He says would you come and see him, it's urgent."

"What can the police want with me? I'm not a hooligan or a thief," said Almazov.

---

* In the Soviet C.P. programme of 1961, it was announced that in view of the imminent advent of Communism the functions of the "State Organs" (e.g. the police) were being gradually taken over by the public.

"I couldn't tell you, I'm afraid. I wasn't told. But as you know, the police is an organ of the State, so you have to come."

Clearly, Almazov was in trouble.

"I'll come with you," said his wife.

"Certainly," said the policeman.

In front of the door was one of the blue cars with a red stripe which—to distinguish them from Stalin's black limousines known as "black ravens"—are popularly known as "plague carts."

At the police station Valentine was asked to wait. His escort had vanished. The policeman at the door was less polite and refused to answer any questions. Needless to say, there was no conversation with the superintendent. At the end of ten minutes, he was taken to a waiting ambulance in the yard. A woman doctor, employed as guard, said:

"You are Valentine Almazov? By order of the chief city psychiatrist you are being taken in for observation."

"Scoundrels!" Almazov muttered to his wife. "They even turn doctors into policemen! But don't worry, it only shows that they're getting frightened. They got me here by a trick. Communist bandits! They'll get what's coming to them in the end—the people will see to it."

He walked to the ambulance. Two young brutes like oxen stood in white overalls watching him.

It was raining. An hour earlier it had been fine, but now the rain drummed on the roof of the ambulance and streamed down the windows. The two brutes sat sniffing; low clouds lumbered across the sky, like the rhinoceroses Valentine as a child had watched at the zoo; the city looked unfamiliar and hostile.

Almazov was brought to the transit point where, day and night, patients from the Moscow mental hospitals waited to be sent home. The two small rooms in the timber barrack were crowded. Clouds of cheap tobacco smoke drifted under the bare planks of the low ceiling. The floor was filthy with mud and spittle. An intolerable stench came from the door of the lavatory, hardly ever closed; an unshaded, fly-blown bulb threw faces into sinister relief; Almazov's wife was quietly weeping, while the doctor on duty—a middle-aged woman with a pained and exhausted expression—was looking past him into space and saying:

"It's too late today...Dr. Yanushkevich has gone home. He won't be in till tomorrow morning. What happened to you? Did you have a row with the neighbors? No? You have your own flat, you say...Is this your wife?...Yes, I see. Yes of course... You aren't the first and you won't be the last...You're lucky to be sent to an asylum. My husband was shot ... The other day the regional party secretary came and condoled, he said the party would never forget what my husband did...That's what they all say...It's astonishing, isn't it?...Do they really think that we, widows and orphans, hundreds of thousands of us, will forget what the Party did to us?..."

Almazov listened in silence. He was not surprised at her frankness. Everywhere—in trams, in trains, especially in the endless queues—he had recently heard people complaining and jeering at the government. The unanimity of which the politicians boasted did indeed exist: the country unanimously abused its leaders, particularly Khrushchev, and more than ever since prime necessities had again vanished from the shops. The more destitute a man looked, the more angrily he cursed the queues and the shortages, the prices, the wages, the inefficiency of the authorities and their ever empty promises.

"Go and sit down, try to rest," said the doctor. "Try to keep your strength, you'll need it. Don't despair. But don't think of staging a protest—going on hunger strike or writing to complain—it won't 'get you anywhere in our country, no one will pay the slightest attention. Even the Turks and the Greeks were moved when Nazim Hikmet and Glesos went on hunger strike, but here they'd only laugh at you. They're made of stone, they aren't human, they're nothing but hangmen..." Almazov sat down on a bench. He felt he must be asleep, and dreaming of Dante's Hell.

3.

It was late. There were already people snoring on the narrow wooden benches; others sat on the floor and ate water melons, spitting out the pips and chucking the husks into the corners of the room. The air was bitter with smoke. Group after group left. Orderlies called out names and people scrabbled for their belongings and went to the ambulances waiting in the yard. The doors were left open and you could hear the sound of the rain.

Almazov was haunted by the illusion that this was the year 1919 and he was waiting at the Kozlov* station; it never left him all through the night. At some time in the early hours he thought that he was having a nightmare; he was choking and tried to wake up. But in fact he was awake all night and spent it pacing cautiously up and down the sleazy floor littered with sleeping figures. Only once, towards the morning, did he find himself sitting on the edge of a bench on which an old man was lying asleep. He wanted to cry and shout, but who would hear a man in hell?

---

* Reference to the Civil War.

That night was the first in a hell which took various forms. He ceased to believe in the possibility of breaking out of it. But he conceived the faith that the hell itself could be destroyed, and the determination to destroy it at whatever cost. He was more and more on fire with hatred.

Everything passes, every feeling dies away. Only hate endures.

All around him were faces exposed by sleep or contorted by nightmares; he alone was awake. It is always hard to be the only one awake, and it is almost unbearable to stand the third watch of the world in a madhouse, especially the first night, when it seems as if the whole world were insane and dragging one down with it into insanity. Only one's thoughts, if they are big and high and strong enough, can lift one like a crane, and that night Valentine's thoughts kept him out of the black slime into which he had been thrown by fate—a fate of which the only aim, so far as he could see, was to annihilate the individual who dared to stray from the herd.

Some philosopher had said that as soon as a man begins to reflect he begins to despise the world. But could anyone bear to despise his home? It occurred to Valentine—and this was the first comfort he received—that his home was a much smaller place than the world. The same fate which had abandoned him in a den of thieves could get him out of it. He knew that he had friends throughout the world, friends who thought of him and sent him their goodwill.

"O God," he thought, "forgive me my presumption. I know that You will forgive me because my mind is indissolubly a particle of Yours. Tell me, so that I may see some light in my utter darkness: in what style have You created Your world? Is it in the style of the terrifying and the grotesque? Are the artists of terror those who are closest to the truth? Are they Your messengers, such men as Dostoevsky, Hoffmann, Gogol, Poe, Dali, Bosch, Grosz?

"I have tried to listen to all those whom You have endowed with reason. They have urged their various convictions upon me, and I have agreed first with one, then with another, but none succeeded in convincing me in the end. And now I am here in Hell, and I have lost the little understanding I had. I can no longer distinguish light from darkness, or Your holy will from the snares of the Devil. Tell me: if the world is evil and we—my masters and myself, sinful though I am—are its predestined victims, why have You bestowed Your reason upon us, to our eternal torment? Or is it better to stop asking questions? Is it better to beat out my brains against the wall so that my soul may fly to You, although You haven't deigned to summon it?

"I hear You. I know Your voice. You order me to live and to struggle against Satan who holds my wretched country in bondage."

341

Camps

Biographies

Born in Budapest in 1905, **ARTHUR KOESTLER** pursued a career as a journalist; he covered several of the century's central stories.

During the Spanish Civil War, Franco's forces sentenced him to death. He served with the French Foreign Legion and the British Army during World War II. Koestler also reported from the Middle East for London's *Times*.

His 1940 novel *Darkness at Noon* won critical acclaim for being perhaps the finest fictional account of Stalin's purges. In later years, he wrote extensively on science and mysticism.

The Yogi and the Commissar, published in the United States in 1946, includes essays he had written for various magazines. Koestler died in 1983.

GUSTAV HERLING was 20 when Germany and the Soviet Union invaded his native Poland; the war interrupted his university studies. In 1940 the Soviets arrested him as he tried to flee to Lithuania. When apprehended he was wearing high leather boots, which identified him to the Soviets as a major in the Polish army—and, therefore, as prisoner of war. He was not: The boots had been a present from his sister.

When transliterated into Russian, his name resembled "Goering." Thus he also fell under suspicion for being related to the German Field Marshal. Although Herling convinced his captors that he was neither an officer nor a Goering, he still was convicted for illegally crossing a border "in order to fight against the Soviet Union."

Hitler's invasion of the USSR led to an amnesty for Polish prisoners in Soviet camps. But Herling did not gain immediate release. He went on a hunger strike and finally won his freedom in January 1942. Herling joined the Polish army in exile and made his way to England.

A World Apart was published in Britain in 1951, with an introduction by Bertrand Russell. It was not published in the United States until 1986. Albert Camus said *A World Apart* "should be published and read in every country…"

For biographical information on **EUGENIA GINZBUR,** see excerpt in the section "Prison."

For biographical information on **VLADIMIR BUKOVSKY,** see excerpt in the section "Apostasy."

For biographical information on **ELINOR LIPPER,** see excerpt in the section "Prison."

For biographical information on **ANATOLY MARCHENKO**, see excerpt in the section "Prison."

For biographical information on **EDWARD KUZNETSOV**, see excerpt in the section "Prison."

For biographical information on **JOHN NOBLE**, sse excerpt in the section "Prison."

Born in 1907, **VARLAM SHALAMOV** was first arrested at age 22. He spent five years in a labor camp. His praise of Nobel Laureate (and anti-Soviet) Ivan Bunin as a classic Russian writer led to his rearrest in 1937. He was sent to Kolyma and stayed there until the 1950s. He died in Moscow in 1982.

For years his stories about camp life circulated in samizdat. Alexander Solzhenitsyn asked Shalamov to work with him on *The Gulag Archipelago*.

"Shalamov's experience in the camps was longer and more bitter than my own," wrote Solzhenitsyn, "and I respectfully confess that to him and not me was it given to touch those depths of bestiality and despair toward which life in the camps dragged us all."

Kolyma Tales, published in 1980, reprints Shalamov's stories as translated and collected by John Glad. A companion volume of Shalamov's stories was published as *Graphite*.

For biographical information on **NATAN SHARANSKY**, see excerpt in the section "Prison."

The Yogi and the Commissar

Arthur Koestler

1.

There is one question connected with the political changes during the past two decades which cannot be satisfactorily answered: the number of Soviet citizens who in connection with these changes lost life or liberty. The wall of silence around Russia which so effectively prevents information even regarding relatively trivial matters from leaking through, is at its densest where this question is concerned. It has been officially admitted by the Soviet government that the White Sea Canal was built entirely, and the Turksib-Railway partly, by Forced Labor Brigades; gigantic enterprises which involved the labor of a million men. But here official information ends; no figures were published and no outsider was ever permitted to visit those camps.

Indirect indications may be gained from Soviet population statistics—or rather the lack of such statistics. In 1930 the Statistical Bureau was purged and it was announced that "Statistics were a weapon in the fight for Communism." They were certainly a silent weapon for, as we saw, the Soviet Union is the only great country in the world which has for years published no standard-of-living index. Likewise, no population census was published between 1926 and 1940. A census was taken in January, 1937, but the results were not published because, according to an official statement, they contained "grave mistakes owing to the activities of enemies of the People." *(Izvestia, 26/3/1939.)* So the Statistical Bureau was once more purged and a new census was undertaken in January 1939. Its results gave the total population of the U.S.S.R. as 170,126,000 souls—roughly 15 millions less than statistical expectation. (Census of December 1926: 147,000,000; official government estimate of 1930: 157,500,000; average yearly increase according to Stalin's statement on October 1, 1935: 3,000,000; minimum estimate for 1939: 185,000,000.) What happened to those at least 15 million "lost souls"? They were not the victims of a sudden increase of birth-control, for contraceptives were practically unobtainable throughout Russia during the whole period. Some millions may have perished during the famine of 1932-33; the number of miscarriages and child-mortality may have increased owing to malnutrition; the others may have perished in the Forced Labor Brigades where eyewitnesses put the mortality among the prisoners at 30 percent per annum. But all this is guesswork. The only certainty is that roughly 10 percent of the Soviet population is statistically missing.

2.

So far, I have relied entirely on official Soviet sources. As to conditions in the Forced Labor Brigades and the total number of the disfranchised people in Russia only private sources are available—the publications of Ciliga, Trotsky, Victor Serge, etc. Among several eyewitness reports of more recent origin in my possession, I wish to quote one, the testimony of Lucien Blit, a leading member of the Bund (the Jewish Socialist Party of Poland). The following facts are based partly on a confidential report delivered by Blit to the "Group of Interallied Socialist Friends" on April 9, 1943, and partly on details related by him to myself.

After the fall of Poland in 1939 Blit, who had taken an active part in organizing the defense of Warsaw, escaped to Vilna, then under Lithuanian rule. From Vilna he was sent by his Party in March 1940, back to Warsaw as a delegate to the Warsaw underground movement. He had a passport issued under the assumed name of Wiscinsky, a Polish accountant. On his way from Vilna to Warsaw he had to cross a stretch of Russian-occupied Polish territory. He was caught by the Russian frontier-guards on May 30, 1940. Arrested, he did not disclose his identity and mission, as the Bund, being a section of the Second International, is illegal in Russia. In those days of chaos, tens of thousands of Poles were escaping from the Germans to the Russian-occupied parts of Poland. Blit pretended to be one of them and shared the average fate of Polish refugees to Russia.

He was brought to the prison of Lomza and kept there for ten months—from May 30, 1940, to March 30, 1941. His cell—No. 81 on the third floor—measured 4.8 square yards, contained one bed and was intended for one prisoner; he shared it for ten months with *seven* others. The first ten minutes' exercise for these eight men took place on January 22, 1941—after 236 days of confinement; the next, a month later, on February 22. They were not permitted to read, to write or to communicate with the outside world.

Disciplinary punishment—inflicted for speaking too loudly, opening the window, making chessmen out of bread crumbs, etc.—consisted in standing for forty-eight hours against a wall in the icy cellar clothed only in a shirt, in more serious cases standing for forty-eight hours in cold water up to the belt. The latter punishment frequently ended in paralysis, insanity or death. Questioning was usually done at night time and as a rule accompanied by beating and threats of execution. Beating was also applied to women, particularly to girls accused of being members of Polish patriotic student organizations.

Cases of insanity and suicide were frequent. In B.'s cell "One night a powerfully built peasant from the region of Kolno woke us up to tell us that he was Jesus Christ and that it was time they took him down from the cross. He was raving for five days, but the wardens only took him away on the sixth....A Jewish boy who had escaped from Nazi-occupied to Soviet territory shouted day and night for a week: 'I am not Trotsky.' "

If the investigation revealed no specific political charge against the prisoner, his case was dismissed and he received the administrative routine sentence of three to eight years' deportation to "Correctional" labor camps for unauthorized entry into Soviet territory. The fate was shared by all Poles who had sought refuge from the Germans in the Soviet Union. In B.'s case the proceeding took the following form:

> In the night of February 26, 1941, I was ordered to collect my belongings and was taken downstairs. After some time I was led with some others into a big dark room. Without any explanations we were each given a slip of paper to sign. The slip contained three typewritten lines to the effect that the OSOB Y SOWYESCENIE (the Special Commission) of the OGPU in Lomza decreed that for the illegal crossing of the State Frontier, M. Wiszynsky was sentenced in accordance with Art. 120 of the Penal Code of the White Russian Republic to three years in a "Correctional" Labor Camp. The only thing left for me to do was to sign, which I did. Later on the Governor of the prison—who was at the same time Chairman of the Special Commission—told me that there were no specific charges against me; that was why I had got away with such a short sentence. Many others, former soldiers of the Polish army, got five years. A Jew whose name I cannot recall and who had been driven over the frontier by the Germans to Kolno got as much as eight years. The Special Commission had the right to inflict sentences up to eight years only. There was no appeal against their decision.

On April 4, 1941, Blit arrived in the labor camp of Plesek on the river

Onega. It contained about 35,000 prisoners. In the subpolar climate where the temperature even in June dropped under zero point Fahrenheit, the men and women had to work twelve to thirteen hours per day, felling trees in the snow-covered Arctic forest. Their food consisted of bread plus two hot soups between 4 and 5 A.M. and between 8 and 9 P.M.; in between, nothing but hot water. Sugar, fruit and vegetables were unknown, and in consequence of this all prisoners were attacked by scurvy; within the first few months they lost their teeth. No clothing, mattresses or blankets were provided; after a couple of weeks suits were reduced to rags, wet on return from works frozen stiff during the night. Each man or woman was assigned the task of cutting 6 cubic meters (8 cubic yards) of wood per day.

A man of average strength could not do much more than half of it; to the women, the same *norms* applied; and the weight of the bread-ration depended on the amount of wood cut. To fall below half the norm meant direct starvation. The younger women supplemented their rations by prostituting themselves to the guards; their price was a pound of bread a time. Prostitution, theft, graft, denunciations, accompanied the struggle for survival. In August of 1941 out of four hundred and fifty Poles in my section a hundred and twenty had swollen bodies and were unable to get up from the barrack-floor. The mortality in the camp was 30 percent per annum. We worked without respite. Sunday was also a working day; even the first of May was a working day. The majority of the Brigades in my camp had had no rest-day throughout the five months which I spent there.

The camp population consisted of criminals and political prisoners. The latter were divided into two groups: "Spies and traitors," and "socially dangerous elements." The second group consisted mainly of people from the national minorities. In my camp for instance there were four hundred Greeks, old inhabitants of Kerch in the Crimea, who had all been arrested on one day in 1938 and collectively sentenced to five years of Forced Labor.

They will never leave the camp. In the U.S.S.R. release after a sentence served is not automatic, but subject to a special decision of the O.G.P.U. For political prisoners this decision never arrives, or arrives in the form of a prolongation of the sentence for a further five years.

B. was released, together with other Poles, after the German attack on Russia in 1941 and the subsequent signing of the Stalin-Sikorsky treaty. He joined the Polish army then under formation in Alma-Ata. For the Soviet citizen no such happy event is possible. Once sent to one of the Arctic labor camps he never returns, doomed to perish in the cold inferno of the polar night.

How many of them? There is no means of ascertaining it; but the estimates by people who have glimpsed behind the Soviet scene suggest about 10 percent of the total population. This is not so fantastic as it seems, since the five million Kulaks officially deported in the years of collectivization already represent a solid core 3 1/2 percent. Then came the crushing of the various oppositions of Left and Right—Trotskyites, Buckarinites, etc., culminating in the purges. And opposition cannot have vanished since, in a people with a great revolutionary tradition, subjected to such sudden and mortal shocks as the arrival of Ribbentrop in Moscow out of the blue sky of an August day in 1939. It would be a miracle if among the 170 million people of the U.S.S.R. there had not been a few hundred thousand who carelessly betrayed their disgust and despair. It is difficult for the Western mind to visualize in a concrete way conditions of life in a country where dissent is officially identified with crime. Once this point is established, the steady trickle of "socially dangerous elements" into the pool of the Forced Labor Battalions and the maintenance of this pool at a level of about 10 percent appears as a logical and inevitable phenomenon.

"I have lived with a number of Russian families," B. says at the end of his narrative, "and there was not a single case in which at least one member among the relatives or friends of the family was not 'absent.' When I spoke to a well-known Soviet journalist in Kuibishev he emphasized, with some pride in his voice, that there were not more than 18 million of them; everything else was exaggeration. Officials of the regime grew very angry at estimates over 20 million; up to that figure their attitude was one of tacit admission."

This is one first-hand report among many, whose authors are personally known to me as reliable and responsible persons. I am fully aware, however, that to the Soviet addict, and also to many uninformed sympathizers, this report will sound like a tale from the moon. One is generally prepared to accept a correction of one's ideas by say, 10 percent; a correction by 1,000 percent is beyond one's capacity of immediate adaptation. Through the cumulative effect of two decades, the gulf between myth and reality has become so great that it requires an equally great mental effort to take the jump and part with one's most cherished illusion.

A World Apart

Gustav Herling

W 1.

hat our work was, or rather what it could be in the hands of those who choose to use it as an instrument of torture, is best shown by this example of a man who, in the winter of 1941, was murdered with work in one of the forest brigades, by a method which was completely legal and only slightly infringed the code of the camp.

A month after my arrival a new transport, containing a hundred political prisoners and twenty bytoviks, came to Yercevo. The bytoviks remained in Yercevo, and the politicals were transported to the other camp sections, with the sole exception of a young, well-built prisoner with the blunt face of the fanatic, called Gorcev, who was detained in Yercevo and directed the forest.

Various strange rumors were current in the camp about Gorcev, for he himself, disregarding the prisoners' time-honored custom, never spoke a word about his own past. This fact alone was sufficient to arouse the prisoners' hostility, for those who guarded closely the secret of their sentence and imprisonment were considered either too proud to be admitted to the solidarity of the prisoners, or else as potential spies and informers. This was not his worst offense, for spying and denunciation were looked upon in the camp as the most natural thing; we were irritated particularly by Gorcev's behavior. His attitude was that of a man who accidentally slipped into the camp, while keeping a firm foothold on freedom. Only the technical experts of the I.T.R.* cauldron were allowed to behave like that, never ordinary prisoners. It was whispered that Gorcev had been an N.K.V.D. officer before his arrest.

He himself—unconsciously, or else through simple stupidity—did everything to confirm this suspicion in our minds. Whenever he opened his

---

* "Iteerovski"—I.T.R.: Engineering and Technical Work.

mouth as the prisoners sat around the fire in the forest, it was to pronounce short, violent harangues against "the enemies of the people" imprisoned in the camps, defending the action of the Party and the Government in placing them out of harm's way. His dull face, with the cunning eyes of a knave and a large scar on the right cheek, lit up with an instinctive smile of humility and subservience whenever he pronounced the words of that magic formula — "the Party and the Government." Once he unwarily revealed that he found himself in the camp only "through error," and that he would soon return to his former "position of responsibility." The other prisoners began to treat him with open and undisguised hatred.

I made several attempts to gain his confidence, not through sympathy but simply from curiosity. I was fascinated by the opportunity of talking to a man who, imprisoned in a labor camp, observed it through the eyes of a free communist. But Gorcev avoided me as he did the others, snubbed me whenever I asked a question, and even provocative jeers produced no reaction from him. Only once did I manage to engage him in conversation, and we discussed capitalist encirclement. This discussion convinced me of the error of the popular belief that the young generation of Soviet communists is only a band of condottieri, who obey their leader but are ready to abandon him at the first good opportunity. For hundreds of thousands of Gorcevs bolshevism is the only religion and the only possible attitude to the world, for it has been thoroughly instilled into them during childhood and youth. Older men like Zinoviev, Kamenev or Bukharin may have looked upon their "ideological deviation" as a great personal defeat which suddenly robbed their lives of meaning, they may have suffered and considered themselves to have been betrayed, they may even have broken down completely—but despite everything they must still have retained enough of their critical faculty to enable them to consider what was being done to them and around them with historical detachment in their sober moments. But for the Gorcevs the breakdown of their faith in communism, the only faith which has directed their lives, would mean the loss of the five basic senses, which recognize, define and appraise the surrounding reality. Even imprisonment cannot goad them into breaking their priestly vows, for they treat it as temporary isolation for a breach of monastic discipline, and wait for the day of release with even greater acquiescence and humility in their hearts. The fact that their period of seclusion and meditation has to be spent in hell does not prove anything for them, or rather it proves only that hell really does exist, and woe to those who suffer expulsion from paradise for sins against the doctrines of the Almighty.

One evening the veil concealing Gorcev's past was lifted slightly. He had

quarreled over some trifle with a group of Mongol nacmeny in the corner of
the barrack, and fell into a rage such as we had never seen in him before. He
seized one of the old Uzbeks by the collar of his robe and, shaking him
furiously, hissed through clenched teeth: "I used to shoot you Asiatic bastards
by the dozen—like sparrows off a branch!" The Uzbek, sitting on his folded
legs on a lower bunk, rattled in his throat in his own language, and his face
changed in a split second so as to become unrecognizable. His eyes darted steel
at the attacker from under his lowered eyelids, his upper lip trembled nervously
under the thin drooping mustache, revealing a row of white teeth. Suddenly,
with a lightning thrust, he knocked Gorcev's hands into the air, and moving his
body slightly forward, spat with all his force in the other's face. Gorcev tried to
throw himself on the old man, but he was held still by the iron grip of two
young Mongols who had jumped down from an upper bunk and caught his
arms. We watched this scene in silence without moving from our places. So it
seemed that he had been employed in suppressing the great native insurrection
of Central Asia; and we knew that this task was entrusted only to those in the
confidence of the authorities, the elite of the party and the N.K.V.D. Gorcev
went to the Third Section with a complaint, but the old Uzbek was not even
summoned for questioning beyond the zone. Perhaps because he had unintentionally confirmed the existence of the rebellion of which it was forbidden
to speak throughout Russia, or perhaps because, despite appearances, he had
no powerful protector beyond the zone, his old connections could not help
him, and he was defenseless before the approaching blow. At any rate, his brigade
took this failure as a good sign. All they wanted was that the Third Section
should refrain from intervention in this matter, that it should throw at least
one of its own people to the wolves, giving him up to the prisoners' revenge.

Some time about Christmas a transport from Krouglitza to the Pechora
camps passed through Yercevo. The prisoners spent three days in the Peresylny
barrack, walking round our barracks in the evenings and looking for friends. It was
one of these who stopped suddenly and went pale as he passed Gorcev's bunk.

"You—here?" he whispered.

Gorcev raised his head, blanched, and backed against the wall.

"Here?" repeated the new arrival, approaching him slowly. Then suddenly
he jumped at Gorcev's throat, threw him down on his back across the bunk, and
pressing his right shoulder into Gorcev's chest, started hammering his head
furiously against the planks.

"So you fell too, did you?" he shouted, punctuating almost every word
with a thud from Gorcev's head. "You fell at last, did you? You could break
fingers in doors, push needles under fingernails, beat our faces and kick us in

the balls and the stomach . . . couldn't you . . . couldn't you? My fingers have grown again . . . they'll choke you yet . . . they'll choke you . . ."

Although younger and apparently stronger than his attacker, Gorcev behaved as if he was paralyzed and did not attempt to defend himself. Only after a few moments did he seem to come to life, and he kicked the other man with his bent knee and fell with him to the floor. Supporting himself on the nearest bench, his face twisted with fear, he got up and started to run towards the barrack door. But there he found a barrier of Uzbeks who had left their corner to prevent his escape. He turned back—his brigade was waiting for him, looking at him with hostility. The attacker now walked towards him, holding an iron bar which someone on an upper bunk had thrust into his hand. The circle began to close round Gorcev. He opened his mouth to shout, but at that very instant one of the nacmeny hit his head with the wooden cover of a bucket, and he fell to the floor, dripping with blood. With the remnants of his strength he raised himself on his knees, looked at the slowly advancing prisoners and shrieked horribly: "They'll kill me! Guard! They'll kill me!"

In the deep silence, Dimka crawled off his bunk, limped over to the barrack door and bolted it. A jerkin, thrown from an upper bunk, fell on Gorcev and immediately the furious blows of the iron bar rained on his head. He threw the jerkin off and, stumbling like a drunkard, rushed towards his own brigade. There he was met by an extended fist, and he bounced off it like a rubber ball, vomiting blood, his legs giving way. He was passed from hand to hand, until he slid to the floor quite helpless, instinctively folding his hands round his head and protecting his stomach with drawn-up knees. He remained crouching like that, crumpled and dripping blood like a wet rag. Several prisoners came up to him and nudged him with their boots, but he made no movement.

"Is he still alive?" asked the one who had unmasked him.

"Examining judge from the Kharkov prison, brothers. He used to beat good men so that their own mothers wouldn't know them. What a bastard, oh! what a bastard . . ." he lamented.

Dimka came up with a pailful of hvoya and threw it over Gorcev's head. He stirred, sighed deeply, and stiffened again.

"He's alive," said the forester-brigadier, "but he won't live long."

The next morning Gorcev washed the dry, congealed blood off his face and crawled to the medical hut, where he was given one day's dispensation from work. He went again beyond the zone, with another complaint to the Third Section, and returned empty-handed. It was now clear to us that the N.K.V.D. was giving up to the prisoners one of its own former men. A strange game, in which the persecutors entered upon a silent gentleman's agreement with their victims, was played out in the camp.

After the discovery of his past Gorcev was given the hardest work in the forest brigade: the sawing of pines with the "little bow." For a man unaccustomed to physical labor, and to forestry in particular, this work means certain death unless he is relieved at least once a day and given a rest at burning cleared branches. But Gorcev was never relieved, and he sawed eleven hours a day, frequently falling from exhaustion, catching at the air like a drowning man, spitting blood and rubbing his fever-ridden face with snow. Whenever he rebelled and threw the saw aside with a gesture of desperate bravado, the brigadier came up to him and said quietly: "Back to work, Gorcev, or we'll finish you off in the barrack," and back to work he would go. The prisoners watched his agonies with pleasure and satisfaction. They could indeed have finished him off in the course of one evening, now that they had their sanction from above, but they would have prolonged his death into infinity to make him suffer the agonies to which he had once condemned thousands.

Gorcev tried to fight back, although he must have known that it was as hopeless as the resistance of his victims had once been at the interrogations. He went to the doctor for a further dispensation, but old Matvei Kirylovich refused to put him on the sick list. Once he refused to march out to work, and was sent to solitary confinement on water alone for forty-eight hours, then driven out to work on the third day. The understanding was working well. Gorcev crawled out every day at the end of the brigade, he walked about dirty and half-conscious, he was feverish, moaned terribly, spat blood and cried like a baby at night, and begged for mercy in the daytime. He received the stakhanovite third cauldron, so that he would not die immediately, for though his work did not entitle him even to the first cauldron, yet the other prisoners did not stint their own percentages to fatten up their victim. Finally, towards the end of January, after a month had gone by, he lost consciousness at work. The prisoners were worried that this time they could not avoid sending him to the hospital. It was agreed that the water carrier who drove out to the forest every day with the stakhanovites' extra portion, and who was friendly with the forest brigades, should take him back on the sledge after the day's work. In the evening the brigade marched slowly off towards home, and several hundred yards behind crawled the sledge with Gorcev's unconscious body. He never reached the zone again, for at the guard-house it was found that the sledge was empty. The water-carrier explained that he had sat in the front of the sledge the whole time, and probably had not heard the fall of the body in the soft snow, piled up on either side of the track. It was not until nine—after the guard had eaten his supper—

that an expedition with a lighted torch set out to find the lost man. Before midnight, through the windows of our barrack, we saw a wavering point of light on the road from the forest, but the sledge, instead of coming straight to the zone, turned off in the direction of the town. Gorcev had been found in a snowdrift two yards deep which was covering one of the frozen streams—his legs hanging out of the sledge, must of course have caught in the rail of the wooden bridge. The body, frozen like an icicle, was taken straight to Yercevo mortuary.

Long after his death, the prisoners still cherished their memories of this revenge. One of my friends among the technical experts, when I had in confidence told him the background of this accident at the forest clearing, laughed bitterly and said: "Well, at last even we can feel that the revolution has reversed the old order of things. Once they used to throw slaves to the lions, now it is the lions who are thrown to the slaves."

2.

"Dom Svidanyi," literally "the house of meetings," was the name which we gave to a newly-built wing of the guard-house, where prisoners were allowed to spend between one and three days with their relatives, who had come from all parts of Russia to the Kargopol camp for this short visit. Its topographic situation in the camp zone was to some extent symbolic: our entrance to the barrack was through the guard-house, from the zone, and the way out was already on the other side of the barbed wire, at liberty. Thus it was easy to think that the house in which the prisoners saw their relatives for the first time after so many years was on the borderline between freedom and slavery; a prisoner, shaved, washed and neatly dressed, having shown his pass and the official permit for the visit, walked through the partition straight into arms extended to him from liberty.

Permission for such a visit was granted only after the most complicated and trying procedure had been undergone by the prisoner as well as by his family. As far as I can remember, every prisoner was in theory allowed to have one visitor a year, but the majority of prisoners had to wait three, sometimes even five, years for it. The prisoner's part was limited: when a year had passed from the moment of his arrest, he was free to present to the Third Section a written request for a visit, together with a letter from his family, which made it quite unmistakably clear that one of them wished to see him, and a certificate of his good behavior, both at work and in the barrack, from the camp authorities. This meant that a prisoner who wanted to see his mother or his wife had to work at the level of at least the second cauldron, or full norm, for a year; the inhabitants of the mortuary were as a rule excluded from the privilege of a visit. The letter from the family was no mere formality. Where the connections between a prisoner and a free person were not those of blood, but of marriage, the greatest pressure was put on those outside to sever all relations with the "enemy of the people", and many wives broke down under it. I read many letters in which wives wrote to their husbands in the camp: "I can't go on living like this," asking to be freed from their marriage vows. Occasionally, when the prisoner had every hope that permission for the visit would be granted, the procedure suddenly stopped dead, and only a year or two later did he learn that his relatives at liberty had thought better of it and withdrawn the original request. At other times, a prisoner who went to the house of meetings was welcomed not by extended arms, trembling with desire and longing, but by a look of weariness and words begging for mercy and release. Such visits confined themselves to the few hours necessary to settle the fate of the children, while the unfortunate prisoner's heart withered like a dried nut, beating helplessly within its hard shell.

The initiative in the efforts to obtain permission naturally belongs to the family at liberty. From letters which I was shown by other prisoners I gathered that the procedure is prolonged, intricate, and even dangerous. The decision does not rest with GULAG (the Central Office of Camp Administration), which is concerned only with the administration of the camps and has nothing to do with the sentences or the indictments which produced them, but nominally with the Chief Prosecutor of the USSR, and actually with the local N.K.V.D. office in the petitioner's place of domicile. A free person who is sufficiently obstinate to persist in his audaciousness, undeterred by the initial obstacles, finds himself the victim of a vicious circle from which he can seldom escape. Only a person with an absolutely blameless political past, one who can prove that he is immune from the germ of counter-revolution, can obtain the precious permission. Now in Russia no one would dare enter a hearing of interrogation even with a totally clear conscience; in this case, too, the certificate of political health is demanded by officials who are the only ones with the authority to give it. Apart from this evident contradiction, we find another, even more fantastic. The presence in one's family of an enemy of the people is in itself sufficient proof of contamination, for someone who has lived with him during many years cannot be free from the plague of counter-revolution.

The N.K.V.D. treat political offenses as a contagious disease. Thus when a petitioner arrives at the N.K.V.D. office for a certificate of health, that in itself is evidence of his probable infection. But let us suppose that the political blood tests have not shown the presence of infection in the organism, and the petitioner has been vaccinated and remains in quarantine for an indefinite time.

If all goes well, he then receives permission for a direct, three-day contact with the sick man, whose very existence seemed at the interrogation to be dangerous even at a distance of several thousand miles. The cruel, discouraging paradox of this situation is that during the hearings at the N.K.V.D. the petitioner must do everything to convince the interrogator that he has broken all relations with the prisoner and eradicated all emotional ties with him. And back comes the obvious question: in that case, why should he be willing to undertake a distant and expensive journey in order to see the prisoner? There is no way out of this conundrum. No obstacle is put in the way of wives who ask for a visit to the camp in order to end their marriages, thus freeing themselves from the nightmare of a life in half-slavery, in an atmosphere of constant suspicion, and with the brand of shared responsibility for the crimes of others. Others either give it up or else take the final, desperate step—a journey to Moscow to obtain the permission through special influence there. Even if they do somehow succeed by this method, they will have to face the vengefulness of the local N.K.V.D. whom they have slighted to achieve their objective, when they return from the camp to their native town. It is easy to guess how many are brave enough to risk asking for permission under these circumstances.

It is natural to ask why these monstrous difficulties and obstacles are put in the way of a visit, since the contingent of workers has already been supplied to the camps, and the costs of the journey there are covered by the visitor himself. I can only suggest three possible conjectures, of which one at least is accurate. Either the N.K.V.D. sincerely believes in its mission of safeguarding the Soviet citizen's political health; or it attempts as far as possible to conceal from free people the conditions of work in forced labor camps, and to induce them by indirect pressure to break off all relations with their imprisoned relatives; or in this way it is putting power into the hands of camp authorities, which during whole years can squeeze from prisoners the remnants of their strength and health, deluding them with the hope of an imminent visit.

When the relative, usually the prisoner's wife or mother, at last finds herself in the Third Section office of the particular camp, she must sign a declaration, promising not to disclose by even one word, after her return home, what she has seen of the camp through the barbed wire; the privileged prisoner signs a similar declaration, undertaking—this time under pain of heavy punishment, even of death—not to mention in conversation his and his fellow-prisoners' life and conditions in the camp. One can imagine how difficult this regulation makes any indirect or intimate contact between two people who, after many years of separation, meet for the first time in these unusual surroundings; what is left of a relationship between two people if an exchange of mutual experiences is excluded from it? The prisoner is forbidden to say, and the visitor forbidden to ask, what he has gone through since the day of his arrest. If he has changed beyond recognition, if he has become painfully thin, if his hair has turned grey and he has aged prematurely, if he looks like a walking skeleton, he is allowed only to remark casually that "he hasn't been feeling too well, for the climate of this part of Russia does not suit him." Having thrown a cloak of silence over what may be the most important period of his life, the regulations push him back to an already distant and dimly-remembered past, when he was at liberty and an entirely different man, when he felt and thought differently; he is in the unbearable situation of a man who should be free to speak, to shout even, and who is allowed only to listen. I have no idea whether all prisoners keep the promise given before the meeting, but, taking into consideration the high price which they would have to pay for breaking it, it may be supposed that they do. It is true that the closeness of the visiting relative may be some guarantee of discretion, but who is to say whether the tiny room, in which the two live together during the whole visit, is not supplied with an eavesdropping microphone, or whether a Third Section official is not listening on the other side of the partition? I only know that I often heard sobbing as I passed by the house of meetings, and I believe that this helpless, spasmodic weeping relieves their tension and expresses for the wretched human tatters, now dressed in clean prison clothing, all that they may not say in words. I think, too, that this is one of the advantages of a visit, for a prisoner seldom dares to cry in front of his companions, and the nightly sobbing in their sleep in the barrack proved to me that it could bring great relief. In the emptiness which sealed lips create between the two people in the house of meetings, they advance cautiously like lovers who, having lost their sight during long years of separation, reassure themselves of each other's tangible existence with tentative caresses until, at the moment when they have finally learnt to communicate in the new language of their feelings, they must part again. That is why prisoners, after their return from the house of meetings, were lost in thought, disillusioned, and even more depressed than before the longed-for visit.

Victor Kravchenko, in *I Chose Freedom,* tells the story of a woman who, after many attempts and in return for a promise of cooperation with the N.K.V.D., was finally given permission to visit her husband in a camp in the Urals. Into the small room at the guard-house shuffled an old man in filthy rags, and it was only with difficulty and after several moments that the young woman recognized her husband. It is more than likely that he had aged and changed, but I cannot believe that he was in rags. I cannot, of course, make a categorical statement about conditions in the Ural camps, and I can only answer for what

I myself saw, heard or lived through in a camp near the White Sea. Nevertheless, I believe that all forced labor camps throughout Soviet Russia, though they differ greatly in various respects, had a common aim, possibly imposed upon them from above: they strive at all costs to maintain, before free Soviet citizens, the appearance of normal industrial enterprises which differ from other sections of the general industrial plan only by their employment of prisoners instead of ordinary workers, prisoners who are quite understandably paid slightly less and treated slightly worse than if they were working of their own free will. It is impossible to disguise the physical condition of prisoners from their visiting relatives, but it is still possible to conceal, at least partly, the conditions in which they live. In Yercevo, on the day before the visit, the prisoner was made to go to the bath-house and to the barber, he gave up his rags in the store of old clothing and received—only for the three days of the visit—a clean linen shirt, clean underwear, new wadded trousers and jerkin, a cap with ear-flaps in good condition, and boots of the first quality; from this last condition were exempt only prisoners who had managed to preserve, for just such an occasion, the suit which they had worn at the time of their original arrest, or to acquire one, usually in a dishonest way, while serving their sentence. As if this were not enough, the prisoner was issued with bread and soup tickets for three days in advance; he usually ate all the bread by himself there and then, to eat his fill just once, and the soup tickets he distributed among his friends, relying on the food which would be brought by the visitor. When the visit was over, the prisoner had to submit all that he had received from his relatives to an inspection at the guard-house, then he went straight to the clothing store to shed his disguise and take up his true skin once more. These regulations were always very strictly enforced, though even here there were glaring contradictions which could at once destroy the whole effect of this comedy staged for the benefit of free citizens of the Soviet Union. On the first morning of a visit the relative could, by raising the curtain in the room, catch a glimpse of the brigades marching out from the guard-house to work beyond the zone, and see the dirty scrofulous shadows wrapped in torn rags held together with string, gripping their empty messcans and swooning from cold, hunger and exhaustion; only an imbecile could have believed that the scrubbed, neat man who had been brought to the house of meetings the day before in clean underwear and new clothes had avoided the fate of the others. This revolting masquerade was sometimes comic despite its tragic implication, and a prisoner in his holiday outfit was greeted by jeers from the others in the barrack. I thought that if someone would fold the hands of these living dead, dressed in their tidy suits, over their chests, and force a holy picture and a candle between their stiffened fingers, they could be laid out in oak coffins, ready for their last journey. Needless to say, the prisoners who were forced to take part in this exhibition felt awkward in their disguise, as if ashamed and humiliated by the thought that they were being made use of as a screen to hide the camp's true face for three days.

The house itself, seen from the road which led to the camp from the village, made a pleasant impression. It was built of rough pine beams, the gaps filled in with oakum, the roof was laid with good tiling, and fortunately the walls were not plastered. We all had occasion to curse the plaster with which the barrack walls in the camp were covered: water from melted snowdrifts, and urine made by prisoners against the barracks at night, disfigured the white walls with yellow-grey stains, which looked from a distance like unhealthy pimples of acne on a pale, anemic face. During the summer thaw the thin plaster peeled off the walls, and then we walked through the zone without looking to right or left—the holes corroded in the brittle crust of whitewash by the climatic scurvy seemed to remind us that the same process was corrupting our bodies. If only because of the contrast, it was pleasant to rest our weary eyes by gazing at the house of meetings, and not without cause (though its appearance was not the only reason) was it known as "the health resort." The door outside the zone, which could be used only by the free visitors, was reached by a few solid wooden steps; cotton curtains hung in the windows, and long window boxes planted with flowers stood on the window-sills. Every room was furnished with two neatly-made beds, a large table, two benches, a basin and a water-jug, a clothes-cupboard and an iron stove; there was even a lampshade over the electric-light bulb. What more could a prisoner, who had lived for years on a common bunk in a dirty barrack, desire of this model *petit bourgeois* dwelling? Our dreams of life at liberty were based on that room.

Every prisoner was given a separate room, but the prison rules broke that intimacy brutally by making clear distinctions between the privileges of free men and the obligations of prisoners serving a sentence of forced labor. The visiting relative was at liberty to leave the house at any time of the day and night to go to the village, but always alone: the prisoner had to remain in the same room during the whole visit, or else, if he so wished, he could return to the zone for a few minutes after first being searched at the guardhouse. In exceptional cases the permission was burdened by an additional provision which confined the visit to the daytime: the prisoner returned to his barrack in the evening, and came back to the house of meetings at dawn (I could never think of a reason for this cruelty; some prisoners believed that it was a form of deliberate persecution, but this was not confirmed by general practice). In the mornings, when the brigades passed the house of meetings on their way to work, the curtains in its windows were usually drawn slightly aside, and we saw our fellow-prisoners inside with strange, free faces. We usually slowed down and dragged our legs in a slightly exaggerated manner, as if to show the "people from over there" to what life behind barbed wire had brought us. We were allowed to give no other sign of recognition, just as we were forbidden to wave to passengers on passing trains as we passed by the railway tracks (the guards had strict orders to drive their brigades into the forest, away from the railway tracks, whenever they heard the sound of an approaching train). The prisoners in the windows of the house of meetings frequently smiled at us and sometimes greeted us by fondly embracing their visitor, as if in this simple and touching way they wanted to remind us that they were human, with well-dressed relatives, free to touch intimately those "from the other side." But more often tears stood in their faded eyes, and painful spasms passed through the haggard faces; perhaps it was our own wretchedness which thus moved those more fortunate prisoners who saw us through the window of a warm, clean room, or perhaps it was only the thought that tomorrow or the day after they themselves would be back in the brigades, hungry and cold, marching off for another twelve hours in the forest.

The situation of those free women who after surmounting countless obstacles have at last succeeded in reaching the camp for a visit is no more enviable. They feel the boundless suffering of the prisoner, without fully understanding it, or being in any way able to help; the long years of separation have killed much of their feeling for their husbands, and they come to the camp only to warm them, during three short days, with the embers of their love—the flame could not be rekindled from the spark hidden in the warm heart of ashes. The camp, distant and barred off from the visitor, yet casts its shadowy menace on them. They are not prisoners, but they are related to those enemies of the people. Perhaps they would more willingly agree to accept the prisoner's burden of hatred and suffering than to suffer in silence the humiliating and equivocal situation of borderland inhabitants. The camp officials treat them politely and correctly, but at the same time with almost undisguised reserve and contempt. How can they show respect to the wife or the mother of a wretch who begs for a spoonful of soup, rummages in the rubbish heaps, and has long since lost any feeling of his own human dignity? In Yercevo village, where every new face left no doubt as to its owner's purpose in the town, visitors to the camp were cautiously avoided. One prisoner told me that when his daughter visited him in the camp she met an old friend, now the wife of one of the camp officials, in the village. They greeted each other with pleasure, but after a while the official's wife drew back anxiously. "What a coincidence, meeting you here! But what are you doing in Yercevo?" "Oh," answered the girl, "I've come to visit my father. You can imagine how unhappy we are!" and added: "Of course, he isn't at all guilty," as if hoping that after breaking the ice she would succeed in obtaining some consideration for her father in the camp. But the other woman left her coldly, saying: "Good. You should write a complaint to Moscow, they will look into it there."

Although, or perhaps because, these visits were so rare and so difficult to obtain, they played a large part in the life of the camp. I became convinced, while I was still in prison, that if a man has no clear end in life—and the ending of his sentence and his final release were too distant and uncertain to be seriously taken into account—he must at least have something to anticipate. Letters were so rare, and their language so commonplace and restricted, that they had no attraction as an object of expectation; only the visits were left to the prisoners. They waited for them with anxiety and joyful tension, and often reckoned the time of their sentences or their lives by those short moments of happiness, or even its very anticipation. Those who still had not been informed of a definite date for their visits lived on hope; they possessed something to occupy them, and perhaps even more, a quiet passion which saved them from utter despair, from the fatal consciousness of their aimless existence. They fed their hope artificially, wrote requests and applications to Moscow, bore the heaviest work manfully like pioneers building their own future; in the evenings they talked to their more fortunate comrades, repeatedly asking what ways there were of hastening that wonderful event; on rest-days they stood outside the house of meetings, as if to make sure that their rooms were reserved and only awaiting the arrival of the guests, quarreled among themselves in advance over the choice of rooms, and endlessly cleaned and darned their best clothes. Lonely prisoners and foreigners were naturally in the worst position, but even they were able to draw some benefit from the visits, sharing as they did in the happiness and expectation of others, or recognizing them to be their only source of information about life outside, at liberty.

Men isolated forcibly, or even voluntarily, from the rest of the world, idealize everything that occurs beyond the frontiers of their solitude. It was touching to hear prisoners, before the expected visit, recalling the liberty whose mere taste they were about to enjoy. It seemed that never before in their lives had they experienced either important events or bitter disappointments. Freedom for them was the one blessed irreplaceable. At liberty one slept, ate and worked differently, there the sun was brighter, the snow whiter, and the frost less painful. "Remember? Remember?"—excited voices whispered on the bunks. "I remember, at liberty, I was stupid and wouldn't eat brown bread." And another would take up: "I wasn't satisfied with Kursk, I wanted Moscow. Just wait till my wife comes, I'll tell her what I think of Kursk now, just wait till I tell her…" These conversations sometimes dragged on till late into the night, but they were never heard on bunks where a prisoner who had recently returned from a visit lay. The illusion had come face to face with the reality, and the illusion always suffered. Whatever the reasons for their disappointment—whether the freedom, realized for three days, had not lived up to its idealized expectation, whether it was too short, or whether, fading away like an interrupted dream, it had left only fresh emptiness in which they had nothing to wait for—the prisoners were invariably silent and irritable after visits, to say nothing of those whose visits had been transformed into a tragic formality of separation and divorce. Krestynski, a joiner from the 48th brigade, twice attempted to hang himself after an interview with his wife, who had asked him for a divorce and for his agreement to place their children in a municipal nursery. I came to the conclusion that if hope can often be the only meaning left in life, then its realization may sometimes be an unbearable torment.

Younger prisoners suffered additional and, at least as far as their neighbors on the bunk were concerned, by no means intimate sexual anxieties before visits from their wives. Years of heavy labor and hunger had undermined their virility, and now, before an intimate meeting with an almost strange woman, they felt, besides nervous excitement, helpless anger and despair. Several times I did hear men boasting of their prowess after a visit, but usually these matters were a cause for shame, and respected in silence by all prisoners. Even the urkas murmured indignantly whenever a guard, who during his night duty at the guard-house had relieved his boredom by listening, through the thin partition, to the sounds of love from the other side, derisively shared his observations with other prisoners in the brigade. Unbridled sexual depravity was the rule in the zone, where women were treated like prostitutes and love like a visit to the latrine, and where pregnant girls from the maternity hut were greeted with coarse jokes. Yet the house of meetings, in this pool of filth, degradation and cynicism, had become the only haven of whatever emotional life memory had brought into the camp from liberty. I remember our joy when one of the prisoners received a letter, telling him of the birth of a child conceived during a visit from his wife. If that child could have been given to us, we would have looked upon it as our common child, we would have fed it, going hungry ourselves, and passed it from hand to hand, even though there were plenty of brats conceived on a barrack bunk. That, for us, was the most important difference: they had been conceived on a barrack bunk in the zone, not in the house of meetings with a free woman and on clean sheets....In that way only did life allow us, dead and forgotten men, to feel a slight bond with freedom despite our incarceration in that earthly tomb.

What else can I say about our house of meetings? Perhaps only that, as a foreigner, I never expected to see anyone there, and possibly that is why my observations about the behavior of my fellow-prisoners, whose joys and disappointments I shared only involuntarily, are so objective and so indifferent even to pain.

Within the Whirlwind

Eugenia Ginzburg

The children's home was also part of the camp compound. It had its own guardhouse, its own gates, its own huts, and its own barbed wire. But on the doors of what were otherwise standard camp hutments there were unusual inscriptions: "Infants' Group," "Toddlers' Group," and "Senior Group."

After a day or two I found myself with the senior group. The very fact of being there restored to me the long-lost faculty of weeping. For more than three years my eyes had smarted from tearless despair. But now, in July 1940, I sat on a low bench in a corner of this strange building and cried. I cried without stopping, sobbing like our old nurse Fima, sniffing and snuffling like a country girl. I was in a state of shock. The shock jerked me out of a paralysis that had lasted for some months. Yes, this undoubtedly was a penal camp hut. But it smelled of warm semolina and wet pants. Someone's bizarre imagination had combined the trappings of the prison world with simple, human, and touchingly familiar things now so far out of reach that they seemed no more than a dream.

Some thirty small children, about the age my Vasya was when we were separated, were tumbling and toddling about the hut, squealing, gurgling with laughter, bursting into tears. Each of them was upholding his right to a place under the Kolyma sun in a perpetual struggle with his fellows. They bashed each other's heads unmercifully, pulled each other's hair, bit each other . . .

They aroused my atavistic instincts. I wanted to gather them all together and hug them tight so that nothing could hurt them. I wanted to croon over them, like my old nurse, "My sweet little darlings, my poor little dears."

I was rescued from my trance by Anya Sholokhova, my new workmate. Anya was the embodiment of common sense and efficiency. Her married name was Sholokhova, but she was a German, a Mennonite, taught as a child that

366

there was a right way to do everything. In the camps they called people like her "sticklers."

"Listen, Genia," she said, placing on the table a pan that gave off a heavenly aroma of something meaty, "if one of the bigwigs finds you behaving like that you'll be packed off to the tree-felling site tomorrow. They'll say you're high-strung, and in this place you need nerves like steel hawsers. Pull yourself together. Anyway, it's time to feed the children. I can't do it all myself."

It would be wrong to say that the children were kept on a starvation diet. They were given as much to eat as they could manage, and by my standards at the time the food seemed quite appetizing. For some reason, though, they all ate like little convicts: hastily, with no thought for anything else, carefully wiping their tin bowls with a piece of bread, or licking them clean. I was struck by the fact that their movements were unusually well coordinated for children of their age. But when I mentioned this to Anya she made a bitter gesture of dismissal.

"Don't you believe it! That's only at mealtime, that's their struggle for existence. But hardly anyone asks for the potty—they haven't been trained to it. Their general level of development . . . well, you'll see for yourself."

I saw what she meant the following day. Yes, outwardly they did remind me painfully of Vasya. But only outwardly. Vasya at four could reel off vast chunks of Marshak and Chukovsky,* could tell one make of car from another, could draw superb battleships and the Kremlin bell tower with its stars. But these poor things! "Anya, haven't they even learned to talk yet?" Only certain of the four-year-olds could produce a few odd, unconnected words. Inarticulate howls, mimicry, and blows were the main means of communication. "How can they be expected to speak? Who was there to teach them? Whom did they ever hear speaking?" explained Anya dispassionately. "In the infants' group they spend their whole time just lying on their cots. Nobody will pick them up, even if they cry their lungs out. It's not allowed, except to change wet diapers—when there are any dry ones available, of course. In the toddlers' group they crawl around in their playpens, all in a heap. It's all right as long as they don't kill each other or scratch each other's eyes out. Well, now you can see how it is. We're lucky if we can just get them all fed and put on the potty."

"But we ought to try and teach them something. Some songs...some poems...tell them stories."

---

* Samuel Marshak (1887-1964): writer of children's verse, satirist, and translator. Kornei Chukovsky (1882-1969): popular and influential writer, critic, translator, and author of children's verse.

"You can always try! By the end of the day I have barely enough strength left to climb into bed. I don't feel like telling stories."

It was true. There was so much work to do that you did not know which way to turn. Four times a day we had to lug water from the kitchen—which was at the far end of the compound—and haul back heavy pans full of food. Then, of course, there was the business of feeding the children, sitting them on their pots, changing their pants, rescuing them from the enormous whitish mosquitoes....But the main preoccupation was the floors. Camp bosses everywhere had a mania for clean floors. The whiteness of the floor was the one criterion of hygiene. The fumes and the stench in the huts might be suffocating, and our rags might be stiff with dirt; but all this would pass unnoticed by the guardians of cleanliness and hygiene. Heaven help us, though, if the floors did not shine brightly enough. The same unblinking watch was kept on the "floor situation" in the children's home; the boards there were not stained, so they had to be scraped with a knife until they shone.

For all that, I did one day try to put into effect my plan for giving lessons to improve the children's speech. I unearthed a pencil stub and a scrap of paper, and I drew for them the conventional picture of a house with two little windows and a chimney with smoke coming out of it.

The first to react to my initiative were Anastas and Vera, four-year-old twins, more like normal mainland children than any of the rest. Anya told me that their mother, Sonya, was doing time as a petty offender and not as a "professional." She was some sort of cashier who had made a mistake with her books—a quiet, decent, middle-aged woman now working in the camp laundry, in other words, in one of the most privileged jobs in the camp. Two or three times a month she used to slip into the children's home, profiting from her contacts with the guards: she had an "arrangement" to launder their clothes. Once inside, sobbing quietly, she would comb Anastas's and Vera's hair for them with the remains of a comb and pop villainously red fruit drops into their mouths straight from her pocket. Outside, in the "free" world, Sonya had been child-less, but here she had acquired from a casual encounter two of them at once.

"She adores her children, but just before you got here the poor girl was caught with one of the free employees. So now she's on detachment, as far away as you can get, haymaking. They've separated her from the children," Anya explained in her calm Mennonite voice.

It suddenly came to me that Anastas and Vera were the only ones in the entire group who knew the mysterious word "Mamma." Now that their mother had been sent elsewhere, they sometimes repeated the word with a sad, puzzled intonation, looking around uncomprehendingly. "Look," I said to Anastas, showing him the little house I had drawn, "what's this?"

"Hut," the little boy replied quite distinctly.

With a few pencil strokes I put a cat alongside the house. But no one recognized it, not even Anastas. They had never seen this rare animal. Then I drew a traditional rustic fence round the house.

"And what's this?"

"Compound!" Vera cried out delightedly, clapping her hands with glee.

One day I noticed the man on duty in the guardhouse playing with two small puppies. They were gamboling around on a sort of bed he had made for them on the guardhouse desk, by the telephone. Our guard was tickling the puppies around their ears and under their neck. There was such a sentimental good-natured look on his peasant face that I plucked up my courage.

"Citizen Duty Officer! Let me have them for the children! They've never seen anything like them. Never in their lives...We'll feed them. Sometimes the group has leftovers...."

Startled by the unexpectedness of the request, he had no time to erase the look of humanity from his face and reassume his customary mask of vigilance. I had taken him by surprise. And so, opening the door of the guardhouse a fraction, he reached out and handed me the puppies and their bedding.

"Just for a week or two till they get a bit bigger. And then you must return them. Working dogs, they are."

On the porch at the entrance to the senior group's hut we created our "pets' corner." The children quivered with delight. The worst punishment imaginable now was the threat: "You are to stay away from the puppies!" And the greatest possible incentive was: "You can help me feed the puppies!" The most aggressive and the greediest of the children gladly broke off a bit of their white-bread ration for "Pail" and "Ladle." These were the names the children gave the puppies—familiar words that they heard regularly in their daily life. They understood the comic quality of these nicknames and giggled over them.

It all came to an end some five days later, amid great unpleasantness. The head doctor of the children's home, a free employee, Eudokia Ivanovna, discovered our pets' corner and was terribly upset.

A source of infection! They'd warned her that the new "fiftyeighter" was capable of anything, and how right they were!

On her orders the puppies were immediately returned to the guards, and for several days we went around with our hearts in our boots, awaiting reprisals— removal from this cushy job and assignment to haymaking or tree felling.

But just then there occurred an epidemic of diarrhea among the infants' group. The head doctor had so much on her mind that she forgot all about us.

"Well," said Anya Sholokhova, "that's over. It's no good grieving. Especially as the little dogs really are working dogs. They're the Alsatians who'll be taking us on parade when they grow up. And if necessary they'll seize any prisoner by the throat..."

Yes, but that would be when they grew up. Till then...I remembered how our children had smiled at them just like mainland children. How they had put food aside for them, saying "that's for Pail" and "this is for Ladle." They had realized for the first time that it was possible to think of someone other than themselves.

The diarrhea outbreak proved very persistent. The infants died off in droves, although they received intensive care from both free and prisoner doctors. The conditions in which the mothers had lived during pregnancy, the high acidity of their milk, and the climate of Elgen had all taken their toll. The main trouble was that there was so little even of this milk—acidulous from their grief—and less of it with each day that passed. A few lucky infants were breast-fed for two to three months. The rest were all artificially fed. But if they were to hold out against toxic dyspepsia, nothing would help as much as even a few drops of mother's milk.

I had to take leave of my senior group. Petukhov, the prisoner doctor who had been called in for consultation, recommended that as a "nurse with a bit of education," I should be transferred to look after the sick infants. He undertook to instruct me himself. For several days I attended the prisoners' hospital, where Petukhov worked, and he hurriedly taught me all I needed to know. I conscientiously worked through *The Medical Assistant's Handbook,* I learned to apply cupping glasses and to give injections, even intravenous solutions. I returned to the children's home a full-fledged "member of the medical staff," much encouraged by Dr. Petukhov's kind words about me.

Dr. Petukhov was rewarded for his goodness, his intelligence, and his decency with a great happiness, a unique event in those days: he was suddenly rehabilitated in that very same year, 1940, and left for Leningrad. People said that the famous flier Molokov, his brother-in-law, had personally interceded with Stalin on his relative's behalf.

The infants' little cots were pushed close together. There were so many children that to change every single diaper in quick succession would have taken an hour and a half. They all had bedsores, they were getting thinner, and they were wearing themselves out with crying. Some of them gave out a thin, plaintive wall, no longer expecting anyone to take notice. Others set up a desperate, defiant howling, vigorously fighting back. And there were those who no longer cried at all. They simply groaned as adults do.

We performed like clockwork. We fed them bottles, administered medicines, gave injections, and—our main activity—changed diapers. We endlessly folded and refolded the still-damp calico diapers. We grew giddy from constant to-ing and fro-ing for fourteen hours at a stretch and from the powerful stench given off by the enormous pile of soiled diapers. We even lost all desire to eat, we who were always hungry. We gulped down with revulsion the watery semolina left over from the children's meal, just to keep body and soul together.

But the most appalling thing of all was the arrival every three hours, with every change of shift, of the nursing mothers to "feed" their infants. Among them there were some of us—political prisoners—who had taken the risk of bringing an Elgen child into the world. They peered in through the door with an anxious question on their miserable faces, and it was hard to tell what they feared more: that the infant born in Elgen would survive or that it would die. But the vast majority of the nursing mothers were professionals. Every three hours they staged a persecution campaign against the medical personnel. Maternal feelings are a splendid rationale for misbehavior. They hurled themselves on our group with unrepeatable language, cursing us and threatening to kill or maim us the very day that little Alfred or little Eleanor (they always gave their children exotic foreign names) died.

When I was transferred to the isolation ward, at first I was even glad. There were, after all, fewer children there; only the complicated and acutely infectious cases. There it would be physically possible to attend to each individual case. But the very first night shift I did there I felt an unbearable spasm of spiritual nausea.

There they lay, little martyrs born to know nothing but suffering. The one-year-old over there, with the pleasant oval face, already had a spot on his lung. He wheezed and made convulsive movements with his hands, which exhibited bright blue nails. What should I say to his mother? She was Marya Ushakova from our hut.

Or take this one, on whom the sins of his father were visited. The progeny of that cursed criminal underworld: a case of congenital syphilis.

Those two little girls at the end would probably die today, while I was there. It was only the camphor that kept them alive at all. The prisoner-doctor, Polina Lvovna, before she went out into the compound, begged me not to forget the injections.

"If they can only hold out until nine in the morning, so that their death throes don't come while we are on duty."

Polina Lvovna was from Poland. She had only been in Russia two years when she was arrested. It may have been from unfamiliarity with our ways, or simply because it was in her nature, but she was scared of her own shadow, poor thing. Scared and absent-minded. She was capable of holding a stethoscope to the chest of a two-month-old baby and instructing it in a matter-of-fact way: "Patient, breathe in. Now hold your breath!" She was a neuropathologist, and not used to treating children.

I particularly recall one night in the isolation ward. Not just an ordinary night but one of those "white nights" you get in the far north. It was almost the last of the year. But it was not at all like the ones in Leningrad: no gold-colored skies and, of course, no huge buildings asleep beneath them. Indeed, there was something primeval about it, a feeling of something deeply hostile to man in that icy white flush in which normal outlines were held in quivering suspense: the bare sugar-loaf hills, the vegetation, and the buildings. And the night was infested with the buzzing of mosquitoes. This buzzing drilled its way not only into our ears but into our hearts. No mosquito net could save you from the poisonous bites of this winged pestilence, which resembled the normal mosquitoes of our mainland about as much as a rabid tiger resembles a tabby cat.

The light suddenly went out, as so often happened, and all that remained was a small night light, dimly winking on the table. By the flickering glow of that night light I administered hourly injections to a dying baby. She was the five-month-old daughter of a twenty-year-old inside for some petty crime. The baby had been in the isolation ward for some time; whoever was on duty would say as she was relieved, "Well, that one will probably go today."

But there was still a spark of life in her. She was a skeleton clad with aged, wrinkled skin. But the face! The baby's face was such that we called her the Queen of Spades. The face of an octogenarian, wise, sardonic, full of irony. As if she knew it all—she who had stopped in our compound, in that little world of hatred and death, for a brief moment of time.

I was using the large needle for her injection, but she didn't cry. She only grunted feebly and looked straight at me with the eyes of an infinitely wise old lady. She died just before dawn, on the very borderline, when the first faint patches of pink are seen against the lifeless backcloth of Elgen's white night.

The dead body became once more that of an infant. The wrinkles smoothed themselves away. The eyes, prematurely initiated into all the mysteries, closed. There lay the emaciated body of a dead child.

"Little Sveta has passed away!" I said to the woman who was taking over from me.

"Sveta? Oh, the Queen..."

She broke off and glanced down at the rigidly extended little body.

"No, she doesn't look like the Queen of Spades any more. And her mother's away. . . . She's been drafted to Mylga."

They are never to be forgotten, those Elgen children. I'm not saying that there is any comparison between them and, say, the Jewish children in Hitler's empire. Not only were the Elgen children spared extermination in gas chambers, they were even given medical attention. They received all they needed by way of food. It is my duty to emphasize this so as not to depart from the truth by one jot or tittle.

And yet when one calls to mind Elgen's gray, featureless landscape, shrouded in the melancholy of nonexistence, the most fantastic, the most satanic invention of all seems to be those huts with signs saying "Infants' Group," "Toddlers' Group," and "Senior Group."

2.

Where had all these children come from? Why were there so many of them? Was it possible in this world of barbed wire, watchtowers, parades, inspections, curfews, solitary confinement cells, and work parties that anyone could still experience love or even primitive sexual attraction?

I remember how excited I had been in my youth—which fortunately was over before the epoch of the sexual revolution—by Hamsun's* definition of love: "What is love? A breeze rustling amid the sweetbrier, or a squall that snaps the masts of boats at sea? It is a golden glow in the blood." By way of contrast, there was this cynical aphorism from one of Ehrenburg's** early characters: "Love is when people sleep together."

For Kolyma in the forties, even the second definition would have been too idealistic. When people sleep together...But this implies that they have a roof over their heads, the same roof; and that they have some sort of couch where they can sleep; and that they belong, in their sleep, only to themselves and to each other.

In the Kolyma camps love meant hasty, perilous meetings in some sketchy shelter at your place of work in the taiga or behind a soiled curtain in some "free" hut. There was always the fear of being caught, exposed to public shame, and assigned to a penal labor brigade, i.e., posted to some lethal spot; you might end up paying for your date with nothing less than your life.

Many of our comrades solved the problem not just for themselves but for everyone else in a ruling the ruthless logic of which showed them to be genuine

---

* Knut Hanisun (1859-1952): Norwegian novelist, awarded Nobel prize in 1920.
** Ilya Ehrenburg (1891-1967): Russian novelist and journalist.

descendants of Rakhmetov.* "Love is impossible in Kolyma," they said, "because here it expresses itself in forms offensive to human dignity. There must be no personal relationships in Kolyma since it is so easy to slip into prostitution pure and simple."

There would appear to be no room here for argument on principle. Nothing, indeed, is to be done except to illustrate the theme with scenes showing the traffic in living human bodies in Kolyma. Here, then, are some such scenes. (I should add that I am writing only of cases concerning women from the intelligentsia, imprisoned on political charges. The professional criminals are beyond the bounds of humanity. I have no desire to describe their orgies, although I had much to put up with as an involuntary witness.)

A tree-felling site at Kilometer 7 from Elgen. Our brigadier, "Crafty Kostya," was doing the rounds, not on his own, but with two of his cronies. They looked us women over as we set to with our saws and axes.

"Goners!" commented one of the cronies, with a dismissive gesture.

"They need fattening up. Where there are bones, there's bound to be some meat," philosophized Kostya.

"What about that young one over there, the small one?"

Seizing their opportunity while the guards were warming themselves at the campfire, they approached two of the youngest girls from our brigade.

"Hey, sweetie! My pal here would like to compare notes with you."

"Compare notes" was a euphemism, a concession to the proprieties. Without it not even the most case-hardened professional would open negotiations. But the fancy talk stopped there. The contracting parties now descended to a form of speech stripped of all euphemisms.

"I'm the forwarding agent at Burkhala" (one of the most terrible of the gold mines), "so I can put you in the way of sugar, butter, and white bread. I'll give you shoes, felt boots, and a really good padded jacket. I know you're a prison detainee. It doesn't matter—we can come to an arrangement with the guards. We'll have to fork out, of course! There's a shack available. About three kilometers from here…It's not too bad; you can toddle that far…"

More often than not merchants such as these went away empty-handed. But occasionally they did get themselves a deal. However sad it may seem, it went like this. From stage to stage: at first tears, terror, indignation; then apathy; then the stomach protested more loudly and not only the stomach but the whole body, every muscle—for trophic starvation leads to the breakdown

---

* Principal male character in Chernyshevsky's novel *What Is to Be Done?* (1863); he represents the embodiment of positive, revolutionary virtue.

of proteins in the body. And sometimes there was the voice of sex too, which made itself heard from time to time despite everything. And above all there was the example of one's neighbor in the bunks who had recovered her health, had acquired some sort of clothing, and had been able to exchange her sodden, tattered sandals for high felt boots.

It is hard to describe the way in which someone ground down by inhuman forms of life loses bit by bit all hold on normal notions of good and evil, of what is permissible and what is not. Otherwise how else could there have been in the children's home infants whose mother might have a diploma in philosophy, and whose father might be a well-known burglar from Rostov?

Some of the women who had short sentences or who had managed to get out of the camps before the outbreak of war but without the right to return to the mainland (often former Communists sentenced for CRTA—counter-revolutionary Trotskyist activity—which in 1935 had meant a mere five-year sentence) rushed headlong into Kolyma marriages as soon as they were through the camp gates, totally disregarding the possibility of mésalliances. I remember one such woman, Nadya, who the day before her release defiantly challenged those of her hutmates who sought to scare her off: "You will all end up as withered old maids, you pinched virgins! I'm damn well going to marry him, whatever you say! I know he spends his time playing cards. I know that he's a yokel and that I am a university graduate in Scandinavian languages. But who needs my Scandinavian languages? I'm tired out. I want my own quarters and my own fireside. And children of my own...New ones...Those back on the mainland we shall never see again. So the thing is to have some more while I can."

Sometimes the result was not heartbreak but a real comic turn. For example, there was the story of Sonya Bolts's "instantaneous" marriage.

Sonya, a quiet, unassuming textile worker from a little town in Byelorussia, had somehow managed to collect a stiff sentence for CRTA—a fact at which she herself never ceased to marvel. She had already served five of her eight years when all of a sudden a paper arrived from Moscow regrading her offense from CRTA to "negligence," and her sentence was correspondingly reduced to three years.

Sonya was beside herself with joy and so overlooked the fact that the document had been two years in transit. The main thing was that she had to proceed immediately to Yagodnoye, which was where people were released. It was there that the sacred rite of "regularizing" one's Form A, which redesignated convicts as "former prisoners," i.e., discharged prisoners, was solemnized.

At the headquarters of the Area Administration for Camps in Yagodnoye a little window like that of a ticket office opened up on certain days of the week. It was from this window that the ex-zek (ex from that very moment) received the hallowed Form A, her hands trembling with happiness. The workers at the gold mines in the vicinity always knew when the release of a contingent of women from Elgen was due to take place, and the suitors would gather there to await the event.

After folding her Form A once and once again, Sonya Bolts reverently tied it up in her kerchief. At that point a large individual in a shaggy fur hat came up to her and said in a hoarse voice: "Beg your pardon, citizen . . . You've been released? Well, that's grand...I'm from Dzhelgala. My own master, as anyone will tell you. I'd like to compare notes with you."

Sonya scrutinized her suitor critically and put to him a somewhat unexpected question.

"Tell me, you are not a Jew, are you?"

"No, citizen, I can't say I am....Mustn't tell a lie...I'm from Siberia myself, from near Kansk."

"Why do I even ask?" sighed Sonya. "Who'd ever expect to find a Polish Jew in this benighted corner of the earth! I suppose it's lucky you're not one of those...Karakalpaks....How should I know?" And after a short pause Sonya said, "I'm willing."

The funniest thing of all was that this couple subsequently lived for many a long year in total harmony, and in 1956, after their rehabilitation, husband and wife left together for Kansk.

There was everything—from comedy to tragedy—to be encountered in our strange, primordial existence.

Love too? Love, as seen by Hamsun, that "golden glow in the blood"? I would maintain that it did sometimes put in an appearance among us. However heatedly, our rigorists (and they were particularly numerous among the Mensheviks and the Social Revolutionaries) denied the possibility of pure love in Kolyma, love there was. It sometimes visited our huts unrecognized by the bystanders, humiliated, abashed, and defiled; but for all that it was love, true love—that very same "breeze amid the sweetbrier."

One of its mysterious visitations took the following form. After roll call one day the list of punishments ordered by Camp Commandant Zimmerman was read out. Zimmerman herself was an educated person, but she merely signed the orders drafted by the chief disciplinary officer. The form of the words varied: "Five days solitary, escort to work"..."Five days solitary, not to go to work."

Finally we heard one extract from the orders of the day which aroused laughter even from our ranks, from those who had been listening despondently with a sinking heart, wondering for which of us that night would mean not the blessed luxury of collective bunks and huts but the stinking frozen planks of the solitary confinement cell.

"...relations between a male and a female convict," the duty guard read out, "Involving a horse standing idle for two hours....Five days solitary, not to be taken to work." Later on the phrase "relations between male and female convicts involving a horse standing idle for two hours" would become a popular joke in the camp. But at the time our laughter quickly died out and gave way to horror. Those two were done for....

He was a former actor, who had worked with Meyerhold.* She was a ballerina. For a time their previous professions had given them a privileged position in the camp. At Magadan they had both been with the "cultural brigade." This was a serf theater that staged shows for the camp officials who were bored in those provincial backwaters. It fed its actor-prisoners on a comparatively generous scale, and under one pretext or another left them more or less free to go around without escort. The two of them managed to meet from time to time outside the camp. What happiness! It was all the more acutely felt, perhaps, for its fragility, its precariousness from one minute to the next. It was to endure for exactly five months. And then she was discovered to be pregnant. There was one well trodden path for pregnant women in the camp; it led to Elgen, to the ranks of the nursing mothers recruited from the criminal riffraff, to the children's home.

They were separated. The convict-nursing mother was now issued with rough boots and a third-hand quilted jacket instead of tutu and ballet slippers. Her little son died in the children's home before he was six months old.

In order to get to see her he pretended to have lost his voice. He was "unable" to act on stage any more, and so the work assigner, whom he knew, after calling him a blockhead, agreed to "fix him up" as one of a prison draft assigned to Burkhala, a gold mine located in the vicinity of Elgen.

And now in place of the happy-go-lucky life of an actor in the serf theater he endured by his own choice all the horrors of the hell on earth that was Burkhala. He worked his insides out at the mine face: he fell ill, he became a goner. After a certain time he succeeded in getting taken into the Northern Camps (Sevlag) Cultural Brigade, which from time to time came to visit us in Elgen to relieve the tedium by entertaining the camp officials with a variety

* Vsevolod Meyerhold (1874-1940): director and drama theorist; from 1923 director of the Meyerhold Theater in Moscow. Arrested and deported in 1937; died in camp.

show. A number of prisoners selected from the trusties and shock workers were allowed into the back rows.

They met! They actually met! Speechless with joy and anguish, she stood there beside him in the wings of the Elgen camp club hall. Old beyond her twenty-six years, all skin and bones, no longer beautiful, his heart's desire was restored to him.

Finding it hard to put the words together, she could only repeat over and over again how their little son had been him to the life, how even the tiny fingernails had been his daddy's all over again, how within three days the baby had succumbed to toxic dyspepsia because she had had no milk to give him and the little mite had had to be fed on artificial milk. She couldn't stop talking and he kissed her hands with their broken, hopelessly grimy nails and implored her to be calm for they would have other children. And he slipped into the pocket of her jacket a crust of bread he had saved up and some sugar lumps with shreds of plug tobacco adhering to them.

He had good contacts in influential trusty circles and he arranged to have her assigned to what by Elgen standards was a plum job—carter at the stables. It was the nearest thing to happiness. Going around without a guard, after all! She started to get well, recovered her looks, and received notes from him regularly. But what had they to look forward to? Each of them had a ten-year sentence plus five years' deprivation of civil rights. But was it so imperative to look forward? She read his notes a hundred times over and beamed with happiness.

So why all of a sudden "five days solitary, not to be taken to work"? It emerged that he, with the help of some people he knew in the camp administration who were patrons of the arts, had contrived to obtain a fictitious work assignment to Elgen and had lain in wait for her and her horse near Volchok, a spot some five kilometers from the camp compound. And then of course the two of them had tethered the knock-kneed, stunted apology for a Yakut horse to a tree. But some wretched creature had spotted them and denounced them to the authorities. Hence the incident, punishable with solitary confinement, "relations between a male and a female convict involving a horse standing idle for two hours."

Roll call was over, and it was time for the guard to arrive to take the culprits off to the punishment cells. "As long as they don't take him," she said, pulling her rags around her more tightly in anticipation of the penetrating dampness of the cell. "As long as they don't take him. He's had chronic pleurisy ever since he was ill the gold mines."

"Where is she? I have a note for her," said a voice.

The voice belonged to Katya Rumyantseva, who was allowed around without an escort. She had the job of bringing in the water supply on her ox. What a splendid girl! She had managed to get a note past the guards.

"Thank God! It's all right!" she exclaimed with joy, scanning the letter. "Tomorrow and the day after they're putting on performances for the camp officers at Yagodnoye. So they're not sending him to the punishment cell after all, merely giving him a reprimand....They need him! And as for me...I can stick it out...."

She was the first of all those sentenced to the cells to arrive at the punishment block, making her way with her graceful ballerina's walk to spend five days in hell.

Who would not envy them!

To Build A Castle

Vladimir Bukovsky

A criminal camp offers you a complete cross section of society, the entire country in miniature, and in camp life you can find a microcosm of the Soviet people's attitude to the law and their social position.

The majority of people in Soviet criminal camps are not degenerates or professional crooks. According to our most accurate estimates, the number of prisoners in the Soviet Union is never less than two and a half million—that is, one percent of the population, every hundredth person. And usually it's more. If you take into account the fact that the average term of imprisonment is five years, and recidivists account for not more than twenty to twenty-five percent of the prisoners, it emerges that almost a third of the Soviet population has passed through the camps.

Such a high percentage of criminality is artificially maintained by the state—above all for economic motives. Prisoners are a cheap (almost unpaid) word force that can easily be moved, at the authorities' discretion, from one branch of the economy to another, sent out to do the heaviest and most unprofitable types of work and into undeveloped territories with a harsh climate, where you can persuade a fee work force to go only by paying extremely high wages. It was no accident that in the Voronezh region when I was there they had only ten camps (one administrative unit). In the Perm region, farther north and closer to the Urals, where I went in 1973-74, there were about fifty camps (five administrative units). There were about the same number in the Kirov, Tyumen, and Sverdlovsk regions and in the Komi Autonomous Republic.*

---

* Kirov and Sverdlovsk are just west of the Urals, in European Russia, while Tyumen is east of the Urals, in western Siberia. The Komi Republic is farther north than any of these, in the extreme northeast corner of European Russia. (Translator's note.)

This was how all the great construction projects of the USSR had been built: dams, canals, roads, polar cities. By forced labor, almost entirely hand labor.

The average camp prisoner's earnings are 60 to 80 rubles a month, compared with 140 rubles for free workers* on similar jobs. Half of this is deducted by the state and another quarter goes to pay for food, clothing, and maintenance. Thus a camp prisoner's real wage is 15 to 20 rubles a month. Out of this he can spend from 3 to 7 rubles a month, depending on what his sentence was, in the camp canteen. His incentives to work are all negative, that is, they consist basically of assorted punishments for evasion of work or failure to fulfill the norm. Furthermore, the workers are removed from the sphere of normal consumption, which, given the Soviet Union's permanent shortage of goods, is very convenient for demand management. Meanwhile, goods that are not in demand by the population (mainly low-grade food products) are unloaded onto the prisoners, who have no choice in the matter. Prisoners also don't need housing—they build their own barrack huts.

In short, if a general amnesty were suddenly called tomorrow, it would precipitate an economic disaster. That is why, since Stalin's time, there have in effect been no amnesties. There have been a few decrees under which almost no one was freed, since all prisoners convicted of the most frequent charges were excluded. In Khrushchev's time, instead of amnesties they developed the concept of early release (and later of suspended sentences) with compulsory assignment "to national economic construction sites," or, as it was called, "to the chemistry." This category of prisoners is altogether unquantifiable. It usually includes short-timers (up to three years) who are directed to the very heaviest and lowest-paid types of work. If a "chemist" commits some sort of misdemeanor, he is despatched to a camp to serve his full time (time served "at the chemistry" doesn't count). It is an extremely convenient form of release.

It is difficult to say whether the State Planning Agency, Gosplan, gives direct instructions to the Ministry of the Interior as to how many offenders should be arrested each month to maintain the national economy at the requisite level. Given the Soviet Union's centralized planning system, this is perfectly feasible. I think, however, that the matter is handled slightly differently. From somewhere up above, from the very highest reaches of the Party, an instruction is handed down: step up the struggle against, let us say, hooliganism. It's not that there are more hooligans around than usual, but

---

* Civilian employees of the camp administration who live outside the camp and come in every day to do their work. (Translator's note.)

rather that at a given stage in the building of communism, their existence suddenly becomes particularly inadmissible. And a nationwide campaign is inaugurated to promote the struggle against hooliganism. The Presidium of the Supreme Soviet publishes a special decree, social institutions are mobilized to assist the overstretched police force, judges are issued with guidelines, and slogans appear all over the place: "NO MERCY FOR HOOLIGANS," MAKE THE PLACE TOO HOT FOR HOOLIGANS." Every province, every region must arrest more hooligans than it did before the "struggle" was "stepped up." How, otherwise, could you report back that you'd done you job?

But at the top, at the point where all these reports converge, they are outraged to discover that as a result of the campaign, the number of hooligans in the country has steeply risen. My word, this hooligan's a pigheaded brute! Won't given in! And there comes another decree—on yet another stepping up of the struggle against hooliganism. More instructions to the police, directives to the local authorities, and clarifications to the judges, and the concept of hooliganism begins to stretch like a rubber band. A man loses his temper and curses someone out—hooliganism. A husband has a row with his wife—hooliganism. Two schoolboys have a fight—hooliganism. And monstrous sentences, up to five years! How else can you prove your zeal and demonstrate that the struggle is truly being stepped up? The statistics for hooliganism start to climb dizzily, the prisons are overflowing, the judges are exhausted, and battalions of provocative young hooligans are being shipped out to work on the Bratsk Hydroelectric Station or the Baikal-Amur Railway. God defend you from falling foul of one of these regular campaigns—you are bound to be dispatched to a far-away construction project for the glory of communism, because one campaign has a fatal way of leading to another.

On the principal of the feedback circuit, this campaign might continue to grow to infinity—after all, it can't be stopped so long as the number of hooligans continues to grow. And you never ever get a directive to "relax the struggle." Instead, they simply choose some other offense to have a campaign about, and the word goes out from high Party circles: "Step up the struggle against embezzlers of socialist property!" And everybody heaves a sigh of relief: at last the hooligans can be left in peace. Their numbers decline sharply, and up at the top somebody registers a victory over hooliganism. The number of prisoners falls slightly until the new campaign gains momentum, and then rises again.

This is approximately how the purges and campaigns against enemies of the people worked in Stalin's time, but now it is inconvenient to have millions of political prisoners, and it makes for a much easier life simply to jail hooligans and plunderers. Thus the people who end up in the Soviet camps are mostly ordinary Soviet people, and it is quite fair to judge by them the state of our society in general.

If you want to live, learn to look sharp! Bribe the guards, swindle, steal, keep on good terms with whoever's in charge of the food. Otherwise you'll end up a stiff. Admin steals everything it can lay hands on in the camp. Bribery is universal—with a bribe you can get anything, from a visit to conditional release. They order entire suites of furniture from the factory and cart if off like offcuts from the sawmill. Not one of them ever buys firewood or building materials. They even steal the food. Between the district depot and the prisoner's bowl the food simply melts away. Admin grabs the choicest tidbits before it even gets to the camp. In the kitchens, it is plundered by the cooks and trusties—the ones who are "on the road to reform"—not only for themselves but for their friends as well. The servers then give bigger portions to their favorites, and the simple con, who honestly believes that honest labor is the road to home, is left with slops.

Almost all of a prisoner's time is taken up looking for food. This is the axis around which camp life turns, and it defines all human relations. You help me and I'll help you. With the help of the guards, the free workers, the drivers of the trucks who come to collect the furniture, you can buy anything you like: vodka, tea, drugs.

And if you remember that millions of people go through this meat mincer, you involuntarily ask yourself: What does the regime want of its people? What sort of citizens is it turning them into? Judging by the established criteria for rehabilitation, the model Soviet citizen is one who is prepared to bend in whichever direction they wish to bend him. Become an informer, do the policemen's job for them, say what you're told to say, and beam with pleasure all the time.

Do the camps teach you to lead an honest life? Just the reverse: an honest man would die of hunger in a camp. They teach you to steal and not get caught. Here is a typical incident: The duty officer makes a deal with a prisoner for the latter to steal an electric drill from the workshop tool store. He promises to bring him ten packets of tea in exchange (that's ten rubles in camp terms). The prisoner carries out his part of the bargain—steals the drill and smuggles it out to the guardhouse without the foreman catching him. The officer carries it out through the camp checkpoint and takes it home, but doesn't bring the tea. A scandal erupts: the con demands his tea and ends up spilling the beans to admin. And what happens? The officer is reprimanded for "acquiring a tool by impermissible means" and the con gets fifteen days in the box for "theft."

It is a deliberate and systematic plan to corrupt the people. And it has been continuing for sixty years. The more honest element in the people is being physically destroyed, while corruptness is encouraged. In effect, the same thing happens outside as well. Wages are beggarly, and everyone steals as much as he can. Is it that the authorities don't know? Of course they know. And they even prefer it that way. A man who steals isn't in a position to *make demands*. And if he does become so bold, he can easily be put away for theft. Everyone is guilty.

I frequently tried to explain this simple truth to my camp companions, but with no success All of them were extremely hostile to the existing regime, and the word "Communist" was the worst insult you could fling at someone—people would immediately attack you for it. Their attitude to me, as an open opponent of the regime, was one of enormous respect. Yet they could never understand that by robbing the state and harming it in that way, they were nonetheless providing it with its greatest support. There were some who seriously regarded themselves as fighting against the regime.

One of them was even insulted when I didn't acknowledge him as one of us. He had robbed a polling station on the eve of the elections and was extremely proud of this fact. But that's the whole point. Until people learn to demand what belongs to them as a right, no revolution will liberate them. And by the time they learn, a revolution won't be necessary. No, I don't believe in revolution, I don't believe in forcible salvation.

It is easy to imagine what would happen in this country if there were a revolution: universal looting, economic collapse, internecine butchery, and in every district a different band of outlaws with its own "gangleader" at its head. And the passive, terrorized majority would gladly submit to the first strong system of government to come along, in other words a new dictatorship.

In the Machinery of Justice

Elinor Lipper

In Vladivostok transit camp the story of Mother D came to its end. But I will tell it here because it throws some light on the motives that make parents and children, brothers and sisters, men and their wives, repudiate one another once either has been arrested. This is not always done out of cowardice; sometimes it is prompted by an unshakable faith in the justice and infallibility of the Party and the NKVD.

I heard the first part of this story from one of the participants, an elderly engineer who was at work building a barrack for women in the transit camp of Vladivostok. The second half of the story I witnessed.

"Are you sure it was my mother?" the young prisoner asked a new arrival in his cell.

"I couldn't possibly be mistaken," the other said. He was an elderly man who made a strange contrast with the other inmates because he was still clean shaven and his suit was carefully pressed. "It was at my last Party meeting. Shortly afterwards I was expelled from the Party because of contact with an enemy of the people—an old schoolmate of mine with whom I exchanged letters once or twice a year. He was an army officer, and when Tukhachevsky fell he was ruined too. Unfortunately one of my letters was found in his possession when he was arrested. There was nothing incriminating in it, but as you see it was enough to send me to prison."

The younger man's haggard features lit up with a sympathetic smile.

"It happens every day," he answered. "If you stay around here any length of time you'll find out that about 90 per cent of the inmates were arrested for similar reasons. I worked as a secretary in our trade mission in Berlin. Kossior, the brother of the People's Commissar, recommended me for the job, and when he was charged with being a German spy, I was arrested too. But tell me about my mother."

"I've known your mother since the Revolution. She was always one of the most active Communists in the textile factory where I worked as an engineer. A person of extraordinary energy. Sometimes I wondered how she managed to do her work and attend so many meetings, and yet have time for a private life."

"She never did have much time to spare for me," the young man said bitterly.

"Recently," the engineer continued, "I'd noticed how changed she was. She seemed to have aged overnight. We couldn't understand this slump until the day she made her statement at the Party meeting. Then we found out for the first time that her son had been arrested. She had made a point of informing the Party secretary at the factory, and I suppose he ordered her to make a statement at the Party meeting."

"And what did she say?" the son asked, trying to make his twitching features expressionless. He thrust his hands into his pockets to conceal their trembling.

"I'm sure she did not speak voluntarily," the engineer said apologetically. "Certainly not, because when she got up on the platform she was so pale that we all thought she was sick. And her voice had none of the warm, enthusiastic quality we were all used to; it could hardly be heard at the back of the room. It must have cost her a great deal to get up on that platform and announce to hundreds of comrades that she must repudiate her own son."

The son listened without a quiver. And for a moment he involuntarily squinted his sharp eyes, beneath which were dark rings from many sleepless nights—although the same naked bulb dangled as ever from the vaulted ceiling of the cell and the corner where the two men were leaning against the wall was in semidarkness as always.

"She said her son had been arrested six months earlier, that all through that time she had been hoping his innocence would be proved and that he would be rehabilitated and released. But he had not come back and she could therefore no longer doubt that he had been proved a traitor. For no innocent person would be kept under arrest in the Soviet Union, and the NKVD did not make mistakes. A Party member who felt an intimate tie with an enemy of the people—even her own son—could not remain a sincere Party member. Therefore she was now publicly declaring that she no longer considered herself related to her son, since he had fallen into the snares of the enemies of the people."

"So she publicly repudiated me," the son murmured.

"How could we on the outside possibly know that there are so many guiltless persons in prison?" the older man apologized, feeling that he had to say something in extenuation. To his own surprise he wanted to justify himself for having taken part in that meeting. Why had it never occurred to him at the time that it was immoral to require a mother to renounce her own child in the name of the Party? What morality remained in the Party when it made such cynical demands upon its members, and made the others applaud such a spectacle?

But before he could fully formulate this startling new thought, he heard the son whispering hoarsely:

"There were two things I formerly believed in: my mother and the Party. I was never in the unhappy predicament of having to choose between the two. When I was put behind these bars it seemed to me a simple thing to prove my innocence. But nobody here is interested in proofs of innocence. Guilty, guilty! the examining judges shout, and they think their shouts are proof of the truth of their silly fabrications. Their blows and kicks were not enough to destroy the image of the Party that I still carried in my heart. I said to myself that the Party and Stalin do not know what is going on here, and in my simplicity I wrote to People's Commissar Yeshov, to the State Prosecutor, to Stalin. I never received any answer. And I came to the conclusion that these intimate associates of Stalin, and Stalin himself, not only know what is going on here, but want it to go on. After all, we are right in the middle of Moscow, a short walk from the Kremlin. And these things do not happen only to little people; they also happen to former close associates of Stalin, to his secretary, to people's commissars, to those who only recently were working on the Constitution with him, like Eiche, Kossior, Postyshev, Sulimov. People are brought to this prison from all parts of the Soviet Union—and in all the prisons in the whole country the scenes are the same. What interest could all these examining judges have in forcing obviously innocent men by extortion, threats and torture to make the most absurd confessions of guilt? These examining judges, or rather torturers, have been trained according to a carefully thought-out system. Only the People's Commissar for the Interior, the State Prosecutor, and Stalin himself could have developed and approved this system which is applied throughout the country.

"When I recognized this, I lost my faith in the Party. It did not happen when I was arrested and my Party book was taken away, but when I realized that the Party spits upon respect for individuals, that it poisons justice and truth with the blood of the innocent. 'You can't make an omelet without breaking eggs.' Human beings, thousands upon thousands of citizens, are not eggs. Yet their skulls are crushed as though they were. So it does not surprise me that the same rulers should demand such sacrifices from a mother. A spectacle as unnatural and repulsive as that characterizes the men who stage it.

387

"But"— his whisper became almost inaudible—"that my mother, my own mother, would betray me, would deny me for the sake of the Party—such a thought never occurred to me, not even here where you learn to believe in nothing and in no one."

The engineer stared at the boy with incredulous horror and raised his arm as though to shake him. But at that moment the slot in the door opened, the military cap of the guard appeared, and a profound silence settled over the cell which a moment before had been buzzing with the whispers of its hundred inmates.

Slowly the soldier spelled out the name of the engineer, who uttered a loud, tense, "Here," and jumped from the boards down to the level of the door. The slot fell shut and with the typical rattle of prison keys the door was opened and the engineer let out. The murmurs and whispers resumed. Toward dawn, hours later, when the engineer staggered back from his interrogation, the younger man who lay sleepless between his neighbors, watching the bugs on the wall, had no need to ask questions. The man who returned was no longer a newcomer. That night he had found out what Soviet justice meant. With a suppressed groan the engineer sat down on the boards and stared at the small patch of stone floor by the door as though it were an open grave into which he had just laid his dearest love.

Although the mother had renounced her son, she remained under suspicion. A few weeks later her house was searched and two overlooked volumes by Bukharin confiscated. And Bukharin had meanwhile been classed as counterrevolutionary.

Here were grounds enough for issuing a warrant for her arrest. The two dust-covered books were proof enough that she was entitled to an eight-year sentence for counterrevolutionary activity. Such is the dictatorship of the proletariat. The woman who was condemned in the name of the proletariat was a textile worker, one of the many women of the people who had believed that the Party would bring light to the workers and carry out the socialist dream to which she had devoted her life. She had believed in this so thoroughly that she had given up any claim to a personal life. Her real life was her life in the factory. She was not ambitious, but she was proud of each promotion to a position of greater responsibility within the factory because it gave her the opportunity to share her knowledge and experience with more people. When she had been offered a better apartment—since her husband's early death she had lived in one tiny room with her son—she had indignantly refused, saying, "The time has not yet come for me to accept privileges when there are many workers' families larger than mine still living all in one room."

It was a real achievement for her when she managed painfully to work her way through a book on Marxist theory. She was always filled with secret awe when she saw her son gobbling book after book, and she felt intense gratitude to the regime which gave him the opportunity to study by daylight in libraries and universities, while she had always had to read at night, laboring through the pages by candlelight after a hard day's work. The mother and son were both proud of one another. But they had no time to give expression to their feelings. Moreover, such emotionality would have seemed improper to both.

Yet the boy knew that he would always give up tempting dates with friends his own age whenever he had a chance to spend an evening with this unassuming woman who wore old-fashioned dresses and a shawl around her plain face with its strong forehead, flat cheekbones, and wide, energetic month. "Mama," he would say to her, "when you laugh the little wrinkles around your eyes are like the corners of Lenin's eyes." Startled, she would protest his irreverence.

For her there was nothing higher, nothing more sacred than Lenin. How could she possibly be compared with Lenin in any way? It was his voice that had called her to the Party and that had aroused in her her unshakable confidence in the Party, a trust to which she clung in spite of developments which were hard to understand. She needed only to remind herself of Lenin to brush away all doubt. Like her fellow members of the Party she did not notice that Lenin's successor had long misused his name to lead the Party away from Lenin's road. To her the Party was still the purest and most just of all parties; to her it had a copyright on all truth and wisdom. When the time came and she was told to testify for the Party against her son, she sacrificed even her child to the Party. Her mother's love, she assumed, must have blinded her—for the Party could not be mistaken.

It was not until after she was in prison that she realized what an injustice she had done her son. The monstrous fact of her own conviction as a counterrevolutionary paled before her despair over what she felt to be her failure as a mother. She who should have tried to defend him when all were against him had instead delivered the last blow with her own hands. And as she rode to the Far East in the cramped cattle car, the rattle of the train murmured incessantly in her ears: my son, my son, my lost child....

Tens of thousands of prisoners passed through the transit camp in Vladivostok every month. The women's barracks are situated on a hill, surrounded by a small area of trodden ground behind the barbed wire. The barracks for the men are somewhat farther down the hill. Once a day a few men are let out of each barrack to fetch water. Then they go up the barren hill, whose only vegetation is barbed wire, and pass close by the women's zone.

Day after day the mother looked for her son, and at last he came. He came in tattered rags which hung upon an emaciated body; his sunken face was rough with whiskers, his shaved head drooped, his eyes were dull and apathetic. Only a mother would have recognized in this stooped shadow of a man her own son. She knelt at the fence, her hands gripping the wire, her face pressed so close to it that the barbs pierced her forehead like a crown of thorns.

"Son! Volodya! My son!" she sobbed.

The man turned. His lifeless eyes gazed indifferently at the tear-stained face of the old woman, and without a word he went on with his burden.

"My son, my son!" she cried when he came slowly back down the hill with the filled pails of water. "Forgive me, forgive your mother!"

For a moment he set down the pails, as though they were too heavy for him, and in a low, calm voice he said, "I have no mother any more. My mother repudiated me." Then he picked up the pails and vanished among the stooped figures at the bottom of the hill.

2.

The lockup, a kind of miniature prison, is an absolute essential of every camp. It is usually without windows, without illumination, and unheated or very inadequately heated. Frozen toes among the prisoners are frequently due to a stay in the lockup. It contains a biggish common cell and a few tiny solitary cells, the usual planks and the usual bedbugs and lice. The daily ration in the lockup is ten and a half ounces of bread and a warm soup. The camp commanders hand out lockup sentences of from one to ten days for a great variety of infractions of camp discipline; only in very severe cases is the sentence for twenty days. You can be sentenced to the lockup with or without permission to work; the latter type is the harsher sentence. If the prisoner is let out to work he can usually manage to get a little more food than he is allotted, and above all, by moving around at work he can warm up more easily than he can in the lockup.

Lockup sentences are given for the following misdemeanors:

Lateness in leaving camp for work; talking while going out to work; impertinence to the guards, camp administrators, or other free citizens; smoking in the barracks; smoking while going out to work; wearing unauthorized clothing (say, private coats or shoes); leaving the place of work without permission; being found with a man, even though it is in a harmless conversation, which it usually is not; entering a house or store in a free settlement; drunkenness; bringing food back into camp; disorder in the barracks; disorderly cot; refusal to work; theft in camp; theft at the place of work; failure to meet labor quota; use of unauthorized places as a latrine; fighting among prisoners (guards who beat prisoners receive no punishment); refusal to take part in extra duty or shock-troop work (udarniki) for the camp, that is, work which must be done after the end of the official twelve-hour working day; leaving the barracks, except to go to the latrine, after the evening roll call; washing laundry in the barracks; washing hair in the barracks; burning holes in clothing; and so forth.

In a camp with several hundred inmates, not a day passes without some sentences to the lockup. At one time or another every prisoner receives a lockup sentence.

My fate caught up with me in the potato fields. It was sowing time. The potatoes had been held over the winter in boxes, between layers of peat, and were now sprouting. We worked in pairs planting them. Now and then we would pause and gobble up one or two potatoes raw. They tasted bitter and scratched the throat, but they gave us the illusion of having something in our stomachs. Besides, raw potatoes were good against scurvy, and all of us had bleeding gums and loose teeth.

The brigadier came along and ordered us to a new job. One of the small wooden bridges across the trench on the edge of the fields had collapsed and would have to be repaired. "The new stringers are lying there already," he said. "Hurry up." Naturally, neither of us had the slightest idea how to build a bridge, but we picked up our jackets and set out.

At my partner's suggestion I quickly stuffed five small potatoes into the sleeve of my jacket, since we had little prospect of being in the potato field again for the rest of the day, and were still hungry for more raw potatoes. When I straightened up I saw standing before me the well-known figure of the administration chief. Even if he had not noticed me pick up the potatoes, my flustered face would have made him suspicious. He said nothing, but I heard his heavy military boots tramping along behind me. My partner reached the fallen bridge first and casually tossed her jacket to the ground. With an elegant flip I threw mind beside it, and at the same time I heard a voice at my side ask, "What have you got in that jacket?" So he had seen after all. There was no point in denying it. "Potatoes," I said.

"Throw them out." My five miserable little potatoes rolled to the ground. Then he began to rage. For about twenty minutes he skillfully rang the changes on all imaginable and unimaginable curses. He swore he would leave me to rot in the forest where I could eat tree trunks; that at least would do no harm to Soviet agriculture. Not enough that we counterrevolutionaries had committed crimes while we were at liberty; even in camp we were determined to undermine socialist agriculture. He would show me. I would remember him.

He kept his word. I remembered him.

During the next few days nothing happened, and I was beginning to hope that his tantrum in the field had been the end of the matter. Then an auxiliary brigade from the main Elgen camp came out to our auxiliary camp. With this brigade was my friend J.W., a German communist girl whose brother died in a Nazi concentration camp.

"Have you been in the lockup?" she asked me excitedly.

"I? Why? Not at all." But I felt a sinking sensation in the pit of my stomach.

"It was announced at evening roll call that you'd been given three days in lockup for stealing potatoes."

Lockup sentences for all prisoners were read out in the main camp as well as in the spur camps. The commandant of our spur camp, a young Russian who tried not to make our lives harder than they already were, knew I was a disciplined worker, and be was aware because of the evening "shakedowns" (searches) that I had never attempted to smuggle so much as a potato into the camp, although this was generally done by the prisoners. And so he had played the part of Providence; since he didn't want me sitting in the lockup he had not read the sentence at roll call. It is hard to imagine what a tremendous feeling of gratitude such evidences of humaneness call forth in a prisoner; years afterward prisoners would talk about such a commandant. Unfortunately they were rare enough. It is not that all of them are inhuman, but they are all afraid of one another.

I breathed a sigh of relief, thinking that the potato affair was over and done with. It was not.

It was the last day of sowing. Brigadiers, guards, mists, and camp commanders swarmed incessantly around us to spur us on to a last outburst of effort. Reeling with weariness, we returned to camp in the evening and threw ourselves down on the planks without washing or undressing. We felt as though we had not the strength to line up for our soup.

I was just dozing off when the group orderly came into the dim barrack with a list of names. Ordinarily, after the sowing incompetent workers were sent by the brigadiers back to the main camp, where they were switched from one job to the other and continually plagued. I had no reason to fear a transfer, and after blinking indifferently once or twice I closed my eyes again. Then I started up in fright as my name was suddenly called.

I had every reason to be frightened, for all the other names on the list were those of notorious criminals who were well known as work shirkers and who had all been caught several times with large quantities of potatoes. I was certainly not in very good company. A great many of the other prisoners had been caught with a few potatoes, of course. But when you have the bad luck to be reported by the administrative chief in person, when in addition it is wartime and you are a foreigner, there is likely to be a big fuss about it.

I packed my mattress sack and went out to join the incredibly ragged group, who greeted me with loud whoops and the amazed, flattering question, "Why is the 'rose' going with us?" The rose silently swung her sack to her shoulder. With a lump in my throat I answered the calls of, "Don't worry about it," from my friends who were staying behind, and for a second I saw the kindly commandant looking at me. Then he turned us over to the guards who were to conduct us the three miles back to the main camp. The guards had dogs, which meant that this was a disciplinary brigade. On the way we met the administrative chief, whose pale gray eyes flickered with satisfaction when he saw me in the company. I answered with a look of hate.

The commandant of the main camp took the list with our names, looked over the human scarecrows with their elbows, shoulders and toes protruding through their rags, and ordered in a loud, contented voice: "Put the whole pack into the disciplinary barrack."

The barrack was low, dark, and crawling with bedbugs. The inmates were all of the same type as those who had marched here with me. The newcomers made themselves at home at once; they were greeted joyfully with filthy curses, and they pointed out with a smirk what a queer bird they had brought along—namely, myself. They made it quite clear from the start that I had no business there. Some of them were lesbians; they lay on the planks, couples sharing one blanket, their faces ashen, dark circles under their eyes, and watched with malicious grins as I tried to find a place. It was hopeless from the start. Wherever I put down my sack someone said, "This place is taken. These planks are broken. Keep out of here. Get going." Or they simply tossed my things back to the floor, and from all corners of the room they hissed, howled and screeched at me, "Rose, rose. . . ."

They might have stripped me and taken away all my things, down to the last foot-rag; I would have been completely defenseless, and they knew it. That was the usual procedure when a solitary contrik fell into the hands of criminals. But they did not do it. They merely made it quite clear to me that I had better get out of here as fast as possible. The reason they did not touch me was that I was after all a foreigner. Toward foreigners Russians feel a certain respect, and this feeling comes out quite clearly in the more primitive and unspoiled of the people. There is in this attitude an element of innate hospitality, the consciousness of their own inadequacies, and the enchantment of the exotic, the fairy-tale quality of the unknown. Every day these people are given their antiforeign inoculation at meetings, over the radio, and in their newspapers. The words "spy" and "fascist" are on everyone's lips—but it is all lip service. Alongside of this artificially created suspicion of foreigners there is an altogether different attitude buried deep inside these people, an attitude passed down from their forefathers; it is an almost childish reverence for people from another world, a world that seems to them as strange and resplendent as the world of the Arabian Nights to us.

A trace of this lingered still in the unconscious minds of this utterly depraved band, and protected me from their fists that night.

The barrack was not yet locked, and I rushed out and sought refuge in the "German" barrack, which was after all also a barrack of outcasts. I cried out to the camp orderly, "Do what you like with me, but you won't get me back into the disciplinary barrack unless you carry me in." Apparently my desperation impressed her, for such outbursts were not usual with me. She quietly legalized the status quo and nothing more was said about the disciplinary barrack.

Next morning, however, I was called out to work as a member of the disciplinary brigade. The scum of the camp were in this brigade; when they marched out to work the strong convoy of guards had wolfhounds with them. Our place of work was five miles from the camp. The road led across the cemetery for free citizens where instead of crosses, wooden pyramids, painted red and tilted by the wind, with Soviet stars on top of them, were slowly decaying. Sometimes a skeletal hand or a well-preserved foot protruded from the grave. It had been heaved to the surface by the thaw, for in winter it was impossible to break through the frozen earth to make a sufficiently deep grave. At the sight, the hardened criminals who were my companions today broke ranks, uttering piercing screams—for all criminals are intensely superstitious. All of them also make a great to-do over their religion, which does not stop them from committing horrible crimes. For that reason they are generally somewhat restrained in their behavior toward the nun prisoners, the *monashki*.

After a march of about two hours we reached the swamps where we were to work. Clouds of mosquitoes instantly fell upon us with enthusiastic buzzing. We could protect our faces against them with the nakomarnik, but not our arms, legs, and the backs of our necks. I often wondered what they lived on before prisoners were brought in to feed them.

In July the sparse swamp grass is mowed. We were supposed to chop out whatever brush might interfere with the scythes and throw it into the pools of water. It was unnecessary work which had been thought up specially for the disciplinary brigade. Lighting smudge fires to drive away the mosquitoes was strictly forbidden. It was impossible to munch so much as a piece of bread throughout the day, for the moment you lifted your netting a horde of mosquitoes settled on your face. The constant pricking and itching of mosquito bites drove you crazy after a short time, but what good was it to run around in a circle like a mad dog—you could not break through the line of guards.

The guards suffered only from boredom, since their good uniforms and top-boots shielded them from the mosquitoes. Now and then one of them would kick a sleeping prisoner; then a furious blob of face, swollen by sleep and mosquito bites, would emerge from under the jacket that covered it. The prisoner would wait until the soldier turned his back; then she would promptly huddle under the jacket again. Hardly anybody worked. Why should they? The labor product was reckoned for the whole brigade together, and the majority of the members of the brigade were inveterate work-shirkers. Besides, who was going to count the number of twigs thrown into the water? We were already sure of the lowest bread ration, fourteen ounces. The prospect before this brigade was transfer to Mylga, the disciplinary camp of Elgen.

The hours crawled by. The day stretched out endlessly. Had the earth forgotten to rotate? Would the sun remain forever in the same spot? The mosquitoes bit, stung, crawled, itched, and burned. No slow darkening of the sky promised the coming of night; the one feature that marked the approach of evening was that the buzzing of the gnats became louder and more threatening. Bright days, ghostly bright nights. Days filled with mosquitoes, nights with bedbugs.

At first I rejected the thought of begging the camp commander for another job. She might sometimes relent if you piteously crawled and confessed your sins to her. I was resolved not to do that. But after several weeks in the swamp I was desperate, and went to her. Several times I turned back at the door of the administrative barrack. Finally I went in. I stood for half an hour in the waiting room, biting my lips, until I was at last called in.

Behind the desk sat Valentina Mikhailovna Zimmermann, known as "the Pike." When I entered and stood waiting at suitable distance, facing the portrait of Stalin which hung on the wall above her head, she threw me a brief, icy glance and bent over her papers again. I stood and waited. I stood looking at the narrow, set face with its hard, unfeminine features, the ugly mouth and the finely shaped brow under smooth dark hair, the trim body in the neat, well-fitting uniform. I was standing there in my oversized shoes and my baggy, stained man's jacket, looking down at the cracked skin of my hands, which were puffy and hideous from mosquito bites. When I looked up again she caught my eye.

"What do you wish?" she asked with cold politeness.

I made my request for transfer to another brigade.

"Where are you working?" She knew perfectly well, since she herself had put me in the disciplinary brigade.

"Clearing the meadows," I answered.

"Oh. Then there's nothing I can do. The other brigades are already full." She maintained the pretense of sticking to regulations, although she knew that I knew that there were daily changes among the personnel of the labor brigades.

"How long must I suffer over a few wretched potatoes?" I said.

She lifted her eyebrows and replied with the complacent contempt of the well-fed: "You might have thought of that before you committed theft."

I turned and left the office.

Nevertheless, after another week she transferred me from the swamps to another brigade.

Afterwards, whenever anyone mentioned the word "potatoes" in my presence, I felt sick.

3.

Work is a matter of honor, the heroism and the glory of every Soviet citizen.
—Stalin

Even in camp we were never spared the banners, slogans, mottos, and quotations from Stalin which are the universal madness of the Soviet Union.

Above the entrance to the dining room were the words: "He who does not work shall not eat."

There was no doubt that you went hungry in camp if you did not work. Unfortunately those who worked also went hungry.

On all the walls were signs: "Place yourself in the ranks of the best workers." The best workers were those who were still fresh, whose energies had not yet been sapped. There was no advice on how a prisoner who had undergone many years of near-starvation was to get up the strength to be a "best worker."

"Two-hundred percenters, teach the others to imitate you!"

The recipe: do as little as possible and bribe the brigadier with money or alcohol, preferably both, so that he will credit others' labor to you, thus making you a two-hundred percenter. Women could repay such a service on the part of the brigadier without money or alcohol.

"Honest work is the way to early release!"

In some countries there are dog races in which the dogs pursue mechanical rabbits running on a track. The moment the first dog reaches the goal, the current is turned off and the rabbit disappears before the eyes of the bewildered racer. It is as easy for a Soviet prisoner who works honestly to win an early release as it is for the dog to catch the rabbit.

"Cleanliness makes for health."

Unfortunately, cleanliness alone won't do it.

Only the doctor can release a prisoner from work. Refusal to work is punished by a sentence in the lockup. A notation of the case is made and signed by the camp commander, the commander of the guard, and the doctor. From three to five such notations are sufficient to bring a work-shirker to trial. In peacetime he was given additional sentences of from five to ten years on the basis of Paragraph 58, Article 14: counterrevolutionary sabotage. During wartime counterrevolutionaries who refused to work were shot; criminals usually got off with an additional sentence of ten years.

In general, cases of refusal to work among the so-called counterrevolutionaries are comparatively rare. It is the criminals who try to evade all kinds of work. They have usually turned to crime because of their dislike for work, and regular work is agony for them. For a few weeks at a time they will pitch in and break all records at work and then they are through with it. They loaf around devising plans for getting into the hospital. Some of them drink salted water. They swell up and are excused from work. Some may steal a syringe from the infirmary and inject kerosene under their skin. This results in bloody boils which keep them in the hospital for weeks.

Or in the morning, before departing for work, others may wrap a wet foot-rag around one of their feet. In the evening they come back with third-degree frostbite in their toes. The same trick can be used on the fingers.

There is another method that many criminals have recourse to. They lay their left hand on a block of wood and with an ax cut off their three middle fingers, leaving the little finger and the thumb. With two fingers they cannot hold a wheelbarrow in the gold mines, but when they are ultimately released they can still do other kinds of work with a crippled hand.

Acid and crayon are rubbed into the eyelids, producing a syndrome similar to that of trachoma. The criminals also have a recipe, which they keep strictly secret, for producing symptoms typical of syphilis.

Out of the stems and roots of *makhorka*, a kind of ersatz tobacco, they make an infusion which produces heart murmurs and fever. They also rub their armpits with onions or garlic before their temperature is taken. This produces a higher reading, but onions are worth fifty rubles apiece in Kolyma and are very rare. Another method to raise the temperature is to rub the mercury end of the thermometer when they are unobserved. The friction heats the bulb and makes the reading higher.

Sciatica is one of the favorite camp sicknesses, but a good many prisoners have to limp dejectedly off to work because they tried to make too much of a good thing and pretended to have sciatica on both sides—which is impossible. A great many prisoners simulate insanity, some for years. There are special insane asylums for prisoners. But even genuine and proved mental disease is no grounds for the release of a prisoner in the Soviet Union.

Prisoners are never informed beforehand when they are being transferred from one camp to another. When the trucks are ready and waiting, the prisoners destined for shipment are brusquely ordered out of the barrack with their bundles and loaded like so much baggage. If a criminal has an idea that the new camp will be worse for him than his present one, he will at the last moment cut open the surface of his abdomen. Criminals are so skillful at this that they never injure their internal organs. In fact, such cases are so frequent that the prisoner is not even sent to the hospital. The gaping wound is sewed up in the camp infirmary, and if the criminal has bad luck he will at most gain half an hour by his self-mutilation. Then he will be tossed into the truck.

Female criminals trying to escape transportation will strip off all their clothes and crawl naked up to the top of the board platforms. Crouching there they will respond to all orders to go to the truck with a torrent of curses. Finally two guards will come, tie the screaming and kicking woman's hands and feet and throw her into the truck. Usually some sympathetic person will toss her clothes in after her, so that she can dress during the ride.

Every prisoner welcomes a broken arm or leg—and the bones of sufferers from scurvy break easily. Here, too, the prisoners will assist chance if they have the opportunity. For example, they will hold their leg between moving hand trucks in the mines.

Especially envied are the prisoners with large trophic boils, which also are common to scorbutics. However, such boils have to be extraordinarily large to win a prisoner release from work. The smaller scorbutic sores, which may persist for years, do not count.

Deafness, dumbness, and paralysis are sometimes simulated for years, since many of the camps are without qualified doctors. In the hospitals false paralysis is uncovered in the following fashion. The malingerer is placed on the operating table and given a slight anesthesia. The moment he wakes up, when he is not yet fully conscious, he is placed on his feet and his name is called. Automatically he will take a few steps. As soon as he becomes fully conscious he will let himself collapse to the floor—but by then it is too late; the doctors have already had convincing proof that his legs are quite capable of supporting him.

Proved cases of malingering and self-mutilation are punishable, and if there is a medical report on the case, the prisoner will have at least two years added to his sentence. But doctors rarely make such a report if there is any way to avoid it. And the regulation that self-mutilators are allowed no more than thirteen days in the hospital is generally evaded.

4.

The last way out is suicide. This is a way never chosen by the criminals, though it is occasionally taken by male counterrevolutionaries and less frequently by female counterrevolutionaries. The chief reason for the relatively low rate of suicides is the fact that prisoners are never alone. In the barracks and at work they are constantly surrounded by other prisoners or by guards. The very fact that thousands of others are enduring the same fate tends to suppress the thought of suicide.

There is an incessant flow of rumors to the effect that revision of cases, amnesty, relaxation of the rules, or improvement in the rations are "on the way." No one believes these rumors; they are laughed at, but they nevertheless leave a lingering spark of hope.

Women are far more enduring than men. A man can reach a point of exhaustion where he no longer recognizes anything but food and sleep. A woman will still try to preserve a remnant of her humanity. And women are also more adaptable to unaccustomed physical labor. Strictly speaking, wood chopping is lighter than the work in the gold mines, from which women are exempt. But the transition from working as a stenographer, housewife, or teacher to wood chopping is no easier than the transformation of an intellectual into a gold miner. In almost every case it was the intellectual who chose voluntary death by freezing, hanging, or plunging from the tower of the refinery into the depths of the mine, rather than endure the slow, deadly torture of the camp.

Members of the family are not informed, no matter whether death is "natural" or violent. The fact is entered into the statistics, and the prisoners' documents are transferred to another file which bears the identifying mark: "File Number 3."

5.

"Petya," the nurse called, laying the used syringe into the sterilizer to be boiled. Petya, the orderly, a pickpocket who was serving his fifth camp sentence, although he was just twenty-five years old, stuck his shorn head with its prominent ears in at the door of the office.

"Petya, Volkov asked me to wish you a long life."

Petya was not particularly shocked at thus learning that Volkov had died. Since he had been working in this ward of the prisoners' hospital, he had seen so many die that death no longer made any impression upon him.

"Shall we take him out tonight, nurse?"

The nurse looked at the clock with its iron weights shaped like pine cones. How had such clocks got to Kolyma, she wondered? It was shortly after midnight.

"Yes, in two hours you can take him to the morgue. Why leave him lying with the patients all night? Where is Nyura?"

"Washing the floor."

"She'll just about finish by then. Bring me a board for Volkov."

While she wrote the dead man's name and dates on the little board, Petya busied himself with the body. The shirt and underwear had to be removed, for they were hospital property—prisoners were buried naked. Then he drew the blanket over the sunken, yellowish face with its closed eyes.

"A good nurse," Petya murmured to himself. "She even closed his eyes. The others don't trouble about it."

Respectfully, he watched her writing the last words on the board. Petya could not write. Then, with a piece of bandage, he tied the slat to the body's big toe. After that he looked around for Nyura.

Nyura was fifteen years older than Petya, but he loved her dearly. She was contrik, not a criminal. All her life she had worked hard. Her youth had been spent in a small village. Later, in the turmoil of revolution and civil war, she came to the city and worked in a factory. By the time of her arrest she was the mother of four children and lived in a small worker's flat in a town in Byelorussia. But her mother was Polish, and in 1938 in the Soviet Union that was as danger as having a Jewish mother in Hitler Germany. Convicted of counterrevolutionary activity and sentenced to ten years in camp, she was transported more than eight thousand miles to Kolyma to pay for a nonexistent crime.

Nyura worked on the assumption that all men were good who did not emphatically prove that they were not. And even when they did, she was still in doubt, still wondered whether she might not have been mistaken. A friendly manner was as much part of her as her pink skin, the wrinkles at the corners of her gray eyes, and the clean shawl which she wore tied with neat severity around her straight blonde hair.

She worked as an orderly in the hospital, but no one ever dreamed of addressing her with the customary, "Sanitarka." Everyone called her Nyanya, the name Russian children give their "nannies"—and to her, all—doctors, patients, and Petya the pickpocket—were her children. Her voice was not especially tender or pleasant, nor were her hands; but it had a kindly sound, as her hands had a kindly touch. Other mothers who had been parted from their children became in their sorrow harsh and embittered. But Nyura, who had wept over her children continually during the first months of her imprisonment, could not lock up her maternal feelings within herself.

Petya was as devoted as a dog to her. Most of the women he had known were prostitutes and thieves. Kicked about from early childhood, without a home or parents, he had spent his boyhood riding the "rods" of railroad cars. He never cared where the trains were going, as long as it was somewhere in the south; he could spend the winter in a warm climate, begging for his food, and if the going got tough he could steal what he needed.

Sometimes he would band together with one or two other boys, until they got separated somewhere in the vast expanses of the country. Once he was caught and taken to a children's colony. But for him the steppes were home, the starry sky a roof; he had spent his days dozing on cliffs above the Black Sea, and the rattling of railroad-car wheels was music to him. He could not endure the monotonous work and discipline of the educational colony, and on the first warm day he ran away.

Next time he was sent to prison for theft, and from prison to a penal colony. Branded as a criminal, he became a criminal. From then on he worked together with members of the profession. Adult criminals taught him the tricks of the trade. Camp was his school, bandits were his teachers. In 1938 he was sent to Kolyma as a recidivist, a criminal with several convictions.

After recovering from an illness he stayed in the prisoners' hospital as an orderly. He was a dour-looking fellow with dark, sullen eyes and a harsh twist to his mouth. He spoke as little as possible—until Nyura came.

Nyura was like a little stove, and like a freezing animal he crept close to her to receive her warmth. Silently he crouched near her, incapable of saying what he felt for her, for this was the first time any human being had been simply good to him. Gradually words came to him, words he had not known were in him; gradually he learned how to smile as he had never smiled before. Petya, who always had shirked work, would run headlong out into a blizzard, eagerly swinging the hated water pail, because Nyura needed water and Nyura must not carry anything if he could do it for her.

Now she was moving along the floor with her scrub cloth, reaching under the cots that stood side by side. The patients were all asleep except for a dropsical cardiac patient who was in a half-sitting position—a block of wood had been placed tinder the straw mattress to prop up his back—and who sat brooding, his inflamed eyes open, his breathing rapid and painful.

401

Opposite him stood the cot with the dead man. Above the table in the center of the barrack hung the burning electric bulb, shielded for the night with a scrap of blue muslin. Now and then the cardiac patient looked at the cot where Volkov lay beneath his blanket. Volkov was so emaciated that only his head made any hump under the blanket. Not that he felt particularly sorry for Volkov; the man had been an unpleasant, quarrelsome patient. But to die like this, in this barrack, all alone, without a single familiar face, a single hand to cling to when the end came—the cardiac patient groaned softly to himself.

Nyura was finished with her work. Petya went out behind the barrack and dumped the dirty water. This was forbidden, but it was snowing anyhow and the spot was almost instantly covered by fresh snowflakes.

Then they placed the dead man on a stretcher, spread the blanket over the stiff, naked body, and carried him out. Only the left foot with the board attached to the big toe showed out of the blanket—but the Kolyma winter could no longer harm Volkov's feet.

They put on their padded jackets and tramped out into the snow. The commander of the guard glanced quickly at the stretcher and let them pass. The morgue was outside the hospital zone. They walked down the deserted road, past the laboratory and a two-story dwelling house, until they came to the small, isolated frame building.

Outside, a figure was leaning against the doorjamb. Petya started in fright: the figure was a corpse. He overcame his fear and knocked. It took some time before Kolya, the convict guardian of the dead, opened the door.

"What kind of helper have you got there?" Petya asked.

Kolya grinned. "That's the best way to keep the guards away. Never fails. Not one of them comes by when I have a cadaver standing out there. They used to come sniffing around here now and then. Now I can have a glass in peace whenever I want, and when Katya is on the night shift and drops by we aren't disturbed when we . . ." Leaving the sentence unfinished, he ran his tongue over his full lips and glanced at Nyura out of the corners of his eyes to see whether she might be interested in having a little love among the dead.

But Nyura's eyes looked past him at the corpses which lay piled up along the walls all around the dissection table. Now Volkov lay there too as though he had never breathed or spoken. His arm dangled down and his head hung over the legs of the corpse beneath him.

"They'll be up for autopsy tomorrow," Kolya said, prodding the pile of frozen corpses with his toe. "I'll have to warm the place up so that they'll be thawed out in time." He busied himself about the small iron stove. "If you want to have a smoke, Petya, you two can stay here a while."

He opened a door which led to a small partitioned-off room behind the dissection room. There was a cot in it. On shelves around the walls stood glass vessels containing hearts, kidneys, and stomachs in alcohol. Kolya closed the door behind them and went back to his corpses.

They were alone. But Petya did not roll a cigarette. He looked at Nyura, then at the closed door and the cot. On the window sill a kerosene lamp was smoking. He blew it out and took hold of the woman. At first Nyura resisted; then she yielded.

When Kolya let them out, Petya mumbled casually, "The lamp went out, Kolya. I guess it's out of kerosene."

"That's all right," Kolya growled understandingly, and he closed the door behind them.

This time, as they passed the corpse leaning again doorjamb, Petya threw it a look of gratitude.

Special Regime

Anatoly Marchenko

1.

Criminal cons often, so to speak, "volunteer" to be transferred to political camps. There is a persistent legend going around the criminal camps that conditions for politicals are not too bad, that they are fed better, the work is easier, they are treated more humanely, the guards don't beat you up and so on. At the root of this legend lies the rumor of an actually existing Mordovian camp for foreigners who have been sentenced for espionage: conditions there are indeed almost like a holiday camp—unlimited parcels, as much food as you can eat, no work norms demanded: if you feel like it—work; if not, you can play volleyball in the zone. Returning home after his time is up the foreigner can find nothing bad to say about our camps and prisons. And among our own people, of course, the newspapers create an impression that every one of our political prisoners is bound to be a spy and a foreign intelligence agent, and so the rumor goes about the camps that politicals live in a kind of paradise. In actual fact conditions in the political camps are far worse than in the criminal ones. But there is also a grain of truth in the legend. Politicals are no longer sent to do logging and lumbering, they are guarded more carefully now, for logging means working almost without guards, and then it also means having axes and saws. Furthermore politicals have different attitudes among themselves: they don't kill one another or slit one's throats, and in general they respect their comrades and do their best to help them out in time of trouble. And this means that the guards in such camps hesitate to beat the prisoners up in public.

And so a criminal resolves to commit a state crime in order to get into a political camp, even if it means getting an extra sentence. He writes a denunciation of Khrushchev or the party—usually half the words are obscenities. Or else he puts some rags together to make an "American flag" drawing as many stars on it as he can manage (he doesn't have a clue how many there are, all he knows is that it's a lot). Then he has to get caught. He hands out copies of his denunciation to the other cons, somebody is bound to inform admin. Or else he sticks it on a wall in the work zone for everybody to see. The flag is hung up in a prominent position or perhaps he parades with it at roll call. Thus a new state criminal is prepared.

In the political camp he starves even worse than in the criminal one. On one occasion or another he gets a spell in the cooler and on the way there gets beaten up in the guardroom by the warders. He starts to write official complaints, but is soon convinced that this is useless. Meanwhile he has a long term ahead of him; and he has brought his own forms of protest with him from the underworld, together with its customs and point of view. And this is where the tattoos come in.

Once I saw two former criminal cons, then politicals, who were nicknamed Mussa and Mazai. On their foreheads and cheeks they had tattoos: "Communists = butchers" and "Communists drink the blood of the people." Later I met many more cons with such sayings tattooed on their faces. The most common of all, tattooed in big letters across the forehead, was: "Khrushchev's slave" or "Slave of the CPSU" (Communist Party of the Soviet Union).

Here in the special regime camp, in our hut, there was a fellow called Nikolai Shcherbakov. When I caught sight of him in the exercise yard through the window I almost collapsed; there wasn't a single clear spot on his whole face. On one cheek he had "Lenin was a butcher" and on the other it continued: "Millions are suffering because of him." Under his eyes was: "Khrushchev, Brezhnev, Voroshilov are butchers." On his pale, skinny neck a hand had been tattooed in black ink. It was gripping his throat and on the back of the hand were the letters CPSU, while the middle finger, ending on his Adam's apple, was labeled KGB.

Shcherbakov was in another corner cell similar to ours, only at the other end of the hut. At first I only saw him through the window when their cell was taken out for exercise. Later, though, we three were transferred to another cell and we often exercised simultaneously in adjoining yards. In secret conversation, unnoticed by the warders, we got to know one another. I became convinced that he was normal and not cracked, as I had thought at first. He was far from stupid, he used to read quite a lot and he knew all the news in the newspapers. Together with him in one cell were Mazai and the homosexual, Misha, both with tattooed faces!

In late September 1961, when our cell was taken out for exercise, Nikolai asked us in sign language whether anyone had a razor blade. In such cases it is not done to ask what for—if somebody asks, it means they need it, and if you've got one you hand it over, with no questions asked. I had three blades at that time which I still had from camp ten, before landing in the cooler, and I had hidden them in the peak of my cap as a necessary precaution; in spite of all the searches they had never been found. I went into the latrines, ripped open the seam under the peak with my teeth and took out one blade. Back in the yard, when the warder's attention was distracted, I stuck it into a crack on one of the wooden fence posts to which the barbed wire was secured. Nikolai watched me from his window. The blade stayed there in the crack all day long. Many other cons saw it—the boys used to scour every corner of the exercise yard while outside, every pebble, every crack, in the hope of finding something, useful. But once a blade has been placed somewhere, that means it already has an owner waiting to pick it up; in such a case nobody will touch it. Furthermore Nikolai spent the whole day at the window, keeping watch on the blade just in case. While exercising the following day he picked out the blade and took it back to his cell.

Later that evening a rumor passed from cell to cell: "Shcherbakov has cut off his ear." And later we learned the details. He had already tattooed the ear: "A gift to the 22nd Congress of the CPSU." Evidently he had done it beforehand, otherwise all the blood would have run out while it was being tattooed. Then, having amputated it, he started knocking on the door and when the warder had unlocked the outer door, Shcherbakov threw his ear through the bars to him and said: "Here's a present for the 22nd Congress."

2.

Here is one out of a number of similar stories, from which it differs only in its originality. It took place before my very own eyes in the spring of 1963. One of my cell-mates, Sergei K., who had been reduced to utter despair by the hopelessness of various protests and hunger strikes and by the sheer tyranny and injustice of it all, resolved, come what may, to maim himself. Somewhere or other he got hold of a piece of wire, fashioned a hook out of it and tied it to some home-made twine (to make which he had unravelled his socks and plaited the threads). Earlier still he had obtained two nails and hidden them in his pocket during the searches. Now he took one of the nails, the smaller of the two, and with his soup bowl started to hammer it into the food flap—very, very gently, trying not to clink and let the warders hear—after which he tied the twine with the hook to the nail. We, the rest of the cons in the cell, watched him in silence. I don't know who was feeling what while this was going on, but to interfere, as I have already pointed out, is out of the question: every man has the right to dispose of himself and his life in any way he thinks fit.

Sergei went to the table in the middle of the room, undressed stark naked, sat down on one of the benches at the table and swallowed his hook. Now, if the warders started to open the door or the food flap, they would drag Sergei like a pike out of a pond. But this still wasn't enough for him: if they pulled he would willy-nilly be dragged towards the door and it would be possible to cut the twine through the aperture for the food flap. To be absolutely sure, therefore, Sergei took the second nail and began to nail his testicles to the bench on which he was sitting. Now he hammered the nail loudly, making no attempt to keep quiet. It was clear that he had thought out the whole plan in advance and calculated and reckoned that he would have time to drive in this nail before the warder arrived. And he actually did succeed in driving it right in to the very head. At the sound of the hammering and banging the warder came, slid the shutter aside from the peephole and peered into the cell. All he realized at first, probably, was that one of the prisoners had a nail, one of the prisoners was hammering a nail! And his first impulse, evidently, was to take it away. He began to open the cell door; and then Sergei explained the situation to him. The warder was nonplused.

Soon a whole group of warders had gathered in the corridor by our door. They took turns at peering through the peephole and shouting at Sergei to snap the twine. Then, realizing that he had no intention of doing so, the warders demanded that one of us break the twine. We remained sitting on our bunks without moving; somebody only poured out a stream of curses from time to time in answer to their threats and demands. But now it came up to dinner time, we could hear the servers bustling up and down the corridor, from neighboring cells came the sound of food flaps opening and the clink of bowls. One fellow in the cell could endure it no longer—before you knew it we'd be going without our dinner—he snapped the cord by the food flap. The warders burst into the cell. They clustered around Sergei, but there was nothing they could do: the nail was driven deep into the bench and Sergei just went on sitting there in his birthday suit, nailed down by the balls. One of the warders ran to admin to find out what they should do with him. When he came back he ordered us all to gather up our things and move to another cell.

I don't know what happened to Sergei after that. Probably he went to the prison hospital—there were plenty of mutilated prisoners there: some with ripped open stomachs, some who had sprinkled powdered glass in their eyes and some who had swallowed assorted objects—spoons, toothbrushes, wire. Some people used to grind sugar down to dust and inhale it—until they got an abscess of the lung....Wounds sewn up with thread, two lines of buttons stitched to the bare skin, these were such trifles that hardly anybody ever paid attention to them.

The surgeon in the prison hospital was a man of rich experience. His most frequent job was opening up stomachs, and if there had been a museum of objects taken out of stomachs, it would surely have been the most astonishing collection in the world.

Operations for removing tattoos were also very common. I don't know how it is now, but from 1963 to 1965 these operations were fairly primitive: all they did was cut out the offending patch of skin, then draw the edges together and stitch them up. I remember one con who had been operated on three times in that way. The first time they had cut out a strip of skin from his forehead with the usual sort of inscription in such cases: "Khrushchev's Slave." The skin was then cobbled together with rough stitches. He was released and again tattooed his forehead: "Slave of the USSR." Again he was taken to hospital and operated on. And again, for a third time, he covered his whole forehead with "Slave of the CPSU." This tattoo was also cut out at the hospital and now, after three operations, the skin so tightly stretched across his forehead that he could no longer close his eyes. We called him "The Stare."

In the same place, in Vladimir, I once happened to spend several days in a cell with Subbotin. This was a fellow the same age as myself and a homosexual. There were few homosexuals in Vladimir and everyone knew who they were. There was nothing they could earn there. He had been classed as a "political" after being in an ordinary criminal camp and making an official complaint—thus "letting the tone down." One day, after having sent about forty or fifty complaints to Brezhnev and the Presidium of the Supreme Council and to Khrushchev and the Central Committee of the Communist Party of the Soviet Union, he swallowed a whole set of dominoes—twenty-eight pieces. When the whole of our cell was being led down the corridor to the exercise yard—he had swallowed the dominoes just before our exercise period—he clapped himself on the stomach and said to one con from camp maintenance who was coming the other way: "Listen, Valery!" I don't know whether Valery really heard the sound of dominoes knocking together in Subbotin's stomach, but he asked him: "What have you got there?" and Subbotin drawled, "Dominoes."

The doctors wouldn't operate on Subbotin. They simply ordered him to count the pieces during defecation, saying that they would have to come out on their own. Subbotin conscientiously counted them each time and on his return to the cell ticked off in pencil on a special chart the number that had come out. No matter how diligently he counted, however, four pieces still remained unaccounted for. After several days of agonizing suspense he washed his hands of them: if they stayed in his stomach it was all right as long as they didn't interfere, and if they were out already, then to the devil with them.

Prison Diaries

Edward Kuznetsov

In 1967 one Lithuanian (I can't remember his name but I remember reading about him in the *Chronicle of Current Events**) who had served 17 out of his 25 year sentence was persuaded by the Cheka to write a request for clemency. He wrote it but nothing happened. His own people had turned their backs on him (if you request clemency you have no choice but to renounce all your ideals and actions and say how much you love the powers-that-be), so he killed himself. In full daylight he jumped into the forbidden zone and made as if he were going to try and climb the fence a few yards from the watch-tower. There could have been nothing simpler than to catch him—there he was, the high fence in front of him, and then the barbed-wire fence, and then one minute's walk from the guard-house which was crowded with soldiers. The sentry stood and fired round after round at him!

When a convict is killed in the forbidden zone, the murderer always receives the gratitude of the authorities and is rewarded with a two-week holiday. I wouldn't say it was for this reason alone that the sentries that guard political prisoners run and bayonet any madman or daredevil as fast as they can.

The authorities tell them the most fantastic and horrifying stories about us and about how cunning and clever we are. It's this which keeps alive in them that vigilance which becomes nervousness at the critical moment and that misinformed comprehension of their duty that turns into the fear that they are committing a crime themselves in allowing a horrible beast to escape, an enemy of the Soviet regime, who, before you know it, will blow up the Kremlin! I know several cases when would-be escapists, surrounded on all sides, and standing with their hands raised, were shot point-blank. This is what happened to Algis Petrosyavichus in 1958—the two men he ran away with were killed—(one of them while climbing up a tree and completely unarmed) while he, twice wounded, was left for dead.

---

* Underground bi-monthly account of trials, imprisonments and illegal acts of the Soviet authorities.

This was the only thing that saved him: the camp hospital was too crowded to finish him off, so all they did was amputate his right arm up to the shoulder, though there was nothing wrong with it (the bone was untouched). He later protested against this "operation" after hearing the surgeon say, "Let's make sure he never forgets this as long as he lives!" He was then 18 years old.

In late summer 1964 I saw Romashev bestially murdered before my eyes. He had served two years of his four-year sentence when he was rejected by his Komsomol wife and Communist Party parents on account of his anti-Soviet views. What had happened was that the authorities had written to them saying he refused to praise the Soviet regime and aid it by spying and informing on his friends. So one day he jumped into the forbidden zone and climbed over the fence only 10 yards from the watchtower. The sentry pointed his submachine gun at him And screamed, "I'll kill you, I'll kill you," but he shot twice in the air, unable to bring himself to shoot a man who was just sitting on the fence waiting to be killed, and making no attempt whatsoever to escape.

A minute or two later a few soldiers ran up and one swine among them cold-bloodedly emptied his gun into the living target, who didn't even blink when the barrel was leveled at him. The body, its legs stuck to the barbed-wire of the fence hung head downwards. Possibly Romashev was still alive but he could well have died in the 10 minutes it took the sergeant (Kiril Yacovlevich Shved) to come. He just tugged one of its arms and the body crashed to the ground. If Romashev had still been alive when he was hanging from the fence, the blow of his head on the ground would have been enough to kill him. The prisoners went wild, nearly rioted and had to be driven back by the guards. Then about 10 of us wrote protests and demanded a public inquiry, but we might as well not have bothered.

And what about Ivan Kochubei and Nikolai Tanashuk, who were slain by soldiers in the very middle of the camp?

Tanashuk had gone out of his mind and so had Kochubei, from all accounts, but this of course didn't prevent them serving out their terms. There was one fellow (I can't remember his name) whom I actually saw jump three times into the forbidden zone; each time he was removed by the guards, who knew he was insane—they never took their eyes off him during exercises and warned the sentry not to fire if the "fool," as they called him, should jump over the wire. In the two weeks I shared with him in the punishment block he jumped over the wire three times. Each time a guard dragged him back from the fence by his feet while the sentry smashed his rifle butt into his forehead. One week after he left the punishment block he was shot down in broad daylight in the forbidden zone. The zone isn't the punishment block, after all— how can you be expected to keep a guard on every "fool"?

I Was A Slave In Russia

John Noble

M 1.

y life in Vorkuta was the closest thing possible to a living death. It was a grueling combination of slow but continuous starvation, exhausting work, killing cold, and abject monotony that destroyed many a healthier man than I.

There was no wasted time in Vorkuta. I went to work producing coal for the Reds the day I got there. The brigadier in charge of surface transportation (hauling coal and slate) at Mine 16 was Politayev, the former Red army political officer who looked me over and picked me for his work brigade. My job was to push a two-ton car full of slate by hand. Some of the others chosen complained that they couldn't handle such heavy work.

"Sukinsin!" ("Son of a bitch!") one disgruntled prisoner yelled at Politayev. Politayev turned and looked disdainfully at the complaining prisoner. Then he pointed out a slave half-propped up on his bunk. I caught some of the conversation and learned later that he was pointing out a mine slave, one of the unfortunates who worked all day in the 2 1/2-foot-high coal tunnels, crawling on their stomachs and knees like rodents, chipping out the coal. He had a blank, animal-like expression on his face, his hair had turned mostly white, and his eyes were sunk deep in his cadaverous face. All his bones showed under a thin skin covering.

I turned away, sick.

For the next fourteen months, though, my lot wasn't much better than his. In fact, I never expected to live through the winter of 1950-1951.

My day began about 4:45 A.M. when a guard came through yelling "Vstan!" ("Get up!"). The first few weeks I washed with the half of a sheet I had taken from Buchenwald. But one morning when the water buckets froze (a common failure) I noticed that some of the prisoners were washing in the snow stripped to the waist. I decided to give it a try. The entire operation had to be done quickly, I learned by experimenting. One minute was fine, but five minutes could produce a bad frostbite. It stung and my face and body turned a beet red, but I was clean.

"Breakfast" was at 5:30. (The first step out of the barracks each morning suffocated me for a moment, the air was so cold and thin.) There were two meals a day, in the morning and evening. Each morning, I received a pound and three quarters of sticky black bread, which was our basic ration for the day. It was baked less than an hour and soaked with sixty percent of water. It was about one-third the size of an American one-pound rye-bread loaf. It was too wet to eat as it was, so I toasted it over the barracks stove, as the others did.

Breakfast consisted of a scoop of kasha (grayish grits) and a small bowl of watery soup with a few cabbage leaves at the bottom. There was nothing to drink except water. Supper, about twelve hours later, was the same kasha and thin soup, plus a thimbleful of sunflower oil to pour over the kasha, a $1\,1/4$ -inch square of fish, and a roll the size of a small egg. Every ten days, instead of the fish, I got two ounces of tough reindeer meat. Once, on May Day, we had pork.

My whole day's food totaled about 1400 calories (so a Russian doctor told me), about half what an office worker usually requires to live. I was continually starved, my stomach in a knot crying for more. It's a feeling you never get used to.

The evening meal was just enough to engender a real appetite. All I could do to relieve the hunger pains back in the barracks was to brew some homemade "coffee," an art I learned by watching the others. You take an inch-square piece of black Russian bread, stick it on a wire, and toast it over a flame until it is pitch black—but you don't allow it to become white-hot ashes. When it's the right color, you quickly dunk the burnt bread into a cup of hot water until it too turns black. This dirty water is Vorkuta coffee. Strangely enough, on cold nights later on, when I had forgotten the aroma of real coffee, it tasted good.

I had heard about the Vorkuta winter, but I never quite believed it until I saw and felt it.

"It gets bad here in winter," my Polish friend had told me. "The cold gets in your bones so bad you don't want to live any more. It gets thirty, fifty, even seventy below zero."

I worked on the surface that first year in the worst Vorkuta winter in a decade. After morning mess, I lined up in excruciating thirty-five-below-zero cold, hopping around from one foot to the other while the plodding MVD guards called the roll. My job was a mile and a half away from the camp. Fifty of us, covered by ten guards and two police dogs, made the trip every morning through a forty-foot-wide corridor connecting Mines 12, 14, and 16 with

Camp 3. The corridor had the same double set of barbed wire on either side, and the same brilliantly lit prohibited zone. About twenty guard towers were alternately spaced on either side of the corridor. Each tower was manned by one guard, with a submachine gun, who was relieved every three hours.

Winter came quickly. By November and December, the mile-and-a-half trip to and from work took us over an hour each way, as we trudged through snow up to my hips. (The corridor had a wooden walk, visible only in July and August.) Every week the thermometer dipped another five degrees. Within a short time, traveling to work under armed guard became a polar expedition—little Arctic safaris of guards, dogs, and slaves braving below-zero temperatures and blinding snowstorms that blew up out of nowhere. Only the MVD police dogs could forecast them. At the approach of a storm they whined pitifully.

I hit an ugly storm not long after I arrived. It snowed all night, and by morning, the twelve-foot barbed-wire fence on the corridor was only a foot above the snow in some spots. I had never seen anything like it in my life. We ran to the mine through the snow (the pace was killing but it was the only way to create warmth). The snow blew up in front of my face in great swirls. At times the visibility was as low as six inches. The wind howled mercilessly. I was one of the few men wearing the face mask issued by the camp; gradually my breath, captured inside it, began to freeze painfully against my face. I ripped it off and threw it into the snow. I pulled my *bushlat* over my head, and staggered with my arm covering my face.

"Don't break out of line or you will be shot," one of the MVD guards yelled.

I could have stepped right over the buried barbed-wire fence at a dozen spots along the corridor, but there was nowhere to escape to except deeper into the snowstorm.

Suddenly the slave next to me tapped me on the shoulder and pointed to my chin. It was a warning that my chin had turned white, the first frightening sign of frostbite. I pulled my hand out from under my jacket and started to rub the circulation back, the only hope of stopping frostbite. It took ten minutes to get my chin red again. I stopped just in time, for the back of my exposed hand had just begun to show small white spots.

Others weren't as lucky. Hundreds of Vorkuta slaves walked around with toes and fingers missing, amputated after a case of frostbite to stop the gangrene from spreading. One coal miner who had been brought up to the surface on a stretcher after a cave-in had crushed his chest, lay on the ground for fifteen minutes before he was taken to the hospital. His chest finally healed but the short exposure to the cold and snow made it necessary to amputate all his toes and nine fingers.

I never noticed the poor condition of the prisoners until later, when I injured myself and had to go to a dispensary. There I saw how skinny they were. Their pelvic bones were actually protruding through the skin, and from this they were seeking relief; all they got was a new bandage; no extra food, no time off from work.

My own injury consisted of a broken rib and two cracked ribs, suffered during work after I had been at Vorkuta for three weeks. The coal car I had been handling hooked into my jacket and pinned me between the car's sharp corner and a pillar in the corridor where the tracks ran.

Luckily, this occurred at the end of a shift, and I was able soon to leave for the camp. I explained to the doctor what had happened. Because it happened at work, he told me, I must have the mine doctor make a report of the accident. So he gave me a day off to get things settled with the mine.

The next day began one of my monthly three-day rests, and I did not go to the mine until the second day after the accident. The report was made out by the mine doctor, without any trouble, and I went to my department boss to have it countersigned. He said to me: "You had an accident and broke a rib, so you cannot work. How long will it take to get better?"

"Maybe three or four weeks," I replied.

He came close to me and said: "I like you, Amerikanitz, and I want you to work for me, but if I sign this for you, then the next thing I do will be to kick you out. Slave 1-E-241 will work and die in the darkest corner of the mine."

"But why?" I asked. "I didn't break my rib intentionally."

"I know," he replied, "but look: if I sign this, the camp will send you to a place to rest, all right, but I am the department boss and I will have to pay for the time you don't work, and the chief engineer won't get his bonus. You have to confess that you injured yourself intentionally and then take an additional sentence. If you don't do this, you will have to find some way out, but not at my expense. I'll help you along and give you a few days' rest at the mine, and some light work to cover a few weeks, but that's all I can do."

I went off to seek advice on how to close the door that I had opened at the dispensary. My brigadier suggested a second accident, not at the mine but in the camp; I then could say that the first injury was only a sprain but that the camp injury did the real damage. In this way, because the time I lost was not the result of an injury during working hours, the department boss would not be personally responsible for the time I lost from work.

I carried out this suggestion, and so had a day's further rest in the camp and a few at the mine. The chief benefit was that I could stay on the surface and have a boss I could get on with.

414

2.

When we arrived at Mine 16 on the bitter day that I narrowly escaped frostbite on my chin, there was another roll call. Mishka, a student from Stalingrad, was missing, lost somewhere in the snow corridor. None of the guards volunteered to search for him. The next day, when the storm subsided, his frozen body was found buried face down in the snow. The cold had frozen a pained, lifelike expression in place.

My job at Mine 16 was pushing a two-ton car full of slate. My partner, a Latvian who had done it before, briefed me in sign language on what I was supposed to do. The waste slate dug up with the coal came up the mine elevator and was dumped into metal cars on tracks.

The two of us were supposed to push the car 160 yards by hand, then tilt and unload the slate into another car below our platform. I had to do this seventy times a day, back and forth.

I looked at the tracks covered with snow and the loaded two-ton car. It's impossible, I thought.

Unfortunately, it was only *nearly* impossible, and I became a human locomotive for the next fourteen months. I pushed with my shoulder, jabbing it against the car until my shoulder turned almost permanently blue. Tilting the car was a superhuman strain. The first time I did it, I felt as if my backbone was bending and ready to snap. I never got used to it.

After I dumped the slate, an American-made electric pulley brought it to the top of a sixty-foot-high heap, where it was dumped again.

Every few days I was assigned to work at the top of the heap. The climate sixty feet up was not unlike that on a 15,000-foot Alpine peak. It was horrible. The icy, pricking wind almost hurled me off the slate mountain with every step. It took hours to do the work of minutes.

I worked without protection against the weather. Our tracks were covered overhead with a thin porchlike roof, but we were usually exposed on both sides to the cold, the snow, and the wind. According to GULAG regulations, we weren't supposed to work on the surface in temperatures lower than forty below zero (work went on at all times in the mine), but that was a joke. Major Tchevchenko was responsible to MGB General Derevyenko, boss of all Vorkuta, who was in turn responsible to the Kremlin for Vorkuta's coal output. They wouldn't countenance a day's stoppage—even, it was said, if the mustache froze on Stalin's statue in Vorkuta. I worked in fifty and sixty below, my head buried against my shoulder in a pitiful attempt to ward off the cold. One day the thermometer dropped quickly to 72 below Centigrade (-90 Fahrenheit), where it stayed for three hours, freezing the axle grease on my car. But there was still no letup in the work.

More than half the time, we worked in almost inky blackness. During January and February, I worked by starlight at noontime—an eerie experience for one still not used to the Arctic.

I had no gloves, but I managed to steal some oil rags out of the mechanic's shop and wrapped them around my hands. I wrapped my feet in large rags, which were actually warmer than socks. (The Red army uses rags too.) But nothing could keep the cold out. After an hour's work, I was so chilled and exhausted, my face, hands, and feet so numb that I cried like a child.

Officially there was no break in our work, not a minute out for rest or lunch (there was no lunch), but the great institutional Russian inefficiency saved my life. One day, the mine elevator stopped working. There was no slate coming up to us to be pushed in my "baby carriage." A Latvian prisoner pointed across a field to a small building, the mine powerhouse. In a combination of sign language, Russian, German, and English, he explained that it would be about ten minutes before the elevator would be fixed. I raced to the powerhouse, where I was greeted by smiling Russian prisoners warming themselves over a stove. I felt great, except that my boots got wet from the melting snow and they froze when I went out again. From the powerhouse I could hear the signals—two bells for coal, five for slate.

Mechanically, the Soviet mines are very poorly equipped. This is because of Russia's backwardness, in part, but also because of another factor which the executive engineer explained to me. While Russia has—both on paper and in "show" mines—the most modern machinery, it would not be possible to put this to use generally. Because a modern machine can be operated by one person, replacing from one hundred to two hundred men, this one person is able, if he is "evil-minded" (anti-Communist), to slow down or stop the work of up to two hundred men as represented in the output of the machine. If you have the people themselves to do the work, little harm results if one or two out of a hundred are evil-minded. Why take the risk of using machines?

The mine elevator was a machine they could not replace by man power. Therefore they used the best one available, an American lock hoister built in Iowa in 1913. Almost all electrical machinery was made in America or Germany.

I felt more and more like a primitive slave, my starving body pushing a two-ton car in an age of mechanization. I did not know the language, and I worked all day without a real friend at my side, for they changed partners regularly. I was sure that slaves in other times and places had a better deal than this.

The first seven months of the winter 1950-1951, I had just enough stamina to make it back to the camp every night. After "supper" in the *stolovaya,* our mess hall, I collapsed on my hard shelf in my filthy, snow-soaked work clothes. My face was a deep red from the cold, and for two hours after coming indoors I felt as if a log fire were six inches from my nose. I could hardly lift my stiff legs. My shoulder was blue from the slate car, and the palms of my hands had turned to elephant skin, each palm a large callous insensitive to cold, heat, or pain.

The starvation, climate and work had eaten away my body fat and left me a skin covering that hung over my bones. My weight had dropped to 95 pounds. Where my bones pushed against the skin, the skin turned a deeper brown than the rest of my yellowing but still not bleeding body. My rear end just disappeared. With the fat eaten away, the skin hung in big folds like a toy accordion.

The lack of oxygen in the Vorkuta air complicated my problems. I longed for sleep, but even sleeping all through my day off (three days a month) couldn't shake that all pervading tiredness.

God, I'm near the end of my rope, I thought to myself desperately one night. If the Reds push me just a little further, I'll break.

The other prisoners were even more wretched looking than I was (although the Russians among us took Vorkuta fatalistically: "What can we do? The regime and I were never friends. The MVD won, so we are here."). They were ill and decrepit far beyond their age. Ninety percent of them suffered from abnormally high blood pressure or heart disease, the blights of the polar region. I had only a slight case of high blood pressure, but my wrists and ankles swelled regularly into puffy masses of skin. Everyone had a cadaverous appearance (average weight was 75-115 pounds), a fact that hit me hard every ten days when we were taken to the camp *banya,* or bath, to get a hot bath and shave and to have our slave's mark of distinction restored—the head shaved down to shiny, hairless scalp. With our clothes off and the filth washed away, the pelvic bones stood out clearly. Only the Baltic prisoners, who received excellent food packages from home when Tchevchenko allowed it, looked any better.

Our teeth rotted from lack of vitamins. There was no dental care—only extractions. Most men had half their teeth missing, especially the lowers. I lost a few, and those I have left are discolored, eaten away, and shaky. Dental problems followed a pattern. The gums around a tooth would start to swell. The expanding fluid inside the flesh gradually pressed against the tooth until it loosened and fell out helplessly—generally while one was eating, especially the leathery reindeer meat served Vorkuta style. Some prisoners frantically tried to stop the inevitable process by puncturing the swelling gums with a needle and draining the fluid.

There was one boon to health. The cold that chilled the life out of us was itself a lifesaver. It was just too cold for most bacteria to live in Vorkuta. Otherwise, epidemics would have destroyed us in a year. Only tuberculosis, probably aggravated by the coal dust, was common.

The heavy labor was almost impossible to avoid. Refusing to work meant time in the cold cell. Prisoners were stripped down to light clothing and put into an unheated stone room, hands chained to the wall, thighs straddled over a concrete block that rubbed the fierce 40- or 50- below cold into the sensitive skin on the inside of the thigh. (Later, a friend, Ivan Simkovich, who had been accused of purposely slowing down his work, was sentenced to five days in the cold cell. "After one night in the cold cell you'll do anything they want," he told me. "It kept preying on my mind. All I wanted to do was get into a warm room.")

No one stood directly over us while we worked, but we had our Communist "norm," more diabolical than any ancient slave master. My "norm" was to transport all the slate that came up the mine elevator. Others had more specific tasks—so many feet of shoring in the main shafts, so many tons of coal to be dug, so many feet of coal-car tracks to be laid. Those of us who didn't fulfill their norms were put on punishment rations of less than half the normal diet. It was a vicious cycle. Those too weak to do their work were put on punishment rations. They became weaker and less able to fulfill their norms. The brigadiers, who are always anxious to get the best workers, shunted these poor starving souls from job to job until their emaciated bodies just expired. Those who were fortunate enough might have a sympathetic *feldshar* (one of the half-trained doctors of Vorkuta) declare him fit for only lighter work.

Conditions in the camp hospital were primitive. According to the theory that sick men weren't working and therefore needed less to eat, patients were given only half the normal ration. Only those who had undergone surgery had real beds—the others slept on shelves as we did. But it was still a sought-after haven, a rest from the grueling work and cold.

The hospital was run by a good-looking twenty-year-old girl, called "Doctor." She was actually a *feldshar* with a year of medical-school training. She cursed like a ten-year veteran of Vorkuta, but basically she was pretty nice. Still she had to turn dying men away from the hospital. According to GULAG regulations, only a very small percentage of the work force could be sick on any given day.

A high fever was the only excuse to get in. In the winter of 1950 a group of prisoners transferred to Vorkuta from southern Russia brought in a virus that infected the entire camp within a few days. Only those with 101 Fahrenheit or higher could be excused from work. My fever got quite high, and I spent a welcome week in the hospital. I was given little medication or care, but it was a chance to sleep.

Some slaves who couldn't take the grind dreamed up elaborate escape plans, but these always failed. Three prisoners in a barracks near the fence dug a tunnel from the drying room under the fence to the outside. They made white capes from stolen sheets and skis from old whittled-down boards. They broke out during a snowstorm, but soon lost track of one another. One fell into the hands of a guard at a neighboring camp. Another wandered in a circle for a day and ended up back at Camp 3. The third was found dead in the snow three days later.

Until 1948, escapees were shot immediately. After that, however, they would be thrown into the cold cell—but not before the MVD guards gave them a going over. Since a successful escape would probably mean death for the guards responsible, they beat up everyone who tried, as a warning to the other slaves. I saw one of the three men who broke out on skis. He was lying limp on the floor of the guards' hut at the main gate, his face bloated from constant bashing.

There was really only one way to beat the Communists, and many prisoners used it. That was to disable yourself so badly that you could only be a floor sweeper or the *sushilchik,* the stoker of the barracks stove.

One evening in the middle of the first winter, I was sleeping on my shelf when a loud yell from the end of the barracks startled me. Quickly jerking myself up off the shelf, I saw an Asiatic Russian prisoner, a fierce-looking Kalmuk, one of the remnants of what was once the Kalmuk Autonomous Soviet Socialist Republic. He had been arrested during World War II resisting the Russian genocide of his entire nation. The Russians killed and imprisoned almost all the 225,000 Kalmuks, including babies and women, and discontinued the "republic" in 1943 when the Kalmuks refused to fight for their Soviet oppressors.

He stood in the center of the aisle. In his left hand was a hatchet he had stolen from the mine. All eyes were on him. He placed his right hand palm down on a stool directly under the naked electric bulb.

"Russki Cherti! [Russian Devils!]" No more work from me" he shrieked at the top of his lungs.

As the words came out, his left hand swung the hatchet down in a resounding blow that struck the hand just above the knuckles, severing his four fingers cleanly from his hand. As he lifted the stump, the blood fountained out and covered his face and clothes. The force of the blow had thrown what once were four fingers onto the floor. His eyes were shining with fierce pride. He wrapped two filthy rags around the remains of his hand to absorb the blood, crawled back onto his shelf, and chanted himself to sleep, cursing the Russians. The Kalmuk spent two months in the camp jail, but he never again did a day's heavy work for the MVD.

Others rubbed dirt into self-inflicted foot or leg wounds and massaged the wounds until they couldn't walk. Some had their friends crush their wrists with six-inch poles. The shrewd ones threw apoplectic fits and tried to simulate high blood pressure by drinking vast amounts of fluids before an examination. Some succeeded, others got time in the cold cell and heavy jail sentences for "sabotage." Tchevchenko blanched and raged with fury at the news of any new self-made cripple. He was deathly afraid the trend would spread and that his wards, Mines 12, 14, and 16, would no longer send enough coal to warm Leningrad.

3.

I lived in this mad world for more than half a year almost entirely alone, and with little to occupy my mind. Playing cards and singing were strictly forbidden. No more than five men were allowed to congregate at one time. Radio Moscow blared out of the barracks loudspeaker in a foreign language I couldn't speak or write, and which I could hardly understand. As I later found out, there were some women, but I was a Vorkuta greenhorn. Each of the nationalities was organized into something resembling community life, but, besides an odd Canadian, I was the only American in my camp. (I had heard rumors about Private William Marchuk, Private William Verdine, and two other Americans, Homer Cox and Towers, as well as many others, but I had no chance to meet them.)

Days passed into weeks, weeks into months. I wondered whether the U.S. government knew where I was. Were they doing anything? I received no mail or packages (Tchevchenko wouldn't let them through even if they arrived), and I wasn't allowed to write my mother and brother George in Detroit, or my father, who I thought was still in a Russian prison in East Germany (actually he was released in 1952 and was back in Detroit), or the U.S. Embassy in Moscow. They even refused me a Red Cross postcard, a basic international right.

But mostly I thought about food—strangely enough, not about exotic dishes or steaks or ice cream, but plain milk and fruit. I saw shining white glasses of milk and clean pears and apples in my dreams. But I never saw them in reality for nine years.

Sitting on my bunk, I watched some of the other lucky ones get packages from home, for them the difference between life and death. The Russian packages from the rural areas were good evidence of the widespread poverty, generally just a bag of onions, some tea leaves, and dried vegetables. Only rarely they included a small piece of bacon. The Latvians, Lithuanians, and Estonians, whose countries' former prosperity hasn't yet been completely destroyed by Red rule, got full, wholesome packages of candies, sugar, bacon, lard, and sausages. Each package was quickly divided among the prisoner's hungry friends, who tried to make the wonderful gifts last a day or two. Unless it was cleverly hidden, though, food or dried bread might not be husbanded. Molkov, a short, hated MVD guard (unlike most others, easy-going slobs who closed their eyes to most things unless another guard was along), regarded food saved for a hungry day as "evidence" that a slave was making "escape preparations." It was worth six weeks in the *bor* for one of our Lithuanians, Scichkauskas.

My stomach envied those who got packages or who had friends who got packages. I had neither. Then I heard there was a chance to pick up bits of leftover food down at the kitchen after the evening meal. One night, before the evening roll call, when we were locked in for the night, I went to the *stolovaya* and approached one of the well-fed cooks.

"Yeda, yeda" ("Food, food"), I begged in rehearsed Russian. I pointed longingly at the discarded fish heads and a small pile of *kasha,* scrapings off the prisoner-officials' plates. The cook looked me over to see if I was a friend, a friend of a friend, or a quick man with substantial *blat* (bribe money). When he decided he didn't know me from Adam, he kicked me out of the kitchen with a menacing wave of his food chopper. I went back to the barracks a little hungrier, lonely, and more disgruntled than usual.

4.

"Johnny, everything in Vorkuta depends on who you know," Vaska, a Ukrainian in my barracks, told me. "With enough *blat* the guards and brigadiers will give you the right job. There are few Russians that can't be bribed. You need friends in the kitchen for a little extra food, and a contact in the hospital will also never hurt you. If you are part of a tight-knit group, not even the *blatnois* will bother you." He was right.

Learning Russian was my first survival project. My teacher was a barracks mate, Ivan, a former student at Moscow University, one of the many disgruntled Soviet intellectuals. Without realizing it, I had already picked up a few words on the slate job—"pull," "stop," and others from the guards' commands. In no time I was making excellent progress. "Soon you will speak better than many of the Ukrainians," Ivan said. I worked at it every spare minute, and in a short time could speak halting, grammatically poor Russian.

Now that I was out of my cocoon, my circle of friends grew rapidly. Three prisoners, Vaska, Ivan, and Alexia, became my closest friends. Vaska, a twenty-five-year-old, short, dark-haired Ukrainian peasant, worked the electropulley that hauled my slate to the top of the heap. A fervent Ukrainian nationalist, Vaska fought with the Ukrainian Banders army during World War II against both the Nazis and Communists. Ivan, a thirty-year-old Ukrainian, had some secondary education—somewhat of a rarity in the rural areas. He hated the Communists with a passion reserved for Ukrainians. Three million of his people died of famine in 1932 during the severe drought. Red troops closed the Russian-Ukrainian border to keep the starving people from leaving, and stole whatever grain existed. Both Ivan's parents had been deported to Siberia.

"Millions were sent to Siberia or killed in the thirties when the Communists forced us to collectivize our farms," another Ukrainian told me. "When Hitler invaded Russia it was a chance to fight back against the Kremlin. We had millions of soldiers ready to destroy Stalin. But when we saw that Hitler was no better—he kidnapped thousands of our people to work in his factories and had no intention of giving us independence—we had to fight on both fronts. We died on the west against the Nazis and on the east against the Communists. It was hopeless."

Alexia was a Russian from Smolensk. He had been arrested in 1946 while a senior high school student, charged with the ubiquitous *Paragraph 58-10*. Agitation, the standard charge for anything from telling jokes about Stalin to intellectual deviationism.

My new friends made life a little more bearable. I shared in their meager food packages sent from home. Sometimes a friend in the kitchen could find a little extra cabbage soup or fat to help protect my 95 pounds against the cold. When I went to the camp hospital later, my friends brought me bread saved from their own rations, and other favors for which I'll always be grateful.

Learning Russian dispelled another fear. The language is so harsh I always thought everyone was screaming at me. Later I realized it was just a way of speaking. Actually the Russians are far from firm. They are masters of bluff—but when you stand up to them aggressively, they invariably back down.

Through my triumvirate and my new command of the language, I came to know the more than one hundred other slaves in my barracks, and others throughout Vorkuta. Vorkuta was a veritable League of Nations, and it contained many notables of the Communist world. The former First Secretary of the Communist Party of Estonia, who had labored to turn his country over to the Soviets, was handing out food in the *stolovaya* of Mine 29.

There were slaves who had been deputy ministers of East Germany and satellite countries, and regional leaders of the Communist Party itself. Gureyvich, a Russian Jew and former Soviet diplomat, was in Camp 3 just a few barracks from me. He had been recalled from France by the Kremlin shortly after World War II (when the "cold war" policy developed) and arrested by MVD agents as he stepped off the plane in Moscow. We had a colleague of Trotsky, who had been in dozens of slave camps for the last nineteen years, a former Professor of History at the University of Leningrad, and many former university students. A barracks mate, Dmitri Bespalo, an active member of the Young Communist League (Komsomol) at the University of Kiev, was serving fifteen years for "agitation."

We had many former CP members from East Germany, who were arrested in periodic purges from 1946 to 1950. There were even two Spanish Communists who had been in Odessa in the thirties expediting war materials to the Spanish Loyalists during the Civil War. They stayed on in Russia after Franco won, and a year later were arrested for "espionage." Most of the ex-Communists were disillusioned with what they consider the Kremlin's perversion of Marxism.

Not everyone in Vorkuta was an ex-Red. We were a polyglot army of slaves from every walk of life and almost every nation in the world. In Camp 3 we had Poles who had served with the Allies in General Anders's army during World War II and were arrested back in Poland when the Communists took full control in 1947. There were hundreds of Baltic people—Lithuanians, Latvians and Estonians, whose nations had been gobbled up in 1940 and made into Soviet republics.

"When the Russians realized they couldn't really "communize us," a Latvian, a former resident of Riga, told me, "they started to bring hundreds of thousands of Russians in to live in our country. They sent our people in exile to Siberia. Those of us who fought the deportation are here in Vorkuta, or in Karaganda or Irkutsk, or other slave camps instead of living in collectives in Siberia. Well, maybe there isn't much difference anyway."

Another Latvian had been a student at the University of Riga before his arrest. A prominent athlete, he had often visited Moscow with various sports groups. He confided to me that a good part of the Russian Olympic teams are actually made up of closely guarded, blond-haired anti-Communist athletes from the Baltic nations.

There were slaves from Iraq, Iran, Italy, Mongolia, China, and Czechoslovakia and later two North Koreans accused of disloyalty to their regime. There were a number of Russian and Ukrainian Jews, victims of Stalin's anti-Semitic pogroms of 1949-1953. In Camp 3 alone there were ten Greeks who had been taken prisoner by the Communists during their civil war. One of my barracks mates was a young Hungarian, James, a former university student in

Budapest. He had been arrested as a "Western agent," allegedly for spreading Colorado potato bugs, thus causing the bad potato crop in Hungary. There were hundreds of Germans, both Communists and Nazis, and some former SS troopers. We had representation from France in one prisoner, René (his wife was in the women's compound), who had been attached to the French government unit in West Berlin; an Englishman named Chapman (in Camp 10), a British army man who had been captured by the Germans in Holland. He was liberated in 1945 by the Russians from a Nazi PW camp, then promptly rearrested by the Reds and sent to Vorkuta. When I met him in mid-1945, his mind had been almost completely destroyed. Eve Robinson, a good-looking blonde Englishwoman, about thirty, was in the women's camp.

A number of my fellow prisoners were clergymen, Catholic priests from Lithuania, Protestant ministers from Latvia and Germany, and Russian Orthodox priests who were the only ones allowed to keep their long beards. Religion was one of the most serious crimes in Vorkuta. Possession of a Bible meant at least a month in jail.

But, despite all controls, religion flourished. Some groups held services at an altar in an unused hallway of the mine. A group of Baptists sat together at the evening meal in the *stolovaya* and prayed. When an MVD guard came over, they said: "There is nothing wrong, *Chort* [devil]. We are just praying." (The guards in Vorkuta took the slaves' imprecations philosophically.)

On free days I sometimes attended Protestant services given by a Latvian minister. It was in a different barracks each time. It was dangerous, but only if two or more guards came along. Individual guards made believe they saw nothing and walked away. A Lithuanian priest in my barracks was arrested regularly. But after two months in the *bor,* he would return each time to minister to his flock.

I was the only American in Camp 3, but I had contact with a few men who claimed to be Americans. In Camp 10, where I lived in 1953 and 1954, there was a William Vlasilefsky, an English-speaking, Russian-born prisoner who claimed to be an American citizen. He said that he lived most of his early life in the Western states and that part of his family was still living in Seattle. According to Vlasilefsky, he was in the United States army in the early thirties, then migrated to China, where he started a successful business. In 1949, the Chinese Reds called him to Peiping, where he was arrested and sent to the Soviet as a slave laborer.

Then there was Roy Linder, in Vorkuta called Adolf Eichenbaum, a prominent Vorkuta citizen. I met him in the hospital in 1950. Later he would come over to my barracks once in a while to talk. He spoke perfect English and, for that matter, equally good Russian, German, Swedish, and Chinese. We reminisced about Detroit (he had been a stunt flier at the Michigan State Fair) and about the States in general. Linder was very tall and balding and had a scarred chin that was twisted to one side, the result, he said, of a plane crash. According to his story, he was born in Vancouver, British Columbia, was an American citizen and a colonel in the United States Air Force, one of our commanding officers at Templehof Airport in West Berlin. During World War II he had been a U.S. army pilot in China, and prior to the war had flown as a "neutral" observer in the Spanish war.

According to Linder's version of his arrest, he had been kidnapped by the Communists in West Berlin in 1949 and dragged over to the eastern sector. After a year in Lubianka prison in Moscow, he had been shipped to Vorkuta as a slave laborer.

His story seemed convincing (except for occasional references to himself as major instead of colonel), but his short sentence of five years for Paragraph 58-6, "Espionage," made everyone suspicious. An American officer (unless he was trusted by the MVD) would undoubtedly have been tagged with a fifteen-to-twenty-five-year sentence. He had a local reputation as a person who might be pro-Communist. He seemed to have more freedom of action than the other slaves, more to eat, and more respect from the guards and MVD officers. My friends warned me not to trust him—that he was probably an MVD *stuckachey*—an informer.

"Don't worry, Johnny. I won't make any trouble for you," Linder once told me in an unguarded moment.

The last time I saw Linder was just before he was released by pardon. He sent me a note a few weeks later, saying that he was in Vorkuta working in the village powerhouse as a free worker. He had a girl friend in Rostov in South Russia and hoped to go and meet her. I have no idea whether he was ever allowed to leave the Vorkuta area, or what has since become of him.

Many other Americans are still in the Soviet, working as slave laborers. I heard that an American engineer, seized while working for the Reds in Vladivostok, is still in Lubianka prison in Moscow. According to newly arrived slaves coming from Moscow, so is Stalin's son, Lt. Gen. Vassily Stalin. But a Yugoslav who had been imprisoned only a hundred miles from Vorkuta told me more startling news.

"I spoke with eight of your countrymen," the Yugoslav told me. "They said they were American fliers who had been shot down by the Russians over the Baltic Sea. The Air Force has, of course, acknowledged that several B-29s and B-50s on routine missions were downed over the Baltic. One of them told me he was afraid they would never get back to America. The Russians had reported them dead, saying there were no survivors of the crash."

Prisoners being funneled into Vorkuta from camps in Tadzhik and Irkutsk in Soviet Asia, Omsk in Siberia, and Magadan in the Far East said there were many Americans, including veterans of the Korean War, both GIs and officers, and South Korean soldiers, working as slave laborers in their camps. From what I heard, they were PWs captured by the Communist Chinese and North Koreans who had been shipped to the Soviet for safe-keeping.

Some of the Ukrainians in our camp literally fell over every newcomer, questioning him on what prison camp he had come from and how many prisoners were there. Through adding, cross-checking, and striking averages, it was possible to establish a fair approximation to the number of people interned in Russia. The total population of the Vorkuta complex lay between four and five hundred thousand working in mines, brick factories, power plants, railroad lines, streets, city and village construction, food transportation, prison help, and hospitals. According to records we were able to piece together, throughout the entire Soviet Union in mid-1954 a total of twenty-five to twenty-eight million people were held in slave-labor camps, concentration camps, secret camps for foreigners, PW camps, repatriation camps, MVD prisons, investigation centers, MGB prisons, juvenile labor camps, and juvenile detention homes. An additional twelve million not in custody were interned in restricted areas. All told, a monstrous mass of slaves and persecuted peoples.

Kolyma Tales

Varlan Shalamov

1.

A lot of time must have passed between the beginning and end of these events, for the human experience acquired in the far north is so great that months are considered equivalent to years. Even the state recognizes this by increasing salaries and fringe benefits to workers of the north. It is a land of hopes and therefore of rumors, guesses, suppositions, and hypothesizing. In the north any event is encrusted with rumor more quickly than a local official's emergency report about it can reach the "higher spheres."

It was rumored that when a party boss on an inspection tour described the camp's cultural activities as lame on both feet, the "activities director," Major Pugachov, said to the guest:

"Don't let that bother you, sir, we're preparing a concert that all Kolyma will talk about."

We could begin the story straightaway with the report of Braude, a surgeon sent by the central hospital to the region of military activities. We could begin with the letter of Yashka Kushen, a convict orderly who was a patient in the hospital. Kushen wrote the letter with his left hand, since his right shoulder had been shot clean through by a rifle bullet.

Or we could begin with the story of Dr. Potalina who saw nothing, heard nothing, and was gone when all the unusual events took place. It was precisely her absence that the prosecutor classified as a "false alibi," criminal inaction, or whatever the term may be in a legal jargon.

The arrests of the thirties were arrests of random victims of the false and terrifying theory of a heightened class struggle accompanying the strengthening of socialism. The professors, union officials, soldiers, and workers who filled the prisons to overflowing at that period had nothing to defend themselves with except, perhaps, personal honesty and naiveté—precisely those qualities that lightened rather than hindered the punitive work of "justice" of the day. The absence of any unifying idea undermined the moral resistance of the prisoners to an unusual degree. They were neither enemies of the government nor state criminals, and they died, not even understanding why they had to die. Their self-esteem and bitterness had no point of support. Separated, they perished in the white Kolyma desert from hunger, cold, work, beatings, and diseases. They immediately learned not to defend or support each other. This was precisely the goal of the authorities. The souls of those who remained alive were utterly corrupted, and their bodies did not possess the qualities necessary for physical labor.

After the war, ship after ship delivered their replacements—former Soviet citizens who were "repatriated" directly to the far northeast.

Among them were many people with different experiences and habits acquired during the war, courageous people who knew how to take chances and who believed only in the gun. There were officers and soldiers, fliers and scouts....

Accustomed to the angelic patience and slavish submissiveness of the "Trotskyites," the camp administration was not in the least concerned and expected nothing new.

New arrivals asked the surviving "aborigines":

"Why do you eat your soup and kasha in the dining hall, but take your bread with you back to the barracks? Why can't you eat the bread with your soup the way the rest of the world does?"

Smiling with the cracks of their blue mouths and showing their gums, toothless from scurvy, the local residents would answer the naive newcomers:

"In two weeks each of you will understand, and each of you will do the same."

How could they be told that they had never in their lives known true hunger, hunger that lasts for years and breaks the will? How could anyone explain the passionate, all-engulfing desire to prolong the process of eating, the supreme bliss of washing down one's bread ration with a mug of tasteless, but hot melted snow in the barracks?

But not all of the newcomers shook their heads in contempt and walked away.

Major Pugachov clearly realized that they had been delivered to their deaths—to replace these living corpses. They had been brought in the fall. With winter coming on, there was no place to run to, but in the summer a man could at least die free even if he couldn't hope to escape completely.

It was virtually the only conspiracy in twenty years, and its web was spun all winter.

Pugachov realized that only those who did not work in the mine's general work gang could survive the winter and still be capable of an escape attempt. After a few weeks in the work gang no one would run anywhere.

Slowly, one by one, the participants of the conspiracy became trusties. Soldatov became a cook, and Pugachov himself was appointed activities director. There were two work gang leaders, a paramedic and Ivashenko, who had formerly been a mechanic and now repaired weapons for the guards.

But no one was permitted outside "the wire" without guards.

The blinding Kolyma spring began—without a single rain, without any movement of ice on the rivers, without the singing of any bird. Little by little, the sun melted the snow, leaving it only in those crevices where warm rays couldn't pierce. In the canyons and ravines, the snow lay like silver bullion till the next year.

And the designated day arrived.

There was a knock at the door of the guard hut next to the camp gates where one door led in and the other out of the camp. The guard on duty yawned and glanced at the clock. It was 5:00 A.M. "Just five," he thought.

The guard threw back the latch and admitted the man who had knocked. It was the camp cook, the convict Gorbunov. He'd come for the keys to the food storeroom. The keys were kept in the guardhouse, and Gorbunov came for them three times a day. He returned them later.

The guard on duty was supposed to open the kitchen cupboard, but he knew it was hopeless to try to control the cook, that no locks would help if the cook wanted to steal, so he entrusted the keys to the cook—especially at five in the morning.

The guard had worked more than ten years in Kolyma, had been receiving a double salary for a long time, and had given the keys to the cooks thousands of times.

"Take 'em," he muttered and reached for the ruler to write up the morning report.

Gorbunov walked behind the guard, took the keys from the nail, put them in his pocket, and grabbed the guard from behind by the neck. At that very moment the door opened and the mechanic, Ivashenko, came through the door leading into the camp.

Ivashenko helped Gorbunov strangle the guard and drag his body behind the cabinet. Ivashenko stuck the guard's revolver into his own pocket. Through the window that faced outward they could see a second guard returning along the path. Hurriedly Ivashenko donned the coat and cap of the dead man, snapped the belt shut, and sat down at the table as if he were the guard. The second guard opened the door and strode into the dark hovel of the guardhouse. He was immediately seized, strangled, and thrown behind the cabinet.

Gorbunov put on the guard's clothing; the two conspirators now had uniforms and weapons. Everything was proceeding according to Major Pugachov's schedule. Suddenly the wife of the second guard appeared. She'd come for the keys that her husband had accidently taken with him.

"We won't strangle the woman," said Gorbunov, and she was tied, gagged with a towel, and put in the corner.

One of the work gangs returned from work. This had been foreseen. The overseer who entered the guardhouse was immediately disarmed and bound by the two "guards." His rifle was now in the hands of the escapees. From that moment Major Pugachov took command of the operation.

The area before the gates was open to fire from two guard towers. The sentries noticed nothing unusual.

A work gang was formed somewhat earlier than usual, but in the north who can say what is early and what is late? It seemed early, but maybe it was late.

The work gang of ten men moved down the road to the mine, two by two in column. In the front and in the rear, six meters from the column of prisoners as required by the instructions, were two overcoated guards. One of them held a rifle.

From the guard tower the sentry noticed that the group turned from the road onto the path that led past the buildings where all sixty of the guards were quartered.

The sleeping quarters of the guards were located in the far end of the building. Just before the door stood the guard hut of the man on duty, and pyramids of rifles. Drowsing by the window the guard noticed, in a half sleep, that one of the other guards was leading a gang of prisoners down the path past the windows of the guard quarters.

"That must be Chernenko," the duty officer thought, "I must remember to write a report on him."

The duty officer was grand master of petty squabbles, and he never missed a legitimate opportunity to play a dirty trick on someone.

This was his last thought. The door flew open and three soldiers came running into the barracks. Two rushed to the doors of the sleeping quarters and the third shot the duty officer point-blank. The soldiers were followed by the prisoners, who rushed to the pyramid of weapons; in their hands were rifles and machine guns. Major Pugachov threw open the door to the sleeping quarters. The soldiers, barefoot and still in their underwear, rushed to the door, but two machine-gun bursts at the ceiling stopped them.

"Lie down," Pugachov ordered, and the soldiers crawled under their cots. The machine gunners remained on guard beside the door.

The "work gang" changed unhurriedly into military uniform and began gathering up food, weapons, and ammunition.

Pugachov ordered them not to take any food except biscuits and chocolate. In return they took as many weapons and as much ammunition as possible.

The paramedic hung the first-aid bag over his shoulder.

Once again the escapees felt they were soldiers.

Before them was the taiga, but was it any more terrible than the marshes of Stokhod?

They walked out onto the highway, and Pugachov raised his hand to stop a passing truck.

"Get out!" He opened the door of the driver's cab.

"But I..."

"Climb out, I tell you."

The driver got out, and Georgadze, lieutenant of the tank troops, got behind the wheel. Beside him was Pugachov. The escapee soldiers crawled into the back, and the truck sped off.

"There ought to be a right turn about here."

"We're out of gas!"

Pugachov cursed.

They entered the taiga as if they were diving into water, disappearing immediately in the enormous silent forest. Checking the map, they remained on the cherished path to freedom, pushing their way straight through the amazing local underbrush.

Camp was set up quickly for the night, as if they were used to doing it.

Only Ashot and Malinin couldn't manage to quiet down.

"What's the problem over there?" asked Pugachov.

"Ashot keeps trying to prove that Adam was deported from paradise to Ceylon."

"Why Ceylon?"

"That's what the Muslims say," responded Ashot.

"Are you a Tartar?"

"Not me, my wife is."

"I never heard anything of the sort," said Pugachov, smiling.

"Right, and neither did I," Malinin joined in.

"All right, knock it off. Let's get some sleep."

It was cold and Major Pugachov woke up. Soldatov was sitting up, alert, holding the machine gun on his knees. Pugachov lay on his back and located the North Star, the favorite star of all wanderers. The constellations here were arranged differently than in European Russia; the map of the firmament was slightly shifted, and the Big Dipper had slid down to the horizon. The taiga was cold and stern, and the enormous twisted pines stood far from each other. The forest was filled with the anxious silence familiar to all hunters. This time Pugachov was not the hunter, but a tracked beast, and the forest silence was thrice dangerous.

It was his first night of liberty, the first night after long months and years of torment. Lying on his back, he recalled how everything before him had begun as if it were a detective film. It was as if Pugachov were playing back a film of his twelve comrades so that the lazy everyday course of events flashed by with unbelievable speed. And now they had finished the film and were staring at the inscription, "THE END." They were free, but this was only the beginning of the struggle, the game, of life....

Major Pugachov remembered the German prisoner-of-war camp from which he escaped in 1944. The front was nearing the town, and he was working as a truck driver on clean-up details inside the enormous camp. He recalled how he had driven through the single strand of barbed wire at high speed, ripping up the wooden posts that had been hurriedly punched into the ground. He remembered the sentry shots, shouting, the mad, zigzag drive through the town, the abandoned truck, the night road to the front and the meetings with his army, the interrogation, the accusation of espionage, and the sentence—twenty-five years.

Major Pugachov remembered how Vlasov's emissaries had come to the camp with a "manifesto" to the hungry, tormented Russian soldiers.

"Your government has long since renounced you. Any prisoner of war is a traitor in the eyes of your government," the Vlasovites said. And they showed Moscow newspapers with their orders and speeches. The prisoners of war had already heard of this earlier. It was no accident that Russian prisoners of war were the only ones not to receive packages. Frenchmen, Americans, Englishmen, and prisoners of all nations received packages, letters, had their own national clubs, and enjoyed each other's friendship. The Russians had nothing except hunger and bitterness for the entire world. It was no wonder that so many men from the German prisoner-of-war camps joined the "Russian Army of Liberation."

Major Pugachov did not believe Vlasov's officers until he made his way back to the Red Army. Everything that the Vlasovites had said was true. The government had no use for him. The government was afraid of him. Later came the cattle cars with bars on the windows and guards, the long trip to Eastern Siberia, the sea, the ship's hold, and the gold mines of the far north. And the hungry winter.

Pugachov sat up, and Soldatov gestured to him with his hand. It was Soldatov who had the honor of beginning the entire affair, although he was among the last to be accepted into the conspiracy. Soldatov had not lost his courage, panicked, or betrayed anyone. A good man!

At his feet lay Captain Khrustalyov, a flier whose fate was similar to Pugachov's: his plane shot down by the Germans, captivity, hunger, escape, and a military tribunal and the forced-labor camp. Khrustalyov had just turned over on his other side, and his cheek was red from where he had been lying on it. It was Khrustalyov whom Pugachov had first chosen several months before to reveal his plan. They agreed it was better to die than be a convict, better to die with a gun in hand than be exhausted by hunger, rifle butts, and the boots of the guards.

Both Khrustalyov and the major were men of action, and they discussed in minute detail the insignificant chance for which these twelve men were risking their lives. The plan was to hijack a plane from the airport. There were several airports in the vicinity, and the men were on their way through the taiga to the nearest one. Khrustalyov was the group leader whom the escapees sent for after attacking the guards. Pugachov didn't want to leave without his closest friend. Now Khrustalyov was sleeping quietly and soundly.

Next to him lay Ivashenko, the mechanic who repaired the guards' weapons. Ivashenko had learned everything they needed to know for a successful operation: where the weapons were kept, who was on duty, where the munitions stores were. Ivashenko had been a military intelligence officer.

Levitsky and Ignatovich, pilots and friends of Captain Khrustalyov, lay pressed against each other.

The tankman, Polyakov, had spread his hands on the backs of his neighbors, the huge Georgadze and the bald joker Ashot, whose surname the major couldn't remember at the moment. Head resting on his first-aid bag, Sasha Malinin was sound asleep. He'd started out as a paramedic—first in the army, then in the camps, then under Pugachov's command.

Pugachov smiled. Each had surely imagined the escape in his own way, but Pugachov could see that everything was going smoothly and each understood the other perfectly. Pugachov was convinced he had done the right thing. Each knew that events were developing as they should. There was a commander, there was a goal—a confident commander and a difficult goal. There were weapons and freedom. They slept a sound soldier's sleep even in this empty pale-lilac polar night with its strange but beautiful light in which the trees cast no shadows.

433

He had promised them freedom, and they had received freedom. He led them to their deaths, and they didn't fear death.

"No one betrayed us," thought Pugachov, "right up to the very last day." Many people in the camp had known of the planned escape. Selection of participants had taken several months, and Pugachov had spoken openly to many who refused, but no one turned them in. This knowledge reconciled Pugachov with life.

"They're good men," he whispered and smiled.

They ate biscuits and chocolate and went on in silence, led by the almost indistinguishable path.

"It's a bear path," said Soldatov who had hunted in Siberia.

Pugachov and Khrustalyov climbed up to the pass to a carto-graphic tripod and used the telescope to look down to the gray stripes of the river and highway. The river was like any other river, but the highway was filled with trucks and people for tens of miles.

"Must be convicts," suggested Khrustalyov.

Pugachov examined them carefully.

"No, they're soldiers looking for us. We'll have to split up," said Pugachov. "Eight men can sleep in the haystacks, and the four of us will check out that ravine. We'll return by morning if everything looks all right."

They passed through a small grove of trees to the river-bed. They had to run back.

"Look, there are to many of them. We'll have to go back up the river."

Breathing heavily, they quickly climbed back up the river-bed, inadvert-ently dislodging loose rocks that roared down right to the feet of the attackers..

Livitsky turned, fired, and fell. A bullet had caught him square in the eye.

Georgadze stopped beside a large rock, turned, and stopped the soldiers coming after them with a machine-gun burst. But it was not for long; his machine gun jammed, and only the rifle was still functioning.

"Go on alone," said Khrustalyov to the major. "I'll cover you." He aimed methodically, shooting at anyone who showed himself. Khrustalyov caught up with them, shouting: "They're coming." He fell, and people began running out from behind the rock.

Pugachov rushed forward, fired at the attackers, and leaped down from the pass's plateau into the narrow riverbed. The stones he knocked loose as he fell roared down the slope.

He ran through the roadless taiga until his strength failed.

Above the forest meadow the sun rose, and the people hiding in haystacks could easily make out figures of men in military uniforms on all sides of the meadow.

"I guess this is the end?" Ivashenko said, and nudged Khachaturian with his elbow.

"Why the end?" Ashot said as he aimed. The rifle shot rang out, and a soldier fell on the path.

At a command the soldiers rushed the swamp and haystacks. Shots cracked and groans were heard.

The attack was repulsed. Several wounded men lay among the clumps of marsh grass.

"Medic, crawl over there," an officer ordered. They'd shown foresight and brought along Yasha Kushen, a former resident of West Byelorussia, now a convict paramedic. Without saying a word, convict Kushen crawled over to the wounded man, waving his first-aid bag. The bullet that struck Kushen in the shoulder stopped him halfway.

The head of the guard detail that the escapees had just disarmed jumped up without any sign of fear and shouted:

"Hey, Ivashenko, Soldatov, Pugachov. Give up, you're surrounded. There's no way out!"

"Okay, come and get the weapons," shouted Ivashenko from behind the haystack.

And Bobylyov, head of the guards, ran splashing through the marsh toward the haystacks.

He had covered half the way when Ivashenko's shot cracked out. The bullet caught Bobylyov directly in the forehead.

"Good boy," Soldatov praised his comrade. "The chief was so brave because they would have either shot him for our escape or given him a sentence in the camps. Hold your ground!"

They were shooting from all directions. Machine guns began to crackle.

Soldatov felt a burning sensation in both legs, and the head of the dead Ivashenko fell on his shoulder.

Another haystack fell silent. A dozen bodies lay in the marsh.

Soldatov kept on shooting until something struck him in the head and he lost consciousness.

Nikolay Braude, chief surgeon of the main hospital, was summoned by Major General Artemyev, one of four Kolyma generals and chief of the whole Kolyma camp. Braude was sent to the village of Lichan together with "two paramedics, bandages, and surgical instruments." That was how the order read.

Braude didn't try to guess what might have happened and quickly set out as directed in a beat-up one-and-a-half-ton hospital truck. Powerful Studebakers loaded with armed soldiers streamed past the hospital truck on the highway. It was only about twenty miles, but because of frequent stops caused by heavy traffic and roadblocks to check documents, it took Braude three hours to reach the area.

Major General Artemyev was waiting for the surgeon in the apartment of the local camp head. Both Braude and Artemyev were long-term residents of Kolyma and fate had brought them together a number of times in the past.

"What's up, a war?" Braude asked the general when they met.

"I don't know if you'd call it a war, but there were twenty-eight dead in the first battle. You'll see the wounded yourself."

While Braude washed his hands in a basin hanging on the door, the general told him of the escape.

"And you called for planes, I suppose? A couple of squadrons, a few bombs here and there...Or maybe you opted for an atom bomb?"

"That's right, make a joke of it," said the general. "I tell you I'm not joking when I say that I'm waiting for my orders. I'll be lucky if I just lose my job. They could even try me. Things like that have happened before."

Yes, Braude knew that things like that had happened before. Several years earlier three thousand people were sent on foot in winter to one of the ports, but supplies stored on shore were destroyed by a storm while the group was underway. Of three thousand, only three hundred people remained alive. The second-in-command in the camp administration who had signed the orders to send the group was made a scapegoat and tried.

Braude and his paramedics worked until evening, removing bullets, amputating, bandaging. Only soldiers of the guard were among the wounded; there were no escapees.

The next day toward evening more wounded were brought in. Surrounded by officers of the guard, two soldiers carried in the first and only escapee whom Braude was to see. The escapee was in military uniform and differed from the soldiers only in that he was unshaven. Both shinbones and his left shoulder were broken by bullets, and there was a head wound with damage to the parietal bone. The man was unconscious.

Braude rendered him first aid and, as Artemyev had ordered, the wounded man and his guards were taken to the central hospital where there were the necessary facilities for a serious operation.

It was all over. Nearby stood an army truck covered with a tarpaulin. It contained the bodies of the dead escapees. Next to it was a second truck with the bodies of the dead soldiers.

But Major Pugachov was crawling down the edge of the ravine.

They could have sent the army home after this victory, but trucks with soldiers continued to travel along the thousand-mile highway for many days.

They couldn't find the twelfth man—Major Pugachov.

Soldatov took a long time to recover—to be shot. But then that was the only death sentence out of sixty. Such was the number of friends and acquaintances who were sent before the military tribunal. The head of the local camp was sentenced to ten years. The head of the medical section, Dr. Potalina, was acquitted, and she changed her place of employment almost as soon as the trial was over. Major General Artemyev's words were prophetic: he was removed from his position in the guard.

2.

Pugachov dragged himself into the narrow throat of the cave. It was a bear's den, the beast's winter quarters, and the animal had long since left to wander the taiga. Bear hairs could still be seen on the cave walls and stone floor.

"How quickly it's all ended," thought Pugachov. "They'll bring dogs and find me."

Lying in the cave, he remembered his difficult male life, a life that was to end on a bear path in the taiga. He remembered people—all of whom he had respected and loved, beginning with his mother. He remembered his school teacher, Maria Ivanovna, and her quilted jacket of threadbare black velvet that was turning red. There were many others with whom fate had thrown him together.

But better than all, more noble than all were his eleven dead comrades. No other people in his life had endured such disappointments, deceits, lies. And in this northern hell they found within themselves the strength to believe in him, Pugachov, and to stretch out their hands to freedom. These men who had died in battle were the best men he had known in his life.

Pugachov picked a blueberry from a shrub that grew at the entrance to the cave. Last year's wrinkled fruit burst in his fingers and he licked them clean. The overripe fruit was as tasteless as snow water. The skin of the berry stuck to his dry tongue.

Yes, they were the best. He remembered Ashot's surname now; it was Khachaturian.

Major Pugachov remembered each of them, one after the other, and smiled at each. Then he put the muzzle of the pistol in his mouth and for the last time in his life fired a shot.

3.

The fresh tractor prints in the marsh were tracks of some prehistoric beast that bore little resemblance to an article of American technology delivered under the terms of Lend-Lease.

We convicts heard of these gifts from beyond the sea and the emotional confusion they had introduced into the minds of the camp bigwigs. Worn knit suits and second hand pullovers collected for the convicts of Kolyma were snapped up in near fist fights by the wives of the Magadan generals.

As for the magical jars of sausage sent by Lend-Lease, we saw them only at a distance. What we knew and knew well were the chubby tins of Spam. Counted, measured by a very complex table of replacement, stolen by the greedy hands of the camp authorities, counted again and measured a second time before introduction to the kettle, boiled there till transformed into mysterious fibers that smelled like anything in the world except meat—this Spam excited the eye, but not the taste buds. Once tossed in the pot, Spam from Lend-Lease had no taste at all. Convict stomachs preferred something domestic such as old, rotten venison that couldn't be boiled down even in seven camp kettles. Venison doesn't disappear, doesn't become ephemeral like Spam.

Oatmeal from Lend-Lease we relished, but we never got more than two tablespoons per portion.

But the fruits of technology also came from Lend-Lease—fruits that could not be eaten: clumsy tomahawk-like hatchets, hand shovels with un-Russian work-saving handles. The shovel blades were instantaneously affixed to long Russian handles and flattened to make them more capacious.

Barrels of glycerin! Glycerin! The guard dipped out a bucketful with a kitchen pot on the very first night and got rich selling it to the convicts as "American honey."

From Lend-Lease also came enormous black fifty-ton Diamond trucks with trailers and iron sides and five-ton Studebakers that could easily manage any hill. There were no better trucks in all of Kolyma. Day and night, Studebakers and Diamonds hauled American wheat along the thousand-mile road. The wheat was in pretty white linen sacks stamped with the American eagle, and chubby, tasteless bread "rations" were baked from this flour. Bread from Lend-Lease flour possessed an amazing quality: anyone who ate it stopped visiting the toilet; once in five days a bowel movement would be produced that wasn't even worth the name. The stomach and intestines of the convict absorbed without remainder this magnificent white bread with its mixture of corn, bone meal, and something else in addition—perhaps hope. And the time has not yet come to count the lives saved by this wheat from beyond the sea.

The Studebakers and Diamonds ate a lot of gas, but the gas also came from Lend-Lease, a light aviation gas. Russian trucks were adapted to be heated with wood: two stoves set near the motor were heated with split logs. There arose several wood supply centers headed by party members working on contract. Technical leadership at these wood supply centers was provided by a chief engineer, a plain engineer, a rate setter, a planner, and bookkeepers. I don't remember whether two or three laborers ran the circular saw at the wood-processing plant. There may have been as many as three. The equipment was from Lend-Lease, and when a tractor came to the camp, a new word appeared in our language: "bulldozer."

The prehistoric beast was freed from its chain: an American bulldozer with caterpillar tracks and wide blade. The vertical metal shield gleamed like a mirror reflecting the sky, the trees, the stars, and the dirty faces of the convicts. Even the guard walked up to the foreign monster and said a man could shave himself before such a mirror. But there was no shaving for us; even the thought couldn't have entered our heads.

The sighs and groans of the new American beast could be heard for a long time in the frosty air. The bulldozer coughed angrily in the frost, puffed, and then suddenly roared and moved boldly forward, crushing the shrubbery and passing easily over the stumps; this then was the help from beyond the sea.

Everywhere on the slope of the mountain were scattered construction-quality logs and firewood. Now we would not have the unbearable task of hauling and stacking the iron logs of Daurian larch by hand. To drag the logs over the shrubbery, down the narrow paths of the mountain slope, was an impossible job. Before 1938 they used to send horses for the job, but horses could not tolerate the north as well as people, were weaker than people, died under the strain of the hauling. Now the vertical knife of the foreign bulldozer had come to help us (us?).

None of us ever imagined that we would be given some light work instead of the unendurable log hauling that was hated by all. They would simply increase our norms and we would be forced to do something else—just as degrading and contemptible as any camp labor. Our frostbitten toes and fingers would not be cured by the American bulldozer. But there was the American machine grease! The barrel was immediately attacked by a crowd of starving men who knocked out the bottom right on the spot with a stone.

In their hunger, they claimed the machine grease was butter sent by Lend-Lease and there remained less than half a barrel by the time a sentry was sent to guard it and the camp administration drove off the crowd of starving, exhausted men with rifle shots. The fortunate ones gulped down this Lend-Lease butter, not believing it was simply machine grease. After all, the healing American bread was also tasteless and also had that same metallic flavor. And everyone who had been lucky enough to touch the grease licked his fingers hours later, gulping down the minutest amounts of the foreign joy that tasted like young stone. After all, a stone is not born a stone, but a soft oily creature.

A creature, and not a thing. A stone becomes a thing in old age. Young wet limestone tuffs in the mountains enchanted the eyes of escaped convicts and workers from the geological surveys. A man had to exert his will to tear himself away from these honeyed shores, these milky rivers of flowing young stone. But that was a mountain, a valley, stone; and this was a delivery from Lend-Lease, the creation of human hands....

And thus from beyond the ocean there had arrived one of those creatures as a symbol of victory, friendship, and something else.

Three hundred men felt boundless envy toward the prisoner sitting at the wheel of the American tractor—Grinka Lebedev. There were better tractor operators than Lebedev among the convicts, but they had all been convicted according to Article 58 of the Criminal Code (political prisoners). Grinka Lebedev was a common criminal, a parricide to be precise. Each of the three hundred witnessed his earthly joy: to roar over to the logging area sitting at the wheel of a well-lubricated tractor.

The logging area kept moving back. Felling the taller trees suitable for building materials in Kolyma takes place along the stream banks where deep ravines force the trees to reach upward from their wind-protected havens toward the sun. In windy spots, in bright light, on marshy mountain slopes stand dwarfs—broken, twisted, tormented from eternally turning after the sun, from their constant struggle for a piece of thawed ground. The trees on the mountain slopes don't look like trees, but like monsters fit for a sideshow. Felling trees is similar to mining gold in those same streams in that it is just as rushed: the stream, the pan, the launder, the temporary barracks, the hurried predatory leap that leaves the stream and area without forest for three hundred years and without gold—forever.

Somewhere there exists the science of forestry, but what kind of forestry can there be in a three-hundred-year-old larch forest in Kolyma during the war when the response to Lend-Lease is a hurried plunge into gold fever, harnessed, to be sure, by the guard towers of the "zones."

Many tall trees and even prepared, sectioned firelogs were abandoned. Many thick-ended logs disappeared into the snow, falling to the ground as soon as they had been hoisted onto the sharp, brittle shoulders of the prisoners. Weak prisoner hands, tens of hands cannot lift onto a shoulder (there exists no such shoulder!) a two-meter log, drag its iron weight for tens of meters over shrubs, potholes, and pits. Many logs had been abandoned because of the impossibility of the job, and the bulldozer was supposed to help us.

But for its first trip in the land of Kolyma, on Russian land, it had been assigned a totally different job.

We watched the chugging bulldozer turn to the left and begin to climb the terrace to where there was a projection of rock and where we had been taken to work hundreds of times along the old road that led past the camp cemetery.

I hadn't given any thought to why we were led to work for the last few weeks along a new road instead of the familiar path indented from the boot heels of the guards and the thick rubber galoshes of the prisoners. The new road was twice as long as the old one. Everywhere there were hills and dropoffs, and we exhausted ourselves just getting to the job. But no one asked why we were being taken by a new path.

That was the way it had to be; that was the order; and we crawled on all fours, grabbing at stones that ripped open the skin of the fingers till the blood ran.

Only now did I see and understand the reason for all of this, and I thank God that He gave me the time and strength to witness it.

The logging area was just ahead, the slope of the mountain had been laid bare, and the shallow snow had been blown away by the wind. The stumps had all been rooted out; a charge of ammonal was placed under the larger ones, and the stump would fly into the air. Smaller stumps were uprooted with long bars. The smallest were simply pulled out by hand like the shrubs of dwarf cedar....

The mountain had been laid bare and transformed into a gigantic stage for a camp mystery play.

A grave, a mass prisoner grave, a stone pit stuffed full with undecaying corpses of 1938 was sliding down the side of the hill, revealing the secret of Kolyma.

In Kolyma, bodies are not given over to earth, but to stone. Stone keeps secrets and reveals them. The permafrost keeps and reveals secrets. All of our loved ones who died in Kolyma, all those who were shot, beaten to death, sucked dry by starvation, can still be recognized even after tens of years. There were no gas furnaces in Kolyma. The corpses wait in stone, in the permafrost.

In 1938 entire work gangs dug such graves, constantly drilling, exploding, deepening the enormous gray, hard, cold stone pits. Digging graves in 1938 was easy work; there was no "assignment," no "norm" calculated to kill a man with a fourteen-hour working day. It was easier to dig graves than to stand in rubber galoshes over bare feet in the icy waters where they mined gold— the "basic unit of production," the "first of all metals."

These graves, enormous stone pits, were filled to the brim with corpses. The bodies had not decayed; they were just bare skeletons over which stretched dirty, scratched skin bitten all over by lice.

The north resisted with all its strength this work of man, not accepting the corpses into its bowels. Defeated, humbled, retreating stone promised to forget nothing, to wait and preserve its secret. The severe winters, the hot summers, the winds, the six years of rain had not wrenched the dead men from the stone. The earth opened, baring its subterranean storerooms, for they contained not only gold and lead, tungsten and uranium, but also undecaying human bodies.

These human bodies slid down the slope, perhaps attempting to arise. From a distance, from the other side of the creek, I had previously seen these moving objects that caught up against branches and stones; I had seen them through the few trees still left standing and I thought that they were logs that had not yet been hauled away.

Now the mountain was laid bare, and its secret was revealed. The grave "opened," and the dead men slid down the stony slope. Near the tractor road an enormous new common grave was dug. Who had dug it? No one was taken from the barracks for this work. It was enormous, and I and my companions knew that if we were to freeze and die, place would be found for us in this new grave, this housewarming for dead men.

The bulldozer scraped up the frozen bodies, thousands of bodies of thousands of skeleton-like corpses. Nothing had decayed: the twisted fingers, the pus-filled toes which were reduced to mere stumps after frostbite, the dry skin scratched bloody and eyes burning with a hungry gleam.

With my exhausted, tormented mind I tried to understand: How did there come to be such an enormous grave in this area? I am an old resident of Kolyma, and there hadn't been any gold mine here as far as I knew. But then I realized that I knew only a fragment of that world surrounded by a barbed-wire zone and guard towers that reminded one of the pages of tent-like Moscow architecture. Moscow's taller buildings are guard towers keeping watch over the city's prisoners. That's what those buildings look like. And what served as models for Moscow architecture—the watchful towers of the Moscow Kremlin or the guard towers of the camps? The guard towers of the camp "zone" represent the main concept advanced by their time and brilliantly expressed in the symbolism of architecture.

I realized that I knew only a small bit of that world, a pitifully small part, that twenty kilometers away there might be a shack for geological explorers looking for uranium or a gold mine with thirty thousand prisoners. Much can be hidden in the folds of the mountain.

And then I remembered the greedy blaze of the fireweed, the furious blossoming of the taiga in summer when it tried to hide in the grass and foliage any deed of man—good or bad. And if I forget, the grass will forget. But the permafrost and stone will not forget.

Grinka Lebedev, parricide, was a good tractor driver, and he controlled the well-oiled foreign tractor with ease. Grinka Lebedev carefully carried out his job scooping the corpses toward the grave with the gleaming bulldozer knife-shield, pushing them into the pit and returning to drag up more.

The camp administration had decided that the first job for the bulldozer received from Lend-Lease should not be work in the forest, but something far more important.

The work was finished. The bulldozer heaped a mound of stones and gravel on the new grave, and the corpses were hidden under stone. But they did not disappear.

The bulldozer approached us. Grinka Lebedev, common criminal and parricide, did not look at us, prisoners of Article 58. Grinka had been entrusted with a task by the government, and he had fulfilled that task. On the stone face of Grinka Lebedev were hewn pride and a sense of having accomplished his duty.

The bulldozer roared past us; on the mirror-like blade there was no scratch, not a single spot.

The Interconnection of Souls

Anatoly Sharansky

On the day of my arrest I weighed sixty-five kilos. When I began my hunger strike I weighed a little over fifty, and by the time it was finally over I was down to thirty-five. As soon as I stopped the hunger strike they immediately began a repair job on me, and the very next day I was moved to a "hospital cell" at the other end of the corridor. Slowly, barely shuffling my feet, and staggering under the weight of the mattress and pillow, I dragged myself past the doors of the seemingly identical cells. But they were different in that various types and amounts of food passed through the food traps of these doors, depending on the behavior of the occupants.

My cell was the most fortunate of all because such rare items as milk, meat, and butter came through the food trap every day. I was also given vitamins in the form of pills and shots. I gained strength daily, and before long I was able to go out for exercise. But it took at least two weeks before I could utilize the entire two hours that were allocated on a hospital regime.

"You have dystrophy of the myocardium—a weakening of the heart muscle," the doctor told me. "It could take months before it goes away."

In reality, it took years before I could lie on my left side. Even now, as I write these words fifteen months after my release, any slightly increased physical activity, such as running or swimming, reminds me of my hunger strike in Chistopol.

"Don't fool around with your heart like that again," warned the doctor. "You shouldn't go even one day without eating."

Perhaps he was right. In the future, even during a twenty-four-hour hunger strike my chest hurt as if I had been fasting for two months. But the doctor's concern had nothing to do with ill health. He was merely conveying the standard KGB message: Stop being a troublemaker.

Despite these warnings I did undertake other hunger strikes. A little over a month after my hunger strike had ended, I heard Anatoly Koryagin scream

444

from the corridor that he had been beaten while being taken to the punishment cell. Our demand that the incident be investigated immediately was rejected, so I joined a group of zeks who carried out a week-long hunger strike as a sign of solidarity with Koryagin.

And what became of my correspondence? As I promised in my note to Mama, ten days after the end of my hunger strike I wrote my first letter, about fifteen pages. A week later I was informed that it was confiscated. This time, it's true, they didn't demand that I reduce everything to a few predetermined words; they merely suggested that I mention nothing about my health. But I knew this was only the beginning, and that once again they were testing my resolve. They undoubtedly assumed that it wouldn't be easy for me to start a new hunger strike now that I had begun to regain my strength and to taste life once more.

Without hesitating, I wrote to the procurator declaring that unless my letter was sent I would renew my hunger strike. A few days later it was sent to Moscow, which initiated a remarkable period of a year and a half when virtually all my letters reached home and their size gradually increased from a few pages to forty. (There were never any specific limits on length, but the longer your letter, the less chance it had of going through.) In these letters I analyzed my entire prison experience, discussed topics that had agitated me over the years, and explained, sometimes allegorically, the reasons for certain decisions I had made. My link with home, with my family in Moscow and Jerusalem, had never been so valuable and so deep as during these months when we reaped the fruits of our victory.

After the hunger strike was over, I was visited by a series of procurators and inspectors. But now they were prepared to admit that mistakes had been made in the past. They even indicated the source of these mistakes—Romanov. The general procurator of the Tatar Republic told me that only someone who was ignorant of Soviet law could demand that a zek reduce his letter to one sentence, and he added that I had every right to send letters abroad.

The most remarkable thing of all was that this said in the presence of Romanov himself, who sat to the side and sullenly looked downward. His days are numbered, I thought, as they assured me that in the future there would be no problems with mail. The authorities also hinted that justice would soon prevail in the case of Koryagin, who had been conducting a hunger strike for several months after his beating.

By May the word was out that Romanov had been fired, and in another few weeks we learned that he had committed suicide. The Andropov purge had swept him away, too. As usual in these cases, when they decide to get rid of someone, they blame him for everything. Among other things, Romanov was

445

blamed for driving me to a hunger strike, although here, as in so many other areas, he was merely the obedient executor of the KGB's will.

In early March the KGB brought me to a special room where Galkin usually talked with political zeks. But today somebody else was behind the desk, a large man with an affable smile. "Hello, Anatoly Borisovich," he said. "I've come from KGB Headquarters in Moscow at your mother's request. I spoke with her at length only yesterday over a cup of tea." He walked toward me and offered his hand.

Naturally, I didn't take his hand. Instead I sat down and said, "I'm listening."

Why didn't I simply turn around and leave as I had been doing all these years? Was I intrigued by his mention of Mama, or was it simply that after my hunger strike I was eager to learn what was going on in the outside world, just as in Lefortovo? It was probably both reasons.

The KGB man sat behind the desk and reached for a package of Validol pills. He put one on his tongue and said something about his heart ailment. Then, showing the sympathy and solidarity of one sick man to another, he switched to the topic of my own heart problems. He told me how anxious and distressed Mama was about me, how she had cried in his office and had begged the KGB to help her obtain a meeting with her son.

"You were deprived of your January meeting," he said, "and the next one is in July. So far it hasn't been canceled. The KGB, however, is willing to be accommodating toward your mother's request and to ask the prison administration for an earlier meeting. Moreover, this year you will complete half of your term, and the Presidium of the Supreme Soviet may review the question of a pardon. This would depend exclusively on your behavior."

He continued: "Why not show some compassion toward yourself? I can understand that you were upset about the lack of correspondence with your mother and your wife, but why must you interfere in the relations between the administration and other prisoners? [This was a clear reference to our recent week-long hunger strike in support of Koryagin.] Why should you care about them? Your term is much longer than theirs and your case is more serious; you should think about your health and your family. Besides, they aren't serious people; they're vain, and their only concern is how to use your fame to their own advantage. The KGB is willing to meet you halfway; what guarantees can you give us?"

All of this was banal and very familiar—the references to family attachments, the attempts to play on my self-esteem, the disparaging references to my fellow zeks, the reminder that I could be deprived of my next meeting. I rose and walked toward the door, telling him, "I have nothing to say to you."

446

My new companion in heart ailments called after me: "If you change your mind, write, and I'll come to you right away."

Had Mama really turned to him? Had she wept in his office and begged? They're lying as usual, I told myself, but there was a bitter aftertaste that wouldn't go away. I had no way of knowing, of course, that Mama had been forcibly brought to the KGB, that they had tried to persuade her to send me a letter and a food package through them, and that she had categorically refused to cooperate. I didn't know any of this, but I hoped this was what had happened. I hoped and I feared.

The visit of this KGB man from Moscow, the new "liberal" attitude toward me on the part of the prison officials, who stopped throwing me into the punishment cell or subjecting me to other harassments even though my conduct hadn't changed at all; the attempts by the procurators and the Interior Ministry to blame Romanov for all previous violations—all this and much more told me that after my hunger strike the ice around me had started to melt. Some kind of game was in the works, but I resolved not to give in to idle fantasies, and used the opportunity to write long and detailed letters home.

The mystery was cleared up on July 5, 1983, at the next two-hour meeting with Mama and Lenya, our first meeting in a year and a half. It had been six months since my hunger strike and I had grown noticeably stronger, but even so, Mama was horrified at how thin I was. And while I tried to put on a good front and not complain about my health, I gave myself away by my habit of lightly massaging my chest with my right hand, which seemed to alleviate the constant chest pains. But not even my health could distract Mama and Lenya from the main piece of information they brought me, which was undoubtedly why our meeting had not been canceled.

"During your hunger strike there were many protests," said Lenya, speaking quickly in case they stopped him. "Some were by heads of state and Party leaders. On January 21, Andropov replied personally to an appeal from Georges Marchais in France, and it was clear that in doing so he was simultaneously replying to all the other leaders as well. He let it be known that you could be released soon, and after that our correspondence was restored."

Lenya continued: "The Helsinki Review Conference is now drawing to a close in Madrid, and the Americans made it clear that they won't sign the final document without a resolution of your problem. The head of the Soviet delegation has informed Max Kampelman, the head of the American delegation, and Kampelman told Avital, that if you sign a statement requesting a release for reasons of health, the request will be granted. In Moscow, the KGB told us the same thing. Kampelman thinks the Soviets are serious, and that this is a major concession. They aren't asking you to admit guilt, or to recant, or to condemn anyone else. Elena Georgievna [Bonner], in the name of herself and her husband [that is, Sakharov], asked me to tell you that in their opinion it's possible to accept this proposal."

I interrupted Lenya: "And what about Natasha? Did Natasha ask me to do it?"

"No, she asked nothing," he said. I sighed with relief, for otherwise it would be the first time I had to disagree with Avital since my arrest, which would have been a terrible blow to our spiritual unity.

"Mama and I won't advise you what to do," said Lenya, "but I must convey your answer to the American embassy in Moscow. They're waiting for it. So think about it and let us know by the end of the meeting."

"I can tell you now," I replied. "I committed no crimes. The crimes were committed by the people who arrested me and are keeping me in prison. Therefore the only appeal I can address to the Presidium is a demand for my immediate release and the punishment of those who are truly guilty. Asking the authorities to show humanity means acknowledging that they represent a legitimate force that administers justice."

Neither of them tried to contradict me, but I could see how Mama's face had fallen. She and Lenya continually brought up Natasha's name, trying to tell me about her tireless struggle, but the guards stopped them every time. At the end of the meeting Mama said timidly, "Well, Tolya, perhaps you'll think about this proposal again anyway?"

My poor old mother! How hard it was to disappoint her. I shook my head, for there was nothing to think about. We agreed that I would send my next letter, the July one, directly to Avital in Jerusalem. We had agreed on exactly the same point at our previous meeting, a year and a half ago, which had led to my hunger strike.

At the end of the meeting the guards demonstrated yet another sign of the Andropovian "thaw" as they allowed me to hug and kiss Mama.

"And now my brother," I said, tearing myself away from my weeping mother.

"No, that's already too much!" The duty officer reacted indignantly to my impudence, and two noncoms grabbed me by the arms and quickly took me to my cell.

The meeting had not been easy. As always, everything became confused in my head and questions emerged from this chaos almost by chance. And with each question, another unasked question: Is this item worth spending precious minutes of a two-hour visit, a visit whose price was a year and a half of my life?

448

As soon as the meeting was over, I began the usual calculation of credits and debts—this I said, that I knew, something else I forgot or didn't understand, and so on. Inevitably I was flooded with thousands of questions that I hadn't been able to ask. I recalled dozens of people I hadn't managed to ask about, and whom I might not learn about for years. The few details I was able to grasp invariably opened up an enormous window to the world, and for months I would review this information. Seeing my family for fleeting moments every year or two was a vivid reminder that time wasn't standing still, that life continued to rush on, that the people I cared about were changing, maturing, growing older. I had to make a continual effort to live my life with these dear, beloved people. This time, however, in addition to everything else there was also Mama's sad face and her half-hoping question "Perhaps, after all?"

I had rejected the KGB's offer outright, without even trying to explain the reason to Mama. But was it really possible to explain such a thing during a brief meeting? And were the reasons impelling me to say no completely clear and comprehensible even to myself? Avital, of course, would understand. But how could she explain rationally what I myself could not?

In Lefortovo they had demanded that I recant and condemn my "accomplices." In exchange they had promised me a speedy release and the possibility that later, in Israel, I could take back my confession. At the time, I formulated three reasons why I couldn't do this: it would weaken the resolve of my comrades; it would sabotage our support in the West; and it would help the KGB prepare new reprisals against dissidents and Jewish activists.

Even then I realized that these rational arguments were only partial answers, and that embedded deep within me was a commitment to resistance that automatically gave a negative answer to every KGB offer. I knew that if I began to bargain with them, to "understand" them, I would inevitably return to that former servile state of doublethink in which I had spent the first twenty-odd years of my life. In an effort to uphold my commitment and to remain beyond the reaches of the KGB, day after day, month after month, I mentally reinforced the bonds with my world, my family, Israel, and Avital.

"We need each other," I had once told her, and after my arrest our interdependence had increased a thousandfold. "The time has come for this little book to be with you," Avital had written on the eve of my arrest, and later I spent many long months in the punishment cell so that our Psalm book really would stay with me. There, in the cold and dark punishment cell, I heard not only Avital's voice but also the singing of King David.

And had King David not expressed himself on this very matter of the KGB's offer? I recalled Psalm 39:

449

I resolved I would watch my step
Lest I offend by my speech;
I would keep my mouth muzzled
While the wicked man was in my presence.
I was dumb, silent;
I held my peace
While my pain was intense.

Back in Lefortovo, Socrates and Don Quixote, Ulysses and Gargantua, Oedipus and Hamlet, had rushed to my aid. I felt a spiritual bond with these figures; their struggles reverberated with my own, their laughter with mine. They accompanied me through prisons and camps, through cells and transports.

At some point I began to feel a curious reverse connection: not only was it important to me how these characters behaved in various circumstances, but it was also important to *them,* who had been created many centuries ago, to know how I was acting today.

And just as they had influenced the conduct of individuals in many lands and over many centuries, so I, too, with my decisions and choices had the power to inspire or disenchant those who had existed in the past as well as those who would come in the future.

This mystical feeling of the interconnection of human souls was forged in the gloomy prison-camp world when our zeks' solidarity was the one weapon we had to oppose the world of evil, and when the defeat of any of us had an immediate and painful effect on the others. It was tempered in the punishment cells, where the supportive voices of my friends reached me only if I summoned them through a mental effort and only if our hearts were tuned to the same frequency. This feeling of our great unity and solidarity that knew neither temporal nor spatial limits crystallized during my hunger strike when the voices from *their* world, the voices of the guards, the doctor, or the radio, hailed me only in order to pour in another portion of the mixture or to remind me it was still not too late to join them. With each round, however, I lingered with them less and less. My eyes would indifferently scan the drab cell, lingering over the picture of Avital at the waterfall of Ein Gedi, and I would happily follow her into our world.

"The time is out of joint," says Hamlet in a moment of despair when he encounters villainy face-to-face. But now I was restoring temporal connections by entering into a fraternal union with those who helped me defend dignity—not my own personal dignity but the dignity of Man, created in God's image and likeness.

Of course the world in which I was immersed was not black and white, or good and evil. In order to divide the entire world into two distinct camps, one had to pass through a long zone of fear, vacillations, and doubts. And there were many people, both real and fictional, who tried to reinforce my doubts.

Above all, there was Galileo, whose name had come up in a conversation with Timofeev, my cell mate in Lefortovo. "Now, there was a smart man," he said. "He recanted to the Inquisition and was able to continue his scientific research with so much benefit to mankind. And at the end of his life, he uttered the eternal words [referring, of course, to the earth], 'And yet it moves,' restoring the truth." Once it was brought up, Galileo's name didn't leave my mind. The authority of that great scientist pressed upon me no less than the arguments of my own inquisitors. In the end, I stood up to debate with Galileo as well, and he and I ended up on opposite sides of the fence.

For me, Galileo was one of the few true giants in history, a scientific pioneer who, among other achievements, discovered the principle of inertia. And yet his very fame undoubtedly multiplied the number of individuals in various times and places who cited his great name in order to justify their own moral failure, caused by an inertia of fear, and who argued that what they told the authorities was less important than the fact that "it moves."

Although Galileo recanted to the Inquisition three and a half centuries earlier, his capitulation was pressing on me, trying to push me into doing likewise. But if I accepted the KGB's proposal, in addition to betraying myself I would be adding to the evil in the world. For perhaps at some future date my own decision would be a harmful influence on some other prisoner.

As I recalled my disputes and conversations with friends and opponents, both real and imaginary, as I thought about those who inspired me in this struggle and inspired me by their very existence, I formulated for myself a new law: the law of universal attraction, interconnection, and interdependence of human souls. I discussed it in a letter to Avital, although from prison, of course, I could explain my position only allegorically: "In addition to Newton's law of the universal gravitational pull of objects, there is also a universal gravitational pull of souls, of the bond between them and the influence of one soul on the other. With each word we speak and each step we take, we touch other souls and have an impact on them. Why should I put this sin on my soul? If I have already succeeded once in tearing the spider's web, breaking with the difficult life of doublethink and closing the gap between thought and word, how is it now possible to take even one step backward toward the previous state?"

A few days after I sent this letter, it was returned to me with words that ominously recalled the terrible events of the previous year: "You are a citizen of the USSR and there is no reason for you to write letters abroad."

451

Romanov, of course, had said exactly the same thing after my last meeting with my family, and I had then embarked on a long struggle that led to the hunger strike. The procurators had blamed Romanov for this situation, but Romanov was dead. Now what? After all that had happened, I had no intention of submitting complaints all over again. I immediately began another hunger strike.

But my heart was clearly unprepared, and within a day I suffered chest pains like those I had experienced in the second month of my longer hunger strike. On the third day the procurator appeared, and I reminded him of all the assurances that he and his superiors had given me.

"You're right, it's scandalous," he said. "I will immediately order them to accept your letter, and you will stop your hunger strike."

"No, first of all, explain to the administration in my presence that they are violating the law. Let them take the letter and show me it was sent, and then I'll stop the hunger strike."

The procurator summoned the censor, and I gave him my letter to Avital. The procurator explained that I had the right to send a letter to Israel, and that he was speaking in the name of the procurator general of the Tatar Autonomous Republic.

"You have your boss," the censor replied, "and I have mine. I have orders not to accept the letter."

I stood up and laughed, saying, "Well, now we can see who wields the real power—the KGB or the procurator's office."

I returned to my cell, leaving the letter with the procurator and the censor. The next morning they brought me a confirmation that my letter had been sent to Israel. I stopped my hunger strike, but it took another three weeks before Mama informed me in a telegram that Avital had received my letter.

After my long hunger strike, the restoration of my correspondence home was the most significant feature of my life in prison, but it wasn't the only change. During a sixteen-month period I wasn't punished even once, nor was I deprived of any meetings. My behavior hadn't changed at all: I maintained intercell communication, continued to write "slanderous statements," and participated in solidarity hunger strikes with other prisoners. As before, the prison officials regularly drew up reports about disciplinary violations, which were normally the harbingers of punishment. I would be caught talking through the radiator or the toilet bowl, and my companions would be punished, but not I. Or we would declare a hunger strike in solidarity with a friend, and my fellow zeks would be deprived of a meeting and switched to a less nutritious diet, while the authorities would pretend not to notice me.

The reader might rationally assume that the policy was related to my health. True, I was plagued by constant chest pains, which intensified with sudden motions and turned me into an invalid in the months following my hunger strike. But anyone who is familiar with the Gulag will understand the absurdity of this assumption. The authorities had their own reasons for being lenient. In response to the wave of protests over my hunger strike, Andropov had promised that I would be released for "good behavior," and apparently he was determined to prove that I had genuinely started on the road to "rehabilitation," no matter how I actually behaved. This hypothesis was confirmed by the fact that my punishments were resumed a few weeks after Andropov's death in February 1984.

Whereas 1983 was a year of "thaw" for me, this wasn't the case for the other politicals in Chistopol. Many zeks waited tensely for the results of the Madrid conference, where, based on the meager reports in the newspaper, we assumed that a struggle was taking place around the issue of human rights. The prison held members of the Moscow, Ukrainian, Lithuanian, and Armenian Helsinki groups, men who had sacrificed their freedom trying to test the willingness of the Soviet Union to observe the agreements it had signed in Helsinki. What would the West do now, when, eight years after Helsinki, the Soviet Union had moved even further along the road of repressions against any citizen who took those agreements seriously? Fragmentary information that reached us during family meetings confirmed that the West was pressuring the Soviets, demanding the release of political prisoners and freedom of emigration. But in the highly isolated environment of prison, encouraging words spoken at international forums were often inflated into significant hints, or even incontestable indications, that there would soon be a change for the better.

The Madrid conference ended, the next declaration was signed, and *Pravda* printed a condensed version of the text. We read it carefully, how all sides obligated themselves, made promises, and so on—just as at Helsinki. So what had the West attained during this period? Prison is the most sensitive barometer of change, and in prison nothing had changed. The politicals did not conceal their disappointment, and one of them began to circulate a new curse: "Madrid, you motherfucker." In Russian the two words are almost identical.

In October 1983, only three weeks after Madrid, the prison bosses went from cell to cell and announced the adoption of a new law, Article 188.3, which stated that the terms of prisoners who violated discipline in prisons and camps could routinely be extended by a court. In the case of politicals, up to five years could be added at once. In other words, if you continued to insist on your views or to protest injustice, they could now give you an additional prison term just as if you had committed a new "crime."

And why not? After all, we were imprisoned in the first place because of our views, so why should the authorities release us if those views hadn't changed? Previously, however, they'd had to invent some kind of provocation to justify their logic, whereas now the law made their job much easier. Rumors about the new law had been circulating for months, but apparently the authorities had waited until after Madrid to avoid giving critics in the West something more to use at the conference.

It is human nature to hope for the best, and after a few months the more optimistic zeks said, "look, they adopted the law, but they aren't in a rush to apply it." Unfortunately, even these hopes proved idle.

When the news came of Andropov's death, I was writing my next letter. As with Brezhnev's death, shouts of joy rang out in the cells, and prison officers and soldiers with German shepherds began making the rounds. I decided not to interrupt my letter. On the one hand, of course, I couldn't be indifferent to the death of a dictator who had headed the KGB for many years and had directed the fabrication of charges against me. On the other hand, I didn't want to think about the possible consequences of Andropov's death either positive or negative, for the country in general or for me personally—at the very moment I was concentrating on communicating with my family.

In March my letter to Avital was confiscated. In April they put me in the punishment cell for throwing a note to another zek in the exercise cell. Punishment is inevitable in such cases, but during the past sixteen months I had gotten away with much more. And so I would have to spend Passover in the punishment cell—the first Passover when I was to have matzoh!

Arkady Tsurkov had received a package of matzoh from home. He divided it into two parts, and for a long time sought an opportunity to send it to me and another Jewish zek. "I don't need it," he said. "After all, I'm going to be released." But instead of release he earned another two years of camp, and he greeted Passover, the holiday of freedom, somewhere far away, among criminals. And now, I, too, at the last moment had lost the opportunity to use Arkasha's matzoh, which I received from a zek who was transferred to my cell. Well, so what? The salted sprats would be my *maror*, the bitter herb, and for the *charoset*, the sweet mixture of nuts, apples, and wine, I would use my cup of hot water. What could be sweeter in the punishment cell? I tried to recall everything I could from the Passover Haggadah, starting with my favorite lines: "In every generation a person should feel as though he, personally, went out of Egypt," and "Today we are slaves, tomorrow we shall be free men. Today we are here; tomorrow in Jerusalem." The thaw was over, the future was fraught with new tribulations, and I hurried to steel myself with the words of the Haggadah.

My mood improved markedly when I left the punishment cell and learned that my April letter had successfully reached home. Good, at least I didn't have to start another hunger strike. I had put a lot of effort into that letter; each one that arrived home was like another part of my life that was saved from imprisonment.

But the KGB was eager to show me that the period of liberalization was over. I soon spent another term in the punishment cell, which was followed by six months of strict regime. In response I increased the length of my letters, bringing them up to forty, even forty-five pages. Still they passed the censor. Evidently the authorities didn't want me to start another hunger strike.

On the strict regime I again wound up with my old camp friend Volodia Poresh. He had gone through work strikes and hunger strikes to get back his Bible, so our astonishment and rapture knew no bounds when, toward the end of 1983, he suddenly received it. What was going on here? Was the KGB playing new games with Poresh? Or had there been a change in attitude at the highest levels?

It was impossible to know, but in any case I decided not to let the occasion pass without trying to obtain a Bible of my own. My efforts were fruitless, but I was still able to enjoy reading the Bible with my Christian friend Volodia.

Every morning after returning from the exercise yard, we began our Bible study. Volodia did the actual reading, as my eyes were again failing me and I couldn't follow a printed text for more than five or ten minutes without pain. Although we knew they could take the Bible away from us at any time, we made no effort to hurry. We decided to read both from the Old Testament and the New, and to discuss what we had read.

We called our sessions "Reaganite readings," first, because President Reagan had declared either this year or the preceding one (it wasn't exactly clear from the Soviet press) the Year of the Bible, and, second, because we realized that even the slightest improvement in our situation could be related only to a firm position on human rights by the West, especially by America, and we mentally urged Reagan to demonstrate such resolve.

As a child I knew almost nothing about the Bible other than Papa's stories about David and Goliath, Samson and Delilah, and Joseph and his brothers. And in the heat of my struggle to become a free person, almost no time was left for contemplating why the biblical tales, which were full of miracles that my skeptical mind refused to believe and accounts that I perceived only as a poetic rendering of history, had such an enormous moral influence on me.

455

My arrest changed everything. When the prison gates closed behind me, the huge world that had opened before me in recent years as the arena of an all-encompassing struggle between good and evil was suddenly narrowed down to the dimensions of a prison cell and my interrogator's office. I had to take everything that was dear to me, everything that had meaning in my life, with me to prison. The world I recreated in my head turned out to be more powerful and more real than the world of Lefortovo Prison; my bond with Avital was stronger than my isolation, and my inner freedom more powerful than the external bondage. Mysticism turned into reality, and through my prayers I seemed to admit the power of an external force that my rational mind had denied.

The Psalm book was the sole material evidence of my mystical tie with Avital. What impelled her to send it to me on the eve of my arrest? And how did it happen that I received it on the day of my father's death? The reading of the Psalms not only reinforced our bond but also demystified their author. King David now appeared before me not as a fabled hero or a mystical superman but as a live, indomitable soul—tormented by doubts, rising against evil, and suffering from the thought of his own sins. He was proud, daring, and resolute, but in order to be bold in combat with his enemies, he had to be humble before the Lord. The fear of God guided David when he entered the valley of death.

When I first came across the concept of *yir'at shamayim* (the fear of God), I automatically understood it as referring to the fear of God's punishment for our sins. But as I read the Psalms it became harder to maintain this narrow, utilitarian understanding of these words. Why had I refused to enter into any discussions with the KGB after my trial? Why was I prepared to die unless they sent my letters? Why did I refuse to ask for a release for reasons of health? Why was it so important for me not to take one step back toward that servile life I had once led? In time I began to understand that *yir'at shamayim* includes both an admiration of the grand divine design and worship of the divine might, as well as man's instinctive fear of being unworthy of his lofty role.

"The fear of the Lord is the beginning of knowledge," Poresh read aloud from the words of King Solomon in the Book of Proverbs, and for me these words seemed to be a natural summation of long years of spiritual search. I wrote in my next letter home:

> Perhaps this feeling is a necessary prerequisite for man's achieving inner freedom, and is also the prerequisite for spiritual resolve. Perhaps the fear of the Lord is the only thing that can conquer human fear, and all that remains for us is to repeat after King Solomon, "The fear of the Lord is the beginning of knowledge."

And if you want my opinion on the origin of this fear of God, whether

456

it was bequeathed from on high or was cultivated by man himself through the course of history, this is essentially a question about the source of religion—that is, a question to which there will never be an answer. And while I am well aware how much blood has been spilled over this question and how important it is to so many people, for me it's immaterial. Having realized there is no answer, I am not even searching for it. Does it really matter where this religious feeling stems from, whether man in some fashion was able to rise above his physical nature, or whether he was created that way? For me, the important thing is that this feeling really exists, that I sense its force and power over me, that it influences my deeds and my life, and that for ten years it has linked me with Avital more concretely than any letters.

Yes, we were bound to each other not merely by memories of the past, or by photographs or a few letters, but precisely by that elevated feeling of freedom from human evil and bondage to God's covenant that lifted us above earthly reality. Volodia read how God's angel instructed the prophet Elijah on how he would hear the divine voice: first there will be a storm that will crush the rocks, but God will not be in it; then an earthquake, but God will not be there; then a fire, but He is not there, either; and finally, a quiet wind—and there you will hear Him. Having passed through the storm of my struggle against the KGB for the right to emigrate, having undergone the earthquake of my arrest and the fire of cold punishment cells, I listened to the words of the Bible and through them Avital and I heard and understood each other.

Volodia and I normally read a book of the Old Testament and a short chapter of the New Testament, but I perceived these texts in different ways. Although I was responsive to the New Testament's concern with not losing the meaning or the spirit of the ritual in the letter of the law, I could not detach myself from its historical context. When my companion read me the parts where the Jews scream, "Let him die! His blood will be on us and our children," I couldn't help thinking how many bloody crimes against my people, how many millions of murders and other violent deeds, had been justified by these words.

Volodia was also aware of it. Tearing himself away from his reading, he suddenly said to me, "You know, I feel like"—and here he named some unfamiliar French Christian philosopher—"who said that persecuting Jews in the name of Christianity is the same as murdering one's parents for the sake of affirming a 'new truth.' There can be no justification for this."

His voice was trembling, and I already knew Volodia well enough to realize that he was speaking from the bottom of his heart.

This marvelous reading continued for an entire month until they put us in different cells, and during that month the feeling grew stronger that no matter how different our paths, or how different our prayers, we were praying to the same God, who instructed us to fear no evil as we entered the valley of death.

Half a year later, in July 1984, I wound up in the same cell as Volodia for the last time, as his five years of imprisonment were due to end on August 1. But would he really be released? In recent months the situation had changed for the worse. New orders had come out, making the conditions in the punishment cell even harsher "with the purpose of intensifying its educative effect." And if you began a hunger strike they put you in the punishment cell immediately.

The main thing, however, was that the authorities began to apply the new law that enabled them to extend a prison term almost automatically for disciplinary violations. Recently, one of the political prisoners, Nikolai Ilishkin, was separated from us and put in the end cell in anticipation of a trial under Article 188.3. In this context, it seemed particularly ominous that in the past two months the prison administration had punished Volodia as often as possible—in the punishment cell, followed by strict regime, followed by another term in the punishment cell—and were probably doing this to justify the application of Article 188.3. It looked as if the KGB was unwilling to accept that yet another zek—especially one who had seemed like easy prey at the time of his arrest—could leave the kingdom of the Gulag undefeated.

Volodia had two lovely daughters. When he was arrested, one was two years old and the other had just been born. Poresh followed their lives through occasional photographs, but the girls lacked even this connection to their father. Their only link to him was through their mother's stories and the reading of his infrequent letters from prison. I remember how long Volodia would sit over each letter, slowly choosing the words to send to his little girls, words that had to take the place of a paternal caress and a father's smile. The last time Volodia had seen his wife was two years earlier, in their native Leningrad, where he had been brought for so-called prophylactic work. The KGB had pressured him and threatened him and suggested that he influence his wife; he had refused. They had pressured his wife, suggesting that she influence her husband; she had refused. They took him to Chistopol and he hadn't seen his wife again. Four times in a row they had denied him his next meeting.

As his final weeks of imprisonment came and went the tension mounted by the day. Would they release him or not? His mail showed that the tension on the outside among Volodia's family and close friends was just as great. In one recent letter from his wife, Tatiana, describing the girls' playfulness, she had written that the time had come for them to have a father: "They need you so much, Volodia…." It was as if she were trying to influence fate.

Volodia's name day—the day of his patron saint—was four or five days before his scheduled release. It was also the name day of our third cell mate, Volodia Balakhanov, whom I had first met back in 1978. His twelve-year term was also coming to an end; only half a year remained. In the current situation, however, given his record of "bad behavior," who knew what awaited him? In order not to give in to anxious thoughts, we decided to use the opportune excuse of the double holiday to enjoy ourselves a little. We decided to hold a feast and to prepare a torte for it.

I had long ago heard tales about prison tortes, but as with the fabulous exotic delicacies of the East, I had never actually eaten one. In order to prepare such a torte you had to accumulate a fair amount of various foods, which was possible only under certain conditions. First, you had to have been on a "normal" diet for a long time; second, you or your cell mates had to acquire an additional three rubles' worth of food products in the prison shop; and third, nobody in your cell could be in such terrible health that it would be immoral to hoard food without feeding him.

All three of us were far from the dietary norm, but our desire to hold a memorable evening before our separation was so powerful that we decided to hoard food anyway. Over the course of two weeks we piled up about two hundred grams of sugar and two kilos of rolls. Moreover, Balakhanov, who had not lost his store privileges, acquired a package of margarine and some candy and a packet of green tea. On the morning Of July 27, we began with pomp and ceremony to prepare the torte.

With the help of bowls and mugs we ground up the rolls—that was our flour. A glass of water into which all the candies had been melted was poured over it and the mixture was stirred; this was our sweet dough. The package of margarine was mixed with the sugar and whipped up—this was the frosting. Now we had only to stick in the matches with their heads up in the shape of the letter V. In the evening an appropriate speech was delivered, and we lifted up our mugs of tea and lit the end match. The flame raced forward, and then we ate.

I ate my portion over three days, as I simply couldn't manage more than two spoonfuls at a time of such a filling, delectable treat. In the end I even shared my portion with my friends, who managed to finish their portions more rapidly. To call the result "tasty" is to demean it. The very word "tasty" seems insipid with regard to this celestial dish.

Before we sat at the festive table, Volodia took out the photograph of his dear ones and put it on the little bedstand together with postcards from home of biblical scenes painted by Raphael and Rembrandt that he used as icons, and he began to pray. He did this every evening, but this time he prayed for an unusually long time and with special passion. An experienced zek respects the right of his cell mate to a personal life, and doesn't violate the temporal and physical bounds that are reserved for his neighbor. I was lying on my cot, engrossed in a book, but when I accidentally turned toward Volodia I saw that he was looking at the photograph of his wife and little girls and his eyes were full of tears. He was praying to God for mercy. His position toward the KGB was like reinforced concrete, but in order to be strong in this world he had to be humble before God.

That evening was also the start of the Sabbath, so when Volodia had finished praying, I sat at the table and began reciting the Psalms. I had long ago become accustomed to reciting twenty or thirty Psalms on the Sabbath, but because they had taken away all the large-print Psalms that I had copied out, I had to read the microscopic text of my tiny Psalm book while ignoring the pain in my eyes. I was reading to myself when I heard a sigh from Volodia Balakhanov, who was pensively squatting and smoking near the cell door.

"O Lord," he said, "give us the strength to preserve the purity of this life in the future!" What awaited us in the future? Volodia Poresh's fate would be decided in a few days, and Balakhanov's in a few months. But what about mine?

On the morning of August first, the final day of Poresh's five-year term, they took us out for exercise. For the last time I repeated to Volodia the messages I wanted him to convey when he was released. I didn't want to mention other possibilities, but Volodia sensed my unspoken question.

"Don't worry, I'm ready for any possibility."

When we returned to the cell, the duty officer said, "Poresh, with your things!"

"Can the bedstand be left with us?" I asked.

"No, let him take everything. Ten minutes to collect your things."

"Everything will be fine, I'm sure," Volodia Balakhanov kept repeating.

I kept silent. I had asked about the bedstand because if they were really taking Poresh out of prison, then he wouldn't need it. This looked like a bad sign, but maybe they were simply playing games with us.

The final embraces. We blessed each other, each with the words of his own prayer. Volodia left, the cell door slammed. I glued myself to the door, and it looked as if they had taken Volodia into the opposite cell, where the administration usually talked with prisoners. The minutes dragged ever so slowly, and a funereal silence reigned in the cell. Finally the door of the opposite cell opened and I heard a hoarse voice, "So, now I'll be with Kolya."

Was that really Volodia's voice? Yes, he was informing us that they were taking him to the end cell, with Nikolai Ilishkin, where he would await a new trial. Soon he received another three years of imprisonment under Article 188.3 for "malicious violation of prison discipline." His violation consisted of the fact that he somehow slept in the cell during the daytime, that on another occasion he didn't sleep at night, and that he was also caught in an attempt to throw a note to a neighboring yard during the exercise period.

For several days I was preoccupied with Poresh's re-arrest. Why did this incident have such an effect on me? Hadn't many dramas unfolded in front of me during these years? I wasn't thinking of Volodia, however. I knew that he wouldn't break, and although it would be very difficult for him, he would take himself in hand. No, I was thinking about his wife and children. How would they bear this blow?

You choose your own path of struggle in this world, but in making choices for yourself you also make them for your family. Do I have the right to do this? I asked myself. The KGB often tried to play on these feelings: "If you don't have compassion on yourself, then have compassion on your mother!" I had long ago learned to reject their conclusions and not to allow their words to enter my heart, but now I couldn't help thinking of Volodia's family—and also of mine.

Shortly before these events, another prisoner gave me a gift of some ragged little pages that had been torn out of a journal many years ago by a zek, and had been passed from hand to hand ever since. It was an excerpt from Camus's essay "The Myth of Sisyphus."

> The gods had condemned Sisyphus to ceaselessly rolling a rock to the top of a mountain, whence the stone would fall back of its own weight. They had thought with some reason that there is no more dreadful punishment than futile and hopeless labor....At the very end of his long effort measured by skyless space and time without depth, the purpose is achieved. Then Sisyphus watches the stone rush down in a few moments toward that lower world whence he will have to push it up again toward the summit....It is during that return, that pause, that Sisyphus interests me....I see that man going back down with a heavy yet measured step toward the torment of which he will never know the end....At each of these moments when he leaves the heights and gradually sinks toward the lairs of the gods, he is superior to his fate....Again I fancy Sisyphus returning toward his rock, and the sorrow was in the beginning. When

the images of earth cling too tightly to memory, when the call of happiness becomes too insistent, it happens that melancholy rises in man's heart: this is the rock's victory, this is the rock itself. The boundless grief is too heavy to bear....But crushing truths perish from being acknowledged....

I read and perceived these words as if each sentence had been written about us zeks. For wasn't this the way we traversed the circles of the Gulag, and having finished one term, began another? Didn't we suffer when "images of earth" became too strong? But what did "too strong" mean? Did feeling pain over loved ones mean we were permitting the victory of the stone?

In my next letter home I wrote:

I felt long ago that the meaning of life can be discovered only when you challenge fate and destiny, when you tear yourself away from the numbing iron embraces of "social, " " historical," and other necessities. In time I also understood what a cunning and deadly enemy even hope can be.... If you don't see the meaning of the life you are leading this very minute, if it appears only when you live on the hope of rapid changes, then you are in constant danger.

It is difficult enough for man to reconcile himself to infinity and to meaninglessness, but it is totally impossible to adjust to infinite meaninglessness. Therefore, if his life today seems meaningless, man inevitably makes himself see the end of it on a near horizon. All you must do is drag the stone one more time to the summit. But in the end, deceptive hope poisons the soul and weakens the spirit.

During these years I have met people who have been weakened from constant disappointments. They continually create new hopes for themselves, and as a result they betray themselves. Others live in the world of illusions, hastily and incessantly building and rebuilding their world in order to prevent real life from ultimately destroying it.

What, then, is the solution? The only answer is to find the meaning of your current life. It's best if you are left with only one hope—the hope of remaining yourself no matter what happens. *Don't fear, don't believe, and don't hope. Don't believe words from the outside; believe your own heart. Believe in that meaning which was revealed to you in this life, and hope that you will succeed in guarding it.*

In Camus's essay, Sisyphus looks calmly at the stone rolling down. Although he has no control over the stone, he is calm. He descends not as a slave but as a man who has risen above his fate. But what if his mother, his wife, and his children are in the way of the stone? That is the real problem here. Simply rising above this suffering means making all your efforts meaningless. If you are going to suffer, then how can you suffer and not flinch? How can you suffer and not be broken by the desire to defend your loved ones from suffering?

There is, of course, one solution—in the complete mingling of two fates into one—together we roll the rock up the mountain, and together we stand under it, like Avital and me.

I thus shared my gloomy thoughts from prison without being able to explain what evoked them. When the opportunity finally arose, and I told Avital about my doubts, she said, "I don't understand the problem. Had you betrayed yourself for my sake, you would have betrayed me as well."